JUST FINANCIAL MARKETS?

Diese Publikation geht hervor aus dem DFG-geförderten Exzellenzcluster "Die Herausbildung normativer Ordnungen" an der Goethe-Universität Frankfurt am Main.

DFG NORMATIVE ORDERS
Exzellenzcluster an der Goethe-Universität Frankfurt am Main

Just Financial Markets?

Finance in a Just Society

EDITED BY
LISA HERZOG

OXFORD
UNIVERSITY PRESS

OXFORD
UNIVERSITY PRESS

Great Clarendon Street, Oxford, OX2 6DP,
United Kingdom

Oxford University Press is a department of the University of Oxford.
It furthers the University's objective of excellence in research, scholarship, and education by publishing worldwide. Oxford is a registered trade mark of Oxford University Press in the UK and in certain other countries

First Edition published in 2017

Published in the United States of America by Oxford University Press
198 Madison Avenue, New York, NY 10016, United States of America

British Library Cataloguing in Publication Data
Data available

Library of Congress Control Number: 2016955406

ISBN 978–0–19–875566–1

Contents

List of Contributors

Anat R. Admati is the George G. C. Parker Professor of Finance and Economics at the Graduate School of Business, Stanford University. She has written extensively on information dissemination in financial markets, trading mechanisms, portfolio management, financial contracting, and, most recently, on corporate governance and banking. Since 2010, she has been active in the policy debate on financial regulation, particularly capital regulation, writing research and policy papers and commentary. She is a co-author, with Martin Hellwig, of the book *The Bankers' New Clothes: What's Wrong with Banking and What to Do about It* (2013). She was also named by *Time* Magazine as one of the 100 most influential people in the world and by *Foreign Policy* Magazine as one of the 100 global thinkers in 2014.

Alan H. Brener is currently undertaking a PhD at the Centre for Commercial Law Studies (CCLS), Queen Mary University of London. He is a member of the Advisory Board of the Centre for Ethics and Law at University College London and a council member of The Chartered Institute of Bankers in Scotland. He is also a qualified Chartered Accountant and member of the Institute of Chartered Accountants in England and Wales and has a LLM from UCL. Prior to starting his PhD, he worked for Santander UK and was responsible, at different times, for the compliance and retail legal departments and regulatory policy. Before joining Santander in 2005, from 1996 he headed the compliance departments for the retail banking divisions of NatWest and RBS banks. From 1989 to 1996 he was a senior prudential and conduct of business regulator for the insurance and collective investments sectors, having previously worked on aspects of public policy at the Department of Trade and Industry. He also helped set up the Banking Standards Board with the objective of improving standards of conduct and professionalism within the banking industry.

Rutger Claassen is Associate Professor of Ethics and Political Philosophy at the Department of Philosophy of Utrecht University. His research centers on three main themes: socio-economic justice (especially the capability approach, on which he is writing a monograph); economic and ethical theories about the concept of the market and the justifications for regulating and limiting markets; and conceptions of freedom, autonomy, and paternalism. He has published in journals such as *Economics and Philosophy, Inquiry, Law and Philosophy, Journal of Social Philosophy* and *Politics, Philosophy and Economics*. He also regularly publishes articles and books in Dutch, to bring philosophy to a broader audience. He is an editor of a public journal (*Filosofie & Praktijk*) and co-organizer of a monthly Philosophical Café in Utrecht.

Jay Cullen is a lecturer in banking and finance law at the University of Sheffield. His main research and teaching interests are banking regulation, shadow banking, and corporate governance of financial institutions. He has been a visiting scholar at Columbia University (2016) and has received research grants from the British Academy and European Commission for work on financial regulation. His work on bank leverage and corporate governance has been quoted by the *Financial Times* and the BBC. In addition, he is an associated expert at the Institute for New Economic Thinking and a member of the Sustainable Market Actors Network, hosted by the Law Faculty at the University of Oslo. His monograph on executive compensation (*Executive Compensation in Imperfect Financial Markets*) was published in 2014. He has published articles in journals such as *The Columbia Journal of European Law* and the *Journal of Financial Perspectives*. His work has been presented at leading academic venues including the Institute for New Economic Thinking, Oxford University, Berkeley, and The National Institute for Economic and Social Research.

Boudewijn de Bruin is Professor of Financial Ethics at the University of Groningen. He held visiting positions at Cambridge University, the Fondation Maison des sciences de l'homme in Paris, and Harvard Business School, and is a Life Member of Clare Hall (Cambridge). With Alex Oliver (Cambridge), he is directing a program on *Trusting Banks* financed by the Dutch Research Council (NWO). De Bruin's research interests are financial ethics, moral, and political philosophy, theory of knowledge, philosophy of mathematics, economics and finance, game theory, and philosophical logic. He is the author of a monograph on *Explaining Games: The Epistemic Programme in Game Theory*, published in 2010, and co-editor, with Christopher F. Zurn, of *New Waves in Political Philosophy* (2008). His monograph *Ethics and the Global Financial Crisis: Why Incompetence Is Worse than Greed* was published in 2015.

Peter Dietsch is Associate Professor in the Philosophy Department at the Université de Montréal. His research interests lie in the domain of economic justice, with a focus on income inequality as well as on normative issues in economic policy, including fiscal and monetary policy. His book *Catching Capital: The Ethics of Tax Competition* was published by Oxford University Press in 2015. Among other journals, he has published in The *Journal of Political Philosophy*, the *Journal of Moral Philosophy*, the *Journal of Social Philosophy*, and *Politics, Philosophy and Economics*.

Lisa Herzog is Professor of Political Philosophy and Theory at the Bavarian School of Public Policy at the Technical University Munich. She works on the intersection of economic and political questions, with a focus on the history of economic and political thought, the normative status of markets, and, most recently, the role of complex organizations in markets and their moral status. She is the author of *Inventing the Market. Smith, Hegel, and Political Theory* (2013) and numerous academic papers in English and German. She also writes for a broader audience, including the monograph *Freiheit gehört nicht nur den Reichen. Plädoyer für einen zeitgemäßen Liberalismus* (2014).

Aaron James is Professor of Philosophy at the University of California, Irvine. He is the author of various papers that have appeared in journals including *Philosophy and Public Affairs* and *Philosophy and Phenomenological Research*, and of *Fairness in Practice: A Social Contract for a Global Economy* (2012). He has been a recipient of ACLS's Burkhardt Fellowship, a fellow at the Center for Advanced Study in the Behavioral Sciences, Stanford University, and Visiting Professor of Philosophy at NYU.

Rosa M. Lastra is Professor in International Financial and Monetary Law at the Centre for Commercial Law Studies (CCLS), Queen Mary University of London. She is a member of the Monetary Committee of the International Law Association (MOCOMILA), a founding member of the European Shadow Financial Regulatory Committee (ESFRC), an associate of the Financial Markets Group of the London School of Economics and Political Science, and an affiliated scholar of the Center for the Study of Central Banks at New York University School of Law. From 2008 to 2010 she was a Visiting Professor of the University of Stockholm. She has served as a consultant to the International Monetary Fund, the European Central Bank, the World Bank, the Asian Development Bank, and the Federal Reserve Bank of New York. From November 2008 to June 2009 she acted as Specialist Adviser to the European Union Committee [Sub-Committee A] of the House of Lords regarding its Inquiry into EU Financial Regulation and responses to the financial crisis. Since 2015 she has been a member of the Monetary Expert Panel of the European Parliament and since 2016 she has been a member of the Banking Union (Resolution) Expert Panel of the European Parliament. She has written extensively in her fields of expertise (central banking, financial regulation, international monetary law, EU law), with several authored and edited books and numerous articles.

Seumas Miller is a professorial research fellow at the Centre for Applied Philosophy and Public Ethics (an Australian Research Council Special Research Centre) at Charles Sturt University (Canberra) and the 3TU Centre for Ethics and Technology at TU Delft (The Hague) (joint position). He is the author or co-author of over 200 academic articles and fifteen books, including

Social Action (2001), *The Moral Foundations of Social Institutions* (2010), *Investigative Ethics* (co-author Ian Gordon) (2014), *Shooting to Kill: The Ethics of Police and Military Use of Lethal Force* (2016), and *Institutional Corruption* (forthcoming).

Katharina Pistor is the Michael I. Sovern Professor of Law at Columbia Law School and the Director of the School's Center on Global Legal Transformation. She previously taught at the Kennedy School of Government, and worked at the Max Planck Institute for Foreign and International Private Law in Hamburg, Germany and the Harvard Institute for International Development. Her research interests include the relation of law and finance, the transformation of economic systems, comparative corporate governance, and law and development. She serves as President of the World Interdisciplinary Network for Institutional Research, and on the editorial boards of the *Journal of Institutional Economics*, and the *Columbia Journal of Transnational Law*, among others. In 2012 she received the Max Planck Research Award for her contributions to international financial regulation. Recent publications include "A Legal Theory of Finance" (*Journal of Comparative Economics*, 2013); "Regulatory Capabilities" (with Fabrizio Cafaggi) (*Journal on Regulation and Governance*, 2015), and a book co-edited with Olivier De Schuttter, *Governing Access to Essential Resources* (2015).

Mark R. Reiff is the author of four books: *On Unemployment, Volume I: A Micro-Theory of Economic Justice* (2015), *On Unemployment, Volume II: Achieving Economic Justice after the Great Recession* (2015), *Exploitation and Economic Justice in the Liberal Capitalist State* (2013), and *Punishment, Compensation, and Law: A Theory of Enforceability* (2005). His papers on issues within political, legal, and moral philosophy have appeared in leading academic journals in the US, the UK, France, and Canada. He has taught political, legal, and moral philosophy at the University of Manchester, the University of Durham, and most recently at the University of California at Davis, and in 2008–9 was a Faculty Fellow at the Safra Center for Ethics at Harvard University. He is also a lawyer, and prior to retuning to academia to obtain his PhD at the University of Cambridge he practiced complex civil trial and appellate litigation in California for many years. He is also admitted to practice as a solicitor in England and Wales.

Roseanne Russell is a Lecturer in Law at Cardiff University. Her research lies at the intersection of company law, employment law, and feminist legal theory. She is a solicitor and practiced in Edinburgh and London before moving to academia.

Charlotte Villiers is Professor of Company Law and Corporate Governance at the University of Bristol. Her research focuses on company law, employment law, and Spanish Law. She studied law at the University of Hull and the London School of Economics and Political Science, and is a qualified solicitor. She has taught at the Universities of Sheffield and Glasgow, and was a Visiting Lecturer at the University of Oviedo in Spain. She was appointed Professor of Company Law in 2005. Her publications include *European Company Law—Towards Democracy* (1998), and most recently, *Corporate Reporting and Company Law* (2006). She has also written extensively on UK industrial relations. Her current research sponsored by the Arts and Humanities Research Council (AHRC) concerns female participation in company boards.

1

Introduction: Just financial markets? Finance in a just society

Lisa Herzog

1.1 INTRODUCTION

Finance has become a serious political affair. In a 2000 newspaper article, the speaker of the board of Deutsche Bank, Rolf-E. Breuer, called financial markets the "fifth power," which, together with the "fourth power" of the media, helped to keep in check the executive, legislative, and judicial branches, the three traditional powers of the state (Breuer 2000). In 2002, Warren Buffet, one of the world's most successful investors, called derivatives "financial weapons of mass destruction," and he has recently confirmed this view (Financial Review 2015). Weapons of mass destruction, if they should exist at all, should certainly not exist in the hands of a small group of private actors—they are a political issue *par excellence*. Some bankers think of their work even more highly: Goldman Sachs's chief executive Lloyd Blankfein once famously told a reporter that bankers are "doing God's work" (Wall Street Journal 2009).

Rhetoric and self-aggrandizing aside, finance has certainly become an issue of utmost importance for capitalist societies. Since the 1970s, the volume of financial services has grown with around twice the speed of GDP growth in both the UK and the US (Turner 2016, 20ff.). The Great Financial Crisis of 2008 has made painfully clear that financial markets are not just markets like any others. Their impact on the lives of numerous individuals is huge: so many jobs, wages, nest eggs, mortgages, and consumer loans depend, directly or indirectly, on what happens on the trading floors of Wall Street, the City of London, and elsewhere, a phenomenon sometimes described as the "financialization" of society. And yet, financial markets are highly abstract entities, and therefore difficult to grasp: all we see are charts on computer screens, in green or red, and maybe some pictures of nervous men (and the occasional woman) in suits shouting orders at each other from their trading desks. The abstractness of financial markets may be one of the reasons why it has been more difficult than with regard to other institutions to address a very simple question to them: are they in line with our considered judgments about how a just society should be organized? After the Great Financial Crisis, political philosophers and theorists[1] have begun to develop an interest in such questions, and a new debate has started.[2] This volume brings together contributions to this debate not only from political philosophy, but also from economics and law. They shed light on a number of interconnected themes that all have to do with the relation between financial markets and justice.

In the last decades, political philosophers have by and large[3] relied on the academic division of labor and mostly left questions about markets to economists, despite the fact that there is a venerable tradition in philosophy—from Aristotle to Montesquieu, Smith, Kant, Marx, and many others—that takes economic questions seriously as genuinely philosophical questions. More recent discussions, in contrast, have started to open up the "black box" of markets (Dietsch 2010) and to look in more detail at the structures of markets: the values they embody, the institutional landscape they are part of, and the impact they have on the distribution of opportunities and resources (see Herzog 2013 for an overview). So far, however, the debate about markets has been limited to considerations about markets in general, and has focused mostly on their moral limits (see notably Anderson 1992, Satz 2010, and Sandel 2012) or on the duties of market participants, which have also been discussed in business ethics (see e.g. Heath 2014). In this volume, in contrast, the focus is on one particular kind of markets: financial markets. As I will

[1] I here use these terms interchangeably.

[2] Contributions that analyze the Great Financial Crisis include Lomansky (2011), Nielsen (2010), Graafland and Van de Ven (2011), Nowak and O'Sullivan (2012), Roemer (2012), and the essays collected in Dobos, Barry, and Pogge (2011). There are now some emerging discussions about "justice in finance," e.g. James (2012, 249–84) or Wollner (2014). Monographs that discuss normative questions about finance, but mostly from a perspective of *ethics* rather than political philosophy—i.e. with a focus on moral agency rather than institutional structures—include Koslowski (2011), Hendry (2013), Boatright (2014); see also the volume edited by Boatright (2010). De Bruin (2015) explores the nexus between epistemology and ethics in financial markets; Emunds (2014) provides a critical account of financial markets from a perspective of global justice. A specific branch of the financial services industry, microfinance, raises questions of justice of its own: often motivated to help the poor by providing them with loans, there has also been some debate about abuses and exploitative practices. For a discussion from a philosophical perspective see for example Sorrel and Cabrera (2015).

[3] There are some exceptions that concern specific aspects of markets—for example the role of luck in markets, or the role of self-interested motives and the role of incentives in a just society—that were discussed in debates about luck egalitarianism and about Rawls's approach (see e.g. Cohen 1997). These debates, however, concerned abstract features of markets rather than markets as concrete institutions.

discuss below, they have specific features that make them particularly interesting for those interested in justice, or in obstacles to justice.

There are good reasons not to leave the consideration of financial markets to economists alone. Much could be said about the way in which economics, with its focus on elegant mathematical models, had smuggled idealized assumptions about human behavior and about the structure of markets into its descriptions of financial markets (see e.g. Krugman 2009a, Shiller 2012, chap. 19). While it might be unfair to expect economists to predict the precise timing and evolution of an event like the Great Financial Crisis, the way in which this crisis took the discipline by surprise speaks volumes. Simplifying models, however, are not the only problem of an exclusively economic perspective.[4] Another one is the almost exclusive concentration on Pareto-efficiency as the only normative criterion, that is, efficiency in the sense that it is impossible to make anyone better off without making someone else worse off. For some markets, it may be a useful strategy to do so: Pareto-efficient markets can help to create a large "pie" that can then be redistributed by other institutions. While much can be said about existing financial markets from a perspective of Pareto-efficiency, it is questionable whether this strategy is sufficient for understanding markets that have become so dominant in our societies as financial markets have in recent years. While some of the chapters in this volume remain tied to a perspective of efficiency, others ask more fundamental questions about the institutional structures of financial markets and the normative values or principles we should draw on when thinking about them.

In the remainder of this Introduction, I will first provide an overview of some of the mechanics of financial markets and the justifications that have traditionally been offered for them.[5] I then present some of the preliminary evidence that suggests that financial markets should be considered not only from a perspective of efficiency, but also from a perspective of justice. This is followed by a more in-depth discussion of how financial markets differ from the markets for apples and oranges that populate economics textbooks.[6] These considerations lead to a strong case for reform. I conclude with a preview of the chapters of this volume, which discuss not only the principles of justice that can serve as guidelines for evaluating financial markets, but also more concrete aspects that are relevant from a perspective of justice, and that

[4] Another problem on which I cannot comment here is the way in which members of the economic profession were coopted by financial institutions and other interest groups. The documentary movie *Inside Job* provides sobering insights into these connections. See also Chapter 13 (by Admati) in this volume.

[5] This section can be skipped by those already familiar with the basic mechanisms of financial markets.

[6] See also Bowles 1991, 15 on the weird fact that textbook examples of markets are often fruit markets, which are very different from more complex markets such as labor markets or financial markets.

provide food for thought about how financial markets could be changed such as to be brought better into line with our considered judgments about what makes a society just.

1.2 FINANCIAL MARKETS—A FEW NUTS AND BOLTS

In a first approximation—and in the view that was, arguably, dominant before the Great Financial Crisis—financial markets are a subgroup of markets in general. Hence, the descriptions and justifications offered for free markets are assumed to apply to them as well. Markets are institutions in which agents exchange goods and services, usually using money as a medium of exchange. Market prices mediate the interplay between supply and demand: if supply is high relative to demand, the price falls, signaling to suppliers that less of the product in question is required (or driving some suppliers out of the market); if supply is low relative to demand, the price rises, signaling to suppliers that they should provide more of the product in question (or attracting new suppliers). Those on the demand side can equally react to changing prices, for example by increasing or reducing their consumption or by switching to other goods or services. There is no need for a central planner who would coordinate the behavior of all these agents; rather, the changes of the price level do so automatically. To be sure, this does not mean that the state has no role at all to play: it has to create a framework of property rights in the first place, and it has to offer the legal infrastructure needed for enforcing these rights and the contracts that right-holders can enter with one another. It may also have to regulate certain aspects of markets, for example in order to prevent market participants from causing "external effects" on third parties, such as environmental pollution. But within this framework, individuals are free to decide according to their own preferences: to buy or to sell at whatever price they find appropriate. Or so the textbook story goes.

Free markets are "competitive" in the sense that on both sides of the market, participants have to compete with one another in order to be successful: those on the supply side have to compete for customers, and those on the demand side have to compete for access to the goods or services in question. Depending on the structures of a market, competition on either side can be stronger than on the other, creating advantages for those on the other side: if there is strong competition among suppliers, customers benefit by receiving lower prices and/or better quality; if there is strong competition on the demand side, suppliers can demand higher prices and/or offer lower quality. In the "perfectly competitive markets" presented in many textbooks, there are large numbers of market participants on either side. This means that all mutually beneficial opportunities for trade will be used, which means that the result is "Pareto-optimal." In more colloquial terms: there is no "waste" from unused opportunities to gain from trade. For this result to apply in practice, however, markets have to come close to the idealized markets of textbooks. For example, all market participants must be fully informed about the products that are traded, they have to be fully rational, and they have to be able to buy and sell whenever they like. There is an extensive literature on "market failures," that is, cases in which these assumptions do not hold and this fact causes inefficiencies.

Financial markets can be understood as markets in which financial products are traded. Sometimes this trade takes place physically, in trading places such as the New York Stock Exchange; increasing amounts of financial products, however, are traded electronically, either on regulated electronic trading platforms or in other trading networks. This holds both for business-to-business trade, in which financial institutions trade with one another, and for business-to-consumer trade, in which private or institutional clients buy or sell financial products from brokers. The products traded in financial markets include various forms of equity and debt contracts. Equity means that investors hold property rights that often come with certain control rights—for example the right to vote at a shareholder meeting—and that involve the full transfer of risk, upwards (gains), and downwards (losses) to the owner. "Capital," in the traditional sense of shares in traded companies that pay a dividend if the company makes a profit, is the prototypical case of equity. The owners of debt contracts, in contrast, do not receive control rights or the right to a dividend; instead, they receive the right to fixed payments. This categorization, however, is only a rough one, as there can be various intermediate forms. Many equity and debt contracts are traded very frequently; what matters to investors is thus not only the profile of payments and risks that they receive, but also the price levels of these assets and in particular the expected future development of their prices.

In addition to company shares and government bonds, a huge number of other products are traded in financial markets. In a first approximation, they can all be understood as bundles of contractual rights that describe payment schedules for different future scenarios. They vary with regard to their risk (how likely is it that their owner will experience gains or losses?), their profitability (how much money can the owner earn in different future scenarios?), and their liquidity (how easy or difficult is it to exchange them for other products, typically, money, in the short term?). Other goods that are traded in financial markets include, for example, insurance contracts or foreign currencies.

It would be impossible to understand modern financial markets, however, if one assumed that the goods traded in them were only the goods listed so far, all of which are relatively closely tied to phenomena in the "real economy"—companies issue shares in order to raise capital, governments issue bonds in order to finance public investment, individuals or companies insure themselves against untoward events such as a natural disaster, companies buy foreign currency in order to trade with business partners in other countries. In addition to these bread-and-butter products, financial markets include large numbers of "derivative" products that are related, in one way or another, to other, underlying financial products. The existence of such products is not new; especially in times of financial manias, derivative products tend to spring up like mushrooms. The amount and the complexity of such derivative products in the last decades, however, beat everything that had happened earlier. The possibility of using computers and IT networks for creating products and keeping track of them allowed for an explosion in derivatives that would have been hard to imagine in a world of paper-based trading.

Derivative products can be relatively simple or they can be very complex, and they all relate, in one way or another, to the fluctuation of prices of other products. Relatively simple products include, for example, options, which give the owner the right to buy or sell a financial product or commodity at a certain price at a certain future date. For example, a wheat farmer might want to buy an option for selling the annual harvest at a certain price; if the demand for wheat at the time of delivery is higher than expected, driving up the price, the farmer does not have to use the option, but if the demand, and hence the price, is lower, he or she can use the option to avoid selling at a lower price. In that way, the option serves as an insurance against losses from price fluctuations. Similarly, forwards and futures are contracts about the obligation (rather than the right) to buy or sell some financial product at a fixed price in the future. Swaps are contracts in which two market participants exchange the future cash flows of different underlying financial products. In addition to these still relatively simple derivatives, there can be combinations or derivatives-of-derivatives of almost unlimited complexity. Often, they are tailor-made between parties and traded "over the counter," that is, in one-on-one transaction outside of regulated exchanges such as the New York Stock Exchange or the Chicago Mercantile Exchange.

Such derivatives can be bought by investors who want to "hedge" risks to which they are exposed in their economic operations. For example, a company heavily trading with companies in other currency areas might want to hedge the risks of currency fluctuations. But they can also be used for speculative purposes. Derivatives are themselves heavily traded, which means that their prices can fluctuate considerably. If a trader expects the price of a certain derivative to rise, he or she might buy a bunch of it in the hope of selling it at a better price in the future—or he or she may buy a derivative that builds on this very price development, for example an option contract that gives him or her the right to buy these derivatives at the current price in the future.[7] If the price

[7] A related practice, which can be described as a "bet" on falling prices, is "short-selling," which means selling financial products one does not currently own (but which one can borrow), and then repurchasing them later.

has by then risen, he or she can make a profit. Sophisticated mathematical models have been developed for calculating the expected profits, and hence the current prices, of options and other derivatives.[8] In the years before the Great Financial Crisis, it seemed that these models were doing a good job at describing the underlying reality. In fact, the very existence of these models—and hence the impression that one could remain in control of all the risks one was exposed to when trading in complex derivatives—contributed to the boom in derivatives trading. The total amount of outstanding derivative contracts, that is, legal claims to certain payments under certain scenarios, had reached a sum of 400 trillion US dollars by 2008 (Turner 2016, 1).

What is the point of all these derivative contracts?, you might ask. Did they all fulfil a useful function in the economy? Why were the markets for derivatives not closely watched and regulated in order to make sure that they would not cause additional risks? To understand why they were seen as harmless, and even beneficial, by many commentators, including academic economists and regulators, it is important to understand the ideological landscape before the Great Financial Crisis. Free markets in general were seen as fundamentally beneficial: the free play of supply and demand enables a process of "price discovery" that supports the efficient allocation of scarce goods. Financial markets were seen as similar to other markets in this respect. In fact, in many macroeconomic models, finance was not even included: it was considered a "veil" that did not change the underlying structures of the real economy, no matter how large it was and what kinds of products were traded in it. Central bank policy did not pay attention to financial markets either, as it focused mostly, and largely successfully, on keeping inflation in check. The possibility that financial markets might create instability from within was simply not on the radar (see also Turner 2016, 38).

This narrowness of vision, however, was no pure dogmatism, but rather based on microeconomic considerations that formed a coherent narrative. According to this narrative, financial markets were basically markets for streams of payments under different future scenarios. Market participants who differed in their estimations about the likelihood of these scenarios, in their demand for liquidity, or in their appetite for risk, could reap gains from trade in those markets. The more fine-grained the products they could buy, the better they could fine-tune their investment strategies, choosing portfolios that exactly matched their preferences. Thus, risks would be carried by those who were able and willing to carry them, and scarce capital would be optimally allocated. Relatedly, it was thought that more efficient financial markets would be able to serve as control mechanisms for those who held control over productive assets—typically the executive managers of companies.

[8] For example, the "Black-Scholes" or "Black-Scholes-Merton" model for option pricing (Black and Scholes 1973).

Share prices provided them with a real-time feedback mechanism on how well they were doing, and the threat of a hostile takeover, by an investor who thought that the stock of capital could be used more efficiently, was seen as a disciplinary mechanism on management not to squander resources (see e.g. Emunds 2014, 70ff.).

Behind these ideas stood the "efficient market hypothesis" (see especially Fama 1970), which holds that in efficient markets, asset prices reflect all available information on a given asset. This hypothesis is based on the assumption that all market participants behave rationally, or if they do not, irrational behavior occurs in a random fashion, and rational arbitrageurs have incentives to correct irrational behavior by betting against it.[9] From this perspective, it cannot be the case that a market *as a whole* deviates from the fundamentals on which it is based; once a deviating movement starts, this immediately creates profit opportunities for rational investors who will bring market prices back to normal, hence there can be no price bubbles. Whether or not the efficient market hypothesis possesses any plausibility is hotly debated among economists; Eugene Fama, one of its most prominent defenders, continued to argue against the possibility of bubbles—or at least against the usefulness of the concept—even after the Great Financial Crisis (Cassidy 2010). Among his most prominent critics are behavioral economists, for example Robert Shiller, who not only takes into account a more empirically robust picture of human nature, but who was also one of the first to warn that the US real estate market might be subject to overheating (Shiller 2007).

Another problem with the efficient-market hypothesis is that, if true, it paradoxically destroys the incentive to acquire information, because market participants must assume that all available information is already reflected in prices (Grossman and Stiglitz 1980). Lomansky (2011, 150ff.) describes this paradox nicely:

> A rational agent will, then, choose to free-ride on the cognitive undertakings of others. The greater the confidence in the overall efficiency of the market, the greater the incentive to take a free ride. At the extreme, everyone is free-riding on everyone else, and no one is actually monitoring the condition of the underlying assets. Well before that stage is reached, however, serious informational distortions will have been introduced. [. . .] The proposition that markets are efficient

[9] It is worth noting that in this case the assumption of human rationality became more than a mere modeling assumption or "heuristic." Many economists, when faced with criticism of "economic man," defend it in this way, admitting that men of flesh and blood often behave differently. But in the case of financial markets, such models were used not only as a basis for regulation (or rather, non-regulation), but were also drawn upon by market participants to describe the behavior of other market participants and to adapt their behavior accordingly in order to make most profit. For a discussion of how economic models, especially models of option pricing, helped to shape the reality they were supposed to describe (their "performativity") see MacKenzie 2006, with the telling title *An Engine, Not a Camera: How Financial Models Shape Markets.*

> tends to be self-refuting. The more it is believed, the less accurate it becomes. The more skeptical market players are of its truth, the more effort they will invest in monitoring their potential investments, the overall effect of which is to enhance efficiency. That will then create conditions under which those who subscribe to the efficient-markets proposition will do better than the skeptics. And the merry-go-round takes another spin.

Nonetheless, the narrative of efficient markets is the narrative that the mainstream of economics had told. At the time, many scholars and practitioners found it sufficiently plausible to base their behavior on it. Some economists focusing on financial markets certainly held more sophisticated pictures that included questions about market failure, stability, or the relation between financial markets and the real economy, but especially in the curricula of undergraduate economics courses, these more nuanced accounts had played a marginal role. In a macroeconomic environment that seemed fairly stable, the narrative of efficient markets seemed accurately to grasp the economic reality. But if one puts together the various idealizations and generalizing assumptions it contains, one arrives at an all-too-rosy picture of what financial markets are and how one should see their role in society. Adair Turner, former head of the UK's Financial Services Authority, provides a good summary of the conclusions that market participants, regulators, and politicians had drawn on the basis of these assumptions:

> A strongly positive assessment dominated among finance academics and at least implicitly among regulators. It reflected the assumption that free competition was bound to result in useful rather than harmful activity, and that increased financial activity, by making more markets complete and efficient, must be improving capital allocation across the economy. (2016, 28)

Important institutions such as the International Monetary Fund shared these views. It was assumed that more efficient financial markets would, in the final analysis, lead to economic growth, which would benefit everyone in society.[10] Almost everyone trusted that the recent "innovations" in risk management had really made the whole system safer and more stable. Critics of this broad consensus seemed outlandish Cassandras.

But then, the Great Financial Crisis happened. It arose around a specific type of financial products: securitized loans. Securitization is a financial practice that had started with Fannie Mae and Freddie Mac, two government-sponsored entities in the US that handled large amounts of mortgages for home purchases. The basic mechanism is to bundle together a certain amount of mortgages into

[10] Empirical studies seemed to confirm that "financial deepening" was related to GDP growth (e.g. Levine 2005, quoted in Turner 2016, 32) and this relation from the past was assumed to also hold in the present and future, despite the fact that the kind of financial products through which the "deepening" had happened were not necessarily the same as were now used.

a portfolio and then to divide it up into different "tranches" with different risk and return structures. The top tranches, whose claims would be given priority in the case of defaults on loans, were considered extremely safe—they received "triple A" ratings from rating agencies, the same investment grade as US treasury bonds. Investors trusted these ratings, because rating agencies had been perceived as doing a good job in the past when evaluating bonds and shares and had thereby acquired a reputation as trustworthy, competent evaluators (Akerlof and Shiller 2015, chap. 2; see also de Bruin 2015, chap. 7). It was also assumed that any remaining risks could be hedged by diversification, because the market as a whole could not go wrong. Credit securities and credit derivatives were often traded many times, between multiple institutions; they seemed to offer what had previously been taken to be an impossible combination: high returns *and* safe investments.

As long as there was general optimism—not to say enthusiasm—and everyone believed in the prevailing narrative, the trade with these products soared. Once market participants started to realize, however, that they had become entangled in a huge speculative bubble, and once it became clear that the US government would *not* bail out all endangered institutions—as evidenced by the fall of Lehman Brothers in September 2008—trust and optimism evaporated overnight (for a summary of the events see e.g. Shiller 2012, chap. 5). It was especially the role of credit default swaps (CDSs)—which magnified the losses from small rises in defaults rates, because numerous traders could insure against each default, and which had been vastly underpriced—that brought the financial system to a halt, because markets for CDSs were extremely complex and lacked transparency, and no one understood any more who had which exposure (see e.g. Reiff 2013, 240ff.).

The Great Financial Crisis showed that the models on which investors had based their decisions, and banks and regulators their risk assessment, had been fundamentally flawed. They had assumed that future events could be described in terms of quantifiable risks, excluding the possibility of nonquantifiable uncertainty (Knight 2006 [1921], III.VII.3), which created a sense of security because quantifiable risks could be "managed" by using other financial instruments. Many models also included an assumption that different events, for example the development of asset prices in different market segments, would be independent from one another. This is a crucial assumption for the strategy of managing risks through diversification: if risks occur *jointly,* spreading one's investments across a large number of assets is of no help. More generally speaking, the likelihood of non-normal events, in the sense of large deviations from the general trend, was underestimated because investors often used normal approximations, rather than functions that allowed for greater "tail risks." Also, the past data on which many calculations were based did not go back very far in time—and many asset prices had been relatively stable within this time window, which also contributed to underestimating volatility. In other words: the techniques used for reducing risks were unable to capture precisely those cases in which risk management would be most needed, that is, a downswing of whole markets. This possibility was conceptually excluded, creating the impression that one had finally mastered the art of risk management.[11]

In hindsight, it seems hard to deny that much of what had taken place in financial markets before the Great Financial Crisis was anything but productive: trading in financial products as such cannot, after all, increase the economic pie; in the best case, it helps to allocate capital and risks efficiently, which can *in turn* benefit the economy. But this does not mean that these benefits continue to be created if trading is blindly expanded—at the very least, one has to ask whether there might also be a price one has to pay for these expanded activities in financial markets, for example in terms of increasing instability. And, as some commentators have pointed out (e.g. Mullainathan 2015, Turner 2016, 27), there is also another price one has to consider from a social perspective: the opportunity costs of resources, and especially the skills of well-educated and highly motivated young people being employed in finance rather than in, say, cancer research, engineering, technology, teaching, or public service. Considerations of counter factual scenarios are, of course, always to some degree speculative, and it is hardly possible to quantify these costs—but this does not mean that they do not exist.

1.3 FINANCIAL MARKETS AND JUSTICE—THE PRIMA FACIE EVIDENCE

Why, then, should one subject financial markets to an inquiry from a perspective of justice? And what is the relevant notion of justice anyway? The chapters of this volume all share a liberal egalitarian perspective, which is based on the assumption of the equal moral value of all individuals. This implies that all members of a society have certain basic rights, and that certain forms of discrimination, e.g. along the lines of gender or race, must be excluded. Based on these shared assumptions, however, different theorists of justice have drawn different conclusions with regard to other features of a just society, and especially with regard to the degree of inequality that is compatible with justice. It is worth noting, however, that the degree of inequality currently prevailing in

[11] Trust in "scientific" expertise seems to have played a role as well, as can be seen from a remark by a former hedge fund employee: "a lot of the Ph.D.-like jobs you can get out there, in finance especially, are window-dressing jobs. It's basically a company where they open their door to the client and then they point to a back room filled with Ph.D.s working furiously; they say: Oh, don't worry about our product; you can have faith; we have Ph.D.s" (Econtalk 2013).

Western[12] societies (see e.g. Piketty 2014) is problematic from the perspective of almost all theories of justice that are discussed in the literature.

There is strong prima facie evidence that much that happened in financial markets in recent years was unjust, no matter how exactly one defines "justice." One could start with the cases of spectacular fraud such as Madoff's Ponzi scheme or the manipulation of the LIBOR. On the one hand, one might say that these cases are theoretically easy to grasp because they violated existing laws. On the other hand, they raise questions that are anything but trivial about the possibility of law enforcement in systems that are as complex as today's financial markets, and in which the likelihood of discovery of fraudulent behavior is therefore lower than in other areas of life. A second fact about financial markets that should catch the attention of those interested in justice is the sheer size of the profits that were made in them, including the size of bonuses for individual traders or managers. Standard economic theory predicts that when high profits are being made in a market, this attracts competitors and profits are driven down again. This did not happen, nor do all those who made a fortune before the Great Financial Crisis seem to have suffered the ensuing losses. Moreover, the group of "winners" did not represent a cross-cutting section of society; for one thing, they were predominantly white and male. While a full analysis of the effects of financial market liberalization and the ensuing Great Financial Crisis on distributive justice would have to take into account numerous complex factors—general economic developments, differential impacts of interest rates and asset prices, effects on unemployment and inflation, etc.—and although claims that make comparisons to counterfactual scenarios face methodological difficulties, it seems fair to say that these effects deserve close scrutiny.

The Great Financial Crisis was, after all, not a natural disaster. Turner puts it starkly: "This catastrophe was entirely self-inflicted and avoidable" (2016, 2). The greatest loss, in his view, was the slowing down of economic growth in the years since the crisis—a view that is probably based on the assumption that higher growth could have benefited everyone in society. The relationship between inequality and financial expansions is a complex one, because inequality arguably also *drove* some of the financial excesses and hindered the economic recovery (Turner 2016, chap. 7). What is especially interesting, from a perspective of justice, is the *structural* impact of financial markets on wider societies and their distributive outcomes. Financial markets do not exist in a void, after all. If they were what they have often been compared to—that is, casinos—they would probably be far less harmful: they would be contained, individuals would—hopefully—know what they are doing when entering them,

[12] I here focus on Western societies because these are the ones that have fully developed financial markets of the kind described earlier. This does not mean, of course, that the *effects* of financial markets could be limited to these societies.

they would play with their own money and, at worst, go bankrupt, which might impose unjust costs on others, but which is still a somewhat limited problem. But today, we are in a situation in which what happens in financial markets has a much broader impact—not only on the distribution of resources, but also on the distribution of opportunities and the distribution of power in society. Almost everyone in society relies on using financial services, after all. Even bread-and-butter financial products are connected to the rest of the financial system; financial markets have become closely interwoven with the fabric of our societies. So it does seem worth asking: do financial markets, in the way in which they are currently organized, make our societies more or less just?[13]

A further point deserves emphasis. There is a broad scholarly consensus that the Great Financial Crisis was not caused exclusively by individual or corporate misbehavior, but also by structural features, for example incentives to take excessive risks because the gains were privatized while losses could be socialized. Otherwise one might think that normative issues in financial markets raise only questions of individual morality or of the morality of financial companies—questions that are addressed mostly in the discipline of business ethics. The perspective taken in this volume does by no means deny the importance of individual behavior. Nonetheless, the focus is mostly on *institutions* and the ways in which they coordinate and regulate behavior. Normative perspectives on institutions are the domain of political philosophy—and more specifically theories of justice—rather than ethics. In recent years, there have been some calls to bring political philosophy and business ethics closer together (e.g. Heath, Moriarty, and Wayne 2010). While there already exist some accounts of business ethics in financial markets, this volume brings the other side, that is, perspectives of justice, to the table.

Before sketching some of the proposals for reforms of financial markets and providing an overview of the chapters of this volume, however, we should subject to scrutiny one of the premises that underlie the very notion of "financial markets"—namely that the financial system as we know it can be described as a subgroup of the institution we call "market."

1.4 ARE FINANCIAL MARKETS—MARKETS?

This question, to be sure, is a polemical one. But it is nonetheless worth asking, given the degree to which financial markets—in contrast to, say, markets in

[13] There is also an international dimension to this question. The high volatility of capital flows in and out of developing countries makes their economic development highly unstable; it is probably not the best way of supporting a form of sustainable economic growth that would benefit the global poor (for a discussion see Emunds 2014).

health care, education, or surrogate motherhood—were seen by many as the prototype of well-functioning, competitive markets. Financial markets have specificities of their own. These can be roughly grouped into three categories: concerning products, concerning participants, and concerning equilibria (or the lack of equilibria, i.e. bubbles).

As already described, many of the products traded in financial markets are highly artificial legal constructs, many of which are several layers away from what happens in the real economy.[14] As such, they obviously do not directly satisfy the preferences of consumers; as Turner puts it: "No one gets up in the morning and says 'I feel like enjoying some financial services today'" (2016, 20). In some markets, such products are traded with a speed that is far beyond anything we can imagine for markets with physical products. In textbook markets, it is usually assumed that participants intend to hold the property rights of products for a certain amount of time; even if they buy for speculative purposes, they have to wait a bit until the price has moved into a certain direction. In many financial markets, participants siphon profits from tiny movements in prices, sometimes—in computerized trading—on a millisecond scale. Computerized or "algorithmic" trading is taking place in many financial markets, despite the fact that it is still rather badly understood. It is unclear, for example, how exactly the numerous "subsecond extreme events" that take place in these markets are related to the stability of the financial system as a whole (see e.g. Johnson et al. 2013).

Another specific feature of the products traded in financial markets—although arguably less specific than the character of these products—is the sheer volume that is traded in financial markets. With these amounts of money being moved around by relatively small groups of traders and financial institutions, we should not be surprised that the temptation to enrich oneself is greater than in many other markets—especially in upswings. As Kindleberger and Aliber drily note: "The supply of corruption increases in a pro-cyclical way much like the supply of credit" (2005, 143). Corruption can mean that market participants use illegal, fraudulent methods for making money, but it can also mean that they increase their efforts to exploit other people's vulnerabilities, for example their ignorance, their fears, or their time-inconsistent preferences. As Akerlof and Shiller argue in their latest book, *Phishing for Phools*, the tendency to exploit such vulnerabilities is not a rare "externality," but rather "inherent in the workings of competitive markets" (2015, 166). It is certainly not exclusive to financial markets, but the high sums at stake in them, and the abstractness and complexity of the products traded in them, may make them a particularly attractive pond for "phishers."

[14] Much more could be said here about the nature of money, money creation, and its role in society, but as this volume focuses on financial *markets*, this is not the place to go into these details. For discussions see e.g. Douglas 2016 or Amato and Fantacci 2012.

A second specificity of financial markets has to do with the agents who participate in them. In standard models of markets, it is assumed that economic agents carry both the upward and the downward risks of their decisions; this is what creates incentives for them to choose carefully between different options, depending on their appetite for risks and/or profits. In financial markets, however, liability is limited in numerous ways, which are often not reflected in prices. For one thing—but which is not too specific to financial markets—many participants in them are corporations, which means that their shareholders enjoy limited liability by definition, because they are only liable with the capital they have invested, not with their private capital (see e.g. Ciepley 2013 on the nature of corporations). The limitations of liability in the financial system, however, go much further. Deposits in banks are often insured by government-run insurance systems that are supposed to prevent "bank runs." A country's central bank serves as "lender of last resort" for banks that run out of liquidity (see e.g. Minsky 1986, chap. 3; Kindleberger and Aliber 2005, chap. 11). And as the Great Financial Crisis has shown, financial markets are marred by the issue of "too big to fail," or "too complex to fail": if financial institutions are so central for the financial system as a whole that their failure would engulf the whole system in the abyss, governments will take steps to prevent such failures. This means that financial institutions benefit from an implicit insurance by the government, which creates problems of "moral hazard": why not choose a somewhat riskier strategy if it promises high profits, and the downward risk is covered by taxpayers' money?

Less attention has been paid to another way in which liability was undermined, or at least reduced, in financial markets: this is the problem of internal control in financial institutions. Within large, complex institutions such as large banks there exist numerous possibilities of covering up wrongdoings or diluting responsibilities. In banks, many tasks are highly specialized and require technical skills that few individuals possess, which means that it is difficult for others to monitor their behavior. It also seems that the compliance culture of many banks was not working very well. Evidence for this is the fact that many cases of wrongdoing by individual employees, for example the unauthorized trading by Jérôme Kerviel at Société Générale, were discovered very late in the day, when huge damage had already been done.[15] The small likelihood of discovery of wrong or questionable behavior, combined with high bonuses tied to short-term profits, created a situation in which the temptation to behave recklessly was presumably far greater than it would

[15] Kerviel was a derivatives trader who was convicted for unauthorized trades that caused losses estimated at €4.9 billion. In the ensuing process, Société Générale claimed that he had traded without authorization, whereas Kerviel claimed that his trading activities had been known and that such practices were widespread in the company.

have been had employees acted in a more transparent context with more possibilities of control, let alone if they had traded with their own money.

A third way in which financial markets are different from other kinds of markets is the question of whether they self-stabilize or whether they can also generate destabilizing dynamics—bubbles instead of a market equilibrium. The dominant pre-Crisis picture assumed the former, holding, as noted above, that movements away from the market equilibrium would attract rational arbitrageurs that would return markets to the equilibrium. But not all economists saw financial markets in this way. John Maynard Keynes had already used the term "animal spirits"—which George A. Akerlof and Robert J. Shiller then picked up in the title of a 2009 book—for describing "a spontaneous urge to action rather than inaction, and not as the outcome of a weighted average of quantitative benefits multiplied by quantitative probabilities" (1936, 161–2). If market participants follow their "animal spirits," markets may not equilibrate, but rather create irrational upswings or downswings. These can lead to massive financial crises like the one we saw in 2008.

Based on earlier work by Hyman P. Minsky (1986), Kindleberger and Aliber provide a good account of financial crises; as their historical work illustrates, these can be based on underlying assets of very different kinds, ranging from tulip bulbs—in the famous "tulipmania" of the 1630s (see also Dash 2001)—to company shares and real estate (see Kindleberger and Aliber's Appendix (2005, 256ff.) for an overview of historical bubbles). Shiller defines bubbles as situations "in which news of price increases spurs investor enthusiasm, which spreads by psychological contagion from person to person, in the process amplifying stories that might justify the price increases and bringing in a larger and larger class of investors, who, despite doubts about the real value of an investment, are drawn to it partly through envy of others' successes and partly through a gambler's excitement" (2000, 2). This definition emphasizes the psychological elements of the phenomenon, which is also present in Kindleberger and Aliber's analysis.

In an upswing—which Kindleberger and Aliber also call a "mania"—an increasing percentage of trade is motivated not by a desire to invest money in the long term or to hedge risks in the real economy, but rather by the hope to gain from short-term increases in price-levels. Attracted by the opportunity to make easy money, many investors buy assets, often financed by credit, in order to find a "greater fool" to whom they can sell them before everyone realizes that the assets have been hugely overpriced (Kindleberger and Aliber 2005, 12). Once an upward movement is on its way, optimism spreads, and it is almost impossible for investors to resist it. Even sophisticated investors may decide to go with the herd, especially if their employers or clients evaluate them in comparison to the trend (see also Turner 2016, 40ff.). This can fuel the movement even more. As Citigroup's CEO Charles Prince famously said: "As long as the music is playing, you've got to get up and dance" (quoted in Lomansky 2011, 151). The question is: what happens when the music stops?

As Kindleberger and Aliber note, in such a mania "asset prices will decline immediately after they stop increasing—there is no plateau, no 'middle ground'" (2005, 10). Once prices have started to fall, everyone realizes that they have to get out as quickly as they can—and the same mechanism that drove prices upwards in the upswing now drives them downwards. For when there is a surplus of sellers in a market, prices fall, which means that other holders of assets also want to sell them before their prices fall even more. This holds in particular when many investors have bought assets with borrowed money. They can quickly get overwhelmed by debt—which they have a fixed, legal obligation to repay—while they see the value of their assets melting down. Some of them will be forced into "fire sales," others will go bankrupt, further driving down prices. In a general climate of panic and disillusionment, lenders have little incentive to hand out further loans. This role of credit for the cyclical instability of financial markets had been emphasized in particular by Minsky; mainstream economics, in contrast, had hardly paid any attention to the role of credit and its expansion.

Some commentators argue that seemingly technical details in the regulation of banks reinforced the pro-cyclicality even more. For each loan they hand out, banks are required to hold a certain amount of capital in their balance sheets. But the value of this capital was calculated in terms of the current value of these assets on the market, rather than historical costs. This meant that in an upswing, the values of the assets in the banks' balance sheets rose, which implied that they had more capital available to fulfil the regulatory requirements for making new loans. Thus, they could provide credit to more investors, who would use it to buy more assets, driving prices up even further—whereas in a crisis, falling asset prices would be directly reflected in the balance sheets, even if banks had no intention of selling an asset. Thus, the use of "value at risk" models functioned as a pro-cyclical amplifier of the price movements (see e.g. Turner 2016, 102ff.). Other factors that fueled the increases of financial crises in the decades since 1980s—documented, for example, by Reinhart and Rogoff (2009)—were the use of credit securitization and of structured financial products, while the free flow of capital in a globalized economy meant that crises in one country or region could lead to international contagion (Kindleberger and Aliber 2005, chaps 7 and 8).

Thus, financial markets have quite specific features, which is why it is worth asking whether we should describe them as "markets" at all. But why does this matter?, you might ask—isn't this just a verbal question, and aren't other markets quite different from the idealized, perfectly competitive markets one finds in textbook models as well? This is true. But if we call the arenas in which financial products are traded "markets," our attention is directed to certain features and distracted from others. Our views about what a *just* regulation of these arenas would be is also likely to be influenced. A widespread view of how markets should be regulated with regard to justice runs, roughly, as follows: markets should have fair rules that create a level playing field, and they also require regulation—and maybe some voluntary ethical commitment on the part of market participants (Heath 2014)—to prevent market failures that arise from unequal access to information, externalities, or other deviations from perfectly competitive markets. Apart from that minimal, procedural account of justice, markets should be left free. This not only makes them maximally efficient, but also maximizes human freedom. Regulation with regard to the justice of distribution kicks in afterwards, usually in the form of redistributive taxation, but it can come at the cost of efficiency (see e.g. Okun 1975; for a critical discussion see Le Grand 1990).

Much could be said about the strengths and weaknesses of this picture, but this is not the place to do so. For it should be clear that if financial markets lack central features that other markets have, we may have to ask much more fundamental questions about them and their relation to justice—questions that are obscured if financial markets are seen as the prototypical case of markets that come quite close to textbook markets, as they were often seen before the Great Financial Crisis. We cannot take for granted that there can be ideal "free" financial markets that are such that all deviations from the model of a perfectly competitive market are corrected by regulation; at least it seems questionable whether such an ideal would be compatible with the monetary systems we currently have, in which money is created by private banks that are backed up by a central bank.[16] In other words, it may be futile to look for regulation that would "repair" financial "markets," so that they become more similar to markets for apples and oranges. We cannot assume that "freer" financial markets also contribute to increasing the freedoms of human individuals; they might, in fact, create threats to these freedoms, e.g. the freedom to plan one's life in a reasonably stable macroeconomic environment. And lastly, we do not have to take for granted that when we regulate financial markets for *justice*, there is necessarily a price to be paid in terms of efficiency

[16] This is why some more radical critics have questioned the current monetary system, for example by proposing to abolish fractional banking and private money creation altogether (e.g. Felber 2014) or by taking up Keynes's proposal of introducing an international monetary unit (the "Bancor") instead of using the dollar or the Euro as lead currencies (Amato and Fantacci 2012). Such proposals seem even more utopian than others that have been brought forward in the debate; they might seem preferable as blueprints for building monetary systems from scratch, but it is unclear how we could get there from where we currently are. It is also unclear whether it is *required*, from a perspective of justice, to adopt such proposals, or whether our current monetary system, suitably amended, could be *sufficiently* just. One of the functions of such proposals, however, is to remind ourselves that the current system is not without alternatives, and to see its strengths and weaknesses in comparison to the strengths and weaknesses of other, theoretically possible, systems.

or the size of the economic pie; this might make regulation for justice easier than it would otherwise be.

Thus, we need to ask questions of justice about the institutional structures of financial markets afresh, without having in mind assumptions about the relation between justice and markets that may not hold in this case. To be sure, for *some* aspects of *some* financial markets it may make perfect sense to try to approximate them as far as possible to textbook markets, and there may also be areas in which there are trade-offs between efficiency and equality. The main lesson to be drawn from these considerations—whether financial markets are markets—maybe is to take seriously the diversity of what financial markets are or can be: the diversity of their products, their participants and their respective liabilities, and their tendency to form bubbles. This means that an evaluation from a perspective of justice also needs to be sufficiently nuanced. Not all dimensions of financial markets are equally problematic from a perspective of justice. Some markets function reasonably well and manage efficiently to allocate capital and risk without doing harm to third parties or the society as a whole. In fact, some parts of financial markets have continued to function largely uninhibited during the Great Financial Crisis.[17]

Financial markets are many different things, and their character can crucially depend on seemingly small technical details that vary from country to country. In theory, one could maybe separate out the financial markets that function reasonably well, from a perspective of efficiency and justice,[18] and one could suggest to simply keep those and shut down the others. In practice, different financial markets are highly interconnected—and the advantages and disadvantages of these various connections would in turn have to be evaluated from the perspectives of justice and efficiency. This is part of what makes the issue so complex. It means that different proposals for reform apply in different degrees to different kinds of financial markets.[19] But if we tried to simplify these complexities further, we would risk ending up with theories that are not sufficiently complex to describe the complex social phenomena we are

[17] E.g. so called "ethical," locally operating banks, see Herzog, Hirschmann, and Lenz 2015.

[18] Depending on one's theory of justice, efficiency might be integrated into one's conception or might be a separate consideration, which might then either pull in the same direction or stand in a conflictual relationship with justice. I assume that for many concrete regulatory questions, considerations of justice (according to different understandings) and considerations of efficiency can travel together a long way, at least if efficiency is defined in a way that includes effects on third parties (e.g. considerations of overall stability).

[19] This also holds for the chapters of this book: while some take on a "global" perspective that looks at the financial system as a whole, others make more specific proposals that apply more or less to different parts of the financial system. For reasons of space, most discussions cannot spell out these more detailed considerations. To get to the level of concrete policy proposals, one would also have to take into account specificities of national legislation and the economic situation of different countries.

faced with—and we have already seen enough of the problems of overly simplistic theories to want to avoid that trap.

1.5 THE CASE FOR REFORM

The picture that the financial system presents us with is not black and white, but rather complex, both from a descriptive and from a normative perspective. This explains why some forms of criticisms seem to go into different directions. For example, we may at the same time argue for more equal—for example gender-equal—access to certain markets, while also criticizing their function from a broader perspective and demand changes in their overall structure.

What seems clear is that leaving the financial system simply as it is would be a bad idea; in fact, there have been numerous proposals for reform, some of which have also been realized in new laws or regulation. For example, higher capital ratios for banks have been proposed (see especially Admati and Hellwig 2013), and reforms in bonus structures have been suggested and in some places implemented. Other new regulation concerns transparency requirements, as well as the various safety mechanisms put in place in the Eurozone in order to stabilize its banking system. Usually, these reforms have been proposed from an economic perspective; political philosophy can endorse some of them, but would want to go further in many cases, based on considerations not only of efficiency and stability, but also of justice. And political philosophy can add reflections on what *kind* of changes are required from a perspective of justice.

After the Great Financial Crisis, the focus of such reform efforts has been on legal regulation: changes in the rules and regulations that govern the financial system. While doubtlessly important, however, one wonders whether such changes in the legal regulation are sufficient, or whether they need to be accompanied by changes in the ethos and the culture of financial markets. In a system as complex as today's financial system, governance by rules requires getting the incentives right, which is no easy task.[20] Rules are, by definition, rather rigid and may not be ideal as the only tool for regulating a wide variety of cases; if circumstances change quickly, rules may become outdated and those setting them may have trouble catching up. Rules need to be applied to concrete cases, which can require some degree of judgment

[20] Some therefore argue that this very complexity should be reduced as far as possible, for example by using simple heuristics instead of complex indicators that can easily be manipulated (e.g. Haldane 2012). Rules that are simple and easy to understand and apply might avoid many of the disadvantages of existing rules.

and a joint understanding of the practices they are supposed to regulate. And last but not least: the control of whether rules are obeyed is time-consuming and costly.

These various factors imply that it is highly desirable that complex systems be regulated not exclusively by rules but also by a joint ethos of those who participate in the systems. In an ideal financial system, one would want market participants to cooperate with regulators on how to best set rules, voluntarily to forgo opportunities of making profit by using loopholes, and to build a culture of co-responsibility for the functioning of the system as a whole. One would want them to develop a professional ethos that embodies an orientation towards the standards implicit in the practices they are active in, whether they are allocating capital, hedging risks, or advising customers (see also van de Ven 2011). One would want them to organize themselves in professional bodies in which they can discuss, and reinforce, ethical norms; such professional bodies might also take on legal liability for certain kinds of risks or harms. One would want them jointly to build and maintain an ethos that is appropriate to the responsibility of an industry that plays a crucial role in modern capitalist societies.

But such an ethos is an elusive affair, and it is anything but clear how it could be implemented in a social sphere that, arguably, had a very different ethos. Awrey et al. (2013) have discussed how the idea of "process-oriented regulation" might help to design concrete steps that would improve ethical standards in the financial industry. Based on the UK's "Treat Customers Fairly" initiative they suggest that similar models—which focus on dialogue, "tone from the top," board-level ethics committees, internal controls, and changes in behavioral norms—could also help to improve the behavior vis-à-vis counterparties and to reduce "socially excessive risk-taking." This would mean that financial companies would be expected to internalize some of the tasks of regulation, and would not be allowed to externalize the negative effects of their actions any more.

Concerning the *aims* of regulation, one can distinguish between specific and integrated approaches.[21] Specific approaches suggest specific measures for addressing specific issues; often, the assumption behind them is that it is useful to have a division of labor between different institutions that are responsible for different tasks. When it comes to markets, this often corresponds to the line mentioned on pp. 4–5, which holds that markets should be made efficient, and regulation concerning justice should take place through

[21] The following considerations concern a more concrete level than that typically considered in "theories of justice." Thus, different theories of justice can have different positions on how, for example, to integrate considerations of efficiency into an account of justice, or how to make trade-offs between different values or principles more generally speaking. They might then *also* differ—or in fact agree—on whether to realize the resulting account of justice in a way that assigns specific tasks to specific institutions or in an integrated way.

other institutions, whether taxation or the welfare state. Such approaches might suggest new institutions in order to address social issues that current institutions do not address. A case in point is Baradaran's proposal to revive postal banking in the US (2015). It is based on an analysis of how current financial markets exclude poorer parts of the population, and on skepticism concerning the possibility of forcing profit-oriented banks to serve the needs of poor clients. Hence, it does not focus on the structures of existing financial markets—although it is quite clear from Baradaran's text that she would welcome changes there as well—but suggests a new solution to a problem that current institutions fail to solve.

Integrated approaches to regulation focus on the interconnectedness of institutions and try to inscribe broader objectives into existing institutions. For example, they might propose regulation for markets that aims not only at maximum efficiency but tries to incorporate considerations of distributive justice as well. This might involve the prevention of certain kinds of market transactions that tend to reinforce inequality (even if they might be Pareto-efficient), or the redesign of existing institutions in ways that better realize normative goals such as the prevention of poverty and the reduction of inequality. For example, Mian and Sufi (2014) argue that the way in which mortgages currently work means that too much risk—notably, the risk of large price swings in real estate markets—ends up on the shoulders of those who are least able to carry it, namely private households. This, they argue, means that when prices in real estate markets fall, these households will cut back their consumption, leading to a slump in overall demand that reinforces the recession. To address this problem, they discuss the possibility of "shared-risk mortgages," in which debtors are somewhat shielded from this risk because payment plans are tied to the local house price index, in exchange for sharing some of the future capital gains with creditors (Mian and Sufi 2015, chap. 12). This proposal is very ambitious, in the sense that it suggests a change at the heart of the legal infrastructure on which certain financial markets are based.

There is no a priori reason for favoring specific or integrated approaches; all depends on which problems one tries to address—and, to be sure, creating additional, specific institutions can also have implications for how existing institutions work, for example because customers now have alternatives and can opt out of existing institutions, which means that the boundary between the two categories can be blurred. Creating specific institutions may seem less risky in the sense that it does not involve quite as many "unknowns" concerning the reaction of a complex system to changes in its core, but it may also appear as a rather helpless second-best that tries to put band aids on wounds that require surgery. Integrated proposals have the potential to be more far-reaching, but might also be more difficult to push through because they impact the vested interests of those benefitting from the current system.

If there is one thing to be learned from the Great Financial Crisis and the regulation (or lack thereof) that preceded it, it is the importance that seemingly technical details, whether in the design of regulation or the use of indicators, can have for the working of the system as a whole. No wonder that such details are the target of intense lobbying by banks and other financial institutions that have to gain or lose from changes.

Although there are certainly many important theoretical questions to be asked about how to regulate better financial markets, the elephant in the room is the question of whether politicians and regulators are actually willing to make the changes that would be required to really improve the situation—or whether the financial industry is successful in resisting real change and can get away with what are, in the final analysis, only cosmetic changes. This is, in the end, a question of power. Much has been written about the problem of lobbyism and the influence of money in politics (e.g. Hacker and Pearson 2010, Gilens 2013, Reich 2015). This issue is, of course, much broader and more fundamental than its implications for the regulation of financial markets. But the latter is a place where the implications of this problem become particularly visible. Another problem is the international dimension of financial markets, which would, ideally, call for an internationally coordinated effort at regulation. Indeed, financial stability has been conceptualized as a global public good (Kaul et al. 1999; see also Emunds 2014, 272ff. for a discussion), with incentives for individual countries to free-ride on the regulatory efforts of others. The problems of the international dimension also raise additional questions of justice—concerning *global* justice, which theorists of justice have just started to explore; these concern not only the structure of international taxation and the legitimacy of international financial flows, but also the governance of institutions such as the International Monetary Fund or the World Bank (see e.g. Wollner 2014, Emunds 2014, Krishnamurthy 2014). These questions are not discussed explicitly in this volume, but some of the chapters have implications for them as well.

1.6 SUMMARY OF CHAPTERS

As an edited volume, this book reflects the views of its different authors who often, but not always, agree about the problems of justice raised by today's financial markets. The three parts cover different deficits and failures concerning the justice of financial markets. The first part discusses what one might call "conceptual failures": failures to use sufficiently broad and nuanced normative frameworks for thinking about justice and financial markets. What unites the chapters in this part—and, in fact, also many of the other chapters—is the rejection of a simplistic free market approach to finance, and a broadening of the perspective from a purely economic to a philosophical-cum-economic one. From such a perspective, we can ask questions about financial markets that go beyond the perspective taken by—even very sophisticated—economists: How do they relate to human rights? Do they support individuals in exercising their capabilities? What is their function in society? Can we assume that incomes in them are deserved, as some economists have claimed?

The second set of chapters looks at the legal framework within which financial markets take place, and analyzes various ways in which this framework is unjustly biased. Such biases can be found both in the legal infrastructures that hold individuals and companies accountable for wrongdoing and excessive risk-taking, and in the underlying system of rights that makes financial markets as we know them possible in the first place.

The third part combines chapters that look at *specific* institutions and practices and their impact on various dimensions of justice—whether distributive justice, epistemic dimensions of justice, or gender justice. These analyses are what economists would call "partial analyses," in the sense that they look at specific institutions or practices from specific perspectives. Even if we could change the general conceptual take on financial markets, and correct the fundamental biases in their legal infrastructure, the questions raised by these chapters would remain open. One important question in this context, addressed by the last chapter, is how the current set of institutions and practices—including mental habits and vested interests—stands in the way of change.

1.6.1 Part I: Normative foundations

Rosa M. Lastra and Alan H. Brener, in Chapter 2, "Justice, financial markets, and human rights," focus on the necessity for social institutions to gain and maintain legitimacy. One source of legitimacy, on a national and international level, is compliance with the human rights frameworks that have been developed after World War II. Lastra and Brener trace some aspects of the history of human rights thinking, notably in the "School of Salamanca," emphasizing the parallels with the development of both conceptions and practices of markets. To gain legitimacy, markets need to remain within a framework of justice, and this can require careful trade-offs and compromises, as the authors show by briefly discussing some of the complexities of payday lending regulation. On an international scale, the United Nations' "Guiding principles on foreign debt and human rights" can be seen as an example of how the gap that has opened between market thinking and market practice and human rights could be closed. Lastra and Brener conclude that only if the compatibility of financial markets with human rights will be secured, financial markets can regain legitimacy and social trust.

Rutger Claassen suggests a unified approach for evaluating and regulating markets, including financial markets, in Chapter 3, "A capability framework for financial market regulation." Reviewing the mainstream approaches to market regulation, he concludes that they separate economic considerations that aim at Pareto-efficiency from social considerations that aim at paternalist protection and distributive justice. This means that no guidance can be provided when these different aims are in conflict. Claassen suggests shifting to a different paradigm: the capability approach developed by Amartya Sen and Martha Nussbaum. Applying this approach to questions of market regulation, Claassen distinguishes participatory capabilities, consumer capabilities, and third-party capabilities. He closes by showing how this approach throws light on three issues discussed by other contributors to this volume: de Bruin's suggestions for how to think about the role of rating agencies, Russell and Villiers's discussion of gender justice in financial markets, and Admati's analysis of failures of reform.

Seumas Miller, in Chapter 4, "Financial markets and institutional purposes: The normative issues," provides a different, but arguably not incompatible, normative account of financial markets: a "teleological" account. Rejecting approaches such as Shareholder Theory and Corporate Social Responsibility theories, Miller argues for taking the *purpose* of institutions seriously when thinking about their proper regulation. Institutions are supposed to provide collective goods for a society. This teleological perspective leads to a number of questions: about the institutional purpose of specific institutions, the formal and informal institutional means for achieving them, and the wider macro-institutional context within which they operate. Miller applies this account to three segments of the financial system: the banking sector, retirements saving schemes, and capital markets. The resulting arguments and calls for reform are intuitively plausible—so much so that one wonders whether some commentators have instinctively been guided by an account similar to Miller's teleological account. Another possibility is that this account converges with other accounts when it comes to practical recommendations. Miller's perspective challenges us to revise traditional notions of how to think about institutions in general, and financial markets in particular.

In Chapter 5, "Can incomes in financial markets be deserved? A justice-based critique," I take up a notion frequently heard in public criticisms of financial markets: that the high incomes generated in them cannot possibly be deserved. In contrast, some economists have used the notion of desert in order to *defend* high incomes. Drawing on the philosophical debate about desert, I defend a modest, institutional notion of desert and apply it to financial markets. Doing so directs our attention to the institutional rules within which markets take place, and which determines whether they are "Mandevillian"—in the sense of rewarding vicious behavior—or "Smithian"—in the sense of rewarding socially useful, if somewhat mundane, forms of behavior.

Modern financial markets, especially in their pre-Crisis form, failed to live up to the idea that the rules of markets should be designed such that they fulfil their role in society and that rewards should go to those who play by the rules. Instead, they were, and arguably still are, marred by problems of market failure and externalities; they are neither efficient nor do they reward desert on any defensible notion of the term. Hence, economists and philosophers can agree on many of the flaws of the financial system that generated undeserved high incomes, and jointly push for reform.

1.6.2 Part II: Legal structures

The next two chapters deal with legal questions that concern the enforcement of law and their impact on the justice of financial markets. Mark R. Reiff, in Chapter 6, "Punishment in the executive suite: Moral responsibility, causal responsibility, and financial crime," argues for a thorough rethinking of the way in which criminal justice in financial markets works. Many debates about justice do not discuss criminal justice, but simply presuppose that once certain rules have been determined and agreed upon, it will be possible to enforce them through law. The Great Financial Crisis throws some doubt upon this assumption: despite some outrageous forms of wrongdoing—at least some of which were also illegal by existing standards—very few individuals went to prison. Enormous fines have been imposed on financial companies, but it is doubtful whether they can serve as a sufficient deterrent that would elicit more responsible business practices in the future. Reiff argues that our traditional ways of thinking about knowledge and intent as a precondition for a criminal conviction is too limited. Instead, he suggests a morally loaded conception of causal responsibility, which needs to be established on a case-by-case basis, depending on the concrete responsibilities of corporate officers. Reiff's discussion suggests that the imposition of terms of imprisonment can be legally and morally justified in a far greater number of cases than the prosecution currently seems to assume.

Jay Cullen takes on questions of legal accountability from a different angle. The central question of Chapter 7, "A culture beyond repair? The nexus between ethics and sanctions in finance," is how sanctions could be designed such that they create a culture in which socially excessive risk-taking is reduced. Cullen argues that banks are special in certain ways: they receive implicit public subsidies and insurance because of their "too big to fail" characteristics, and there are also numerous asymmetries of knowledge and conflicts of interest in banking that are hard to regulate. This limits the effectiveness of self-regulation, which is why questions of culture and ethics as alternative ways of regulating behavior come to the fore. But the character of modern financial markets with anonymous, IT-based interaction makes it difficult to find an anchor for an ethics of responsibility. Cullen therefore suggests taking a closer look at the relation between ethics and sanctions, emphasizing the role of the latter for creating accountability, a key component of the former. He describes the UK's new "Senior Managers' Regime" as a promising approach that could help to bring about a change in the fundamental assumptions that drive the culture of financial markets.

In contrast to Reiff, Cullen prefers an approach to legal justice in financial markets that relies mostly on civil law, quoting both systematic and pragmatic reasons for doing so. He is more optimistic than Reiff that monetary sanctions could be effective, and less optimistic about how criminal law could be used in the context of financial markets. Both agree, however, that individual liability needs to be strengthened. Both also emphasize the importance of sanctioning not only *actions*, but also *omissions*, specifically failures by managers to understand and properly supervise the behavior of their team members. This points to the problem of epistemic responsibility in financial markets, which de Bruin also discusses in Chapter 11.

Katharina Pistor opens up a road rarely traveled by political philosophers, but therefore all the more interesting for them: questions of justice that lie at the very core of the social ontology of finance, namely the legal construction of money. In her "legal theory of finance" (2013), Pistor has developed an intriguing account of how finance is legally constructed. In Chapter 8, "Moneys' legal hierarchy," Pistor pursues this line further and explores the unequal treatment that these legal structures imply for market participants at the "apex" and at the "periphery" of financial markets. As the historical development of means of payments shows, financial markets, despite a rhetoric to the contrary, are anything but a "level playing field," because the legal claims on which they are built are of different strengths. Pistor thus challenges the view that whereas firms are hierarchical, markets consist of horizontal relationships. The legal claims on which they are built include not only the structures of payment systems, but also trust law and corporate law, which can serve to insulate assets from legal claims. Pistor ends by pointing out one of the main obstacles to creating a more impartial system: government finance, which makes governments dependent on private money creation. This theoretical approach helps us to understand the legal and hence structural injustices of the current financial system at a fundamental level. The questions raised by those structures are no legal technicalities, but political questions that concern both the control of hierarchies and their distributional consequences.

Aaron James, in Chapter 9, "Investor rights as nonsense—on stilts," challenges a legal practice that has become widespread in recent years: the use of bilateral or multilateral investment treatises that provide special protection to international investors. Today's financial markets are perhaps *the* most globalized institution (maybe in a tie with organized crime). Hence, the legal apparatus that undergirds them is of utmost importance for questions of global justice. Investment treatises give foreign investors—whether they invest in physical or financial capital—the right to sue governments in front of special arbitration tribunals. James dissects the arguments that seem to support such treatises: neither consequentialist nor social contract arguments can justify the robust rights that they give to investors. Drawing on his practice-dependent account of international trade, James argues that these rights are based on a misunderstanding of the social practice in which international financial flows are embedded. This is an instance of how the rights of participants in financial markets can be distorted, and questions of structural justice arise: these markets are no level playing fields, but rather privilege certain parties. Exposing the flawed arguments and undermining the narratives brought forward in support of these legal structures is a first step toward change.

1.6.3 Part III: Institutions and practices

The first two chapters of the third part look at two specific institutions, central banks and rating agencies, from a perspective of justice. With the question raised in Chapter 10, "Normative dimensions of central banking: How the guardians of financial markets affect justice," Peter Dietsch breaks what seems to have been a taboo: he discusses monetary policy not from a technical perspective, but from a perspective of distributive justice and legitimacy. Central banks play a crucial role at the interface of public policy and financial markets. Dietsch provides an overview of monetary policies, distinguishing conventional from unconventional measures. The latter, which include so-called "quantitative easing," have been chosen by many central banks after the Great Financial Crisis in an attempt to kick-start the economy. But there is evidence that these unconventional policies have increased inequality, which is problematic from a number of theories of (distributive) justice. With regard to legitimacy, Dietsch discusses how the reactions of financial markets have become a powerful force that can influence monetary policies. This is problematic not only because it gives capital undue leverage on policy-making, but also because the economic self-determination of countries can be undermined.

Boudewijn de Bruin, in Chapter 11, "Information as a condition of justice in financial markets: The regulation of credit-rating agencies," discusses an important dimension of justice in financial markets: the epistemic dimension. In the past, important epistemic tasks in financial markets were "outsourced" to credit agencies. When these agencies failed to accurately rate the risks of complex structured financial products, they were criticized not only on economic, but also on ethical grounds. De Bruin points out, however, that the origins of the problem lie in the fact that states started to consider ratings as official stamps of approval on tradeable assets and drew on them in the regulation of financial companies. Drawing on minimal assumptions about the justice of markets, de Bruin argues that rather than attempting to "regulate away" problems such as oligopolistic power and conflicts of interest, policy-makers should undertake steps that bring epistemic responsibilities back to where they belong in the financial system. The responsibility for evaluating the risks of different financial products must be carried by those who trade them. The added value of rating agencies does not justify a legal endorsement of their judgments. This argument runs counter to the instinctive reaction many theorists of justice have to problems in markets, namely to think about *more* regulation. With regard to the epistemic dimensions of financial markets, a high degree of regulation in the wrong place—where it would allow outsourcing epistemic responsibilities—was part of the problem, not the solution, de Bruin argues. While this conclusion may appear radical to some, it receives support from the fact that financial markets are not markets in which normal goods are traded; rather, many trades express different estimations about the future and the likelihood of certain economic outcomes. The task of processes information is subverted if epistemic responsibilities are outsourced to other institutions.

The last two chapters discuss not specific institutions but specific practices, or dimensions of practices, in today's financial markets. In Chapter 12, "Gender justice in financial markets," Roseanne Russell and Charlotte Villiers explore a question of justice that is independent from, but arguably no less urgent than, the questions of justice discussed so far: gender justice. The dominance of the male gender in financial markets—and in the boardrooms of corporations in general—has not gone unnoticed. There have been various initiatives for empowering women, but they have often been based not on considerations of human rights or gender justice but rather on arguments from "diversity" or the "business case" for including women. These arguments, Russell and Villiers show, lack a secure foundation. But it is not necessary to resort to them in order to argue for the fair representation of women and other minorities in the corporate world and in financial markets. The authors call for more sincerity in the debate, and for recognizing that current calls for more female participation are often instrumentalist; instead of challenging existing power structures, they target privileged women who can afford to outsource care work to less privileged ones. As an alternative, Russell and Villiers suggest a greater emphasis on a form of feminism that includes considerations of social justice from the start, overcomes an individualistic mindset, and builds on loyalty with other groups in order to attain sustainable, structural change.

Anat R. Admati's concluding chapter, "It takes a village to maintain a dangerous financial system" (Chapter 13), addresses a question that many members of the general public have probably asked themselves after the Great Financial Crisis: which steps will regulators and politicians take, and will they be sufficient? Based on her earlier work (notably Admati and Hellwig 2013), Admati argues that the regulatory steps taken so far are insufficient to address the inherent instability of the financial system, which has to do with the low equity ratios of banks. She compares the financial system to aviation: in aviation, "it takes a village" to make sure that passenger and crew members will arrive safely. In finance, however, it is the collaboration of many actors that does the opposite: keep in place a system that is inherently unstable and that relies on being bailed out by the public if necessary, whereas profits are reaped privately, which makes it deeply unjust. Admati analyzes the confluence of ignorance, confusion, willful blindness, and lack of accountability that keep the current system in place. There are numerous conflicts of interest that keep those who should know better, including many academics, from explaining basic problems and mechanisms to the public. One can only hope that Admati's gloomy analysis will one day become obsolete. As she points out, similar phenomena could be observed when other industries, for example the tobacco industry, faced public criticism. Change is possible, but it also "takes a village" to bring it about.

1.7 CONCLUSION

Today's financial markets fail to be just in many ways. They continue to be based on an overly optimistic view of free markets and their self-regulating features. They thereby fail to fulfil the functions they are supposed to fulfil in a just society, whether these are captured in terms of human rights or capabilities. Their legal framework has not only too many loopholes, but also a general bias in favor of powerful players, which distorts their distributive outcomes. Many specific institutions and practices fail to be just along a number of dimensions, including gender justice, but powerful interest groups and powerful social and psychological mechanisms concur to prevent substantial change.

Paul Volcker, ex-Chairman of the Federal Reserve, said in 2009 that "The only useful thing banks have invented in 20 years is the ATM" (New York Post 2009). This may be an exaggeration, but the message is clear: not all financial "innovations" are socially useful and worth endorsing. Finance is, after all, an *instrument* for doing other things, and whereas trade in goods and services can generate "gains from trade" by bringing together individuals with different preferences and skills, much financial trade is, in Turner's words, "driven by differences in expectations, reflecting either different analysis or different sources of information" (2016, 43). In the final analysis, the value of financial trading—whether through "price discovery," the allocation of capital and risk, or the provision of liquidity—stems from its ability to help the real economy become more efficient; all else is a zero-sum game (Turner 2016, 105). Financial markets need to be refocused towards their role in the real economy, and their relation to justice needs to be evaluated with this role in mind.

Maybe there can be a future world in which theories of justice do not have to deal with financial markets—because they are functioning smoothly, contained by policies that regulate inequality and secure justice in our societies. Theorists of justice do not, after all, write about the details of traffic regulation or the design of water supply and sewage systems, which are also public tasks, in which the well-being of individuals is at stake, and which have distributive dimensions. But many societies have found ways of regulating them reasonably well, so that we do not have to pay special attention to them from a perspective of justice; exceptions, such as the scandal around the contamination of drinking water in Flint, Michigan, confirm the rule.[22] In many countries, one cannot earn huge fortunes in the provision of such services—again, exceptions confirm the rule—and it is not clear a priori why it should be different in finance. It may be advisable for a society to reward genuinely socially useful innovations, but it is unclear whether finance is the first and foremost area where we should look for such innovations—they are likely to be more required in other areas, for example with regard to technical innovations that make our economy more climate friendly.

Keynes, in his 1930 essay on "Economic Possibilities for Our Grandchildren," expressed the hope that one day, economic problems would become simple, technical problems, to be dealt with by "humble, competent people, on a level with dentists" (Keynes 1963, 373). Economists had thought that they had understood financial markets well enough to leave them to technical experts—and have failed spectacularly in doing so, thereby raising all the questions of justice discussed in this volume. But we should not give up the hope that it might be possible, with a deeper understanding of the economic phenomena and their normative dimensions, to arrive at better regulation, better practices, and a stronger moral ethos of financial markets, that would indeed make them more similar to an area of public infrastructure than to the juggernauts they have become. After the Great Financial Crisis, Paul Krugman called for "making banking boring" (2009b). We should indeed aim at making financial markets boring—ideally, they are boring, and are no obstacle to justice. In other words: just financial markets are probably those financial markets that are just—i.e. nothing but—financial markets.[23]

[22] See https://en.wikipedia.org/wiki/Flint_water_crisis%20for%20an%20overview.

[23] I would like to thank Mark Reiff, Tom Parr, and Gabriel Schor for valuable comments on earlier drafts.

REFERENCES

Admati, Anat, and Martin Hellwig. 2013. *The Bankers' New Clothes: What's Wrong with Banking and What to Do about It*. Princeton and Oxford: Princeton University Press.

Akerlof, George A., and Robert J. Shiller. 2009. *Animal Spirits: How Human Psychology Drives the Economy, and Why It Matters for Global Capitalism*. Princeton and Oxford: Princeton University Press.

Akerlof, George A., and Robert J. Shiller. 2015. *Phishing for Phools: The Economics of Manipulation and Deception*. Princeton and Oxford: Princeton University Press.

Amato, Massimo, and Luca Fantacci. 2012. *The End of Finance*. Cambridge: Polity Press.

Anderson, Elizabeth. 1992. *Values in Ethics and Economics*. Cambridge, MA: Harvard University Press.

Awrey, Dan, William Blair, and David Kershaw. 2013. "Between Law and Markets: Is There a Role for Culture and Ethics in Financial Regulation?" *Delaware Journal of Corporate Law* 191, and http://at%20papers.ssrn.com/sol3/paers.cfm?abstract_id=2157588.

Baradaran, Mehrsa. 2015. *How the Other Half Banks: Exclusion, Exploitation, and the Threat to Democracy*. Cambridge, MA and London: Harvard University Press.

Black, Fischer, and Myron Scholes. 1973. "The Pricing of Options and Corporate Liabilities." *Journal of Political Economy* 81(3), 637–54.

Boatright, John, ed. 2010. *Finance Ethics: Critical Issues in Theory and Practice*. Chichester: Wiley-Blackwell.

Boatright, John. 2014. *Ethics in Finance*, 3rd edition. Chichester: Wiley-Blackwell.

Bowles, Samuel. 1991. "What Markets Can and Cannot Do." *Challenge* 34(4), 11–16.

Breuer, Rolf-E. 2000. "Die fünfte Gewalt." *Die Zeit*, April 27. http://www.zeit.de/2000/18/200018.5._gewalt_.xml/komplettansicht.

Cassidy, John. 2010. "Interview with Eugene Fama." *The New Yorker*, January 13. http://www.newyorker.com/news/john-cassidy/interview-with-eugene-fama.

Ciepley, David. 2013. "Beyond Public and Private: Toward a Political Theory of the Corporation." *American Political Science Review* 107(1), 139–58.

Cohen, G. A. 1997. "Where the Action Is: On the Site of Distributive Justice." *Philosophy and Public Affairs* 26(1), 3–30.

Dash, Mike. 2001. *Tulipomania: The Story of the World's Most Coveted Flower and the Extraordinary Passions It Aroused*. New York: Broadway Books.

De Bruin, Boudewijn. 2015. *Ethics and the Global Financial Crisis: Why Incompetence is Worse than Greed*. Cambridge: Cambridge University Press.

Dietsch, Peter. 2010. "The Market, Competition, and Equality." *Politics, Philosophy and Economics* 9(2), 213–44.

Dobos, Ned, Christian Barry, and Thomas Pogge, eds. 2011. *The Global Financial Crisis: The Ethical Issues*. Basingstoke: Palgrave Macmillan.

Douglas, Alexander X. 2016. *The Philosophy of Debt*. London: Routledge.

Econtalk. 2013. "Cathy O'Neil on Wall St and Occupy Wall Street." February 11. http://www.econtalk.org/archives/2013/02/cathy_oneil_on.html.

Emunds, Bernhard. 2014. *Politische Wirtschaftsethik globaler Finanzmärkte*. Wiesbaden: Springer Gabler.

Fama, Eugene. 1970. "Efficient Capital Markets: A Review of Theory and Empirical Work." *Journal of Finance* 25(2), 383–417.

Felber, Christian. 2014. *Geld. Die neuen Spielregeln*. Vienna: Deuticke Verlag.

Financial Review. 2015. "Warren Buffett Still Says Derivatives Are 'Weapons of Mass Destruction'." June 17. http://www.afr.com/markets/derivatives/warren-buffett-still-says-derivatives-are-weapons-of-mass-destruction-20150617-ghpw0a.

Gilens, Martin. 2013. *Affluence and Influence: Economic Inequality and Political Power in America*. Princeton: Princeton University Press.

Graafland, Johan, and Bert van de Ven. 2011. "The Credit Crisis and the Moral Responsibility of Professionals in Finance." *Journal of Business Ethics* 103: 605–19.

Grossman, Sanford J., and Joseph E. Stiglitz. 1980. "On the Impossibility of Informationally Efficient Markets." *The American Economic Review* 70(3), 393–408.

Hacker, Jacob S., and Paul Pearson. 2010. *Winner-Take-All Politics: How Washington Made the Rich Richer—and Turned Its Back on the Middle Class*. New York: Simon & Schuster.

Haldane, Andrew G. 2012. "The Dog and the Frisbee." Speech at the Federal Reserve Bank of Kansas City's 366th economic policy symposium, "The Changing Policy Landscape," Jackson Hole, Wyoming, August 31. http://www.bis.org/review/r120905a.pdf.

Heath, Joseph. 2014. *Morality, Competition, and the Firm: The Market Failures Approach to Business Ethics*. Oxford: Oxford University Press.

Heath, Joseph, Jeffrey Moriarty, and Wayne Norman. 2010. "Business Ethics and (or as) Political Philosophy." *Business Ethics Quarterly* 20(3), 427–52.

Hendry, John. 2013. *Ethics and Finance: An Introduction*. Cambridge: Cambridge University Press.

Herzog, Lisa. 2013. "Markets." In *The Stanford Encyclopedia of Philosophy* (Fall 2013 edition), edited by Edward N. Zalta. http://plato.stanford.edu/archives/fall2013/entries/markets/.

Herzog, Lisa, Edgar Hirschmann, and Sarah Lenz. 2015. "'Ethische Banken'—Nische oder Avantgarde?" *WestEnd. Neue Zeitschrift für Sozialforschung* (1), 85–94.

James, Aaron. 2012. *Fairness in Practice*. New York and Oxford: Oxford University Press.

Johnson, N., G. Zhao, E. Hunsader, H. Qi, N. Johnson, J. Meng, and B. Tivnan. 2013. "Abrupt Rise of New Machine Ecology beyond Human Response Time." *Nature Scientific Reports* 3, 2627. http://www.nature.com/articles/srep02627.

Kaul, Inge, Isabelle Grunberg, and Marc Stern, eds. 1999. *Global Public Goods: International Cooperation in the 21st Century*. Oxford: Oxford University Press.

Keynes, John M. 1936. *The General Theory of Employment, Interest and Money*. London: Macmillan.

Keynes, John M. 1963. *Essays in Persuasion*. New York: W. W. Norton & Co.

Kindleberger, Charles P., and Robert Z. Aliber. 2005. *Manias, Panics and Crashes: A History of Financial Crises* edition. Hoboken, NJ: Wiley.

Knight, Frank. 2006 [1921]. *Risk, Uncertainty, and Profits*. Mineola: Dover Publications.

Koslowski, Peter. 2011. *The Ethics of Banking: Conclusions from the Financial Crisis*. Dordrecht: Springer.

Krishnamurthy, Meena. 2014. "International Financial Institutions." In *The Routledge Handbook of Global Ethics*, edited by Darrel Moellendorf and Heather Widdows. London and New York: Routledge, 230–50.

Krugman, Paul. 2009a. "How Did Economists Get It So Wrong?" *New York Times*, September 2.

Krugman, Paul. 2009b. "Making Banking Boring." *New York Times*, April 9.

Le Grand, Julian. 1990. "Equity Versus Efficiency: The Elusive Trade-Off." *Ethics* 100(3), 554–68.

Levine, Ross. 2005. "Finance and Growth: Theory and Evidence." In *Handbook of Economic Growth*, edited by P. Aghion and S. Durlauf (North Holland: Elsevier), volume IB, pp. 865–934.

Lomansky, L. E. 2011. "Liberty after Lehman Brothers." *Social Philosophy and Policy* 28(2), 135–65.

MacKenzie, Donald. 2006. *An Engine, Not a Camera: How Financial Models Shape Markets*. Cambridge, MA: Harvard University Press.

Mian, Atif, and Amir Sufi. 2014. *House of Debt*. Chicago: University of Chicago Press.

Minsky, Hyman P. 1986. *Stabilizing an Unstable Economy*. New Haven and London: Yale University Press.

Mullainathan, Sendhil. 2015. "Why a Harvard Professor Has Mixed Feelings When Students Take Jobs in Finance." *New York Times*, April 10.

New York Post. 2009. "The Only Useful Thing Banks Have Invented in 20 Years is the ATM." December 13. http://nypost.com/2009/12/13/the-only-thing-useful-banks-have-invented-in-20-years-is-the-atm/.

Nielsen, Richard. 2010. "High-Leverage Finance Capitalism, the Economic Crisis, Structurally Related Ethics Issues, and Potential Reforms." *Business Ethics Quarterly* 20(2), 299–330.

Nowak, Alojzy, and Patrick O'Sullivan. 2012. "Ethical Issues in the Policy Response to the 2008 Financial Crisis: Moral Hazard in Central Banking and the Equity of Bailout." In *Business Ethics: A Critical Approach: Integrating Ethics Across the Business World*, edited by Patrick O'Sullivan, Mark Smith, and Mark Esposito. London: Routledge, 147–66.

Okun, Arthur M. 1975. *Equality and Efficiency: The Big Tradeoff*. Washington: Brookings Institution Press.

Piketty, Thomas. 2014. *Capital in the 21st Century*. Cambridge, MA: Belknap Press.

Pistor, Katharina. 2013. "A Legal Theory of Finance." *Journal of Comparative Economics* 41(2), 315–30.

Reich, Robert B. 2015. *Saving Capitalism: For the Many, Not the Few*. New York: Alfred A. Knopf.

Reiff, Mark R. 2013. *Exploitation and Economic Justice in the Liberal Capitalist State*. Oxford: Oxford University Press.

Reinhart, Carmen M., and Kenneth S. Rogoff. 2009. *This Time Is Different: Eight Centuries of Financial Folly*. Princeton: Princeton University Press.

Roemer, John. 2012. "Ideology, Social Ethos, and the Financial Crisis." *Journal of Ethics* 41(2), 315–30.

Sandel, Michael J. 2012. *What Money Can't Buy: The Moral Limits of Markets*. New York: Farrar Straus Giroux.

Satz, Debra. 2010. *Why Some Things Should Not Be for Sale: The Moral Limits of Markets.* Oxford: Oxford University Press.

Shiller, Robert J. 2000. *Irrational Exuberance.* Princeton and Oxford: Princeton University Press.

Shiller, Robert J. 2007. "Bubble Trouble." *Project Syndicate*, September 17. https://www.project-syndicate.org/commentary/bubble-trouble?barrier=true.

Shiller, Robert J. 2012. *Finance and the Good Society.* Princeton and Oxford: Princeton University Press.

Sorrel, Tom, and Luis Cabrera, Luis, eds. 2015. *Microfinance, Rights, and Global Justice.* Cambridge: Cambridge University Press.

Turner, Adair. 2016. *Between Debt and the Devil: Money, Credit, and Fixing Global Finance.* Princeton and Oxford: Princeton University Press.

van de Ven, Bert. 2011. "Banking after the Crisis: Towards an Understanding of Banking as a Professional Practice." *Ethical Perspectives* 18(4), 541–68.

Wall Street Journal. 2009. "Goldman Sachs' Blankfein on Banking: 'Doing God's Work'." November 9. http://blogs.wsj.com/marketbeat/2009/11/09/goldman-sachs-blankfein-on-banking-doing-gods-work/.

Wollner, Gabriel. 2014. "Justice in Finance: The Normative Case for an International Financial Transactions Tax." *Journal of Political Philosophy* 22(4), 458–85.

Part I

Normative Foundations

2

Justice, financial markets, and human rights

Rosa M. Lastra and Alan H. Brener

2.1 INTRODUCTION

In the wake of the Great Financial Crisis there has been a plethora of both "hard" and "soft" rules ranging from the Financial Stability Board recommendations on cross-border resolution (an example of "top down" soft law rule) to the EU Capital Requirement Directive (an example of "top down" hard law rule) as well as revised codes of practice, such as those promulgated by the International Swaps and Derivatives Association, ISDA (an example of "bottom up" soft law rule). There is a risk, however, that in drafting these rules and codes experts may view their work as solely a technical task, correcting some market malfunction or increasing financial resilience.

Instead, this chapter puts forward the view that the process of preparing and implementing both hard and soft law needs to be grounded in establishing, or re-establishing, the legitimacy of financial markets and the institutions which operate in and govern these areas. None exists in a vacuum; all should have a social purpose. As John Rawls says, "How men work together to satisfy their present [economic] desires... affects the kind of person they will be... Choice[s] must, therefore, be made on moral and political as well as economic grounds. Considerations of efficiency are but one basis for decision and often relatively minor at that" (1999, 229). Paraphrasing Grotius: there is no justice if every being seeks only to advantage themselves. Man lives in society and desires the society of others and therefore "it cannot be conceded that everyone is impelled by nature to seek only their own good" (2012 [1625], 2).

In order to exist and prosper, financial institutions and markets need to establish and maintain their legitimacy in the eyes of those they affect. Often this sense of legitimacy is founded on the legal concepts of justice and human rights buttressed by notions of ethics. This chapter also considers the consequences of a failure to acknowledge, develop, and nurture this perception of legitimacy, based on a conception of mutuality ("we are all in this together"), which may lead to societal disconnection and/or to a swing toward extremes. Consequently, both financial institutions and markets need to engage more closely with the communities they affect and explain their rationale in creating wealth in the interests of society as a whole and not merely a privileged few.

Section 2.2 presents an account of social legitimacy as based on social purpose[1] and the acceptance of self-restraint. We then discuss under what conditions financial institutions and markets are considered legitimate in the views of theorists such as Rawls and Raz, who to some degree "proceduralize" the requirements of legitimacy. We exemplify the kinds of trade-offs and institutional solutions that need to be sought from a perspective of justice by briefly discussing the issue of payday lending regulation. Not only on a national, but also on an international level, a shared basis for legitimacy are human rights, which are deeply rooted in the history of Western thought and whose development shows interesting parallels to the growth of markets. We trace some historical steps in this development, focusing on the "School of Salamanca" and the reassessment of legal positivism after World War II, which led to the creation of the modern human rights regime. But in today's world there is a gap between the acceptance of human rights as a basis for legitimacy and the way in which markets, especially financial markets, operate, breeding a sense of injustice and social distrust. We turn to the United Nations' "Guiding principles on foreign debt and human rights" as an example for how this gap could be closed, and conclude by emphasizing the need for financial markets to regain and maintain their social legitimacy.

2.2 THE SOCIAL LEGITIMACY OF INSTITUTIONS

The functions and privileges that society grants to financial institutions and markets, via the law, should not be taken for granted. It may be said that "social actions which involve relationships may be [based on] . . . a belief in the existence of a legitimate order[ing]" (Weber 1947 [1915], 124). It has been described as the acceptance of integrity in that "each citizen accepts and makes demands on others which 'extend the moral dimension' and 'fuses citizens' moral and political lives" (Dworkin 1986, 189). This implies at least the concept of reciprocity in that being a member of society and playing a role in it requires "special responsibilities of membership" based on "reciprocity" in which membership involves showing "roughly the same concerns" for other members of society (ibid., 198–201). Rather than describe it as a social

[1] On the notion of institutional purpose see also Chapter 4 by Miller in this volume.

contract in the Hobbesian sense, it may be better to view this relationship as a sense of morality which is demonstrated in how we act in relationship to others (Guest 2013, 160–2).

This morality requires a sense of self-discipline or restraint, otherwise the perceived abuse of power, whether political or economic, may undermine the whole (Dunn 1999, 324). Bracing markets and financial institutions with detailed regulations may not be sufficient. In addition, a level of moral restraint may be necessary in order to ensure that markets serve the "public good" (Sandel 2012, 14).

This means that the legitimacy of financial institutions and markets is based on their social purpose coupled with a form of "self-denying ordinance," not simply embedded in law, but rather in a sense of personal and institutional morality (O'Neill 2000, 60).[2] If the social purpose of these markets and institutions is made clear and an element of self-restraint is evident, then they may be considered to be trustworthy and their role in society accepted.[3] Without this level of trustworthiness and legitimacy all that is left is the increasing use of more coercive rules and restrictions. Section 2.3 considers how financial markets and institutions can demonstrate this social purpose based on a sense of perceived justice.

2.3 THE PURPOSE OF FINANCIAL INSTITUTIONS AND MARKETS, AND THEIR SOCIAL LEGITIMACY

St Thomas Aquinas, quoting Aristotle, describes justice as "the most distinguished virtue and neither the evening nor the morning star is so wonderful" (1918 [1485], Justice, Question 58, Twelfths Article, 134). Justice,

[2] O'Neill sees a role for institutions, other than those acting on behalf of the state, as institutionalizing justice. This could include financial markets and institutions and goes beyond law making.

[3] This is also the position of the Catholic Church. In "Caritas in Veritate" ("Charity in Truth"), Pope Benedict XVI (2009) states: the exclusively binary model of market-plus-state is corrosive of society, while economic forms based on solidarity, which find their natural home in civil society without being restricted to it, build up society. Pope Benedict calls for a new model in which the global "market-state" is re-embedded within a wider network of social relations and governed by virtues and universal principles such as justice, solidarity, fraternity, and responsibility. The dignity of the individual and the demands of justice require, particularly today, that economic choices do not cause disparities in wealth to increase in an excessive and morally unacceptable manner and that we continue to prioritize the goal of access to steady employment for everyone. All things considered, this is also required by "economic logic." Through the systemic increase of social inequality, both within a single country and between the populations of different countries (i.e. the massive increase in relative poverty), not only does social cohesion suffer, thereby placing democracy at risk, but so too does the economy, through the progressive erosion of "social capital": the network of relationships of trust, dependability, and respect for rules, all of which are indispensable for any form of civil coexistence.

and its perception, are fundamental to the establishment of a belief in the legitimacy of financial markets and institutions. For Hume justice was not some vague ideal but part of the "glue" which held society together since it is in our own self-interest to act in a way to each other perceived as just (see Penelhum 1992, 135–6). He gives, as an example, two rowers who, although they have no contractual relationship, must row to synchronize their strokes in their common interest (1978 [1738], Book III.II, 490).

However, John Rawls sees the connection between justice and markets as one of fair process (1999, 242; see also Martin 1985, 157–74 for a discussion). This is similar to the empirical findings of Tom Tyler on why people obey the criminal law.[4] As part of his views on the need for fair process Rawls sees markets as needing to have fair and open access (1999, 240ff.). However, Rawls acknowledges that markets may frustrate fairness of process and consequently, while markets are the central economic mechanism, they need to be supplemented by institutions that ensure fair access and are also aligned with his two principles of justice, especially the second one that refers to economic justice (see Martin 1985, 161). It can be summarized as holding that, first, there is equality of access to economic opportunity (e.g. to training or positions which may "generate income and wealth"), and second, inequality is only acceptable "if it improves the situation of everyone (including the least advantaged)" in that particular area where it exists (ibid., 64 and 67). It is possible to misinterpret Rawls and to see his views as providing a rationale for any form of inequality. Alternatively, the better view may be to see Rawls as recognizing that inequality inevitably exists but that in these circumstances a duty should be imposed on both the beneficiaries of this inequality and on the institutions and markets that profit from it not just to alleviate the circumstances of those who are disadvantaged, but actively to improve their position.

Rawls sees justice as closer to a contractual arrangement in the mold of Locke and others. For Rawls, justice has a social role, which is "to enable all members of society to make mutuality acceptable to one another their shared institutions and basic arrangements by citing what is publicly recognized as sufficient reasons" (1980, 540–2). This perception of justice as a mechanism for "working out" issues of conflict within a society is taken further by Joseph Raz. Raz sees it as requiring those that do not agree to all or part of these common values either to suppress their views in the interest of a higher good or, by definition, no longer to be included in this community (Raz 1986, 127). In Raz's view the more likely issues within a community are the methods and trade-offs necessary to achieve a shared view of justice; in practice, the members of the community engage in a "process of bargaining" and compromises to achieve "a less than perfect doctrine as the optimally realizable second best" (ibid., 129). The results

[4] Tyler 1990, 178; in his discussions he considers the importance of "perceptional legitimacy" as crucial in terms of individuals' acceptance and compliance with the law (see 19–30).

may be seen to be just presumably because the process is fair and seen to be so. However, justice as a series of compromises may not be acceptable since the result may not be unqualifiedly good (ibid., 129f.).

The role of payday lenders provides an example of where a balance needs to be struck and where there are limits to "black and white" judgments. These types of very high-cost lenders can be seen as immoral providers of credit to those at the bottom end of society who cannot get by without borrowing to live. They charge usurious rates of interest for small short-term loans and advertise extensively, particularly on primetime television, with enticing advertisements offering to complete the transaction within a few minutes and to provide the loan almost instantaneously. In the UK they have recently become subject to statutory regulation and the expectation is that the new regulatory requirements will put most of them out of business.[5] There has been considerable support for tough action on capping interest rates and restricting advertising (see e.g. Cooper and Purcell 2013).

The most authoritative, independent report to date in the UK was issued in 2013 based on work by a team at Bristol University led by Professor Elaine Kempson (Personal Finance Research Centre University of Bristol 2013). This report saw the need to balance restriction on payday lending with concern that

> access to credit may reduce, particularly for low income or other vulnerable consumers... Most would either go without or turn to a friend or relative for help. A small number would try and borrow from somewhere else, including from another short-term lender... going without the money they borrowed from a short-term lender would potentially mean defaulting on other financial commitments (especially household bills). (vii)

There is also a risk of some borrowers turning to illegal "loan shark" lenders. However, while payday lenders may be complying with increased regulation, it is not clear that they are acting with any sense of morality. Consequently, it behooves the wider community to help low-income borrowers find other sources of credit who share a belief in the wider sense of mutuality. A potential avenue is to develop the scope of credit unions and credit cooperatives. However, while these may wish to help, they are largely staffed by volunteers and do not have the ability to advertise or attract members on the necessary scale. This may be an area that collective communal action can address.[6] These broad

[5] See Financial Conduct Authority 2014. The then Chief Executive of the FCA said that "strict new rules on payday loans could force a quarter of lenders out of business... it will probe lenders on "how they make their money, where they make their money" and whether "they can only make their money by abusing clients".... "Within this market there are some appalling practices" (Financial Times 2014).

[6] See *Archbishop's Task Group on Responsible Credit and Savings "To Our Credit"* (2016), recommending Church community support, debt "signposting" to responsible institutions and new savings programs and clubs.

themes are taken forward in Section 2.4, which considers how financial markets apply justice in the context of human rights.

2.4 HUMAN RIGHTS AS A BASIS OF LEGITIMACY AND THEIR HISTORICAL DEVELOPMENT

In the context of financial markets and human rights, striving to do right may be seen as progress since, at least, the underlying concepts exist, even as progress toward them is made in a series of incremental steps. Financial markets are based on a series of relationships and promises that are enforced both by mutual interest and by the law. Similarly, law itself is founded on a series of understandings between individuals and the state and its agencies and is itself founded on shared values and a level of trust (see for example Arendt 1958, 243ff.). There is extensive academic literature on the relationship between the state and individuals, extending through Hobbes and Locke and onwards via Carl Schmitt and Hans Kelsen through to Ronald Dworkin. It is beyond the scope of this chapter to cover this lengthy debate.[7] However, central to this chapter is the concept of legitimacy as based on shared values that bind a community together. "Community" in this sense extends beyond the nation state.

As Hannah Arendt explains, key understandings such as those relating to human rights transcend national boundaries. Rather, "human rights become the rights of world citizens" (Volk 2015, 195ff.). In this understanding, human rights are not created by law; instead, the purpose of law is to proclaim these rights, which are broadly accepted, and to set out how they should be put into effect (Raz 2015). Michael Sandel develops this idea by saying that not only must a community have a shared understanding but, in addition, these must be "embodied in their institutional arrangements" (2012, 173).[8] It is worth looking at earlier thought on human rights that has contributed to our broader understanding of the subject matter.

The concept of human rights is, according to St Thomas Aquinas, derived from natural law with law being based on justice that includes serving the common good and sharing burdens fairly.[9] The Christian tradition of respect

[7] See for example Jacobson and Schlink 2002. See also Hayek 1973, 91–3 on "allegiance and sovereignty" and the need for laws to be consistent with "a universal rule of just conduct."

[8] See also Sandel 1998, 172–4; he views a community's shared understanding as insufficient in recognizing a right. Reform of rights may require a "challenge to prevailing practice." However, the reforming motive may "recall a community to itself" and appeal to "ideals implicit but unrealized in a community" (ibid., x–xi).

[9] Aquinas 1918 [1485], 215, Question 95, Second Article. This puts forward the proposition that it is not possible for man to be virtuous acting alone. It requires a community acting together for the common good (see also Loughlin 2010, 215).

for the individual is rooted in a belief in the sanctity of the human soul and can be traced to the biblical relationship between man and God.[10] While private law deals with the relations between individuals, or bodies with the persona of an individual, human rights are much broader and also encompass the relationship between individuals and the state. Medieval Spanish scholarship developed the concept of the juxtaposition between the rights of the individual and that of the political community (Freeman 2006, 11). These concepts are subsequently taken forward in the sixteenth and seventeenth centuries in northern Europe by, among others, Grotius, Pufendorf, Hobbes, Locke, and later Kant. For example, both Pufendorf and Grotius draw heavily on the works of, among others, Francisco Suárez (see e.g. Crowe 1999, 10–20; Carr and Seidler 1999). The latter was part of a group of Spanish philosophers in the sixteenth century, particular from the so-called "School of Salamanca," who developed earlier medieval thinking in which they based natural rights on natural law.[11]

One can draw historical parallels between the development of the market, both in practice and as a concept, and the understanding of rights and freedoms.[12] Issues relating to markets, setting value and the freedom of exchange and money and the effects on the poor concerned at least two thinkers of the "School": Domingo de Soto and Francisco de Vitoria, who considered and developed their thinking on the need to promote relief for the poor, not as an act of charity but rather to "[uphold] the poor man's right to liberty of person and action" (Grice-Hutchinson 1952, 43; Kamen 1997, 24). This was set out in a treatise by de Soto and submitted to Spanish king Philip II in 1545; in that same year he became the emperor's confessor and

[10] See e.g. Buber 2013 [1937]. Buber describes the "I" as working in the sphere of economics while "Thou" belongs in the world of the spirit (ibid., 47–51 and Part III, where the author develops the "I–Thou" relationship of God to man).

[11] The "School of Salamanca" is the name applied to a group of Spanish jurists, theologians, and philosophers who created a body of doctrine on natural, international, and economic law, rooted in the intellectual work of Francisco de Vitoria, who started teaching in Salamanca in 1526 on the "catedra de prima," the most important chair of theology at the university. Other distinguished members of this school were Domingo de Soto, Fernando Vázquez de Menchaca, Diego de Covarrubias, Luis de Molina, Juan Ginés de Sepúlveda, and Francisco Suárez (see Lastra 2014, 129–38). The role of the School of Salamanca in the development of early monetary theory has been documented in Grice-Hutchinson 1952.

[12] For example, the rapid growth of the Flemish towns in the thirteenth and fourteenth centuries reflects both their level of independence and free thought and their roles as centers of trade, exchange, and banking (see Murray 2005, 77–8). The roles of, for example, Bruges and Ghent in developing international markets moved, in due course, to Antwerp (Gelderblom 2013). The group of thinkers in Salamanca corresponded with merchants and clerics in Antwerp in the sixteenth century as the great influx of gold and, particularly, silver flowed in from the New World. At the same time interest increased in how best to govern these new lands (Grice-Hutchinson 1952, 40–2). It is also worth noting that Gonzalo Pérez, who served as Phillip II's personal secretary during the latter's youth and later his reign, had studied at the University of Salamanca through the key period of the "school's" development (Kamen 1997, 27).

subsequent representative at the Council of Trent. Thus, theories on natural law resulted in important parallel developments in the concepts of markets and human rights. However, the economic analysis of markets subsequently took a different path and a gap in this relationship developed (see Section 2.5).

The subsequent development by Grotius and others of a modern school of international law was reassessed in the twentieth century in the context of the legal responses to the atrocities—violation of human rights and the genocide of the Jewish people[13]—perpetrated by Nazi Germany. This led to a re-examination of the justification of positive law when it becomes dissociated from natural law. These debates clearly showed that legal positivism, which had been influenced by the work of Hans Kelsen (1967 [1934]) and taken up by thinkers such as H. L. A. Hart in its contrasting form of Anglo-American legal positivism, has its limits (see e.g. Bodanksy and Watson 1992 on the limits of state consent).

A recent book by Philippe Sands (2016) weaves together the contributions by a generation of outstanding scholars—including Hersch Lauterpacht and Raphael Lemkin—to illuminate this recent chapter in the development of international law in response to the Nazi atrocities. As acknowledged, Lauterpacht, a Cambridge professor of International Law and one of the outstanding legal scholars of the 1940s, became a key figure in the development of the international rights regime. Raphael Lemkin, a Polish Jewish lawyer, coined the term "genocide."

What is at stake is the fact that the state cannot suppress human rights, and that the recognition and protection of human rights are inviolable. This led to the adoption of the Universal Declaration of Human Rights by the General Assembly of the United Nations on December 10, 1948 (UDHR 1948). As the Preamble states:

> Whereas recognition of the inherent dignity and of the equal and inalienable rights of all members of the human family is the foundation of freedom, justice and peace in the world,
>
> Whereas disregard and contempt for human rights have resulted in barbarous acts which have outraged the conscience of mankind, and the advent of a world in which human beings shall enjoy freedom of speech and belief and freedom from fear and want has been proclaimed as the highest aspiration of the common people,
>
> Whereas it is essential, if man is not to be compelled to have recourse, as a last resort, to rebellion against tyranny and oppression, that human rights should be protected by the rule of law,

[13] The Nazi regime targeted many groups for extermination, including gypsies, Slavs, the disabled, and homosexuals. However, the scale of persecution and murder of Jews was on a scale without comparison. More than six million Jews were killed in the Holocaust.

Whereas it is essential to promote the development of friendly relations between nations,

Whereas the peoples of the United Nations have in the Charter reaffirmed their faith in fundamental human rights, in the dignity and worth of the human person and in the equal rights of men and women and have determined to promote social progress and better standards of life in larger freedom,

Whereas Member States have pledged themselves to achieve, in co-operation with the United Nations, the promotion of universal respect for and observance of human rights and fundamental freedoms,

Whereas a common understanding of these rights and freedoms is of the greatest importance for the full realization of this pledge,

Now, Therefore THE GENERAL ASSEMBLY proclaims THIS UNIVERSAL DECLARATION OF HUMAN RIGHTS as a common standard of achievement for all peoples and all nations, to the end that every individual and every organ of society, keeping this Declaration constantly in mind, shall strive by teaching and education to promote respect for these rights and freedoms and by progressive measures, national and international, to secure their universal and effective recognition and observance, both among the peoples of Member States themselves and among the peoples of territories under their jurisdiction.

2.5 ECONOMICS, FINANCIAL MARKETS, HUMAN RIGHTS, AND JUSTICE IN TODAY'S WORLD

While the recognition and protection of human rights is widely recognized as an intrinsic element of the rule of law as we understand and defend it nowadays, the debate about the relationship between markets (including financial markets) and the state continues to change. It frames current and historical policy debates and influences the electoral agenda of diverse political parties. Issues of social justice cannot be disentangled from questions about markets in the construction of a fair and just society. This has important consequences in terms of the design of adequate national and international policies and institutions.

An innate and intensely felt sense of injustice after the Great Financial Crisis triggered protests around the world from New York ("Occupy Wall Street") and London to Spain ("Indignados") and the subsequent development of political movements/parties that have gained prominence in some countries in the Eurozone (notably Syriza in Greece and Podemos in Spain). What lies underneath this development is a re-examination of the relationship between justice and markets (in particular financial markets) from the perspective of equality and inequality.

While this debate has contemporary manifestations, the issues at stake are not new. Indeed, debates about social justice, solidarity, social policy, and social security permeate the history of the design of the welfare state in Europe in the twentieth century.

William Beveridge,[14] widely considered as the "father of the Welfare State" in the UK, was the main author of the eponymous Beveridge Report (officially the Social Insurance and Allied Services Report) published on December 7, 1942, which formed the basis of the 1945–51 Labour Government's legislation program for social reform. Comprehensive social insurance (with a free national health service) has become since then a feature of the social policy in the UK, and a feature that exists in many other Western European countries from Sweden to Spain. However, many of these social security systems have been downsized and are now endangered in their very existence, given the fiscal necessities of nation states across the developed world, in particular in the aftermath of the Great Financial Crisis, but also considering the demand of public pensions and defined benefit systems in the light of demographic, financial, and fiscal developments (see Davis and Lastra 2016).

Coming back to the debate about human rights, in a Hohfeldian sense they exist at a nation state level in that a state owes or grants rights to its citizens in exchange for correlative duties such as obligations to obey the laws of the state, pay taxes etc. (Hohfeld 1913, 1917). However, financial markets and institutions cross borders and operate internationally. Consequently, there is an issue to what extent, if any, there is an interaction between human rights and global financial markets and institutions. This problem is exacerbated by the development, in economic thinking, of "homo economicus."

In conceptual analysis it is possible to view man as a purely economically oriented being.[15] However, while it may be useful for economic modeling purposes to construct "homo economicus" as a representation of some aspects of reality, it is also necessary to stand back and to consider the human being as a whole.[16] With this perspective comes the concept of "human dignity." This latter idea encompasses the view that each person has a range of potentialities and that society has a responsibility to develop these both for the benefit of the

[14] William Henry Beveridge was Director of the London School of Economics from 1919 to 1937 (see the report published in *LSE Connect*, Winter 2012, 21ff.). The economic details of the Beveridge Report were worked out in collaboration with John Maynard Keynes and Lionel Robbins.

[15] For example, John Stuart Mill holds that "political economy... is concerned with [man] solely as a being who desires to possess wealth, and who is capable of judging the comparative efficacy of means for obtaining that end" (1874 [1836], essay 5, 137). "Homo economicus" is and remains a prevalent concept in economic theorizing.

[16] It is possible to view economic analysis as "consequentialist" in that economic policies can be assessed by empirical evaluations of the results (i.e. "outputs focused"). However, concepts such as human rights are seen as "strongly deontological" in that they are based on absolute principles (Freeman 2006, 22). In a Kantian sense the outcome of the action is less important than the motive with which it is undertaken and that the action that is morally good is good within itself (see Kant 1997 [1785], 60, "The good will and its results," chap.1).

individual and of the community as a whole.[17] Unfortunately, as discussed in Section 2.3, this broader perspective is often omitted from economic and financial market analysis. It is not surprising that the institutional designs that result from such analyses have brought about a loss in societal trust.

The global dislocation experienced in the wake of the Great Financial Crisis, coupled with long periods of low growth, high unemployment especially among the young, restricted access to housing, and specific issues within the Eurozone, have generated political instability with considerable disillusionment with existing political and financial institutions and a popular move towards more extreme political parties. There are a range of reasons for this, but central among them is the perceived failures of previous economic certainties and a growing distrust in financial institutions and markets, not least because of the failure of financial markets to create wealth for society as a whole.

In part this may be seen as a failure of a technocratic approach to economics and markets in communicating with and engaging a wider population. Hitherto trust had been placed in a relatively small group of experts to guide and manage these areas. The Great Financial Crisis and its aftermath revealed severe deficiencies in this approach, which were made worse by a number of political failures. There is a growing concern that many financial markets have lost touch with the societies to which they belong. It is likely that trading securities has become an end in itself, failing to satisfy societal needs (e.g. Turner 2016, 42ff.). The result has been manifest in a perception of increasing inequality, injustice, and the failure to engage and develop a sense of community.

Many citizens see themselves as subject to "unjust" forces. Often, this perception is viewed through the prism of conspiracy theories and similar fantasies frequently disseminated through social media. This dislocation is blamed on the "other," with a consequential rise in disaffection, extremism, and a failure to discern individual worth.

To a considerable extent the concerns involved may be expressed as a feeling of "loss of control." There is a perception that there has been a loss of predictability and individual choice. Powerful market and economic forces, which had always existed, appear to have been suddenly unleashed. Many of these changes have been beneficial and over a number of decades have benefited many, lifting, for example, millions of individuals in India and China out of poverty. Sanitation and medical progress together with urban growth and agricultural improvements have expanded the options available to many. However, these developments have not been consistent and not all have benefited at the same pace, or at all, and, in many areas, the certainties and

[17] These concepts can be traced back to Aristotle and St Thomas Aquinas. See, for example, Nussbaum 2000, 106 and 112. See also Lee and George 2008.

support derived from communities or welfare state institutions have unraveled. This has led to questions about the nature of economic change and its relationship to human dignity and social equality.[18]

Ronald Dworkin sought to divide "equality" into those forms that require treating people as part of a "common humanity" and those that relate to "attributes of a person that are capable of development and fulfillment" (Guest 2013, 197). The first is addressed by freedom of access to resources, while the latter leaves individuals free to choose how they wish to live (Dworkin 2011, 356–63), where he considers issues relating to "equality of resources." Dworkin sees the search for justice as requiring an "inclusive theory of ethics and morality" (ibid., 419). Assessing how people live their lives, including their relationships within the economy, requires "some effective ethical conviction... [which] is essential to responsibility in living" (ibid., 420).

Taking this forward and connecting it to the previous discussion, it is important to consider which human rights are most relevant for this analysis. Human rights are often classified into two main groups: those that are absolute (e.g. rights to life, freedom, and fear of physical violence) and those that are relative (e.g. rights to free education, access to clean water, adequate food etc.) (see e.g. Raz 2015, 225 and 229–31, in which Raz questions whether the second group are actually "human rights"). This second group has been described as requiring "compossible duties" as the counterparty to rights, in that absolute rights can be satisfied by forbearance and restraints while relative rights require "positive actions" on those that bear the duty (O'Neill 2015, 77ff.). This latter set of rights may be described as "aspirational" and the duty to satisfy these rights as dependent on the relative ability of the agencies involved to achieve the satisfaction of these rights. However, this form of conceptualization may be too limited. It seems to be grounded in a form of economic analysis that obscures both what is important and what is possible.[19]

This criticism has also been expressed by Amartya Sen, who is critical of a narrow economic focus on income and wealth; although these are important, he views the creation of "capabilities of people to lead the kind of lives they value" as more relevant (Sen 1999, 18). Individual and community capabilities are increased by a number of "freedoms" including the alleviation of disease and improved health, education opportunities and an ability to participate in the economic and political world (ibid., 15–17).[20] It is about giving people

[18] See e.g. Piketty 2014, for a modern examination of the effects of income inequality.

[19] Contrary views have been expressed by, for example, Nickel 2006, 7, and Griffin 1986, 284–312.

[20] See also Nussbaum 2007, 69ff., where she expands the use of the term "capabilities" as a way to measure "what people are actually able to do and to be in a way informed by an idea... of life that is worthy of the dignity of the human being."

choices: increased capabilities provide opportunities for individuals and societies, as a whole, to help themselves in accordance with their human dignity. If they are able to participate in developing these capabilities, they, in turn, influence the areas to which they are connected (ibid., 15). Being able to participate in a market is in itself a "freedom" and an aspect of a human right and to be viewed as liberating.[21]

Consequently, the right and ability to engage with markets, both financial and otherwise, is fundamental to individual capabilities and human rights. The failure of markets to engage both individuals and communities and to support the development of their capabilities may breed distrust and alienation. As mentioned earlier, this is particularly true of financial markets following the Great Financial Crisis. Markets need to be perceived as fair and connected and supportive of the society in which they operate. This means that individuals in markets need to operate ethically, and the culture of markets needs to include clear and understandable explanations of their social purposes, their transparency, and their relevance to society with clear lines of accountability. These key factors are well set out in the 2012 United Nations "Guiding principles on foreign debt and human rights," to which we now turn.

2.6 UNITED NATIONS "GUIDING PRINCIPLES ON FOREIGN DEBT AND HUMAN RIGHTS"

The Report of the Independent Expert on Foreign Debt and Human Rights (2011) sets out the guiding principles in this area. They are based on the Universal Declaration of Human Rights (UDHR) covering civil, political, economic, social, and cultural rights of all people, and are the foundation for the international system for the recognition and protection of human rights.[22] The structure of the Declaration mirrors that mentioned earlier by Raz and reflects elements of Sen's focus on enhancing capabilities. For example, Articles 3–21 refer to the rights of individuals to life, liberty, security and property, freedom of expression, freedom from torture, right to due process and equality

[21] Sen discusses this in the context of female education and workforce participation (Sen 1999, 115–16). See also Chapter 3 by Claassen in this volume.

[22] The "International Bill of Human Rights" is formed by the "UN General Assembly, Universal Declaration of Human Rights," December 10, 1948, GA res. 217 A (III), http://www.unhchr.ch/udhr/lang/eng.htm, the "International Covenant on Civil and Political Rights," New York, December 16, 1966, 999 UNTS 171, http://www.ohcr.org/Documents/ProfessionalInterest/ccpr.pdf, and the "International Covenant on Economic, Social and Cultural Rights," New York, December 16, 1966, 993 UNTS 3, http://www.ohcr.org/Documents/ProfessionalInterests/cescr.pdf.

before the law, while Articles 22–7 set out the importance of economic, social, and cultural rights which provide the path for development, such as the right to education, work, and a healthy and working environment.

The United Nations' "Guiding principles on foreign debt and human rights" have, for example, as their "Foundation Principles" the need for UN Member States to ensure the "primacy of human rights" (11–12), equality and non-discrimination (12), the shared responsibilities of debtors and creditors (14), and the need to ensure "transparency, participation and accountability" (14–15).

These principles resonate and inspire. Financial markets and institutions need to engage with society. Financial law needs to function within an ethical framework of accepted values and principles. At a time in which the European Union confronts numerous political, economic, and existential challenges, it is worth recalling that human rights, democracy, and the rule of law are core values of the European Union. Embedded in the founding treaty, they were reinforced when the EU adopted the Charter of Fundamental Rights in 2000, and strengthened still further when the Charter became legally binding with the entry into force of the Lisbon Treaty in 2009. Countries seeking to join the EU must respect human rights. And all trade and cooperation agreements with third countries contain a clause stipulating that human rights are an essential element in relations between the parties.[23]

2.7 CONCLUSION

Financial markets and institutions need to re-establish and maintain their legitimacy to operate. Detailed regulations may be necessary, but they are not sufficient. It requires those who run and participate in these markets to consider their ultimate purpose and their need to satisfy the needs of society. This means operating in an ethical manner with a culture that understands the wider purpose of the financial market and in particular the creation of wealth for the benefit of society and not just a privileged few. While all elements of human rights are important, in this context financial markets should especially seek to engage and to promote enhancing societal capabilities ensuring transparency, participation, and accountability.

[23] See also http://www.consilium.europa.eu/uedocs/cms_data/docs/pressdata/EN/foraff/131173.pdf.

REFERENCES

Aquinas, St Thomas. 1918 [1485]. *Summa Theologiae,* Part II (Second Part), Justice, R&T Washbourne, London, 113–35. http://www.newadvent.org/summa/3058.htm#article1.

Archbishop's Task Group on Responsible Credit and Savings "To Our Credit" (2016). http://static1.squarespace.com/static/5406dac3e4b02d18666bcb68/t/56b9bff9c2ea513afa7d2be3/1455013883903/Task+Group+Final+Report.pdf (accessed June 16, 2016).

Arendt, Hannah. 1958. *The Human Condition.* Chicago: University of Chicago Press.

Bodansky, Daniel, and J. Shand Watson. 1992. "State Consent and the Sources of International Obligation." *Proceedings of the Annual Meeting* (American Society of International Law) 86, 108–13.

Buber, Martin. 2013 [1937]. *I and Thou.* London: Bloomsbury.

Carr, Craig, and Michael Seidler. 1999. "Pufendorf, Sociality and the Modern State." In *Grotius, Pufendorf and Modern Natural Law,* edited by Knud Haakonssen. Aldershot: Dartmouth Publishing, 133–57.

Cooper, Niall, and Sarah Purcell. 2013. "Stopping the Pay-day Loan Rip-off" (Church Action on Poverty, October). http://www.church-poverty.org.uk/news/pressroom/resources/reports/paydayloanreportpdf (accessed June 16, 2016).

Crowe, M. B. 1999. "The 'Impious Hypothesis': A Paradox in Hugo Grotius." In *Grotius, Pufendorf and Modern Natural Law,* edited by Knud Haakonssen. Aldershot: Dartmouth Publishing, 3–34.

Davis, E. Philip, and Rosa M. Lastra. 2016. "Pension Provision, Care and Dignity in Old Age: Legal and Economic Issues." *Brunel Economics and Finance Working Paper* No. 16–06. http://ssrn.com/abstract=2780484 (accessed October 24, 2016).

Dunn, J. M. 1999. "'Bright Enough for All Our Purposes': John Locke's Conception of a Civilized Society." In *Locke's Moral, Political and Legal Philosophy,* edited by J. R. Milton. Aldershot: Dartmouth Publishing, 315–35.

Dworkin, Ronald. 1986. *Laws' Empire.* Oxford: Hart Publishing.

Dworkin, Ronald. 2011. *Justice for Hedgehogs.* Cambridge, MA: Harvard University Press.

Financial Conduct Authority. 2014. "PS14/16: Detailed Rules for the Price Cap on High-cost Short-term Credit—Including Feedback on CP14/10 and Final Rules." https://www.fca.org.uk/news/ps14-16-detailed-rules-on-the-price-cap-on-high-cost-short-term-credit (accessed June 16, 2016).

Financial Times. 2014. "FCA Rules Could Force Quarter of Payday Lenders Out of Business." April 1. http://www.ft.com/cms/s/0/39745222-b967-11e3-957a-00144feabdc0.html#axzz4BkYjpmS6 (accessed June 16, 2016).

Freeman, Michael. 2006. "Beyond Capitalism and Socialism." In *Human Rights and Capitalism: A Multidisciplinary Perspective on Globalisation,* edited by Janet Dine and Andrew Fagan. Cheltenham: Edward Elgar Publishing, 3–27.

Gelderblom, Oscar. 2013. *Cities of Commerce: The Institutional Foundations of International Trade in the Low Countries, 1250–1650.* Princeton, NJ: Princeton University Press.

Grice-Hutchinson, Marjorie. 1952. *School of Salamanca, Reading in Spanish Monetary Theory, 1544–1605.* Oxford: Clarendon Press. https://mises.org/system/tdf/The%20School%20of%20Salamanca_3.pdf?file=1&type=document (accessed June 4, 2016).

Griffin, James. 1986. *Well-being.* Oxford: Clarendon Press.

Grotius, Hugo. 2012 [1625]. *On the Law of War and Peace.* Cambridge: Cambridge University Press.

Guest, Stephen. 2013. *Ronald Dworkin*, 3rd edition. Stanford: Stanford University Press.

Hayek, F. A. von. 1973. *Law, Legislation and Liberty.* London: Routledge.

Hohfeld, Wesley. 1913. "Some Fundamental Legal Conceptions as Applied in Judicial Reasoning." *Yale Law Review* 23, 16–59.

Hohfeld, Wesley. 1917. "Fundamental Legal Conceptions as Applied in Judicial Reasoning." *Yale Law Review* 26, 710–70.

Hume, David. 1978 [1738]. *A Treatise of Human Nature.* Oxford: Oxford University Press.

Jacobson, Arthur, and Bernhard Schlink. 2002. "Hans Kelsen" and "Carl Schmitt." In *Weimar: A Jurisprudence of Crisis*, edited by Arthur Jacobson and Bernhard Schlink. Berkeley and Los Angeles: University of California Press, 67–109, 280–312.

Kamen, Henry. 1997. *Philip of Spain.* New Haven: Yale University Press.

Kant, Immanuel. 1997 [1785]. *The Groundwork of the Metaphysic of Morals.* Translation by H. J. Paton. London: Routledge.

Kelsen, Hans. 1967 [1934]. *Pure Theory of Law.* Berkeley and Oakland: University of California Press, Berkeley, Oakland.

Lastra, Rosa. 2014. "Global Financial Architecture and Human Rights." In *Making Sovereign Financing and Human Rights Work*, edited by Juan Pablo Bohoslavsky and Jernej Letnar Černič. Oxford: Hart Publishing, 129–38.

Lee, Patrick, and Robert George. 2008. "The Nature and Basis of Human Dignity." *Ratio Juris* 21(2) (June), 173–93.

Loughlin, Stephen. 2010. *Aquinas' Summa Theologiae.* London: T&T Clark.

Martin, Rex. 1985. *Rawls and Rights.* Kansas: University of Kansas Press.

Mill, John Stuart. 1874 [1836]. "On the Definition of Political Economy, and on the Method of Investigation Proper to It." In *Essays on "Some Unsettled Questions of Political Economy,"* 2nd edition. London: Longmans, Green, Reader & Dyer, 120–64.

Murray, James. 2005. *Bruges, Cradle of Capitalism 1280–1390.* Cambridge: Cambridge University Press.

Nickel, James. 2006. *Making Sense of Human Rights.* Hoboken, NJ: Wiley-Blackwell.

Nussbaum, Martha. 2000. "Aristotle, Politics, and Human Capabilities: A Response to Antony, Arneson, Charlesworth, and Mulgan." *Ethics* 111(1) (October), 102–40.

Nussbaum, Martha. 2007. *Frontiers of Justice.* Oxford: Oxford University Press.

O'Neill, Onora. 2000. "Bounded and Cosmopolitan Justice." *Review of International Studies* 26, 45–60.

O'Neill, Onora. 2015. "Response to John Tasioulas." In *Philosophical Foundations of Human Rights*, edited by S. Cruft, Matthew Liao, and Massimo Renzo. Oxford: Oxford University Press, 71–8.

Penelhum, Terence. 1992. "Hume's Moral Psychology." In *The Cambridge Companion to Hume*, edited by David Norton. Cambridge: Cambridge University Press, 117–47.

Personal Finance Research Centre University of Bristol. 2013. "The Impact on Business and Consumers of a Cap on the Total Cost of Credit." https://www.gov.uk/government/uploads/system/uploads/attachment_data/file/136548/13-702-the- impact-on-business-and-consumers-of-a-cap-on-the-total-cost-of-credit.pdf (accessed June 16, 2016).

Piketty, Thomas. 2014. *Capital in the Twenty-First Century*. Cambridge, MA: Harvard University Press.

Pope Benedict XVI. 2009. Encyclical Letter "Caritas in Veritate" ("Charity in Truth"). http://w2.vatican.va/content/benedict-xvi/en/encyclicals/documents/hf_ben-xvi_enc_20090629_caritas-in-veritate.html (accessed June 16, 2016).

Rawls, John. 1980. "Kantian Constructivism in Moral Theory." *Journal of Philosophy* 77, 515–72.

Rawls, John. 1999 [1971]. *A Theory of Justice*. Oxford: Oxford University Press.

Raz, Joseph. 1986. *The Morality of Freedom*. Oxford: Clarendon Press.

Raz, Joseph. 2015. "Human Rights in the Emerging World Order." In *Philosophical Foundations of Human Rights*, edited by Rowan Cruft, S. Matthew Liao, and Massimo Renzo. Oxford: Oxford University Press, 217–31.

Report of the Independent Expert on Foreign Debt and Human Rights (2011). "Report on the Effects of Foreign Debt and Other Related International Financial Obligations of States on the Full Enjoyment of all Human Rights, Particularly Economic, Social and Cultural Rights. Cephas Lumina: Guiding Principles on Foreign Debt and Human Rights." April, A/HRC/20/23. https://documents-dds-ny.un.org/doc/UNDOC/GEN/G12/128/80/PDF/G1212880.pdf?OpenElement (adopted July 18, 2012 (A/HRC/RES/20/10)).

Sandel, Michael. 1998. *Liberalism and the Limits of Justice*, 2nd edition. Cambridge: Cambridge University Press.

Sandel, Michael. 2012. *What Money Can't Buy: The Moral Limits of Markets*. London: Allen Lane.

Sands, Philippe. 2016. *East West Street: On the Origins of Genocide and Crimes Against Humanity*. New York: Weidenfeld & Nicolson.

Sen, Amartya. 1999. *Development as Freedom*. Oxford: Oxford University Press.

Turner, Adair. 2016. *Between Debt and the Devil*. Princeton, NJ: Princeton University Press.

Tyler, Tom. 1990. *Why People Obey the Law*. New Haven: Yale University Press.

UDHR. 1948. "The Universal Declaration of Human Rights." http://www.ohchr.org/EN/UDHR/Documents/UDHR_Translations/eng.pdf. Adopted by the United Nations General Assembly on December 10, 1948 http://www.un.org/en/documents/udhr/index.shtml (accessed October 24, 2016).

Volk, Christian. 2015. *Arendtian Constitutionalism*. Oxford: Hart Publishing.

Weber, Max. 1947 [1915]. *The Theory of Social and Economic Organization*. New York: Free Press.

3

A capability framework for financial market regulation

Rutger Claassen

3.1 INTRODUCTION

In the aftermath of the global financial crisis, questions about when, why, and how to regulate financial markets have received renewed attention. Answers to such regulatory questions rely—implicitly or explicitly—on a *normative theory of market regulation*: a theory that justifies certain reasons as valid reasons for the state to interfere with the freedom of individuals to act on markets (in the following, "regulation" will be used as shorthand for "state regulation of markets"). This chapter is concerned with one specific approach, that is, the so-called capability approach to justice, which has been developed by Amartya Sen, Martha Nussbaum, and others. It asks whether this approach can provide a better basis for such a normative theory of regulation than the currently prevailing mainstream economic theories.

How the capability approach relates to markets and their regulation seems to be an open question, in the sense that the approach does not take an a priori positive or negative stance towards markets. As an introductory handbook on the capability approach notes:

> the human development and capability approach is neither pro-state nor pro-market, nor does it favour any particular economic system of material provisioning. The essence of the approach is that the success of social and economic processes should be assessed according to whether they expand valuable freedoms. That these processes are state or market-led does not matter, provided that two conditions are met: people's agency and well-being ... should be both promoted and respected.
> (Johnson 2009, 179)

This passage admirably expresses the *independence* of the normative criterion (assess outcomes according to how they score on capabilities) on the one hand and the institutional arrangement (markets or alternatives) that are to bring about these outcomes on the other hand. Competing normative theories (say, utilitarianism, or Rawls's theory) are equally independent: normative theories endorse specific institutional arrangements only contingently, to the extent that they happen to lead to the desired outcomes. This chapter can be seen as an exercise in thinking about how, given the initial distance, the capability approach bridges this gap to institutional conclusions and assesses the desirability of markets and their regulation. It will especially concentrate on how this compares to standard economic or utilitarian ways of bridging the same gap.

The chapter starts with a brief overview of the state of the art on regulation. It argues that the currently dominant approach is to distinguish economic from social regulation, where the first refers to efficiency considerations and the second to considerations of distributive justice and paternalism. No unified idea is available to ground these different types of regulation (Section 3.2). Moreover, a discussion of the justice literature will lead us to conclude that the utilitarian theory that underlies the economic justifications for regulation cannot provide a basis for thinking about social regulation (Section 3.3). To solve this problem, I argue that the capability approach has the potential to provide a unified theory of regulation. It shows how considerations of allocative efficiency, distributive justice, and paternalism all are related to a concern for the development of the agency of market participants and of citizens more generally (Section 3.4). To cash out this potential, the chapter proposes a capability framework for market regulation (Section 3.5). Finally, it discusses how using a capability approach would impact on our view of financial market regulation (Section 3.6).

3.2 THE STANDARD VIEW OF MARKET REGULATION

Standard handbooks of regulation show a remarkable convergence in their set-up. They generally divide justifications for regulation into three categories: one economic and two social justifications for regulation (Sunstein 1990, Barr 2004, Ogus 2004, Morgan and Yeung 2007, Stiglitz 2009, Baldwin, Cave, and Lodge 2012). In this section I will present these categories. This is meant to evoke an uncontroversial picture that is hopefully familiar to most of those who think about normative justifications for regulation.

1. Economic justification: efficiency. The economic justifications for regulation are often lumped together under the heading of "market failures" (Bator 1958, Cowen 1988, Den Hertog 1999). The guiding idea is that perfectly competitive markets are characterized by *allocative efficiency*. The more specific criterion of efficiency that is used in this context is that of Pareto-optimality.

This criterion holds that a state is efficient when no one can be made better off without making others worse off. The starting point of the economic analysis (as expressed in the First Fundamental Theorem of Welfare Economics) is that: on a perfect market all voluntary transactions are exhausted—no one is able to improve his or her position through further trades without making others worse off. However, in reality various market failures upset this efficiency property of perfect markets. Market failures include cases where markets do not provide for certain goods because of free rider problems (public goods), cases where market production involves negative spillovers to third parties (externalities), cases where imbalances in information between parties make transactions voluntary in name only (information asymmetries), and cases where parties gain large market shares and are able to dictate prices and reap economic rents (monopolistic or imperfect competition). In all these cases, there is at least a prima facie case to think that government regulation can enhance efficiency. Governments are required to regulate so as to restore Pareto-optimality, or at least bring the economy as close as possible to the Pareto-frontier. Allocative efficiency therefore is the guiding normative value for all forms of intervention in this category. Since an efficient economy does better at satisfying consumer preferences, the term "efficiency" should here be understood as a placeholder for the ultimate value: welfare, understood in terms of the satisfaction of preferences.

When other justifications for regulation are presented, these are usually labeled "social," to mark the contrast with these economic grounds for regulation. Unlike the economic theory of market failure (which is more or less standardized), there is nothing approaching consensus on the main features of social justifications for regulation. Authors endorsing social justifications are usually dissatisfied with the narrow confines of the economic focus on efficiency. They normally do not reject economic justifications, but want to supplement them with social justifications. How this is worked out, however, depends on the specifics of each author's theory. One finds a bewildering variety of proposals, with much less standardization than is usual in economics (Stewart 1982, Sunstein 1990, Trebilcock 1993, Bozeman 2002, Soule 2003, Prosser 2006, Feintuck 2010). Nonetheless, two broad types of social justifications can be singled out as particularly prominent, which are added to efficiency grounds in the standard views of regulation in the handbooks mentioned at the start of this section:

2. Social justification (1): distributive justice. Here, the general idea is that efficiency can never replace considerations of equity. Indeed, *if* one deems equity reasons valid reasons for regulation at all (which, it is stressed by the handbooks, is politically contested), then one cannot incorporate them into economic ones but needs to add them separately. Analytically, the distinction is based on the equity/efficiency split. The market can be considered as a game in which players have different starting positions, depending on their endowments, both external ones (monetarily valuable assets) and internal ones (marketable talents). Some theories of justice (of a broadly libertarian flavor) would hold that any initial allocation of endowments that happens to arise is just. Absent "force and fraud," individuals are entitled to their endowments and have to play the market game with the endowments they can get a hold on. Transactions starting from this baseline are just. Most other theories of justice disagree and want to place constraints on these endowments. A general intuition is that redistribution is necessary to enhance the bargaining power of vulnerable parties and may thus be necessary to make their transactions voluntary in a more than formal sense. This can be cashed out in different ways. For example, one familiar type of egalitarian theory, luck egalitarianism, holds that inequalities in endowments between individuals that have arisen out of unchosen circumstances can be a reason for compensation by government. This is only one example: different theories of justice diverge widely in the amount and specific justificatory rationales for redistribution.

3. Social justification (2): paternalism. A third reason for regulating is *paternalism*. Traditionally, this category was treated with suspicion by economists and (liberal) philosophers alike. Government regulations interfering with the choices of individuals, for the sake of their own well-being, both violate individual freedom and disrespect revealed preferences. The individual who is allowed entry into the market is supposed to have the status of an autonomous agent who can choose what is best for him or her. Nonetheless, with the advent of behavioral economics, which has shown how irrational human decision-making can often be, it has become more accepted to think that some forms of intervention (especially milder ones, leaving choices open while nudging behavior in the "right" direction) may be necessary to prevent gross deviations from the welfare-maximizing choices people would make if they were fully rational. Protecting weaker parties on the market can thus also be understood as a matter of protecting people from falling prey to their own cognitive biases, such as when they would be prepared to contract higher wages to work in a physically hazardous working place out of over-optimism ("this won't happen to me"). This is the rationale behind a lot of health and safety regulation as well as consumer regulation. Note that for this diagnosis of paternalism the deficiencies in the formation of one party's preferences are coupled with the inequality between parties. It is the threat of the other party, having market power because of its superior information position, abusing the weaker party, which makes paternalist intervention by a third party (i.e. governments) necessary.

Obviously, there can be interaction effects between the different types of justification in practice. The most familiar one probably is that redistribution in the name of justice may have negative effects on efficiency; there may be an efficiency price to more equality (today's final allocation is tomorrow's initial allocation—in reality there is a constant sequence of market games). This does not invalidate the general observation, however, that the three main categories for regulating markets are distinct and provide diverging reasons for interfering with market processes. This state-of-the-art makes one wonder whether a unified perspective is possible. This seems desirable, not only for reasons of theoretical elegance, but also precisely because of the cases where the different justifications lead to conflicting prescriptions. Some idea of how they hang together is needed for deciding how to deal with these conflicts.

3.3 JUSTICE AND THE EQUITY/EFFICIENCY SPLIT

To approach a unifying perspective, I first want to steer the conversation to the field of justice as the field on which to search for such a perspective. This may seem counterintuitive (given the association of the norms of justice with one of the three specific justifications for regulation, as described above). Let me explain why this is nonetheless warranted, through a small excursion into intellectual history.

The search for justifying grounds for regulation has traditionally been a preoccupation of both political philosophy and economics. The two disciplines have handled the matter very differently. From a political philosophical perspective, the split between the state (public domain) and markets (private domain) forms the basis of the theory of liberalism. A liberal understanding of society as consisting of these two domains has informed political thinking since the political revolutions of the eighteenth and nineteenth centuries and the advent of capitalist markets. In this liberal understanding, private freedom to act on markets has an a priori justified status, and interventions with market freedom require justification. From an economic perspective, the market sphere was often conceptualized as a self-standing sphere which, if left to its own devices (i.e. the automatic processes of adjustment steered by the price mechanisms mediating supply and demand), would bring maximal welfare to all citizens. This welfare-maximizing property of markets was and remains its justifying basis from an economic perspective (see also Sen 1985). Underlying this perspective often is a utilitarian view in which individual preferences form the justified basis for market decisions. Respecting these preferences is the economist's way of respecting individuals themselves.

This raises the question of how these liberal freedom-based considerations and economic welfare-based considerations relate to each other. The economic view of respecting market-based preferences in practice often supported liberalism's a priori defense of individual freedom, even if it was based on a very different—namely utilitarian—philosophical theory. But the two may also come apart on certain occasions, and regulation, I think, is one of them. The highly sophisticated philosophical literature that has arisen since the 1970s on the question of social *justice* is, in my view, the best place to discuss this issue, because liberal, utilitarian, and other normative theories can be understood as specific conceptions of justice, as so many different and competing interpretations of what justice requires. This quest for the right conception of justice, in turn, has been interpreted as underlying the quest for the legitimate limits of state action: the state should restrict itself to establish justice, whatever that requires. For the purposes of this chapter, therefore, we may work within this justice literature and treat economic and philosophical answers to the regulation question as competing answers to the same question: how markets need to be regulated as a part for the larger quest of realizing a just society.

The importance of this move is that the general philosophical literature on justice throws doubt on the use of the equity/efficiency split that underlies the distinction between economic and social justifications for regulation mentioned in the previous section (we leave out the separate role of paternalism for the moment, but will come back to it later). It forces one to think about how a unified measure of efficiency/justice can be constructed.

The justice literature thinks about justice in distribution in terms of two parameters: a *metric* that specifies the object of distribution, and a *distributive rule* that specifies how the objects are to be distributed to individuals (E. Anderson 2010). Both parameters are a necessary input to answer the first question of (philosophically informed) policy-making: according to justice in distribution, which state of affairs ought to be reached? Answering this question requires having a theory of justice (both a metric and a distributive rule). It gives us the target we want to reach. The second question is, assuming that means are scarce, how to reach this distribution as efficiently as possible? The salient point is that when we represent things in this way, then we do not face an efficiency/equity trade-off in the sense described above. We have a fixed end-point, which is a matter of justice, followed by an efficiency question, which relates to how to reach this end-point. Efficiency is thus about how to realize in practice what justice requires in theory with as few means as possible.

Why then do regulation theories posit an efficiency/equity trade-off and set allocative efficiency and distributive justice apart? My suggestion is that this comes naturally because of the set-up of our social institutions: we are accustomed to thinking about society as consisting of a private domain of free interactions (the market) and a public domain of collective action. Regulation theories reflect this division, by using a different criterion of justice for each realm. The market game is supposed to generate a maximal satisfaction of consumer preferences. Efficiency is then—often tacitly—related to a specific theory of justice, with its own metric and rule: utilitarianism. The metric is subjective well-being, the distributive rule is Pareto-optimality. Equity should characterize the initial allocation of resources (hence: whatever is done by public institutions, outside of the market), while efficiency should characterize the market process played on the basis of that initial allocation. This requirement on the market process is most often characterized as allocative efficiency, and rarely recognized as a distributive theory in itself. Nonetheless, it is. As Julian Le Grand has aptly remarked (1990, 566):

> Investigations of the trade-offs between various interpretations of equity and Pareto-optimality are not really concerned with the trade-off between equity and efficiency at all. Instead they are investigating what is, at least in part, actually a trade-off between two different kinds of equity: that whose properties are being explored and that embodied in the Pareto social welfare function.

However natural, the tendency to equate efficiency with the objective of welfare maximization (in its Pareto form or otherwise) should be resisted. Efficiency denotes not one social objective, but a relation between social objectives that are each part of one's theory of justice. An economy is efficient to the extent that it is able to reach as many of these objectives as possible, given available resources, and subject to a decision about how to make trade-offs between these objectives.[1]

Given these insights, the position of the handbooks of regulation is not merely theoretically inelegant (in presenting a disparate set of justificatory grounds for regulation), but incomprehensible. The economic justifications are backed up by a utilitarian theory, but the social justifications cannot be grounded in utilitarianism.[2] For consider the *utilitarian view of the person*. According to standard utilitarianism, the person participating in market transactions is deemed to be a person who holds his or her preferences and endowments legitimately. This is the reason why regulatory interventions with these preferences (paternalism) or these endowments (distributive justice) on the market are deemed to be an interference with the free, spontaneous forces of supply and demand. This intervention is seen as lowering social welfare. The individual coming to the market is already constituted as a person, a participant whose holdings and preferences are to count as legitimate input for the game. Any doubts about this view must be dismissed since the utilitarian

[1] Trade-offs, then, are not between "efficiency" and "equity," but either between justice-related and other goals, or between several parts of one's scheme of justice. In the latter case multidimensionality in one's distributive scheme (e.g. separate capabilities) requires to somehow weigh these dimensions even if they are separately important for justice (hence, to some extent, incommensurable).

[2] I here use the label "utilitarian." Some would object since Pareto-optimality does not require interpersonal comparisons of utility and does not allow maximization across persons (and utilitarianism only exists where the rule is to maximize utility). Nonetheless, I use the label, given that the nature of the underlying metric of the Pareto-criterion remains utility, in terms of satisfaction of preferences. Note that in practice, a lot of regulation does aim at utility maximization: standard cost-benefit analysis makes use of the criterion of potential Pareto-improvements (Kaldor-Hicks compensation criterion).

believes in utilitarianism not just on the market but everywhere in social life. The utilitarian cannot admit that this is intuitively unattractive because preferences are not well formed or because some inequalities are not fair. For this would render his or her theory a problematic hybrid of non-utilitarian and utilitarian distributive rules (leaving open which metric the utilitarian would adopt for the social, non-market part). Given the entanglement of the "before," "during," and "after" the market processes in practice, the position will be indeterminate in its prescriptions.[3]

Hence, we face the choice between either rejecting social regulation and identifying justice with market efficiency, or finding a common normative basis for the traditional social and economic justifications for regulation (and the latter option requires showing how economic regulation can be understood on a non-utilitarian basis). It is here that the capability approach comes in.

3.4 THE CAPABILITY APPROACH AND THE MARKET

In this section, I first introduce the essentials of the capability approach and then show how the use of a capability approach is able to unify the trichotomy of justifications that has haunted us so far. This provides the philosophical basis on which, in Section 3.5, I will propose a concrete capability framework for market regulation.

The basis of the capability approach is the distinction between capabilities and functionings. Functionings are defined as "doings" or "beings": to have good health, to be well educated, to write a book, to drink a coffee, are all examples of functionings. Capabilities refer to the ability to do these things or to be in these states. When a person has a capability, say to drink coffee, then the person can "convert" this capability into a functioning, by choosing to act in the way that is open to him or her. An essential element is thus that when individuals are provided (by society or by government) with a set of capabilities, they have the freedom to decide for themselves which ones to convert into functionings. The terminology of functionings and capabilities is extremely flexible, so much depends on the level of generality at which one defines these capabilities. In any case, each capability has an internal and an external aspect. The internal aspect refers to the developed abilities of the person to act in the way the capability indicates: the presence of the required capacities, dispositions, or skills in the person. The external aspect refers to the options open to the agent, for example the legally permitted access to higher

[3] To be consistent, such a position needs a meta-criterion to decide trade-offs between utilitarian and non-utilitarian distributions.

education or the health care system. Both aspects can come in degrees, so it is a matter of further normative decisions when we are prepared to say that a person "has the capability to *x*": this depends on how many capacities and options are necessary to judge that this is the case.

The term "capability to function" indicates a metric of justice. Amartya Sen has argued that any view about justice provides an answer to the "equality of what" question (Sen 1979, 1992, 2009). In contrast to resourcist and utilitarian metrics (see below) the capability approach proposes to conceive of a just society as one in which citizens have "equality of capabilities," or more precisely, an equal right to a set of basic capabilities. To develop this general starting point into a fully fledged theory of justice, however, two further decisions need to be made. First, a selection of a set of basic capabilities needs to be made. Martha Nussbaum has argued, based on her neo-Aristotelian criterion of human flourishing (later, human dignity), for a set of ten basic capabilities, such as the capability to life, bodily integrity, senses, imagination and thought, play, practical reason, affiliation, and others (Nussbaum 2000, 2006, 2011). Other criteria for the selection of basic capabilities have also been explored. Elsewhere, I have argued for using a criterion of free and autonomous agency as the basis for the capability approach to justice. The basic idea here is that of positive freedom: if individuals are to be truly free, they need to become persons who have sufficient capacities and options to choose and realize their own goals in life. This requires both non-interference from others with one's options and positive contributions to enhance one's capacities to make use of these options (Claassen 2017a).

Second, which distributive rule would fit the capability approach? In the justice literature, many distributive rules have been proposed: (luck) egalitarian, prioritarian, sufficientarian, or maximizing rules, all subject to countless variations. The capability metric itself does not dictate any distributive rule. Nonetheless, many authors have employed the capability approach in combination with a sufficientarian rule (Nussbaum 2006, Schuppert 2014, Axelsen and Nielsen 2014). Each capability should be provided up to a threshold level. Below this level, citizens are in need. Above this level, the political community has no role to play for its citizens (these are luxury levels of functioning). Elsewhere, I have argued for a qualified defense of this sufficientarian position (Claassen 2017b). The general idea of setting thresholds will prove to be important for a theory of regulation.

Properly worked out, a capability theory of justice would be a competitor to its two main rivals: resourcist and utilitarian metrics. The capability metric can best be thought of as intermediate between these two. On the one hand, resources provide the input for capabilities. The resource bundle at someone's disposal is a major determinant of this person's capability set. However, various social, personal, and environmental conversion factors determine how many resources one needs to reach a certain capability level. Thus, a physically disabled person may need more resources to reach the same level of, say, mobility, than a physically healthy person. Capability theorists have argued that resources are mere means, while capabilities present goals in life; thus justice should be defined in terms of the latter. This is important given the fact that—due to differences between people in conversion factors—a purely resourcist approach that gives people equal bundles of resources may give some too much while giving others too little. On the other hand, after a person has converted certain capabilities into functionings, he or she experiences a certain feeling of well-being, happiness or satisfaction of his or her preferences, as attached to his or her functioning in a certain way ("listening to music makes me happy"). These utility levels (output), however, are also variably related to functionings. Those with a more pessimistic character will need more or higher-level capabilities or functionings to experience the same utility level as those with a more optimistic character. Here the capability theorist argues that people should be responsible for their own subjective well-being. This is especially important because otherwise some might claim that they need higher capability levels (hence more resources) than others in order to reach the same level of well-being (expensive tastes problem), while others might claim too little because they have become accustomed to be satisfied with very little (adaptive preferences problem). Thus, being positioned in between resources and utility, capability is the right metric for defining social justice.

Let us now turn to the question of regulation. A capabilitarian evaluates social states with respect to the question of whether the set of basic capabilities is realized up to the threshold level. In contrast to the economic approach described earlier, there is no distinction between pre-market allocations and market-based outcomes. The sufficientarian capability criterion is used to assess the normative rightness of both. The sufficiency threshold does institute a dichotomy, between below-threshold distributions and above-threshold distributions. If a person or group of persons is below a capability threshold, some form of government action is needed to bring them above that threshold. If a person or group is above the threshold, no action is needed. This means that these persons can act freely above the threshold. Since I identify the bundle of capabilities with a view to their contribution in rendering people free and autonomous agents, we can state this dichotomy as follows: below the threshold a person is not yet *constituted as an agent*, above the threshold he or she is. We may think of this by analogy to legal capacity, which is not granted to minors and persons with severe mental disabilities, but is granted to all others. Similarly, a capability theory of justice looks at the agency required to be able to live a free and autonomous life. Below the threshold individuals are still *developing* their capacity for agency, above the threshold they are *exercising* their agency in freely chosen activities which bring them enjoyment, well-being, or anything else they wish for (Claassen 2016).[4] The dichotomy of agency development/exercise is orthogonal to the state/market dichotomy. The capability theory does not have an a priori view of markets as good or bad institutions, but rather evaluates markets' contributions to capabilities enhancement from this dual agency perspective.

On the one hand, markets, like other institutions, may be *instruments* in the service of capability justice. Markets may be the most efficient institutions for the production of certain resources which are in turn necessary for giving people basic capabilities. Food markets may be the most efficient way to produce food for the population; hence they enable their basic capability for nutrition. If, and to the extent that, a particular market is thus a necessary condition for the realization of one or more basic capabilities, it is placed under scrutiny. What is at stake is the *constitution of agents in general* via their market-based roles (producers, consumers). To do so, markets need to function well, and this requires that the market failures familiar from economic theory be addressed. From a capability perspective, however, the reason to remedy market failures is not to maximize welfare, but to realize basic capabilities. Since the normative criterion is different, we can expect that this will lead to different diagnoses of these market failures than those available in mainstream economic theory. Markets need participants which can play the market game well, but what playing well means depends on the outcomes one envisages for the game (more on this in Section 3.5).

On the other hand, to the extent that a market is not necessary as an instrument of capability justice, it is a social domain which is *intrinsically* valuable, for the free exercise of one's agency. Here market activity is on a par with activity in other parts in the private sphere: with the activities in the home or in civil associations. No conditions are put on such activity, except for the negative one of not harming the basic capabilities of others (i.e. making them fall below the threshold). Note that although the capability theory does not put any positive requirements on actions above the threshold, it is crucial that there is an above-threshold domain of action. If not, the whole point of developing agency would become redundant. Government regulation here has a role which is not interfering with the market, but enabling the constitution of the market itself. The protection of the market as such an arena is emphasized by all those who defend economic liberties as basic liberties (Tomasi 2012). In capability terms, these liberties are capabilities which serve the *constitution of persons as market participants*, which is a specific social role (see p. 67). This requirement is analytically distinct from the previous one, and both are relevant for a capability theory. In reality both

[4] For another influential view which evaluates markets from the angle of agency, see Satz 2010 and my review (Claassen 2012).

are considerations that have to be weighed where they come together on specific markets.

This section has shown how the capability approach to markets starts from a fundamental concern for the *constitution of agency* in individuals. Such a concern is able to integrate the elements of allocative efficiency, distributive justice, and paternalism, which are often mentioned as grounds for market regulation. Corrections on pre-market endowments and preferences are warranted to the extent that they are necessary to realize basic capabilities. Enhancing "market efficiency" (the market's ability to satisfy consumer demand) is valuable, to the extent that it is, for the same reason. Overall, the difference with the utilitarian-economic theory of regulation is deeper than it may appear if we only look at the reasons usually quoted to prefer capability metrics to utility metrics, such as adaptive preferences or expensive tastes. The difference lies in how these approaches perceive the constitution of persons as agents. For utilitarians/economists, a person's preferences and endowments are leading, since the person is deemed to be already fully constituted as an autonomous agent. For the capability theory, a person's preferences and endowments can only determine his or her free actions to the extent that his or her agency is sufficiently developed, which may or may not be the case at the point where he or she is engaged in a market transaction. Corrections on preferences and endowments are warranted where this is not (yet) the case.

3.5 A CAPABILITY FRAMEWORK FOR MARKET REGULATION

This section will provide the outlines of a capability framework for market regulation. The first and biggest part is to identify whose capabilities are at stake when regulating markets. The second part is about setting thresholds and dealing with conflicts.

I propose to identify three types of capability interests that may be at stake when assessing a specific (set of) markets. I will call these participatory capabilities, consumptive capabilities, and third-party capabilities. *Participatory capabilities* are the capabilities of those acting as market participants. This category relates to the intrinsic valuation of markets mentioned in the previous section. The economic liberties mentioned above are, roughly, the capability to hold and use property and the capability to make contracts. Following the standard perspective on economic liberties, the aim of enhancing participatory capabilities is to allow maximal freedom to hold property and make contracts. *Consumptive capabilities* are the capabilities that agents have as consumers of goods which they have bought on the market. This is connected to the instrumental perspective: people often value their participation in markets for the goods it brings them, and the general agency (basic capabilities) which they gain by having access to these goods. Markets are in the business of providing nutrition, mobility, education, health, and many other important basic capabilities. Markets can be assessed according to how they enable consumers to enhance their access: this requires strengthening their position on the market itself (as a participant) so that they can better enjoy the results of such participation. Finally, *third-party capabilities* refer to the capabilities of those who are affected by market exchanges even if they are not connected to them as producers or consumers. This category needs to be included because of the ability of markets to produce negative externalities. Neighbors suffering damages, future generations being harmed by present production, etc. all are third parties whose capability interests need to be included in an assessment of markets.

For all these capabilities, thresholds need to be set. There is very little that can be said about this task in general. The normative criterion for selecting capabilities is crucial in setting thresholds as well. If—as I would propose—the criterion is (some form of) free and autonomous agency, then for every capability one would have to ask: how much of this capability does a person need, in terms of the potential of this capability to contribute to the person's ability to act autonomously? For some capabilities the answer may require adequate biological information (for example, assessing the capability of nourishment requires information about human metabolism and caloric intake); for other capabilities social and cultural information is crucial (for example, the capability for mobility depends on available technologies and networks of transportation). In all cases a margin of judgment is unavoidable. Once capability thresholds are established, judgment is also required when different capabilities conflict, to weigh the respective importance of each capability appropriately. Although little can be said in general about setting thresholds and weighing conflicting capabilities, there is one marked difference that can be identified in general between the capability framework and alternative approaches with an aggregative structure (such as most forms of utilitarianism): given its sufficientarian structure, further increases in one capability above the threshold will be (sharply) discounted against subthreshold levels of other capabilities. This can have important practical implications that differ from standard economic theories of regulation.[5]

[5] For example, in competition law, we argued that certain agreements between corporations, which raise prices for consumers (who remain, however, above the threshold for the relevant goods which are at stake) and would therefore be forbidden as market-distorting under an economistic approach, may need to be allowed if they bring third parties above the threshold. See Claassen and Gerbrandy 2016.

Let us now see in more detail how this general framework affects market regulation. Here we can build upon work already being done. I will discuss two examples of areas of market regulation where the capability approach has been applied: those of property law and contract law.

1. Property law. Gregory Alexander defends the position that property should be understood as a coin that has two sides. On the one hand a property owner has the right to exclude others from (unconsented) uses of his or her property. Property rights protect a zone of individual discretion. On the other hand, a property owner has social obligations that restrict the use of his or her property. The idea that a property right would only be characterized by the exclusionary side of the coin is a myth. There have always been restrictions on property. Both the granting of the exclusionary right and the imposing of social duties emanate from the same source: the decision-making authority of the relevant political community (Alexander 2009a). The question is not whether communities have the right to impose restrictions, but how to determine which restrictions are legitimate. Alexander rejects the law-and-economics scholarship that uses utility (welfare) as the decisive criterion for determining the legitimacy of restrictions. Instead, he proposes that this role should be fulfilled by the concept of human flourishing: "[t]he very factor that makes the institution of private property a social good is also the very factor that renders its limits, i.e. human flourishing" (Alexander 2009b, 750; similarly Alexander and Penalver 2012, 80–101). From this premise he derives the most general formulation of what he calls a *social-obligation norm*: "[a]n owner is morally obligated to provide the society of which the individual is a member those benefits that the society reasonably regards as necessary for human flourishing" (Alexander 2009b, 774). To develop this view, Alexander turns to Nussbaum's capability theory, applying it to two types of limits on property: expropriations and restrictions on use.

In the first category an example is the expropriation of a large landowner's piece of land by the South African state after several hundreds of poor black citizens had invaded the land and refused to leave. The Court refused to send these citizens back into homelessness and accepted the expropriation. At the same time it ordered compensation of the landowner, because the enormous problem of homelessness in South Africa should not fall disproportionally on this landowner, but as far as possible on the community as a whole. Alexander defends this ruling, appealing to capability theory:

> The squatters' access to land for dwellings is surely a component of the minimal material conditions for human flourishing, on almost any conception. The capabilities of life and freedom, for example, are virtually meaningless if one does not have a place one is entitled to be. (Alexander 2009b, 790)

In the second category a good example is the right to public access to beaches that are privately owned. In several cases courts have granted such a right (without compensation). Alexander defends this practice, in those cases where there are no public beaches available in the surrounding areas. He does so by referring to Nussbaum's capabilities for affiliation and recreation:

> recreation is not a luxury, especially for the poor. It is an important aspect of the capabilities of both life and affiliation. With respect to life as a good, ample and growing medical evidence indicates that recreation and relaxation contribute importantly to good health, reducing the risk of diseases ranging from depression to heart disease. ... The requisite socializing activity—affiliation—often, though not always is site-specific. It cannot be carried on just anywhere but must be done in a particular venue or at least at a particular type of venue. Baseball must be played on an open (hopefully) grassy area, whereas beachcombing requires an unobstructed beach. (Alexander 2009b, 805, 809)

These examples show how in the area of property law the capability approach pays attention to the freedom both of the property-owner (a participatory capability) and of the specific parties that are barred from access to vital consumptive capabilities: housing (for the squatters) or recreation (for those without access to the beach). Of course the judgments made in these contexts are highly context-dependent. The assessments Alexander makes are contingent upon (a) the specific capabilities he treats as basic (following Nussbaum), and (b) the thresholds he—or the judges in the South African case—set in assessing these capabilities. Such weightings are the bread and butter of legal cases, but this does not make them less controversial. The capability approach can here be seen as underlying and acknowledging these controversial assessments. It offers a common language to identify these interests, but cannot decide between them unless a more specific view is offered of how to select basic capabilities and determine thresholds.

2. Contract law. Simon Deakin has, in collaboration with others, applied the capability approach to contract law (Browne, Deakin, and Wilkinson 2002, Deakin and Browne 2003, Deakin 2006, 2010). He starts from the observation that contract law has developed considerably from its classical foundations in the eighteenth and nineteenth centuries. The classical view of contract law was built on a notion of (legal) "capacity." It is a vital precondition of a market economy to determine which contracts will be enforced and for this it is crucial to see who is legally able to make a contract. The doctrine of capacity excluded several categories from this ability. Normal adult citizens are supposed to be able to assess whether the contract they are making is in their own interests. In history, several groups were excluded (think of married women), but now only minors and those with grave mental illnesses are excluded from this contractual capacity. The assumption of having contractual capacity is now more widespread: most people are assumed to be able to make appropriate judgments (Deakin 2006, 322). However, Deakin argues, at the same time more and more restrictions have been placed on specific types of contracts. His central example is that of labor law. In the twentieth century, more and more mandatory and default terms have been introduced, designed mainly to protect laborers against the bargaining power of employers (Deakin 2006, 352).

For Deakin, these legal interventions are not distortions of the market process, but rather enhance the capacity of market participants, "endowing them with the resources needed to participate in market exchange in more than a purely formal or procedural sense" (Deakin 2006, 333). To theorize this legal change in economic terms, he argues, we have to switch from a standard economic framework to a capability approach. The crucial point is to see contract law as one of the conversion factors. These are the factors that determine how an individual is able to convert a resource bundle into a set of capabilities. The abilities of persons are a function both of resources and of the quality of institutional rules—hence the idea that "institutional rules do not simply constrain, they also empower" (Deakin 2006, 336). A case in point is discrimination law. Against the standard economic view of Gary Becker and others that persisting discrimination may be an efficient response of employers to market circumstances (if they are left unpunished by their customers), Deakin argues that discrimination unjustifiably excludes participants from the market. Anti-discrimination laws are necessary to make sure that markets empower individuals. Elsewhere, he argues that in a more general sense, the capability approach helps to see that social rights need to be inserted into rules structuring market exchanges, rather than being left exclusively to public systems of social provisioning (Deakin and Browne 2003, 39).

In terms of the capability framework presented above, Deakin's position strongly emphasizes the participatory capabilities of (potentially excluded) market participants, such as groups that are threatened with marginalization on the labor market. He never explicitly trades these off against the capabilities of other groups. His argument may be understood as implicitly claiming that these groups suffer from subthreshold levels of labor market participation (where such participation may be both intrinsically valuable and valuable for the instrumental benefits it brings, such as a wage). On the other side of the equation, there are the capabilities of employers who have to carry costs to comply with anti-discrimination laws and see their freedom of contract restricted, and the capabilities of consumers, who may have to pay for these costs in terms of increased prices. The framework invites us to balance benefits and costs in capability terms, under the crucial presupposition that improving the position of groups whose capabilities are in a subthreshold state should be prioritized to improving the position of groups whose capabilities are already at an above-threshold level.

Both illustrations from existing work in property and contract law show how the capability approach can be fruitfully applied to market regulation. It provides a paradigm shift compared to the standard (law-and-)economics approach. The framework in this section structures these applications by pointing to the need for a systematic inventory of all relevant capabilities and clarity about thresholds and weightings of these capabilities. Most importantly, the applications show that these types of regulation are not simply about "redistribution" between groups or "paternalism" vis-à-vis individuals, but ultimately about ensuring the capabilities necessary to act as autonomous agents, both on the market and outside of it.

3.6 REGULATING FINANCIAL MARKETS

The capability framework outlined above can also be applied to financial markets. Indeed, very often criticisms of standard economic approaches to financial markets can be systematized by making use of this framework; something like a capability approach can be reconstructed as a necessary ground for these moral evaluations. Let me close this chapter by illustrating this point with respect to the arguments of three of the chapters included in this volume.

In Chapter 13 Anat Admati argues that financial market regulation after the Great Financial Crisis of 2007–9 continues to be inadequate, so that too many risks remain hidden in the system. She attributes this to a misalignment between the interests of those working in the system and the interests of the public at large. The latter can best be understood along the lines of what I called *consumptive capabilities*, in so far as consumers of financial products often have a very basic interest in access to the financial system in order to buy a house or take out a small business loan, and *third-party capabilities* in as far as they relate to people who do not consume financial products themselves but whose interests are nonetheless negatively affected by a financial crisis (as taxpayers, as workers who lose their jobs, etc.). These capabilities have to be set against the *participatory capabilities* of bankers and others working in the system, who value maximum freedom to arrange transactions as they see fit. As with many other instances of consumer regulation, these serve the purpose of protecting consumers who suffer from information asymmetries (stretching, in some cases, into deception, manipulation, and fraud). The ultimate moral value at stake here is not consumer welfare, but the basic functionings of consumers. Given the necessity of taking out credit for many normal life plans, autonomous agency requires a financial system serving consumers well. These capabilities need to be balanced, and the sufficientarian framework advocated here suggests that consumers' capabilities are more basic for agency than the participatory capabilities of bankers who would like to take high risks.[6]

[6] Elsewhere, I argued that this requires a new social contract between the financial industry and society, determining the appropriate level of risk within the system. See Claassen 2015.

What is striking about Admati's text is that it then moves the discussion to a higher level: why does regulation continue to fail consumers and the public? Her suggestion is that regulatory capture, inadequate media coverage, and corporate lobbying are an important part of the answer. This points us to the political game about market regulation. This suggests an even further extension of the capability framework offered here, in two senses. One is that the level of *financial literacy* of consumers needs to be raised, so that they can adequately evaluate offers by the financial industry. Financial literacy (like literacy generally) is a capability in its own right. While general literacy is a basic capability (in Nussbaum's sense), financial literacy can best be reconstructed as part of consumers' participatory capabilities. For consumers to be able to act as agents on financial markets, they need this kind of training. A second extension is to the political process. In the end, all the capabilities of individuals on financial markets mentioned so far are determined by the political system—hence citizens' *political capabilities* to organize themselves and to provide a counterweight to the lobbying of financial corporations are crucial. This may be reconstructed as instrumental to their first-order market-based capabilities, but is crucial nonetheless.

In Chapter 12 Roseanne Russell and Charlotte Villiers discuss the issue of gender justice in financial markets. This is a topic also regularly discussed within the capability approach (e.g. Robeyns 2003). Russell's and Villiers's main target is an economic approach that aims to enhance women's participation in corporate decision-making just because this kind of diversity maximizes profits: women in the boardroom are "good for business." This "business case" for gender equality is problematic, they hold, because it focuses on individuals instead of groups, and because it instrumentalizes the issue of social justice between the groups of men and women (equal opportunity on the labor market). As a result, gender justice as a whole may not be served by having more women in leading positions, since these are currently coopted by male elites and may therefore tend to adopt masculine norms and remain passive about the rights of women lower down the chain (there is no "trickle down" of gender concerns). Instead, Russell and Villiers advocate an approach that broadens attention beyond the quota for women in the boardroom, toward the corporation as a whole where women need to be included at all levels. Moreover, they advocate focusing on empowerment and representation of women as a group instead of the "1% feminism" which characterizes the business case for gender diversity.

These concerns align very well with the capability approach advocated here. Three steps are necessary for the framework to apply to these issues. One is that the labor market, given its specific nature, requires special conceptualization. People's own time, energy, identity, and need for recognition are at stake in work; work is much more than financial remuneration (Gheaus and Herzog 2016). Laborers' "consumptive capabilities" here refer to these material and immaterial things they get out of work; since the laborer is the supplier of work we could better call this *productive capabilities*. Moreover, the chapter focuses on the subcategory of women laborers and their demands for equal inclusion (like that of other groups demanding equal opportunity), which can best be conceptualized as a participatory capability. To be able to effectively participate in the labor market, the male-dominated social norms within this market need to be transformed. In the capability approach, these social norms are one of the conversion factors that make it the case that an equal bundle of resources can nevertheless translate into unequal capabilities sets for individuals. It should be noted, however, that although the sociological analysis of these conversion factors needs to be sensitive to the stigmatizing effects on groups as a whole, the ultimate moral concern in the capability approach remains with the individual and his or her equal opportunities. There is a difference between ethical and methodological individualism—the capability approach adopts the first but not the second. Third and finally, the issue of gender equality also points us to the need for adequate *political capabilities* to bring about change (Russell and Villiers briefly discuss this need for a reinvigorated social movement and collective action).

Finally, in Chapter 11 Boudewijn de Bruin discusses the role of justice with respect to rating agencies. He observes that they have received much criticism after the financial crisis, but ultimately finds this to rest on a faulty ascription of responsibilities. As private agents, businesses should be responsible for their own risk assessments. They should not rely on rating agencies, who have no moral duty to provide accurate information. Likening this to a newspaper which only publishes gossip, De Bruin qualifies such behavior as unvirtuous, but not violating any moral rights. The investors (buyers of bonds or securities) should beware of the risks they run. In addition, De Bruin criticizes the US government for having required many institutional investors to take the information of rating agencies into account, and to disinvest when ratings drop below a certain level. This has gained the agencies an audience that should have remained free to decide whether or not to take the agencies' information into account. The right approach to risk assessment on financial markets, then, is deregulation instead of more regulation.

De Bruin's chapter raises crucial questions about what I have called participatory capabilities. In particular, the question is whether every citizen in a society has a right to be included in every market. This question necessitates making a distinction between *general* participatory capabilities—to be able to hold property and make contracts in ways protected by the general civil code—, and *particular* participatory capabilities which are only relevant for certain markets. While we need to accept the equality of citizens in terms of these general capabilities, this is an open question for the specific capabilities. The concept of agency goes beyond merely formal freedoms to require that people actually have the capacities for autonomous decision-making in the relevant context. However, people may suffer from "autonomy gaps," that is, gaps between what the policy requires from them and what capacities they have. At least two solutions offer themselves: either a policy to enhance people's capabilities or a policy that requires suppliers to lower the complexity of their products (J. Anderson 2014). De Bruin opts for a third option: letting these gaps subsist. This hands-off approach may be justified if a specific market does not fulfil a vital interest (i.e. in terms of necessarily contributing to a basic capability), so that participation is truly optional. Whether this is the case for rating agencies would require more discussion about the specific content and weight of these capabilities. At any rate, the capability framework does not point to any of these three options as the a priori best one.

This brief overview is far from conclusive with respect to the specific arguments made in the financial context. It does however show that the capability framework can be fruitfully linked to issues within concrete markets. Moreover, as the discussion shows, consideration of these cases has helped us to refine and extend the framework, including new capabilities and subdivisions within existing ones (see Table 3.1). More applied work on financial markets could help to bring out this potential even further. In this chapter I have tried to clear the theoretical ground for this, by trying to show how the capability approach can help us to frame the existing normative grounds for regulating markets into a unified and powerful normative framework.

Table 3.1. Framework of capabilities relevant to market regulation

1. Participatory capabilities—i.e. capabilities to participate on the market as agents
   a. general: capability to hold property and contract (as protected by civil law)
   b. market-specific capabilities, e.g. financial literacy
2. Instrumental capabilities:
   a. Consumptive capabilities—i.e. capabilities of consumers (e.g. to housing, as dependent on the financial system)
   b. Productive capabilities—i.e. capabilities of laborers (e.g. women laborers in financial organizations)
3. Third-party capabilities—e.g. those of citizens not directly involved in the financial system but suffering from the economic consequences of financial crises
4. Political capabilities—i.e. capabilities for political action to influence regulation about the other categories of capabilities

REFERENCES

Alexander, Gregory. 2009a. "The Complex Core of Property." *Cornell Law Review* 94(4), 1063–71.

Alexander, Gregory. 2009b. "The Social-Obligation Norm in American Property Law." *Cornell Law Review* 94(4), 745–819.

Alexander, Gregory, and Eduardo Penalver. 2012. *An Introduction to Property Theory*. Cambridge: Cambridge University Press.

Anderson, Elizabeth. 2010. "Justifying the Capability Approach to Justice." In *Measuring Justice: Primary Goods and Capabilities*, edited by Harry Brighouse and Ingrid Robeyns. Cambridge: Cambridge University Press, 81–100.

Anderson, Joel. 2014. "Regimes of Autonomy." *Ethical Theory and Moral Practice* 17, 355–68.

Axelsen, David, and Lasse Nielsen. 2014. "Sufficiency as Freedom from Duress." *Journal of Political Philosophy* 23(4), 406–26.

Baldwin, Robert, Martin Cave, and Martin Lodge. 2012. *Understanding Regulation: Theory, Strategy, and Practice*, 2nd edition. Oxford: Oxford University Press.

Barr, Nicholas. 2004. *Economics of the Welfare State*. Vol. 4. Oxford: Oxford University Press.

Bator, Francis M. 1958. "The Anatomy of Market Failure." *The Quarterly Journal of Economics* 72(3), 351–79.

Bozeman, Barry. 2002. "Public-Value Failure: When Efficient Markets May Not Do." *Public Administration Review* 62(2), 145–61.

Browne, Jude, Simon Deakin, and Frank Wilkinson. 2002. "Capabilities, Social Rights and European Market Integration." *ESRC Centre for Business Research, University of Cambridge* Working Paper 253.

Claassen, Rutger. 2012. "Review of Debra Satz's Why Some Things Should Not Be for Sale." *Business Ethics Quarterly* 22(3), 589–601.

Claassen, Rutger. 2015. "Financial Crisis and the Ethics of Moral Hazard." *Social Theory and Practice* 41(3).

Claassen, Rutger. 2016. "Justice in Regulation: Towards a Liberal Account." In *Theorizing Justice: Novel Insights, Future Directions*, edited by Jay Drydyk and Krushil Watene. London: Rowman & Littlefield.

Claassen, Rutger. 2017a. "An Agency-Based Capability Theory of Justice." *European Journal of Philosophy* forthcoming.

Claassen, Rutger. 2017b. *Navigational Agency: A Capability Theory of Justice*. Monograph in preparation.

Claassen, Rutger, and Anna Gerbrandy. 2016. "Rethinking Competition Law: From a Consumer Welfare to a Capability Approach." *Utrecht Law Review* 12(1), 1–15.

Cowen, Tyler. 1988. "Public Goods and Externalities: Old and New Perspectives." In *The Theory of Market Failure: A Critical Examination*, edited by Tyler Cowen Fairfax, VA: George Mason University Press, 1–26.

Deakin, Simon. 2006. "'Capacitas': Contract Law and the Institutional Preconditions of a Market Economy." *European Review of Contract Law* 2(3), 317–41.

Deakin, Simon. 2010. "Contracts and Capabilities: An Evolutionary Perspective on the Autonomy-Paternalism Debate." *Erasmus Law Review* 3(2), 141–53.

Deakin, Simon, and Jude Browne. 2003. "Social Rights and Market Order: Adapting the Capability Approach." In *Economic and Social Rights under the EU Charter of Fundamental Rights: A Legal Perspective*, edited by Tamara Hervey and Jeff Kenner. Portland, OR: Hart Publishing, 27–43.

Den Hertog, Johan. 1999. "General Theories of Regulation." In *Encyclopedia of Law and Economics, Volume III. The Regulation of Contracts*, edited by B. Bouckaert and G. de Geest. Cheltenham: Edward Elgar, 223–70.

Feintuck, Mike. 2010. "Regulatory Rationales Beyond the Economic: In Search of the Public Interest." In *The Oxford Handbook of Regulation*, edited by Robert Baldwin, Martin Cave, and Martin Lodge. Oxford: Oxford University Press, 39–63.

Gheaus, Anca, and Lisa Herzog. 2016. "The Goods of Work (other than Money!)." *Journal of Social Philosophy* 47(1), 70–89.

Johnson, Susan. 2009. "Institutions, Markets and Economic Development." In *An Introduction to the Human Development and Capability Approach*, edited by Séverine Deneulin. London: Earthscan, 162–84.

Le Grand, Julian. 1990. "Equity versus Efficiency: The Elusive Trade-Off." *Ethics* 100(3), 554–68.

Morgan, Brownen, and Karen Yeung. 2007. *An Introduction to Law and Regulation*. Cambridge: Cambridge University Press.

Nussbaum, Martha. 2000. *Women and Human Development: The Capabilities Approach*. Cambridge: Cambridge University Press.

Nussbaum, Martha. 2006. *Frontiers of Justice*. Cambridge, MA: The Belknap Press.

Nussbaum, Martha. 2011. *Creating Capabilities: The Human Development Approach*. Cambridge, MA: The Belknap Press.

Ogus, Anthony. 2004. *Regulation: Legal Form and Economic Theory*. Oxford: Hart Publishing.

Prosser, Tony. 2006. "Regulation and Social Solidarity." *Journal of Law and Society* 33(3), 364–87.

Robeyns, Ingrid. 2003. "Sen's Capability Approach and Gender Inequality: Selecting Relevant Capabilities." *Feminist Economics* 9(2–3), 61–90.

Satz, Debra. 2010. *Why Some Things Should Not Be for Sale: The Moral Limits of Markets*. New York: Oxford University Press.

Schuppert, Fabian. 2014. *Freedom, Recognition and Non-Domination: A Republican Theory of (Global) Justice*. Dordrecht: Springer.

Sen, Amartya. 1979. "Equality of What." *The Tanner Lectures on Human Values*. http://tannerlectures.utah.edu/.

Sen, Amartya. 1985. "The Moral Standing of the Market." *Social Philosophy and Policy* 2(2), 1–19.

Sen, Amartya. 1992. *Inequality Reexamined*. Cambridge, MA: Harvard University Press.

Sen, Amartya. 2009. *The Idea of Justice*. Cambridge, MA: The Belknap Press.

Soule, Edward. 2003. *Morality and Markets: The Ethics of Government Regulation*. Lanham: Rowman & Littlefield Publishers.

Stewart, Richard. 1982. "Regulation in a Liberal State." *Yale Law Journal* 92, 1537–90.

Stiglitz, Joseph. 2009. "Government Failure vs. Market Failure: Principles of Regulation." In *Government and Markets: Toward a New Theory of Regulation*, edited by Edward Balleisen and David Moss. New York: Cambridge University Press, 13–51.

Sunstein, Cass. 1990. *After the Rights Revolution: Reconceiving the Regulatory State*. Cambridge, MA: Harvard University Press.

Tomasi, John. 2012. *Free Market Fairness*. Princeton: Princeton University Press.

Trebilcock, Michael. 1993. *The Limits of Freedom of Contract*. London: Harvard University Press.

4

Financial markets and institutional purposes: The normative issues

Seumas Miller

4.1 INTRODUCTION

The massive economic, social, political, and other harms caused by the Global Financial Crisis, the Sovereign Debt Crisis, and the Great Recession have generated considerable scrutiny of financial markets and financial institutions, notably banks, and a variety of defects have been identified (see e.g. Garnaut 2009, MacNeil and O'Brien 2010, Dobos et al. 2011, Gilligan and O'Brien 2013, Morris and Vines 2014). These include structural problems (e.g. "too big to fail"[1] systemically important financial institutions), regulatory inadequacies (e.g. enabling regulatory arbitrage), criminal and unethical behavior indicative of corrupt cultures (e.g. benchmark manipulation), and short-termism (e.g. in equity markets). Accordingly, a wide variety of structural, regulatory, and culture-change reforms have been proposed and, in some cases, implemented (see e.g. UK Financial Services Authority 2009). These include increased capital ratios for banks, splitting retail/investment banking conglomerates into utilities, and market-based investment-only institutions,[2] providing government with the legal power to convert bank debt into equity (Financial Stability Board 2014), simplifying and harmonizing the regulatory architecture, redesigning oversight bodies and increasing their investigative and other powers, overhauling the administrative arrangements and methodologies in relation to financial benchmarks,

[1] See, for example, US Attorney General Eric Holder's answers to the Senate Judiciary Committee as reported in Sorkin (2013).

[2] Perhaps in accordance with the so-called Volcker Rule originally within the Dodd-Frank Wall Street Reform and Consumer Protection Act, but subsequently watered down.

strengthening the licensing requirements of financial institutions and occupations, banning "unsafe" financial products (e.g. various complex derivatives), curtailing executive remuneration, realigning the incentive arrangements for fund managers with the long-term interests of savers and companies, introducing legally based fiduciary duties for financial service providers, drafting codes of ethics, and embedding educational and other professionalization processes, and so on and so forth.

Whatever the virtues of many of these suggested reforms[3]—and, arguably, their main shortcoming is their failure to be implemented in the face of opposition from powerful financial interests[4]—they do not for the most part address the matter of institutional *purpose*. Institutional purpose has tended to be neglected in the reform process.[5] However, it is one of the principal tasks of those who regulate markets, principally legislators, and regulators, to ensure that the ultimate institutional purposes of markets, be they financial or otherwise, are in fact achieved (Miller 2010, chaps 2 and 10).

The notion of institutional purpose in play here is normative: the purposes that financial markets and financial institutions *ought to have*. Naturally, these purposes vary, or ought to vary, from one kind of financial market to another and from one kind of financial institution to another. Thus the institutional purpose of equity markets is not the same as that of foreign exchange markets. Again, the institutional purpose of pension funds is not the same as that of banks, and that of retail banks not the same as that of investment banks. Moreover, if one looks, for example, at the objectives of many regulators of financial markets one typically finds only limited aims, e.g. to reduce crime and protect consumers, and procedural concerns, e.g. to promote competition and efficiency. There is little or no reference to the ultimate institutional purposes or ends of particular financial markets. Accordingly, there is a pressing need for an adequate *general* normative account or "theory" of financial markets, and for adequate *special* normative "theories" of particular financial markets, e.g. equity markets.

In this chapter I discuss various currently influential normative theories of markets and market-based institutions, and reject them (Section 4.2). I go on to elaborate my own normative *teleological* account of social institutions

[3] For an overview of the global regulator's (IOSCO—International Organization of Securities Commissions) conception see Medcraft (2014). Medcraft is the current Chair of IOSCO.

[4] See, for example, Miller (2014c). See also note 2 regarding the Volcker Rule.

[5] This is not always the case. For example, Mark Carney, Governor of the Bank of England, implicitly recognizes institutional purpose in Carney (2014), and at the time of writing there is a somewhat belated discussion in Australia whether or not the purpose of Australia's compulsory retirement scheme (superannuation) ought to be specified and enshrined in law (Corporations Act 2001); and specified, in particular, as the purpose of providing an adequate income stream for retirees as opposed to, say, a pool of savings for investment by government or savers. Even an institution that was designed and constructed by government did not have its institutional purpose specified and agreed upon. See, for example, Mather and Rose (2016).

(Section 4.3) and apply it to financial markets, specifically, the banking sector, retirements saving schemes, and capital markets (Section 4.4).

4.2 NORMATIVE THEORIES OF MARKETS AND MARKET-BASED INSTITUTIONS

On one normative conception of markets, including financial markets, market actors act and ought to act in their self-interest and are entitled to do so on broadly libertarian grounds. In short, markets are, or ought to be, an expression of individual freedom (on the part of both buyers and sellers) and that is the end of the matter. On this radical free market conception the normative structure of markets consists essentially in procedural requirements, notably free and fair competition. So there is no moral requirement that markets serve larger collective purposes, such as maximizing overall utility.

Such radical free market enthusiasts—market fundamentalists[6]—argue that any institutional purposes of markets ought to be subservient to or, indeed, ought to be merely an expression of, the freely made choices of market actors (Miller 2011). Here there is often a conflation of organizations and individuals. Doubtless, the protection and promotion of individual freedom is a good thing, but large corporations are far from being individual human beings and, therefore, maximizing the freedom of the former is not necessarily maximizing the freedom of the latter. Indeed, the reverse is likely to be the case; increasing the freedom to act of large and powerful organizations often comes at the expense of the freedom of relatively powerless individuals, such as individual employees, consumers, and clients. The excesses of banks and other financial institutions in the Global Financial Crisis, and the consequent harm done to individual consumers, homeowners, retirees, investors etc., graphically illustrate this point.

Moreover, this unqualified belief in free markets ignores the problem of the massively harmful effects of many free market practices, such as large-scale speculative trading, on nonparticipants in those markets; for example, the creation of cycles of bubble and bust that have undermined financial stability and significantly contributed to severe economic downturns. As J. S. Mill (1859) and others of a liberal persuasion stress, it is good to exercise one's freedom of choice, but bad—and likely morally wrong—to cause harm to others in doing so. Moreover, many, if not most, financial and other institutions operating in financial markets are not private sector firms in the sense

[6] Soros (2009) refers to such adherents as market fundamentalists and subjects them to sustained pejorative criticism.

required by the premise of this fundamentalist argument. Firstly, financial institutions, such as banks and pension funds, are dependent on governments to an extent and in a manner that other market actors are not. For example, governments (implicitly, if not explicitly) guarantee the deposits of (at least) systemically important banks; moreover, governments have established central banks to function as lenders of last resort to banks. It is fanciful to think that the retail banking sector, in particular, could operate without these safeguards provided by governments. Again, pension funds in many countries depend on compulsory savings and, therefore, on government policies and enforcement thereof. Secondly, many organizations operating in financial markets are corporations and, as such, the institutional creations of governments; they are not the pre-existing market actors of the ideology of market fundamentalism. Governments have granted special *privileges* to corporations (notably, the limited liability of shareholders) for a reason (Ciepley 2013). Presumably, the reason for granting this privilege is that corporations will have the general institutional purpose of serving the community at large. At any rate, morally justifiable granting by governments of special privileges must serve *some* defensible social purpose. Thirdly, financial markets are in part constituted by financial infrastructure, such as interest rate and currency benchmarks, which provide public goods upon which market actors rely. At the core of competitive financial markets is infrastructure serving collective purposes (Miller 2014a). Fourthly, even if financial institutions, such as insurance companies, are not directly dependent on governments in the manner that, for example, banks are nevertheless, many of these institutions are corporations: they typically rely on financial benchmarks (e.g. in the case of derivative contracts that provide insurance against financial loss), and they depend in various ways on financial institutions which are directly dependent on governments (such as banks). In short, the freely acting, rationally self-interested, institutionally prior, human individual of the ideology of market fundamentalism is a myth, and a self-serving and harmful myth at that.

On a second normative conception, markets—including, presumably, financial markets—do serve, or ought to serve, larger collective purposes. This second normative conception is surely more plausible than the first, given that the first denies, in effect, that markets have any institutional purpose at all. However, this second conception is a very broad church and it includes a number of quite different, indeed often opposing, normative "theories." In relation to markets in general, there is the appeal to the workings of the so-called "invisible"[7] hand; each market actor pursues their individual rational

[7] My use of scare quotes is to imply that the so-called invisible hand is, and ought to be, more visible than sometimes assumed, especially to legislators, regulator, and industry leaders.

economic self-interest and, by means of the "invisible" hand, the common good is maximized. There are also normative theories of the corporation, such as the Shareholder Value Theory (SVT)[8] and Corporate Social Responsibility (CSR) theories.[9] SVT holds that the ultimate institutional purpose of corporations is to maximize profits and, thereby, maximize shareholder value. Since many financial institutions are corporations, their ultimate purpose must also, presumably, be to maximize profits and shareholder value. CSR theories canvass a wider range of "stakeholders," such as employees, customers, and the community, and emphasize the so-called triple bottom line of "Profit, People, and Planet." However, none of these currently influential normative theories of the individual corporation or of the markets in which they compete is compelling.

The idea of the "invisible" hand mechanism, while important, needs to be put on a narrower and more sound footing than a general appeal to the amorphous notions of maximizing utility (however utility is understood, e.g. happiness, pleasure, preference satisfaction), optimizing welfare or the like. Moreover, it is far from obvious that in all, or most, markets the pursuit of individual rational self-interest, even in the context of free and fair competition, actually maximizes overall utility. Whether it does or not is an empirical question. Our concern is with financial markets. So let us consider occupational groups in the financial sector with fiduciary duties to their clients (Miller 2014b): occupations such as banker, fund manager, financial planner, and so on. Evidently, the pursuit of individual rational self-interest, notably profit maximization, by the members of these occupational groups, far from maximizing overall utility, has been extraordinarily harmful to clients and highly damaging to the markets themselves.

For its part, SVT confuses (part of) the means (shareholder value) with the end (e.g. an adequate quantum of some good or service). Evidently financial rewards such as wages, executive remuneration, and dividends are proximate, not ultimate, purposes; they are part of the reward system and, as such, the means to an end. The *raison d'être* for the establishment of retail banks is not to maximize shareholder dividends, much less enrich bankers, but rather to provide a secure place for depositors' funds, enable payments to be made, and the like. If a retail bank consistently fails to realize these latter purposes then it is failing as an institution, even if for some reason it continues to make a profit and, thereby, benefits shareholders. Again, the ultimate purpose of insurance companies is to provide insurance rather than to maximize shareholder

[8] See Friedman (1970). For criticisms, albeit different from the ones I make here, see Stout (2012). Importantly, Stout argues that there is no legal obligation on the part of CEOs and other managers to maximize shareholder value; this is a myth.

[9] For an elaboration and criticisms (again, different from the ones I make here) of these various theories, including CSR theories, see Audi (2008).

dividends; the latter are a means to the former. If an insurance company makes a profit but consistently fails to pay out when it should, then it is failing as an institution; it is not providing actual (as opposed to promised) insurance, notwithstanding the benefits to shareholders. Moreover, SVT unacceptably narrows the list of stakeholders so that it consists only in shareholders (or are at best rendered entirely subservient to the interests of shareholders); remarkably, the interests of customers and clients, in particular, are omitted!

CSR theories, on the other hand, cast the net of stakeholders too wide and, thereby, dilute institutional purpose. CSR theories provide long lists of stakeholders, including not only shareholders, managers, employees, customers, and clients, but also suppliers, other industry players, the environment, the wider society, and so on. No doubt, firms need from time to time to attend to a wide range of parties who are affected, positively or negatively, by their activities, as we all do. Certainly, they ought to avoid harming people and damaging the environment (and ought to provide compensation if they do). But the content of a normative theory of the corporation or of a particular industry or market cannot simply consist of a long list of affected parties, on pain of having provided little more than an unhelpfully general prescription to avoid harm and to be beneficent wherever possible. Aside from the absence of clear direction provided by such a prescription, it may tend to encourage window-dressing (e.g. minor charitable donations), at the expense of focused attention on what ought to be the core activity of an industry, and scrutiny of the manner in which that activity is undertaken. In short, CSR loses sight of the main game in any given industry: the producers or providers of the product or service and their customers or clients.

In the light of the above deficiencies in prevailing normative accounts of markets and market-based institutions, I have proffered a general normative teleological theory and derived special normative theories. On this conception, which I have elaborated in detail elsewhere (Miller 2010), markets are social institutions and, as such, ought to serve collective ends and, specifically, generate collective goods. However, the collective goods in question are narrowly specified. It is not a matter of maximizing general utility, however defined, but rather of market actors competing with one another under conditions of free and fair competition and in doing so jointly producing an adequate and sustainable quantum of some specific good or service at a reasonable price and of reasonable quality. In the case of capital markets, the good in question is an adequate supply of financial capital for investment by productive enterprises; in the case of pension funds it is an adequate quantum of funds to provide for workers' post-retirement; and so on. In what follows I develop and argue for this conception. I begin with an elaboration of my teleological normative account of social institutions.

4.3 A TELEOLOGICAL, NORMATIVE ACCOUNT OF SOCIAL INSTITUTIONS

Our first task is the provision of a viable account of social institutions. In fact, the term, "social institution," is somewhat unclear both in ordinary language and in the philosophical literature. However, contemporary sociology is rather more consistent in its use of the term. Typically, contemporary sociologists use the term to refer to complex social forms that reproduce themselves, such as governments, universities, hospitals, business corporations, markets, and legal systems. A typical definition is that proffered by Jonathan Turner: "a complex of positions, roles, norms and values lodged in particular types of social structures and organizing relatively stable patterns of human activity with respect to fundamental problems in producing life-sustaining viable societal structures within a given environment" (Turner 1997, 6). Notice that some social institutions are market-based, some are not.

Social institutions need to be distinguished from less complex social forms such as conventions, social norms, roles, and rituals. The latter are among the constitutive elements of institutions. Social institutions also need to be distinguished from more complex and more complete social entities, such as societies, polities, or cultures, of which any given institution is typically a constitutive element. A society or polity, for example, is more complete than an institution since a society—at least as traditionally understood—is more or less self-sufficient (e.g. in terms of its capacity to provide for the full range of the basic needs of its members), whereas an institution is not.

Social institutions are often organizations. Moreover, many institutions are *systems* of organizations. For example, capitalism is a particular kind of economic institution, and in modern times capitalism consists in large part in specific organizational forms—including multinational corporations—organized into a system. Further, some institutions are *meta-institutions*: they are institutions (organizations) that organize other institutions (including systems of organizations). For example, governments are meta-institutions (Miller 2010, chap. 12). The institutional end or function of a government consists in large part in organizing other institutions (both individually and collectively); thus governments regulate and coordinate economic systems largely by way of (enforceable) legislation. Note that in the modern world many global social institutions (e.g. the global financial system) transcend in various respects the boundaries and jurisdictional and/or enforcement reach of the meta-institutions (e.g. national governments) that regulate and coordinate their activities.

On this teleological (from the Greek word *telos* meaning point or purpose) account of social institutions, collective ends are collective goods by virtue of their possession of the following three properties (Miller 2010, chap. 2): (1) they are produced, maintained, or renewed by means of the *joint activity* of members of organizations, e.g. schools, hospitals, welfare organizations, agribusinesses, electricity providers, police services, banks, insurance companies, pension funds, superannuation trusts, i.e. by institutional role occupants; (2) they are *available to the whole community*, e.g. clean drinking water, clean environment, basic foodstuffs, electricity, banking services, investment services, legal services, education, health, safety, and security, and (3) they *ought* to be produced (or maintained or renewed) and made available to the whole community since they are desirable (as opposed to merely desired), and such that the members of the community have an *(institutional) joint moral right* to them. (See p. 90 for more on the notion of a joint right.)

Note that our notion of a collective good, as defined, is different from standard notions of so-called public goods deployed by economists and others. Economists typically define public goods as being non-rival and non-excludable. If a good is non-rival then my enjoyment of it does not prevent or diminish the possibility of your enjoyment of it, e.g. a street sign is non-rival since my using it to find my way has no effect on you likewise using it. Again, a good is non-excludable if it is such that if anyone is enjoying the good then no-one can be prevented from enjoying it, e.g. national defense. However, our notion of a collective good is defined not in terms of non-rivalness or non-excludability but in terms of its being jointly produced and having an explicitly normative character as the object of a joint moral right. As such, it is available for use in relation to market-based institutions that produce goods that are rival and/or excludable, as well as in relation to non-market-based institutions.

An important underlying assumption here is that *contra* much economic theory, human beings are not always and everywhere motivated by individual rational self-interest, albeit self-interest is a powerful and pervasive driver.[10] However, moral beliefs and, specifically, doing one's moral duty for its own sake—as the German philosopher Immanuel Kant stressed—are an important additional motivation for action, and one not reducible to self-interest at the expense of the goals of others (Sen 2002) (no matter how self-interest is conceived, e.g. self-centeredness, pursuit of one's own goals or preferences—whatever they might be). Here it is important to note that the duties constitutive of professional and institutional roles (see pp. 89–90) are often also *moral* duties and, therefore, doing one's professional and/or institutional duty is often also discharging one's moral duty. Moreover, it is the mark of members of the professions, and mature institutional actors more generally, that they internalize the constitutive principles and purposes of their role in a manner that enables them to transcend their prior and limited, individually rational self-interested goals and interests.

The rational choice model assumes rational self-interested individuals in competition with one another. This is fine as far as it goes. However, as

[10] The relationship between self-interest and morality is, of course, complex. See Bloomfield (2008).

Amartya Sen and others have argued, it is far from being the whole of the story (Sen 2002). Specifically, it does not leave room for rational individual action performed in the collective self-interest and/or in accordance with socially engendered moral principles and purposes (see Elster 1989, Miller 2001, chap. 6); yet the latter are ubiquitous features of human collective life, including in the economic sphere.

What is needed at this point is the acceptance that individual human agents can, and often do, engage in action-determining reasoning from collective goals and interests to individual actions: collective goals and interests to which members of social groups and organizations are strongly committed. On this view of individual reasoning from common goals and collective interests to their own individual action, what is called for is a conception of an individual human agent *qua member of an occupational group or organization*, for example qua banker or qua financial planner. In short, the individual internalizes the collective goals and interests of the occupational group or organization to which he or she belongs. Crucially, these collective goals and interests can, and often do, transcend the role occupant's prior and limited, individually rational self-interested, goals and interests. Moreover, the collective goals and interests in question can be, and often are, embraced by the individuals in question on the grounds that they are desirable from an impartial or, at least, a collective standpoint.[11]

A further point regarding the individual rational self-interest model is one typically made by behavioral economists, namely, that human beings are often irrational, in terms of both their individual and their collective self-interest. Consider the phenomena of herding and cognitive bias evidenced in booms and busts on the share-market. Consider also the lack of knowledge and the unwillingness or inability to acquire it, on the part of so-called unsophisticated investors.

So institutional design needs to proceed on the assumption that rational self-interest, irrationality, and morality are all important drivers of, and motivations for, human action, and that none of them necessarily dominates the others when they come into conflict, as they often do.

In the light of the above, it is clear that on the normative teleological account of social institutions, institutions, including financial markets, ought to achieve particular institutional purposes in the overall macro-institutional moral and legal framework setting in which they exist. Moreover, they do so by means of specific institutional structures and, for that matter, cultures.

[11] This capacity of individuals to reason from, and act in accordance with, collective goals and interests is not without its problems. For example, the collective goals in question might be inherently morally problematic (e.g. those of the Third Reich), or the collective interest of the members of an organization in question might be at variance with the interests of the wider society (e.g. the members of an investment bank with a business model based on constructing and on-selling toxic financial products).

Accordingly, there are at least three salient *general* normative issues that arise, namely:

(1) *Institutional purpose*: What *ought to be* the principal institutional purposes of the various financial markets?

(2) *Institutional means:*

  (a) *Structure, including individual rights and duties*: Is the market-based industry structured so as to adequately realize its institutional purposes. For example, are there "too big to fail" institutions? Is the structure of institutional duties (e.g. fiduciary duties) and rewards (e.g. remuneration packages) morally acceptable? More specifically, does the structure comply with relevant moral principles and does it facilitate the principal institutional purposes of the financial market in question?

  (b) *Culture*: Is the organizational culture morally problematic? More specifically, does it comply with relevant moral principles and is it conducive to the realization of the principal institutional purposes of the financial market in question?

(3) *Macro-institutional context*: What role ought the financial market in question play in the larger economic order and, more specifically, what ought its relationship be to relevant other socio-economic institutions? Should Wall Street serve Main Street?

4.3.1 Institutional purpose: collective goods

The basic normative question that needs to be asked of a business organization, financial market, or financial occupation, I suggest, is the same as for any other social institution, namely: What *collective good(s)* does it exist to provide? Consider capital markets. The most salient—if not the only (see pp. 98–9)—collective good that capital markets exist to provide is an adequate and sustainable supply of capital at a reasonable price. I note the distinction between proximate and ultimate institutional purposes or ends: collective goods are the ultimate purposes of social institutions, but not necessarily their proximate purposes.

In the case of business organizations and markets these collective goods include: (1) the coordination of buyers and sellers of goods and services, and (2) a quantum of a product or service sufficient to meet the relevant aggregate needs of the population in question.[12] Here Adam Smith's "invisible" hand mechanism is salient (Smith 1776).[13] The outcome (a collective good) of the

[12] For the developed version of the material in this section see Miller (2010, chaps 2 and 10). Some of the material in this section is drawn from that volume.

[13] In fact the notion of an invisible hand, while famously attributed to Smith, is scarcely to be found in his writings. See Rothschild and Sen (2006, 363).

workings of the invisible hand is the ultimate purpose (collective end) of this institutional mechanism (e.g. an adequate supply of houses, or of auditing services, or of retirement savings, or of capital etc.); profit maximization is the proximate end.

The existence of profit maximization adds a complication in the case of market-based organizations that is not present in the case of other social institutions. In the case of market-based organizations, but not necessarily other social institutions, there are *three* collective ends, namely, the constitutive collective end (e.g. the production of cars, the accumulation of depositor funds in banks, the accumulation of savings for investment, the accumulation of savings for future use); the collective good (e.g. transport, security of savings, investment of funds in infrastructure, income stream for retirees); and (thirdly) profit maximization.

Notice that a constitutive collective end is not necessarily a collective good. Consider so-called toxic financial products, for example packages of sub-prime mortgages. The production of these financial products was the (realized) collective end of the members of investment banks. However, as it turns out, these products contributed significantly to the global financial crisis; they caused great harm to many groups, including ultimately to taxpayers when banks holding these "assets" were bailed out by governments. So the realization of this collective end was not a collective good; quite the reverse.

Moreover, we can now see that there are two potentially competing collective ends, namely, collective goods and profit maximization (in the case of corporations: profit maximization in order in turn to maximize shareholder value). By the lights of our account of social institutions, the claim must be that the pursuit of the collective end of profit maximization as an end will, as a matter of contingent fact—and by virtue of the "invisible" hand—realize the collective good definitive of the social institution in question. Unfortunately, the empirical claim upon which the efficacy of the "invisible" hand is predicated is contestable and, in some cases (as we saw in Section 4.1 in respect of occupations with fiduciary duties) evidently false. For example, the reliance on wholly market-based mechanisms for the provision of investment funds for much needed infrastructure in Australia has been a failure.

4.3.2 Institutional means

4.3.2.1 Structure, rights, and duties

Thus far we have focused on one dimension of the normative character of social institutions, namely, institutional purpose and, specifically, the collective goods that institutions produce (or ought to produce). However, there are two other normative dimensions worthy of note here. Firstly, there are the moral constraints on institutional activity. In this regard institutional activity is no different from non-institutional human activity; the prohibitions on murder, fraud, and theft, for example, constrain institutional activities.

Secondly—and more importantly for our concerns here—there is the structure of particular institutions, bearing in mind that institutional purpose ought to give direction to structure. At a general level, there is the question of whether an institution ought to be a market-based institution at all. This ought not to be a question of ideology but rather an empirical question: what structure, be it market-based or non-market-based, best realizes institutional purpose?

Here it needs to be noted that the distinction between market-based and non-market-based institutions is not necessarily a strict dichotomy; there is also the possibility of hybrid institutions: institutions that utilize the mechanism of the market but are not wholly market-based. As we have seen, compulsory retirement savings systems and financial benchmarks upon which capital markets depend are cases in point; and there are many others. But to reiterate: by the lights of our normative teleological account of social institutions, whether an institution ought to be wholly market-based, non-market-based, or a hybrid of both, is a matter to be settled by recourse to collective goods: it is a matter of which of these three models most efficiently and effectively enables the collective good in question to be produced.

Further structural issues pertain to the size of market actors (e.g. "too big to fail" banks), structural conflicts of interest (e.g. ratings agencies that rate the financial products of investment banks, which in turn fund the ratings agencies), and regulators who are themselves "players in the game," e.g. the UK's Financial Conduct Authority pursues the particular interests of the City of London, potentially at the expense of other financial centers. Again, by the light of my normative teleological account these matters of structure ought to be settled by recourse to the collective goods that the markets in question, including global markets, ought to be realizing. "Too big to fail banks" are obviously unacceptable, given the threat they pose to the international financial system and, therefore, to the collective goods which that system ought to be realizing. For the same reason, structural conflicts of interest need to be removed. Regarding regulators who are not impartial, the point to be made is that the collective good of a global financial market cannot merely be the interests of the City of London.

Thirdly, there are, as already noted, a variety of *institutionally relative* moral rights and duties (as opposed to moral rights and duties that are logically prior to all institutions (i.e. natural rights and duties) or otherwise transcend particular institutions) that are derived at least in part from institutionally produced collective goods and, indeed, that are constitutive of specific institutional roles, e.g. the rights and duties of a fire officer or of a banker or of a fund manager or of a financial advisor. These institutional rights and duties (which are also moral rights and duties) are constitutive of institutional roles and, therefore, are in part constitutive of the structure of specific institutions. And since the structure of an institution is, or ought to be, an important part of the means by which its institutional purposes are achieved, so it is that these institutional moral rights and duties are part of the means and hence, in part, derived from the institution's large purpose—its defining collective good. Thus debates about whether financial advisors ought to have the institutional right to charge commissions as opposed to, say, fees for services ought, on this view, to be settled by recourse to the relative contributions of these two competing structures of occupational rights and duties to the larger institutional purpose (viz. efficient and effective provision of retirement savings).

These structured sets of moral rights and duties are institutionally relative in the following sense. Even if they are in part based on an institutionally prior human right (e.g. the human need of the elderly for food, clothing, and shelter), their precise content, strength, context of application (e.g. jurisdiction, national territory, particular economy), and so on can only be determined by reference to the institutional arrangements in which they exist and, specifically, in the light of their contribution to the collective good(s) provided by those institutional arrangements. Thus the specific needs-based rights of an elderly person in contemporary Australia to be paid a certain sum of money during the period of their retirement is institutionally relative to the Australian pension and superannuation system (and to the specific contributions that that elderly retiree made during their period in the workforce).

There is a further distinction that we need to invoke at this point, namely, that between *individual* institutional (moral) rights and *joint* institutional (moral) rights. Joint moral rights are moral rights that attach to individual persons, but do so jointly. For example, the joint owners of a house might have a joint right to occupy the house; that is, each has an individual right to occupy the house, but each only has this right conditionally on the other likewise having it. Joint rights need to be distinguished from universal individual human or natural rights (as opposed to individual *institutional* rights). The right to life is an example of a universal individual human right. Each human being has an individual human right to life. However, since one's possession of the right to life is wholly dependent on properties one possesses as an individual, it is not the case that one's possession of the right to life is dependent on someone else's possession of that right.

As we have seen, sometimes the end realized in joint action is not merely a collective end, it is also a collective *good*. (By *collective* good I simply mean that the good is collectively or jointly produced; I do not mean to imply that it is collectively or jointly consumed—it might be, and often is, individually consumed.) If so, then a joint right may well be generated. What is the relationship between joint moral rights and collective goods? The good is a realized collective end; and the participants in realizing that collective end, that is, the contributors to the production of that good, possess a joint right to this collective good.

It is easy to see why these persons, and not some other persons, would have a right to such a good: they are the ones responsible for its existence, or continued existence. In this connection consider the shareholders, members of the board of directors, managers, and workers (shareholders, officers, and employees) in a company that builds blocks of apartments that are sold for profit. Board members, managers, shareholders, and construction workers have a joint right to be financially remunerated from the sales of the apartments that they have jointly produced (albeit the amount of money to which each has an individual right may vary from one individual to another, depending on the nature and extent of their individual contribution). Moreover, if a component of the financial benefits to which they have a joint right is channeled into, say, a pension fund then they have a joint right to these funds (albeit, again, the amount of money to which each has an individual right may vary from one individual to another, depending on the extent of their individual contributions over time). It is also clear that if one participating agent has a right to the good, then—other things being equal—so do the others. That is, there is interdependence of rights with respect to the good. The same point holds of workers (who provide labor), managers (who provide leadership), and investors (who provide capital): they have joint rights with respect to the financial benefits arising from the goods or services produced (e.g. whether in the form of wages, salaries, dividends etc.).

Naturally, the remuneration is in many cases dependent on the specific legal contracts that have been entered into, including contracts of employment. However, these joint moral rights are not equivalent to, or reducible to, moral rights based on legal contracts. Rather, normatively speaking, these contracts presuppose the joint moral rights in question; it is because a construction worker, for example, has contributed (jointly with others) to the construction of the apartment buildings that he is morally entitled to a wage (whatever the legal situation might be). Moreover, this normative relationship between contracts and underlying joint moral rights is in evidence when it is claimed that a specific contractual payment was fair or unfair. For a contract might or might not reflect a person's contribution to the production of a collective good, depending on a host of contingencies (notably relationships of power). Consider in this connection the extraordinarily generous executive compensation packages on offer in some corporations, including investment banks which have had to be bailed out with taxpayers' money. In many cases there is no correlation between executive compensation and contribution to the collective goods produced by the corporation or even to the profits generated by the corporation (Gregg and Tonks 2005).

4.3.2.2 Culture

It is increasingly recognized by regulators and others that institutional culture is an important determinant of individual behavior.[14] However, these discussions are typically focused on unethical or illegal behavior and on the malign influence of culture, for example the culture of traders in recent cases of benchmark manipulation. What is missing from these deliberations is the relationship, or lack thereof, between culture (including both ethical and unethical dimensions of culture) and institutional purpose. Whether or not the members of some organization internalize the *desirable* ends and principles of an organization—as opposed to undesirable ones—is in part a matter of structure, e.g. eliminating structural conflicts of interest, but it is also in part a matter of institutional culture. Institutional culture is in turn dependent on the extent to which the collective moral responsibility (see Miller 2015) to achieve desirable ends, and eschew corrupt practices, is embedded in the organization by way of explicit institutional mechanisms (e.g. formal continuing education programs in professional ethics, whistle-blower protection schemes, remuneration systems that do not encourage excessive risk taking) and implicit practices (e.g. managers who acknowledge their mistakes, employees who are unafraid to voice their concerns).

If, on the other hand, the prevailing ethos or culture of an organization, and perhaps even ideology of central elements of a sector, downplays desirable institutional goals and other ethical considerations in favor of the pursuit of individual self-interest then it should hardly surprise when individual self-interest overrides compliance with ethical principles, even ones enshrined in the law. This is no doubt especially the case in a context of high temptation and opportunity, on the one hand, and low risk of detection and conviction, on the other, e.g. LIBOR manipulation by bank traders motivated by large bonuses in a context of an oversight body with a structural conflict of interest.

4.4 FINANCIAL MARKETS AND INSTITUTIONAL PURPOSES

4.4.1 Banking sector

As mentioned above, on this teleological account, both organizations and markets are essentially complex structures of joint action and, as such, have collective ends that are also collective goods. Financial institutions, such as banks, are no different from any other social institution in this respect; that is,

[14] For example, Greg Medcraft (2015), the current head of IOSCO, has stressed this point.

there is a need to identify collective ends that are collective goods and, as such, provide the *raison d'être* for their existence. However, evidently in the case of the banking sector, as elsewhere in the financial system, the prior fundamental ethical question as to the ultimate institutional purposes (collective goods) of this sector remains unanswered or is, at least, contested. Yet, as argued above, without an answer to this question governments, regulators, and policy-makers cannot give appropriate rational direction to the banking sector.

On the teleological account of the market mechanism there is an outcome which ought to be aimed at, if not necessarily by all market actors, certainly by legislators, regulators, and, I suggest, responsible representatives and members of the industry. The latter are well aware of the market as a whole and the need to regulate and, if necessary, redesign and restructure it to achieve desirable outcomes.[15] To this extent the "invisible" hand is to an important extent visible. Moreover, normatively speaking, this outcome is, to reiterate, a collective end that is also a collective good. Further it is an end that is realized by the market as whole and not simply by a single market actor. I have suggested above that the collective end in question is an adequate and sustainable supply of some good or service. Moreover, the good or service in question should be of reasonable quality and available at a reasonable price.

If this is correct then there are a number of questions to be addressed in relation to any given market or market-based institution, including financial institutions such as banks. First, is the product or service actually a good, normatively speaking; is it worthy of production? Presumably, as is the case with unsafe foodstuffs, "innovative" financial products that are, nevertheless, unsafe ought not to be produced. Second, is the good or service offered at a reasonable price? The oligopolies in banking in the UK, EU, Australia, and elsewhere are problematic in this regard. Third, is the supply sustainable? Short-termism driven by the desire to maximize profits as reflected in quarterly returns is a problem in terms of this long-term yardstick (Kay 2013). Fourth, is the quantum of the good or service in question adequate? Here we can distinguish between different segments of a consumer or client group; specifically, we can distinguish between higher-income earners, middle earners. and low-income earners. The housing market, for example, would be inadequate if it only provided a stock of expensive mansions affordable by high-income earners; likewise a housing mortgage market which did not cater for low-income earners.

Moreover, on my normative teleological account, financial rewards such as wages, executive remuneration, and dividends are proximate, not ultimate, purposes; they are part of the reward system and, as such, the means to an end. The end in question on this account is, of course, the provision of an adequate

[15] There is, of course, often disagreement in relation to specific regulatory and other proposals.

and sustainable supply of some good or service (of reasonable quality and at a reasonable price).

Let me now turn directly to the matter of the institutional purposes of banking. I do so from the standpoint that the ultimate institutional purpose of the banking and finance sector is to provide for the needs of the non-financial productive sector and, ultimately, the aggregate rights-based needs of human beings (as opposed to, say, corporations) (Miller 2010). Normatively speaking, banking and finance are a derivative second order form of economic activity. In short, Wall Street exists or, at least, ought to exist, to provide for the needs of Main Street. Thus the institutional purpose of capital markets is to provide an adequate quantum of capital at a reasonable interest rate (directly or indirectly) for the productive sector. Again, the institutional purpose of derivatives markets (e.g. swaps, options, futures) is to mitigate risk (provide financial insurance); often, admittedly, for actors in the financial sector, but not only for them because financial stability is a necessary condition for the productive sector to function effectively.[16]

On this normative teleological account it is of the first importance to specify the specific institutional purpose or purposes of the banking sector. I take it that core institutional purposes of the banking sector are the provision of the following (Kay 2010):

1. secure locations for depositors to deposit and withdraw their funds;
2. payments system;
3. an adequate supply of reasonably priced loans of reasonable quality (i.e. based on safe assets) for homeowners and for small and medium sized businesses (SMBs or SMEs).

Following John Kay's terminology, let us refer to institutions which have these purposes as narrow banks.[17] According to Kay, in recent times "retail savings institutions metamorphosed from the purpose of meeting routine financing needs of everyday banking into functions that were treated as profit centres in their own right" (Kay 2010, 224). Kay goes on to argue that narrow banks should be regarded as utilities. Currently existing retail/investment banking conglomerates should be split into utilities and market-based investment-only institutions. Moreover, narrow banks, and only narrow banks, should be deposit-taking institutions with depositors' funds guaranteed.

Viewed from this perspective an important question arises in relation to speculative trading, e.g. speculative trading on currencies, commodities, and derivatives. Arguably, speculative trading is for the most part a market-based

[16] It is an empirical question as to whether or not they actually achieve this purpose. Clearly so-called toxic financial products did the reverse.

[17] Kay might not have had this precise set of purposes in mind; no matter for my purposes here, for example, perhaps not the business loans.

method of redistributing funds from one party to another. Moreover, large-scale speculative trading can create bubbles which burst and lead to stock market crashes, banking collapses, unemployment, shortages, and/or over-priced goods and services, and so on. Perhaps, therefore, speculative trading ought to be curbed, for example by placing limits on speculative positions in commodity markets.[18] At any rate, the point to be made here is that high-risk activities, such as speculative trading, are highly problematic for deposit-taking institutions. Hence, the soundness of Kay's recommendation that such activities not be allowed in narrow banks.

A further issue in the global banking sector pertains to institutional structure. As already noted, an important macro-institutional feature of the global banking sector is the phenomenon of global financial institutions that are "too big to fail." Thus there were a number of bailouts of major banks and other financial institutions following the decision in 2008 to allow Lehman Brothers to fail; a decision that is thought to have virtually brought the international financial system to its knees. Importantly, for our concerns here, the phenomenon of banks that are "too big to fail" has morphed into the phenomenon of banks that are "too big to regulate." For example, there is the recent money-laundering case of the multinational bank HSBC (Treanor and Rushe 2012). HSBC received a US$1.9 billion fine for failing to have in place effective anti-money-laundering measures and for failing to conduct due diligence on some of its account holders. Criminal negligence notwithstanding, HSBC retained its license to operate, having in effect been deemed by the regulators "too big to fail." However, the inference that is being drawn from HSBC's retention of its license in these circumstances is that it is, in effect, too big to regulate.

According to the Financial Stability Board (2011) there are twenty-nine systemically important financial institutions; in effect, twenty-nine institutions that are too big to fail and, therefore, too big to regulate or, at least, to regulate effectively. Evidently, corruption, instability, and other harms arising from commercial competition between the investment arms of banks in a market context in which there is an overriding imperative to maximize profit and in which many of these banks are "too big to fail" look to be too great to be overcome, other than by substantial institutional redesigning and restructuring. This would involve splitting the investment from the retail arm of banks to form two separate institutions, as recommended by Kay—or, at the very least, iron-clad segregation within one institution, if that is possible—and "downsizing" banks "too big to fail" and, therefore, "too big to regulate" (Miller 2014c). A market in which an individual market actor cannot fail is a contradiction in terms and is, in any case, intolerable in the global banking sector, given what is at stake, namely, global financial stability.

[18] We return to the issue of speculation below.

4.4.2 Retirement savings schemes

Retirement savings schemes, including many pension schemes and so-called superannuation funds, have as an institutional purpose to provide for the financial needs of retirees. In some such schemes, payments are voluntarily made by a person into a retirement fund during the person's working life, for the purpose of being withdrawn as an income stream during retirement. In other schemes, employers are required to make contributions on behalf of their employees, equivalent to some percentage of their wages or salary.[19] So the contributions to a future pension or income stream upon retirement are largely (compulsorily) made by employers. Arguably these contributions should be understood as a component of the benefits paid by employers to employees for the work that they do for the employers. In short, the employers paying the monies into the employees' funds is simply the mechanism by means of which employees self-fund their retirement. So the money taken out of the employees' salary or wage during their working life is directly related to the income available to them when they retire.

An alternative, but not mutually exclusive,[20] arrangement is one in which salary and wage earners (and other taxpayers) are taxed with a view to generating a pool of funds to be paid out at a later date as a pension in the context of a universal pension scheme. Under this arrangement every retiree is entitled to a pension, irrespective of how much tax they might have paid, or other contribution they might have made to the pool of funds from which pensions are drawn, during their working life. At any rate, my concern here is only with schemes in which monies are paid by a person (whether compulsorily or voluntarily) into a fund which is invested during the person's working life and drawn upon during retirement. I will refer to these as retirement savings schemes.

The constitutive collective end and resulting collective good of retirement savings schemes, whether compulsory or not, is in essence an aggregate of savings that have been produced by the retirees themselves during their time in the workforce. Accordingly, they have a joint right to that collective good, albeit one consisting of a differentiated set of individual rights to specific monetary amounts depending in large part on the amount of savings each individual initially made, but also, to some extent, on the performance of the particular fund to which they have contributed. To be sure, there are other contributors, for example fund managers. For the savings in question are held in trust funds, and are invested in, for example, a portfolio of cash,

[19] Compulsory retirement schemes raise particular moral issues. See Miller (2017).

[20] Australia has such a hybrid system, i.e. it has both a pension scheme and a retirement savings (so-called superannuation) scheme.

bonds, and shares and, as a consequence, should increase in monetary value. However, it is presumably the case that any rights of, for example, financial intermediaries, such as fund managers, to financial reward (in the form of fees or commissions) should be taken out of the monetary value added to these initial savings by these professionals, and not out of the initial savings themselves. Evidently, this is something that in many cases has not been happening; rather there have been excessive fees and commissions (Cooper 2011).

Moreover, the persons who operate the trust funds in which these savings are held, and the fund managers who invest these savings, also have moral obligations: it is, after all, other people's money that has been entrusted to them, other people's money that they have undertaken to invest for them. This raises important ethical questions. The relationship between someone who manages a trust and the beneficiary is a fiduciary relationship, both morally and legally. But is the relationship between someone who invests a person's savings (perhaps under general directions, but perhaps not, e.g. a banker), and the person who provides the savings, a fiduciary relationship (Berry 2011), morally, if not legally? Moreover, what are the ethical implications if the managers of a trust outsource the management of the investment of these savings to a third party who is remunerated partly on the basis of the profitability of their investment decisions? After all, this third party has an incentive to make more profitable, but also more risky, investments (say in equities as opposed to bonds); yet this seems inconsistent with the overriding moral obligation of those who hold others' money in trust to ensure its preservation. Moreover, here there is an issue concerning the specific horizon of this obligation and the impact this ought to have on any investment strategy. Clearly, there ought to be a much longer-term investment strategy for a 20-year-old than a 60-year-old. Thus it may be permissible to invest in assets with a relatively high short-term risk (but low long-term risk) in the case of the 20-year-old but not in the case of the 60-year-old. A further issue here pertains to the ambiguity surrounding the trustee role when members do in fact make choices about their retirement savings. For there is a lack of clarity about how much responsibility they are taking and how much the trustee is looking after them.

The answer to these questions is in part to be found by recourse to our notion of institutional purpose. In the case of retirement schemes, the institutional purpose (the collective good, in my parlance) is the provision of an adequate income stream for retirees (derived from savings generated during their time in the workforce). Evidently, therefore, there is, or at least ought to be, a fiduciary relationship between the investors of those funds and those whose funds they manage; and fund managers should be appropriately risk averse. Accordingly, retirement savings schemes should be differentiated from wealth creation schemes; the latter being schemes in which the constraints (e.g. of risk adversity) derived from the institutional purpose of retirement savings schemes do not necessarily obtain. Nor are these constraints necessarily simply a matter of choice for those whose savings are being invested. For if these savings are dissipated as a result of risky investments then it is very likely the taxpayer, that is, the saver's fellow citizens, who will be expected to step up to the plate and provide an income (e.g. a pension) for the unfortunate saver when he or she retires.

4.4.3 Capital markets

As noted above, the Global Financial Crisis, the Sovereign Debt Crisis, and the Great Recession—which recession appears to be continuing in one form or another at the time of writing, at least in Europe, Japan, and in some of the so-called emerging economies, such as Brazil—have revealed various deficiencies in equity markets, in particular. These include short-termism (driven by the desire to maximize profits as expressed in quarterly returns) (Kay 2013), an excess of purely speculative trading of shares, and massive and harmful capital outflows (e.g. from developing economies). These deficiencies have been exacerbated by the advent of high-speed trading (Lewis 2014) and unregulated so-called "dark pools" (Clarke 2014).

According to Kay, for example, the decline of major British companies, such as ICI and GEC, was in large part a consequence of the replacement of the conception of the corporate executive not as efficiently and effectively managing a producer of goods and services but rather as a "meta-fund manager, acquiring and disposing of a portfolio of businesses rather as a fund manager might view a portfolio of shares" (Kay 2012, 9). Kay goes on to say, "The central issues for this Review [Kay Review of Equity Markets] arise from the replacement of a financial services culture based on trust relationships by one based around transactions and trading. We can see that shift in the management preoccupations of ICI and GEC, and in the development of a market place in which hedge funds and high frequency traders account for a majority of turnover on the London exchange even though they hold an insignificant proportion of the stock" (Kay 2012, 9).

As already emphasized, by the lights of my teleological normative account of social institutions, capital markets have as their institutional purpose (collective good) to provide an adequate and sustainable supply of financial capital to (especially non-financial) productive firms at a reasonable cost. Moreover, the productive firms in question are ones that meet aggregate human needs (e.g. for food, clothing, shelter), including, indeed especially, in impoverished countries where these needs are greatest.

Capital markets characterized by short-termism and dominated by speculative trading are at odds with this collective good since such markets are not focused on long-term investment in productive firms. Moreover, as Kay indicates, these untoward features of capital markets have infected even the management of the firms themselves. In short, the tail (Wall Street) is now wagging the dog (Main Street).

Ironically, the problem is compounded by free markets. For example, the absence of control over capital outflows enables massive and harmful inflows and outflows of capital from one economy to another based on speculation, e.g. on fluctuations in commodity prices, currencies, and interest rates and, in particular, on the likely actions of other traders, rather than a consideration of the likelihood of the long-term productivity of firms. Here, as elsewhere, the groups most harmed tend to be the less well-off.

There are a raft of reforms that have been suggested to deal with these deficiencies in capital markets. These range from redesigning corporate governance structures and regulating "dark pools," through to the reintroduction of capital controls under some circumstances and innovative proposals such as a radical extension of the concept of Special Drawing Rights to create a new global reserve currency to help stabilize global financial markets and make reserves available for investment in productive enterprises in impoverished countries (Stiglitz 2006, 206–8).

As noted above, an important macrostructural feature of the global financial sector pertains to the legislators and regulators. National governments and regulators have an ambiguous role in relation to global financial markets. For national governments and their regulators are to some extent partisan, and (understandably) seek to look after the interests of their own banking sector (e.g. the "City" in the case of UK regulators). This is especially the case if, as in the case of the UK, the finance and banking sector is of major importance to the economy as a whole. Moreover, in the absence of a uniform set of global regulations and a single global regulator with real authority, regulators operating at a national level can be played off against one another by multinational corporations. Evidently, there is a need to redesign the global regulatory structure to deal with this problem. John Eatwell has suggested that a World Financial Authority should be established on the grounds that the domain of the regulator should be the same as the domain of the market that is regulated (Eatwell 2000, Eatwell and Taylor 2000). This is surely correct, at least in theory. However, it faces prodigious practical difficulties, such as from nation states unwilling to cede authority to such a body. Eatwell, however, has argued that it is possible to establish such a body, given the degree of mutual self-interest in play.

At any rate, the general point to be stressed here is that any such proposals need to be adjudicated by recourse to institutional purpose: are they efficient and effective in relation to the realization of the collective good that should be provided by capital markets?

4.5 CONCLUSION

In this chapter I have proffered my normative teleological account of social institutions and applied it to financial markets. In doing so, I have distinguished the general normative "theory" of financial markets from special normative "theories" of particular financial markets and their constitutive market-based institutions. The applications in question were in respect of the banking sector, retirement savings schemes, and capital (specifically, equity) markets. I identified manifest deficiencies in these financial markets and mentioned various proposed remedies. I argued that these deficiencies were deficiencies, and these remedies were remedies, principally in the light of the (normatively understood) institutional purposes of these financial markets and market-based institutions.

REFERENCES

Audi, R. 2008. *Business Ethics and Ethical Business.* Oxford: Oxford University Press.

Berry, Christine. 2011. *Protecting Our Best Interests: Rediscovering Fiduciary Obligations.* London: Fair Pensions.

Bloomfield, Paul, ed. 2008. *Morality and Self-interest.* Oxford: Oxford University Press.

Carney, Mark. 2014. "Inclusive Capitalism: Creating a Sense of the Systemic." Inclusive Capitalism Conference, London, 27 May. http://www.bankofengland.co.uk/publications/Documents/speeches/2014/speech731/pdf (accessed October 25, 2016).

Ciepley, David. 2013. "Beyond Public and Private: Toward a Political Theory of the Corporation." *American Political Science Review* 107(1), 139–58.

Clarke, Thomas. 2014. "High Frequency Trading and Dark Pools: Sharks Never Sleep." *Law and Financial Markets Review* 8(4), 342–51.

Cooper, Jeremy. 2011. *Review into the Governance, Efficiency, Structure and Operation of Australia's Superannuation System.* Canberra: Australian Government.

Dobos, Ned, Christian Barry, and Thomas Pogge, eds. 2011. *The Global Financial Crisis: The Ethical Issues.* Basingstoke: Palgrave Macmillan.

Eatwell, John. 2000. "The Challenge Facing International Financial Regulation." Speech given at Queens' College, Cambridge, 1–20.

Eatwell, John, and Lance Taylor. 2000. *Global Finance at Risk: The Case for International Regulation.* New York: New Press.

Elster, Jon. 1989. "Rationality and Social Norms." *Studies in Logic and the Foundations of Mathematics* 8, 531–52.

Financial Services Authority. 2009. *Turner Review: A Regulatory Response to the Global Banking Crisis.* London: FSA. http://www.fsa.gov.uk/pubs/other/turner_review.pdf (accessed October 25, 2016).

Financial Stability Board. 2011. "FSB Announces Policy Measures to Address Systemically Important Financial Institutions (SIFIs) and Names Initial Group of Global SIFIs." Press release, November 4. http://www.fsb.org/wp-content/uploads/pr_111104cc.pdf (accessed October 25, 2016).

Financial Stability Board. 2014. *Adequacy of Loss-absorbing Capacity of Global Systemically Important Banks in Resolution.* Basel: FSB. http://www.fsb.org/2014/11/adequacy-of-loss-absorbing-capacity-of-global-systemically-important-banks-in-resolution (accessed October 25, 2016).

Friedman, Milton. 1970. "The Social Responsibility of Business is to Increase Profit." *New York Times Magazine*, September 13.

Garnaut, Ross. 2009. *The Great Crash of 2008.* Melbourne: Melbourne University Press.

Gilligan, G., and J. O'Brien, eds. 2013. *Integrity, Risk and Accountability in Capital Markets: Regulating Culture.* Oxford: Hart Publishing.

Gregg, Paul, and Ian Tonks. 2005. "Executive Pay and Performance in the UK 1994–2002." *Centre for Market and Public Organisations Working Paper Series* 05/122. http://www.bris.ac.uk/Depts/CMPO/workingpapers/wp122.pdf.

Kay, John. 2010. "Should We Have Narrow Banking?" In *The Future of Finance: The LSE Report.* London: London School of Economics and Political Science.

Kay, John. 2012. Speech at *Kay Review of UK Equity Markets and Long-Term Decision Making* Launch, Department for Business Innovation and Skills. London, July 23.

Kay, John. 2013. *Kay Review of UK Equity Markets and Long-Term Decision Making.* London: UK House of Commons. https://harr123et.files.wordpress.com/2010/07/futureoffinance5.pdf (accessed October 25, 2016).

Lewis, Michael. 2014. *Flash Boys: Cracking the Money Code.* London: Penguin.

MacNeil, Iain, and Justin O'Brien, eds. 2010. *The Future of Financial Regulation.* Oxford: Hart Publishing.

Mather, Joanna, and Sally Rose. 2016. "Low Tax Sought for $2.5m Super." *Australian Financial Review* 11 (March), 6.

Medcraft, Greg. 2014. "Extending the Regulatory Perimeter: Mapping the IOSCO Agenda." *Law and Financial Markets Review* 8(2), 95–7.

Medcraft, Greg. 2015. "Corporate Culture and Corporate Regulation." Law Council of Australia BLS AGM seminar, Melbourne, November 20.

Mill, J. S. 1859. *On Liberty.* London: Parker and Son.

Miller, Seumas. 2001. *Social Action: A Teleological Account.* New York: Cambridge University Press.

Miller, Seumas. 2010. *The Moral Foundations of Social Institutions: A Philosophical Study.* New York: Cambridge University Press.

Miller, Seumas. 2011. "Global Financial Institutions, Ethics and Market Fundamentalism." In *The Global Financial Crisis: The Ethical Issues*, edited by Ned Dobos, Christian Barry, and Thomas Pogge. Basingstoke: Palgrave Macmillan, 24–51.

Miller, Seumas. 2014a. "The Corruption of Financial Benchmarks: Financial Markets, Collective Goods and Institutional Purposes." *Law and Financial Markets Review* 8(2), 155–64.

Miller, Seumas. 2014b. "Trust, Conflicts of Interest and Fiduciary Duties: Ethical Issues in the Financial Planning Industry in Australia." In *Capital Failure: Rebuilding Trust in Financial Services*, edited by Nicholas Morris and David Vines. Oxford: Oxford University Press, 305–31.

Miller, Seumas. 2014c. "'Trust Me.... I'm a (Systemically Important) Bank!': Institutional Corruption, Market-Based Industries and Financial Benchmarks." *Law and Financial Markets Review* 8(4), 322–5.

Miller, Seumas. 2015. "The Global Financial Crisis and Collective Moral Responsibility." In *Distribution of Responsibilities in International Law*, edited by Andre Nollkaemper and Dov Jacobs. Cambridge: Cambridge University Press, 404–33.

Miller, Seumas. 2017. "Designing-in-Ethics: A Compulsory Retirement Savings System." In *Designing-in-Ethics*, edited by J. van den Hoven, Seumas Miller and Thomas Pogge. Cambridge: Cambridge University Press. Forthcoming.

Morris, Nicholas, and David Vines, eds. 2014. *Capital Failure: Rebuilding Trust in Financial Services*. Oxford: Oxford University Press.

Rothschild, Emma, and Amartya Sen. 2006. "Adam Smith's Economics." In *The Cambridge Companion to Adam Smith*, edited by Knud Haakonssen. Cambridge: Cambridge University Press, 319–65.

Sen, Amartya. 2002. *Rationality and Freedom*. Cambridge, MA: Harvard University Press.

Smith, Adam. 1776. *An Inquiry into the Nature and Causes of the Wealth of Nations*. London: Strahan and Cadell.

Sorkin, Andrew Ross. 2013. "Realities Behind Prosecuting Big Banks." *The New York Times*, March 12, B1.

Soros, George. 2009. *The Crash of 2008 and What it Means*. New York: Perseus.

Stiglitz, Joseph. 2006. *Making Globalisation Work: The Next Steps to Global Justice*. London: Penguin.

Stout, Lynn. 2012. *The Shareholder Value Myth*. San Francisco: Berrett-Koehler.

Treanor, J., and D. Rushe. 2012. "HSCB to Pay 1.2 Billion Pounds over Mexico Scandal." *Guardian*, December 10. http://www.guardian.co.uk/business/2012/dec/10/standard-chartered-settle-iran-sanctions.

Turner, Jonathan. 1997. *The Institutional Order*. New York: Longman.

5

Can incomes in financial markets be deserved? A justice-based critique

Lisa Herzog

5.1 INTRODUCTION

In a 2015 speech, President Obama noted that the twenty-five most highly paid hedge-fund managers in the US earned more than all kindergarten teachers of the country combined (Washington Post 2015). A frequent reaction to such comparisons is disbelief, mixed with outrage: "How can they deserve these incomes?" Defenders of these high incomes, however, also draw on the notion of desert. A prominent example is Gregory Mankiw, winner of the Nobel Memorial Prize in Economics, who, in a recent set of papers, developed a "Just Desert Theory" of wages and and defended the "1%" of top earners in terms of desert (2010, 2013). We can assume that he is not alone among economists in thinking that incomes earned in financial markets are just because they are deserved. Can such a claim be justified? Can we think about justice in financial markets by drawing on the notion of desert at all? As I will argue in this chapter, we ultimately cannot—but picking up the gauntlet thrown down by Mankiw offers an excellent opportunity for reflecting on some of the ongoing institutional problems of today's financial system.

In moral and political philosophy, desert has been a continuing topic of debate at least since the 1970s (for an overview see McLeod 2008). Many thinkers have rejected the notion altogether: it leads to various conceptual puzzles, and it is a prime candidate for ideological abuse by those who are economically privileged (von Hayek 1978, 74ff.). While I am sympathetic to many arguments against the notion of desert, I nonetheless suggest retaining a notion of *institutional desert*—similar to Rawls's notion of "legitimate expectations" (1971, 273)—that can help us to diagnose problems from a specific perspective: a perspective of normatively informed institutional design.

In recent years, there has been increasing interest in the institutional design of markets as an instrument for making societies more just (e.g. Dietsch 2010). A notion of institutional desert can serve as a heuristic for thinking about such questions, especially if one is interested in non-ideal theorizing that starts from the here and now. It can also help to integrate moral and economic perspectives on financial markets. Moral philosophers are probably far more likely than economists to reject the notion of desert, especially as applied to markets. But the economic perspective is, arguably, based on a view of markets that sees them in a rather rosy light, based on assumptions that go back to Adam Smith, but that seldom hold in practice—and admitting the discrepancies between idealized and real markets can bring economists and philosophers closer to one another. Analyzing financial markets through the lens of institutional desert can help to overcome the unproductive standoff between them that often blocks constructive debate about the justice of economic institutions. As we will see, the moral intuition that high incomes in the financial system are not deserved can be made sense of in terms that philosophers and economists can agree on.

I first revisit the philosophical debate about desert in order to carve out a working notion of "institutional desert" that can throw light on financial markets. I then ask whether and how this notion can be applied to labor incomes in financial markets.[1] To do so presupposes an analysis of the character of financial markets, which, however, shows that they are marred by numerous internal problems: forms of market failure that lead to inefficiencies. When pursuing this line further, reflections on one kind of market failure, namely externalities, show that we cannot limit our argument to this "internal" perspective. Instead, we also need to consider the place and role of financial markets in society. This will throw further doubt on the idea that incomes in financial markets can be described as deserved—even on the modest notion of institutional desert I develop earlier—and instead points to various problems in the institutional design of today's financial markets. I conclude by briefly hinting at some proposals that would address these problems.

I hasten to add that my analysis is based on a more generous attitude toward the defenders of desert than some readers might want to grant. Many more questions and criticisms about this notion could be raised. My aim is to show, however, that even if one puts these aside, the notion of desert, mostly used by those who want to *defend* high incomes in financial markets, backfires against their intentions. It shows, instead, how many of the conditions for the notion

[1] The focus on labor incomes implies that the question of whether income that derives from *ownership* (whether of financial assets or of computers that are used for high frequency trading) can be justified is beyond the scope of my discussion. See Herzog 2014 for a critical discussion of whether our traditional notion of ownership can be applied to financial markets at all.

of desert to be applicable are not fulfilled in financial markets. Given that these conditions can also be endorsed for other reasons, those who want to apply the notion of desert to financial markets—or at least the subset of those who are willing to engage in a discussion about this notion and accept its implications—and those who criticize financial markets from other perspectives of justice can travel a long way together.

5.2 DESERT AS AN INSTITUTIONAL NOTION

Desert claims usually take a tripartite form: person A deserves outcome x in virtue of y. Y has often been called the "basis" of desert, and it is usually taken to be something that person A can be held responsible for in a meaningful way. The notion of desert is used in two areas: retributive justice, i.e. just punishment—a topic I here put aside—and distributive justice, where there is an on-going debate about whether or not desert can and should play any role at all. Social scientific evidence shows that many individuals do draw on a notion of desert when thinking about justice in distribution (for an overview see Miller 1999, 64ff.).

Some scholars have completely rejected the notion of desert in distributive justice. Barry, for example, denounces the "cult of personal responsibility," which he takes to be built on wrong assumptions about the degree to which people can be held responsible for their choices (2005, chap. IV). Others have argued that it is not so clear how we can consistently hold people responsible in legal affairs, e.g. in criminal and civil law, but reject any notion of responsibility, and hence desert, in other areas of life (see e.g. Moriarty 2003). But one does not have to reject the possibility of responsible moral agency to be skeptical about the role that desert claims can play in distributive justice: one can instead ask whether the *institutions* in which this agency takes place are such that it makes sense to apply a notion of desert (cf. similarly Dick 1975, 262, Kernohan 1993, 202, Scheffler 2000). In what follows, I assume, for the sake of argument, that we can ascribe at least *some* elements of human behavior to conscious choices and hold people responsible for them, so that finding bases of desert is not impossible *in principle.*

A second important question with regard to desert is whether it is understood in an institutional or a pre-institutional sense (Kleinig 1971). Some scholars have described desert as an elementary building block of morality, and hence as prior to institutions or practices (e.g. Feinberg 1963, Pojman 1997, 1999). The basic argument for a pre-institutional account is that if desert were nothing but an institutional notion, it would boil down to entitlement: what people deserve is what they are entitled to according to the rules of the institution in question. But, the argument goes, there can be cases in which desert and entitlement come apart, for example when a candidate who deserves to win a competition because of her outstanding talents is, by some streak of bad luck, defeated by a much less deserving competitor, who is nonetheless formally entitled to the victory. Against this, other scholars have held that unless it is tied to institutions, the notion of desert is too vague and indeterminate, or even evaporates in some general notion of "goodness" (see e.g. Brigati 2014, 3, similarly Garcia 1988, Lamont 1994).

A solution on which many scholars have concurred is to see desert as referring to institutions, but as nonetheless not boiling down to entitlement, because it is tied to an idealized notion of the institution and of what it *should* achieve. As Cummiskey puts it: "Desert is logically prior to institutions in the same way that the point of the institutions is prior to the institutions" (1987, 19; cf. similarly Holmgren 1986, 226). If entitlements and desert are systematically decoupled, so this argument goes, this shows that something is wrong with an institution, and that its rules should probably be changed.

This strategy, however, leads to questions of the *criteria* we should use for describing this idealized notion of an institution. If our answer involves, in one way or another, a claim about "giving people what they deserve," we are back where we started: at a pre-institutional notion of desert. We thus need different criteria, and these are likely to include some claims about the function an institution should fulfil and the principles of justice it should realize or contribute to realizing. This is also the strategy pursued by Rawls, who replaces the notion of *moral* desert—which he rejects for distributive justice (1971, 73ff., 104)—with a notion of "legitimate expectations" within just institutions (1971, 273, for a discussion see O'Neill 2014). As O'Neill explains, this notion avoids tying individual rewards to "morally (or metaphysically) controversial, or unknowable, or impracticable, standards of individual virtue or worth" (2014, 430). It is nonetheless compatible with an understanding of "giving people what they deserve" within just institutions, because such institutions *define* what forms of behavior can serve as bases of desert and should be rewarded accordingly. The fit between behavior and reward does not have to be, and often cannot be, too fine-grained—for example, luck can always interfere—but it should hold approximately.

5.3 DESERT AND MARKETS

In what follows, I draw on this notion of institutional desert and ask whether it can be applied to markets. It is worth noting, however, that this is a rather modest notion of desert: it does not carry any "moral glamor" in the sense that it would reward some high-flying ideal of virtue; in fact, it remains silent on the degree to which the behavior that is rewarded can be ascribed to the choice of an agent or to luck in the sense of having a rare talent that is in high demand and earns a premium. But it is sufficiently robust to be applied to the question of what it means to call labor incomes, and more specifically labor incomes in financial markets, deserved.

Markets, to be sure, are institutions of a special kind: they do not directly assign rewards to individuals. Rather, prices and wages are determined by the free play of supply and demand, which is supposed to lead to efficient outcomes.[2] As such, markets are supposed to lead to an efficient allocation that helps to maximize the "pie" of economic goods and services that is available in a society. Philosophers have often treated markets as "black boxes" (see also Dietsch 2010), focusing, instead, on the justice of the overall distribution in a society, *post* tax and transfers. The assumption in Rawls's theory of justice, and arguably also in many others, is that markets should indeed be evaluated according to an economic notion of efficiency, whereas questions of justice are to be answered at the level of the "basic structure" of a society, which comprises markets as well as other institutions. This would imply that an institutional notion of desert for markets should be tied to their role in creating a large "pie": rewards should go to those who act in ways that help to achieve this aim.[3] Holding that they "deserve" a high market income is compatible, however, with holding that they do *not* deserve to keep all of it—the market is, after all, only one institution in a whole web of institutions, in which it plays an instrumental role, but does not determine the overall distribution on its own.

This account is immune to one argument that has been brought forward against the application of any notion of desert to distributive questions. Thus, Scheffler has held that distribution is a "holistic" problem, in which "the justice of any assignment of economic benefits to a particular individual always depends—directly or indirectly—on the justice of the larger distribution of benefits in society" (2000, 984). One consequence of this holistic character is that we lose any notion of individual behavior or action that could, on its own, serve as the basis for desert claims. In markets individual behavior *on its own* does not determine rewards; they also depend on the play of supply and demand, temporal dynamics of scarcity and abundance, and sheer luck.

But the fact that markets do not achieve a direct, one-to-one match between behavior and reward—because other factors can intervene—does not mean

[2] I here abstract from the many questions about how *labor* markets differ from markets in other goods and services. My intention is not to deny the importance of these difference, but to focus on the specificities of *financial* markets and their normative deficits. This strategy can also be justified by the fact that labor markets in the financial system are probably *less* plagued by typical labor market problems (for example the lack of exit options) than other labor markets, as employees tend to be highly skilled.

[3] Note that this is *not* the same as attempting to justify free markets on the basis of a notion of desert; as Olsaretti has convincingly shown, this is an impossible task (2004, esp. chap. III).

that they could not be integrated into a broader set of social institutions that *together* determine the distributive results in a society. There are, after all, no "free" markets, independent of any other institutions, in which anonymous forces beyond human control are at play. Markets function within a framework of rules, regulations, and social norms, and their outcome is also co-determined by the surrounding institutions, for example the provision, or lack of provision, of public infrastructure (cf. also Herzog 2013b). Depending on how the rules of the game are set, the play of market forces rewards different things, for example socially desirable or less socially desirable forms of behavior. One can reap profits by creating genuinely useful products and services, or by polluting the environment and exploiting workers. This is a question of what standards regulate the behavior of businesses, and how well they are enforced.[4]

If we could regulate markets such that they resemble the textbook model imagined by economists, we would probably be able to kill two birds with one stone: we would achieve maximum efficiency, and we would end up with markets that reward forms of behavior that can be called "deserved." The latter might seem to follow by definition, as I have argued for an institutionalized notion of desert. But it would also correspond, at least roughly, to certain moral intuitions about what markets should reward. This is the case because in perfectly competitive markets, as described in textbook models, typical forms of behavior that are *both* morally problematic *and* economically inefficient could simply not happen. For example, in the absence of market power individuals could not coerce others to do things against their will. If all market participants possessed full information and were perfectly rational, attempts to deceive or seduce others would also fail. Instead, only transactions that are genuinely beneficial to both sides would take place—and providing goods or services that are genuinely beneficial to others seems a reasonable, if somewhat mundane, basis for institutional desert in markets.

This is how defenders of markets since the days of Adam Smith have seen their benign potential. Whereas Bernard de Mandeville had seen an irreducible tension between morality and efficiency—expressed in the famous line about "private vices, public benefits" (1924 [1714])—Smith argued that they would reward the provision of useful goods and services, as well as certain secondary virtues such as "industry, prudence, and circumspection" (Smith

[4] The problem of enforcement has received little attention in normative theorizing, where it is standardly assumed that rules, once in place, can also be effectively enforced. But it is a well-known problem that it is difficult to punish corporations (see notably Coffee 1981); after the Great Financial Crisis, there have been additional questions about corporations "too big to jail" (Garrett 2014), or "too complex to jail," i.e. about the problem of whether prosecutors are in a position to adequately enforce existing rules. Chapter 6 of this volume considers the problem of enforceability and argues for a new understanding of legal accountability in order to make it possible to enforce existing rules.

1976a, III.V.8, see Herzog 2013a, 85ff. for a discussion). These virtues are socially useful because they make it more likely that individuals indeed make valuable contributions in markets. To be precise: Smith's point is not that markets are so perfect that these virtues would become superfluous. Rather, these virtues can help to overcome small market imperfections, for example some asymmetry of information between buyers and sellers, and if markets are sufficiently close to the ideal, they would be rewarded because they would, by doing so, increase efficiency. For example, a buyer who sees that his imperfect knowledge is not exploited by a seller would return to this seller rather than switch to a less honest one. While the correlation would not necessarily hold in every instance, it would hold in the long-term average.

Thus, if this picture is true, certain virtues are indeed rewarded in markets. Under certain circumstances, what we would want markets to reward—in the sense of institutional desert—is also something we could morally praise. If market participants offer genuinely valuable goods and services in an honest and reliable way, this is also efficient. To be sure, the kind of behavior rewarded in markets is not the highest form of virtue. But this is not surprising if we consider that markets are only *one* social institution, in which *one* form of behavior is rewarded. Von Hayek famously noted that markets reward the supply of matches rather than of wisdom (1978, 76)—but this is fine as long as everyone understands that this is their role, and as long as there are other institutions in which wisdom has its place.[5]

Whether or not such a Smithian match of morality and efficiency can be brought about depends to a large degree on the institutional framework within which markets take place. Hardly any market—let alone a market as complex as today's financial market—is "Smithian" on its own. Therefore, if we think about desert as an institutional notion applied to markets, we are inevitably led to questions about the institutional framework within which they take place, because this framework is decisive for determining whether markets take on a more "Smithian" or a more "Mandevillian" character. Ceteris paribus, we want markets to set incentives for reliability, honesty, and the provision of socially useful services—and we want these incentives to hold for each individual. We want individuals to generate an income by playing a fair game, not by using various loopholes, building up one-sided market power, or exploiting forms of market failure. In a well-functioning market, high incomes serve as a signal that there is high demand and insufficient supply for some goods or services—and they should quickly attract competitors, thereby lowering incomes (Smith 1976b, I.VII.12). If high incomes persist, this should be a reason for alarm: such incomes are likely to be caused by some form of market failure or

[5] Similarly, contemporary authors who defend desert as one element of distributive justice hold that it is only *one* among a plurality of considerations, which are specifically tied to specific institutions (e.g. Miller 1999, Honneth 2014, 223ff.).

other—and often, the form of behavior that such market failures make possible is not only inefficient, but also morally problematic, for example if it exploits one-sided dependencies.[6]

So, with regard to markets, the idea behind the notion of institutional desert can be summarized as follows: *markets should be such that rewards go to those who play by the rules, and the rules should be designed such that markets fulfil their role—of creating a large pie of socially useful goods and services—within a broader set of just institutions.* Such a notion of institutional desert can serve as a "critical" notion (as Miller puts it, 1999, 123, 127, 140ff.) that can help us to detect two kinds of problems: problems concerning rewards that go to those who do *not* play by the rules of the game—which is often a matter of criminal justice, and which I here put to one side—and problems concerning the design of the rules. Thus, with regard to high incomes in financial markets, these are the questions to which the question about desert leads us. In the following sections, I discuss some elements of an answer.

5.4 INTERNAL PROBLEMS: MARKET FAILURES

Even a cursory view of today's financial markets—especially in their pre-crisis instantiation—reveals numerous problems that throw doubt on the claim formulated above: either because market participants have not played by the rules, or because these rules have been badly designed, failing to prevent market failures. In neither case can we say that they deserve their income, although we might want to differentiate the degree of personal blame we attribute to them. In what follows, I treat these two problems together, because the relevant differences should be sufficiently clear.

I first look at "internal" problems that are located within the financial system; these considerations, however, quickly lead to a broader, "external" perspective. From the internal perspective, we can point to a number of market failures that have come about by a lack of attention to the rules, by bad rules, or by both. Importantly, the effects of such problems in one part of the financial system—for example in one specific market, for a specific kind of financial product—are not necessarily limited to this part, but can spill over to others and "infect" them, as it were. This is the case because financial markets are highly interconnected and their prices are interrelated. Therefore, problems that distort the prices in one market can affect the prices in other

[6] Heath (2006, 2014) has used market failures as a starting point for business ethics, in the sense that businesses should not try to profit from market failures. My focus, in contrast, is on institutional design (without denying that ethical behaviour is an indispensable element for "moralizing" markets).

markets, affecting claims of desert there as well. Thus, problems in markets that sell financial products to consumers and in markets in which financial agents trade with one another have an impact on the labor market in the financial system, where incomes are earned. Let me pick out some problems of these markets, without any claim to completeness—a complete list could hardly be compiled within the scope of a single chapter.

One obvious source of market failures in financial markets are information asymmetries. If information asymmetries exist, we cannot be sure any more whether the transaction in question is mutually beneficial, because one party might have made her decision on the basis of insufficient information. Information asymmetries mar the whole "value chain" in the financial system—from inexperienced customers taking out sub-prime loans they had insufficient information about (cf. e.g. Bitner 2008), to an unjustified trust in the labels provided by rating agencies,[7] or the tricks played on market participants that took themselves to be finance-savvy, but were much less so than others. Here, better regulation—and maybe also more "epistemic virtue" on the part of market participants (de Bruin 2015)—is needed.

A second problem concerns the availability of "exit options" or reasonable alternatives, without which market competition does not work efficiently, and without which markets lack the character of voluntariness that their defenders praise them for. The degree of voluntariness and the availability of alternatives vary in different parts of the financial system. But it seems clear that they are rather limited at the far end of financial intermediation, when it comes to private customers and their need for loans and other financial services. In times of a receding welfare state, many customers depend on loans, and are sometimes also locked into contracts that they cannot exit. Others may be able to switch between different financial providers, but which are run according to similar principles and offer little variation when it comes to the terms of business. The degree of choice and voluntariness for different market participants is ultimately an empirical question, but it seems fair to say that financial markets are at quite some distance from the idealized model of markets suggested by Smith and endorsed by many economists. And even if involuntariness should only exist in certain pockets of the financial system, these are likely to have a distorting influence on prices in other parts of the financial system.

It is illuminating, in this respect, to compare financial markets to other markets in which highly unequal incomes are generated. Defenders of high incomes in financial markets often point out that most people do not resent sports stars or movie stars for their high incomes (e.g. Mankiw 2010, 293ff.).[8]

[7] See Chapter 11 by de Bruin.

[8] In the philosophical debate, Nozick used the example of Wilt Chamberlain for suggesting that high incomes in sports are just, without taking into account the specificities of this case (Nozick 1974, 156ff., 161; for a discussion see Herzog 2013a, 89f., 117f.).

But the structure of the markets in which these incomes are earned is somewhat different. A well-functioning financial system is an essential element of a modern economy, and many individuals depend on it, directly or indirectly, in ways that suggest less than complete voluntariness. Sports and movies, in contrast, are markets with a high degree of voluntariness on the part of buyers. Ceteris paribus, it seems less problematic if high incomes are generated in markets with high degrees of voluntariness, as a high willingness to pay is then more likely to express a genuine appreciation of the goods or services in question, rather than a lack of alternatives. Thus, the analogy between financial markets and the markets for sports stars or movie stars is misleading.

A third kind of market failures that is relevant for our purpose are externalities: negative effects on third parties that are not "priced into" the prices of assets. The standard example of an externality is environmental pollution that results from the production process of goods: while the production of these goods is useful for the buyers who can purchase them and the sellers who gain by producing them, there is a cost to the general public. Similarly, some financial transactions are beneficial for buyers and sellers, but have an externality on others, for example in the form of decreased stability of the financial system as a whole. And while we can apply the conceptual distinction between transactions and externalities to financial markets, the nature of financial products should make us think twice about what it is that we are conceptually distinguishing.

In the case of environmental pollution, we assume that the goods in question are useful for individuals and society, whereas the pollution is harmful. If we look at the financial system, we might wonder whether we can so easily draw the distinction between what is useful and what is harmful. After all, *all* financial products only have instrumental value; as Turner puts it: "No one gets up in the morning and says 'I feel like enjoying some financial services today'" (2016, 20). The point of a financial system is to ensure liquidity, to facilitate transactions, to allocate capital, and to provide mechanisms for ensuring risk. While we can put some of these functions into the category of "useful products" and others into the category of "harmful externalities," we also need to consider their *net* effect, that is, the overall contribution the financial system makes to the economic well-being of a society. This question is particularly relevant for the numerous transactions in the financial system that are highly "derivative," in the sense that they are several levels away from processes in the real economy, while at the same time contributing to "systemic" developments in the financial system that might have problematic consequences for whole societies.

If we want to understand how to delineate the "externalities" of financial markets from their useful products, we thus need to ask about the role and function of the financial system as a whole—and this is a question we cannot answer by a purely "internal" consideration of financial markets. To answer the question of what good rules for financial markets are, we cannot limit our discussion to the avoidance of market failures, as we might be able to do in the case of other markets, in which goods or services that directly satisfy people's needs are traded. To be sure, there are financial products, for example insurance products for end consumers that are quite close to the direct satisfaction of needs and which therefore seem to be quite similar to other products we buy. But the role and function—and also the price—of such products is intertwined with the role and function of other parts of the financial system, which have mostly a systemic role. Thus, we cannot avoid asking: what is the financial system *as a whole* contributing to the economic well-being of our societies? Only then can we complete the discussion about institutional desert and its implications for financial markets.

5.5 EXTERNAL PROBLEMS: SOCIAL DYSFUNCTIONALITIES

Financial markets have a specific role to play in a modern economy. They provide loans and opportunities for investment, and facilitate the allocation of capital and of risks.[9] By its very nature, finance cannot be an end in itself, but must be a means to other ends. Innovations in financial markets are supposed to contribute, in some way or other, to the development of the economy. Some scholars have indeed suggested that the provision of a well-functioning financial system has the character of public infrastructure (e.g. Pettifor 2014), a thought that goes back to Smith, who once compared the availability of money to the availability of a highway (1976b, II.II.86).

The question thus is whether the financial system has indeed played this role as a socially useful infrastructure—or whether the risks it has imposed on societies have in fact outweighed its benefits. It is clear that many financial services have played, and continue to play, an important role for our economies. But if we look at the developments of the last decades before the financial crisis, and the "innovations" in finance they brought, there are reasons for doubt about their specific contributions—and it was, after all, the trade with such "innovative" financial products that generated many of the exorbitantly high incomes with which we started this inquiry.

The grand post-World War II narrative about free markets, including free financial markets, was that they would generate economic growth that would, in the end, be beneficial to everyone in society, including its poorest members.

[9] My perspective here is similar to that of Miller in Chapter 4 of this volume.

More "complete" financial markets were understood as providing more liquidity and, by offering better "price discovery," as improving the allocation of capital and risks, thus contributing to making the economy more efficient and more stable (cf. Turner 2016, 27ff.). Various empirical studies seemed to confirm that "financial deepening" contributed to economic growth: there was a positive correlation between measures of financial deepening, such as loans to the private sector or stock-market turnover, and economic growth (see e.g. Levine 2005 for an overview).

But at least since the Great Financial Crisis we have learned that this picture has been too rosy: it is unclear *both* whether financial innovation has contributed to economic growth *and* whether economic growth has been beneficial for societies.

The most straightforward way in which financial innovation was *harmful* to society was by creating a crisis in which the financial sector had to be bailed out by huge sums of public money and that caused a prolonged recession. The sanitized account of financial markets based on rational economic man that prevailed before the Great Financial Crisis implied that financial markets could only *reduce* risks. But real financial markets, with human participants with human psychologies, can exhibit various "irrational" features, for example herding behavior. They are driven not only by fundamentals, but also by sentiments and expectations, including expectations about the behavior of others. This means that there can be self-referential processes in which prices in financial markets deviate more and more from what is going on in the real economy. When the huge bubble that had built up in the American sub-prime market burst, panic raged. It was only by massive public interventions that sufficient confidence could be restored to prevent a complete breakdown. Some players, notably large financial corporations, could in fact anticipate that they would be "bailed out" in case they ran into liquidity problems. This meant that they had "soft budget constraints" (Kornai 1980), and could cream off upside profits, while the downside risk fell to the general public. In hindsight it seems only logical that this created problems of "moral hazard" and led to excessive risk-taking. Ultimately, taxpayers paid the bill—a fact that flies in the face of anyone who tries to defend the high incomes generated in financial markets as "deserved," even on a minimalist notion of desert.

But even apart from these post-crisis problems, it is not clear whether the expansion of financial markets has been as beneficial for society as their proponents claimed. Evidence from various studies suggests that the enthusiasm for "financial deepening" was premature. More liquidity is not necessarily "limitlessly valuable," as Turner puts it—for example if high-frequency trading leads to "an arms race of expenditure on technology and skilled people for an activity with no social value" (2016, 42, 44). Cecchetti and Kharroubi (2012) find a U-shaped relationship: up to a point, financial development, measured as the relation of private credit to GDP or as the share of financial intermediation in total employment, is beneficial; beyond that point, it is negatively correlated with aggregate economic growth. As they summarize their findings: "Overall, the lesson is that big and fast-growing financial sectors can be very costly for the rest of the economy. They draw in essential resources in a way that is detrimental to growth at the aggregate level" (ibid., 13; cf. similarly Arcan et al. 2012; for a theoretical model of the conflictual relationship between "Main Street" and "Wall Street" see also Korinek and Kreamer 2014).

And last but not least, the second part of the claim—that economic growth is good for societies and benefits everyone—can also be questioned based on empirical data. For example, a study by Tcherneva (2013) shows that whereas in the postwar years the bottom 90 percent of the income distribution benefited from economic expansions, this trend has turned since the 1970s. Until then, the bottom 90 percent benefited more from economic expansion than the top 10 percent. Since the 2000s, the bottom 90 percent have hardly benefited from expansion, and between 2009 and 2012, the returns were negative, whereas they skyrocketed for the top 10 percent.[10] If one assumes that growing inequality has harmful effects, one arrives at the startling conclusion that contrary to widely held opinions, economic growth itself—or at least the statistical artifacts we got used to calling "growth"—may be at best a mixed blessing for societies (for a discussion see also Herzog 2016).

Thus, the financial system we have seen in the last decades, with its extremely high incomes, has been dysfunctional in many ways. This does not mean that all financial transactions were equally questionable with regard to their social value—the "financial system" is, after all, extremely heterogeneous, including everything from small local banking coops to global banks with balance sheets larger than the social products of many countries. But it seems fair to assume that some parts of the financial system are at best useless and at worst dangerously dysfunctional for the societies within which they operate and maybe even for the global economic system as a whole. We will probably never be able to quantify their opportunity costs because we do not know what would have happened if the human and financial capital that went into these parts of the financial system had been used in more socially useful ways. There are massive opportunity costs if talented people work on Wall Street instead of working in research or creating new enterprises (or, one hardly dares to mention it: become good public servants) (cf. e.g. Mullainathan 2015). Even Mankiw himself, the defender of high incomes on the basis of desert, holds that "The last thing we need is for the next Steve Jobs to forgo Silicon Valley in order to join the high-frequency traders on Wall Street" (2013, 24).

[10] As Piketty 2014 shows, the general trends in different Western societies are structurally similar.

What should be clear, thus, is that claims about institutional desert in the financial system run up against huge justificatory obstacles that stem from the failure of the financial system to fulfil its role in society. Maybe we should not be too surprised by this. The picture of institutional desert I have developed earlier assumes that the rules of the game are designed by a democratic process, with the public good in mind. But the rules of the financial system seem to have been set at least in part by those who were supposed to be regulated by them. How much influence financial lobbies had—and continue to have—on the legislative and regulative process is, ultimately, a question that historians will have to answer. But we already know that in some cases, private interests played a central role. For example, Pistor (2013, 318) describes the process of the legal creation of global markets for over-the-counter (OTC) derivatives. The International Swaps and Derivatives Association (ISDA), which is a private organization, was critical for standardizing contracts and for ensuring their legal validity in different countries (Morgan 2008). Without any assurance that the rules of the game are set as part of a process that creates and maintains just institutions that serve the society as a whole, all talk about desert rings hollow.

5.6 CONCLUSION: GETTING BEYOND MARKET FAILURE AND DYSFUNCTIONALITIES

In this chapter I have followed the argumentative path suggested by those who want to defend high incomes in financial markets as "deserved." Doing so leads one to the opposite of what they intended to claim. Instead of proving market participants to be morally justified in receiving high incomes, taking the notion of desert seriously reveals the massive flaws of today's financial system. An institutional notion of desert—the only one that can plausibly be defended—draws our attention to the ways in which financial markets work. If we use such a notion of desert, we cannot ask only whether market participants are playing by the rules, but we also need to ask whether the rules are any good—otherwise it can only be legal entitlement, but never desert, that we are talking about. Doing so reveals both internal problems of market failures and external problems of social dysfunctionality. It is high time to address these problems by putting in place better rules for financial markets. This would probably have the side-effect of considerably shrinking the high incomes they had generated. If it did not, this might be seen as a reason for caution: maybe some forms of market failures had been overlooked and further regulation is required.

Of course, financial markets are not the only institutions in our societies that stand in need of repair from a perspective of justice. Some might ask whether it is worthwhile to consider specific institutions and how they could be improved, instead of thinking about overall distributive justice. This choice may, to some degree, depend on optimism or pessimism about what kinds of reforms are possible. Focusing on specific institutions suggests itself in cases in which there is hope that concrete steps to reform might be feasible, and where these steps would not block the path to more radical reforms concerning overall justice. I take it that this is the case with regard to today's financial system. I also take it that such reforms might play a role for creating momentum toward further reforms that would make our societies more just.

The flaws of today's financial system—of which the exorbitantly high incomes are a symptom—are such that economists and moral philosophers can agree that something is wrong. Many parts of the financial system are *both* inefficient *and* unjust. This means that economists and philosophers can form alliances with regard to the pressure for reform. Philosophers may in fact be the junior partner in such alliances, because the voices of economists tend to find a more sympathetic ear in the public and with politicians. But this should not stop philosophers from weighing in with their arguments. Many members of the general public felt not only anger about the inefficiencies of the financial system, but also moral outrage at its injustices and in particular at the exorbitantly high incomes it generated. Philosophers can address the normative dimensions of these debates, which go beyond considerations of efficiency.

In recent years, economists have proposed a number of reforms to the financial system and to the ways in which financial markets function. The most important one is probably to put more "skin into the game," and thus to force market participants to be liable for downward risks, rather than just creaming off upward opportunities (cf. especially Admati and Hellwig 2013). Others have suggested that the culture in the financial system needs to change (cf. e.g. Salz 2013, 76ff., 177ff.). Work on financial institutions that have an explicitly ethical mission suggests that their employees are motivated by shared values and by a desire to contribute something useful to society (see e.g. Herzog, Hirschmann, and Lenz 2015). If the financial system were reoriented to fulfilling a useful role in society, supporting sustainable and socially just forms of economic development, such a sense of purpose could also help motivate employees in other financial institutions. This would provide an answer to the worry, sometimes raised by defenders of the financial system, that without high incomes and bonuses, employees would not be motivated to work hard any more.

Some might fear that high payments might nonetheless be indispensable for motivating participants in financial markets. But ethnographic evidence suggests that what mattered most among those who received high bonuses in the financial system was their relative position, not the absolute amount they received (Luyendijk 2011, cf. also Lamont 1997 for a discussion of the distinction between incentives and economic rents). If it turned out that monetary incentives were necessary for motivating market participants, they could be offered on a much smaller scale. Thus, there is no reason to think that it is impossible to create a financial system that could be more efficient *and* more just, by correcting the flaws that allow for today's undeserved incomes. The greatest obstacles, it seems, is not the lack of reasonable proposals but the political will to implement them.

Repairing the financial system is only one among the many steps it will take to make our societies more just. In today's situation of glaring inequality, theorists of justice from many different camps agree that this must mean: more equal. Rousseau held that "no citizens should be so rich that he can buy another, and none so poor that he is compelled to sell himself" (1997, II.11.2). By these standards, we have a long way to go. While the notion of desert is helpful for analyzing current flaws, in the long run we might hope that it could be one of those Wittgensteinian ladders that one throws away once one has used them. For the more we think about the notion of desert, the more we will probably see how much of what we like to describe as deserved is, in reality, a matter of luck—not only because the conditions in which the notion of desert could be applied do not hold, but also because one of the assumptions that I made in this chapter does not stand up to scrutiny: what we take to be morally responsible agency probably falls far less within the scope of our control than we often think. This concerns not only the "natural lottery" of talents and character traits (Rawls 1971, 73f., 104), but also the "lottery" concerning the country we are born in, whose institutional structures have a huge influence on the productivity of our efforts. And in many cases there may simply be epistemic barriers to distinguishing plausible bases of desert from other factors (see also Moriarty 2006).

Acknowledging the great influence of luck on incomes might help, in the long run, to lead to cultural change in the sense that individuals feel less entitled to the income they end up with. This might open up new possibilities for egalitarian policies. More just economic structures would probably still include a financial system and probably also certain types of financial markets.[11] But it is unlikely that they would generate huge incomes. The momentum created by the moral outrage against undeserved incomes in the financial markets may help us to push for much-needed reforms, and for longer-term changes towards more equal social structures.[12]

[11] As Carens (1981) has shown, markets can be used as instruments of coordination, even if they do not determine overall distribution.

[12] I would like to thank Barry Weingast as well as the participants of the Economic Ethics Network Meeting in Berlin and of the workshop "Finance, Taxation and (Global) Justice" at the Ethikzentrum Zürich for very helpful discussions. I owe special thanks to Felix Koch, who was my discussant in Zürich.

REFERENCES

Admati, Anat, and Martin Hellwig. 2013. *The Bankers' New Clothes: What's Wrong with Banking and What to Do about it.* Princeton and Oxford: Princeton University Press.

Arcan, Jean-Louis, Enrico Berkes, and Ugo Panizza. 2012. "Too Much Finance?" *IMF Working Paper WP/12/161*, June.

Barry, Brian. 2005. *Why Social Justice Matters.* Cambridge: Polity.

Bitner, Richard. 2008. *Confessions of a Subprime Lender: An Insider's Tale of Greed, Fraud, and Ignorance.* Hoboken: Wiley.

Brigati, Roberto. 2014. "Desert as a Principle of Distributive Justice: A Reconsideration." *Philosophy and Social Criticism* 40(7), 705–22.

Carens, Joseph H. 1981. *Equality, Moral Incentives, and the Market: An Essay in Utopian Politico-Economic Theory.* Chicago and London: University of Chicago Press.

Cecchetti, Stephen G., and Enisse Kharroubi. 2012. "Reassessing the Impact of Finance on Growth." *Bank for International Settlements Working Paper* No. 381, July.

Coffee, John C., Jr. 1981. "'No Soul to Damn: No Body to Kick': An Unscandalized Inquiry into the Problem of Corporate Punishment." *Michigan Law Review* 79(3), 386–459.

Cummiskey, David. 1987. "Desert and Entitlement: A Rawlsian Consequentialist Account." *Analysis* 47, 15–19.

De Bruin, Boudewijn. 2015. *Ethics and the Global Financial Crisis: Why Incompetence is Worse than Greed.* Cambridge: Cambridge University Press.

Dick, James C. 1975. "How to Justify a Distribution of Earnings." *Philosophy and Public Affairs* 4(3), 248–72.

Dietsch, Peter. 2010. "The Market, Competition, and Equality." *Politics, Philosophy & Economics* 9(2), 213–44.

Feinberg, Joel. 1963. "Justice and Personal Desert." In *Nomos VI: Justice*, edited by C. J. Friedrich and J. W. Chapman. New York: Atherton Press.

Garcia, J. L. A. 1988. "A Problem About the Basis of Desert." *Journal of Social Philosophy* 19(3), 11–19.

Garrett, Brandon L. 2014. *Too Big to Jail: How Prosecutors Compromise with Corporations.* Cambridge, MA: Belknap Press.

Heath, Joseph. 2006. "Business Ethics Without Stakeholders." *Business Ethics Quarterly* 16, 533–57.

Heath, Joseph. 2014. *Morality, Competition and the Firm.* Oxford: Oxford University Press.

Herzog, Lisa. 2013a. *Inventing the Market: Smith, Hegel, and Political Theory.* Oxford: Oxford University Press.

Herzog, Lisa. 2013b. "Markets." In *The Stanford Encyclopedia of Philosophy Fall 2013 edition* [online], edited by Edward N. Zalta. Stanford: Stanford University Press.

Herzog, Lisa. 2014. "Eigentumsrechte im Finanzsystem. Rechtfertigungen und Reformimpulse." *Deutsche Zeitschrift für Philosophie* 62(3), 415–42.

Herzog, Lisa. 2016. "The Normative Stakes of Economic Growth: Why Adam Smith Does Not Rely on 'Trickle Down.'" *Journal of Politics* 78(1), 50–62.

Herzog, Lisa, Edgar Hirschmann, and Sarah Lenz. 2015. "'Ethische Banken'—Nische oder Avantgarde?" *WestEnd. Neue Zeitschrift für Sozialforschung* 1, 85–94.

Holmgren, Margaret. 1986. "Justifying Desert Claims: Desert and Opportunity." *Journal of Value Inquiry* 20, 265–78.

Honneth, Axel. 2014. *Freedom's Right: The Social Foundations of Democratic Life*. New York: Columbia University Press.

Kernohan, Andrew. 1993. "Desert and Self-Ownership." *Journal of Value Inquiry* 27, 197–202.

Kleinig, John. 1971. "The Concept of Desert." *American Philosophical Quarterly* 8, 71–8.

Korinek, Anton, and Jonathan Kreamer. 2014. "The Redistributive Effects of Financial Deregulation: Wall Street versus Main Street." *Bank for International Settlements Working Paper* no. 468, October.

Kornai, J. 1980. "'Hard' and 'Soft' Budget Constraint." *Acta Oeconomica* 25(3/4), 231–45.

Lamont, Julian. 1994. "The Concept of Desert in Distributive Justice." *The Philosophical Quarterly* 44, 45–64.

Lamont, Julian. 1997. "Incentive Income, Deserved Income, and Economic Rents." *Journal of Political Philosophy* 5, 26–46.

Levine, Ross. 2005. "Finance and Growth: Theory and Evidence." In *Handbook of Economic Growth*, edited by P. Aghion and S. Durlauf (North Holland: Elsevier), volume IB, 865–934.

Luyendijk, Joris. 2011. "Voices of Finance: MD, Corporate Finance, at a Major Bank." *Guardian*, September 15.

McLeod, Owen. 2008. "Desert." In *The Stanford Encyclopedia of Philosophy Winter 2008 edition* [online], edited by Edward N. Zalta. Stanford: Stanford University.

Mandeville, Bernard. 1924. *The Fable of the Bees, Part I (1714), Part II (1729)*, edited by F. B. Kaye. Oxford: Clarendon Press.

Mankiw, N. Gregory. 2010. "Spreading the Wealth Around: Reflections Inspired by Joe the Plumber." *Eastern Economic Journal* 36, 285–98.

Mankiw, N. Gregory. 2013. "Defending the One Percent." *Journal of Economic Perspectives* 27(3), 21–34.

Miller, David. 1999. *Principles of Social Justice*. Cambridge, MA: Harvard University Press.

Morgan, Glenn. 2008. "Market Formation and Governance in International Financial Markets: The Case of OTC Derivatives." *Human Relations* 61, 637–60.

Moriarty, Jeffrey. 2003. "Against the Asymmetry of Desert." *Noûs* 37(3), 518–36.

Moriarty, Jeffrey. 2006. "The Epistemological Argument against Desert." *Utilitas* 172, 205–21.

Mullainathan, Sendhil. 2015. "Why a Harvard Professor Has Mixed Feelings When Students Take Jobs in Finance." *The New York Times*, April 10.

Nozick, Robert. 1974. *Anarchy, State, and Utopia*. New York: Basic Books.

Olsaretti, Serena. 2004. *Liberty, Desert and the Market*. Cambridge: Cambridge University Press.

O'Neill, Martin. 2014. "Legitimate Expectations." In *The Rawls Lexicon*, edited by Jon Mandle and David Reidy. Cambridge: Cambridge University Press, 428–30.

Pettifor, Ann. 2014. *Just Money: How Society Can Break the Despotic Power of Finance*. Kent: Commonwealth Publishing.

Piketty, Thomas. 2014. *Capital in the 21st Century*. Cambridge, MA: Belknap Press.

Pistor, Katharina. 2013. "A Legal Theory of Finance." *Journal of Comparative Economics* 41, 315–30.

Pojman, Louis. 1997. "Equality and Desert." *Philosophy* 72, 549–70.

Pojman, Louis. 1999. "Merit: Why Do We Value It?" *Journal of Social Philosophy* 30(1), 83–102.

Rawls, John. 1971. *A Theory of Justice*. Cambridge, MA: Belknap Press of Harvard University Press.

Rousseau, Jean-Jacques. 1997. *The Social Contract and Other Later Political Writings*, edited by Victor Gourevitch. Cambridge: Cambridge University Press.

Salz, Anthony. 2013. "Salz Review: An Independent Review of Barclay's Business Practices." http://online.wsj.com/public/resources/documents/SalzReview04032013.pdf (accessed October 25, 2016).

Scheffler, Samuel. 2000. "Justice and Desert in Liberal Theory." *California Law Review* 88(3), 965–90.

Smith, Adam. 1976a [1759/90]. *The Theory of Moral Sentiments*, edited by D. D. Raphael and A. L. Macfie. Oxford: Clarendon Press; New York: Oxford University Press.

Smith, Adam. 1976b [1776]. *An Inquiry into the Nature and Causes of the Wealth of Nations*, 2 vols, edited by R. H. Campbell and A. S. Skinner; textual editor W. B. Todd. Oxford: Clarendon Press; New York: Oxford University Press.

Tcherneva, Pavlina R. 2013. "Reorienting Fiscal Policy: A Critical Assessment of Fiscal Fine-Tuning." *Levy Economics Institute Working Paper* No. 772.

Turner, Adair. 2016. *Between Debt and the Devil: Money, Credit, and Fixing Global Finance*. Princeton and Oxford: Princeton University Press.

von Hayek, Friedrich August. 1978. *Law Legislation and Liberty, ii: The Mirage of Social Justice*. Chicago: University of Chicago Press.

Washington Post. 2015. "The Top 25 Hedge Fund Managers Earn More than All Kindergarten Teachers in the U.S. Combined." May 12.

Part II

Legal Structures

6

Punishment in the executive suite: Moral responsibility, causal responsibility, and financial crime

Mark R. Reiff

6.1 INTRODUCTION

In 2014, the US Justice Department collected a record $24.7 billion in fines and penalties from banks and other financial institutions for fraud and misconduct in connection with the 2008 financial crisis, and this was on top of the $21 billion it had already collected from 2012 through 2013 (Reuters 2014). During the same period, other federal and state law enforcement agencies also collected eye-popping amounts, and from many of the same institutions (Silver-Greenberg and Eavis 2013, 2014). The fines kept coming in 2015 (Protess 2015a and b; Protess and Ewing 2015), and by October the grand total collected by US federal and state authorities since the financial crisis began had risen to a whopping $204 billion (Cox 2015). And this does not include the fines imposed by various European regulators, which have also been substantial (see Sterngold 2014). Even now, early in 2016, the grand total continues to grow by leaps and bounds, with huge new fines being assessed against or agreed to by Goldman Sachs, Wells Fargo, and Morgan Stanley (Goldstein 2016, Koren 2016, Popper 2016a). Obviously, the fallout from the financial crisis is not over yet.

What the enormity of these fines and penalties reflects—as if it were not already obvious—is both the extent of the losses flowing from the financial crisis and the widespread nature of the misconduct that surrounded it. Yet despite the undeniable seriousness of what occurred in our financial institutions, no high-ranking corporate executive has been criminally prosecuted for any of this misconduct, much less actually gone to prison (Eisinger 2014a and c, Stewart 2015a and b, Morgenson and Story 2011). Very few mid- to low-level employees have been criminally prosecuted either.[1] Much criticism has been directed at the relevant authorities for this, and I think it is fair to say that many members of the public are incredulous about what seems to be the authorities' reluctance to prosecute senior executives for passively allowing if not actively encouraging globally significant acts of financial wrongdoing—that is, conduct that should be treated as legally criminal and not merely morally wrong if it is not (and this is debatable) technically a crime already (see generally Eisinger 2014b, Morgenson 2014a, Office of Inspector General 2014).[2]

There has been some indication recently that this criticism may be leading the relevant authorities to confess that they have not been using the legal tools currently available to them as fully as they could, and to profess a change in attitude and approach (Apuzzo and Protess 2015, Cohen 2015, Henning 2015c, Morgenson 2015b). But there is also reason to worry that real change is unlikely (Protess and Apuzzo 2015, Henning 2015a).[3] Although the current lack of criminal prosecutions has been particularly disappointing, hesitance on the part of the relevant authorities to prosecute those engaged in financial crimes is nothing new. Revelations of widespread financial fraud by leading financial institutions seem to occur periodically, but senior corporate officers often escape prosecution in these cases, as they have done now. And while there are always calls to prosecute those involved more vigorously whenever this occurs (see e.g. Fisse and Braithewaite 1994), these prior calls have obviously failed to have the desired effect.

Indeed, if anything we seem to be going backwards. Over 1,000 bankers were convicted by the US Justice Department following the Savings and Loan (S&L) crisis in the 1980s, and even so, many people felt that too many bankers got away then too lightly (Breslow 2013, The New York Times 2011).[4] True,

[1] There have, however, been a few exceptions at this level. See Bray (2016c and 2015a, b, c, and d) and Smith (2015).

[2] To cite just one example, no criminal charges have yet been brought against senior executives at Deutsche Bank despite a finding by the German bank regulator that then co-CEO Anshu Jain had "ignored signs of misconduct by traders and failed to investigate thoroughly when allegations of wrongdoing came to light," and "had created a corporate culture that allowed the wrongdoing to take place" (Ewing 2015). See also *In the Matter of Deutsch Bank* 2015. For similar findings (or agreed statements of fact) against other financial institutions, see Dealbook 2015.

[3] See also Protess and Eavis 2015 (SEC abandons litigation against former Freddie Mac executives despite a promise that "all individuals, regardless of their rank or position, will be held accountable for perpetuating half-truths or misrepresentations"); Morgenson 2015e (criticizing the settlement between the SEC and Citigroup that holds no one at the bank accountable for behavior that caused investors to lose an estimated $2 billion); Eisinger 2016 (criticizing the SEC for going easy on senior executives at Goldman Sachs and Paulson and Company because these were just "good people who had done one bad thing").

[4] Indeed, as one US senator put it in the course of voting for tougher provisions that he thought would ensure that future prosecutors would bring more cases and be able to convict more of those who committed fraud at insured financial institutions, "the American people have made it very clear that if they are being asked to foot the bill for the S&L crisis, at the

the institutions involved in that crisis were both more numerous and far smaller, none was systemically significant, and many of the bankers charged were principal owners or otherwise had effective control of their respective institutions.[5] Given what was often the brazen looting of these institutions, perhaps prosecutors had fewer obstacles to overcome in going after these senior executives.[6] But even so, the reaction to the S&L crisis shows that senior executives can be and sometimes are actually held accountable.

Indeed, what we are experiencing now is even worse than what happened after the Great Depression of the 1930s. Then, as now, virtually no bankers were convicted of wrongdoing. But in reaction to this, Congress produced a tidal wave of prophylactic legislation. Unfortunately, many of the key provisions of this legislation were eliminated in the run up to the S&L crisis, and even more in the run up to the 2008 financial collapse. And while a good argument can be made that this is what allowed if not encouraged the rate of institutional misconduct to rise again, the re-regulation triggered by the 2008 collapse has been rather modest, and the safeguards reinstituted strictly limited (see generally Reiff 2013, 253–4, 256 n. 188, Morgenson 2015a, Weisman and Lipton 2015).[7] This makes it doubly important that we take steps to ensure that senior executives face the possibility of criminal prosecution if we are to have any hope they will be more proactive in their efforts to ensure that widespread misconduct in their institutions does not happen yet again. At the very least, this is an objective upon which all those interested in promoting justice in the financial markets should be able to agree.

The purpose of this chapter is to provide an explanation of why the attitudes of the public and the public prosecutor about what justice requires here have gotten so out of sync, and offer some new suggestions on how to think about the responsibilities of senior corporate executives that make it easier to say why their conduct should be seen as both morally wrong and legally criminal regardless of its allegedly more ambiguous legal status now. In Section 6.2, I put the current dearth of criminal prosecutions in its proper context and discuss what seems to be at the root of this problem—the perceived difficulty in proving that senior officers had the requisite knowledge and criminal intent that is supposedly required to support an imposition of criminal liability as

very minimum the Government owes them swift and tough action to put those responsible in jail" (Sanford 1990).

[5] Consider, for example Charles Keating of Lincoln Savings & Loan, which Keating used as if it were "his own personal cash machine" (McFadden 2014).

[6] But see Heath (2011), suggesting that the absence of prosecutions is the result of law enforcement's recent practice of not investigating financial misconduct in large institutions unless the institution has affirmatively "turned itself in."

[7] See also Kashkari (2016): "While significant progress has been made to strengthen our financial system, I believe the [Dodd-Frank] Act did not go far enough. I believe the biggest banks are still too big to fail and continue to pose a significant, ongoing risk to our economy."

either a legal or a moral matter. In Section 6.3, I argue that the imposition of criminal liability is indeed appropriate in these cases as a prima facie matter even in the absence of the usual proof of knowledge and intent because the underlying rights at issue here would otherwise be rendered unenforceable, and it is enforceability, not morality, that determines the scope of sanctions available in the first instance. In Section 6.4, I argue that even in the absence of the usual proof of knowledge and intent, as long as there is sufficient proof to establish *causal* responsibility on the part of the individuals involved we have done all we need to do to establish their *moral* responsibility for these offenses as well, and as long as the relevant individuals are morally responsible there is no moral impediment—and under existing law there is no legal impediment either, although things could be more clear—to imposing criminal sanctions upon them. Finally, in Section 6.5, I discuss how causal responsibility in these cases is to be assessed, and how we might amend existing law to make the applicable standard in these cases clearer. My hope is that once the correct standard is identified we can see how a wide variety of past financial misdeeds can be punished and therefore future financial misdeeds deterred with the threat of criminal sanctions.

6.2 WHY PROSECUTING FINANCIAL CRIME CAN BE PROBLEMATIC

Senior managers of major financial institutions are not the only ones to have escaped charges of criminal liability for their role in the 2008 financial crisis: criminal prosecutions against financial institutions themselves have also been pretty thin on the ground.[8] Not because the legal tools do not exist to charge an institution with a crime even though it is not an independent moral agent in the way a person is: the legal tools for prosecuting corporate entities for crimes are well established. Of course, establishing what a corporate entity "knew" and what it "intended" and sometimes even what "it" did—all prerequisites for proving criminal conduct in most cases—can sometimes pose difficulties given that groups do not possess a single mind that has knowledge, intentions, and makes decisions in the way individuals do (see Reiff 2008, 220–3). But the reluctance to prosecute financial institutions for their latest round of crimes has not been driven by concern about these difficulties. Instead, it has been driven by the fear of upsetting a fragile economic recovery by throwing some of our most systemically important financial institutions

[8] For one of the few exceptions, see Eavis (2015) and *Federal Housing Finance Agency v. Nomura Holding*, 2015 WL 2183875 (S.D.N.Y.).

into turmoil, for criminal conviction can result in the revocation of the licenses required for these companies to do business.[9]

But I do not intend to discuss whether this fear is justified—that is, whether it represents a correct application of the relevant consequentialist concerns. Because even if it does, this is beside the point. After all, we do not usually relieve *people* of criminal responsibility just because punishing them will have bad consequences for others, which it often does, especially for their families.[10] And even if there is something to be said in favor of caution when it comes to criminal prosecution of systemically important financial institutions, this does not explain the reluctance to prosecute high-ranking *individuals* at those institutions. On the contrary, such prosecutions would signal a seriousness about ensuring the rule of law that could only strengthen trust in these financial institutions and therefore in the market as whole, and this is good for everybody (see Morgenson 2016b). Mere fines, unfortunately, cannot do this. Corporations can act only through agents, and there is substantial evidence that despite the imposition of even enormous fines, a large number of these agents are still inclined to engage in criminal behavior (Sorkin 2015). Indeed, according to one recent survey of the financial industry completed after a good portion of these fines had already been imposed, "more than one third of those earning $500,000 or more [report that they] have witnessed or have first-hand knowledge of wrongdoing in the workplace" (Tenbrunsel and Thomas 2015, 3). Not only does such wrongdoing continue to be widespread despite the imposition of substantial fines, those with knowledge of this wrongdoing also remain unwilling to report it: internally due to fear of retaliation; externally because they have signed confidentiality agreements with their employers that prohibit them from doing so (ibid.). Clearly, whether we focus on deterring future misconduct or punishing past misconduct, the use of fines alone has not been enough.

There are no doubt a variety of factors contributing to this failure to impose more serious sanctions, but in this chapter I intend to focus on just one: when it comes to prosecuting management for massive frauds committed by

[9] For numerous examples of how this fear discourages criminal prosecutions of financial institutions, see Garrett (2014). For an individual case study (in this instance HSBC), see Morgenson 2016d. Note also that even when a financial institution is prosecuted, the target is usually small and insignificant or a holding company or subsidiary that can be convicted with minimal collateral consequences for the principal business entity. (See Editorial 2015a, Protess and Corkery 2015, Henning 2015b, and Morgenson 2015d (noting that the only mortgage-fraud related prosecution brought by Manhattan DA Cyrus Vance was against a small minority-owned bank based in NYC's Chinatown), and Finkle 2016 (noting that only executives at small institutions ever seem to go to jail.)

[10] The argument that we should consider such "collateral consequences" when contemplating criminal prosecution of corporations, at least in recent times, is usually attributed to a memo written by former Attorney General Eric J. Holder in June 1999 when he was Deputy Attorney General of the United States. See Holder (1999, sec. 9).

otherwise legitimate business organizations in which no one seems to have played a central "mastermind" role but large numbers of people (including those ostensibly "in charge") have played necessary and therefore not insignificant contributory parts, it seems wrong—that is, both morally and legally questionable—to subject individuals to criminal charges and penalties unless it can be proved that they individually harbored the requisite knowledge and intent to defraud. This, however, can be very difficult to prove, especially when the fraud requires the passive (if not active) cooperation of large numbers of people, all of whom have varying responsibilities and none of whom has complete information (see Wang 2011, Reckard 2011, Taibbi 2012). For example, in a September 2015 report examining the difficulties prosecutors face in these kinds of cases, US Deputy Attorney General Sally Quilliam Yates (2015) stated:

> There [are] many substantial challenges unique to pursuing individuals for corporate misdeeds. In large corporations, where responsibility can be diffuse and decisions are made at various levels, it can be difficult to determine if someone possessed the knowledge and criminal intent necessary to establish their guilt beyond a reasonable doubt. This is particularly true when determining the culpability of high-level executives, who may be insulated from the day-to-day activity in which the misconduct occurs.

Now some of those most familiar with how these cases are put together and tried have expressed skepticism that intent would really be as difficult to prove as those currently in charge of doing so claim (Rakoff 2014, Steinzor 2015, esp. 217–19). Knowledge and intent can be proved indirectly, inferred from other evidence, meaning there is no need to produce a "smoking gun" that establishes exactly what a particular executive knew and when.[11] Smoking guns are rarely available in other kinds of criminal prosecutions and yet this does not deter prosecutors from stepping up in those cases. And in the cases we are examining here, there is a substantial degree of evidentiary material suggesting that senior executives did indeed know what was going on. Even some outsiders who had no access to inside information knew. Indeed, with regard to most of the misconduct relating to the 2008 financial collapse, especially the mispricing of risks associated with mortgage-backed securities and credit default swaps, the problems were apparent enough to some outsiders that they took huge positions betting the whole enterprise would collapse, just as it eventually did (see Lewis 2010). While the number of short sellers here was relatively small, their positions were large, and one of the principal justifications for allowing this kind of short selling is that it is

[11] But see the very recent and heavily criticized decision in *United States v. Countrywide*, Docket Nos. 15-496 and 15-499 (2d Cir, May 23, 2016), which held that there can be no fraud if at the time a promise is made there is no intent to defraud even though intent to defraud is present when the promise is performed. For a discussion of this decision, see Hiltzik 2016.

supposed to provide an early warning of fraud, a justification that is rendered meaningless if the warning bells this generates can be ignored with impunity by senior management. The fact that some outside investors were betting the farm on such a collapse should have led company insiders to at least engage in some introspection and internal re-evaluation of the risks involved within their own institutions, but it did not.

That they failed to do so is not surprising, perhaps, given the amount of profit that questionable transactions were generating for their institutions as well as for the senior officers themselves. But this does not excuse them. Indeed, there is a legal doctrine already in place to deal with exactly this kind of conduct. This is the doctrine of "willful blindness" (sometimes called "willful ignorance"), the idea that those who deliberately avoid investigating suspicious activity occurring right in front of their faces can be charged with knowledge of what they would have found out if they had been more careful, and can thereby be found to have constructive knowledge of the wrongdoing and have effectively intended it to occur even if they did not actually know what was going on.

Not that willful blindness is itself always easy to prove. According to the Model Penal Code § 2.02(7), willful blindness is "almost knowledge" and certainly more than negligence. Beyond that, exactly what constitutes willful blindness can be controversial (see Charlow 1992, Husak 2010, Lynch 2015). But it is still easier to prove than intent, so the willful blindness doctrine should have given prosecutors all they needed to charge senior executives with criminal wrongdoing even if the available amount of direct or inferential evidence of criminal intent was less than ideal.

Why prosecutors have been so reluctant to use this tool is not entirely clear. The most cynical explanation is that prosecutors think that making out a case of willful blindness is still too difficult, and they are reluctant to bring high-profile cases against well-funded defendants when the case might be lost, for losing makes promotion and an eventual move to higher office more problematic. We could, of course, try to encourage prosecutors to be less risk averse, but risk aversion is a common feature of human nature and is difficult to change (see Tversky and Kahneman 1991). So even though there is good reason to believe that it would have been nowhere near as difficult to prove willful blindness if not intent in these cases as the relevant prosecutors' offices seem to have feared (but cf. Bray 2016a and b), we need to give prosecutors tools they can employ with greater confidence if we want to ensure that senior executives are held accountable for what seem like obvious cases of criminal wrongdoing.

Before we can see what kinds of additional tools prosecutors need in these cases, however, we need to get clear on how the moral and legal aspects of these cases interrelate. For what I intend to argue is that the failure to prosecute senior executives in these cases stems not just from a lack of adequate legal tools but from a misunderstanding of how the moral and legal responsibility of these executives should be assessed. And I will begin my exploration of this issue by examining whether the decision to make criminal sanctions available to deter and punish a particular kind of conduct is, in the first instance, even a moral matter.

6.3 ENFORCEABILITY AND CRIMINALIZATION

There are many ways of characterizing the issue that is facing us when we ask whether senior executives can be held criminally responsible for the financial crimes committed by those within their organization or by the organization as a whole. One might even contend that phrasing the issue in this way amounts to begging the question, for what we should be asking is whether what the entity has done should be treated as a "crime" or not; we cannot simply assume that a crime has been committed, especially if no individual or entity has been convicted of criminal conduct or at least admitted that criminal conduct has occurred. And unless knowledge and intent or at least willful blindness can be ascribed to certain individuals and through them to the entity as whole, one of the traditional elements of criminal conduct seems to be missing. With regard to the liability of senior executives, then, shouldn't the issue be whether something less than willful blindness can be deemed criminal?

This latter way of phrasing the question is what we might call "the conventional view or criminalization." This view holds that wrongs should be divided into two categories: the civil and the criminal. Civil wrongs are to be compensated; only criminal wrongs are to be punished. True, there is some disagreement on how to decide whether a wrong should be placed in one category or the other. Some argue that this depends on whether the wrong in question is sufficiently serious in terms of its broader societal effects to be the public's business; others argue that instead of focusing on the societal effects of a particular class of conduct, we ought to focus on the intrinsic nature of the wrong itself. But the same factors seem to come into play under either approach so the difference between them may be merely semantic. In any case, under the conventional view, determining what sanctions are available for any particular alleged wrong depends on how that wrong (if it even is a wrong) is categorized, for determining what kind of sanctions are available naturally flows from this (see generally Duff 2010, Husak 2008).

But I think this is a mistake. The question should never be whether such and such conduct constitutes a criminal wrong or a civil wrong or no wrong at all. This way of phrasing the issue begs the question in another way: it assumes that there are different kinds of wrongs—civil and criminal—and that some higher standard is required in order to characterize something as a criminal rather than merely a civil wrong, when this is the very question that is at stake. Indeed, the whole enterprise of thinking about categorizing wrongs is misplaced, for wrongs are derivative of rights, and it is the nature and scope of the rights at issue on which our attention should be focused. And there are not two kinds of rights—civil sanctions and criminal sanctions are different kinds of *remedies* for the violation of any right, not different kinds of *wrongs*. In the first instance the only question is whether the remedy of criminal sanctions is required to make whatever underlying right is at issue enforceable. I say in the first instance for it may be the case that even if criminal sanctions are necessary for a certain right to be enforceable, there are moral limits that apply to how we may punish people, and it may be that in this particular case those moral limits will be transgressed if we impose criminal sanctions, especially if we are talking about terms of imprisonment. But I will treat this as a separate issue, to be decided after we consider the question of enforceability. For if we conflate these questions now, we effectively assume that a higher degree of scienter—that is, the mental state accompanying whatever conduct is being treated as a potential wrong—is required for criminal sanctions to apply, and that is the very notion I want to challenge. This does not mean I will be assuming that a stringent scienter requirement does not apply, merely that the question of what level of intent is required should arise in a different place in our moral reasoning (and therefore in our legal reasoning too) than we tend to place it now. So for the time being, I will consider only the question of enforceability—we will get to the moral question that may be raised when we seek to impose criminal sanctions later.

Of course to even get to the question of enforceability, we have to have a right in mind that we are seeking to enforce. Is there a moral and a legal right not to be injured in the way that those who were injured by financial institutions leading up to and coming out of the financial crisis claim? Was it a wrong to issue loans to borrowers with no proof of income or ability to pay? Was it a wrong to construct mortgage-backed securities using exclusively or largely sub-prime loans yet claim the upper trenches of these securities were no riskier than US Treasury securities, which are as risk free as one can get? Was it a wrong to sell these mortgage-backed securities as AAA, yet bet that they would fail and not disclose these bets to the clients who were buying them? Was it a wrong for rating agencies to rate these securities AAA without examining the underlying loans of which they were composed? Was it a wrong to foreclose on many of these loans even though proper documentation that they were in default did not exist? Was it a wrong for firms to manipulate the rate for Libor, the London Interbank Offered Rate upon which so many interest rates are based? I could go on, but I hope I do not have to. The evidence is overwhelming that all these acts occurred, and the firms involved have by and large admitted that they occurred, although not always that they were illegal (see Financial Crisis Inquiry Commission 2011, Dealbook 2015). Nevertheless, given the size of the fines agreed to by these firms, it would be the height of obstinacy to insist that without an admission of guilt or prosecution and conviction we cannot conclude that something illegal happened here. And the immorality of these acts is self-evident. I will therefore take it as given that the kind of conduct at issue in these cases, conduct that in total (that is, taken together as a whole rather than just individual actor by individual actor) has caused serious and substantial class-wide economic injury (as opposed to merely individual economic injury, no matter how large) violates something we could safely call both a moral and legal right, even though it may still be unclear at this point whether individual executives as well as the institution as a whole is legally and morally responsible. The only other option is to argue that the enormous fines and settlement payments being extracted here are in fact a massive injustice, and I know of no one worthy of being taken seriously who argues this. The question, then, is what kind of sanctions should be available in order to ensure that this underlying moral and legal right is actually enforceable.

Drawing on my work in *Punishment, Compensation, and Law: A Theory of Enforceability* (Reiff 2005), I contend that criminal sanctions against senior executives and officers are indeed necessary in these cases to make this underlying right enforceable. The test I articulate in that work is twofold: one for the previolation state of affairs, and one for the postviolation state of affairs. The threatened amount of punishment that must be available in order to a make a right enforceable in the previolation sense is an amount sufficient to make the beneficiaries of that right rationally believe that potential violators will prefer to remain in the previolation state of affairs (ibid., 87–8). The test for determining enforceability in the postviolation sense, however, is somewhat different: the amount of punishment that must be available to make a right enforceable once a violation has occurred is the amount necessary to make the violator's suffering equivalent to the uncompensated suffering of the right's beneficiary (ibid., 133). Interestingly, this amount—the amount of retributive punishment enforceability requires—is not the same amount that rights beneficiary might have expected to be available when they were in the previolation state of affairs—it merely has to be enough to maintain their expectations, and for a variety of reasons these measures turn out to be very different. What these reasons are, why they lead to different tests for the previolation and the postviolation state of affairs, and how these different tests interrelate and support one another are important issues, but they are far too involved to discuss further here.[12] Given these tests, however, I think it is

[12] For a full discussion of these issues, see Reiff (2005).

obvious that the availability of civil sanctions and fines—even in the staggering amounts we are talking about here—is insufficient to make the rights at issue enforceable in either the pre- or the postviolation sense. What is necessary, if we are to make these rights enforceable, is that senior executives have to face a realistic threat of—and on occasion must actually go to—jail.

First, it is not even clear these fines, enormous as they are, actually exceed the profits generated by the relevant wrongdoing. Analysis of this is rarely made in the course of determining the amount of these fines or otherwise settling the cases from which they arise and when it is it is not made public (see Protess 2014). This allows and perhaps even encourages potential future violators to believe that even if they are caught they can still end up profiting from their wrongdoing. For no matter how big the fines imposed or settlements extracted are, if they are not bigger than the amount of profit generated by this activity they are neither sufficient to deter similar misconduct in the future nor likely to be sufficient to satisfy the demands of retribution—they are simply one more cost of doing business, of no more significance than any other (see Becker 1968, Coffee 1980).[13] This is especially true when these costs can be deducted from the corporation's taxes and therefore subsidized by the taxpayer, as is often the case (see Baxandall and Surka 2015, Moyer 2015), or the fines levied are subject to various credits for "good behavior" the corporation can claim to reduce the amount it actually pays, which is often the case too (see Popper 2016b). In any event, to the extent these fines are *actually* paid by the corporation involved, they are *effectively* paid by the corporation's shareholders, and not the actual wrongdoers themselves. And while there could be collateral consequences for these wrongdoers, in most cases there are none. Indeed, avoiding such collateral consequences seems to be the major impetus for the corporation to agree to these fines in the first place, and so far, the relevant authorities have largely gone along with this on the grounds they would rather have an agreed fine than an imposed one which could be challenged in the courts (see Morgenson 2016a).

Second, even if the fines levied and settlement amounts agreed did exceed the profits generated by this activity, it seems unlikely that they could equal the *harm* caused by this activity, which is the traditional measure of damage for moral wrongs. This measure would almost certainly be far greater than the disgorgement of profits given the potential of consequential damage to those that have been injured. The problem here is that the harm caused is likely to be so great that many of the financial institutions involved would not have sufficient resources to fully compensate those injured by their conduct and remain in business. Yet their failure to survive as viable parts of the economic

[13] Indeed, in order to have a sufficient deterrent effect they would have to be substantially bigger than the profit generated by the wrongdoing, in order to account for the possibility that the misconduct would not be identified and punished.

system would only serve to exacerbate the consequential financial injury already inflicted by their wrongdoing. This is why it is so difficult to achieve justice if we are having to rely on monetary sanctions alone to keep financial wrongdoing under control: we cannot compensate people for their injuries because attempting to do so would only make their injuries worse. Which means that we have to prevent such injuries from occurring, and when they do occur, we have to impose real punishment on the bad actors involved if we are going to make the relevant rights enforceable (see Reiff 2005).

Third, even if fines were levied on the individuals involved, as some suggest they should be (see e.g. Hill and Painter 2015), payment of these fines is often covered by insurance or the individual involved is otherwise directly or indirectly indemnified by the corporation, thereby effectively making the payment no different than if it had been made by the corporation itself (see Morgenson 2015c and 2016c). Even when this is not the case, the individuals involved are extremely high-income earners, so fines may simply act as another cost of doing business for them just as they do for the corporation, to be offset by even larger amounts of future compensation. In this case, why should we expect fines to have any greater effect on their behavior than on that of their corporate employers? Indeed, shareholders have long been able to bring civil suits for damages against senior executives for their misconduct and yet such misconduct has continued to flourish. And bringing such suits has recently been made significantly more difficult, so corporate executives are even less likely to be subjected to these suits than they used to be.[14] Which means that substituting individual fines for corporate fines would at best serve to maintain the status quo. If we are going to make the underlying right against being subject to such financial injury from corporate misconduct enforceable, we are accordingly going to have to do so by using a sanction other than the payment of money (see Rakoff 2015). Only if those in the upper echelons of the corporation face personal criminal conviction and imprisonment can the relevant rights be enforceable in the previolation sense, and only if they sometimes go to prison when they are not deterred can we support these previolation expectations, deliver the requisite amount of retribution, and make these rights enforceable in the postviolation sense.

In some sense the law already recognizes this through what is called the "responsible corporate officer" (RCO) doctrine.[15] Under that doctrine, an individual may be convicted of a regulatory offense even if he had no direct knowledge of the relevant facts and did not intend that the offense occur as long as he or she is a "responsible corporate officer." Exactly what it takes to be a "responsible corporate officer," however, remains vague. Is only the most

[14] Shareholders who sue top executives for misconduct and do not prevail now have to pay the defendants' attorneys' fees, making shareholder suits much riskier (see Morgenson 2014b).

[15] For a recent discussion of the RCO doctrine, see Sepinwall (2014).

immediate supervisor of those with the requisite knowledge and intent the "responsible corporate officer," or can liability flow all the way up to the most senior executives and even the corporate boardroom? And the question of the level of scienter required for conviction under the doctrine is also unclear: some think that proof of individual negligence on the part of the officer is required (in other words, even if the officer did not know what was going on he should have); others claim that the doctrine effectively creates a strict liability offense, although some think that the underlying bad actor must at least be shown to have acted with the requisite intent, while others think strict liability is possible all the way down. Some of those in each camp, in turn, think that whatever standard the RCO doctrine creates it is unjust, for only knowledge and intent can support criminal liability as a moral rather than a legal matter.[16]

Regardless of how one thinks the RCO doctrine should be cashed out, however, and regardless of whether this can be done in a way that satisfies the demands of justice, the doctrine has rarely been applied since it was formulated some fifty years ago. When it is applied, moreover, its violation only leads to criminal liability for a misdemeanor. This is a serious defect, for given the enormous profits that such misconduct can generate, a very small chance of a misdemeanor conviction hardly seems sufficient to deter the kind of misconduct we are trying to suppress. Nor does a misdemeanor conviction seem sufficient to impose the requisite amount of retributive punishment given the severity and scope of the injury this misconduct has caused, even if a misdemeanor conviction were to have collateral consequences such as the loss of one's job or disbarment from the industry, which unfortunately it rarely does (see Havian 2015). And even if it did—even if it meant the individual involved could never work in the industry again—the individuals involved are almost always rich enough already to continue to live comfortably for the rest of their lives. Which means the personal upside of doing nothing to stop the misdeeds at issue here would remain substantial and consequences of not doing so marginal. In any event, the long-standing existence of the RCO doctrine obviously did nothing to ensure that those with supervisory responsibility would make themselves aware of what their underlings were doing and stop any wronging going on below them in the run up to the financial crisis. So still more needs to be done to make the underlying right here enforceable in

[16] For recent criticism of the RCO doctrine along these lines, see e.g. Copeland (2014); Petrin (2012). Note that Congress is currently considering a proposal put forward by the National Association of Criminal Defense Lawyers and Koch Industries, the conglomerate owned by David and Charles Koch, that would restrict the RCO doctrine by requiring proof of knowledge of wrongfulness before any individual could be criminally convicted under it (see Editorial 2015b; Taub 2015). Of course if this proposal were to become law, the RCO doctrine would become mere surplusage, for proof of this level of knowledge and intent already subjects one to aiding and abetting liability. See Securities Act of 1933, 15 U.S.C. § 77*o*(b).

either the pre- or the postviolation sense. Prison is what those in a position to prevent this kind of misconduct fear, and given the enormity of the financial injury that can result from this kind of misconduct, only prison can put the scales of justice back in balance.[17]

6.4 MORAL RESPONSIBILITY AND CAUSAL RESPONSIBILITY

Now that we have decided that criminal sanctions against individual corporate employees are necessary to make the rights at issue here enforceable and therefore genuine rather than merely nominal (again, see generally Reiff 2005), we need to consider whether criminal sanctions such as imprisonment are morally permissible. This is because morality places limits on who we can punish and what kind of punishments we can impose even if such punishments are necessary to make a particular right enforceable. No matter what, we cannot impose certain kinds of punishments, we cannot impose an amount of punishment that is out of proportion to the wrong, and we cannot punish people who are not in some way morally responsible for the wrong itself (see Reiff 2005, esp. 133–4). This is the second problem we must overcome if we are to punish executives at corporations that have (or whose employees have) committed serious financial crimes. While we can (indeed we often must) prove intent to defraud by the corporation as a whole by aggregating what its individual employees knew and intended, if we cannot prove that the particular senior executive in question had the requisite knowledge and intent to defraud—even when willful blindness can be considered tantamount to intent—we may be forced to leave these executives both legally and morally off the hook. After all, no less an esteemed figure than H. L. A. Hart argued that there can be no moral responsibility without fault (Hart 1994, 173).[18] And imposing criminal sanctions on corporate officers without proof of individual fault looks uncomfortably like employing a doctrine of collective responsibility, triggering many familiar objections.[19] To make things even more difficult, many people think that proof of intent, not simply negligence—in other words,

[17] For a similar sentiment from a federal district judge who has tried a lot of these cases, see Scheindlin (2015): "Frankly, these people do not want to go to jail . . . and that's what they care about. The money part is the cost of doing business—it's trivial!" See also Tillman and Pontell (2016).

[18] And there are many other scholars who take a similar position. See e.g. Alexander 1990. Of course, there are also others who argue against this and assert that there can be moral responsibility without fault. See e.g. Kramer (2005, esp. 328–31).

[19] For a discussion of these, see Reiff (2008). Nevertheless, there are still some theorists who advocate the imposition of collective responsibility here. See e.g. Sepinwall (2015); Miller (2014).

a particularly serious degree of fault—is required for the just imposition of criminal (as opposed to merely civil) sanctions, especially imprisonment.

But there are so many exceptions to such a requirement (if it even is one) in the law already that it is hard to see how this could really represent a correct statement of our moral beliefs. We accept transferred intent (intent to kill A suffices as intent to kill B), temporally shifted intent (intent to drive drunk suffices as intent to injure someone later while driving drunk), inferred intent (intent to sell is inferred from the quantity possessed), willful ignorance as intent (the failure to investigate highly suspicious circumstances is deemed intent to further the conduct that one would have known about if one had investigated), shared intent (intent to join a conspiracy is deemed intent to commit any acts done in furtherance of the conspiracy even if done without knowledge or even hypothetical approval by other members of the conspiracy), and so on. We also believe that ignorance of the law (or of the requirements of morality) is no excuse (in other words, you do not have to intend to do wrong, just to intend to do what you did to trigger either legal or moral liability). True, some people raise moral objections to all these legal fictions for discovering intent, and along the edges of some of these cases there may indeed be good reason for concern. But look at the number of them—our legal practice suggests we do not take straightforward proof of intent as morally required and it seems likely that if we did, we would almost never be able to justifiably imprison anybody for anything, at least with regard to white-collar crimes, and *that* would be contrary to most people's moral intuitions. So unless we are willing to claim that morality simply prohibits the imposition of imprisonment in the absence of direct proof of actual intent to commit an act or omission the defendant knew was a crime—and I do not think many people's moral intuitions run this way—we should stop inconsistently paying lip service to the idea that only direct proof of intent will morally suffice to trigger criminal liability.

More importantly, while we often do require proof of fault in order to subject a rights violator to criminal sanctions, we find negligence sufficient for this on enough occasions in the law already that it seems far too late in the day to argue that as a moral matter negligence will not do. Even the traditionally conservative Model Penal Code accepts that negligence alone (and not just intent, recklessness, and *gross* negligence) can lead to criminal liability (see American Law Institute § 2.02(2)(d)).[20] True, most cases that lead to criminal liability for negligence involve serious *physical* injury. But the financial injuries inflicted by the conduct at issue here are also serious and they affect such a large number of people that treating these as morally different merely because

[20] While some scholars continue to claim that the imposition of criminal liability for negligence is unjust, I will not re-argue the issue here, for there is enough material on this elsewhere (see e.g. Huigens 1998).

they are not *initially* physical makes little sense. Those who lose their homes, their jobs, and their savings are obviously going to suffer greatly, as much if not more than many of those who sustain serious physical injuries, and many will suffer consequential physical injuries such as strokes or heart attacks or may even commit suicide as a result of the stress arising from these situations. In any event, negligence clearly is a form of moral wrongdoing, so there seems to be no moral impediment to holding senior executives criminally liable if they can be found to have been negligent in exercising their supervisory duties in this class of cases even if this has left them with no actual knowledge of the wrongdoing of their underlings and they did not specifically intend that this wrongdoing occur.

Note that this is effectively what we do already when we find senior executives *civilly* liable as "control persons" under Section 15 of the Securities Act of 1933, 15 U.S. § 77*o*(a).[21] Our reluctance to apply the same standard when it comes to imposing terms of imprisonment instead of the payment of money is simply a side-effect of addressing the question of the morality of criminal sanctions incorrectly. Rather than ask whether negligence in this context is an independent criminal wrong we should be asking whether the threat of imprisonment is necessary to make the underlying right against negligent injury enforceable and if so, whether morality permits this, for this leads to a result that is more in line with our moral intuitions. If the underlying right of people not to be injured by acts of class-wide corporate fraud requires holding senior executives criminally liable in order to make these rights enforceable—and we have already established that it does—and we hold them liable only if they are found to have exercised their supervisory duties negligently—something which would have to be proved beyond a reasonable doubt for criminal conviction to occur—there seems to be no basis for asserting a moral objection here.

The evidence of negligence among senior executives in these cases actually seems overwhelming—after all, do we really think that the global financial system could collapse because of the nature of the investments made without *anyone* in a senior position failing to exercise reasonable care? More likely, this was only possible because *everyone*, or at least a great many people, failed to exercise reasonable care. The widespread nature of this misconduct, however, is not a reason to let anyone off the hook. Nevertheless, I do not want to rest my argument here, for as I have already made clear, the legal tools to bring prosecution on these grounds were already arguably in place yet prosecutors did not use them. Apparently, even the burden of proving negligence is seen by prosecutors as too difficult to meet when they are concerned about bringing cases that might adversely affect their conviction rate and therefore their

[21] See *Federal Housing Finance Agency v. Nomura Holding*, 2015 WL 2183875 (S.D.N.Y.), 102–10.

chances for promotion. If we are going to overcome their reluctance to bring high-profile cases in financial cases against well-funded defendants, we are going to have to make the requirements even more manageable than this.

Whether something *less* than standard negligence could ever morally justify the imposition of criminal sanctions, however, is a much more difficult question. We sometimes do impose criminal liability for what we call strict liability offenses, of course, so our practice does suggest that criminal sanctions can sometimes be imposed even without proof of negligence. But the morality of doing so is sufficiently controversial that I do not intend to rely on the argument that our current practice settles the matter.[22] Instead, my argument is this: there is *always* moral fault whenever we find a senior executive causally responsible for widespread and severe class-wide financial injury. Whether the law currently recognizes this or not (and under the RCO doctrine it might), it should do—the current fear that this would somehow transgress applicable moral limits is misplaced. Accordingly, instead of separately considering what level of fault is present in any particular case, all we need to consider is whether the executive in question is causally responsible for the loss, at least in part. His level of what we might call "traditional" fault (knowledge, intent, or negligence) is a *factor* in determining his causal responsibility, for our sense of causal responsibility tends to expand and contract with the degree of wrongfulness we attribute to an actor. But traditional wrongfulness is neither a necessary nor a sufficient factor for a finding of causal responsibility.[23] In other words, causal responsibility is not simply a metaphysical determination—it is also a moral determination, and so anyone found causally responsible is necessarily morally responsible too, and as long as there is moral responsibility the imposition of a term of imprisonment is not unjust.

I realize this is a controversial claim, and so much needs to be said to defend it. Much of this has been said in my "No Such Thing as Accident: Rethinking the Relation between Causal and Moral Responsibility" (Reiff 2015), which focused on the relation between moral and causal responsibility in cases of serious physical injury. I now extend the claims made there to cases of serious class-wide economic injury—that is, injury that is suffered by a large number of similarly situated clients, customers, creditors, debtors, shareholders, counterparties, investors, or depositors, as opposed to injury to just one individual or entity or a few. The essence of these claims is as follows. Causal responsibility is not some junior, broader inquiry that identifies a pool of candidates among whom a more senior concept of moral responsibility allows

[22] For some relatively recent discussions of this issue, however, see Thomas (2012), Hamdani (2007).

[23] For further discussion of how we are willing to treat more remote causes as responsible causes when the seriousness of the conduct is particularly high, albeit in a slightly different context, see Reiff (2005, 135–6).

us to pick and choose when deciding who will be assigned to the category of wrongdoer, be it civil or criminal.[24] Rather, causal responsibility is itself a moral inquiry. And not merely because there are moral elements to any causal inquiry, both at the actual or cause-in-fact level and the legal or proximate or cause-in-law level, something that I think it fair to say is no longer subject to reasonable dispute.[25] It is a moral inquiry because causal responsibility is itself a moral determination, at least when we are looking for the cause of the serious class-wide economic injuries at issue here. Someone found causally responsible for these injuries (as opposed to being a mere causal condition, a distinction I shall say more about in a moment) is therefore *necessarily* morally responsible too even in the absence of proof of traditional fault. In these cases, fault is effectively an *output* of our causal determination rather than an input.[26]

Note that I am not arguing that criminal sanctions may be imposed even in the absence of fault. What I am arguing is that whenever we find someone causally responsible, at least in this particular class of cases, *fault is always present*, for this is built into our conception of causal responsibility itself. If we then subject those found causally responsible to criminal sanctions only when we also find them guilty of traditional moral fault, we have engaged in a moral double-counting, and we risk allowing some of those who are morally responsible to escape punishment merely because their moral responsibility has not been proven twice. From the victim's point of view this would obviously work an injustice, as great an injustice as prosecuting those who are not in any way morally responsible for a wrong. To prevent this former type of injustice from arising out of financial cases we accordingly need to reorient our examination of the conduct at issue so that we focus on what I call *comprehensive* causal responsibility—a kind of causal responsibility that includes moral responsibility but is not subservient to it—rather than afford those already found causally (and therefore morally) responsible an escape from liability unless we are also able to show they took a second and even larger bite out of the moral apple. If we have found a particular senior executive causally responsible for a particular wrong (such as fraud in the creation or sale of a mortgage-backed security), then we have already done all we need to do to find him morally responsible too.

[24] For an example of how the hierarchical ordering of inquiries I am challenging here is often simply assumed to be self-evidently appropriate, even by those who argue for more vigorous prosecution of corporate wrongdoing, see Pettit (2007, 173): "holding someone responsible, then, is different from the mere assignment of causal responsibility."

[25] For a discussion of these moral elements, see Reiff (2015, 380–3).

[26] Not only is a finding of traditional fault not a necessary element of causal responsibility, it is not a sufficient one either, for someone may be at fault yet not causally responsible if there was someone much closer down the chain of causation to the actual injury who was a supervening or overwhelming cause (see Reiff 2015).

6.5 ESTABLISHING CAUSAL RESPONSIBILITY

What factors besides those relevant to a finding of traditional fault are relevant to an assignment of causal responsibility to senior executives for the acts or omissions of their employees? Merely because the particular senior executive we are investigating happens to be higher up in the chain of command is not enough to establish this. After all, it is necessarily true that all those in a supervisory role failed to prevent the wrongdoing of all those beneath them. So lack of action on behalf of a supervisor is always a causal condition of every wrong. But identifying a causal condition is a different enterprise than identifying causal responsibility. There are potentially an infinite number of causal conditions for every act of misconduct but only a few of them are ultimately assigned causal responsibility. Deciding which causal conditions will be assigned causal responsibility is a comparative process, involving consideration of a wide range of factors, including the degree of remove between the factor under consideration and the harm, the extent to which the contribution of that particular factor to the ultimate harm is especially significant in comparison to other causal conditions, and the ease at which those at a supervisory level could have intervened and prevented the wrong from occurring. The comparative scienter of the various actors involved up and down the causal chain is relevant too, for a particularly high degree of scienter can turn a causal condition further down the chain into an intervening cause and relieve those higher up the chain of causal responsibility if this intentional wrongdoing was not foreseeable. Other considerations may also be relevant. Unfortunately, there is no strict formula for making this comparative calculation; it is an all-thing-considered inquiry, just like the assignment of moral responsibility is said to be. But a useful way of thinking about what we seem to be doing here is this: when we are seeking to assign causal responsibility we are trying to identify the place or places in the chain of causation where human intervention is most likely to significantly reduce the chances of a similar injury happening again (Reiff 2015, 391–2).

One obvious factor in these cases is the degree to which the senior executives had reason to pay attention to the activity of a subordinate. As part of a traditional moral inquiry, what we would be looking for here is whether the executive acted reasonably in discharging his or her supervisory responsibilities. But this would require consideration of the standard of care, and if supervisory personnel in the financial industry typically do not exercise the kind of supervision that those unfamiliar with the industry might expect, this mitigates against a finding of actual negligence, even though we could impose a standard of care that exceeded the actual standard. This, however, is not a problem when it comes to assigning causal responsibility. While negligence presents an objective standard, the comparative causal standard assesses responsibility on the facts as it finds them. And if we find causal responsibility then this means that this particular actor's causal contribution to the injury was unreasonable *by definition*. So, for example, a subordinate's prior acts of wrongdoing would not only trigger a heightened expectation that the relevant supervisor would have done more to ensure there was no wrongdoing currently going on, these prior bad acts also make it clear that the supervisor's failure to intervene was causally responsible for the wrong and not merely a causal condition.

Factors that indicate the employee's performance was outside the norm, *in either direction*, have a similar effect. Indeed, one common quip within the financial world is that "when someone is doing well, give them a bonus, but when they are doing extraordinarily well, fire them, for the only reason this could be happening is that something illegal is going on." This is meant to be a joke, of course, but there is a kernel of truth in the principle it reflects. When an activity is generating huge amounts of profits (or losses, but we needn't worry about heightened supervisory scrutiny when losses are occurring—this always seems to get people's attention), those higher up in the chain of command are supposed to be aware of this, and the degree of supervisory activity we expect from them increases. The failure to pay close attention to those generating what appear to be "cowboy capitalist" profits may not amount to willful blindness, but it certainly is a factor in deciding whether a particular supervisor was at least in part causally responsible for any resulting avoidable injury to others. And if we are willing to assign causal responsibility, a sufficient degree of moral responsibility has been found to justify the imposition of criminal sanctions.

The degree of remove, a traditional factor for causal responsibility, is also relevant here. We are not trying to hold chief executives criminally responsible for determining whether some entry-level administrative assistant is cheating on his or her expense reports. But the activities at issue here were such a huge part of the economic activity of these companies that we should naturally expect all those in the supervisory chain to exercise much greater control over these activities than they otherwise might. More direct supervisors might have more responsibility, of course, but given the amount of money at stake and the potential that more direct supervisors will have their judgment clouded by the personal financial benefits these activities typically generate, it is not unreasonable to expect even those at the highest corporate level to pay close attention to what is going on.

Also relevant is whether the particular individual signed any document found to have contained misrepresentations. Corporate agents should not be able to lend their name to a statement and then deny that they had sufficient knowledge to know that it was false. When one makes a representation, one also makes an implied representation that one has made a reasonable investigation to ensure the representation is correct.[27] The greater the potential

[27] A principle now expressly codified by section 302 of the Sarbanes-Oxley Act of 2002, 15 U.S.C. § 7241(a).

harm that might result if that representation is untrue, the greater the amount of investigation required to ensure that it is true. Even when an executive relies on underlings to do this investigation for him, he has no more protection than he would had he done the investigation himself. And if the potential harm of the representation is serious enough, the only amount of investigation that is reasonable is enough to determine whether the representation is in fact true. Or, to put it in causal terms, when one sends a misrepresentation out into the world that foreseeably causes widespread and severe financial harm one is morally responsible for the injury this misrepresentation creates.

The nature of the financial product itself may also make supervision by those further up the chain of command more essential. When these products are especially dangerous—as were the mortgage-backed securities and credit default swaps that led to the 2008 financial collapse—it is not unreasonable to expect more extensive supervisory scrutiny and control.[28] We are therefore much more likely to place causal responsibility on senior executives in these cases than we might with respect to the handling of some more conservative financial product. After all, if financial services and products can cause widespread and severe financial injury just like non-financial products can cause widespread and severe physical injury, why should we not treat the provision of these financial products as sufficiently causally important that we place responsibility for the injuries those products cause squarely on those who provide them, just as we do in the case of non-financial products?[29] Changing the law to provide for this would not only make the law accord better with our current moral notions, it would also make it clear to senior executives that a great deal more is going to be required of them in the future if they want to avoid criminal liability for this kind of wrongdoing.

Another factor is the corporate culture those at the top establish. A corporate culture that puts enormous pressure on underlings to bring good news to their supervisors and punishes them if they bring bad news is another factor that goes to whether we should charge those at the top with causal responsibility for a wrong they could have prevented or stopped had a different corporate culture been in place.[30] "Firms with a strong ethical culture and senior leaders who set the right tone, lead by example and impose

[28] See Buffet (2002), referring to these derivatives as "financial weapons of mass destruction."

[29] Note that even though the responsibility placed on manufacturers of non-financial products is commonly referred to as "strict liability," this does not mean there is no moral component to it. While recovering for injuries caused by defective consumer products does not require proof of traditional fault, it does require proof that the product was defective, and proof of this does indeed require proof of a kind of unreasonable conduct, and therefore moral fault nonetheless. For further discussion of this point, see Reiff (2014, 245).

[30] For a discussion of the relation of corporate culture to bank performance, see McNulty and Akhigbe (2015). For an example of how corporate culture facilitated misconduct at one bank (Citibank), see Waytz (2015).

consequences on anyone who violates the firm's cultural norms are essential to restoring investor confidence and trust in the securities industry," says the chairman of the Financial Industry Regulatory Authority (Morgenson 2016a).[31] And an ethical corporate culture is something that is very difficult to impose from the outside—only if firm leadership adopts this approach are things likely to change, making their causal responsibility for any losses that result from a less-than-ethical culture and their corresponding moral responsibility for these losses abundantly clear.

There are a myriad of other factors that could also be relevant. Did the senior executives in question profit personally from the wrongful activity, directly, or indirectly? The more they did, the more they are causally responsible for that activity if they did not look into how these profits were being generated. Were the corporate controls in place sufficient for senior executives to rely on them to bring any misconduct to their attention? If not, and the particular senior executive was in a position to have improved these controls, this also supports a finding of causal responsibility. Were any other "red flags" present in this case that should have led those in charge to subject the conduct of their underlings to greater scrutiny, making their failure to do so an even more significant causal factor in the injury the misconduct of those underlings ultimately inflicted?

I do not mean to suggest that this brief list is exhaustive. I am merely trying to make the point that we can easily find those in charge causally responsible even without a finding of traditional fault. And once this is done, our concern that there may be additional limits morality places on our ability to impose criminal liability in these cases is misplaced. The problem is not that we are going beyond what morality allows and holding people criminally liable when this is unjust, as some seem to contend (e.g. Husak 2009).[32] The problem is that we are not following morality and holding people criminally liable when the *failure* to do so is unjust. This is why the public is so outraged by the failure to prosecute in these cases.

So how do we fix this? Prosecutors can already allege willful ignorance even when they cannot prove intent, and legal tools such as the RCO doctrine already exist to allow them to prosecute senior executives even when they cannot prove willful ignorance. Nevertheless, it is obvious that the current state of the law regarding both these doctrines is more ambiguous than it

[31] See also Moyer (2016).

[32] Note that Husak does not address the example of financial crimes, but he does suggest that something important may be lost by holding people criminally liable without an adequate showing of criminal intent. I agree that intent is always relevant to determining criminal liability; I just contend that its absence is not determinative of either the legal or the moral question of whether such liability should attach.

should be. It is also obvious that the misdemeanor liability available under the RCO doctrine is not sufficient to deter the kind of misconduct that is occurring here given that it has clearly failed to do so to date. And while there is no reason why the RCO doctrine could not be interpreted to lead to felony liability when the underlying violation is serious enough, no one has ventured to argue for this so far. If we want to ensure that prosecutors are not so reluctant to use the tools available to them in the future, we must accordingly try to correct this by providing additional tools through legislative action. Whether we do so by enacting and then more aggressively using a more expansive version of the RCO doctrine[33] or by enacting something like a financial products safety law that parallels the provisions of consumer products safety law but provides criminal as well as civil sanctions, is not important.[34] What is important is that we act quickly if we do not want financial history to repeat itself yet again, and that we recognize there are no moral impediments to such action in the way.

I am under no illusion that proving the causal responsibility of senior executives in these cases will always be an easy task, although it will be an easier task than proving intent or willful blindness. Whenever we are talking about financial fraud, the activities in question often exhibit what we might call "causal complexity" (see generally Fisch 2009). This complexity, in turn, can express itself in a variety of ways. No single actor may be a "but for" cause, while many may be significant contributing causal factors. Deciding which causal factors should be assigned causal responsibility is ultimately a judgment call.[35] But I do not see this as a bad thing—on the contrary, it is this complexity, this requirement to consider a myriad of factors and to balance what actually happened against various counterfactual scenarios, that makes the ultimate determination of causal responsibility a moral determination and gives the assignment of causal responsibility its moral force. In any event, easy or not, this is simply what justice requires if we are to address the moral and legal breakdown that the 2008 financial crisis has brought to light.[36]

[33] Note that the argument often made against the RCO doctrine—that it is unjust to hold responsible officers "strictly liable" (if this is what the RCO doctrine does) when the underlying regulatory offense does not itself require knowledge and intent or even negligence—simply has no force under my analysis because causal responsibility satisfies the requirement of moral responsibility at all levels. As long as the underlying wrong requires proof of causal responsibility, it contains enough of an element of moral responsibility to justify criminal sanctions, and therefore the causal responsibility of supervisory personnel does as well.

[34] For an argument that it is the RCO doctrine that should be expanded, see Schuck (2010).

[35] For a discussion of some of these causal complexities and how we might deal with them, see Reiff (2015).

[36] An early version of this chapter was presented at the Manchester Workshops in Political Theory. My thanks to all those in attendance for their comments and suggestions. Thanks also to Amy Sepinwall for her comments on a somewhat later draft, and to the editor of this volume, Lisa Herzog, for her comments, suggestions, and support.

REFERENCES

Alexander, Larry. 1990. "Reconsidering the Relationship Among Voluntary Acts, Strict Liability, and Negligence in Criminal Law." *Social Philosophy & Policy* 7, 84–104.

American Law Institute. 1985. *Model Penal Code.*

Apuzzo, Matt, and Ben Protess. 2015. "Justice Department Sets Sights on Wall Street Executives." *The New York Times,* September 9.

Baxandall, Phineas, and Michael Surka. 2015. "Settling for a Lack of Accountability? Which Federal Agencies Allow Companies to Write Off Out-of-Court Settlements as Tax Deductions, and Which Are Transparent About It." US Public Interest Research Group Education Fund (December). http://uspirg.org/sites/pirg/files/reports/USPIRG_SettlementsReport.pdf (accessed October 25, 2016).

Becker, Gary S. 1968. "Crime and Punishment: An Economic Approach." *Journal of Political Economy* 76, 169–217.

Bray, Chad. 2015a. "Former Citigroup and UBS Trader Convicted in Libor Case." *The New York Times,* August 3.

Bray, Chad. 2015b. "Trial Opens for 6 Brokers Accused of Rigging Libor." *The New York Times,* October 6.

Bray, Chad. 2015c. "British Authorities Accuse 10 of Rigging Benchmark Interest Rate." *The New York Times,* November 13.

Bray, Chad. 2015d. "Court Reduces Ex-Trader's Sentence in Libor Case." *The New York Times,* December 21.

Bray, Chad. 2016a. "5 Ex-Brokers Cleared in London Libor Trial." *The New York Times,* January 27.

Bray, Chad. 2016b. "Sixth Ex-Broker Cleared in London Libor Trial." *The New York Times,* January 28.

Bray, Chad. 2016c. "British Court Convicts Former Barclays Employees over Libor Rigging." *The New York Times,* July 4.

Breslow, Jason M. 2013. "Were Bankers Jailed in Past Financial Crises?" Frontline (January 22). http://www.pbs.org/wgbh/frontline/article/were-bankers-jailed-in-past-financial-crises (accessed October 25, 2016).

Buffet, Warren. 2002. Berkshire Hathaway Annual Report. http://www.fintools.com/docs/Warren%20Buffet%20on%20Derivatives.pdf (accessed October 25, 2016).

Charlow, Robin. 1992. "Willful Ignorance and Criminal Culpability." *Texas Law Review* 70, 1351–429.

Coffee, John Collins, Jr. 1980. "Corporate Crime and Punishment: A Non-Chicago View of the Economics of Criminal Sanctions." *American Criminal Law Review* 17, 419–76.

Cohen, William D. 2015. "Justice Dept. Shift on White-Collar Crime Is Long Overdue." *The New York Times,* September 11.

Copeland, Katrice Bridges. 2014. "The Crime of Being in Charge: Executive Culpability and Collateral Consequences." *American Criminal Law Review* 51, 799–836.

Cox, Jeff. 2015. "Misbehaving Banks Have Now Paid $204B in Fines." *cnbc.com* (October 30). http://www.cnbc.com/2015/10/30/misbehaving-banks-have-now-paid-204b-in-fines.html (accessed October 25, 2016).

Dealbook. 2015. "Reports from the Libor Investigations." *The New York Times,* April 23.
Duff, Antony. 2010. "Towards a Theory of the Criminal Law?" *Aristotelian Society Supplementary Volume* 84, 1–28.
Eavis, Peter. 2015. "Judge's Ruling Against 2 Banks Finds Misconduct in '08 Crash." *The New York Times,* May 11.
Editorial. 2015a. "Banks as Felons, or Criminality Lite." *The New York Times,* May 22.
Editorial. 2015b. "Don't Change the Legal Rule on Intent." *The New York Times,* December 5.
Eisinger, Jesse. 2014a. "Why Only One Top Banker Went to Jail for the Financial Crisis." *The New York Times,* April 30.
Eisinger, Jesse. 2014b. "Wall Street Prosecutors Bare Their Teeth, but Still Lack Bite." *The New York Times,* August 27.
Eisinger, Jesse. 2014c. "In Turnabout, Former Regulators Assail Wall St. Watchdogs." *The New York Times,* October.
Eisinger, Jesse. 2016. "Why the S.E.C. Didn't Hit Goldman Sachs Harder." *The New Yorker,* April 21.
Ewing, Jack. 2015. "Deutsche Bank's New Profit More than Tripled in Second Quarter." *The New York Times,* July 30.
Federal Housing Finance Agency v. Nomura Holding, 2015 WL 2183875 (S.D.N.Y.).
Financial Crisis Inquiry Commission. 2011. *The Financial Crisis Inquiry Report.* New York: Public Affairs.
Finkle, Victoria. 2016. "The Big Fish Seen Escaping an Agency Pursuing Bank Fraud." *The New York Times,* July 27.
Fisch, Jill E. 2009. "Cause for Concern: Causation and Federal Securities Fraud." *Iowa Law Review* 94, 811–72.
Fisse, Brent, and John Braithewaite. 1994. *Corporations, Crime, and Accountability.* Cambridge: Cambridge University Press.
Garrett, Brandon L. 2014. *Too Big to Jail: How Prosecutors Compromise with Corporations.* Cambridge, MA: Harvard University Press.
Goldstein, Matthew. 2016. "Goldman to Pay Up to $5 Billion to Settle Claims of Faulty Mortgages." *The New York Times,* January 14.
Hamdani, Assaf. 2007. "Mens Rea and the Cost of Ignorance." *Virginia Law Review* 93, 415–58.
Hart, H. L. A. 1994. *The Concept of Law,* 2nd edn. Oxford: Oxford University Press.
Havian, Eric R. 2015. "How to Punish Corporate Fraudsters." *The New York Times,* October 22.
Heath, David. 2011. "Too Big to Jail? Executives Unscathed as Regulators Let Banks Report Criminal Fraud." *Huffington Post Investigative Fund,* May 25.
Henning, Peter J. 2015a. "Financial Crisis Cases Sputter to an End." *The New York Times,* April 20.
Henning, Peter J. 2015b. "Guilty Pleas and Heavy Fines Seem to Be a Cost of Business for Wall St." *The New York Times,* May 20.
Henning, Peter J. 2015c. "The Prospects for Pursuing Corporate Executives." *The New York Times,* September 14.
Hill, Claire A., and Richard W. Painter. 2015. *Better Bankers, Better Banks: Promoting Good Business through Contractual Commitment.* Chicago: University of Chicago Press.

Hiltzik, Michael. 2016. "The Legal Technicality that Let BofA Skate on an Alleged Billion-Dollar Fraud," *Los Angeles Times,* May 24.

Holder Eric J. 1999. "Federal Prosecution of Corporations." US Department of Justice (June 16). http://www.justice.gov/sites/default/files/criminal-fraud/legacy/2010/04/11/charging-corps.pdf (accessed October 25, 2016).

Huigens, Kyron. 1998. "Virtue and Criminal Negligence." *Buffalo Criminal Law Review* 1, 431–58.

Husak, Douglas. 2008. *Overcriminalization: The Limits of the Criminal Law.* Oxford: Oxford University Press.

Husak, Douglas. 2009. "The Costs to Criminal Theory of Supposing that Intentions Are Irrelevant to Permissibility." *Criminal Law and Philosophy* 3, 51–70.

Husak, Douglas. 2010. "Willful Ignorance, Knowledge, and the 'Equal Culpability' Thesis: A Study of the Deeper Significance of the Principle of Legality." In *The Philosophy of Criminal Law: Selected Essays.* Oxford: Oxford University Press, 200–32.

In the Matter of Deutsch Bank. 2015. Consent Order under New York Banking Law §§ 44 and 44-a. New York State Department of Financial Services (April 23). https://www.documentcloud.org/documents/2062812-deutsche-bank-settlement-with-new-york-regulator.html (accessed October 25, 2016).

Kashkari, Neel. 2016. "Lessons from the Crisis: Ending Too Big to Fail." Federal Reserve Bank of Minneapolis, February 16. https://www.minneapolisfed.org/news-and-events/presidents-speeches/lessons-from-the-crisis-ending-too-big-to-fail (accessed October 25, 2016).

Koren, James Rufus. 2016. "Wells Fargo to Pay $1.2 Billion over Bad Government-Backed Mortgages." *Los Angeles Times,* February 3.

Kramer, Matthew H. 2005. "Moral Rights and the Limits of the Ought-Implies-Can Principle: Why Impeccable Precautions Are No Excuse." *Inquiry* 48, 307–55.

Lewis, Michael. 2010. *The Big Short: Inside the Doomsday Machine.* New York: Allen Lane.

Lynch, Kevin. 2015. "Willful Ignorance and Self-Deception." *Philosophical Studies* 173, 505–23.

McFadden, Robert. 2014. "Charles Keating, 90, Key Figure in '80s Savings and Loan Crisis, Dies." *The New York Times,* April 2.

McNulty, James E., and Aigbe Akhigbe. 2015. "Corporate Culture, Financial Stability, and Bank Litigation." October. 333 https://www.newyorkfed.org/medialibrary/media/research/conference/2015/econ_culture/McNulty_CorporateCultureandFinancialStability.pdf (accessed October 25, 2016).

Miller, Seumas. 2014. "The Global Financial Crisis and Collective Moral Responsibility." SHARES Research Paper 52. Amsterdam Center for International Law, University of Amsterdam. http://www.sharesproject.nl/wp-content/uploads/2014/07/SHARES-RP-52-final.pdf (accessed October 25, 2016).

Morgenson, Gretchen. 2014a. "A Loan Fraud War That's Short on Combat." *The New York Times,* March 15.

Morgenson, Gretchen. 2014b. "Shareholders Disarmed by a Delaware Court." *The New York Times,* October 25.

Morgenson, Gretchen. 2015a. "Kicking Dodd-Frank in the Teeth." *The New York Times,* January 10.

Morgenson, Gretchen. 2015b. "S.E.C. Wants the Sinners to Own Up." *The New York Times*, March 14.

Morgenson, Gretchen. 2015c. "Ways to Put the Boss's Skin in the Game." *The New York Times*, March 21.

Morgenson, Gretchen. 2015d. "A Tiny Bank's Surreal Trip through a Fraud Prosecution." *The New York Times*, July 17.

Morgenson, Gretchen. 2015e. "An S.E.C. Settlement with Citigroup that Fails to Name Names." *The New York Times*, August 28.

Morgenson, Gretchen. 2016a. "Fining Bankers, Not Shareholders, for Banks' Misconduct." *The New York Times*, February 6.

Morgenson, Gretchen. 2016b. "Battered Bank Stocks Reflect Not Just Jitters, but Mistrust." *The New York Times*, February 12.

Morgenson, Gretchen. 2016c. "Countrywide Mortgage Devastation Lingers as Ex-Chief Moves On." *The New York Times*, June 24.

Morgenson, Gretchen. 2016d. "A Bank Too Big to Jail." *The New York Times*, July 15.

Morgenson, Gretchen, and Louise Story. 2011. "In Financial Crisis, No Prosecutions of Top Figures." *The New York Times*, April 14.

Moyer, Liz. 2015. "Tax Deductions Blunt Impact of Large Corporate Settlements, Report Says." *The New York Times*, December 3.

Moyer, Liz. 2016. "Finra Begins a Review of Brokerage Firm Culture." *The New York Times*, February 23.

The New York Times. 2011. "Two Financial Crisis Compared: The Savings and Loan Debacle and the Mortgage Mess." *The New York Times*, April 13.

Office of the Inspector General, Audit Division US Department of Justice. 2014. "Audit of the Department of Justice's Efforts to Address Mortgage Fraud." Audit Report 14–12 (March). https://oig.justice.gov/reports/2014/a1412.pdf (accessed October 25, 2016).

Petrin, Martin. 2012. "Circumscribing the 'Prosecutor's Ticket to Tag the Elite'—A Critique of the Responsible Corporate Officer Doctrine." *Temple Law Review* 84, 283–324.

Pettit, Philip. 2007. "Responsibility Incorporated." *Ethics* 117, 171–201.

Popper, Nathaniel. 2016a. "Morgan Stanley to Pay $3.2 Billion Over Flawed Mortgage Bonds." *The New York Times*, February 11.

Popper, Nathaniel. 2016b. "In Settlement's Fine Print, Goldman May Save $1 Billion." *The New York Times*, April 11.

Protess, Ben. 2014. "Justice Department Sued Over $13 Billion JP Morgan Pact." *The New York Times*, February 10.

Protess, Ben. 2015a. "S.&P.'s $1.37 Billion Reckoning over Crisis-Era Misdeeds." *The New York Times*, February 3.

Protess, Ben. 2015b. "Commerzbank of Germany to Pay $1.5 Billion in U.S. Case." *The New York Times*, March 12.

Protess, Ben, and Matt Apuzzo. 2015. "Justice Dept. Vow to Go after Bankers May Prove a Promise Hard to Keep." *The New York Times*, September 10.

Protess, Ben, and Michael Corkery. 2015. "5 Big Banks Expected to Plead Guilty to Felony Charges but Punishments May Be Tempered." *The New York Times*, May 13.

Protess, Ben, and Peter Eavis. 2015. "Ex-Freddie Mac Leaders Reach Deal with S.E.C." *The New York Times*, April 14.

Protess, Ben, and Jack Ewing. 2015. "Deutsche Bank to Pay $2.5 Billion Fine to Settle Rate-Rigging Case." *The New York Times*, April 23.

Rakoff, Jed S. 2014. "The Financial Crisis: Why Have No High Level Executives Been Prosecuted?" *The New York Review of Books*, January 9.

Rakoff, Jed S. 2015. "The Cure for Corporate Wrongdoing: Class Actions vs. Individual Prosecutions." *The New York Review of Books*, November 19.

Reckard, E. Scott. 2011. "U.S. Drops Criminal Probe of Former Countrywide Chief Angelo Mozilo." *Los Angeles Times*, February 18.

Reiff, Mark R. 2005. *Punishment, Compensation, and Law: A Theory of Enforceability.* Cambridge: Cambridge University Press.

Reiff, Mark R. 2008. "Terrorism, Retribution, and Collective Responsibility." *Social Theory and Practice* 34, 209–42.

Reiff, Mark R. 2013. *Exploitation and Economic Justice in the Liberal Capitalist State.* Oxford: Oxford University Press.

Reiff, Mark R. 2014. "Incommensurability and Moral Value." *Politics, Philosophy, and Economics* 13, 237–68.

Reiff, Mark R. 2015. "No Such Thing as Accident: Rethinking the Relation between Causal and Moral Responsibility." *Canadian Journal of Law and Jurisprudence* 28, 371–97.

Reuters. 2014. "Justice Department Sets Record in Penalties for Fraud." *The New York Times*, November 19.

Sanford, Terry. 1990. Statement of Senator Sanford. *Congressional Record* 136, July 11: S9488.

Sarbanes-Oxley Act of 2002, section 302, 15 U.S.C. § 7241(a).

Scheindlin, Judge Shira A. 2015. "Random Thoughts of a Federal District Judge." *Loyola University Chicago Law Journal* 46 (Spring), 453–8.

Schuck, Christina M. 2010. "A New Use for the Responsible Corporate Officer Doctrine: Prosecuting Industry Insiders for Mortgage Fraud." *Lewis & Clark Law Review* 14, 371–95.

Securities Act of 1933, Section 15, 15 U.S.C. § 77*o*(a) and (b).

Sepinwall, Amy J. 2014. "Responsible Shares and Shared Responsibility: In Defense of Responsible Corporate Officer Liability." *Columbia Business Law Review* 2014, 371–419.

Sepinwall, Amy J. 2015. "Crossing the Fault Line in Corporate Criminal Law." *Journal of Corporation Law* 40, 439–82.

Silver-Greenberg, Jessica, and Peter Eavis. 2013. "Wall Street Predicts $50 Billion Bill to Settle U.S. Mortgage Suits." *The New York Times*, January 9.

Silver-Greenberg, Jessica, and Peter Eavis. 2014. "Morgan Stanley Reaches $1.25 Billion Mortgage Settlement." *The New York Times*, February 4.

Smith, Randall. 2015. "Two Former Traders Found Guilty in Libor Manipulation Case." *The New York Times*, November 5.

Sorkin, Andrew Ross. 2015. "Many on Wall Street Say It Remains Untamed." *The New York Times*, May 18.

Steinzor, Rena. 2015. *Why Not Jail? Industrial Catastrophes, Corporate Malfeasance, and Government Inaction.* Cambridge: Cambridge University Press.

Sterngold, James. 2014. "For Banks, 2014 Was a Year of Big Penalties." *The Wall Street Journal*, December 30.

Stewart, James B. 2015a. "In Corporate Crimes, Individual Accountability Is Elusive." *The New York Times,* February 19.

Stewart, James B. 2015b. "Convictions Prove Elusive in 'London Whale' Trading Case." *The New York Times,* July.

Taibbi, Matt. 2012. "Goldman Non-Prosecution: AG Eric Holder Has No Balls." *Rolling Stone,* August 15.

Taub, Jennifer. 2015. "Going Soft on White-Collar Crime." *The New York Times,* November 20.

Tenbrunsel, Ann, and Jordan Thomas. 2015. "The Street, the Bull and the Crisis: A Survey of the US & UK Financial Services Industry." University of Notre Dame and Labaton Sucharow LLP (May). http://www.labaton.com/en/about/press/Historic-Survey-of-Financial-Services-Professionals-Reveals-Widespread-Disregard-for-Ethics-Alarming-Use-of-Secrecy-Policies-to-Silence-Employees.cfm (accessed October 25, 2016).

Thomas, W. Robert. 2012. "On Strict Liability Crimes: Preserving a Moral Framework for Criminal Intent in an Intent-Free Moral World." *Michigan Law Review* 110, 647–76.

Tillman, Robert H., and Henry N. Pontell. 2016. "Corporate Fraud Demands Criminal Time." *The New York Times,* June 29.

Tversky, Amos, and Daniel Kahneman. 1991. "Loss Aversion in Riskless Choice." *The Quarterly Journal of Economics* 106, 1039–61.

Wang, Marian. 2011. "Why No Financial Crisis Prosecutions? Ex-Justice Official Says It's Just Too Hard." *ProPublica,* December 6. http://www.propublica.org/article/why-no-financial-crisis-prosecutions-official-says-its-just-too-hard (accessed October 25, 2016).

Waytz, Adam. 2015. "How Citibank's Culture Allowed Corruption to Thrive." *Kellogg Insight.* Kellogg School of Management, January 5. http://insight.kellogg.northwestern.edu/article/how-citibanks-culture-allowed-corruption-to-thrive (accessed October 25, 2016).

Weisman, Jonathan, and Eric Lipton. 2015. "In New Congress, Wall St. Pushes to Undermine Dodd-Frank Reform." *The New York Times,* January 13.

Yates, Sally Quilliam, Deputy Attorney General. 2015. "Memorandum on Individual Accountability for Corporate Wrongdoing." U.S. Department of Justice (September 9). http://www.justice.gov/dag/file/769036/download (accessed October 25, 2016).

7

A culture beyond repair? The nexus between ethics and sanctions in finance

Jay Cullen

7.1 INTRODUCTION

The Great Financial Crisis (GFC) of 2008 revealed massive deficiencies in modern financial risk management paradigms. It has shaken faith in the efficiency of markets and the power of market discipline. The losses from the crisis, the ongoing occurrences of serious professional misconduct, and the compliance failures at financial institutions, manifested in the subsequent billions of dollars paid in fines and compensatory damages since have resulted in the financial industry losing the trust of large swathes of the public.[1]

The severity and perceived drivers of these episodes have ensured that considerable focus has been placed on both bank business models and the internal cultures of large financial institutions.[2] A substantial proportion of the analysis to emerge posits that a gradual ethical erosion has taken hold in financial markets and, as might be expected, discussions concerning "culture" and "ethics" have dominated large parts of the vast majority of recent enquiries into the causes of these crises. Indicatively, the US Financial Crisis Inquiry Commission concluded that prior to the GFC there had been "a systemic breakdown in accountability and ethics" in banking (US Financial Crisis Inquiry Commission 2011, 8). Similarly, the UK Parliamentary

[1] For illustration, a 2012 US poll found that 42 percent of people responded either "somewhat" or "a lot" to the statement that Wall Street "harms the country"; furthermore, 68 percent disagreed with the statement: "In general, people on Wall Street are as honest and moral as other people." See Dudley (2014).

[2] Global banks have been accused of all manner of illegal activities over the last few years, including money laundering for drugs cartels, breaking economic sanctions, rigging currency and interest rate markets, and facilitating the funding of terrorism.

Commission on Banking Standards (PCBS), established to investigate banking practices over the previous decade, found that "[b]ankers [have] prioritised short term personal gain over their customers and shareholders and recklessly failed to prevent wrongdoing... [there was] a failure of professionalism and ethics" (UK PCBS 2013, 48). Ethicist Michael Sandel (2010, 4) has gone so far as to argue that financial markets have "become detached from fundamental values."[3] Key questions for policy-makers, regulators, and citizens are what ought those values to be and how might they be enforced?

Thanks to the aforementioned cultural and ethical failures across global financial markets, the view that an ethical discourse in shaping new laws and regulations is required has gained considerable traction (Blair 2016). Yet, in spite of widespread reforms to corporate governance and compensation systems at financial institutions, criticisms abound that many of the global initiatives since 2008 have largely failed to address the ethical deficit in finance culture. The question of *how* values ought to be enforced, other than through appeals to the financial community itself, remains largely unanswered. Instead, in common with other crisis response episodes, we have barely progressed from the "stopgap" phase of recapitalization of the financial system, which has simply imbedded a sense that reputational preservation is paramount, and simultaneously increased moral hazard.[4] Moreover, the task of reforming micro-structures governing conduct has been left largely to financial markets themselves, even in an era where financial fragility, in the context of the size and structure of institutions which may cause systemic collapse, is arguably on the rise.[5]

A key theme to emerge from the debates concerning banking activities is the role of regulatory sanctions in deterring and punishing individuals who misbehave in financial markets. Recently, Kay (2015, 275) has argued that "obligations of high standards of behaviour... should be enforced by criminal and civil penalties, directed primarily to individuals rather than to organisations. While the culture of organisations is of central importance, culture is the product of individual behaviour." I take up this mantle in this chapter,

[3] By one estimate, ten of the world's largest banks between them have paid over $300 billion in conduct-related fines and settlements since 2008. See London School of Economics (2014). Some $60 billion of that amount has been levied for "lying to clients either in reporting or in describing the quality of loan securitizations" (Kane 2016b).

[4] An exception to this has been the reforms made to compensation incentives, especially in the EU. I have written about this extensively elsewhere—see Cullen (2016) and Avgouleas and Cullen (2015).

[5] According to Vice-Chairman Thomas Hoenig (2016) of the Federal Deposit Insurance Corporation, in April 2016: "[Systemic financial] firms are generally larger, more complicated, and more interconnected than they were [in 2008]. They control assets equivalent to approximately 60 percent of GDP... The average notional value of derivatives for the three largest derivative dealers among these GSIBs [global systemically important banks] was approximately $50 trillion at year-end 2015, about a 30 percent increase over their level at the start of the crisis."

arguing that the measures taken thus far in many jurisdictions remain largely insufficient and often ignore the crucial role of sanctions in deterring both unethical conduct and excessive risk-taking, as well as providing framing for corporate behavior through the setting of parameters for acceptable conduct.

I frame this discussion around the concept of *accountability*. In ethics and governance, accountability is often used synonymously with "answerability," "blameworthiness," "liability," and the "expectation of account-giving" (Dykstra 1939). In this chapter, I use accountability in its simplest sense, which "entails a relationship in which people are required to explain and *take responsibility* for their actions" (Sinclair 1995, 220–1).[6] As shall be explained, combating corporate misconduct is made more effective by demanding accountability from individuals who engage in wrongdoing. This is important for several reasons: "it deters future illegal activity, it incentivizes changes in corporate behavior, it ensures that the proper parties are held responsible for their actions, and it promotes the public's confidence in [the] justice system" (Yates 2015, 1). As I shall explain, ethical norms of behavior are mostly too amorphous to be precisely defined in the context of banking; the very nature of financial markets—in particular the manner through which financial commitments are organized via complex and innovative products and long chains of intermediation—make "ethical conduct" a highly slippery concept to define. And yet, without imposing accountability for individual actions, the forms of conduct witnessed across financial markets in recent years are likely to continue. Moreover, in light of the widespread failures of industry-led initiatives to improve behavior in banking, accountability must necessarily flow from the imposition of credible regulatory constraints on *individual* conduct. Sanctions for non-compliance with established rules and norms are therefore a vital component of ensuring this accountability. They are required in order to discourage behavior that can be described as unjust not only because it allows some individuals to benefit at the cost of others or a society as a whole, but also because it arguably contributes to distributive injustice through its tendency to widen inequality.

In advocating this, I recognize the practical difficulties that may be faced by authorities in ascribing liability for such conduct, especially under criminal law principles (not least the high burden of proof required in criminal law trials). To give legal traction to these positions and to ensure they address the most damaging forms of abusive conduct in financial markets, in common with Kane (2016a), I argue that charges of unethical (and therefore proscribed) conduct ought to encompass cases in which bankers take *excessive* risk from a societal perspective, or omit to prevent their divisions from so doing, as well as those instances in which bankers engage in fraudulent or overtly exploitative

[6] This is often expanded to include requiring the relevant actor to "the giving and demanding of reasons for conduct" (Roberts and Scapens 1985, 447).

behavior. Crucially, as I shall explain, the *form* of sanction (criminal[7] or civil), provided it is of a sufficiently serious nature, is less important in improving accountability, than *to whom it is directed* (whether individual or corporation).

Against this backdrop of the normative case for greater accountability, this chapter introduces the new UK regulatory regime, which applies to all members of senior management at financial institutions, and suggests that it—whilst imperfect—provides an easily replicable model for other global financial centers to follow. The prescriptive nature of the rules it promulgates regarding conduct, the heavy sanctions it imposes in cases of non-compliance with behavioral norms, and, importantly, its requirement that managers undertake to account for the conduct which occurs in key business areas for which they are responsible (a so-called "Statement of Responsibilities") hold considerable promise for greater personal accountability. They provide credible signals that authorities regard excessive risk-taking in the same way they regard other forms of market abuse. Widespread implementation of these mechanisms would arguably assist financial institutions—in an admittedly ultra-competitive and fast-paced financial environment—to navigate effectively between the exploitation of the benefits of free market capitalism and the need to do the right thing.

In Section 7.2 I outline the limits of self-regulation in financial markets, which is followed by a discussion of the problem of tackling the negative externalities that excessive risk-taking or other forms of misconduct in financial markets can impose on society. I argue that the lack of effectiveness of an approach based exclusively on moral insight means that the imposition of individual liability is justified, whether on the basis of civil or criminal charges. I describe the UK's new "Senior Managers' Regime" as a way forward in solving the problem of accountability.

7.2 THE LIMITS OF SELF-REGULATION IN FINANCIAL MARKETS

It may be argued that the prevailing economic orthodoxy of the last century has, at its core, the belief that self-interest is the crucial virtue in the operation of efficient markets. The Friedmanite[8] view of human behavior notably spawned the shareholder value model; a model which makes equity returns

[7] On *criminal* liability in the context of the financial system see also Chapter 6 (Reiff, in this volume).

[8] Although this approach to corporate governance predated Milton Friedman, he is arguably the economist most closely associated with its message and ideals, famously arguing that "the social responsibility of business is to increase its profits" (Friedman 1970).

on investment the operative principle for corporate managerial focus. This reductionist canon eschews everything but metrics relating to market (equity) prices in its assessment of performance, requiring corporations to be run with a view toward enhancing corporate profit and shareholder returns. The economics discipline has provided theoretical sustenance to this reductionism: the assumptions of all orthodox financial models hold that individuals are simplistic hyper-rational profit-seekers who single-mindedly maximize utility in the same way that firms maximize profit. In this synthesis there is little room for ethical considerations in financial decision-making at the individual or aggregated levels, beyond the potential effects on the eventual (economic) payoff from the course of behavior in question.[9] Indeed, arguably the most influential theory of the firm—agency costs theory—assumes that managers are unethical by nature and need to be controlled to prevent them from expropriating wealth that properly belongs to their principals (Jensen and Meckling 1976).

And yet, it is widely recognized that banking remains a quasi-public activity; financial firms exist, in part, to benefit the public, not simply their shareholders, employees, and corporate clients (Dudley 2014). Financial institutions need a *social license* to operate, and they earn this through a track record of exemplary conduct and a reputation for integrity and prudence, as well as a demonstration that their duties to customers and counterparties are based on not simply a contractual obligation, but an ethical one as well. The maintenance of a banking license in most major jurisdictions, for instance, is contingent on financial institutions abiding by conduct rules and refraining from the violation of laws designed to tackle illegal or unethical financial activity. In return, banks are provided with generous public subsidies, emergency support mechanisms and special powers to issue liabilities at will (bank deposits).

In the presence of these benefits, any upside benefits accrue to top executives and shareholders by virtue of the positive effect on stock prices that high risk-taking has on bank value, whereas downside costs are borne by taxpayers and governments. In this context, the singular focus on returns to stockholders by industry participants and, to an extent, regulators, appears misplaced. Whilst many analyses posit that market discipline may act as a brake on behaviors in financial markets which do not generate profit, as strong-form utility-maximizing market participants respond best to financial (price) incentives, it is not clear that this will lead to improved outcomes from a societal perspective. Despite constantly uprated standards of governance demanded across financial markets over the past twenty years, a considerable

[9] The infamous admission of Alan Greenspan following the GFC concerning his "flawed view" of the way the financial markets operate is testament to the limits of this view. See Andrews (2008).

body of research suggests that corporate governance reform itself—in terms of altering structures or introducing new processes—is limited in preventing excessive risk-taking in the financial markets (Avgouleas and Cullen 2014). In fact, there is scant evidence that corporate governance has weakened over the last thirty years; most indicators instead show that governance has considerably strengthened over this period (Holmstrom and Kaplan 2001, Hermalin 2005).[10] And yet, the incidence of severe banking crises is increasing, and the footprints of the largest financial institutions continue to expand.

7.3 CONDUCT REGULATION AND THE LIMITS OF ETHICS

Organizational theory emphasizes that an organizational culture must fit with the organization's strategy and environment. The focus on the organizational environment here is vital, as for a good organizational culture to emerge key values such as trust and integrity must be in place and practiced. O'Toole and Bennis (2009) observe that "[e]thical problems in organizations originate not with 'a few bad apples' but with the 'barrel makers.'" If we examine the "barrel makers" cultures, according to Schein (2010) we will discern three hierarchical layers—artifacts (which are apparent and discussable), espoused values and beliefs, and, at root, the underlying basic assumptions that its members share: every set of behaviors incorporates a view about the way the world works. When aggregated, these three layers represent the collective rules of organization, which both direct and guide internal relationships and govern interactions with external parties. Over time, basic assumptions (the "third layer") in particular inform habitual behavior—"a set of routines, procedures and rules which define us" (Salz 2013)—which eventually becomes institutionalized, and plays a key role in defining organizational *identity*. This identity, according to Salz (ibid., 182), is something "everyone defends." Ethicality and its application to the financial industries is a microlevel (the individual

[10] As Roe (2014) notes, neither the usual corporate governance assumptions nor discipline from the market for corporate control apply to financial firms because of the artificially low funding costs large banks enjoy. Whilst large financial institutions may be more efficient if split into smaller, more manageable, units, the loss of the too-big-to-fail subsidy embedded in firm funding costs would negatively impact the newer, smaller units' level of performance, and without the normal pressure from the market to reform internal processes and ensure maximal standards of governance, the incentives generated to assume excess risks place bank executives and shareholders in conflict with those who bear the costs of deposit insurance and the too-big-to-fail-subsidy—namely taxpayers. On this basis, one option for regulation would be to withdraw state-backed support for all financial market activities, although there is an acknowledged trade-off between the loss of implicit and explicit guarantees and overall economic performance.

executive(s)) as well as a macrolevel (regulator or policy-maker) issue, and research demonstrates the cardinal importance of social structures in developing virtues and traits of character. Ethics is not something remote to human behavior; it is everyday stuff (see e.g. Singer 2003, 1).

Traditional ethics teaches that popular motives, underscored by virtue, are driven by regard for the *common* good. One purpose of regulation is to ensure the ethical character of markets, by equally orienting them toward this purpose. But the difficulty with many modern forms of regulation in this context is that they emphasize the means, rather than the ends, which then results in an "undue emphasis on the setting up of structures and the design of processes" instead of governing the firm well within the wider context of society (Sison 2008, 222). This may allow individuals to escape liability for reckless actions, so long as they can demonstrate that proper processes were followed and appropriate governance structures had been established across the relevant firm(s).

Support for this trend is certainly apparent if one examines the general regulatory response to the Great Financial Crisis, which has been characterized by the promulgation of a greater number of internally constructed—largely voluntary—codes of conduct as well as the introduction of a plethora of new "soft" regulation of governance structures and processes. The continued dominance of the principal-agent axiom elevates internal hierarchical oversight and control to prevent self-regarding activities—with the regulator or "club rules" at the top, shareholders, the board, executives, and, lastly, managers and employees at the bottom.[11] These "club rules" cross Schein's taxonomic boundaries: they represent both "shared assumptions and beliefs" and "values and norms," and are often manifested in the membership rules of relevant professional organizations or in codes of conduct and behavioral guides. Events in financial markets over recent years naturally cast doubt as to the fitness for purpose of this internalized hierarchical oversight and its capability in checking unethical conduct. This is why there has been renewed interest in other ways of regulating behavior, including trust and ethics.

The financial markets are in many ways schizophrenic on the importance of these concepts. Trust, for example, is widely regarded as a vital feature of any market economy, including the financial system, and has been described as the "link" between organizational theory and ethics (Hosmer 1995). Indeed, the very word "credit" is derived from the Italian word for trust ("credito"). In spite of the raw belief that rugged individualism always delivers optimal

[11] Perhaps most instructive was the Walker Review of Corporate Governance at UK Banks (Walker 2009), which concluded that the existing UK Code of Corporate Governance "remain [ed] fit for purpose"—overlooking, in an instant, the fact that the code was proven wholly ineffective when the financial world crashed. For discussions of the (many) limits to corporate governance reform to counteract risk-taking at banks, see Avgouleas and Cullen (2014).

resource allocation and prosperity, even in a market economy trust is the grease that allows society to function. The reason that certain communities emerged as global merchants and financiers is that the members of the community trusted each other. During the financial crisis, our highly complex financial markets broke down when banks stopped trusting each other, and the financial system froze.

On the other hand, as markets become more globalized and financial deepening results in fragmentation and specification, notions of trust, honor, and virtue become much less salient. In the world of transactional banking, for example, where a good deal of contracts remain faceless, one-time encounters with unknown counterparties, and increasingly are automated, trust and goodwill may become largely irrelevant. As these qualities become less valued assets in financial market transactions, the importance of ethical conduct arguably degrades; in its absence, actors retreat to rules and legal provisions which, whilst facilitative of increasing volumes of trade and efficiency, are eminently more malleable.[12] Much discussion about conduct then becomes framed in terms of "what *can* I do?" or "what will regulators do to stop me?", which are not questions of normative ethics but of pragmatism.

Against this backdrop it is perhaps unsurprising that many high-profile reviews have concluded that redefining duties and obligations of bankers in their working environment(s) is a fruitless endeavor. Indeed, whilst there have been concerted calls for the reinvention of professional ethics at financial institutions, considerable doubt has been expressed as to whether there is any such thing as a "banker" and whether there exists a single set of employees capable of being unified by professional values or beliefs. The core function(s) of senior bankers differ widely in substance, resulting in a wide degree of functional separation between different areas of banking activity (Gapper 2014). On this basis, banking is unique precisely because it cannot be defined narrowly; if it cannot be defined narrowly, core generalized behavioral qualities are also incapable of precise definition and/or are inapplicable. Seemingly confirming this view, the UK PCBS opined that:

> [I]t is questionable whether the business of banking possesses sufficient characteristics of a profession to lend itself to direct control through a professional body. "Banking" involves a wide range of activities and lacks the large common core of learning which is a feature of most professions. *It is a long way from being an industry where professional duties to customers, and to the integrity of the profession as a whole, trump an individual's own behavioural incentives*... If a unified professional body for banking... is to emerge, the onus should lie on the industry itself to maintain the impetus for its development. (UK PCBS 2013, 597, 599)

[12] Indeed, some have characterized the financial crisis as a triumph of clever lawyering. For a discussion see Schwarcz (2010).

There is compelling evidence that senior bankers and traders see themselves as very different from other employees in the bank, such as retail bankers, back office staff, accountants, and compliance officers (Ho 2009). The trading divisions of banks have traditionally been the domain of high-powered incentives as well as the main source of bank profits. Indeed, bankers working in these divisions regard themselves as an "elite," and often disparage those lower down the corporate food chain. Bankers in senior positions tend to be thrust into close-knit, intense and social circles (Mandis 2013), which, when coupled with decline in the relationship banking model, results in an absence of socialization amongst traders (Wexler 2010). This is evident in contemporary inquiries into banking culture, which recount how traders at large, sophisticated banks "had a singular view of their role and operated outwith what others saw as the prevailing organizational culture" (Wheeler 2016, 86).

As a normative question, moreover, many rightly claim that culture cannot be "regulated for" and there remain significant practical hurdles to be overcome in reshaping something so amorphous as ethical conduct across a constellation of financial firms (Campbell and Loughrey 2013). This is reinforced in the case of large organizations, where the duties that managers owe to others are extensive and often conflict. In the event of damage to one or more parties, managers may always revert to the default defense that the inevitable trade-off between different parties' interests was impossible to negotiate, even honestly. The consequences of this dilemma are that managers retreat to rules they construct to guide their working behavior. Yet, the relative morality of these rules derives not from principles or internally held convictions, but rather from "ongoing albeit changing relationships with some person, some coterie, some social network, some clique that matters to a person [whilst] independent morally evaluative judgments get subordinated to the social intricacies of the bureaucratic workplace" (Jackall 1988, 101, 105, cf. Kane 1994, 2–3). In these circumstances, employee behaviors are shaped largely by what is perceived to be rewarded. If rewards become contingent only on financial outcomes, employees will come to believe that these outcomes are what their organization values. One consequence which flows from this is that in the absence of any prescriptive guidelines on proper and ethical behavior or credible sanctions for non-compliance, culture will shape itself, with the danger that the behaviors produced will not be those desired.

Empirically, it is apparent that the dominant norms of pre-crisis banking continue to inform behavior and in fact may be becoming *more* prevalent. Consider the following survey results of 1,200 finance professionals concerning workplace ethics. They conclude that, despite the constant appeals to the banking industry to tackle the ethical problems it faces, "a culture of integrity has failed to take hold. Numerous individuals continue to believe that engaging in illegal or unethical activity is part and parcel of succeeding in this highly competitive field" (Labaton Sucharow 2015, 3). Specific conclusions include, *inter alia*:

1. 47 percent of respondents find it likely that their competitors have engaged in unethical or illegal activity in order to gain an edge in the market...a spike from the 39 percent who reported as such when surveyed in 2013. This figure jumps to 51 percent for individuals earning more than $500,000 or more per year.
2. More than one-third (34 percent) of those earning $500,000 or more annually have witnessed or have first-hand knowledge of wrongdoing in the workplace.
3. 23 percent of respondents believe it is likely that fellow employees have engaged in illegal or unethical activity in order to gain an edge, nearly double the 12 percent that reported as such in 2012.
4. 25 percent would likely use non-public information to make a guaranteed $10 million if there was no chance of getting arrested for insider trading. Employees with less than 10 years' experience are more than twice as likely as those with over 20 years' experience, reporting 32 percent and 14 percent respectively.
5. In the UK 32 percent of individuals said they would likely engage in insider trading to earn $10 million if there was no chance of getting arrested, compared to 24 percent of respondents from the US.
6. Nearly one in five respondents feel financial services professionals must at least sometimes engage in illegal or unethical activity to be successful.
7. 27 percent of those surveyed disagree that the financial services industry puts the best interests of clients first. This figure rises to 38 percent for those earning $500,000 or more per year.
8. Nearly one-third of respondents (32 percent) believe compensation structures or bonus plans in place at their company could incentivize employees to compromise ethics or violate the law.
9. 33 percent of financial service professionals feel the industry has not changed for the better since the Great Financial Crisis.

7.4 TACKLING NEGATIVE EXTERNALITIES FROM EXCESSIVE RISK-TAKING

If we accept for the moment that directly regulating for culture or ethics is not a worthwhile endeavor, but equally that the relative efficacy of the status quo is also inevident, we must consider whether other mechanisms exist which may be used to remedy these defects. Under a Coasean (Coase 1960) analysis, if one assumes that negative externalities imposed by financial institutions are inadequately dealt with by current regulation and, moreover, the spillover effects of financial firm distress caused by bankers' activities are outsized in comparison to the private benefits enjoyed by insiders, there are three broad baskets of regulatory options available: (1) taxation; (2) property right assignment; and (3) regulation. Many, including the IMF and FSB, have advocated for the first of these options; namely, the imposition of financial institutions of a so-called "financial stability contribution," as a way of restricting bank size and mitigating the costs associated with bank failure. Indeed, many jurisdictions with large banking sectors levy such taxes as a matter of course.[13] Yet taxation in this context will not address individual conduct, beyond making it (more) expensive to engage in certain financial activities.

Scholars and policy-makers have also approached the issue from the second angle, and base their regulatory solutions upon the assignment of property rights. In the context of bank resolution, Connor and O'Kelly (2012) emphasize the public dimension of banking and the externality costs of bank recovery and resolution. Because banking authorities own the "right" to control and prevent public externalities associated with bank distress (through the authorities' willingness to guarantee a proportion of bank liabilities) and their assumption of the bailout costs, they should be allowed to override existing (creditor) bank liability contracts in certain circumstances, that is, in times of systemically dangerous crises. More relevant to this chapter is the proposition by Kane (2016a) for the explicit recognition of the implicit equity stake enjoyed by taxpayers in every large financial firm. Banks benefit from a coercive shareholder put on taxpayer funds (in the form of deposit guarantees and other insurance programs). Legally enshrining taxpayer property rights in financial institutions which benefit from public support (in the form of subsidies and insurance costs) and subjecting the management of those rights to exacting fiduciary and prudential standards could mitigate some of the inherent incentive conflicts. Importantly, Kane holds that it is unethical to take reckless tail-risks which have a propensity to call upon taxpayer-sponsored safety nets, and that abusers of the safety net must be subjected to personal (including criminal) sanction.

Other scholars have instead focused on solutions belonging to the third basket of options; namely, at the macro- and microlevels of regulation. The case for macro-regulatory changes to force internalization of the loss externalities from banking has been led by the likes of Admati et al. (2013) who argue forcefully for much higher capital requirements for banks in order to reduce the probability of damaging bank failures. Yet, like options favoring taxation of externalities, these mechanisms may not internalize all of the costs

[13] Sixteen European countries impose bank levies on financial institutions, although they differ in size and are applied on varying calibrations.

of excessive risk-taking and would not necessarily have an effect on molding *individual* behavior or discourage executives from following strategies which carry the risk of ruin.[14]

From the perspective of regulating individual conduct and incentives, there has been a variety of suggestions. Awrey, Blair, and Kershaw (2013) examine the role that law and markets may play through "process-oriented regulation" in engendering ethical cultures within financial institutions. They view public enforcement and reputational sanctions as crucial to these processes and recommend a more instrumentalist role for board-level ethics committees, changes to remuneration, and the consideration of corporate law reforms to reduce shareholder influence over corporate strategy at banks. Erhard and Jensen (2015) explore the wider applications and interpretations of integrity and ethics in corporate decision-making and produce a positive model of virtuous behavior. Armour and Gordon (2014) argue for a relaxation of the shareholder value norm at systemic firms, and for the introduction of "softer" officer and director liability rules as a complement to (and substitute for) the prescriptive rules that have emerged from the financial crisis. Schwarcz (2016) calls for the introduction of a "public governance duty" at financial firms not to engage in excessive risk-taking that could systemically harm the public. Interestingly, Schwarcz (2016, 6) suggests that any "[r]egulation implementing a public governance duty might even impose an obligation on managers involved in the risk assessment to inform government officials of their firm's noncompliance," a theme which resonates with the thrust of my later discussions. Analyses which emphasize the role of compensation reform—as well as its limits—in improving cultural conditions across financial markets include Cullen (2014, 2016) and Avgouleas and Cullen (2015), each of which analyses the limitations of compensation mechanisms in shaping behavior in financial markets. In the following section, I outline the significance of individual accountability and explain how regulatory sanctions directed toward individuals may complement the methods surveyed above to address externalities caused by excessively risky behavior.

7.5 THE ROLE OF SANCTIONS IN PREVENTING UNETHICAL CONDUCT

The ethical significance of law and regulation, is, as noted by Hall (1961, 119), "a phase of the larger problem of discovering the soundest values, i.e., the best

[14] Indeed, there is significant evidence to suggest that higher capital requirements, in the absence of the control of bankers' activities, would incentivize riskier investments, to compensate for the lower returns generated by identical yet less-leveraged investments. For a discussion see Chason (2013).

answers to social problems."[15] Under any legitimate economic or legal system individuals need to be held accountable for actions which breach the "no harm" principle, which in turn raises presumptively the traditional spheres of responsibility and blame, and the moral connotations of punishment (Hall 1961). The "harm" principle exists as a function of two maxims, namely: (1) first, that the individual is only accountable insofar as her actions affect the interests of others; and (2) that when actions are prejudicial to the interest of others (i.e. cause harm), the individual is held accountable, and subject either to social or legal punishment (Mill 1859).

Loughrey (2014) points out that accountability as a concept is elusive, in particular because the meaning may be affected by both the context it is used in and the relevant discipline's perception of its role and importance.[16] Accountability in the context contemplated here looks outward: it requires the relevant actor to give *an account* for his or her conduct and, where required, be subjected to sanctions for violation of legal rules and/or ethical norms. Importantly, as noted by Loughrey (2014, 735) "[w]hat is important is the possibility of consequences being visited upon the actor, rather than their actual imposition: it is the former that makes the difference between non-committal provision of information and being held to account." Sanctions applied at the individual level are a fundamental element of this process, and support for their use is increasingly found in regulatory policy announcements. The US Justice Department for example:

> [r]ecognizes the inherent value of bringing enforcement actions against individuals, as opposed to simply the companies that employ them. We believe that doing so is both important—and appropriate—for several reasons: First, it enhances accountability... [because] corporate misconduct must necessarily be committed by flesh-and-blood human beings... Second, it promotes fairness—because, when misconduct is the work of a known bad actor, or a handful of known bad actors, it's not right for punishment to be borne exclusively by the company, its employees, and its innocent shareholders. And finally, it has a powerful deterrent effect. (Holder 2014)

Accordingly, a central quality of the law is found in its capacity to achieve corrective justice, the principles of which are invoked where societal wealth patterns are disturbed through injury to one person caused by the actions of

[15] At the same page, Hall goes on to say: "In sum, the legal institution does not direct conduct into right channels merely by blocking action in wrong directions. To determine what are the right goals, with coercion and feasibility held in view, and the construction of the channels to reach them are legal tasks; and the concomitant influence of legal institutions on action is 'positive' in any jurisprudential sense."

[16] For example, in the context of public governance, accountability has two basic qualities: (i) answerability (the obligation of officials to explain their actions); and (ii) enforcement (the capacity of accounting agencies to impose sanctions on those who have violated their duties) (Schedler 1999).

another. Legal and regulatory sanctions are in most cases designed to operate at the residual level; that is, at the point where all other forms of private behavioral control have been exhausted and other applied sanctions (such as reputational) are deemed inadequate.[17] There is a considerable body of research that suggests that proper enforcement of sanctions contributes enormously to shifts in social norms, particularly where channels are available for the reporting of non-conforming behavior and those in positions to report are themselves compliant (Acemoglu and Jackson 2015). This suggests that the introduction of "hard" accountability mechanisms, such as a positive obligation to report non-conforming behavior, would help facilitate sustained changes in expectations and behavior. Commenting on regulatory paralysis relating to failures of accountability in the banking sector, the PCBS (2013, 8) observed:

> Too many bankers, especially at the most senior levels, have operated in an environment with insufficient personal responsibility. Top bankers dodged accountability for failings on their watch by claiming ignorance or hiding behind collective decision-making. They then faced little realistic prospect of financial penalties or more serious sanctions commensurate with the severity of the failures with which they were associated. Individual incentives have not been consistent with high collective standards, often the opposite.

It is easy to sympathize with this view: the abuse of the legal fiction of separate corporate personality has shielded those guilty of malfeasance from personal responsibility for banking practices which caused loss to others.[18] The effects of unethical risk-taking commonly observed at large financial institutions in the recent past were often too (legally) remote to justify regulatory attention; yet, their character was both harmful and, in some instances, reckless (Ferguson 2013).

The optimality of the use of law or moral and ethical mores—or a combination of both—to shape behavior rests on a calculus involving the following factors: the level of private benefits available from committing bad acts; the adequacy of internal and external moral sanctions to counter the said private

[17] For example, where contractual or tortious obligations are breached, parties may access the law to achieve redress in the form of damages or compensation. Or, where moral and ethical restraints are not sufficient to prevent objectively "bad" behavior, that behavior may be criminalized and the person responsible subject to punishment.

[18] Phil Angelides, chair of the US Financial Inquiry Commission, regards this as an "immaculate corruption": "I ask a simple question: how could the banks have engaged in such massive misconduct and wrongdoing without a single individual being involved? In a sense, it's the immaculate corruption... It defies common sense, and the people of America know this... Someone conducted this behaviour, someone approved this behaviour, and I think what is required is a bottom-to-top inquiry at each of these institutions as to who knew what, and who sanctioned this material representation. Frankly, the small fry, the mice have been prosecuted but not yet one lion" (McLannahan 2016).

benefits; the presence (or not) of amoral subgroups, and the dilutive effects of employment by a firm (in other words, the notion that a firm rather than an individual is held morally and legally accountable for actions committed in a corporate setting (Shavell 2002)). Legal and regulatory sanctions are normally to be preferred where the private expected gains from undesirable conduct are large, and the expected harms due to such conduct are also large. Where the private gains available are substantial, moral or ethical incentives may be unable to prevent it; whilst, if the potential damage done by such conduct is great, recourse to the law is justified. Of course, in applying this model to the events and conduct structure(s) of Western financial markets, it is difficult to argue against the case that these factors apply—in total or in part.

Even ignoring, for the time being, the moral and ethical advantages which may flow from the imposition of personal liability, several studies further demonstrate that the availability of sanctions available to punish *individuals* for legal transgressions leads to welfare efficiency gains. In relation to the optimal design of liability schemes—either at the corporate or individual level—as is intuitive, sufficiently high individual sanctions allow society to achieve the best outcome (Argenton and van Damme 2014). Polinsky and Shavell (2000) demonstrate that in the absence of absolute control by the firm of its employees (and hence the existence of imperfect incentives), individual liability will be required to deter violations of rules. The state has recourse to public sanctions, fines, and/or imprisonment which may exceed the highest sanctions that a firm itself can impose on its employees. Fabra and Motta (2013) show that in the presence of firm bankruptcy risk, large corporate fines might not induce optimal deterrence, requiring instead the use of individual sanctions. Therefore, the threat of public sanctions can induce employees to exercise greater and socially more appropriate levels of care than they otherwise would.

Interestingly, sanctions may be more effective in shaping behavior in financial markets than in other areas of society. The path-breaking work of van der Weele (2012) is instructive in this regard. His research investigates the optimal level of law and regulation, and focuses specifically on the most efficient use of sanctions in markets populated by agents who exhibit heterogeneous compliance levels. The agents in these experiments are termed "conditional cooperators" (those who will cooperate with prescribed laws if they witness a sufficient proportion of others complying) and "rational egoists" (who feel no shame in ignoring those same laws ("defecting")). In this analysis, levels of agents' compliance with the law will be reflected in the relative proportions of "conditional cooperators" and "rational egoists" spread across the relevant market. Where there is objective information available to a central authority as to the fraction of "rational egoists," low sanctions can be optimal because they signal that there are few defectors and thus "crowd in" trust and cooperation between agents. Accordingly where norms of cooperation exist between conditional cooperators, optimal sanctioning levels may be lower than those found in a "Hobbesian" setting where all agents are egoistic.[19] On the other hand, where there is a high proportion of egoists who are prepared to break the rules for their own ends, high sanctions may be effective in deterring non-compliance. Whilst high sanctions crowd out the belief that others are of a cooperative tendency, there is no crowding out on the behavioral level, because the coercive power of the sanctions compensates for the effect of decreased trusts in others.

In wider society, of course, the relative proportions of "conditional cooperators" and "rational egoists" is by implication stable. Indeed, in spite of recent events in financial markets, there is ample evidence to suggest that prima facie the ethical standards of bankers are no different to those of professionals in comparable industries (Van Hoorn 2015, Rusch 2015). However, as demonstrated by Cohn et al. (2014), as soon as bankers' professional identities become engaged, they become considerably more dishonest, a finding not replicated across other industries. Importantly, this tends to suggest that "rules of morality" or codes of ethics in financial markets may be ineffective in regulating conduct at the aggregate level. If there are enough individuals in a population for whom moral incentives are unimportant (in other words, "amoral" people), sanctions which invoke moral or ethical justifications will fail to prevent bad behavior. As research suggests that bankers are more amoral than others, internally derived ethical codes are likely to be less successful in deterring reckless conduct. Indeed, as these individuals will themselves be unlikely to impose moral sanctions called for by the (immoral) conduct they observe, the breakdown of moral incentives is exacerbated. In these circumstances, legal, rather than moral, rules are to be preferred (Shavell 2002).[20] Sanctions therefore play an instrumental function in signaling to market participants that particular forms of conduct are unethical. Importantly, they may also act as a deterrent to amoral subgroups who cannot be persuaded to act ethically by appeals to internally derived ethical mores.[21]

[19] A "Hobbesian setting" fulfils the following three conditions: (i) agents are constrained by superior force (i.e. the state); (ii) agents are entirely self-interested; and (iii) the concepts of "right" and "wrong" are non-existent until provided for by agreement of civil society.

[20] This is even more salient in relation to the particular case of financial markets, which are prone to episodic bouts of manias and crashes, during which times financial market participants are more prone to disobeying financial market rules or standard norms of ethical conduct. The abrogation of rules during booms may be a perfectly rational response to euphoric financial conditions: boom periods provide the opportunity for immediate economic benefits with remote (and uncertain) legal liability. As dubious conduct becomes more widespread across markets, participants may come to believe that under-resourced regulators will have little chance of catching them. Gerding (2014) terms this process "compliance rot."

[21] The deterrent feature of sanctions is debated, although most scholars conclude that properly applied penalties may deter certain forms of conduct. In this vein, the Bank of England (2014, 209) opined recently that: "[T]he principal purpose [for] impos[ing] sanctions [is] to promote high standards of regulatory and/or market conduct by deterring persons who have committed breaches from committing further breaches and helping to deter other

7.6 THE FORM AND REACH OF SANCTIONS

As I emphasized in the introduction, the substance rather than the form of sanction, as well as at whom the penalties are targeted, are the more significant considerations in developing a regime capable of enforcing ethical conduct. Notwithstanding this, a brief discussion concerning the form and reach of any conceptualized sanctioning regime is warranted at this juncture.

Taleb and Sandis (2014, 115) claim it is "unethical to drag people into exposures without incurring losses," particularly as the losses in the context of financial markets are acknowledged to have the potential to lead to systematic collapse. There must therefore be a perception that regulators and lawmakers are willing to tackle individual lapses in behavior. As was outlined earlier, the credibility of the new regime lies to some extent in the capacity of the regulations in question to be applied successfully to cases in which bankers take socially *excessive* risk, as well as in cases of overt criminality. In the absence of credible individual penalties for violations of particular norms, it is to be expected that excessive risk-taking will continue. A fundamental concern is that bankers across financial markets have repeatedly demonstrated that the usual rules of the game—higher capital requirements, resolution planning, and compensation controls—may only *temporarily constrain* excessive risk-taking (Kane 2016b), even where the consequences of this risk-taking involve huge social cost. Of course, the credibility of sanctions in molding behavior is contingent upon the perceived likelihood of detection of breaches. In the presence of timid or under-resourced regulators, financial market participants may rationally come to the conclusion that the likelihood of sanctions is minimal. This will lead—even in the presence of heavy sanctions—to failure in the translation of espoused values into action, and may contribute to a breakdown in integrity of the third layer of Schein's taxonomy, discussed above, the so-called "shared assumptions and beliefs": the bounds of acceptable conduct are determined largely by the basic assumptions of the relevant organization, which have a direct and determinative effect on behavior.

Sanctions are properly conceived as having two distinct purposes: to "price" or to "prohibit" (Coffee 1991). Pricing sanctions typically belong to the civil law, whilst prohibitory sanctions exist generally in the criminal domain, although there are some cases which are not easily reconcilable to categorization. On the one hand "pricing" behavior is designed to force the internalization of social costs of particular activities by the actors concerned, as well as preventing defendants from gaining personally from socially useless activities. Coffee (1992, 1875) points to the example of civil pricing sanctions being

persons from committing similar breaches, as well as demonstrating generally the benefits of compliant business."

applied to industrial polluters, which are designed not to prohibit industrial activities which pollute, but to incentivize cleaner production. In contrast, criminal sanctions are used to prohibit some activities entirely (for example, theft or fraud), which sees the victim as having a (moral) right to be free of the offending behavior, regardless of the social utility to either the defendant or society as a whole from the activity concerned.

Many scholars have used the pricing analogy in the context of financial institutions, regarding them as "financial polluters" whose activities are often socially useless whilst creating a systemic externality. This places an onus on regulators to ensure that the sources of damaging financial market activities shoulder the burden of their social costs (Haldane 2010). However, tackling excessive risk-taking in the financial system from this perspective would in practice be difficult. For starters, financial institutions cannot by definition fully internalize all of the social costs involved in their activities, or there would be no need for the myriad insurance programs and guarantees they currently enjoy. Moreover, under this model, agents would still not individually internalize the costs of their actions: no financial market participant could remedy the harm caused by systemic harm generated, for example, through tail-risk. This is one reason why the current regulatory focus on monetary incentives in banking to mitigate short-term risk-taking in financial markets is limited because (in the absence of negative bonuses) there remains an incentive to bury risks in the tails of distribution, and thereby delay ruin. This inquiry tends to suggest that the "price-prohibit" distinction may not be particularly clear-cut in relation to certain financial market activities and makes the choice of tool(s) to tackle socially damaging financial market risk-taking extremely significant.

Much of the reluctance to address this sort of behavior through the regulatory system arguably emanates from the notion that the risks involved are difficult either to envisage or to quantify, and therefore ascribing legal culpability to individuals might be unfair. Certainly, this is true of *criminal* liability.[22] Criminal law is adept at punishing transgressions that are thought to be too serious to be pursued civilly, and there is some evidence that they act as a deterrent to certain behaviors. Criminal penalties are also not dependent for their effectiveness on the perpetrator's solvency (Posner 1985). Yet the use of criminal law entails serious burdens on public resources and significant social loss (Becker 1976).[23] Of course, establishing intention in criminal proceedings, normally understood as requiring an intention to cause harm, or dishonesty, on the part of the perpetrator of the relevant act, is also extremely difficult. Perhaps most significantly, the injudicious

[22] But see the arguments put forward in Chapter 6 (Reiff, this volume).

[23] These costs are often tolerated because of the retributive qualities of criminal sanction, and in the case of imprisonment, also for the (temporary) prevention of repeat offending.

use of the criminal sanction is not without social cost itself, including excessive individual risk-averseness bred out of the fear and anxiety of being exposed to the denial of liberty for violations that may, in fact, be unintentional (Buell 2007).[24]

In most common law jurisdictions a legal standard of recklessness substitutes where direct evidence of criminal intent is absent. Yet, this too requires satisfaction of a high threshold. Moreover causation (in a criminal sense) must be taken into account. In any conceptualized sanctions regime based on a legal standard of criminal recklessness (as is the current UK law in the case of financial institution failure) it is unclear how this would be applied even to individual decision-making at banks, or how it will be demonstrated that the said recklessness was causative of any subsequent distress and therefore warrant the ascription of criminal liability.[25] For example, how any prosecuting authority will prove, in any case other than one involving truly exceptional circumstances, that the act of a manager "caused" the failure of her bank, is unclear.

One response may be to replace any standard of recklessness with the (lower) negligence standard in criminal cases. Negligence standards are not entirely unheard of for corporate individual crimes. Yet, the introduction of this standard would also be problematic: the (very low) negligence standard would in all likelihood act as a deterrent to individuals taking up senior positions in financial institutions, which may drain the financial markets of competence and talent. As noted by Black and Kershaw (2013) this could lead to one of two perverse outcomes: (1) excessive risk-aversion from corporate managers who fear being judged ex post for decisions they take which at the time they consider to be reasonable; or (2) a more extreme scenario in which truly risk-averse managers refuse to serve entirely, leaving the (self-selecting) risk-takers to join boards and senior management teams, resulting in a negative effect on bank conduct from a societal perspective. Even in extreme scenarios, under general common law principles applicable to negligence, a course of conduct is assessed by reference to the standards of one's peers (and in some instances by reference to acceptable industry standards). If everyone

[24] As explained by Coffee (1992, 1881–2): "Additional costs [to deterrence of criminal law use] need to be considered, including the fear and anxiety imposed on risk-averse individuals forced to live under constant threat of draconian penalties... Ultimately, if we measure the success of the criminal law exclusively in terms of the number of crimes prevented, we could wind up, in Herbert Packer's memorable phrase, 'creating an environment in which all are safe but none is free.'"

[25] The UK authorities have for example cautioned that the relevant thresholds to be met in any prosecutions under the new regulatory regime shall be very high and that sanctioning powers are expected only to be utilized in very limited circumstances, namely "in cases involving only the most serious of failings, such as where a bank failed with substantial costs to the taxpayer, lasting consequences for the financial system, or serious harm to customers" (UK PCBS 2013, 244).

in a particular market is behaving in the same way, a court is unlikely to judge behavior to be (criminally) negligent, no matter what outsiders may believe.[26]

For these reasons (strong) civil sanctions—which by definition do not require the use of the criminal justice system—might be preferred. There are several justifications for this preference. First, thanks to the (normally) lower enforcement costs attached to regulatory investigations, regulators enjoy significant economies of scale vis-à-vis criminal prosecutors. The lower burden of proof to be attained does not pose the same disincentive that attaches to decisions whether to embark upon a criminal prosecution. Second, the flexibility of a civil penalty regime stands in marked distinction to that of the criminal law. In civil law, individuals are not only held accountable in law for the known effects of their actions, but also for the effects of those they ought reasonably to be aware of—even when they are not (Taleb and Sandis 2014, 131).[27] Liability could be imposed on any individual or groups of individuals who embark upon the conscious adoption of a strategy which poses a risk—however small—of total ruin, if the persons in question ought to have reasonably known of its possibility. In this vein, Taleb and Sandis (2014, 115) argue for a "global morally mandatory heuristic that anyone involved in an action which can possibly generate harm for others, even probabilistically, should be required to be exposed to some damage, regardless of context." In cases of professional negligence, courts must consider whether a defendant who has engaged in a particular course of conduct ought to have objectively foreseen any potential dangers inherent in that conduct and, if so, whether the actions in question ought to be considered unreasonable. Indeed, civil liability under an analogous recklessness standard is not unknown in corporate law.[28]

Of course, establishing this requires an assessment of relevant evidence on the balance of probabilities, but the obstacles in evaluating this hypothetical legal standard in the context of finance—despite frequent claims to the contrary—are not insurmountable. Courts are of course permitted to consider the opinions of experts in determining liability. "Tail-risk," for example, is not immeasurable. Moreover, tail-risk within financial systems is *endogenous*—created by

[26] In the case of the Great Financial Crisis, for example, it is clear that many of the decisions taken by senior managers which eventuated in their banks collapsing—such as the investments they made in mortgage-backed securities—were at the time regarded as not excessively risky, although financial modeling is now somewhat more circumspect with regard to tail-risk.

[27] Both Kane (2016a) and Taleb and Sandis (2014) offer the example of drivers' obligation not to drive in a reckless manner, even though damage to third parties is not always inflicted in cases of reckless driving. Kane especially holds that banking must be regulated for the same reason as traffic is regulated: to coordinate potentially chaotic activity and to make all drivers behave more safely.

[28] In Delaware corporate law, for example, a finding of liability under the civil standard applied to the duty of care for directors of corporations requires it to be shown that there was a "reckless indifference to or deliberate disregard to the whole body of stockholders or actions which are without the bounds of reason."

financial market participants themselves—which has important implications for regulatory control and for individual and group liability.[29] Indeed, Taleb and Sandis note (2014, 116) that "tail events are not predictable, not measurable statistically unless one is *causing* them, or involved in increasing their probability by engaging in a certain class of actions with small upside and large downside." Causation in this context therefore warrants a demand for accountability.

Finally, civil sanctions may be just as effective in terms of deterrent force as the threat of criminal liability. Posner (1980, 74) holds that "the economic rationale for punishment is not that it undoes the bad effects of the crime but that, by placing a price on crime, it affects people's incentives to engage in criminal activity in the future." Accordingly, where the "price" of a sanction is sufficiently large, whether criminal or not, it will have the capacity to deter the conduct in question. There is nothing to suggest that punishments such as large fines, industry bans, or disqualifications from office would not deter excessive risk-taking. In terms of signaling power, there is substantial research to suggest that civil sanctions carry significant deterrent force to "white-collar criminals" who are (generally) more sensitive to both monetary sanctions (thanks to their greater financial wealth) and the reputational damage which may be caused by regulatory censure (Avgouleas 2005).

Moreover, a draconian civil remedy such as a permanent suspension from a particular industry carries for transgressors the threat of professional extinction, which is a daunting prospect to highly skilled but non-diversifiable labor (Berg 2003). Making individuals liable under a civil standard also avoids the moral hazard associated with the collapse of criminal trials, which are often high-profile, widely reported and entail significant public cost. Where criminal trials collapse or result in "not-guilty" findings, this of course adds weight to the signal market participants receive indicating the credibility or otherwise of a sanctioning regime. A civil sanctioning regime partially avoids this dilemma. In these circumstances, regulatory sanction may provide a next-best option for both deterrence and efficiency.

Taking into account the bounded knowledge and informational constraints affecting regulators, and the incentives for managers to under-report problems, axiomatically those in positions of responsibility must also be held *accountable* if they are aware, or ought to be aware, of the potential for harm to be committed and fail to act (often termed a "duty-to-supervise-and-report"). Conceivably, then, this obligation would need to be enshrined in any efficacious sanctioning regime. In senior management or leadership roles, this form of accountability refers to the acknowledgment and assumption of

[29] Haldane (2010) argues that: "In the run-up to [the Great Financial Crisis], examples of such risk-hunting and regulatory arbitrage were legion. They included escalating leverage, increased trading portfolios and the design of tail-heavy financial instruments."

responsibility for actions, decisions, and policies within the scope of the role or employment position and including the obligation to report, explain, and be answerable for resulting consequences (Weber 2009, 155).

The importance of this form of mechanism in reducing recklessness or unethical conduct cannot be stressed strongly enough. In the past, legislative programs such as mandatory protection for whistleblowers have been designed to counter some of these dangers. However, there is compelling evidence that protections for corporate employees who engage in whistleblowing are extremely weak.[30] The obvious flaw in these programs (aside from the natural behavioral tendency to fear reprisals and future career damage) is that they do not, in general, mandate a *positive* obligation to report material breaches; they merely provide protection for employees who decide *voluntarily* and *without obligation* to come forward to report violations to the relevant authorities. For accountability to be effective and for a sanctioning regime to be credible, it is imperative that senior staff have the incentive to know what is happening in their organizations—not simply an incentive to plead (deliberate) ignorance if and when there is a regulatory investigation.[31] A mechanism such as this is supported by the reasoning of Schwarcz, whose argument on reassigning corporate responsibility is worth quoting at length:

> The increasingly decentralized nature of decision-making at firms makes it difficult to impose personal liability, which gives little incentive for risk-taking managers to change their behavior. Yet excessive risk-taking has been identified as one of the primary causes of the financial crisis. Reassigning corporate responsibility would make it easier to impose personal liability for engaging in—which in turn would help to discourage—excessive risk-taking... There... has been discussion of making senior managers responsible for their subordinates' actions under a "failure to supervise" theory... under which supervisory managers could be held liable for illegal activities that they were in a position to prevent... [o]ne such approach might be regulation requiring systemically important firms to specifically designate one or more risk managers; to adopt both proactive and review-oriented protocols designed to identify and deter excessive risk-taking. (Schwarcz 2015, 572–3)

[30] For example, despite the much vaunted and uprated protections for corporate whistleblowers provided under the Sarbanes-Oxley Act 2002 (SOX), most studies demonstrate that the laws concerned, such as mandatory anti-retaliation provisions, are poorly enforced and grant inadequate relief to employees (Moberly 2007, Earle and Madek 2007).

[31] As noted by the UK PCBS (2013, 17): "One of the most dismal features of the banking industry to emerge from our evidence was the striking limitation on the sense of personal responsibility and accountability of the leaders within the industry for the widespread failings and abuses over which they presided. Ignorance was offered as the main excuse. It was not always accidental. Those who should have been exercising supervisory or leadership roles benefited from an accountability firewall between themselves and individual misconduct, and demonstrated poor, perhaps deliberately poor, understanding of the front line. Senior executives were aware that they would not be punished for what they could not see and promptly donned the blindfolds."

7.7 REGULATING AGAINST UNETHICAL CONDUCT: THE UK APPROACH

The UK has been at the forefront of initiatives to tackle the various forms of abusive conduct mentioned above and now boasts arguably the most prescriptive regulatory regime in financial markets insofar as individual penalties for misconduct are concerned. A principal motivation of the legislature in drafting these laws was that "holding individuals to account is a key component of effective regulation... Clearer individual responsibilities coupled with enhanced enforcement powers for the regulators should give senior management a robust set of incentives and deterrents. This should improve corporate governance and encourage individuals to behave appropriately and accept greater responsibility for their actions" (Bank of England 2014, 8). Significantly, perhaps, criminal sanctions comprise only a small element of the new regulatory regime, although their signaling power may be significant.[32]

At the center of these initiatives is a new "Senior Managers' Regime" (SMR) applicable at certain (large) financial institutions. This was established by the 2013 Financial Services (Banking Reform) Act, and applies to any person who performs a "Senior Management Function" (SMF) at a relevant firm, and requires those firms to take reasonable care to ensure that no employee performing a "significant harm function" as specified by the regulators does so unless the firm has certified them as "fit and proper" to do so. Members of the SMR are subject collectively to an exhaustive list of prescribed behaviors and responsibilities, with no permitted derogation(s) from the provisions.[33]

[32] There have been many recent stories which claim that UK bankers regard the threat of sanction for their individual or collective conduct as serious. According to one UK banker, "What we worry about is being able to properly control activity... You become liable for everything delegated under your areas of activity... You're putting all your assets at risk" (Noonan and Binham 2015). Recently, a *Financial Times* headline claimed that UK bankers were "terrified" by the prospective penalties under the SMR (Arnold and Binham 2016).

[33] According to the Prudential Regulatory Authority, Prescribed Responsibilities of SMRs and firms include: "1. Performance by the firm of its obligations under the senior management regime, including implementation and oversight; 2. Performance by the firm of its obligations under the Certification Rules; 3. Compliance with the rules relating to the firm's management responsibilities map; 4. The induction, training and professional development of all persons performing senior management functions on behalf of the firm and all members of the firm's management body; 5. Ensuring and overseeing the integrity and independence of the internal audit function in accordance with... internal audit; 6. Ensuring and overseeing the integrity and independence of the compliance function...; 7. Ensuring and overseeing the integrity and independence of the risk function...; 8. Ensuring and overseeing the integrity, independence and effectiveness of the firm's policies and procedures on whistleblowing and for ensuring staff who raise concerns are protected from detrimental treatment; 9. Allocation of all prescribed responsibilities; 10. Leading the development of the firm's culture and standards in relation to the carrying on of its business and the behaviors of its staff; 11. Embedding the firm's culture and standards in relation to the carrying on of its business and the behaviors of its staff in the day-to-day management of the firm; 12. The development and maintenance of the firm's business

The SMR at banks constitutes: the relevant firm's board, and at larger and more complex firms the executive committee; heads of key business areas satisfying certain quantitative criteria; individuals in group or parent companies exercising significant influence on the firms' decision-making; and, where appropriate, individuals not otherwise approved as Senior Managers but ultimately responsible for important business, control, or conduct-focused functions within the firm. Any application to perform an SMF must be accompanied by a "Statement of Responsibilities," the purpose of which is to designate the aspects of the bank's business affairs that a senior manager will be responsible for managing. *Individual* members of the SMR are personally liable for any firm conduct which occurs in the area designated as their responsibility and which constitutes a regulatory breach. Offending members of the SMR are subject to a wide range of civil remedies, including fines, restrictions on responsibilities, and industry bans. Importantly, the Act imposes strict obligations of reporting, which requires both members of bank SMRs and, specifically, the SMF with responsibility for regulatory contact to report to the regulator on breaches of conduct or any other matter that it is reasonable to assume would be of material significance.[34] Finally, in cases of financial institution failure, the Act reserves power for regulators to charge or indict members of the SMR with the offense of "reckless misconduct," subjecting them to *individual* criminal liability for taking a decision which leads to the failure of a bank, or failing to prevent such a decision being taken, if the

model; 13. Management of the allocation and maintenance of capital, funding and liquidity; 14. The firm's treasury management functions; 15. The production and integrity of the firm's financial information and its regulatory reporting in respect of its regulated activities; 16. The firm's recovery plan and resolution pack and overseeing the internal processes regarding their governance; 17. If the firm carries out proprietary trading, the firm's proprietary trading activities." (See Norton Rose Fulbright 2014.)

[34] During the Act's implementation, the Bank of England stated that: "Senior managers will be held individually accountable if the areas they are responsible for fail to meet our requirements. Our new accountability regime will hold all senior managers, including non-executive directors, to a clear standard of behaviour and we will take action where they fail to meet this" (Bank of England 2015). The *individual* senior management conduct rules state that "[the manager] must disclose appropriately any information of which the FCA or PRA would reasonably expect notice." This would, of course, include any material conduct breaches. Indicatively, a firm must report to the regulator: (i) if they suspect or are aware that a person has breached a conduct rule; (ii) if, having previously notified the regulators of a known or suspected breach, they reach a subsequent or different determination; and (iii) if they have issued a formal written warning to an employee, suspended or dismissed, or reduced or recovered remuneration from an employee as a result of conduct which amounts to a conduct rule breach. These rules therefore to a degree mimic those which apply to UK law firms, where compliance officers are obliged to report material failures direct to the regulator as soon as reasonably practicable and make a record of non-material failures in order to assess whether a pattern of compliance failures is occurring which might become material as "a failure may be material either taken on its own or as part of a pattern of failures to comply." Any such report may trigger a regulatory intervention and, ultimately, a sanction for both the entity and the individual held to be responsible for the breach.

member of the SMR in question was aware of a risk that the implementation of the decision may have caused failure. SMR members found guilty of this offense may be jailed for up to seven years.

The Bank of England concludes that "by strengthening individual accountability mechanisms ... there are likely to be beneficial changes in behaviour across all relevant sectors and a reduction in non-compliance, misconduct and excessive risk-taking" (Bank of England 2014, 71). The "duty-to-supervise-and-report" ascribed to members of the SMR goes some way to addressing concerns about the potential compromise of internal communication channels: in the absence of a positive duty to report material infractions, senior managers—in control as they are of information flows and with informational advantages over regulators—may choose not to report material breaches, thus allowing damaging or unethical conduct to perpetuate, or obfuscating the precise roles of those involved in particular conduct to impede external investigations, thus reducing the likelihood of sanctions (Velikonja 2011). By making liability for these actions "strict," in the sense that the SMR in financial institutions could not avoid responsibility for reporting and/or acting on regulatory failings, incentives are created against placing obstacles in the way of full disclosure of information. Taking this analysis a step further, managers fulfilling this role would be actively incentivized to prevent serious ethical breaches or excessive risk-taking from occurring *in the first place.*

The threat of such a reporting mechanism may counteract the cognitive bias and self-interest that impair reflective informed decision-making (Loughrey 2014),[35] including the self-serving bias which leads people to interpret information in a manner favorable to them, or in a manner that avoids confrontations with key superiors or clients and to disregard or fail to recognize the significance of information that indicates problems. Moreover, in light of the widespread failure of regulators to prosecute individuals for want of legal proximity or culpability for particular conduct, it shall prevent senior managers from absolving themselves from responsibility for activities that occur on their watch. It shall provide strong incentives to monitor and mitigate excessive risk-taking by subordinates. Institutionalizing these processes over time would assist in providing ethical signposting to financial market participants and thereby avoid the "organizational drift" which afflicted pre-GFC financial institutions (Mandis 2013). Moreover, in line with Schein's teachings, the "shared assumptions and norms" of the relevant organizations could (slowly) be changed.

[35] Loughrey discusses similar regulatory mechanisms in the context of legal compliance officers who are subject to a similar reporting obligation; specifically, UK legal compliance officers (who hold very senior positions) are under a separate obligation to report material breaches of any regulatory requirement by a firm, its managers, employees, or those holding an interest in it (such as shareholders) to the relevant regulator as soon as reasonable.

7.8 CONCLUSION

Ultimately, financial institutions must themselves remain a significant part of the process that is required to get culture right: a good culture cannot simply be mandated by law or imposed by supervisors. Yet, the dual realization that much financial activity remain bankrolled by taxpayers, whereas financial scandals show no sign of dissipating, adds to the confusion over the reticence to regulate the banking profession more closely; it is left to the judiciary to mourn the paucity of regulatory enforcement actions,[36] whilst regulatory reticence to tackle these problems for what they are—failures of professional ethics—continues to prevail.

Contrary to the protestations of some, cultures and ethics can be developed, and sanctions pursued proactively by an intrusive regulator are a vital instrument in this endeavor. I have argued that *individual accountability* is the key to this process. In this sense, this requires obliging individuals to take responsibility for activities which may cause harm, and in the event that harm is caused, to be held accountable for that harm. As I have argued, civil sanctions and regulatory regimes based upon civil standards of proof hold considerable promise in furtherance of this objective.

Accordingly, it is time to end discussions about both the "specialness of banking" and the supposed inadequacy of sanctions for individuals in delivering behavioral change. Regarding bankers a priori as some kind of "other," immune to the standards expected of talented professionals in equally responsible positions, is at best unhelpful and at worst excusatory. Much of the unethical conduct which has happened in financial markets over the past decade occurred precisely because of an overly permissive regulatory culture, which did not apply to bankers the same standards as expected of other highly skilled employees.[37] Moreover, the special quality of excessive risk-taking in financial markets, which may have systemic consequences, arguably demands a looser interpretation of what forms of conduct constitute unethical behavior. In the absence of fraud, it is impossible for most current criminal sanctions regimes at the individual level to adequately cater for instances in which bankers' excessively risky activities cause severely injurious financial loss to markets or to taxpayers. Any regulatory regime must necessarily regard excessive risk-taking as a damaging and unethical practice, worthy of sanction.

[36] Raymond (2013) quoting Federal Judge Rakoff: "The failure of the government to bring to justice those responsible for such a massive fraud speaks greatly to weaknesses in our prosecutorial system that need to be addressed."

[37] For example, lawyers, medical practitioners, and other finance professionals, each of whom also subsists in a high-functioning and skills-portable market landscape and whose activities—even in the aggregate—are unlikely to cause systemic economic harms.

By characterizing excessive risk-taking in this way, the harm posed by those activities may be adequately addressed and remedied.

Therefore, a robust regulatory approach to excessive risk-taking behavior will be required. There are some signs that this has been recognized in jurisdictions beyond the UK: in September 2015, the US Attorney General issued a memorandum which explicitly addressed the failure of regulators and prosecutors to ensure individual accountability in financial markets and demanded a more intrusive approach to regulatory investigations.[38] Targeting high-level managers in a personal capacity would lend support to these initiatives: direct reform of sanctions for non-compliance (as in the UK financial markets), supplemented by uprated roles and responsibilities for risk professionals (with non-delegable duties to report excessive risk-taking and/or unethical behavior), have the capacity to produce an environment in which compliance with ethical norms and restraint from excessive risk-taking by banking professionals is more likely. With the suggested approach, the underlying assumption(s) of financial market culture—that excessive risk-taking will not result in individual liability to account—have a credible chance of being changed.[39]

REFERENCES

Acemoglu, D., and Matthew O. Jackson. 2015. "History, Expectations, and Leadership in the Evolution of Social Norms." *Review of Economic Studies* 82(2), 423–56.

Admati, A. R., P. M. DeMarzo, M. F. Hellwig, and P. Pfleiderer. 2013. "The Leverage Ratchet Effect." Rock Center for Corporate Governance at Stanford University Working Paper No. 146.

Andrews, E. 2008. "Greenspan Concedes Error on Regulation." *New York Times*, October 23.

Argenton, C., and E. van Damme. 2014. "Optimal Deterrence of Illegal Behavior under Imperfect Corporate Governance." TILEC Discussion Paper No. 2014-053 http://ssrn.com/abstract=2540155 (accessed October 26, 2016).

[38] The September 2015 "Yates Memo," as the document is popularly referred to, contains the following directions to prosecutorial staff conducting investigations into alleged financial misconduct: "1. To be eligible for any co-operation credit, corporations must provide to the Department all relevant facts about the individuals involved in corporate misconduct... 2. Both criminal and civil corporate investigations should focus on individuals... 3. Criminal and civil attorneys handling corporate investigations should be in routine communication with one another... 4. Absent extraordinary circumstances, no corporate resolution will provide protection from criminal or civil liability for any individuals... 5. Corporate cases should not be resolved without a clear plan to resolve related individual cases... 6. Civil attorneys should consistently focus on individuals as well as the company... "

[39] The author would like to thank Tony Harvey and Ed Kane for their valuable input.

Armour, J., and J. Gordon. 2014. "Systemic Harms and Shareholder Value." *Journal of Legal Analysis* 6(1), 35–85.

Arnold, M., and Binham, C. 2016. "Bankers 'Terrified' at New Regulations." *Financial Times*, London, March 8.

Avgouleas, E. 2005. *The Mechanics and Regulation of Market Abuse: A Legal and Economic Analysis*. Oxford: Oxford University Press.

Avgouleas, E., and J. Cullen. 2015. "Excessive Leverage and Bankers' Pay: Governance and Financial Stability Costs of a Symbiotic Relationship." *Columbia Journal of European Law* 21(1), 35–80.

Avgouleas, E., and J. Cullen. 2014. "Market Discipline and EU Corporate Governance Reform in the Banking Sector: Merits, Fallacies, and Cognitive Boundaries." *Journal of Law & Society* 41(1), 28–50.

Awrey, D., W. Blair, and D. Kershaw. 2013. "Between Law and Markets: Is There a Role for Culture and Ethics in Financial Regulation?" *Delaware Journal of Corporate Law* 38(1), 191–245.

Bank of England. 2014. "Strengthening Accountability in Banking: A New Regulatory Framework for Individuals." PRA Consultation Paper CP14/14.

Bank of England. 2015. "News Release: Prudential Regulation Authority Sets Out How It Will Hold Senior Managers Accountable for Failure to Meet Its Requirements." February 23.

Becker, G. 1976. *The Economic Approach to Human Behavior*. Chicago: University of Chicago Press.

Berg, P. F. S. 2003. "Unfit To Serve: Permanently Barring People from Serving as Officers and Directors of Publicly Traded Companies After the Sarbanes-Oxley Act." *Vanderbilt Law Review* 56, 1871–906.

Black, J., and D. Kershaw. 2013. "Criminalising Bank Managers." LSE Law and Financial Markets Project Briefing 1/13.

Blair, W. 2016. "Between Law and Markets: Is There a Space for Ethics in Financial Regulation?" In *Reconceptualising Global Finance and its Regulation*, edited by D. Arner, E. Avgouleas, and R. Buckley. Cambridge: Cambridge University Press, 442–54.

Buell, S. W. 2007. "Reforming Punishment of Financial Reporting Fraud." *Cardozo Law Review* 28(4), 1611–52.

Campbell, D., and Loughrey, J. 2013. "The Regulation of Self-interest in Financial Markets." In *Integrity, Risk and Accountability in Capital Markets: Regulating Culture*, edited by J. O'Brien and G. Gilligan. Oxford: Hart, 65–90.

Chason, E. D. 2013. "The Uneasy Case for Deferring Banker Pay." *Louisiana Law Review* 73(4), 923–77.

Coase, R. 1960. "The Problem of Social Cost." *Journal of Law and Economics* 3, 1–44.

Coffee, J. C. 1991. "Does 'Unlawful' Mean 'Criminal'?: Reflections on the Disappearing Tort/Crime Distinction in American Law." *Boston University Law Review* 71, 201–52.

Coffee, J. C. 1992. "Paradigms Lost: The Blurring of the Criminal and Civil Law Models—And What Can Be Done About It." *Yale Law Journal* 101(8), 1875–93.

Cohn, A., E. Fehr, and M. A. Marechal. 2014. "Business Culture and Dishonesty in the Banking Industry." *Nature* 516, 86–9.

Connor, G., and B. O'Kelly. 2012. "A Coasean Approach to Bank Resolution Policy in the Eurozone." LSE Financial Markets Group Special Paper 214.

Cullen, J. 2014. *Executive Compensation in Imperfect Financial Markets*. Cheltenham: Elgar.

Cullen, J. 2016. "Culture as Cash: From Bonus to Malus." In *Controlling Capital: Public and Private Regulation of Financial Markets*, edited by N. Dorn. Oxford: Routledge, 97–125.

Dudley, W. C. 2014. "Enhancing Financial Stability by Improving Culture in the Financial Services Industry." Remarks at the Workshop on Reforming Culture and Behavior in the Financial Services Industry, Federal Reserve Bank of New York, New York City, October 20.

Dykstra, C. A. 1939. "The Quest for Responsibility." *American Political Science Review* 33(1), 1–25.

Earle, B. H., and G. A. Madek. 2007. "The Mirage of Whistleblower Protection Under Sarbanes-Oxley: A Proposal for Change." *American Business Law Journal* 44(1), 1–54.

Erhard, W., and M. Jensen. 2015. "Putting Integrity Into Finance: A Purely Positive Approach." Harvard NOM Unit Research Paper No. 12-074.

Fabra, N., and M. Motta. 2013. "Antitrust Fines in Times of Crisis." CEPR Discussion Paper No. DP9290. http://ssrn.com/abstract=2210260 (accessed October 26, 2016).

Ferguson, B. 2013. "Sanctions, Incentives and Better Behaved Banks." In *Integrity, Risk and Accountability in Capital Markets: Regulating Culture*, edited by J. O'Brien and G. Gilligan. Oxford: Hart, 66–85.

Friedman, M. 1970. "The Social Responsibility of Business is to Increase its Profits." *The New York Times Magazine*, New York, September 13.

Gapper, J. 2014. "There Is No Such Thing as the Banking Profession." *Financial Times*, London, February 12.

Gerding, E. F. 2014. *Law, Bubbles and Financial Regulation*. Oxford: Routledge.

Haldane, A. G. 2010. "The $100 Billion Question." Speech given at the Institute of Regulation & Risk, Hong Kong, March 30.

Hall, J. 1961. "Legal Sanctions; Note." *Natural Law Forum. Paper* 63, 119–26.

Hermalin, B. E. 2005. "Trends in Corporate Governance." *Journal of Finance* 60(5), 2351–84.

Ho, K. 2009. *Liquidated*. Durham, NC: Duke University Press.

Hoenig, T. M. 2016. "FDIC Board Meeting Statement Regarding 2015 Title I Plans Submitted by the Eight Domestic GSIBs." April 13. https://www.fdic.gov/news/news/speeches/spapr1316a.html (accessed October 26, 2016).

Holder, E. 2014. "Remarks on Financial Fraud Prosecutions." New York University School of Law, September 17.

Holmstrom, B., and Kaplan, S. N. 2001. "Corporate Governance and Merger Activity in the U.S.: Making Sense of the 1980s and 1990s." *Journal of Economic Perspectives* 15, 121–44.

Hosmer, L. T. 1995. "Trust: The Connecting Link between Organizational Theory and Philosophical Ethics." *Academy of Management Review* 20(2), 379–403.

Jackall, R. 1988. *Moral Mazes: The World of Corporate Managers*. New York: Oxford University Press.

Jensen, M. C., and Meckling, W. H. 1976. "Theory of the Firm: Managerial Behavior, Agency Costs, and Ownership Structure." *Journal of Financial Economics* 3, 305–60.

Kane, E. J. 1994. "Ethical Conflicts in Managing the S&L Insurance Mess." In *Social Economics: Premises, Findings and Policies*, edited by Edward J. O'Boyle. Oxford: Routledge, 125–44.

Kane, E. J. 2016a. "A Theory of How and Why Central-Bank Culture Supports Predatory Risk-Taking at Megabanks." *Atlantic Economic Journal* 44(1), 51–71.

Kane, E. J. 2016b. "Ethics Versus Ethos in US and UK Megabanking." unpublished manuscript.

Kay, J. 2015. *Other People's Money: Masters of the Universe or Servants of the People?* London: Profile Books.

Labaton Sucharow. 2015. "The Street, the Bull and the Crisis: A Survey of the US and UK Financial Services Industry." www.secwhistlebloweradvocate.com/LiteratureRetrieve.aspx?ID=224757.

London School of Economics CCP Research Foundation. 2014. "Conduct Cost Results 2014." http://conductcosts.ccpresearchfoundation.com/conduct-costs-results (accessed October 26, 2016).

Loughrey, J. 2014. "Accountability and the Regulation of the Large Law Firm Lawyer." *Modern Law Review* 77(5), 732–62.

McLannahan, B. 2016. "Charge Senior Bank Bosses, Says Former Commissioner." *Financial Times* London, February 9.

Mandis, S. 2013. *What Happened to Goldman Sachs?* Cambridge, MA: Harvard Business Review Press.

Mill, J. S. 1859. *On Liberty*. Oxford: Oxford University Press.

Moberly, R. 2007. "Unfulfilled Expectations: An Empirical Analysis of Why Sarbanes-Oxley Whistleblowers Rarely Win." *William & Mary Law Review* 49, 65–155.

Noonan, L., and Binham, C. 2015. "Bankers Seek Ways Round Bonus Clawbacks." *Financial Times*, London, June 26.

Norton Rose Fulbright. 2014. "The New Accountability Regime: Key Things You Should Know." December. http://www.nortonrosefulbright.com/knowledge/publications/123899/the-new-accountability-regime (accessed October 26, 2016).

O'Toole, J., and W. Bennis. 2009. "A Culture of Candor." *Harvard Business Review* June, 1–8.

Polinsky, M. A., and S. Shavell. 2000. "The Economic Theory of Public Enforcement of Law." *Journal of Economic Literature* 38, 45–76.

Posner, R. A. 1980. "Retribution and Related Concepts of Punishment." *Journal of Legal Studies* 9(1), 71–92.

Posner, R. A. 1985. "An Economic Theory of the Criminal Law." *Columbia Law Review* 85(6), 1193–231.

Raymond, N. 2013. "Judge Criticizes Lack of Prosecution against Wall Street Executives for Fraud." *Reuters*, November 12.

Roberts, J., and R. Scapens. 1985. "Accounting Systems and Systems of Accountability—Understanding Accounting Practices in their Organisational Contexts." *Accounting, Organizations and Society* 10(4), 443–56.

Roe, M. J. 2014. "Structural Corporate Degradation Due To Too-Big-To-Fail Finance." *University of Pennsylvania Law Review* 162, 1419–64.

Rusch, H. 2015. "Do Bankers Have Deviant Moral Attitudes? Negative Results from a Tentative Survey." *Rationality, Markets and Morals* 6, 6–20.

Salz Review. 2013. *An Independent Review of Barclays' Business Practices.*

Sandel, M. 2010. *Justice: What's the Right Thing to Do?* London: Penguin.

Schein, E. 2010. *Organizational Culture and Leadership*, 4th edn. San Francisco: John Wiley & Sons.

Schwarcz, S. L. 2010. "Keynote Address: The Role of Lawyers in the Global Financial Crisis." *Australian Journal of Corporate Law* 24, 214–26.

Schwarcz, S. L. 2015. "Excessive Corporate Risk-Taking and the Decline of Personal Blame." *Emory Law Journal* 65, 533–79.

Schwarcz, S. L. 2016. "Misalignment: Corporate Risk-Taking and Public Duty." Unpublished manuscript.

Shavell, S. 2002. "Law versus Morality as Regulators of Conduct." *American Law and Economics Review* 4(2), 227 57.

Sinclair, A. 1995. "The Chameleon of Accountability: Forms and Discourses." *Accounting, Organizations and Society* 20(2), 219–37.

Singer, P. 2003. *A Companion to Ethics.* New York: John Wiley & Sons.

Sison, A. J. G. 2008. *Corporate Governance and Ethics: An Aristotelian Perspective.* Cheltenham: Elgar.

Taleb, N. N., and Sandis, C. 2014. "The Skin in the Game Heuristic for Protection Against Tail Events." *Review of Behavioral Economics* 1, 115–35.

UK Parliamentary Commission on Banking Standards (UK PCBS). 2013. *Changing Banking for Good, Volume I: Summary, and Conclusions and Recommendations.* HL Paper 27–I; HC 175–I.

US Financial Crisis Inquiry Commission. 2011. *The Financial Crisis Inquiry Report: Final Report of the National Commission on the Causes of the Financial and Economic Crisis in the United States.* Submitted Pursuant to Public Law 111–21, January.

van der Weele, J. 2012. "The Signaling Power of Sanctions in Social Dilemmas." *Journal of Law, Economics and Organizations* 28(1), 103–26.

Van Hoorn, A. 2015. "The Global Financial Crisis and the Values of Professionals in Finance: An Empirical Analysis." *Journal of Business Ethics* 130, 253–69.

Velikonja, U. 2011. "Leverage, Sanctions, and Deterrence of Accounting Fraud." *UC Davis Law Review* 44, 1281–345.

Walker, D. 2009. *A Review of Corporate Governance in UK Banks and Other Financial Industry Entities: Final Recommendations.* HM Treasury, 26 November.

Weber, R. H. 2009. "Accountability in Internet Governance." *International Journal of Communications Law and Policy* 13, 152–67.

Wexler, S. 2010. "Financial Edgework and the Persistence of Rogue Traders." *Business and Society Review* 115(1), 1–25.

Wheeler, S. 2016. "Reconstruction of Ethical Conduct in Financial Firms." In *Controlling Capital: Public and Private Regulation of Financial Markets*, edited by N. Dorn. Oxford: Routledge, 77–96.

Yates, S. Q. 2015. "Individual Accountability for Corporate Wrongdoing." US Department of Justice Office of the Deputy Attorney Memorandum, Washington D.C, September 9.

8

Moneys' legal hierarchy

Katharina Pistor

8.1 INTRODUCTION

In its broadest sense, the term "money" refers to widely accepted means of payment. It is usually associated with state-issued money. Following Mehrling (2012) and others, I use the term money to refer to both state and private money, where private money consists of private claims to future payments that can be used as means of payment in their own rights. Classic examples include notes or bills of exchange, but also commercial paper and securitized assets. State and private moneys of different kinds form an interdependent hierarchical system. State money invariably occupies the apex of that system, because it can always be traded at face value. All other moneys are issued by private entities. Unlike states, private entities cannot manipulate their own survival constraint and the moneys they issue are therefore not as safe as state money. Holders of these moneys therefore find themselves on the periphery of the hierarchical money system compared to holders of state money.

This chapter addresses how the structures of financial markets affect actors and entities on the periphery of the financial system. The hierarchy of moneys, I will argue, is largely a function of law. Law enhances predictability and the credibility of commitments and thereby helps scale up financial markets, because those who have been able to shift risk to others are willing to take on even more risks. By the same token, when too many actors rely on credible commitments that can no longer be upheld because the assumptions that informed them were misguided, law can lead to the system's self-destruction from which it can be rescued only by the temporary suspension of the full force of the law, a phenomenon I have termed elsewhere the "law–finance paradox" (Pistor 2013). At this point, a financial system that expanded by betting on the enforceability of claims irrespective of changes in the environment will go into reverse. In order to live up to their legal commitments, debtors will have to spend down their cash reserves, and when this does not suffice, they will have to sell their assets. The more debtors have to resort to these measures, the more asset prices fall, the faster the downward spiral, and the closer the system will come to the abyss.

Retreat from these downward dynamics requires the suspension of the full force of the law and/or liquidity assistance by states or central banks. Preference will usually be given to entities that are critical for the survival of the system. This implies that rescue efforts will focus on entities closer to the system's apex. Those on the periphery will feel the full force of the law and many will be forced into liquidation.

The periphery benefits from such a system on the upside. The firmer the legal commitments, the more credible they are at least ex ante, and the more finance will be forthcoming—but also the more relentless the enforcement will tend to be on the downside. Critically, the tides of financial expansion are not natural phenomena, but are the result of the specific structure of a financial system coded in law. We therefore need to take a closer look at where and how the legal commitments are constructed and who has the power to suspend the full force of the law when things go wrong.

Others in this volume grapple with more comprehensive notions of justice. Therefore, it may be helpful to define the scope of the justice inquiry in this chapter. Hierarchy as such, including the humanly constructed hierarchy of legal claims, is not incompatible with justice. After all, it is a critical component of most, if not all, systems of social order. Some have stronger rights than others; in case of conflict, those with weaker rights must yield. For example, if one person has property rights in an object, another person has no right to use it unless this right is granted to her by the first person. Suppose the second person is leasing a home from the first. She can now exclude even the owner from access. However, the owner can evict her in the event that she fails to pay her rent.

Problems of justice, as understood in this chapter, arise when the rules that determine the hierarchy are biased in one way or another, or when the making or the contents of the rules are rigged to systematically advantage some over others. Things get worse when the disadvantaged are left with few or no options to alter their position or the contents of the rules. Further, hierarchy determines not only who can call the shots, but also who foots the bill when things go wrong. A system that tolerates, perhaps even promotes, a structural mismatch between those who control the rules of the game and those who bear the inevitable costs condones injustice.

The claim advanced here is that the rules that configure our money systems are biased toward those at the top of a hierarchical system. The apex has become increasingly entrenched, thus giving those on the periphery few opportunities to change the rules or to escape the costs of the system. This applies both to domestic financial systems and to the global financial system.

The following sections explain how legal hierarchies emerge in financial markets in which participants have differential access to safe and liquid assets in times of a crisis. I will introduce several legal devices that are commonly used to differentiate access rights: property rights, as in the example above; collateral rights, which allow the secured creditor to enforce against an asset; trust and corporate law, which delineate pools of claims from competing creditor claims. In addition, legal protections have been used to insulate payment claims from other rights and obligations arising out of contracts, which makes them fully fungible, or money-like. Together, these institutions create a system that is unjustly biased in the very way in which it legally constructs the entity around which it turns—money.

8.2 MONEYS' LEGAL HIERARCHY

Economic and financial activities can take different forms. Markets and hierarchies are often depicted as occupying two polar ends of a continuum, with networks located in between (Powell 1990). Markets are places where individuals and entities meet and exchange goods and services and, of course money. Participating in exchange of goods and services can be regarded as an expression of freedom (Sen 1999).

Perhaps a world in which all economic transactions were organized as exchanges would be both freer and flat. That, however, is not the world we live in. Economic systems consist of not only horizontal relations of exchange, but also organizations that embody hierarchies, such as firms. Coase (1937) famously posed the question why firms exist at all. His answer, and that of the "theory of the firm" that he initiated, is that under certain conditions hierarchy can produce outcomes that are superior to markets. The difference between markets and firms, in Coase's view, is that under certain conditions authority and coordination are more efficient than a multiplicity of horizontal transactions. Much of institutional and transaction cost economics is built around the argument that firms are alternatives to markets and that the reason for their existence can be found in transaction and information costs.

This picture assumes that only firms embody hierarchies, whereas markets are horizontal, or flat. In reality, markets in general, and credit-based financial markets in particular, are also hierarchically structured. They are typically not centrally organized. Rather, their hierarchy is determined by the relative elasticity of the survival constraints that different market participants face. Those with the most rigid survival constraints and no place to go to receive an additional credit line in times of stress are at the bottom of this hierarchy, while those who are assured such a lifeline are closer to the top. The apex itself is occupied by whatever entity can manipulate its own survival constraint.

Some economists have broken out of the paradigm that markets are flat. Perry Mehrling (2012) posits that money systems are "inherently hierarchical." In a system in which many actors issue a variety of private and public forms of money, the critical question always concerns the price at which one form of money can be exchanged for another. This is the core question of finance. Hierarchy in finance is not a question of fundamental values, but of structures rooted in law and power: in the legal qualities of different moneys and the money issuing entities; in the legal conditions for access to a lender or dealer of last resort; and in the last instance in the willingness of that lender or dealer to step into the void and offer liquidity support at least to some, even in the absence of legal commitments.

To illustrate, individuals and households deposit cash into their bank accounts. In doing so they relinquish ownership over the money. It now belongs to the bank and depositors are left with an unsecured claim against the bank. They have a legal right to exchange book money into cash, or state money, but no guarantee that they will always be able to enforce this contract. They sleep calmly only because their deposits are insured, usually by a government-run insurance system. This insurance moves them one step closer toward the apex of the system, but only as long as their deposits stay below the insurance ceiling, and only as long as the insurer, for example the national government, commands sufficient resources to meet its liabilities. If the insurer itself has only limited funds, then the system will break down whenever these funds have been exhausted. Purely private and capped insurance schemes are therefore always only stopgap measures. They work as long as the demand for insurance does not exceed the stipulated supply. When demand exceeds supply, which is difficult if not impossible to predict, the insurance becomes worthless and a run on banks, assets, or entire markets ensues.

Turning back to the money deposited in the bank account: The bank in turn takes what is now "its" money and uses it to acquire shares, bonds, notes, or asset-backed securities issued by other entities. These assets will produce different returns. However, the bank cannot (or rather should not) maximize returns alone. The bank also needs to make sure that it can meet the demands of its creditors for cash. This implies that it needs to hold on to enough cash or to ensure that it can quickly liquidate investments and turn them into cash to meet these demands. Banks thus find themselves in a precarious position: Their shareholders demand high returns, but their depositors prefer liquid assets, ideally cash, which can be quickly turned around even as it does not yield high returns. To bridge these conflicting demands, regulated banks are required to maintain reserves with central banks. They also have access to special lending facilities (the discount window, or emergency lending) at central banks to bridge inevitable liquidity squeezes that may occur along the way. Last but not least, banks pay an insurance fee so that the government will insure depositors up to a stipulated ceiling.

When a liquidity crunch turns into a financial crisis—that is, when a certain percentage of banks, beyond some critical threshold, face problems meeting the demands of their depositors or other creditors—a "flight into safety" sets in: all market participants attempt to buy secure assets and to sell less secure ones. This is when the hierarchy of money comes into its own: Unsecured creditors will seek assets that offer security; holders of asset-backed securities will seek to convert them into assets whose value is more reliable, and at the end of the day all will try to hold state-issued money, or cash. Not everyone, however, has a legally enforceable claim to obtain cash whenever he or she needs it. Those who cannot obtain the cash they need will be forced to exit from the market; those who can will survive.

Allowing a rule-bound system to run its course puts it on auto-pilot to self-destruction. To avoid this outcome, public authorities, e.g. central banks, often feel compelled to offer more liquidity than is owed, at least to some market participants. They may be allowed to do so under emergency lending rules; but they may go beyond such legal constraints if they feel that they need to do "whatever it takes," in Fed Chairman Bernanke's famous words, to rescue the financial system from self-destruction. In either case, it is now in the hands of these authorities to determine who will survive. They are not exactly God, but they wield enormous power. What is more, the need to exercise this power is a function of the legal qualities of assets and entities, because these legal qualities determine the hierarchical relations between them.

8.3 MONEYS'? HIERARCHY AS A FUNCTION OF ECONOMIC AND POLITICAL POWER

Hierarchy may be "inherent" to finance, as Mehrling suggested, but the form it takes is constructed in law; it is part of the "rules of the game" for the financial system (North 1990). They are neither of divine nor of natural origin, but man-made. How, where, and by whom the rules are made shape the relative steepness of the hierarchy, and also determine who will be on the periphery and who will be closer to the apex. From a perspective of justice it is critical to determine who makes decisions, who is affected by them, and to whom decision-makers are ultimately accountable.

Spot markets are often depicted as ideal markets. Buyer and seller meet and exchange goods or services, typically for money defined as a means of exchange. More often than not, however, the debtor does not have the money on hand that the seller demands. The buyer will then need to find out whether the seller will take something else and at what price, or "discount." Likewise, a seller who accepts an "I owe you" (IOU) in lieu of cash will have to ask whether she can use it to pay her own bills, and at what discount. Should the seller refuse to take anything but cash, the buyer will be out of luck. Without access to the form of money sellers are willing to take, he cannot participate in an exchange.

This is obvious, and the unequal distribution of resources for making ends meet has been discussed at length. On its own, this may not be enough to condemn markets as unjust, especially as they can be supplemented by other institutions such as social insurance schemes or a minimum income. It turns into a question of justice, however, when some have systematically better access than others to money that is most in demand, without having to pay a price for it. Clearly, not everyone can afford to accept whatever money a buyer has on offer, as this may threaten their own survival. Some, however, may always find ready takers for the money they themselves issue, which puts them in a much better position to accept other money as well. Why so? They are held in high esteem because of economic or political power, or because of legal protections to which we will turn in Section 8.4.

Economic or political power signals that issuers are able to redeem their debt in the future either by the sheer amount of resources they control, or by their power to extract resources from others if necessary. Some private entities, for example large financial companies, can command more resources than small nation states. Their credibility as debtors emanates from these resources, but dwindles when their resources decline. The reason is that private entities ultimately operate under a binding survival constraint. They will be forced to exit the market if they can no longer balance their liabilities and go bankrupt. Some entities, however, can mobilize additional resources by imposing liabilities on others, sometimes even by force. The best example are nation states. They can use military power for foreign conquest and local policing powers to impose taxes to increase revenues (Levi 1988). Private entities can impose liabilities on others only indirectly: By threatening to blow up the system they can force states to help them out.

8.4 FINANCIAL HIERARCHIES WITH LEGAL "COMPLICATIONS"

Horology is the art of building mechanical watches that tell the time with great accuracy—not only hours and minutes, but also seconds. Adding "complications"—chronographs, calendars, or alarms—to these mechanical wonders turns simple horology into a craft, even an art. In a similar vein, complications can be added to a simple exchange of IOUs along a chain of buyers and sellers to stabilize the chain or fortify its apex.

In a simple payment chain every taker of an IOU or "note" along the chain has recourse to the original debtor, and possibly his own counterparty; but not to anybody else in the chain. He has to carry the risk that on payday the original issuer or his contracting party might raise objections arising out of the contract that gave rise to the obligation to pay: The goods may not have been delivered; they may have been defective; or someone else may have raised claims to them.

This creates instability in payment chains. Historically, the problem was addressed by making IOUs or notes legally enforceable against any member of the chain and immune from counter claims. These legal protections turned simple notes into bills of exchange ("negotiable instrument" in technical legal parlance) and the pieces of paper on which they were written and endorsements were made into a command to pay cash upon presentation of such a piece of paper. These legal steroids enhanced the liquidity of bills and put them on an almost equal footing with state money. Bills of exchange became a private payment system that sustained long-distance trade throughout Europe and beyond (Rogers 1995).

Critically, these changes required more than a simple contractual agreement between buyer and seller. The agreement "I will pay not only you, but any note holder, and I will not raise any objections out of contract" had to be enforceable by any holder against any previous holder (or endorsee) regardless of location. Since location typically implied different laws and different courts, backing by legal authorities in the relevant trade centers was needed—and was indeed forthcoming. In the second half of the seventeenth century, city after city throughout Europe enacted a statute on bills of exchange that assured their enforceability. In many cities merchants were controlling the city council and they made sure that their preferred business customs were respected when casting them into formal law. Merchant law was law made by and for merchants and backed up by public authorities. Other members of society benefited from the rise of long-distance commerce and finance. This, however, should not distract from the fact that not everyone obtained a contractual right that could be enforced against any other but the immediate contracting party.

Adding legal complications to what used to be personalized credit relations among merchants transformed them from reciprocal relations to arm's-length investments, and—in the US—eventually from merchants to consumers. Consumers were turned into issuers of notes. This meant that investors who later bought the bills could demand payment from them, even if they had valid claims against the loan originator. The very point of negotiability is to free the bill from such contractual claims. It makes bills more akin to money, while exposing debtors to the full risk of having to pay even if they have contractual rights not to (Manne 1996). Loan originators in turn could sell the bills to investors. The better the legal enforcement guarantees, the more willing investors were to buy; and the greater their demand, the greater the supply by loan-originating intermediaries. It was only when consumers defaulted en masse during the financial downturn in the 1920s that the scheme collapsed.

The story of expanding credit to consumers, while minimizing the risk of the intermediaries that originated or held it, was repeated on a much larger scale when the securitization of mortgages became all the rage. Securitization is a legal technique by which claims to payment (loans, receivables, etc.) are pooled in a "special purpose vehicle" (SPV), which takes the form of a trust or corporate entity. The claims are now separated from the originators of the loans and the trust or corporation can issue certificates to investors who will get their proportionate share of all the payments made to satisfy the loans.

A mass securitization market developed in the US since the 1970s with the help of government-sponsored entities, known as Fannie Mae, Ginnie Mae, and Freddie Mac. They bought mortgages private intermediaries had originated, put them into SPVs, and sold shares in the SPVs to investors (Hyman 2011). When private intermediaries came to realize that securitization was an ingenious device for designing financial assets that had the appearance—and the official AAA stamp from rating agencies[1]—of sovereign debt, if not state money, but with greater returns, the stage was set for rapid expansion. Following the example set by the government-sponsored entities, the new private money minters used off-balance-sheet structures to pool assets, to separate them legally from other activities and indeed their own default risk, and last but not least to avoid regulatory charges. Indeed, regulators privileged these structures precisely because the assets in an off-balance-sheet structure were removed from other credit and default risks. Asset-backing and other credit-enhancement devices were used to lure investors into believing that these assets were as safe as riskless assets, but with higher returns.

For the system to work, the privately minted assets had to be convertible into cash at all times. Indeed, the claims to future pay were expressed in dollar terms. In other words, securitization practices relied on "free liquidity" (Mehrling 2000). Liquidity, however, is not a free good (ibid.) and tends to become scarce precisely when everybody wants it. When all seek to convert their claims into cash at the same time, the hierarchy of moneys comes into its own and investors that relied on free liquidity must collapse. The reason is that in a world where private actors can freely issue their own moneys, private money will vastly exceed state money.

The second complication built into law was the fortification of the system's apex. This was easier to achieve in the sense that at the time when negotiable instruments came into use, an apex existed already. The rulers of emergent nation states were interested not only in control over people and territory; they also established control over the mint that coined the money they authorized.

[1] See also Chapter 11 (de Bruin, this volume).

This is not surprising. As Charles Tilly (1985) has suggested, like thugs, rulers of emergent states have three major tasks: they must fight external enemies, fight internal enemies, and please their friends. All three tasks require resources and ideally in a form that gives the ruler flexibility as to how to spend them. This was done by stipulating an exclusive form of money in which taxes and other levies could be settled: coins, such as sterling, issued by the ruler's mint (Desan 2015). As *the* means of final settlement, that form of money also served as the reference currency for all other IOUs.

Controlling the money at the apex of the system put the ruler in a position of power over others. He could refuse all other means of payment and seize the defaulting debtors' assets instead. But he could also extend a credit line or accept alternative means of payment to settle tax and other debt. State money was not only a means of settling; it also became a tool for conferring favors on some and withholding them from others. To be sure, money is a double-edged governance tool. Its efficacy depends on credibility, not crude force. Taking measures that might undermine money's credibility can leave an emperor, quite literally, without clothes.

Recoining money with a lower silver or gold content was an earlier version of turning on the printing press, and had similar effects: inflation, which operates as a tax on all holders of money claims, and in a worst-case scenario deprives them of the entire value of their claims. The debtors win, but in the extreme case, when money loses all its value, they lose out, too. Rulers therefore had to find a way to carefully balance the credibility of money and their need to expand resources. Raising taxes was not always an option, and became even more difficult once the major taxpaying classes obtained a voice in the matter. Debt finance was the obvious alternative, but debt had to be paid back even by a sovereign, at least in principle.

Suppose the Crown has two sources of revenue: tax and debt. Both have to be paid in silver or gold coins, but coins are limited and not evenly distributed throughout the country. Suppose also that private financiers have two sources of funding: deposits taken from customers and debt issued as notes. Goldsmiths, the early bankers, can accept anything as means of payment and will do so as long as they can be reasonably sure that they will be able to convert it into the money they need to pay off their own debt. If the Crown was able to make it attractive for goldsmiths to buy government debt and goldsmiths were allowed to pay their taxes with government debt, the monetary base could be expanded without debasing coins—with benefits for the Crown and the goldsmiths and, at least on the upside, for others as well, because access to credit becomes easier. For the scheme to work, the Crown had to enhance the attractiveness of its debt by making it freely transferable (it was issued in wooden "tallies"). In addition, tax collectors had to be assured that they could settle taxes with tallies rather than coins.

This is the system of interdependent public and private money that emerged in England over the course of the seventeenth century (Quinn 1994). It had to overcome a binding legal constraint, however: the tellers at the Exchequer's office were instructed to accept only coins for the settling of all taxes. The keepers of the Crown's books, the Treasury and its auditors, however, recorded payments in tallies as payments in coin (ibid., 120)—an "error" that was discovered only much later. Lastly, a financial intermediary was needed who enjoyed the trust of the leading tax collector. He would issue notes and use the proceeds to acquire government tallies. Holders of the goldsmiths' notes used them to settle the tax collectors' claims, who converted them into government tallies, which were presented for settling outstanding tax claims.

On the upside, all participants benefited from the scheme. However, it was not immune to distress. It had to collapse when the Crown defaulted on its debt. At this point, the tax collector would revert to a policy of "coins only" and anybody unable to pay was in default. The first ones to fall were taxpayers at the bottom of the hierarchy without a cushion of coin reserves. To add insult to injury, the notes issued by goldsmiths would also lose in value now that the Crown had defaulted, leaving them with worthless private money on hand. Those higher up in the hierarchy had more wealth and thus could better cushion the blow. More importantly, they would invariably be first in line to benefit from a relaxation of the rules of the game. For if they fell, the Crown would be in even deeper trouble. And so, on the occasion of the "Stop of the Exchequer" in 1672—technically a default of the Crown on its debt—the Crown advised its bookkeepers to accept private debt issued by certain goldsmiths for settling taxes (Quinn 1994, 26).

From here it was only a small step to create a payment system that dispensed with coins as means of payment and instead used paper notes backed by gold. England pegged its currency to gold in the early nineteenth century and gave the Bank of England, a private bank that had been established in 1694, the monopoly to issue notes (Knafo 2006). All other financial intermediaries that had previously competed with the Bank of England in issuing private moneys were nudged into becoming deposit-taking "commercial banks." The carrot used to induce them was the corporate form, which allowed the banks' owners to limit their liability and, by the same token, protect the banks' assets from the shareholders' creditors. Critically, the notes became the new currency in which taxes could be settled, and debt payments made.

Karl Marx (1867, chap. 31) saw clearly what an ingenious system had been created:

> The Bank of England began with lending its money to the Government at 8%; at the same time, it was empowered by Parliament to coin money out of the same capital, by lending it again to the public in the form of banknotes. It was allowed

> to use these notes for discounting bills, making advances on commodities, and for buying the precious metals. It was not long before this credit-money, made by the bank itself, became the coin in which the Bank of England made its loans to the State, and paid, on account of the State, the interest on the public debt. It was not enough that the bank gave with one hand and took back more with the other; it remained, even whilst receiving, the eternal creditor of the nation down to the last shilling advanced. Gradually it became inevitably the receptacle of the metallic hoard of the country, and the centre of gravity of all commercial credit.

The relations between the Bank of England and the Crown were crafted in law. Handing the monopoly for issuing the official note to this institution was meant to enhance financial stability. By the same token it institutionalized the close relation between states and banks. The practice of states financing banks and banks financing states is often condemned as an aberration of how finance ought to be conducted. Independent central banks and arm's-length regulation are meant to sever the cozy relation between states and banks, and public and private money, and create a truly private financial system, relying on the free exchange of moneys. Yet, it seems that our complex system of private and state moneys was begotten in sin—and would not exist in its current form without it. We can tweak it to give private parties more wiggle room (at the risk of having to bail them out ex post), or expand the scope of state money, thereby reducing the ability of private parties to place bets on the central banks' balance sheets. But without state money, private money systems would be too volatile to be scaled to national, much less global, size. And without private money, financial intermediation would be cut back from a money-generating, credit-expanding enterprise, to a simple payment system.

8.5 WEALTH INCUBATORS MADE IN LAW

Earlier we established that economic and political power can enhance the credibility of debtors. A similar outcome can be achieved with the help of legal devices that insulate assets from competing claims and thus protect them from economic downturns. The most common devices are trust and corporate law. They are devices that shield assets from different groups of claimants and thereby offer them a lifeline, whereas ordinary assets lack similar protection (Hansmann and Mattei 1998, Hansmann and Kraakman 2000). Most importantly, like property rights and negotiable instruments, these devices can be enforced against third parties that were not part of the deal when they were set up and may not even have heard about them. If recognized by law, the state's coercive powers can be brought to bear on enforcing them. States, in other words, are critical handmaidens in the production of wealth and the accumulation of capital.

By placing assets into a trust, a settlor removes them from his estate as a matter of law, even though he or she might still use them; the asset is now managed by the trustee, but creditors are barred from seizing them, because the settlor exercises only formal ownership rights without reaping their economic returns; and the interests of the beneficiary have not yet matured so that the creditors cannot put their hands on the asset either. In short, assets are insulated from all conceivable creditor claims; they can multiply without the kind of disturbances (claims, seizures, enforcement, etc.) that other assets face on a regular basis. The official life and role of the trust has been the protection of family wealth and the organization of funds that were devoted to philanthropic purposes. The "secret" life of the trust, however, is the field of commerce and financial investment (Langbein 1997).

Corporate law exerts similar effects. Shareholders who invest in a corporation lose control over these assets. They are now owned by the corporation, which is a legal entity in its own right. Shareholders can sell their shares (at least in publicly traded entities) but cannot take their money out. This also implies that the assets (not the shares) are now beyond the reach of their personal creditors. The corporation can have its own creditors, but does not have to worry about shareholders taking "their" money out, nor about the shareholders' creditors trying to enforce against them (Hansmann and Kraakman 2000, Ciepley 2013).

Trust and corporate law have become widely available legal devices. This was not always the case. Until well into the nineteenth century, establishing a corporation required special approval from state authorities (Pistor et al. 2002). This fact certainly limited access to the corporate form. In some countries minimum capital requirements are still in place. Even in the absence of quantitative barriers of this kind, the benefits of asset shielding and limited liability accrue primarily to those with access to lawyers and the ability to pay them.

This holds for the common law trust even more than for the highly standardized corporate form (or for statutory business trusts). The reason lies precisely in the lack of standardization, making those who seek legal protection more dependent on legal experts. For a long time, trusts were used primarily by wealthy elites. In England, the trust became more widely used only in the nineteenth century (Anderson 2010, Chesterman 1984). Still, to ensure compliance with the law, legal advice is often needed. And when trusts are put to new use—as has been done in asset securitization, the construction of collateral mortgage, debt, or loan obligations—more may be needed: active lobbying of legislatures to change trust or tax law to accommodate these changes.

Exemption from taxation is, of course, a key privilege. Historically, trusts were not taxed, because the value of the assets did not accrue to anyone in real time. Only at a future date would the beneficiary lay his hands on it, which became a taxable event. Even when trusts became widely used as commercial securitization vehicles, they remained tax-exempt. The reason was that the trusts served as simple pass-through-vehicles that left the investors (the beneficiaries) with the economic gains. In 1985, the US Congress extended this benefit to trusts used in securitization structures, even after the tranching of assets held by the trust left it to carry both risks and potential economic benefits (Bordon and Reiss 2014). Many observers have argued that absent this tax privilege, many securitization structures would have been non-viable. More generally, the past several decades have seen extensive changes of trust law in core jurisdictions around the globe to make it fit for the financial sector, most importantly to deflect liability of the trustee and ensure the longevity of the trust (Hofri-Winogradow 2015).

8.6 THE POWER OF LAW

The analysis so far suggests that different forms of money and the hierarchy they form are made in law, even if, in the last instance, discretionary power is needed to avoid the consequences of its tendency to self-destruct in financial crises.

Social systems of limited size can be successfully governed by informal systems of social norms or conventions established in trade and commerce (Greif 2006). More complex systems may require a central authority that promulgates the rules even if it lacks enforcement capacity (Hodgson 2009). Law differs from such systems in its scaling capacity: It helps standardize rights and obligations and enforces them well beyond closely knit communities, including among complete strangers. Law can even be scaled beyond the jurisdiction that first breathed life into it by transplantation (Berkowitz, Pistor, and Richard 2003), or by one state recognizing foreign law and offering its enforcement apparatus to enforce it (Watt 2010).

These mechanisms were already at play prior to the rise of nation states. As we have seen earlier, similar statutes on bills were enacted throughout Europe in the seventeenth century, and courts in faraway places recognized and enforced them. The rise of nation states and the establishment of national legal orders resulted in the harmonization of law within countries. However, it did not eliminate the need to standardize law across countries, or, alternatively, to ensure that one country's law would be recognized and enforced by the courts of a different country. As it turns out, recognizing foreign law and lending enforcement powers, as it were, is a much more powerful device for reducing the number of legal systems that are in play for certain activities.

An early example is the case of "regulatory competition" over corporate law in the United States. Corporate law is a matter of state law; states increasingly recognized the benefit of attracting corporations to their shore even if they did not do business in the state (Cary 1974). In the twentieth century, the small state of Delaware, which had few other constituencies but a legal bar with good connections to law firms in New York, took the lead in incorporation. Most of the largest companies in the country and many foreign firms are today incorporated in Delaware. In fact, the state charges corporations a higher franchise fee than what they would pay elsewhere. This is not all that surprising. What they receive in return is a corporate law that is made for business (Macey and Miller 1987). Delaware is an ideal hub for such a law, because it has no major constituencies, such as labor unions, who might have stood in the way of creating a law that placed managers in the driver's seat to further the interests of shareholders (Becker 1969).

The general lesson here is that laws can be dislodged from the polity that begets them. While states are territorially bounded and cannot unilaterally impose their laws extraterritorially, nothing prevents them from making their legal systems available for willing takers. All that these takers then have to do is to make sure that legal systems on foreign shores will recognize and enforce the choices they have made. These devices give ample room to avoid legal obligations across a range of issues, including tax law and financial regulation, without having to move operations. This is all done on paper by moving the place of incorporation or choosing the legal system that shall govern a set of transactions.

8.7 "WHERE IS MY SWAP LINE"?

No other sentence captures the view from the periphery—where market participants are *not* granted additional liquidity in financial crises—better than this question, posed in the middle of the Great Financial Crisis (Sester 2008). Sester, a senior fellow at the Council on Foreign Relations, was referring to the swap lines that the five major central banks (from the US, the UK, the Eurozone, Switzerland, and Japan) granted one another and some of them granted to selected central banks from emerging markets.

The underlying rationale for the swap lines that a handful of central banks (the C5—which morphed into the C6 when Canada joined the club) created in the midst of the crisis makes perfect sense. In a world of global trade and investments many entities owe payments in currencies other than their domestic currencies. To be able to pay, they must have access to foreign currencies. By entering into swap agreements, the five central banks (Canada was later added as number six) were able to signal to these entities that they would not run out of foreign exchange reserves, thus avoiding a run on the limited amount they themselves controlled. But the swap lines were not made available to everyone—only economies deemed sufficiently important to the country that offered the swap line received one. Swaps may be bilateral agreements, but the choice of partners is a unilateral, discretionary decision.

The same logic applies to domestic financial systems. The liquidity facilities that the US Federal Reserve Bank created during the Great Financial Crisis, based on its emergency lending powers, map exactly the hierarchy of moneys as viewed from the apex of the system: The first ones to receive access to this additional liquidity were the primary dealers that invested in US sovereign debt, followed by intermediaries that invested in sovereign debt, then followed by the intermediaries that provided much of the financial system with a stream of funding, namely the money market funds and so forth (Pistor 2013). Only in 2012 did the Federal Reserve start to pay attention to the periphery of the system: it announced a program to acquire mortgage-backed securities, offering relief to intermediaries holding securitized mortgages, and indirectly to homeowners as well.

An argument has been advanced that offering relief to homeowners should have been given priority over bailing out banks: highly levered households are unlikely to begin spending again, which is deemed critical for putting the economy back on track (Mian and Sufi 2014). In other words, giving those at the periphery of the system some financial wiggle room, for example by allowing them to restructure their mortgages and forcing banks to accept this, would have strengthened aggregate demand, and the economy as a whole would have left the recession faster. Larry Summers, a key advisor to President Obama during the critical period of crisis management, was candid about the reason for why this did not happen: it was politics, not economics (Summers 2014). Neither was it law, because with the right political backing a legal basis could have been created—indeed, this had to be done for banks as well once the discretionary emergency lending powers had been exhausted and longer-term measures, including the recapitalization of banks, were needed.

As compared to banks, homeowners found themselves in a bad spot in the crisis. Yes, they had taken on too much debt, but so had virtually every other market participant (Dynan and Kohn 2007). This is what happens in a system that churns out debt instruments en masse designed for mutual funds, pensions funds, and other intermediaries hungry for cheap, high-yielding assets. In the end, the legal structures that stratified claims and entities ex ante did not keep what they had promised when asset prices deteriorated across the board. Intermediaries holding too many assets that had turned toxic failed. The only safe asset at the end of the rope was state money, preferably issued by solvent states. No market participant had a legal right to be rescued, but some were while others were not.

In what order then should debtors be rescued in a crisis? Several options are conceivable. First, bailouts could be randomized. This certainly would avoid problems of moral hazard—the fear that actors would bet on another bailout next time around. It would also counter accusations of bias. On the downside, a randomized bailout strategy would disregard the priority of rights that private parties created earlier, for which at least some had paid a higher price in the expectation that certain rights would be stronger than others.

Therefore, a better strategy might be for bailouts to follow the order of legal entitlements that had been created earlier. Liquidation in bankruptcy can serve as a model for ranking the creditors of a defaulting debtor. As a general rule, in bankruptcy owners can pull out their assets from the debtors' possessions right away; secured creditors will be next, and among them those who secured an asset earlier come first. Unsecured creditors would receive only the leftovers. If this is what parties bargained for ex ante, it is not only fair but also efficient to enforce this ranking ex post.

The problem with this strategy is that the risk of some of the superior rights had been seriously underpriced. The financial intermediaries that produced and disseminated the new financial products, also referred to as the "sell-side" in contrast to the investors on the "buy-side," had been given subsidies in the form of tax exemptions, exemptions from bankruptcy rules, and implicit guarantees by the government-sponsored entities that invested heavily in these products. Unlike formal banks that have to pay for liquidity support in times of crisis, in the form of regulation and deposit insurance, the intermediaries that used structured finance to engage in off-balance-sheet banking never paid an insurance premium. They effectively free-rode on the balance sheets of financial intermediaries with access to the central banks that backed them with credit lines, guarantees, and went even beyond what they were legally obliged to do in an attempt to prevent the system's self-destruction. And since regulated banks had access to the balance sheet of the Fed, they effectively free-rode on the Fed's unlimited access to high-powered money.

8.8 THE QUESTION OF JUSTICE

As suggested earlier, legal hierarchies as such are not necessarily a challenge to justice. They become one, however, if they go unchecked and if their distributional consequences are unjustified. As the above analysis suggests, our legally constructed money system is beset by unchecked hierarchies and unjustified distributions of the losses that are inherent to the system's operation.

Even if any system of interlocking credit relations is hierarchical, the system that imploded in the Great Financial Crisis had, and arguably still has, peculiar features. It has given private actors ample opportunity to choose the legal systems and the rules that best fit their needs; it has backed up the development of highly speculative markets in new types of financial assets by granting them subsidies in the form of exemptions from laws that everybody else must comply with; and it has outsourced the determination as to what constitutes a priority right for purposes of special treatment in the law to the private sector. A staff report published in 2006 by the Federal Reserve Bank of St Louis estimates that the contingent liability of mortgage-backed assets alone amounted to US$288 billion at the time (Quigley 2006). No wonder the system overheated.

When the system imploded, its costs were born neither by those who caused the implosion nor by those who had benefited most, that is, the private intermediaries and their employees who had received high-powered, incentive-boosting bonuses. Rather, the costs were socialized. It is often argued that the US government actually made a profit from the securities it acquired from the entities it bailed out when it later sold them back to the market. That, however, is a highly skewed calculation. It does not account for the many entities that did not get liquidity support and did in fact fold, and for the economic and social losses that resulted from their collapse. It includes no estimate for the costs of moral hazard. Most importantly, it ignores the effect that the selective liquidity support has on the structure of the system. It benefits the players at the apex of the system—which happen to overlap largely with its greatest beneficiaries—and leaves a disproportionate share of the costs for the periphery to deal with. In effect it vindicates practices designed to allow some to free-ride on the liquidity support that only central banks can provide.

In short, the hierarchy manifested in the Great Financial Crisis and in the response to it is unjustified. The distribution of liquidity boosts that were supposed to mitigate the crisis followed the hierarchical patterns that had been established with the help of the legal subsidies described earlier. No real justification has been provided for why these, rather than more peripheral market participants, were given priority. Last but not least, the agents determining who deserved a lifeline exercised unchecked discretionary powers.

Central banks, of course, have been constructed as independent agencies. Their major task is price stability, with employment added in some statutes.[2] The major villain from the perspective of price stability were spend-drift governments. When the major lubricant for economic growth is not (moderate) inflation but aggressive credit expansion, watching over the public printing press of money, however, is no longer sufficient. Instead, the private money-creation machine needs to be brought under control. Moreover, independence from political interference is not sufficient; impartiality in exercising the powers of central banking is of equal importance.

[2] See also Chapter 10 (Dietsch, this volume) on the distributive consequences of central bank policies.

Inflation has been successfully fought by establishing independent central banks that prevent governments and ministries of finance from turning on the printing press when it best fits their need. What prevents us from designing governance structures that would ensure not only the independence, but also the impartiality, of central banks? The answer to this question brings us back to the original sin: it is government finance. Ultimately governments depend on private money creation for two reasons: to fund the government itself and to provide an alternative to inflation for keeping economic growth on track, namely credit expansion. Financial intermediaries can provide both, but they are not offering this for free. The price they demand is yield and safety, and ideally a combination of both. This makes little sense economically or from a perspective of justice, but governments have agreed to this Faustian bargain mostly for political reasons. In the end, governments, and the ones whom they will hold liable for standing in for their debt with their tax money, will have to foot the bill for a system that is bound to leave a lot of damage in its trails.

The reforms that have been put in place since the beginning of the Great Financial Crisis have closed numerous gaps that previously provided the niches for rapid private credit expansion. But they have also failed to address many structural features of our financial system that are bound to be exploited for private gain and wealth creation. The primary target of financial regulation are still banks. Only at the level of systemically important entities are non-bank financial intermediaries brought into the fore. That leaves ample room for non-banks below this threshold to continue to offer banking services without facing the regulatory costs of banking. Financial regulators have coordinated rule-making in the Financial Stability Board, thus reducing the scope for regulatory arbitrage. They are, however, fighting a difficult battle as the private sector is at least equally well organized, speaks with fewer voices, and retains control over one of the most powerful toolboxes: to relocate activities to jurisdictions that are willing to accommodate them if not now, then in the future.

The real battle, however, is fought not at the rule-setting stage, but when it comes to implementation. Even when rules have been standardized, states retain substantial discretion in interpreting these standards when transposing them into local law and enforcing them—or failing to do so. We know from the experience with Basel I, the first attempt to standardize prudential regulation for banks, that even standardized rules leave ample room for regulatory arbitrage. Although Basel III is tighter than its predecessors, there is simply no legal system without gaps and room for interpretation (Pistor and Xu 2003). This is where the next battles will be fought. Not everyone will be able to participate, and most of the deals will once more take place not in the bright daylight of parliamentary sessions or courts, but behind closed doors, in the neon-lit offices of law firms and regulators.

REFERENCES

Anderson, J. Stuart. 2010. "Trust and Trustees." In *The Oxford History of the Laws of England: 1820–1914 Private Law*, edited by William Cornish, J. Stuart Anderson, Ray Cocks, Michael Lobban, Patrick Polden, and Keith Smith. Oxford: Oxford University Press, 232–94.

Becker, Loftus E. 1969. "Law for Sale: A Study of the Delaware Corporation Law of 1967." *University of Pennsylvania Law Review* 117, 861–98.

Berkowitz, Dan, Katharina Pistor, and Jean-François Richard. 2003. "Economic Development, Legality, and the Transplant Effect." *European Economic Review* 47, 165–95.

Bordon, T. Bradley, and David J. Reiss. 2014. "REMIC Tax Enforcement as Financial-Market Regulator." *University of Pennsylvania Journal of Business Law* 16, 663–736.

Cary, William L. 1974. "Federalism and Corporate Law: Reflections upon Delaware." *Yale Law Journal* 83, 663.

Chesterman, M. R. 1984. "Family Settlements on Trust: Landowners and the Rising Bourgeoisie." In *Law, Economy and Society, 1750–1914*, edited by Gerry R. Rubin and David Sugarman. Oxford: Oxford University Press, 124–67.

Ciepley, David. 2013. "Beyond Public and Private: Toward a Political Theory of the Corporation." *American Political Science Review* 107(01), 139–58.

Coase, Ronald H. 1937. "The Nature of the Firm." *Economica* 4(16), 386–405.

Desan, Christine. 2015. *Making Money: Coin, Currency, and the Coming of Capitalism*. Oxford: Oxford University Press.

Dynan, Karen E., and Donald L. Kohn. 2007. "The Rise in U.S. Household Indebtedness: Causes and Consequences." *Finance and Economic Discussion Series, Federal Reserve Board, Washington DC* (37).

Greif, Avner. 2006. *Institutions and the Path to the Modern Economy: Lessons from Medieval Trade*. Cambridge: Cambridge University Press.

Hansmann, Henry., and Ugo Mattei. 1998. "The Functions of Trust Law: A Comparative Legal and Economic Analysis." *New York University Law Review* 73(2), 434–79.

Hansmann, Henry, and Reinier Kraakman. 2000. "The Essential Role of Organizational Law." *Yale Law Journal* 110, 387–475.

Hodgson, Geoffrey M. 2009. "On the Institutional Foundations of Law: The Insufficiency of Custom and Private Ordering." *Journal of Economic Issues* 43(1), 143–66.

Hofri-Winogradow, Adam S. 2015. "The Stripping of the Trust: A Study in Legal Evolution." http://ssrn.com/abstract=2441709 (accessed October 26, 2016).

Hyman, Louis. 2011. *Debtor Nation: The History of America in Red Ink*. Princeton and Oxford: Princeton University Press.

Knafo, Samuel. 2006. "The Gold Standard and the Origins of the Modern International Monetary System." *Review of International Political Economy* 13(1), 78–102.

Langbein, John L. 1997. "The Secret Life of the Trust: The Trust as an Instrument of Commerce." *Yale Law Journal* 107(1), 165–89.

Levi, Margaret. 1988. *Of Rule and Revenue*. Berkeley: University of California Press.

Macey, Jonathan, and Geoffrey Miller. 1987. "Toward an Interest-Group Theory of Delaware Corporate Law." *Texas Law Review* 65, 469–523.

Manne, Ronald J. 1996. "Searching for Negotiability in Payment and Credit Systems." *UCLA Law Review* 1996–7, 951–1007.

Marx, Karl. 1867. *Capital.* Vol. I: http://www.marxists.org/archive/marx/works/1867-c1/ch31.htm (accessed October 26, 2016).

Mehrling, Perry. 2000. "Minsky and Modern Finance: The Case of Long Term Capital Management. " *Journal of Portfolio Management* 26(2), 81–9.

Mehrling, Perry. 2012. "The Inherent Hierarchy of Money." In *Festschrift for Duncan Foley*. New York, NY, 394–404.

Mian, Atif, and Amir Sufi. 2014. *House of Debt: How They (and You) Caused the Great Recession, and How We Can Prevent It from Happening Again*. Chicago: University of Chicago Press.

North, Douglass Cecil. 1990. *Institutions, Institutional Change, and Economic Performance*. Cambridge: Cambridge University Press.

Pistor, Katharina. 2013. "A Legal Theory of Finance." *Journal of Comparative Economics* 41(2), 315–30.

Pistor, Katharina, Yoram Keinan, Jan Kleinheisterkamp, and Mark West. 2002. "The Evolution of Corporate Law." *University of Pennsylvania Journal of International Economic Law* 23(4), 791–871.

Pistor, Katharina, and Chenggang Xu. 2003. "Incomplete Law." *Journal of International Law and Politics* 35(4), 931–1013.

Powell, Walter W. 1990. "Neither Market nor Hierarchy: Network Form of Organization." *Research in Organizational Behavior* 12, 295–336.

Quigley, John M. 2006. "Federal Credit and Insurance Programs: Housing." *Federal Reserve Bank of St. Louis Staff Reports* (July/August).

Quinn, Stephen Francis. 1994. "Banking Before the Bank: London's Unregulated Goldsmith-Bankers, 1660–1694." PhD thesis, University of Illinois at Urbana-Champaign.

Rogers, James Steven. 1995. *The Early History of the Law of Bills and Notes: A Study of the Origins of Anglo-American Commercial Law* Cambridge: Cambridge University Press.

Sen, Amartya K. 1999. *Development as Freedom*. New York: Random House.

Sester, Brad. 2008. "Where Is My Swap Line? And Will the Diffusion of Financial Power Balkanize the Global Response to a Broadening Crisis?" *Council on Foreign Relations Follow the Money Blog* (October 18).

Summers, Larry. 2014. "Summers on House of Debt." *Financial Times*, 6 June.

Tilly, Charles. 1985. "War Making and State Making as Organized Crime." In *Bringing the State Back In*, edited by Peter Evans, Dieter Rueschemeyer, and Theda Skocpol. Cambridge: Cambridge University Press, 169–91.

Watt, Horatia Muir. 2010. "'Party Autonomy' in International Contracts: From the Makings of a Myth to the Requirements of Global Governance." *European Review of Contract Law* 6(3), 250–83.

9

Investor rights as nonsense—on stilts

Aaron James

> [T]here are no such things as natural rights ... anterior to the establishment of government ... [T]he expression is merely figurative; ... the moment you attempt to give it a literal meaning it leads to error, and to that sort of error that leads to mischief—to the extremity of mischief.
>
> Jeremy Bentham, "Anarchical Fallacies," 1843

9.1 INTRODUCTION

To invest in a foreign country is to take a gamble for profit. To take a gamble for profit is to assume the risk of suffering a loss, with a certain upshot for one's rights. In assuming the risk voluntarily, one forgoes any claim to be compensated, should one's luck go south. So we assume, at the blackjack table, and in speculative trading. The same goes, it would seem, in the global marketplace, in investment relationships across borders, whether by way of foreign direct investment (FDI) or financial investment, including investment in foreign government bonds. The foreign investor voluntarily assumes the risk of suffering a loss, and forgoes all claims to compensation when expected profits fail to materialize.

Things look different if the risks and prospects turned out not to be as they were made to seem, ex ante—if "the game" was rigged, or changed unfairly, without "fair warning," beyond what could be expected in the kind of gamble being taken. Then either the gambler or the investor could reasonably claim compensation, ex post, on grounds of infidelity.

This difference is important. If someone were so bold as to claim a right of compensation after his luck went sour—as against the casino, the market maker, or the foreign government—when he did indeed assume the risks voluntarily, with no unfair play afterward, that, I must say, would be rather rich. It would also be confused: the man would exhibit a certain confusion about the nature of the risks he took, in view of the social understandings and expectations that give them a proper place. (The casino head might say, "Sorry, sir, this *is* a casino, you understand.") To press a claim in legal proceedings, while demanding cash compensation of tens or hundreds of millions of dollars, for example, would be to speak, as Jeremy Bentham might say, a sort of confused "nonsense."

Just such nonsense has come to pervade international economic law, in the recent proliferation of investment treaties.[1] In the new investor-state dispute settlement (ISDS) systems, foreign firms are granted a special legal privilege to initiate proceedings against a government before a tribunal of private lawyers, in order to press demands for cash compensation (of millions or billions of dollars) for an alleged failure of the government to fulfill its treaty obligations, in ways that diminish the value of the firm's investments. The new agreements go beyond the general principles of customary international law, which already ban the direct expropriation of tangible property. They add a broad prohibition on the "indirect expropriation" of foreign investor profits—even when a government never seizes an asset,[2] and even when the alleged losses result from regulation for the public interest, on environmental, health, or safety matters (e.g. toxin bans, nuclear power bans, natural resource policies, plain packaging rules for cigarettes, etc.).[3] The "safeguard" provisions that allow public interest regulation are vaguely formulated and readily open to dismissal (perhaps as "diplomatic" language rather than "law"). When such regulations are deemed not to have been adopted appropriately, consistent with "due process" and "fair and equitable," "non-arbitrary," "non-discriminatory" treatment of foreign investors, governments can be and often are required to pay huge sums in compensation for alleged damages. Ecuador, for example, was asked to pay $2.3bn to a US oil firm in 2013 in part to compensate for lost expected profits.

Many lawyers have argued that investor-state arbitration is a travesty of procedural justice.[4] Domestic courts can be ignored, or their decisions

[1] The move to go beyond the World Trade Organization's (WTO) Trade Related Investment Measures (TRIMS) started with the North American Free Trade Agreement (NAFTA), which then gave rise to numerous follow-up bilateral investment treaties (BITs) or regional agreements, the latest of which is the proposed Trans Pacific Partnership (TPP) and Trans Atlantic Trade and Investment Partnership (TTIP). The emergent investment agreements amount to something of a "regime," because they have much the same NAFTA-like content, and have been crafted chiefly around rich world (especially US) preferences and "offered" to developing countries.

[2] "Indirect expropriation" can apply to any number of assets. The US Supreme Court limits compensable expropriation under the US Constitution's Fifth Amendment "regulatory takings" to real property (such as real estate).

[3] Some proposed annexes seek to limit "indirect" expropriation to either indefinite or severe deprivations of property. A clearer proposal simply states that policies designed and applied to achieve public benefit do not constitute indirect expropriation.

[4] See e.g. this open letter to US officials regarding TPP and TTIP: http://www.afj.org/wp-content/uploads/2015/03/ISDS-Letter-3.11.pdf (accessed October 26, 2016).

superseded, often with no further appeals process, and little oversight or public accountability of the private lawyers that serve as arbitrators, many of whom are of questionable impartiality, for rotating between roles as arbitrators and corporate attorneys.[5] The proceedings and settlements are often kept secret, without public reference to established jurisprudence, or indeed expertise directly relevant to public interest regulation.[6] Could this be a first step toward the rule of law? Not without the exhaustion of domestic remedies and, ultimately, proper courts, an independent judiciary, the full due process of law, along with a right of appeal (perhaps first to any federal or regional courts, and then to the World Trade Organization (WTO) Appellate Body, as the final arbiter).[7]

Procedural justice aside, why should governments be obliged to tailor public interest regulations with a concern for investor losses, at a risk of paying compensation? Although investment rules now come packaged in trade agreements, from a legal perspective, they have different historical and political rationales. Investment treaties typically protected tangible foreign property holdings against direct expropriation (e.g. of extractive industry assets). And until recently, trade agreements were about increasing the flow of goods, services, and capital. Why link them? Some lawyers find a rationale in the supply chains that cross borders, which often work within the multinational corporation: if the firm lacks assured property holdings under a foreign government, it will not keep trade flows flowing. While this rationale has limitations (it applies to China, but less well to Africa), I will suggest a similar way of evaluating them: the two regime types are expressions of a common underlying economic practice. As joined within regional or mega-regional agreements, the new agreements thus raise larger questions of justice in global finance. With capital markets having gone global, a flaw in their legal structures can itself be a distributive injustice, as well as exacerbate further injustices in the way wealth is distributed within and across societies.

In this chapter, I argue that certain ideas of moral "investor rights" exhibit a confusion about the nature of an investment, and the social relations of international trade that give such risk-taking its social purpose. Insofar as foreign investors lack independent rights, this amounts to a partial challenge to a "cosmopolitan" vision—perhaps of a Lockean or libertarian variety—that

[5] Arbitration is regulated either within the Convention on Settlement of International Investment Disputes (the ICSID Convention), or under the UNCITRAL Rules, where the New York Convention provides an enforcement mechanism. This usually affords only modest process checks, for example against obvious bias, insufficient preparation time, and annulment of awarded damages on technical grounds.

[6] Though some tribunals choose to allow expert testimony and accept amicus briefs.

[7] For a similarly broad challenge to arbitration in domestic legal systems, see Fiss (1984). For further criticism, see Van Harten (2007).

would abstract away from the national and international social relations that embed the global economy as we know it.

Some lawyers note that the investment agreements do not treat investment losses, per se, as a cause of legal action.[8] Loss of profits is simply a measure of the damage done by an alleged independent breach of treaty obligations. When damages are awarded, it is a remedy for breach of a prior agreement. Fidelity to prior agreements is the only issue: investors only have a right not to have the promised investment "game" changed in the course of play. It is only when such unfaithfulness can be proven that compensation can be demanded in practice.

This picture invites a misleading degree of clarity about what states can be said to have "promised" ahead of time in generally framed treaty provisions. The tribunals decide the scope and content of state obligations, by deciding what treatment of foreign firms is "fair and equitable," or "arbitrary," "discrimination," or a failure of "due process." Such open-ended provisions must be interpreted, and whether because any interpretation must express a personal preference, or draw from a personal sense of principle, we should ask whether a panel of private lawyers, sympathetic to corporate interests (because at other times working for them), could perchance entertain what they might call "the rights of investors." This reasoning, I claim, is a kind of confused nonsense. As long as it remains a live possibility (it may in fact explain any number of recent awards[9]), there is a standing risk of what Bentham calls the "sort of error that leads to mischief—to the extremity of mischief."

The picture just suggested is open to a natural rights interpretation. Promises and contracts—especially sovereign debt contracts—may seem to give rise to natural rights and obligations. I will develop this thought in detail later. For the moment, I assume there are no such natural investor rights. I consider both utilitarian and social contract theory conceptions, and argue that the appeal to fidelity is insufficient to justify the new investment treaties. I then return to the question of whether natural rights might make up the difference.

9.2 AN ERROR OF PRESUPPOSITION

We can begin by granting key elements of any investment regime. Let us assume the importance of strong domestic property rights, legal rights against direct expropriation without compensation, and equal treatment of nationals and foreigners within jurisdictions. We can even grant that strong investment

[8] See https://www.mcgill.ca/fortier-chair/isds-open-letter (accessed October 26, 2016).

[9] As one sympathetic summary of tribunal interpretations put it: "The power to regulate operates within the limits of rights conferred upon the investor" (Dolzer 2014, 21).

treaties are essential in certain special cases. Certain countries, for instance, may require a treaty in the recent style in order to attract capital for essential infrastructure. Perhaps domestic legal reform that would reassure investors is not in the cards, at least in the short run. While such cases may once have been common, if they have since become exceptional (as I suggest below), the question is whether recent investment regimes are rightly interpreted and enforced by appeal to any pre-agreement investor rights to compensation.

Even Bentham would admit that foreign investors "have rights" under the recent investment agreements, in an institutional sense of the phrase. In a legal sense, firms now can gamble for profit in foreign countries without forgoing all claims to compensation when their gambles go sour, provided an appropriate cause of legal action. It is only talk of pre-agreement rights that Bentham would call "nonsense" of the sort that leads to mischief. In the present context, I side firmly with Bentham: talk of pre-agreement investor rights is not simply mistaken, but confused. That is to say, any putative "investor rights," in *a pre-agreement sense that would call for such agreements in the first place, or, once established, partly settle their content in legal practice,* are confused about the nature of an investment and the social context in which investment proceeds.

Bentham is of course not one for understatement, and it turns out he was behind the times about rights discourse in general, which has become the defining discourse of modernity. But we needn't follow his blanket denial of all non-institutional rights to see his point about foreign "investor rights" in particular. Even for Bentham, talk of pre-institutional "rights" is not *unintelligible.* Unlike words that simply lack meaning (e.g. "a round square"), Bentham himself was able to say what propositions would be implied if rights talk were "meaningful." In his famous animadversions against rights, Bentham called the French Revolution's Declaration of Rights "a perpetual vein of nonsense, flowing from a perpetual abuse of words," by which he meant, "words without a meaning, *or* with a meaning too flatly false to be maintained by anybody" (1843, 497).

The phrase "a meaning too flatly false" suggests an error of presupposition. A particular rights claim (e.g. "The ACME corporation has a right against Uruguay to compensation") need not be unintelligible ("words without a meaning"). Instead, it can have certain moral and social presuppositions, whether in the existence of legal institutions, as Bentham held, or some other moral and social backdrop (e.g. the practices and expectations specified later), which turn out to be false. For when a claim's presuppositions are false, the claim itself is not either true or false, but rather lacking in a truth-value (Frege 1980). So the statement "ACME has a right to compensation for its losses against Uruguay" may be "not true," either by being false, or by lacking a truth-value, for a presuppositional error. And if calling an error of presupposition "nonsense" seems overstated, one might simply call it "bluff," or what Harry Frankfurt calls "bullshit": a way of speaking without regard for the truth, perhaps for reasons of power and interest (Frankfurt 2005).

It would matter if talk of special pre-legal, foreign "investor rights" is a style of nonsense. No right would then be infringed if established investor provisions were abolished, or eviscerated, or simply ignored. Countries could rightly refuse to sign investment agreements in the first place; or withdraw from prior commitments (as South Africa and Indonesia have); or add reservations to various provisions (as Australia has in regards to the Trans-Pacific Partnership); or simply reinterpret prior agreements in the service of their respective publics, if withdrawal or renegotiation is not presently an option. Investors may protest in the name of their "rights." But Bentham will have offered an apt riposte: "reasons for wishing there were such things as rights, are not rights;—a reason for wishing that a certain rights were established, is not that right—want is not supply—hunger is not bread" (1843, 501).

For Bentham the utilitarian, what institutional rights foreign investors have should depend entirely on whether their establishment would promote overall welfare. Yet quite aside from his utilitarianism, I take his suspicions of rights-talk to capture something important, which I hope to articulate without his strident rejection of the meaninglessness of anything non-utilitarian. To that end, I explain why the Bentham-style critique is better posed from a social contract perspective, in view of a practice-based conception of fairness in international trade (James 2012). I set out a positive view of moral and social presuppositions of investor rights claims, and explain how such claims could exhibit a presuppositional error. This in turn has critical force against natural rights conceptions of investor rights. The idea of natural investor rights can gain strength from the limitations of utilitarianism, and a social contract alternative undercuts this source of support. Its idea of fairness also absorbs the force of any further talk of "natural rights," which in turn raises the question of what, if anything, calling them "natural" might add.

9.3 EXPEDIENCY

For the utilitarian, there is a balance to strike between justice and the general welfare, or what J. S. Mill called "expediency." In domestic society, a special judicial system for investors would introduce an intolerable inequality into what Mill calls the basic rights and liberties that define the "groundwork" of our common existence (1987). Yet international investment agreements operate at a different level than a domestic legal system. They relate foreign investors to governments and their whole publics, and they could in theory pose no direct challenge to the basic rights and liberties of individuals (perhaps with further procedural reforms). As Mill would agree, there is then at least room to consider whether special legal provisions are justifiable on grounds of general social welfare. And indeed this seems to be the central rationale for their widespread adoption. Foreign direct investment is by all accounts key for development. The confidence gained from special privilege may thus serve the larger system of international trade, by tending to induce foreign investment and larger economic benefits, especially for developing countries, but also for the greater wealth of nations.

But do the new investor privileges advance social welfare in general, aside from special instances? In fact, there is little reason to expect them to redound to overall economic benefit to most if not all societies. The benefits are negligible or modest, despite significant costs, or at least the claim that they bring significant net benefits is unsupported in historical experience and of dubious merit in the overall cost-benefit analysis (Sachs and Sauvant 2009, chaps 12–16).

For starters, the costs are significant. Governments face large legal expenses (they are often asked to share tribunal costs, to the tune of many millions of dollars, even when they win), and must make huge compensatory payments when they lose. For many developing countries, these can amount to a considerable portion of their national budgets. Ecuador's $2.3bn settlement (since renegotiated) equaled its yearly national health care budget. For developing countries, payment often must come with cuts in services to very poor people. In addition, investor provisions arguably bring a "regulatory chill," for fear of corporate displeasure, even when laws or regulations are agreed to be in the public interest (Tienhaara 2011). The mere risk of expensive legal action—with corporate heads brandishing the threat of arbitral action—may hobble the formation of an effective political consensus. While some studies suggest that government officials pay little attention to international law, and so are not deterred in the slightest, this cannot be expected to continue, as arbitration cases receive greater attention. Perhaps some forms of "accountability" are productive. Yet in the present case, the risks of regulatory chill are significant for the public interest, and often for poor people, who suffer dearly in both losses and forgone benefits. Those costs could of course be offset by large enough benefits, once summed or averaged, from a utilitarian perspective. Yet, crucially, marginal benefits in increasing long-term investment of the new investor privileges are not significant, if there are such benefits at all. For the imposition on their politics and the cost of paying damages, there is little reason not to expect many or most societies to suffer net losses, or at best break even (Hallward-Driemeier 2003).

Here, again, the general utility of maintaining a secure system of property and of strong domestic judicial systems is not in question. Such systems would include firmly enforced rules against arbitrary expropriation of tangible and perhaps some financial property. While not all capital flows are productive (a point now widely recognized after the 2008 crisis), historical experience suggests that foreign direct investment in longer-term ventures, in countries with high-quality institutions, is very important for economic development. This is a key rationale for maintaining a world of relatively free trade. The present question is only whether the new investor privileges can be expected to increase longer-term investment *as compared to the investments that would be undertaken anyway, under relatively free trade.* We have a robust global economy, and we can expect a good measure of foreign investment for reasons of profit opportunity and comparative advantage. The question is how much *more* investment, of the beneficial variety, if any, is attracted *simply* by establishing special investor provisions.[10]

The provisions hope to increase investor "confidence" of profitable opportunities. Little is to be gained, however, simply by reducing the risk of direct government expropriation. This is true even where firms may have little recourse in weak domestic courts, which may be biased against foreigners. For direct expropriation is relatively rare (Minor 1994), and limited to especially weak governments with a poor public track record, which investors can readily peruse. Among investors that survey general investment conditions, there will be little improvement in their confidence.

Recent investment provisions go beyond this: in effect, governments also assume part or all of the risk of failure, or performance below expectations, because of regulatory changes. This will surely ease investor jitters. Yet the question is still why the marginal gain in investor confidence should translate into a significant economic difference for a country, by motivating investment decisions that would not otherwise be taken. There might be no such translation.[11] Indeed, some developing countries, such as Ecuador and South Africa, have withdrawn from investment treaties and seen FDI inflows hold steady or even increase.

Surely the prudent foreign investor will not need to look beyond a prospective country's economic fundamentals, growth prospects in favored industries, and its general regulatory environment, in view of its recent history. If the profit opportunities are not evident, or plainly less attractive than an alternative opportunity elsewhere, the investment presumably should not be undertaken, as even an ISDS will not assuredly spare one from a losing venture.

But perhaps the opportunity to profit is merely doubtful, or as likely to bring losses or merely break even. Even here, surely the prudent investor would

[10] Here the evidence is mixed and inconclusive. According to Aisbett (2007), even when increased FDI flows correlate with participation in bilateral investment treaties (BITs), they are not caused by it, since governments with increasing flows are more likely to enter investment agreements. Some studies do find a positive correlation between FDI flows and BIT participation, for example Egger and Merlo (2007), Lesher and Miroudot (2006), Neumayer and Spess (2005). For a skeptical reply to the latter study, see Yackee (2007).

[11] For a skeptical assessment see Yackee (2010).

not be so reassured as to opt for a very costly enterprise, simply for knowing he or she could seek arbitration, in hopes of *some* measure of compensation. Very good prospects of significant net benefit should be in the cards already, simply on economic fundamentals and the quality of the general regulatory environment.[12]

Many firms will not be so prudent, and bet poorly on profit opportunities. Perhaps special legal privileges will add to their confidence, allowing them to let loose on a gamble. But why seek to attract *them*? Why create an incentive for bad gambles, with the public potentially on the hook for the firm's losses? Or worse: predatory firms may seek to exploit the privileges of investor-state arbitration, by hiring the right lawyers; or activist firms may relish having a "veto" over unwanted regulation for the public interest, for being able to credibly threaten a legal challenge. The social costs of such profiteering and meddling may outweigh the modest benefits of additional investment. Given the risks of imprudence, herd behavior, groupthink, and information cascades, the cautious course is to not encourage the wrong sorts of investors while trying to attract firms seeking mutually advantageous economic gain in the long run. And one can best do that by improving the general quality of the country's institutions, and by strengthening the courts and the rule of law with no special regard for anyone.

Investor provisions do, on the other hand, bring gains to firms, to the benefit of managers, workers, shareholders, savers, and retirees. Yet even relatively large money values spread across many people who are relatively rich by global standards will translate into only slight marginal welfare benefits in the aggregate. Given the diminishing marginal utility of any economic value, benefits to richer people will be steeply discounted and then outweighed by large costs to large numbers of poor people, in wage, pension, or services cuts.

If indeed the rising tide of investment treaties does not best advance the cause of overall human well-being, the utilitarian will conclude that special provisions for foreign investors should simply be abolished, and in the meanwhile disregarded, in favor of more productive institutional and judicial measures. For all we have said so far, no moral right of the investors would be infringed. According to the (act or rule) utilitarian, once everyone's interests are counted, there are no moral rights against what (acts or institutions) would bring about the greatest overall welfare. As Bentham says, "there is no *right*, which ought not to be maintained so long as it is upon the whole advantageous to the society that it should be maintained, so there is no right

[12] There is limited evidence that BITs substitute for institutional quality (Neumayer and Spess 2005, 85). Salacuse and Sullivan (2005, 139) suggest that BITs mainly reflect quality of institutions.

which, when the abolition of it is advantageous to society, should not be abolished" (1843, 501).

9.4 FROM WELFARE TO FAIRNESS

This argument simply assumes a general utilitarian rejection of non-institutional rights, but that may seem rather implausible. Do we not, for example, have moral rights against any number of kinds of theft (not to mention not being kicked, deceived, etc.), at the very least? While the utilitarian might agree for instrumental reasons, it does not seem that a person's claim against theft so directly depends on potential changes in aggregated (summed or averaged) welfare. Might foreign investors then have moral rights as well (if not the firm itself, then its beneficiaries), quite aside from what promotes general welfare? Specifically, why see any very sharp difference in "direct" and "indirect" expropriation with respect to people's rights? If people have a moral right, in some sense, against arbitrary or unfair treatment, why couldn't foreign investors have a moral right, in some sense, against the government actions that investment treaties are supposed to prohibit, including "indirect expropriation" of the value of their investments, and/or any failure of "fair and equitable treatment"? Perhaps they simply have basic moral rights of property like anyone, but face special vulnerabilities under a foreign sovereign government, which can often act with impunity. If the new special investment provisions were the *only* way to protect them against such special vulnerabilities, and they came at a modest societal cost, couldn't they be morally necessary, out of due respect for the investors themselves, quite aside from general welfare in the final tally?

We might elaborate this possibility within a contractualist moral theory, in the style of T. M. Scanlon (1998). In considering a question of "what we owe to each other," we compare the various interests or claims of different parties, as they are each affected under different institutional arrangements. We consider the force of their different potential objections, founded on those interests or claims, comparing each affected party's objections serially, taking each one by one—without summing or averaging the total gains or losses across the different lives affected (except under special conditions). We then make a judgment of which objection is the strongest (the "reasonable" complaint). A proposed institution (such as an investor treaty) is justifiable to all affected if no one could reasonably reject it in favor of some feasible alternative (such as having no treaty)—which is to say, if any objection to the proposed treaty would be weaker than any objection to the alternatives.

In the present context, then, foreign investors would be owed special investment provisions under certain conditions. They are worse off without them, and insofar as this opportunity cost can be considered a morally relevant interest or claim, they may be said to have an objection to their absence. This objection could also be decisive, and the provisions owed to them, if no other affected party has a comparatively strong objection to their establishment, in view of the institutional alternatives (e.g. strengthened domestic and international courts).

Do foreign investors thus have "moral rights," in a non-institutional sense that Bentham would deny? Not necessarily. Scanlon himself (2003, 4, 99) suggests an "instrumentalist" view of rights, in which rights are conclusions of the foregoing moral reasoning rather than its starting points. What I called a *relevant* interest or claim, in contrast with a mere interest or preference, might be called "a right," in a weak sense, if it is admitted that rights are to be balanced or compared in the way interests or claims are to be compared.[13] But then such rights would not necessarily require special protections: the case for that would still have to be made; the above form of argument would still have to be filled in. Alternatively, the term "a right" might be reserved for only those relevant interests or claims that suffice to ground a moral obligation (Raz 1984), in the present context, by presenting the strongest complaint. But then the question is again whether foreign investors can indeed reasonably complain of being denied of the new special investment provisions, perhaps given their special vulnerabilities to mistreatment by a sovereign state.

The answer, I take it, is that they cannot: they have no reasonable objection to an alternative legal regime. They have no *relevant* claim to investor-state arbitration, per se, as against an alternative regime of domestic, regional, and international courts, which affords the full due process of law without special legal privileges. They may be less likely to win compensation for damages against governments, and they may well lose advantages of credibly threatening arbitration. Yet it is hard to see how this power advantage, per se, is morally relevant, without further consideration of some more substantive material or political interests; might, after all, does not make right. And even if we give some weight to their economic and reliance interests, as we should, it is nevertheless governments and their publics that have the weightier objection, for they are in effect asked to pay for the privilege of passing laws in the public interest.

Procedure aside, the main argument for special legal rights is substantive. Investors might indeed have grounds to reasonably complain of their absence if (1) the risks and prospects presented to them, ex ante, turned out not to be as they were made or allowed to seem, and (2) "fair warning" of a consequential change was not provided, when investors had a chance to avoid suffering

[13] Thompson (1992) treats "claims" in this potentially unweighty way (without the contractualist backdrop).

significant loss.[14] Perhaps a firm did voluntarily assume the risks initially, with a reasonable alternative option (investing elsewhere, or saving instead). Yet this fact may lose its significance, not because of changing market conditions, but because of a regulatory change that adversely affected the firm's industry or relative position among its competition. When reasonably presumed circumstances of choice were altered, the fact that a firm *initially* assumed a risk, voluntarily, may not then entail liability for the resulting outcomes, after the dust settles. In theory at least, it could then legitimately press a claim to compensation for any damage done, and for enforcement mechanisms that award damages such as an investor-state arbitration system.

Call this the *infidelity scenario*. The scenario certainly seems possible in principle. Whether it is *actual*, rather than hypothetical, or, even if actual, *typical enough* to justify the rising tide of investment treaties, is a further question, and indeed a question of crucial importance. If the imagined possibility is to be applicable to any real world policy decision, in the normal course of international political economy, it matters what the global economy is generally like, in the expectations it creates, and in what foreign investors can be expected to expect in their risk-taking. The imagined scenario stipulates that the risks and prospects presented, ex ante, turned out not to be as they were made or allowed to seem, and that "fair warning" of a consequential change was not provided, when investors had a chance to avoid suffering significant loss. Which is to say that it was not the sort of policy change one could anyway have been reasonably expected to expect, simply in appreciating the kind of gamble being taken in a foreign investment decision. But is that at all representative of the casino that is global markets?

Surely investing in a foreign country for profit is a kind of gamble. No government can be expected not to make regulatory decisions on a full range of issues, on an ongoing basis, many of which can be presumed to adversely affect the value of a firm's investments eventually, whether in diminished profits or outright losses. In *Occidental vs. Ecuador*, which proceeded under the US-Ecuador BIT, a tribunal ruled on grounds of "reasonable expectations" that "there is certainly an obligation not to alter the legal and business environment in which the investment has been made." The supposed reason for this was "stability":

[14] In Scanlon (1998), condition (1) might fail his principle that forbids the manipulation of intentionally created expectations (p. 298), or his principle that requires due care in creating expectations, however negligently (p. 300). Condition (2) could fail a requirement to take reasonable steps to prevent losses that someone might suffer as a result of one's having intentionally or negligently led him or her to believe one would follow a certain course of action (pp. 300ff.). This does not require that losses actually be prevented, and even when it does, the choice of means is open; the principle is neutral between warning, fulfillment, and compensation.

> Although fair and equitable treatment is not defined in the Treaty, the Preamble clearly records the agreement of the parties that such treatment "is desirable in order to maintain a stable framework for investment and maximum effective utilization of economic resources" The stability of the legal and business framework is thus an essential element of fair and equitable treatment.[15]

This is overstretched. As the US government successfully argued in rebuffing one investor-state attack, "[I]f States were prohibited from regulating in any manner that frustrated expectations—or had to compensate for any diminution in profit—they would lose the power to regulate."[16] The power to regulate would certainly be hobbled without the freedom to let losers lose, or be compensated only eventually or indirectly. "Regulatory chill" could easily become a deep freeze.

Especially in countries with weak institutions or relatively unregulated industries, the prudent investor will have to adjust expectations to local conditions and prospects and place his or her bets accordingly. In the normal case, a firm can be expected to expect ongoing adjustments to law and policy, and seek "sovereign risk" assessments by advisory firms. It will thus have no claim to have been given notice before new regulations in the public interest are announced or debated publicly. Most important, it will have no claim of equity not to be asked to suffer losses from regulatory action, even as a "minimum" standard of fair treatment. However unfair Lady Luck may have been, if the firm indeed voluntarily assumed the investment risks initially, with a reasonable range of alternatives (and any investor can always simply "hold," or place his or her bets elsewhere), it will be fully liable for the outcome. Indeed, it will be the host countries that could mount a reasonable objection to being asked to pay compensation—and, a fortiori, to an ISDS system that induces such objectionable payments. In panel jurisprudence, then, "fair and equitable treatment" provisions should be interpreted with a strong presumption against costs to the public. Damages might be awarded only in exceptional circumstances. And when they are otherwise awarded, unfairly, countries could fairly refuse to pay.

9.5 THE EMBEDDED ECONOMY

In short, the infidelity scenario is not fitted to economic reality—which is to say, to the general realities of political economy that organize real international commerce, including its generally understood expectational circumstances. In the global economy as we know it, foreign investors generally have fair

[15] *Glamis Gold, Ltd vs. United States of America.* [16] Ibid.

warning in the kind of gamble being undertaken, in which case paying compensation is unnecessary and objectionable.

This conclusion is not supplied by the abstract contractualist moral reasoning outlined earlier (which could also support the infidelity scenario). The issue is also one of morally informed social interpretation, about the nature of the social practices that organize global economic relations (James 2005, 2013). A casino is organized by certain expectations for risk-taking, which are set in view of its larger social purposes (i.e. the fun of harmless gambling). In many instances, a particular gambling act is "embedded" and organized within a certain social practice, which in turn shapes our sense of its moral justification, and the rights that may be legitimately or justly claimed of it. In the context of international commerce, it is on the basis of those (perhaps implicit) social understandings that the act of claiming a right to compensation for losses, in judicial or arbitration proceedings, can be said to be confused, about the nature of an investment. The claim exhibits a failure to register social understandings in which its kind of risk-taking has a proper, socially beneficial place.

Elsewhere I have offered a general account of fairness in the global economy that turns on an interpretive characterization of the kind of social structure that organizes international commerce (James 2012). The global economy as we know it is not only organized within the modern territorial state system, in which default rights of non-interference are assigned to political units over different territorial jurisdictions. In light of the standard economic case for free trade, the assurance problems of the interwar years, and the postwar history of international economic politics, trade is best understood as "embedded" within an international social practice, specifically, a social practice in which different countries mutually rely on common markets (in goods, services, and capital), for the sake of augmenting their national incomes (by way of specialization to comparative advantage, economies of scale, and the spread of technology) (James 2012, chap. 2). Countries that participate in the practice of mutual market reliance, by opening borders and more or less complying with market reliance expectations, enjoy a claim to a fair share of the national income gains created by international cooperation (James 2012, chap. 6).[17]

By way of contractualist reasoning, tailored to the foregoing constructive interpretation, I then defend three general principles of "structural equity," which concern how international and domestic law, expectations, and policy

[17] The present argument is consistent with contractualism's general ban on interpersonal summation or averaging, except under certain special conditions. On my account, societies have national economic interests in augmenting the national wealth (or, alternatively, persons have societal interests in augmenting their country's national wealth). This is factored in as the grounding complaints of a single party, which are to be compared, pairwise, to the complaints of other parties, without direct utilitarian aggregation.

distribute the gains from trade, across countries and within their respective classes (James 2012, chap. 7). The principles have an international rather than "cosmopolitan" structure, as befits the international nature of trade law and practice, and its organizing aim of *national* income augmentation. Gains from international cooperation are, in the first instance, to be divided among countries, with citizens receiving a fair share of their country's fair share.[18]

Accordingly, insofar as the very understood purpose of trade is for countries to augment their national incomes, investors can fully expect governments to adopt both trade and domestic policy that advances this end. When or if it is wise for governments to offer foreign investors special assurances in investment treaty provisions, the basic rationale for such measures is to facilitate commerce, over the longer run, for the country's national economic good. And because investors can be reasonably expected to expect ongoing regulation in the public interest, they assume the risks of loss from regulatory adjustment. For the investor to demand compensation anyway, quite aside from what serves a country's overall good in the longer run, is to fail to appreciate the very social purpose according to which cross-border investment is allowed and legitimate in the first place.

This is true, not as a mere abstract moral truth, but because of the social understandings that constituted trade practice. Could such understandings change, perhaps with enough expectation-shaping investor agreements? Perhaps, but not easily in a global economy embedded within a state system. Despite increasing transnational relations, it will remain basic and predominant for the foreseeable future. So if investment treaties themselves shape investor expectations at the surface of international commerce, the underlying social practice takes interpretive and normative precedence, leaving its expression in so many treaties open to sweeping criticism.

Because investors voluntarily assume the risks of foreign investment, they can be expected to understand that any claim to "non-discrimination" or "fair and equitable treatment" must be subservient to the country's greater good. Under relatively free trade, firms are welcomed to take their chances, but the risk of loss is fairly shifted on to the investor and away from the public.[19] When or if it is wise for governments to assume some of those risks, to further encourage investment that serves the national good, the risks are only assumed to the degree necessary for that social objective. Investors can always avoid going to the trouble of investing abroad, so it is perfectly equitable for those that do invest to bear the full risks of their gamble.

[18] For discussion beyond James (2012), including replies to objections, see James (2014a, 2014b).

[19] I believe the distribution of risk is intrinsically significant, aside from what costs or benefits actually ensue, as I argue in James (forthcoming).

We might add that ISDS facilities create asymmetrical power relations, and that these come with special responsibilities, as an expectation of reciprocity.[20] The state, as the basic repository of public power, has certain primary responsibilities, and any transfer of the state's public power to regulate (or in many cases deregulate) to a third-party beneficiary such as a firm must carry at least some responsibility for relevant governance functions. A firm can at least be asked to accept liability to suffering losses for the sake of government regulations that pose any reasonable connection to the public interest. Even if it did have further claims of fairness, it already benefits in power and its privileges, which may compensate for economic losses, even with no payment of damages. Fair benefits have, as it were, already been paid.

Thus in tribunal jurisprudence what is "fair and equitable," even by "minimum standards," should be heavily weighted in the public's favor, with a strong presumption against what would create any risk of failure to regulate for public objectives. Even "non-discrimination," for all its centrality to international law, must be read accordingly. Trade law is but one part of international trade practice. Its non-discrimination norms (the most favored nation rule and the rule of national treatment) are but one of its instruments. To instead take "non-discrimination" to imply the *same* or *similarity* of treatment between foreign and domestic investors, rather than what is merely fair and equitable, is to elevate an instrument of policy to the level of principle, or, as Bentham might say, to confuse law for morality.

9.6 NATURAL RIGHTS

Let us return to the suggestion that investors have natural rights, prior to any such social understandings or agreements. Bentham is famously dismissive in this connection: "Natural rights is simple nonsense: natural and imprescriptible rights, rhetorical nonsense,—nonsense upon stilts.... So much for terrorist language" (1843, 501). Yet his point might be put more modestly. Suppose investors do not have especially weighty claims to special protections *within* trade practice as we know it, as I have claimed. Why then should calling such claims "natural rights" change the balancing equation? What, beyond rhetorical puffery, is added?

Let us assume that foreign investors have morally relevant interests or claims, in their economic and reliance interests. The question is then whether such a "claim" comes to little more than a relevant interest, or *mere* claim, with no special gravity. Similarly, we can assume investors have what Rawls calls

[20] Topal (MS); see also Stiglitz (2008) and Kobrin (2009).

"legitimate expectations," a claim to receive awards one was led to expect within a system of conduct if one undertook certain actions—in this case, investing abroad (Rawls 1971, 311, James 2012, 239–41). Even so, such claims do not bear on how the larger system of incentives is to be designed in the first instance. And in an unfair system, they provide only one *pro tanto* consideration of fairness among many.

Perhaps in some situations a relevant interest or claim would be decisive. Yet context matters, and the self-same interest or claim might vary and weaken in its relative force in a different setting. In what I called the infidelity scenario, I granted that an investor's claim might indeed weigh decisively in favor of special investor protections, provided several assumptions. Even here, little is added in calling this claim a "natural" right, since it is decisive already. The question is then whether any difference is made if we shift to the modern conditions of international political economy, in a very different "expectational situation." If, as I argued, investors voluntarily assume risks of failure, even as a consequence of government actions, our question remains: why would an appeal to "natural rights" to compensation add anything? Why would the relevant interests or claims suddenly become decisive?

9.7 PROMISES

Our main question so far has been whether current investment agreements should have ever been made in the first place. The strongest natural rights argument, from fidelity, begins from agreements already made. However unjust existing investment treaties may be, and however unwise it may be to continue them, as long as they are not rescinded, states have a natural duty to perform as promised, and investors have a right to the promised compensation for losses given a favorable arbitral ruling. Are we not back in the infidelity scenario?

Not necessarily. Even if states do have a natural promissory duty to fulfill treaty agreements, it will be owed to other *states*, the parties with whom the agreements have been made, and not to any foreign investor. When an investor is not treated as promised under an interstate agreement, even with considerable investment losses, the wronged party is nevertheless a state from which the investor originates or is otherwise (somehow) associated.

Foreign direct investment often does not come with government contracts, and so would not create such promissory rights and obligations. Sovereign debt contracts, when treated as investments, are perhaps an exception.[21] Governments borrow from firms or individuals and enter highly specific

[21] Because some recent treaties count sovereign debt as an investment, debt restructuring can qualify as "indirect appropriation."

contracts with them to repay the loan with interest, on a specified time frame. Does this entail a promissory obligation of repayment? Not on some analyses; the contractor is required only to *either* perform *or* be held liable, for some appropriate remedy, if any (Holmes 1897, 457, 462). Argentina would have been quite right to restructure its debt obligations in the wake of its 2001 financial crisis, with or without the permission of foreign bondholders, and may or may not owe full compensation.

But let us grant that contracts are indeed promises (Shiffrin 2007, 2012a), as assumed by one US ruling against Argentina ("We hold that Argentina breached its promise").[22] Why would they create promissory obligations? One answer appeals to expectation creation. According to Scanlon's principle of fidelity ("principle F"), it is wrong to intentionally create expectations about one's future conduct, with the aim of giving others assurance, and then disappoint those expectations, without having been released (Scanlon 1998, 304). Investment treaties arguably create expectations, in which case governments would owe performance as promised to investors, absent special justification. Some philosophers doubt whether this gives rise to full-fledged promissory rights, in the sense of "right" that involves a proper duty-to and claim-against (Gilbert 2004, Owens 2012). But let us grant that we can thus speak, in some apt sense, of an investor's "right to rely" on government-created expectations, because it would be wrong for a government not to perform.

Does this imply a right to compensation? It does not. Even with ISDS systems created, and with investor expectations cemented, the mere fact that a state has a duty of fidelity to agreements and an investor a right to reliance would not settle what should be done in breach. If a state fails to comply, nothing follows for how or even whether a legal system should address this failure—at least not without further argument.[23] A court or tribunal could adopt any number of remedies, on grounds of efficiency, the good of a trading country, or structural equity. Even in breach of a highly specific sovereign debt contract, when a court determines that the contractual and promissory obligation had not been fulfilled, it still needs further grounds for requiring repayment on the terms originally promised. The "background rules" for remedy may be sensitive to further considerations of societal fairness (e.g. the enormous costs of a recent financial crisis, and the need to meet prior wage or pension commitments).[24]

[22] *NML Capital, Ltd vs. Republic of Argentina.*

[23] Craswell (1989). Keating (2012) makes this point about all rights: what to do post-infringement is a separate question of the second-best. Even views that argue from the point and value of promising to an obligation to compensate in breach might come to very different substantive compensatory obligations, because they differ on the question of point and value.

[24] Giving priority to domestic bondholders may well be necessary to address a financial crisis or protect wages and pensions. Even non-discrimination, *subject to fair and equitable treatment*, may thus permit substantial "haircuts."

Promises and contracts nearly always have excusing limitations. When special or extenuating circumstances justify non-performance, there is no cause for remedy, because no unjustifiable breach. Or perhaps a promise was never successfully made, despite certain public statements or written agreements, for being immoral, or in conflict with a prior promissory obligation (Shiffrin 2012b). But even when a promise is made, and an obligation successfully created, a promissory right may still be justifiably infringed. On some views, the original obligation then disappears, without moral remainder. But the point holds even if, as some theorists claim, a genuine promissory right continues to provide a relevant and perhaps important consideration—even, perhaps, when the promise was wrongfully made in the first place. All the same, the infringement may be justified under the circumstances, all things considered (Thompson 1992, Gilbert 2006). So even if investment treaties give rise to genuine promissory rights, for reasons of societal fairness, they can still be void, rightly infringed, or unenforceable. And even if the right is not simply void, but in some sense continuing, it may call for little or even no compensation.

Here one might add that parties that break their promises have a natural remedial duty to pay compensation to those injured in expectational damages (Fried 1981). Here again investment treaties present a mismatch problem: if the "injured" party is the *bearer* of the promissory right, that party would be the investor's home *state*, rather than the persons or firms that suffer economic losses. And if the state has a right to be compensated for the wronging, it might elect not to have due payment flow to the investor, for reasons of welfare, efficiency, or fairness. But let us set this problem aside. Unfaithful states, let us assume, have a duty to compensate the *harmed* parties, and investors can thus "have a right" to compensation for economic harm done to them. The question remains: Would such a right be weighty enough to make a difference under the normal circumstances of international political economy? Why take it to prevail over considerations of welfare, efficiency, or fairness?

Why it would prevail in full force is hard to see. A variety of considerations shapes ideas of due compensation in practice. For starters, although monetary compensation is at best a very imperfect approximation of repair for any real harm done, we presume the matter is settled once an approximate figure is determined. This shows the relevance of practicability to what is owed. Yet even less may be required if payment would impose an undue burden on the unfaithful party. More generally, the level of damages is rightly assessed in view of what is fair, and it will surely then be relevant if all parties are part of an ongoing, generally beneficial relationship. What burden is "undue" would then be shaped by any background considerations of fairness in the larger relationship, in which case we are back where we started: investors voluntarily assume risks of investment losses, and so should accept liability for losses instead of expecting compensatory payments. Perhaps some measure of compensation is appropriate, in special cases. Even so, when the risks are voluntarily assumed, and losses come "fair and square," the normal presumption is that no compensation is necessary.

This brings us to the investor's last stand. Why not claim that people have strict or "absolute" natural rights to compensation in breach, which can be weakened only by waiver, with the injured party's authorization? Yet here we should simply balk: it is extremely implausible to in effect assign such "rights" infinite weight, as against any possible competing consideration.

Surely it is not always and everywhere wrong for states to proceed without explicit waiver, if they *do* pay compensation, or if they have some other sufficient justification.[25] While this raises familiar questions about the force of rights relative to other values, the present issue can be expressed in terms of conflicting rights (Waldron 1989, 508ff.). Why would such rights take precedence over what might be said to be the equally or more stringent rights of a society's members, as established in its social contract? For a government entrusted with the authority to make decisions on its members' behalf, however undemocratically, the choice between paying off investors and cutting essential social services need not be seen as simply a question of equity; it is (perhaps also) a clash of rights. So even if all rights silence all claims of welfare or equity, the question would remain: why should the rights of investors have such great weight as against the rights of a society's members?

Again, foreign investment is voluntary. It is relatively easy to consent not to gamble with one's money abroad (much easier than avoiding a domestic casino). Few if any members of society have a real choice in whether to pay off investors, who may have an outsized influence on their politics. If the investor can be careful in his or her risk-taking, the citizen must often simply live with the risks he or she is given. (And if he or she quits the country, will a destination country's government do things any differently?)

9.8 CONCLUSION: SPEAKING NONSENSE

To claim absolute natural rights, on behalf of investors, is, arguably, to call for philosophical anarchism—a rejection of the very state system and international relations needed to constitute and embed a global economy of the sort we are familiar with.[26] Yet if some sort of spontaneously ordered market relations might somehow emerge and span the globe anyway, this is not a credible possibility for our future, however often we entertain the philosophical fiction.

[25] As Nozick (1974) admits, even in treating rights as "side constraints."
[26] Simmons (2009) would simply reply: "so much the worse for the state."

This raises the question: are such strong claims then even meaningful as claims of right, when voiced in the context of the contemporary global economy?

Their practical meaning is rather unclear. When voiced in contemporary life, they seem to presuppose going trade practice, as an embedding condition for the very possibility of investment flows across borders. And yet that very practice is potentially called into question, and so also not presupposed. Which is it? Presupposed, or not?

To be sure, a person can stand up (on the street corner, or in an arbitration meeting) and make a clear-headed claim to absolute "investor rights," while noting—for the sake of clarity—that the mooted claim is, as Bentham says, "imprescriptible." One could specifically note (in a caveat) that one's claim is *not* addressed to going trade practice. It is not specifically a claim against law and governance as we know it, concerning the normal exercise of its powers, and, if it calls for anything, it is for a radically unknown and perhaps unimaginable state of the world, which no one in particular would know how to implement or even advance in practice. One surely can meaningfully cry from the wilderness without purporting to speak to going practice, from within its understandings. But for being "imprescriptible," or at any rate not prescribed to anyone who might see how to take action, it surely is not *practically* meaningful, in a certain important sense. Instead of speaking of "rights," one would court less confusion by simply speaking of what is "ideal." Perhaps one is demanding an "ideal world," an investor utopia, in which investors are reliably afforded the putative weighty rights.

And what if such a speaker forgets the caveat? A claim of investor "right" is offered with weighty, supposedly decisive significance (e.g. by a tribunal lawyer in internal deliberations), but also addressed specifically *to* international legal systems in real trade practice, being offered on its face as argument about how its normal powers should be exercised (the tribunal should order a government to pay damages). Well, this *is* confused, in a way, if the call is equally for the very abolition of those systems. Consider how one might follow up the speech act, with certain questions of clarification. Are legal powers to be used, not by their understood purposes but to arrange their own undoing, perhaps to sow seeds of revolution? But if so, the natural counter is that the claim is misdirected or has no addressee. "Your beef isn't with this government, or this tribunal," it might be said. "You should speak to God, or all of humanity, if you're speaking to anyone."

One can meaningfully address a claim of right to a practice by speaking within its social understandings. The understandings set presuppositions that give the rights claim a potential truth-value. The present sort of rights claiming calls for the rejection of those very understandings, undercutting a condition of its own meaning. When presented at the very same time as a claim within practice, in the heat of tribunal deliberations, the claim courts a kind of confused nonsense. The claimant speaks, purporting to truth, but then undercuts the very conditions needed for that very claim to have a truth-value. To carry on speaking, with any awareness, is to speak without regard for the truth, to bluff, or to bullshit.

Which of course may do the bidding of power and interest rather nicely. It may help to speak loudly, and angrily, in solemn tones (wearing a fine suit), so to elevate one's rhetoric. Nonsense can be best served "on stilts." Multinational corporations and their lawyers are not so bashful as to offer careful caveats and clarification of what they are, or are not, claiming, for fear of abusing plain moral meaning. But neither then must the lawyer or the policy-maker listen—not to nonsense, not even to nonsense on stilts.[27]

REFERENCES

Aisbett, Emma. 2007. "Bilateral Investment Treaties and Foreign Direct Investment: Correlation versus Causation." CUDARE Working Paper 1032. Berkeley. University of California.

Bentham, Jeremy. 1843. "Anarchical Fallacies." In *The Works of Jeremy Bentham*, vol. 2, edited by John Bowring. Edinburgh: William Tait.

Craswell, Richard. 1989. "Default Rules, and the Philosophy of Promising." *Michigan Law Review* 88(3), 489–529.

Dolzer, Rudolf. 2014. "Fair and Equitable Treatment: Today's Contours." *Santa Clara Journal of International Law* 12(1), 7–33.

Egger, Peter H., and Valeria Merlo. 2007. "The Impact of Bilateral Investment Treaties on Foreign Direct Investment." *Journal of Comparative Economics* 30(10), 1536–49.

Fiss, Owen M. 1984. "Against Settlement." *The Yale Law Journal* 93(6), 1073–90.

Frankfurt, Harry. 2005. *On Bullshit.* Princeton: Princeton University Press.

Frege, Gottlob. 1980. "On Sense and Reference." In *Translations from the Philosophical Writings of Gottlob Frege*, edited and translated by P. Geach and M. Black. Oxford: Blackwell Press, 157–77.

Fried, Charles. 1981. *Contracts As Promise.* Cambridge, MA: Harvard University Press.

Gilbert, Margaret. 2004. "Scanlon on Promissory Obligation." *Journal of Philosophy* 101(2), 83–109.

Gilbert, Margaret. 2006. *A Theory of Political Obligation: Membership, Commitment, and the Bonds of Society.* Oxford: Oxford University Press.

Hallward-Driemeier, Mary. 2003. "Do Bilateral Investment Treaties Attract FDI: Only a Bit.... And They Could Bite." World Bank Policy Research Paper 3121–2003, Washington, DC.

[27] For their comments I am grateful to Margaret Gilbert, Bob Goodin, Jeff Helmreich, Caroline Henckels, Jarrod Hepburn, Lisa Herzog, Matt Lindauer, Greg Shaffer, Nic Southwood, and L. K. ("Lulu") Weis. I also thank my discussants at Melbourne Law School, Australian National University, and McGill's GRIPP, as well as the students in my 2014 seminar at UC Irvine.

Holmes Jr., Oliver Wendell. 1897. "The Path of the Law." *Harvard Law Review* 10, 457–78.

James, Aaron. 2005. "Constructing Justice for Existing Practice: Rawls and the Status Quo." *Philosophy and Public Affairs* 3(33), 281–316.

James, Aaron. 2012. *Fairness in Practice: A Social Contract for a Global Economy.* New York: Oxford University Press.

James, Aaron. 2013. "Why Practices?" *Raison Politiques* 51, 43–62.

James, Aaron. 2014a. "A Theory of Fairness in Trade." *Moral Philosophy and Politics* 1(2), 177–200.

James, Aaron. 2014b. "Reply to Critics." *Canadian Journal of Philosophy* 44(2), 286–304.

James, Aaron. Forthcoming. "The Distinctive Significance of Systemic Risk." *Ratio Juris.*

Keating, Greg. 2012. "The Priority of Respect over Repair." *Legal Theory* 18, 293–337.

Kobrin, Stephen J. 2009. "Private Political Authority and Public Responsibility." *Business Ethics Quarterly* 19(3), 349–74.

Lesher, Molly, and Sébastien Miroudot. 2006. "Analysis of the Economic Impact of Investment Provisions in Regional Trade Agreements." OECD Trade Policy Working Paper No. 36. Paris: OECD.

Mill, John Stuart. 1987. *Utilitarianism and Other Essays.* New York: Penguin.

Minor, Michael S. 1994. "The Demise of Expropriation as an Instrument of LDC Policy, 1980–1992." *Journal of International Business Studies* 25, 177–88.

Neumayer, Eric, and Laura Spess. 2005. "Do Bilateral Investment Treaties Increase Foreign Direct Investment to Developing Countries?" *World Development* 33(10), 1567–85.

Nozick, Robert. 1974. *Anarchy, State, Utopia.* New York: Basic Books.

Owens, David. 2012. *Shaping the Normative Landscape.* Oxford: Oxford University Press.

Rawls, John. 1971. *A Theory of Justice.* Cambridge, MA: Harvard University Press.

Raz, Joseph. 1984. "On the Nature of Rights." *Mind* XCIII(370), 194–214.

Sachs, Lisa, and Karl P. Sauvant, eds. 2009. *The Effect of Treaties on Foreign Direct Investment: Bilateral Investment Treaties, Double Taxation Treaties, and Investment Flows.* New York: Oxford University Press.

Salacuse, Jeswald W., and Nicholas P. Sullivan. 2005. "Do BITs Really Work? An Evaluation of Bilateral Investment Treaties and Their Grand Bargain." *Harvard International Law Journal* 46, 67–129.

Scanlon, Thomas M. 1998. *What We Owe to Each Other.* Cambridge, MA: Harvard University Press.

Scanlon, Thomas M. 2003. *The Difficulty of Tolerance.* Cambridge: Cambridge University Press.

Shiffrin, Seanna. 2007. "The Divergence of Contract and Promises." *Harvard Law Review* 120, 708–53.

Shiffrin, Seanna. 2012a. "Are Contracts Promises?" In *Routledge Companion to Philosophy of Law*, edited by Andrei Marmor. New York: Routledge, 241–58.

Shiffrin, Seanna. 2012b. "Immoral, Conflicting, and Redundant Promises." In *Reasons and Recognition: Essays on the Philosophy of T. M. Scanlon*, edited by R. Jay Wallace, Rahul Kumar, and Samuel Freeman. New York: Oxford University Press, 155–78.

Simmons, A. John. 2009. MS. "Philosophical Anarchism" (February 16). http://ssrn.com/abstract=1344425 (accessed October 26, 2016).

Stiglitz, Joseph E. 2008. "2007 Grotius Lecture Regulating Multinational Corporations: Towards Principles of Cross-Border Legal Frameworks in a Globalized World Balancing Rights with Responsibilities." *American University International Law Review* 23(3), 450–558.

Thompson, Judith Jarvis. 1992. *The Realm of Rights*. Cambridge, MA: Harvard University Press.

Tienhaara, Kyla. 2011. "Regulatory Chill and the Threat of Arbitration: A View from Political Science." In *Evolution in Investment Treaty Law and Arbitration*, edited by C. Brown and K. Miles. Cambridge: Cambridge University Press, 606–28.

Topal, Julien. MS. "Grounding Corporate Responsibilities."

Van Harten, Gus. 2007. *Investor-State Arbitration and Public Law*. Oxford: Oxford University Press.

Waldron, Jeremy. 1989. "Rights in Conflict." *Ethics* 99(3), 503–19.

Yackee, Jason. 2007. "Do BITs Really Work?: Revisiting the Empirical Link Between Investment Treaties and Foreign Direct Investment." Legal Studies Research Paper Series, Paper No. 1054. Wisconsin: University of Wisconsin Law School.

Yackee, Jason W. 2010. "Do Bilateral Investment Treaties Promote Foreign Direct Investment? Some Hints from Alternative Evidence." *Virginia Journal of International Law* 51, 397–442.

Part III

Institutions and Practices

10

Normative dimensions of central banking: How the guardians of financial markets affect justice

Peter Dietsch

10.1 INTRODUCTION

It is a constitutive feature of central banks to play an interface role between governments and financial markets (Singleton 2010, 4ff.). They set monetary policy on behalf of the government, provide banking services to the latter, and often play a role in managing the public debt; at the same time they act as a bank for commercial banks, serve as a clearing house for the balances of the private banking sector, and have important supervisory functions in the banking sector. Given this role of central banks as one of the principal guardians of financial markets, any account of just financial markets naturally includes subjecting the role and actions of central banks to normative scrutiny.

Two roles of central banks should be distinguished in this context. First, the role of central banks as regulators—or macroprudential policy-makers, in today's terminology—who are charged with promoting financial stability, that is, reducing the risk of financial crises; and, second, the central bank's task of ensuring price stability in the economy, that is, monetary policy more narrowly defined. The exercise of both of these functions is intertwined with the functioning of financial markets and both of these aspects of central bank activity raise normative questions. Even though it is impossible to disentangle the two roles entirely, this chapter will focus on the second aspect.

Monetary policy has moved off the radar of normative discussion in recent decades.[1] Normative scrutiny has focused on the other pillar of macroeconomic policy, fiscal policy. Institutionally, this situation is reflected in the

[1] But see Fontan et al. (2016) for a recent assessment of the relationship between central banking and inequality.

doctrine of central bank independence. Monetary policy has come to be perceived as a technocratic exercise that is best left to a group of experts, whose mandate might be formulated by politicians, but who operate at arm's length from the latter.

In light of the events since the onset of the financial crisis in 2008, it seems no longer appropriate to exempt monetary policy from normative scrutiny in this way. With the room for manoeuvre in fiscal policy heavily constricted due to both external constraints such as tax competition for capital (e.g. Dietsch 2015, Dietsch and Rixen 2014) and the self-imposed policy of austerity to contain the further growth of public debt (Blyth 2013), monetary policy has become the prime tool of macroeconomic policy today. This is a source for concern for prudential as well as for broader, normative reasons. While it might have been plausible to argue in the pre-crisis world that monetary policy was relatively benign in its impact on the distribution of income and wealth as well as from a perspective of democratic self-determination, this is arguably no longer true for the unconventional monetary policies employed in recent years. In addition, as for instance the minutes of Federal Reserve Board meetings in 2008 reveal, there is significant theoretical and practical uncertainty about both the effectiveness of unconventional policies and their impact on other social objectives.

In particular, we can distinguish three normative dimensions of monetary policy. First, the distributive dimension: does monetary policy have a significant impact on the distribution of income and wealth and, if so, how should this impact influence policy-making? Second, the democratic dimension: when tensions arise between the monetary policy that best serves the economic interests of the citizens living in the currency area in question on the one hand, and the monetary policy that is optimal considering the response of global financial markets on the other, how should we arbitrate tensions of this kind? Third, the cross-border dimension: when the monetary policy of one country, via international capital flows, has an impact on people elsewhere, should central banks take this impact into account in their policy-making and, if so, how?

This chapter concentrates on the first two of these dimensions.[2] While the third dimension is by no means less relevant today—as demonstrated for instance by the capital outflow from emerging markets in reaction to the discussion of "tapering" of asset-purchases by the Federal Reserve in 2013 (Wigglesworth et al. 2013)—the international issues raised by monetary policy are distinct from domestic ones.

The chapter is structured as follows. I start off in Section 10.2 with a primer on monetary policy for those unfamiliar with it, setting out its goals as well as

[2] For a pioneering discussion of the third dimension, see Reddy (2003).

the means employed to pursue these goals. This preliminary section fills in the empirical and conceptual premises that my subsequent argument will rely on. I then discuss the distributive dimension of monetary policy (Section 10.3). This section is divided into first the factual question of how monetary policy impacts inequality, which then feeds into the normative and institutional questions of how we should respond to this impact. Finally, Section 10.4 of the chapter addresses a tension between monetary policy and democratic legitimacy.

10.2 ENDS AND MEANS OF MONETARY POLICY

What are the primary objectives of monetary policy? Phrased in economic jargon, what should be the objective function of the central bank? Governments delegate some aspects of the social welfare function they pursue to central banks. They formulate the objective function in the mandate they hand to central banks. But what exactly does this mean in practice? What are the concrete social objectives that economic welfare can be broken down into in the context of monetary policy? We need to be clear on how the objective function is defined in modern monetary theory before we can ask whether it should include other social objectives and, if so, how.

For many, the first goal of monetary policy that comes to mind is price stability, which means promoting low inflation while avoiding deflation. Why is low inflation a goal worth pursuing? Several reasons can be invoked here.[3] First, since inflation effectively represents a tax on nominal assets—that is, assets that are not indexed to inflation—it creates distortionary effects; people will hold less nominal assets than they would in a situation without inflation. Second, inflation is bad because it creates uncertainty. Especially at higher rates of inflation, which have historically tended to be subject to bigger fluctuations, economic agents will be uncertain about the future value of money. This complicates their decision-making and may, for example, discourage them from making long-term investments. Third, even when abstracting from uncertainty, inflation creates relative price dispersion; given that people enter economic contracts with variable durations, only some of them will be able to adjust their contracts when inflationary expectations change. Those who cannot will be stuck with inefficient prices for the duration of their contract.

Conversely, monetary policy aims to avoid deflation, because it creates distortionary effects in the opposite direction. When money gains in value

[3] For a representative statement of the importance of price stability from the perspective of contemporary monetary theory see Woodford (2003, chap. 6).

compared to other assets, people have an incentive to hold cash rather than to invest or consume.[4] This has a negative impact on economic growth.[5]

Price stability is the first and often the only item in the mandate of central banks. A second item, the promotion of employment, is an explicit objective only in some countries. The US is the most prominent example. The ECB, despite its reputation of focusing exclusively on price stability, is also required by Art. 127(1) of the Treaty on the Functioning of the European Union to "support the general policies in the Union"—including the promotion of employment—provided that there is no "prejudice to the objective of price stability." In general, even where employment does not figure in their list of competences, central bankers know that neglecting high rates of unemployment might lead to a change in their mandate.

Finally, financial stability is the third task of central banks.[6] They are supposed to help commercial banks overcome liquidity bottlenecks due to maturity transformation,[7] to ensure that banks do not take excessive financial risks, and to identify and prevent potential asset price bubbles. This third goal of monetary policy has taken center stage since the onset of the financial crisis; the ECB, for instance, has acquired formal responsibility for aspects of financial stability (Fontan 2013).[8]

In sum, I think it is fair to say that price stability, employment, and financial stability are perceived to be the main objectives of monetary policy today, with price stability as the *primus inter pares*. How do central banks pursue these three objectives?

Central banks have two principal, and interconnected, policy instruments at their disposal.[9] They set interest rates and they conduct open-market operations (OMOs). We need to distinguish two kinds of interest rates. First and most importantly, central banks set a target for the *money market rate* (or federal funds rate in the United States) at which banks and other financial institutions lend funds to each other. The central bank then uses open-market

[4] Statistics show, for instance, that the Japanese, given their bad experiences with deflation, tend to hold a large proportion of their savings in cash deposits (see Saiki and Frost 2014, 5).

[5] Austrian economists disagree with this view. They hold that deflation when due to technological progress rather than insufficient demand is not problematic and quite compatible with economic growth.

[6] There is a heated debate among academics and central bankers as to whether financial stability *should be* among the objectives of central banks or not. Some argue that an effective promotion of price stability presupposes a narrow mandate that excludes other objectives (e.g. Issing et al. 2001), others maintain that the stabilizing function of the central bank's liquidity management constitutes the essence of central banking (Goodhart 2010, 9) and thus favors a broader mandate. I set aside this debate for the purposes of this chapter.

[7] That is, the fact that under fractional reserve banking, commercial banks tend to *borrow* money for relatively short periods while they *lend* money for relatively long periods.

[8] As indicated in the introduction, this chapter is only concerned with financial stability to the extent that it is conducted through monetary policy, but sets aside macroprudential policy.

[9] I thank Alex Barkawi for his comments on this section.

operations, that is, the buying and selling of short-term government bonds, to influence this interbank interest rate.[10] Second, central banks set the *discount rate* (or the rate for the marginal lending facility as the ECB calls it), that is, the interest rate at which banks can borrow money from the central bank. Short-term loans from the central bank notably form part of commercial banks' strategy to meet their reserve requirements.

Quantitative easing, which refers to the unconventional monetary policy employed in response to the financial crisis, differs from what happens in normal times in the following ways. The first distinguishing feature is the duration and permanent *versus* temporary character of the OMOs deployed. In normal times, OMOs involve the buying or selling of short-term government bonds and are temporary in that they involve repurchase agreements. Since the financial crisis, OMOs have targeted longer-term government bonds,[11] their repurchase agreements have covered longer and longer time-spans,[12] and/or they have dropped the repurchase agreement from the contract altogether. It is the latter permanent OMOs or outright purchases of securities that has led to a ballooning of central bank balance sheets since the crisis.[13] In some cases of quantitative easing, a second difference to normal times lies in the asset classes of securities that are bought and sold in the OMOs. Especially when the goal of the central bank is to repair banks' balance sheets, its quantitative easing programme is likely to target assets that have turned sour such as mortgage-backed securities.[14]

Before turning to the question of how monetary policy impacts inequalities in income and wealth, three remarks are in order on the effectiveness of central bank policy in achieving the above objectives. First, in normal times, the leverage of central bank policy over the money market has arguably declined in recent years. Why? Growing Repo and Eurodollar markets give commercial banks alternative ways to meet their reserve requirements. As Mehrling (2011, 25) argues, the fact that central banks are only a small player in those markets means that their capacity to tighten or loosen credit availability has declined over time.

[10] When the central bank buys government bonds, this props up their price and, through the inverse relationship between price and yield, keeps their yield and thus the money market interest rate low. Conversely, when the central bank sells bonds, this raises the money market rate.

[11] When the central bank buys long-term government bonds, whose prices correlate with future short-term government bonds, they are sending a signal to investors that interest rates will *stay* low for a while.

[12] See for instance the 6-month, 12-month, and finally 36-month long-term financing operations (LTROs) introduced by the ECB in the wake of the crisis.

[13] For the case of the Fed, see for instance Mehrling (2011, 3).

[14] The first rounds of quantitative easing by the US Federal Reserve, for instance, included a significant amount of mortgage-backed securities.

Second, the issue of how effective monetary policy is at promoting employment has always been controversial. Optimists maintain that lowering interest rates will translate into private investment, which in turn will promote employment. By contrast, economists who believe that private investment is largely exogenously determined question this link. First and foremost, John Maynard Keynes argued that when economies find themselves in a so-called "liquidity trap," lowering interest rates will not trigger private investment but merely induce agents to hold more cash (Keynes 2007 [1936], chap. 13).

Third, in order to assess how well a central bank is doing at promoting financial stability, it is crucial to distinguish between liquidity crises and solvency crises. By the former, we refer to a situation in which a bank is unable to meet its current obligations due to the maturity transformation between its assets and liabilities. By the latter, we mean a situation where the assets have lost so much value that this puts in jeopardy the meeting of liabilities as such—independently of the term structure. While an expansionary monetary policy of the kind we have seen since 2008 can be an effective tool for stemming a liquidity crisis, it is less certain whether it is an effective tool for combating solvency issues. One successful model for the latter is the Sveriges Riksbank's response to the financial crisis in Sweden in the 1990s, when all banks were nationalized. Following an analysis of their balance sheets, those with liquidity problems received funds to meet their liabilities, while those with solvency problems were wound down (Englund 1999).

These questions of effectiveness will take center stage when weighing different policy objectives against each other.

10.3 MONETARY POLICY AND INEQUALITY

With the nuts and bolts of monetary policy laid out, we can now pass on to the analysis of monetary policy through the lens of justice. The present section will focus on the impact of monetary policy on inequalities in income and wealth, whereas Section 10.4 will probe the democratic legitimacy of monetary policy.

In both cases, it is crucial to keep in mind that monetary policy is always mediated through the reaction of financial markets to the actions of central banks. It is the *combination* of monetary policy and the reaction by financial markets to it that generate consequences that might concern us from the viewpoint of justice. Different market reactions to the same monetary policy might lead to a more or less unequal outcome or to one that is more or less in line with democratic preferences in the monetary zone in question. Thus, the questions raised here are inherently linked to the regulation of domestic and international financial markets, which circumscribes the set of possible reactions available to financial markets in response to monetary policy.

10.3.1 The factual question

Does monetary policy have implications for inequalities in income and wealth and, if so, what does this empirical link look like? The literature concerned with this question has distinguished a number of different channels or transmission mechanisms through which monetary policy affects inequalities.[15] Some of these suggest that expansionary monetary policy will tend to exacerbate inequalities. For example, since people's primary sources of income differ, expansionary monetary policy interventions that raise profits more than wages will benefit capital owners relative to workers. By contrast, other transmission channels work in the opposite direction. For example, if expansionary monetary policy succeeds in integrating previously unemployed individuals in the labor market, this will tend to decrease inequality.[16]

Complementary research has focused instead on the impact that monetary policy has on inequality via promoting its above-mentioned objectives of low inflation, employment, and financial stability. Beyond the well-established point that inflation favors debtors and harms creditors, a number of recent papers that look at the relationship between the inflation rate and inequality have come to diverging conclusions.[17] At first glance, the link between employment and inequality seems to be a straightforward inverse relationship, but its strength in part depends on the structure of unemployment benefits of a country. Finally, certain monetary policy interventions that target financial stability, especially the decision regarding which banks to bail out and which ones to let fail, clearly have distributive implications, even though in this case it is difficult to identify systematic trends.

In sum, I think it is fair to say that the jury is still out on the relationship between *conventional* monetary policy and inequality. In fact, given that the composition of different transmission channels and of the causal factors at work varies over time, it seems unlikely that there is a stable relationship between the two at all.[18]

However, we can arguably have more confidence when making claims about the impact of certain kinds of unconventional monetary policy on inequality (see also Fontan et al. 2016, section 5). With interest rates at

[15] For a good overview, see the five transmission channels identified by Coibion et al. (2012).

[16] Coibion et al. (2012, 2) call the first transmission mechanism the "income composition channel" and the second the "earnings heterogeneity channel."

[17] Jovanovic (2014) suggests that higher inflation tends to reduce inequality, Albanesi (2007) argues that the opposite is true, while Monnin (2014) holds that there is a U-shaped relationship between the two, with inequality high at both very low and high rates of inflation, whereas it tends to be lower at moderate rates of inflation.

[18] I thank Nancy Cartwright for pushing me to make this explicit. I am bracketing here the idea that the very fact of money creation in an economy might have inegalitarian consequences (e.g. Baeriswyl 2015).

historical lows in recent years, capital owners have the opportunity to engage in carry trades and increase their wealth with little risk: they can borrow at a relatively low interest rate and invest at a relatively high one, without there being a significant risk attached to the investment. This observation holds in particular for large, active investors who can afford the financial services necessary to reap these benefits—smaller investors, by contrast, have suffered from the low-interest environment, which is preventing them from building up retirement savings. Karl Marx put his finger on it when he said that "[t]he antithesis between capitalist and worker, between big and small capitalists, becomes still greater since credit is only given to him who already has, and is a new opportunity of accumulation of the rich man" (Marx in McLellan 1977, 114). Many commentators argue that the low interest rates in the wake of the crisis of 2008, rather than triggering productive investment, have by and large fueled asset price bubbles (Jones 2013).

The same argument applies to the long-term refinancing operations (LTROs) of the ECB conducted in December 2011 and February 2012. Under these schemes, the ECB offered commercial banks credits of up to three years at 1 percent. The programs turned out to be very popular, especially since they offered low-risk arbitrage opportunities. A bank would take the money and buy slightly higher yielding government bonds with it, thus making a nice profit at negligible risk. Whereas LTROs might conceivably have been defended in the immediate aftermath of the crisis by arguing that they were necessary to prevent money markets from freezing up, this argument is less plausible at the time when they were actually employed and when the pressure on banks' balance sheets had already eased considerably. Here, the goal was presumably to incentivize banks to pass on loans to corporations and thus to stimulate productive investment. This goal was not attained. In fact, the ECB implicitly acknowledged that the first two rounds of LTROs had failed: for the third round of so-called TLTROs (targeted LTROs) in June 2014, it imposed explicit criteria to focus on the funding of loans to the non-financial private sector (excluding loans to households for house purchases).[19]

These examples show that when it comes to some of the unconventional tools of monetary policy deployed in response to the crisis, we clearly face trade-offs between some of the standard goals of monetary policy on the one hand—employment and financial stability in particular[20]—and containing inequality on the other. Especially if one is sceptical about the employment effect of expansionary monetary policy in a crisis like the present one, or if one thinks that financial stability could be promoted equally well or even better through alternative means, then one is likely to think, for example, that the price of LTROs in terms of increased inequality is not worth paying.

[19] I thank Alex Barkawi for helping me to make this point more precise.
[20] Trade-offs between inflation and inequality seem to be rarer or less obvious.

It is worth highlighting one particularly tricky aspect of these trade-offs. Most policies will have both a *direct* impact on inequality—LTROs for example give capital holders cheap arbitrage opportunities and thus increase inequalities—and an *indirect* impact on inequality—if it were true, for instance, that in the absence of a particular LTRO program, credit markets would have ground to a halt and sent the economy back into recession, then deploying them will arguably decrease inequalities (or at least keep them at a lower level compared to the relevant counterfactual). The counterfactuals required to weigh these different considerations will always both depend on the reaction of financial markets to monetary policy, as highlighted at the outset of this section, and be hotly contested (see also Section 10.4). However, this is not an excuse not to engage in them.

10.3.2 The normative question

Should we care about the impact of monetary policy on inequality? (See Fontan et al. 2016, section 4.) This depends on what theory of justice we endorse, and what kind or what level of inequalities this theory deems unjust. If you think that current inequalities of income and wealth are problematic from the perspective of justice, then you should be concerned about monetary policy that exacerbates these inequalities.

It is not my goal in this chapter to defend any particular theory of justice. I merely intend to point out how a number of commonly held theories of justice might react to the empirical link between monetary policy and inequality we have analyzed in the previous section. The following theoretical positions are discussed in ascending order from less demanding and more consensual theories, to more demanding and also more controversial theories of justice.

Consider first a rights-based theory of justice that holds that inequalities in income and wealth are problematic only to the extent that they lead to the transgression of political rights.[21] Second, think of a needs-based theory of justice that requires a level of sufficiency in the standard of living for everyone to be met (e.g. Frankfurt 1987). Both of these first theories are relatively minimalist in their demands of justice. Any inequalities in income and wealth that do not violate these criteria, and by extension any inequalities of this kind that result from monetary policy, would be deemed acceptable.

Third, consider a Rawlsian argument defending the idea that inequalities are acceptable provided they benefit the least advantaged members of society (Rawls 1999). Think back to the LTRO programs I discussed in the previous

[21] For a classic statement of this kind of position, see Okun (1975, chap. 1). Michael Walzer's (1993) theory of *spheres of justice* can also be interpreted in this way.

section, which disproportionately benefit capital owners who tend to be rich. As long as they do not worsen the absolute position of the least advantaged in society, they would satisfy Rawls's difference principle.[22] Let me add two observations here. First, as G. A. Cohen (2008, especially chap. 1) has argued in a poignant critique of Rawls's reasoning, it is not clear whether incentive payments to the rich are actually compatible with a just society. Second, even if one thinks that the difference principle survives the critique formulated by Cohen, it is worth noting Rawls's particular way of conceiving the relationship between efficiency and equity. Rawls assumes that the two values are compatible, and that the difference principle serves to pick out one particular distribution among a series of Pareto-efficient distributions (Rawls 1999, section 12). This perspective assumes away potential trade-offs between equity and efficiency. More realistically, however, the relationship between the two values is more complex and does involve trade-offs. The same is true for the relationship between equity and the standard goals of monetary policy introduced in Section 10.2. In this chapter, I will not defend a particular way of arbitrating these trade-offs, but merely argue that we have to take them seriously.

Fourth, post-Rawlsian liberal egalitarians defend the idea that all undeserved inequalities should be compensated for (e.g. Dworkin 1981). Notably, they argue that the distribution of income and wealth should be insensitive to both natural and social endowments. If it turned out that monetary policy undermined this ideal, liberal egalitarians of this stripe would consider it problematic.

Fifth, some theories of justice appeal to an independent standard of merit to determine what levels of inequality are just. For example, one might argue that today's incomes are out of sync with the economic contributions of the individuals that earn them.[23] If monetary policy accentuates this discrepancy, then trade-offs of the type discussed above arise. If the theory of justice turns out to be less tolerant of inequalities than a Rawlsian position, then it would arbitrate these trade-offs in a different way.

The above theories of justice and their respective tolerance of inequalities are summarized in the following table (Table 10.1).

At this point, you might object that there is an argumentative gap between the various theories of justice invoked in this section and the empirical link between monetary policy and inequality discussed previously. This is a fair point. All of the theories of justice discussed here are ones that address

[22] At least on a relatively weak interpretation of the difference principle. A more demanding interpretation requires that the inequality in question *better* the position of the least advantaged, rather than merely *not worsen* it. Thanks to Lisa Herzog for her suggestion to clarify this point.

[23] Within this family of views, we again find different levels of demandingness. For a radically egalitarian position on the distribution of labor incomes, see for example Dietsch (2008).

Table 10.1. Different normative positions on the acceptability of inequalities

What kind/level of economic inequalities is unacceptable, and why?		
Transgression of political rights view	Only inequalities that undermine political rights are problematic	Increasing demandingness ↓
Sufficientarian view	Above a minimum threshold of material resources for everyone, inequalities are unproblematic	
Rawlsian incentives view	Inequalities are unproblematic provided they improve the situation of the least advantaged	
Liberal egalitarian views	Inequalities that reflect natural or social endowments are problematic	
Desert views (contribution, effort, etc.)[a]	Inequalities are acceptable only to the extent that they track an underlying criterion of desert	

[a] Whether desert views are more demanding than liberal egalitarian views is an open question.

inequalities of income and wealth in general, rather than specifically inequalities that arise from monetary policy. What consequences does this have for the assessment of monetary policy from a normative viewpoint? First, it means that this assessment will be context-dependent. In a society with low levels of inequality or with a relatively undemanding conception of justice, a particular monetary policy intervention and its effects might be considered acceptable, whereas the very same intervention might be deemed problematic in a society that starts from a higher level of inequalities or that has a more demanding conception of justice, or both. Similarly, under one set of regulations of financial markets, a particular monetary policy might generate fewer inequalities than under another, presumably laxer, set of regulations. From the perspective of inequality, the monetary policy in question might well be problematic in the latter context, but acceptable in the former.

Second, note that even if one accepts my argument so far—both the empirical claim that there is a link between monetary policy and inequality, and the normative claim that these inequalities should be weighed against traditional objectives of monetary policy—this does not yield any action-guiding conclusions as to what monetary policy should look like. In particular, someone might argue that the best way to arbitrate the trade-offs highlighted above is to have central banks pursue their mandate as currently defined, while the task to address any resulting inequalities falls to the fiscal and social policy of the government, for example through progressive taxation or unemployment benefits. This leads us to the institutional question to which we now turn.

10.3.3 The institutional question

Assuming we care about inequalities stemming from monetary policy, what should we do about this fact? We have two basic options. First, we could pursue what one might call an *integrated approach*. From this perspective, distributive concerns should be part of the central bank's objective function, which itself is informed by the overall social welfare function. When the chairwoman of a central bank is asked what the impact of her policy is on inequalities, neither "I don't know" nor "This falls outside my mandate" would be acceptable answers.[24]

Second, we could adopt a *division of labor approach*. Under this arrangement, the central bank pursues its traditional mandate as discussed in Section 10.2, while questions of distributive justice are taken care of by the government through its tax and transfer policies. Economists and central bankers tend to favor a division of labor of this kind.

However, any introductory economics course will tell you that such a division of labor is inefficient, at least in principle. How so? Well, the division of labor will lead to two local optima—a monetary policy one pursued by the central bank, and a social justice one pursued by government—which will clearly *not* result in a global optimum with respect to the overall social welfare function.

Granted, the advocate of the division of labor approach might concede, the global optimum will be out of reach, but as the experience of the 1970s onwards shows, the same holds for an integrated approach. When monetary policy is "politicized," it tends to lose credibility—in part, because politicians cannot resist the temptation to use it to promote their prospects of getting re-elected (Kydland and Prescott 1977). Thus, so the argument runs, even though a division of labor might be inefficient in the way I pointed out, it is a second-best solution to a problem the first-best solution to which is out of reach.

This comeback by the defender of a division of labor approach is well taken, but three observations need to be added here. First, the idea of conducting monetary policy and then correcting for any undesired inequalities afterwards comes with serious drawbacks itself. Once people receive a given pre-tax income, they tend to develop a sense of entitlement to this income—a phenomenon Murphy and Nagel (2002) have called the "myth of ownership." This imposes serious feasibility constraints on the redistribution required by the division of labor approach.

Second, the argument for a division of labor concedes that it is ultimately an empirical question which institutional set-up for monetary policy best balances

[24] For an in-depth analysis of the discourse of central bankers about inequalities, see Fontan et al. (2016).

our different social objectives. I do not have the evidence at hand to decide which of the two ideal-type institutional arrangements discussed here is preferable today. I merely want to point out the following: If it is true that unconventional monetary policies today have more inegalitarian consequences than traditional monetary policy did twenty or thirty years ago, then this might well reopen the question of whether monetary policy should be conducted in isolation from other policy objectives. Today, the costs of an integrated approach and the political temptations it brings might well be smaller than the costs of a division of labor approach in terms of rising inequalities.

Finally, there may be a third way between the integrated approach and the division of labor approach, namely one that requires central banks to be sensitive to distributive considerations not as a matter of principle but when pursuing certain kinds of monetary policy that are known to have particularly inegalitarian consequences. Fontan et al. (2016, section 6) defend such a view when they argue that central banks should have to factor distributive effects into their decision-making when adopting extraordinary policy instruments of the kind we have seen since the 2008 financial crisis.

This section has not yielded any action-guiding conclusions about how to make monetary policy sensitive to inequality. This might be considered unsatisfactory. However, any stronger conclusions are unwarranted without further empirical analysis.[25] Moreover, I believe that the mere framing of the issue in the above terms is a worthwhile exercise. Those making monetary policy today do not tend to think in the categories employed here.

10.4 OPTIMAL MONETARY POLICY, BUT OPTIMAL FOR WHOM?

In addition to its impact on inequalities of income and wealth, I will now argue that contemporary monetary policy raises questions of democratic legitimacy. On paper, there is no ambiguity. The mandate of central banks requires them to pursue some particular mix of the standard objectives—low inflation, employment, and financial stability—for the polity of the state or currency union in question. The rhetoric of central bankers confirms this picture. For example, when asked to take into account the impact of Federal Reserve policy on developing countries, Janet Yellen stated in February 2014 that US monetary policy will only take into account economic conditions in the US (Financial Times 2014).

[25] For an important step in this direction, see Fontan et al. 2016.

Yet, even though monetary policy is thus made *for* the polity in question, it is not made *by* the polity in question in the sense that central bankers are not democratically elected officials but appointed on the basis of their expertise. There is merely an indirect kind of democratic accountability, in the sense that governments are free to change the mandate of central banks.[26]

Despite the fact that central banks thus operate at arm's length from democratic control, the notion of optimal monetary policy is built on the implicit premise that the policy is optimal for the polity in question. Does this premise hold in practice? Arguably, monetary policy today also serves a "second constituency" (Streeck 2013, 118ff.). One can easily see what this means by looking at whom central bankers address in their policy statements: the "confidence" and reaction of financial markets play an important role in monetary policy setting. Central bankers do not want to upset financial markets, because they need the cooperation of markets to achieve their policy objectives. In particular, they need markets to invest capital in order to promote employment.[27] As highlighted from the very beginning of this chapter, monetary policy is thus mediated by the reaction of financial markets, or, put differently, markets have considerable leverage over monetary policy. It is in the influence that financial markets have over policy agendas as well as outcomes that this influence is most markedly visible. To capture this idea, let us say that *financial markets act as a filter for monetary policy*.

Consider the following examples. First, it is plausible to think that in the absence of the strong reaction from financial markets to the mention by the Fed in May 2013 of the mere possibility of tapering asset purchases, the Fed would have tapered sooner and more decisively. Second, the leverage of markets over policy can be witnessed in appointment procedures for positions at central banks, notably for the position of chairman. For example, when Bill Clinton considered Alan Blinder as a possible replacement for Alan Greenspan in the 1990s, the markets sent a clear signal that they would disapprove of this change. Presumably, we can interpret this as a sign that as chairman of the Fed Blinder would have given the employment objective more weight than Greenspan, thus strengthening the position of labor vis-à-vis capital.

Someone might raise the following objection to the idea of financial markets acting as a filter. Contrary to my claim, what best serves the economic interests of the citizens living in a currency area clearly has to take into account the

[26] When we speak of independent central banks, we need to distinguish between goal independence—which is constrained by the government's capacity to change the mandate—and instrument independence, which refers to the freedom of central banks to use the instruments at their disposal—setting interest rates as well as conducting open-market operations—as they see fit. The "independence" of central banks usually refers to the latter.

[27] Even where employment is not officially part of the mandate of the central bank, a slump in employment poses a deflation risk, which *is* part of the mandate.

reaction of financial markets.[28] If the citizens are worse off, given the financial markets' reaction, in an early-taper world or in a world with Blinder as Fed chairman, then my claim that they would be better off in those scenarios is simply nonsense. To rebut this objection, we need to draw a distinction between a locally optimal policy *versus* a globally optimal policy. The Fed believed, I take it, that the early-taper or Blinder-as-chairman scenario would better serve the social welfare function of Americans, *ceteris paribus*. However, given that financial markets react differently to the various policy options, *ceteris* are not *paribus*. The globally optimal policy would be an early-taper or Blinder-as-chairman scenario in which financial markets react in the same way as in a late-taper or Greenspan-as-chairman world. By contrast, the locally optimal policy, taking into account the response of financial markets, is the late-taper or Greenspan-as-chairman.

My critic will interject that the globally optimal policy world was simply not accessible for the Fed at the time. Now, I agree that it would be nonsense to designate an unfeasible policy option as the globally optimal one. However, I contest that the globally optimal policy is unfeasible in a strict sense. The reaction of financial markets is conditioned on the regulation of the latter. Central banks, through and with the help of governments, can modify this regulatory framework. If it is possible, through regulatory reform, to reduce the set of possible responses by financial markets in order to better serve the social welfare function and get closer to the global optimum, then this is what should be done. In other words, the reaction of financial markets should not be taken as an exogenous parameter, but should be an endogenous variable of policy design.[29]

Why should we think the fact that financial markets act as a filter for monetary policy poses a problem from a normative perspective? There are two complementary answers to this question. First, since it is fair to assume that financial markets represent the interests of capital, their leverage over monetary policy is likely to exacerbate inequalities in income and wealth. This may well be considered problematic for the reasons discussed in Section 10.3. Second, if one accepts economic self-determination as a value to underpin the idea that monetary policy is made for the polity of the state or currency union in question—and I grant that I have not justified here why one should accept this value—then any bias that is introduced into monetary policy from the outside is problematic.[30]

[28] I thank Alex Barkawi for raising this objection.

[29] A parallel can be drawn here to international tax governance, where "market reaction" in terms of tax evasion or tax avoidance can and should be controlled by government policy rather than taken as given in tax setting (Slemrod 1994; Dietsch 2015, chap. 3).

[30] Due to space constraints, I bracket the question of whether there is a difference between domestic *versus* foreign capital exercising this influence. Przeworski and Wallerstein (1988, 24) argue that the state is structurally dependent only on foreign capital, whereas a variety of redistributive policies is compatible with continued domestic investment.

Where the interests of the second constituency of monetary policy—financial markets—are in conflict with those of the first—the polity—and end up trumping them, this undermines economic self-determination in a problematic fashion (see also Dietsch 2016).

Let me add a clarification as to what I am *not* claiming when characterizing financial markets as filters. I am not defending some kind of conspiracy theory suggesting that central banks covertly promote the interests of capitalists. Instead, the claim is that global capital, via financial markets, has undue leverage to set the agenda when it comes to choosing the means from the policy menu to promote domestic welfare. The notion of what constitutes an undue leverage here needs to be specified further. For now, let us say that the members of a subgroup of a constituency have undue leverage when they have sufficient influence to lock the polity into a suboptimal policy. This seems to be the case with regard to financial markets and monetary policy.

Finally, what should be done about this problem? Giving governments more control over monetary policy is not a promising solution. Against the background of increasing public debt, governments would be just as much hostage to financial markets as central banks, if not more so. Take the example of the US: Despite the fact that US officials often complain that China's buying of US treasury bills amounts to a competitive devaluation of the Renminbi, the US would be left high and dry without the constant Chinese demand for its debt.

(Financial) markets acting as a filter for (monetary) policy represents the type of scenario that Karl Polanyi's (2001 [1944]) critique of market liberalization issued a powerful warning of. Polanyi argued that when pushed into a corner by the forces of deregulated markets, societies would inevitably take measures to protect themselves. In the pessimistic scenario, which is the one that played out in Polanyi's time, they protect themselves against the market by sacrificing freedom. In the optimistic scenario, which is still possible but once again on the back foot today, they protect themselves through a coordinated regulation of the market. Multilateral regulation is a necessary condition for attaining the globally optimal policy discussed above. Unilateral efforts by central banks or governments are trapped in locally optimal policy sets, exacerbating the tension between the two constituencies of the demos and the market.

10.5 CONCLUSION

In an era where monetary policy has become the primary tool of macroeconomic policy, it is natural to subject it to normative scrutiny. This chapter has done so from two complementary angles. First, I have shown that unconventional monetary policy instruments of the kind employed today have an exacerbating impact on inequalities in income and wealth. Depending on their demandingness, theories of justice will consider this impact problematic to varying degrees. However, this normative conclusion leaves the institutional response to it underdetermined. The costs of having an independent central bank with a narrow mandate that fuels inequalities in this way will have to be weighed against the costs of a more integrated approach to public policy, where monetary policy is coordinated with other measures.

Second, the sensitivity of central banks' policy-making to financial markets raises the question of whether financial markets introduce a bias into monetary policy. More specifically, is it the case that financial markets act as a filter for monetary policy? If it is empirically adequate to say that financial markets have enough leverage over monetary policy to take policy options off the menu that would better promote the interests of the polity of the country or monetary union in question, then this raises questions of democratic legitimacy. Any effective remedy to this second issue requires multilateral reform.

Finally, it is worth highlighting again another important upshot of this chapter. When thinking about normative dimensions of monetary policy, we should not take the reaction of financial markets as given, but rather treat it as an endogenous variable that can itself be modified by monetary policy and by the regulatory framework more generally.[31]

REFERENCES

Albanesi, Stefania. 2007. "Inflation and Inequality." *Journal of Monetary Economics* 54(4), 1088–114.

Baeriswyl, Romain. 2015. "Intertemporal Discoordination in the 100 Percent Reserve Banking System." *Procesos de Mercado: Revista Europea de Economia Politica* 12(2), 43–80.

Blyth, Mark. 2013. *Austerity: The History of a Dangerous Idea*. Oxford: Oxford University Press.

Cohen, Gerry A. 2008. *Rescuing Justice and Equality*. Cambridge, MA: Harvard University Press.

[31] Previous versions of this chapter have been presented at a workshop on "Normative Dimensions of Monetary Policy" at the Centre de recherche en éthique (CRÉ) in Montréal in April 2014, at the conference "Monetary Policy and Sustainability," organized by the Council on Economic Policies (CEP) in Bellagio in June 2014, and at the workshop "European Central Banking after the Global Financial Crisis" at the European Union Center of Excellence at McGill University in September 2014. I thank participants at these events, in particular Alexander Barkawi, Romain Baeriswyl, François Claveau, Clément Fontan, Frank Garcia, Aaron James, Juliet Johnson, Laurence Kotlikoff, Marco Meyer, Pierre Monnin, Martin O'Neill, Sanjay Reddy, Tom Sorell, and David Woodruff for their comments.

Coibion, Olivier, Yuriy Gorodnichenko, Lorenz Kueng, and John Silvia. 2012. "Innocent Bystanders? Monetary Policy and Inequality in the U.S." *NBER Working Paper* No. 18170.

Dietsch, Peter. 2008. "Distributive Lessons from Division of Labour." *Journal of Moral Philosophy* 5(1), 96–117.

Dietsch, Peter. 2016. "The Ethical Aspects of International Financial Integration." In *Global Political Theory*, edited by David Held and Pietro Maffetone. Cambridge: Polity Press.

Dietsch, Peter, and Thomas Rixen. 2014. "Tax Competition and Global Background Justice." *Journal of Political Philosophy* 22(2), 150–77.

Dworkin, Ronald. 1981. "What is Equality? Part 2: Equality of Resources." *Philosophy & Public Affairs* 10(4), 283–345.

Englund, Peter. 1999. "The Swedish Banking Crisis: Roots and Consequences." *Oxford Review of Economic Policy* 15(3), 80–97.

The Financial Times. 2014. "Yellen Should Look Beyond the US." February 20.

Fontan, Clément. 2013. "Frankenstein en Europe: l'impact de la Banque centrale européenne sur la gestion de la crise de la zone euro." *Politique Européenne* 42, 10–33.

Fontan, Clément, François Claveau, and Peter Dietsch. 2016. "Central Banking and Inequalities: Taking Off the Blinders." *Politics, Philosophy & Economics*, published online before print June 7, doi: 10.1177/1470594X16651056.

Frankfurt, Harry. 1987. "Equality as a Moral Ideal." *Ethics* 98(1), 21–43.

Goodhart, Charles. 2010. "The Changing Role of Central Banks." Bank of International Settlements Working Paper 326, November.

Issing, Ottmar, Vitor Gaspar, Ignazio Angeloni, and Oreste Tristiani. 2001. *Monetary Policy in the Euro Area: Strategy and Decision-Making at the European Central Bank*. Cambridge: Cambridge University Press.

Jones, Claire. 2013. "Did QE Only Boost the Price of Warhols?" *Financial Times*, October 18.

Jovanovic, Branimir. 2014. "Inflation and the Rich After the Global Financial Crisis." *Luxembourg Income Study (LIS) Working Paper Series* No. 613, June.

Keynes, John Maynard. 2007 [1936]. *The General Theory of Employment, Interest and Money*. Basingstoke: Palgrave Macmillan.

Kydland, Finn E., and Edward C. Prescott. 1977. "Rules Rather than Discretion: The Inconsistency of Optimal Plans." *The Journal of Political Economy* 85(3), 473–92.

McLellan, David. 1977. *Karl Marx: Selected Writings*, Oxford: Oxford University Press [*On James Mill*, 1844].

Mehrling, Perry. 2011. *The New Lombard Street: How the Fed Became the Dealer of Last Resort*. Princeton and Oxford: Princeton University Press.

Monnin, Pierre. 2014. "Inflation and Income Inequality in Developed Economies." *Council on Economics Policies (CEP) Working Paper* 2014/1.

Murphy, Liam, and Thomas Nagel. 2002. *The Myth of Ownership*. Oxford: Oxford University Press.

Okun, Arthur M. 1975. *Equality and Efficiency: The Big Trade-Off*. Washington, DC: Brookings Institution.

Polanyi, Karl. 2001 [1944]. *The Great Transformation: The Political and Economic Origins of Our Time*, 2nd edition. Boston: Beacon Press.

Przeworski, Adam, and Michael Wallerstein. 1988. "Structural Dependence of the State on Capital." *American Political Science Review* 82(1), 11–29.

Rawls, John. 1999. *A Theory of Justice*, 2nd edition. Oxford: Oxford University Press.

Reddy, Sanjay. 2003. "Developing Just Monetary Arrangements." *Ethics & International Affairs* 17(1), 81–93.

Saiki, Ayako, and Jon Frost. 2014. "How Does Unconventional Monetary Policy Affect Inequality: Evidence from Japan." De Nederlandsche Bank Working Paper 423 (May).

Singleton, John. 2010. *Central Banking in the Twentieth Century*. Cambridge: Cambridge University Press.

Slemrod, Joel. 1994. "Fixing the Leak in Okun's Bucket: Optimal Tax Progressivity when Avoidance Can Be Controlled." *Journal of Public Economics* 55(1), 41–51.

Streeck, Wolfgang. 2013. *Gekaufte Zeit—Die vertagte Krise des demokratischen Kapitalismus*. Berlin: Suhrkamp.

Walzer, Michael. 1993. *Spheres of Justice*. New York: Basic Books.

Wigglesworth, Robin, Amy Kazmin, and James Crabtree. 2013. "Emerging Markets Pay the Price of the Advent of the Taper." *Financial Times*, June 20.

Woodford, Michael. 2003. *Interest and Prices: Foundations of a Theory of Monetary Policy*. Princeton and Oxford: Princeton University Press.

11

Information as a condition of justice in financial markets: The regulation of credit-rating agencies

Boudewijn de Bruin

11.1 INTRODUCTION

Steven Scalet and Thomas Kelly (2012, 489) make a strong case for the relevance of credit-rating agencies to questions of justice in financial markets:

> Reasonably accessible investing information is not merely a public good... but an important component for creating conditions of justice in a capitalist society, akin to making voting reasonably accessible to all in a democratic society. One can be understood as a demand of justice in capitalism; the other as a demand of justice in democracy.

Credit-rating agencies are supposed to contribute to the informational needs of investors trading bonds. They provide ratings of debt issued by corporations and governments (countries, states, territories, provinces, municipalities, regional water authorities, etc.), as well as of structured debt instruments (mortgage-backed securities, collateralized debt obligations, etc.). With letters ranging from top rank AAA (or *triple A*) to D (for default or bankruptcy), their ratings are intended to capture the risk that the issuer will be unable to repay the debt or will refuse to do so. Besides ratings, the agencies also produce so-called *outlooks* and *watchlists*, which are statements intended to reflect their views about the likely medium and short-term development of the rating of a given bond or structured security.

Many commentators agree with Scalet and Kelly that credit-rating agencies are essential to achieve justice and fairness in financial markets; indeed, many have provided far-reaching regulatory recommendations. In this chapter I argue that the role of credit-rating agencies in achieving justice in finance is not as great as these commentators believe. I argue instead for deregulation. My argument is that lawgivers have unjustifiably elevated the credit-rating agencies into official, legally binding sources of information concerning credit risk, thereby forcing many institutional investors to *outsource* what I call *epistemic responsibility*, that is, their responsibility to investigate credit risk themselves.

This is not to deny that credit-rating agencies can be criticized. As many ethicists, economists, government agencies, regulators, and commentators have pointed out, the credit-rating agencies were the primary source of information about the credit risks attached to such structured instruments as asset-backed securities, but, unlike corporate and sovereign bond ratings, when the sub-prime mortgage meltdown started in 2007 these ratings turned out to be highly inaccurate. Structured securities with triple A ratings defaulted with much higher frequency than the ratings had suggested. The Financial Crisis Inquiry Commission (Financial Crisis Inquiry Report 2011, xxv) concluded that "this crisis could not have happened without the rating agencies," while the US Senate Permanent Subcommittee on Investigations (2011, 6) stated that "inaccurate AAA credit ratings introduced risk in the U.S. financial system and constituted a key cause of the financial crisis." Mario Draghi, in his capacity as chairman of the Financial Stability Forum, stated in 2008 that "poor credit assessments" of complex structured credit products by credit-rating agencies "contributed to the build-up of the financial crisis."[1] The US Department of Justice even went so far as to claim, in 2013, that they "played an important role in helping to bring our economy to the brink of collapse," and decided to bring suit against a company involved.[2]

Despite the criticism, rating agencies are still among us—and perhaps ever more vigorous than before, as witnessed by a near doubling by 2015 of the value of Moody's equity since the outbreak of the crisis in 2007. To see why this is not too surprising, let us briefly consider part of the history of the agencies. Their ancestry goes back to the credit-*reporting* agencies of the nineteenth century, which provided information on the creditworthiness of firms ranging from small and medium-sized businesses to large companies such as those described in Henry Varnum Poor's famous *History of Railroads and Canals of the United States* (Poor 1860), which, despite its name, is a rating manual. Around the turn of the nineteenth century, however, bond rating was still a "fledgling activity" (Sinclair 2008, 97). This all changed through legislation with roots that lie in the regulatory response to the crash of 1929. Ratings soon achieved the status of official stamps of approval

[1] http://www.fsb.org/wp-content/uploads/st_080412.pdf (accessed November 14, 2016).

[2] These words should be attributed to Acting Associate Attorney General West. See https://www.justice.gov/opa/pr/department-justice-sues-standard-poor-s-fraud-rating-mortgage-backed-securities-years-leading (accessed November 14, 2016).

that institutional investors are required to use to justify their investment strategies—that is, to make them legal. To avert another crash, the American government and regulators developed prudential regulation for banks and pension funds, and introduced the distinction between investment and non-investment grade securities, the actual rating of which was to be carried out by the rating agencies, not the government. The Office of the Comptroller of the Currency, for instance, ruled in 1931 that bonds with ratings lower than BBB must be written down to market value. Moreover, from 1936 onwards banks were outright prohibited from investing in what today are called *junk bonds*, bonds of high perceived credit risk. Banks, insurance companies, pension funds, local and national governments, and many others are legally obliged to pay heed to what the agencies say, and to divest once a rating falls below a certain predefined minimum level. The bond-rating agencies, that is, are government-designated sources of information, with ratings obtaining "the force of law" (White 2010, 213).

Three other bits of history are also worth recalling. The first is a change in the 1970s in the business model of the rating agencies. Initially, the agencies charged subscribers for obtaining the ratings. A number of events—the advent of the photocopier might be one of them—led the industry to change to an issuer-pays model where issuers pay the agencies to obtain a rating, and subsequently decide to publish the rating—or not. The second is the establishment in 1975 of a registry of Nationally Recognized Statistical Rating Organizations, the ratings of which were recognized for the purposes of prudential regulation. This clearly strengthened the position of credit-rating agencies as gatekeepers of the financial markets. And thirdly, in the 1990s credit-rating agencies became involved in rating—and consultancy—services concerning structured debt securities, entering a wholly new market.

This chapter critically evaluates the contribution these agencies make to achieving justice. Some preliminary remarks are perhaps in order. The aim of this chapter is not so much to examine credit-rating agencies using a particular view of justice. Rather, by making assumptions that are as minimal as possible, I hope to defend normative conclusions that are acceptable to philosophers and policy-makers with a wide diversity of political convictions. One basic assumption is that individuals in just capitalist societies have interests deriving from their status as free and equal human beings. It is this status that endows them with human rights; but equally, it regulates their behavior as market participants. The presumption against monopoly or oligopoly, to which I turn later, is often motivated by a concern for justice understood in this way, and this is true of the proscription of conflicts of interest too, despite the fact that some views of justice (e.g. libertarianism) may disagree. Regulating away conflicts of interests and market concentration are, then, praiseworthy pursuits for most policy-makers with a concern for justice. But while several commentators have suggested that oligopoly and conflicts of interest in the rating industry are two important obstacles to justice, I argue that the problem lies elsewhere.

A second, but related, assumption is that the central question about justice in financial markets as we know them is not about the distribution of goods, but about the distribution of responsibilities. In words that go back almost two centuries, finance is an industry in which losses are socialized, and profits privatized. From the armchair of the political philosopher, this is deeply unjust, but easily resolved by aligning liability and responsibility, that is, by making people pay for the damage they do. Hardly any economist or policy-maker has suggested what would doubtless be a necessary element in returning responsibility where it belongs, for this would likely lead them to advocate abolishing the status of the central bank as lender of last resort. The consensus seems to be that while a more just financial system might require either the complete socialization of banking (with state banks, etc.) or their complete privatization (with free banking, etc.), it would be foolishly irresponsible to take a principled stance here, as a policy-maker or politician. Rather, what is needed are concrete stepwise regulatory improvements.

That is what the present chapter seeks to do. It argues that the responsibilities for gaining information about bonds and structured securities must be brought back to the people trading them. I argue against what I call *outsourcing epistemic responsibility*, when such outsourcing is unjustifiable. Credit-rating agencies investigate the risks attached to certain securities and publish their opinions. One might think that this fosters an autonomy interest of investors. If investors are to be in the position to make autonomous decisions, then they need not only freedom of choice; they also need information about the products they can choose. Providing such information therefore contributes to informed, autonomous choice. This line of argument has much to recommend it, and has been suggested by many policy-makers exploiting the analogy with the concept of informed consent in medicine. This analogy is spurious, though. If A sells medical drugs (or clothes) to B, then nothing prevents A and B from agreeing about all of the characteristics of the product (e.g. how effective, waterproof, or fashionable it is). But if A sells shares, bonds, or other securities to B, then in the overwhelming majority of cases, if A and B have such views, then A and B will have diametrically different views about the characteristics of the products. (Exceptions are of course when concerns about diversification, etc. play a role.) A will, then, not sell a security S to B unless A thinks that S will drop in price. And B will not buy a security S from A unless B thinks that S will rise in price. If most traders agreed on the characteristics of most securities, there would be no trade. Traders, consequently, disagree about the prospects of securities in many cases, or have no genuine doxastic attitudes at all. If that is true, I argue, a model derived from medicine is unhelpful. Hence it does not make sense to design financial analogs of the US Food and

Drug Administration or the European Medicines Agency, as has been popularly suggested.

The chapter is structured as follows. Section 11.2 reviews some empirical research about the role of bond-rating agencies in financial markets. Section 11.3 discusses, as a starting point, a prominent form of criticism to the effect that justice in financial markets suffers at the hands of rating agencies embroiled in conflicts of interests, but ultimately rejects this criticism. Section 11.4 moves on to examine a number of potential regulatory responses. The main argument here is that the informational added value of the rating agencies is far less unambiguously clear than would be necessary to justify granting their ratings "force of law," and that regulation should not encourage, let alone prescribe, the outsourcing of epistemic responsibilities. In other words, the regulatory response advocated in this chapter is deregulation rather than tighter regulation.

11.2 HOW CREDIT-RATING AGENCIES WORK

What explains the demand for credit ratings? Do ratings live up to what the agencies promise, and if so, do they offer value for money? If all goes well, a rating provides accurate information concerning the probability that the issuer of debt will be unable or unwilling to repay. There is significant agreement in the economics literature that ratings of corporate and sovereign bonds can be linked fairly robustly to default probabilities. A triple A rating, for instance, represents a 0.005 default probability, while a B-corporate bond is scarcely more than 50 percent likely to be repaid (Jorion and Zhang 2007, Zhou 2001). Or, as Moody's, one of the big rating agencies, states in their 2009 annual report (quoted by White 2010, 219):

> The quality of Moody's long-term performance is illustrated by a simple measure: over the past 80 years across a broad range of asset classes, obligations with lower Moody's ratings have consistently defaulted at greater rates than those with higher ratings.

This perhaps sounds reassuring, yet we ought to tread with care, for in reality this is nothing more than claiming that the letter ratings can be given fairly precise meaning. In particular, the correlation does *not* support the conclusion that rating agencies offer services worth paying the price they ask. You can predict with certainty that the sun will rise tomorrow, and you can give an approximate time. But no one will pay you for that bit of information as long as predictions with much higher accuracy can be obtained from internet sites for free. Credit-rating agencies claim to be in a better position than others because they use private and confidential information from the issuers; it may well be, though, that private information does not make their estimations of credit risk more accurate.

Since rating a company is, in essence, nothing other than determining the probability of bankruptcy, studying publicly available information about determinants of the latter provides some insights into the added value of using private information to rate debt. Traditional approaches to bankruptcy by researchers such as Altman (1968) find that financial ratios and data such as leverage, liquidity, and firm size are correlated with default probability. A more recent body of literature studies corporate governance measures (ownership structure, board independence, etc.), finding, for instance, that firms in which CEOs have greater decision-making powers have lower credit ratings (Liu and Jiraporn 2010). Thirdly, macroeconomic factors have a clear impact on ratings. While this last conclusion might not be too surprising, given the difficulties of disentangling fundamental and business-cycle effects, it goes against the official doctrine among the agencies to adopt a through-the-cycle approach based on fundamentals only.

Economists such as White (2010, 219) interpret these and other findings as supporting the claim that so far no unambiguous evidence has been adduced that credit-rating agencies are delivering a service that their customers could not do all by themselves:

> The question of what true value the major credit rating agencies bring to the financial markets remains open and difficult to resolve.

Bond-rating agencies sing the praises of their "privileged" relationship with the issuers. But fixed income analysts working for bond mutual funds and hedge funds arrive at credit-risk estimations without such "privileged" positions. Moreover, as White (2010, 219) continues his argument, the correlation that Moody's refers to in the above quote "could equally well arise if the rating agencies arrived at their ratings by, say, observing the financial markets' separately determined spreads on the relevant bonds (over comparable Treasury bonds), in which case the agencies would not be providing useful information to the markets."

Nor is the accuracy of the ratings always uncontested, witness the failures in the ratings of structured securities. To provide some background (based on Pagano and Volpin 2010), a simplified picture of how mortgage-backed securities work is this. An *originator* (say, New Capital Financial) lends money to someone that wants to finance a house. An *arranger* (e.g. Goldman Sachs) buys some 4,000 mortgages from the originator. A *Special Purpose Vehicle* is created (e.g. GSAMP-Trust 2006-NC2, just to name one of them), buying the portfolio of 4,000 mortgages from the arranger. And the Special Purpose Vehicle, in turn, issues mortgage-backed securities to finance this purchase. It is these things—or more precisely, their various tranches—that credit-rating agencies rate.

But how do they accomplish this? As Pagano and Volpin (2010) argue, to value a mortgage-backed security one needs more than the prospectus and the annual reports that the Special Purpose Vehicle produces, because these documents only publish summary statistics rather than information at the level of individual loans. It is true that companies such as Loan Performance and McDash Analytics provide such detailed information about the underlying loans, such as the borrower's debt-to-income level, the loan-to-value ratio, and the borrower's FICO score, which are completely standard ratios to calculate the risks attached to a particular mortgage. As Pagano and Volpin (2010) note, however, Moody's only started requesting such detailed information in 2007, and Fitch and Standard & Poor's seem to have been no different in this respect. Of course this is only one example; but the impression is confirmed by other studies: the methodology used to rate structured debt was suboptimal, to say the least.

To give a second example, an important part of rating structured securities is to estimate the correlation of default on assets underlying the security; it matters, that is, whether the underlying assets are likely to default simultaneously (if they default), or whether one asset's default is independent of another's. One might expect that credit-rating agencies develop sufficiently subtle measures of default correlation. Based on information provided by Standard & Poor's, however, Benmelech and Dlugosz (2009) report that, quite to the contrary, fairly blunt assumptions were being made to the effect that two corporate securities from the same sector have a correlation of 0.15, and two such securities from different sectors have a correlation of 0.05. It may be reasonable to make such assumptions when times are normal. In times of crisis, however, they are likely to be wide of the mark.

It might be objected that the responsibility for buying securities ultimately lies with the investor. Should the investors have known that ratings of structured debt securities were of lesser quality than ratings of plain vanilla corporate and sovereign bonds? Here is what Standard & Poor's wrote in 2007: "[o]ur ratings represent a uniform measure of credit quality globally and across all types of debt instruments." And, as if this were not clear enough: "[i]n other words, an 'AAA' rated corporate bond should exhibit the same degree of credit quality as an 'AAA' rated securitized issue" (quoted by Pagano and Volpin 2010, 407).

Some people in global finance knew that what Standard & Poor's said was implausible. Lloyd Blankfein, CEO of Goldman Sachs at the time, for instance, once stated that

> too many financial institutions and investors simply outsourced their risk management. Rather than undertake their own analysis, they relied on the rating agencies to do the essential work of risk analysis for them... This overdependence on credit ratings coincided with the dilution of the coveted triple A rating.

> In January 2008, there were 12 triple A-rated companies in the world. At the same time, there were 64,000 structured finance instruments, such as collateralized debt obligations, rated triple A (quoted by Pagano and Volpin (2010, 404)).

Yet many investors thought that all securities with the same rating were identical in terms of credit risk; so to determine the value of an AAA rated tranche of a mortgage-backed security for which a price quotation is unavailable, such an investor would consider comparable AAA rated securities with quoted prices. Jorion (2009, 929), for instance, shows that the loss of $19 billion that UBS, the Swiss bank, incurred on mortgage-backed securities positions in 2007 alone, should be attributed to exactly this ultimately unjustified mapping of triple A rated tranches to yield curves of triple A rated corporate debt. He dubs it "an act of blind faith in the credit rating."

11.3 A JUSTICE-BASED CRITICISM: CONFLICTS OF INTEREST

Credit-rating agencies have been the target of intense and multifarious criticism. They have been accused of an absence of transparency and a lack of competence. They have been said to be involved in unfair competition through such practices as *tying*—where an agency tells the issuer it will give a lower rating if they do not buy other services; *notching*—where the agency tells the issuer it will only rate a large number of securities so that they can only place a bulk order; and *rate shopping*—where issuers request ratings from a variety of agencies and only make the highest rating public. Yet the most frequently heard argument against the credit-rating agencies is that they have unfairly exploited conflicts of interest. Authors such as Duff and Einig (2015), Scalet and Kelly (2012), and Strier (2008) argue that conflicts of interest arise out of the issuer-pays model that characterizes much of the industry: issuers of securities pay the credit-rating agencies to rate them and subsequently decide whether or not to publish the rating. Conflicts of interest are also said to arise out of the fact that in addition to rating services, the agencies offer consultancy services to the issuers, as a result of which they may see products twice, as consultants in the production process, and later as raters. And the governance model of some agencies is also mentioned in relation to conflicts of interest. Selig (2008), for instance, provides evidence that Moody's introduced a new model to rate structured debt securities: it simply relaxed the ratings (the new model led to higher ratings of collateralized debt obligations). Selig explains this by referring to Moody's experiencing serious pressure from the investors after it had become listed on the stock market in 2000.

Under most conceptions of justice, what one gains through exploiting conflicts of interest is an unfair advantage. Justice-based arguments about conflicts of interest are therefore prominent, and if they work here, they are likely very powerful. On closer inspection, however, they turn out to be less than convincing.[3] According to a standard definition developed by John Boatright (2000, 219), a conflict of interest exists whenever

> a personal or institutional interest interferes with the ability of an individual or institution to act in the interest of another party, when the individual or institution has an ethical or legal obligation to act in that other party's interest.

To show that credit-rating agencies have a conflict of interest, we have to do three things: (1) single out the relevant parties or stakeholders and their personal or institutional interests; (2) demonstrate that some interests of the credit-rating agencies interfere with their ability to serve the interests of these other parties; and (3) show that there is an ethical or legal obligation on the part of the agencies to act in the interests of these other parties. (It may be thought that the third condition is redundant, and that the mere existence of two conflicting interests is sufficient for there to be a conflict of interest. But that would widen the concept implausibly to incorporate ethically irrelevant cases in which interests are incompatible.) Relevant stakeholders include the rating agencies, their shareholders, employees, and clients, and not unimportantly, the parties that make use of the ratings in their investment decisions.

Typically, conflicts of interest involve a clash between the interests of a service provider and the interests of their clients. Banks, insurance companies, financial advisers, and many others in the financial services industry have interests the furtherance of which would stand in the way of optimally serving their clients' interests. When credit-rating agencies are described as "conflicted," one hardly ever singles out the clients (that is, the issuers of the rated securities) as potential victims (or for that matter the shareholders and employees). What the critics mean is that there is a conflict between the interests of the rating agencies and the interests of the beneficiaries of the information they provide, that is, the investors (and indirectly, those affected by the actions of these investors). The interests of these and other stakeholders are fairly unambiguous: the investors have an interest in published ratings that estimate credit risk as accurately as possible; the owners of the agencies (shareholders) have an interest in maximizing shareholder value; and the clients of the credit-rating agencies (issuers of securities) have an interest in receiving high ratings.

Unsurprisingly, these interests are far from well-aligned. Yet as long as we have not shown that there are ethical or legal obligations to serve particular

[3] The argument provided here extends an earlier one advanced by de Bruin (2015).

interests, interfering interests do not entail the existence of a conflict of interest. A discussion about *legal* obligations is quickly exhausted. In the United States, credit-rating agencies are protected by the First Amendment; they are seen as publishers of opinions concerning the creditworthiness of issuers, with extensive freedom of speech. Legal complaints about inaccurate ratings have hardly ever stood a chance of being successful. Consequently, American courts do not recognize a legal obligation on the part of the rating agencies to serve the interests of investors.

What about an *ethical* obligation? As the quotation with which this chapter began makes clear, Scalet and Kelly (2012) believe that investors, or civil society at large, have a right to obtain accurate information concerning securities that is not very different from the right to vote. When pressed, they would perhaps not go so far as to consider this to be a genuine human right; but they do seem to consider the right to accurate investment information to be an essential citizenship right, violations of which endanger democracy and justice. Bond-rating agencies, in their view, are an important beacon in developing and maintaining a just society.

Apart from the fact that this argument presupposes a potentially unjustified belief in the added informational value of ratings—as we have seen, the price paid for the ratings may be much too high if ratings can just as easily and accurately be derived from publicly available information—this argument fails to distinguish between (political or social) rights, on the one hand, and the way in which they are secured, on the other. It may well be true that in a given society investment information plays a role in securing certain human rights. The right to security in the event of old age, for instance, counts as a human right according to the Universal Declaration of Human Rights; and as it stands, in many countries this right is guaranteed by pension funds that arguably need adequate information about the creditworthiness of issuers they consider investing in. Yet this does not turn the possession of accurate investment information into a human right, because the right to security in the event of old age can be realized by a very different system that does not need to rely on investment information (e.g. a pay-as-you go pension scheme where current pensioners are financed by taxes on current workers). In other words, information about the creditworthiness of issuers may be useful to guarantee certain human rights in certain ways, but this does entail that there is a human right to such information.

One might suspect that an alternative, more consequentialist, argument could attempt to show that information about credit risk is a public good, for instance on the grounds that inaccurate ratings were a causal factor in the global financial crisis; for clearly, accurate ratings have the potential to prevent much future mishap and to contribute to financial stability. Just as the rights-based argument, however, such an argument will founder on its neglect of alternative courses of action that may be equally well or better suited to achieve the desired consequences. It may be that some of the effects of the crisis would have been less pronounced had the credit-ratings agencies focused more on the interests of investors. That credit-ratings agencies have played a causal role in the global financial crisis must, as we have seen, to a large extent be attributed to existing regulatory frameworks, however. And since abolishing rating bounds for institutional investors may well have the same, or better, results, the consequentialist argument that rating agencies serve the realization of public good fails to do what it is supposed to.

A tempting third line, however, may be to argue that rating agencies have a *conditional* ethical obligation to serve the interests of investors. Given that the agencies do the things they do, their beneficiaries have, according to this line of argumentation, a right to get the best possible service. This surely is a very common line of argumentation. Children, for instance, do not have an absolute right to play with game computers, but they do have the conditional right that if a game computer is marketed to them, it must be sufficiently safe. The traditional model of consumer ethics centered round the tenet of *caveat emptor*, according to which it was up to the consumer to find out whether a product fulfilled the specifications it was claimed to meet. Gradually, however, the ethics of *caveat vendor* has taken over, with countless legal prescriptions about design, production, marketing, and sales.

This strategy does not work for credit-rating agencies, though, for they publish unambiguous disclaimers about the intended use of their ratings. If you visit the website of Moody's, for instance, you thereby agree to its terms of use (Moody's Investors Service n.d.), including the provision that you will

> expressly agree that... the credit ratings and other opinions provided via [Moody's website] are, and will be construed solely as, statements of opinion of the relative future credit risk... of... securities and not statements of current or historical fact as to credit worthiness, investment or financial advice, recommendations regarding credit decisions or decisions to purchase, hold or sell any securities, endorsements of the accuracy of any of the data or conclusions, or attempts to independently assess or vouch for the financial condition of any company;

and that

> you will accordingly, with due care, make your own study and evaluation of each investment decision or security, and of each issuer and guarantor of, and each provider of credit support for, each security or credit that you may consider purchasing, holding, selling, or providing.

Moreover,

> you expressly agree that any tools or information made available on [Moody's website] are not a substitute for the exercise of independent judgment and expertise. You should always seek the assistance of a professional for advice on investments, tax, the law, or other professional matters.

Whoever is in finance is in the business of risk. Moody's terms of use are crystal clear that their "opinions of risk" are what they say they are: mere opinions. Moreover, they are targeted at professionals, not laypeople who may be unable to understand the concepts to which the terms of use refer. *Caveat vendor* does not support the claim that credit-rating agencies have an ethical obligation needed to establish a conflict of interest.

It might be objected that since numerous investors as a matter of fact use ratings in their investment decisions, they have a right to accurate ratings. This argument, however, fails. Consider horoscopes. (This is not to suggest that the added value of the opinions produced by the credit-rating agencies is comparable to the added value of horoscopes, but it is instructive to compare credit rating and astrology.) Some newspapers publish them every week. It may well be true that readers make some daily decisions dependent on them. Readers complaining about inaccurate horoscopes cannot base their complaint on the newspaper's having infringed a right, though. That a group of people uses your publications for particular means does not give them a right over you. This also applies to a variant of this objection to the effect that many investors are legally obliged to use the ratings for investment decisions. As long as the agencies have not signed contracts with the lawgiver about the accuracy of their ratings, what the lawgiver does is no different from, say, the General Medical Council requiring doctors to consult with astrologists before deciding hard medical cases. This would be a reprehensible action for the Council to take; but it would not create new obligations for astrologists.

There are, then, no conflicts of interest. As I argue below, what should worry us most from the point of view of justice is the role of government. Citizens ought to be able to trust that governments and regulators only legally compel individuals and companies to outsource certain of their activities to designated parties when the quality and added value of what these parties do is beyond any reasonable dispute. To avoid misunderstanding, it should be stressed that this does not mean that the rating agencies are off the hook entirely. Imagine a newspaper, used by politicians, policy-makers, and politically interested citizens for its depth, originality, and high-quality investigative journalism. It figures as an important source of information in parliamentary debate, and it indirectly influences law making, both because of the sorts of fact it uncovers and because of its thoughtful editorials. Now the newspaper adopts a new business model. It is bought by a large media conglomerate that owns the largest tabloid in the country, and it switches from a subscriber-pays to an advertiser-pays business model. Soon after, the quality of the newspaper starts to deteriorate. Instead of new investigative stories and constructive editorials, the newspaper rehearses press releases and news from news agencies verbatim. Surely readers will have reason to complain about the greed of the owners (who sold their company) and the meekness of the editor-in-chief (who compromised their high standards of journalism). It is a sad story, and the original owners and the editor-in-chief should not have squandered the newspaper this way; one may even describe their behavior as *unvirtuous*. But they have not infringed on the rights of their readers.

11.4 REGULATORY RESPONSES

While the 2010 *Global Financial Stability Report* of the International Monetary Fund (2010, 111) speaks of "overreliance on ratings in legislation, regulations, and private sector contracts," the changes that the Fund and other organizations suggest are exceedingly mild. A "mechanistic" use of ratings must be discouraged, it writes (ibid., 112), but all the same it should be recognized that "smaller and less sophisticated investors and institutions that do not have the economies of scale to do their own credit assessments will inevitably continue to use ratings extensively." Steps ought to be taken to increase oversight of credit-rating agencies, and in particular they should be required to provide information about the success rates of their ratings.

The US Securities and Exchange Commission (2008) has suggested that credit-rating agencies must disclose the information on which they base their ratings. Referring to the different characteristics of corporate and sovereign debt ratings, on the one hand, and ratings of structured debt, on the other, the Commission has suggested that there is a need for different rating instruments for different categories. Observing the enormous market concentration in the industry (with a Herfindahl-Hirschman index of around 3,000 ranking higher than almost any other industry), the European Commission wants to increase competition among credit-rating agencies. Some have even floated the idea of launching a European credit-rating agency to combat the American oligopoly (Atkins and Tait 2011).

11.4.1 Added value of ratings

These suggestions ignore the fact that it is far from unambiguously clear that credit-rating agencies fulfill a function worth paying for. In contrast to what the International Monetary Fund recommends, for instance, "smaller and less sophisticated investors and institutions" should be discouraged just as much as larger investors from making their investment decisions "mechanistically" dependent on credit ratings. Lack of size or sophistication offers no ground for special access to information; quite to the contrary, it disqualifies you for particular businesses. If a company is too small or unsophisticated to assume responsibility for the risks of certain trades, it should be discouraged from carrying out the trades. (Compare the peripheral hospital, which must focus on routine medical procedures and refer patients requiring more sophisticated treatment to specialized hospitals. Or take the small chemical start-up that should not be allowed to work under relaxed safety procedures just because it cannot afford the legally required level of safety.) As a matter of fact, ratings of structured finance instruments have contributed significantly to a demand for them among investors lacking sufficient expertise (Benmelech and Dlugosz 2009). The regulatory relevance of this bit of empirical evidence cannot be overestimated: without regulation, the sub-prime mortgage bubble might not have been so large. Justice, therefore, is served better by returning the responsibility where it belongs, namely, to the investors themselves.

11.4.2 Information disclosure

The suggestion of the Securities and Exchange Commission that credit-rating agencies must disclose information is equally problematic from the point of view of justice. Some might think that the amount of information the prospectus gives about a particular mortgage-backed security, say, is insufficient in light of the autonomy interests of potential buyers. As we saw above, for consumers to be in the position to make an autonomous decision, they need information concerning the products they can buy. And it is often assumed to be the responsibility of the manufacturer or salesperson to provide this information. Such an argument would be plausible if buyers of structured securities were like patients. Patients typically lack the knowledge to critically assess even the simplest statements made by doctors or pharmaceutical companies. Buyers of structured finance instruments are not patients, though. Even the least sophisticated buyers have sufficient financial knowledge and expertise to know that the information contained in the prospectus is rather useless to determine the relevant risks, and consequently, they can make the autonomous decision to buy or not to buy something of which they do not know enough. Such autonomous decisions were indeed made by many buyers prior to the global financial crisis. Lack of information does not always mean lack of autonomy. To be sure, buyers typically benefit when information about products becomes available; but then on most counts the preferred model is to make the producers or service providers responsible for the provision of such information, rather than the indirect route via costly intermediaries, the rating agencies.

It might be objected that this promotes the exclusion of less informed, potentially poorer participants from a highly profitable market, thereby compromising justice. To begin with, however, these market participants are typically not individuals but institutional investors such as pension funds or banks. Their profits will spread among individuals of very different degrees of wealth, and because of their size these investors are generally capable of doing the research themselves, or they can autonomously decide to hire others to do so. Moreover, it is important to bear in mind that even if certain poorer individuals would not end up profiting from investments in structured finance (for instance because their pension funds were really too small), this need not constitute an injustice.

To see this, let me return to the analogy between finance and medicine. At first sight, it may seem that just as it would be unfair to deny certain poorer patients particular advanced forms of treatment, it is unfair to deny poorer individuals the profits of structured finance. But profit is not the only thing to which buying structured finance may lead; investments may also lead to losses. Now, in contrast to medicine, losses are not mere "side effects" of an otherwise effective treatment; quite to the contrary, downside risks are part and parcel of investing. It seems perfectly reasonable to hold the view that individuals that are too poor to cover these risks should not be exposed to them in the first place, even if it means that of necessity they will also forego potential upside risks. If we find that this results in a skewed distribution of wealth, it is for the state, not the finance industry, to develop *post hoc* redistributive policies.

11.4.3 Different rating systems

As we have seen, UBS, the Swiss bank, lost around $19 billion on positions in structured securities in 2007 alone: they gave the same interpretation to ratings of structured debt and corporate debt. Taking the ratings too literally, they essentially made a mistake that some investors make when they interpret analyst recommendations. It is instructive to consider this briefly. Analyst recommendations range from "strong buy" and "buy," via "hold," to "sell" and "strong sell." Taking these recommendations at face value would be an error, because in about 95 percent of the cases analysts give a "strong buy," "buy," or "hold" recommendation, reflecting a strong bias towards the positive. Malmendier and Shanthikumar (2007) show that individual investors do not discount for this bias. Institutional investors, by contrast, discount the bias and *sell* their shares when they are assigned a "hold" recommendation.

One might object that analysts might be legally proscribed from using the word "hold" when they mean to recommend selling the shares, and that similarly regulators could force a new vocabulary on the rating agencies to deal with the different asset classes (corporate, sovereign, and structured debt). This falsely suggests, however, that it is difficult for the intended users of the recommendations or ratings to discover that terms may mean different things in different contexts; and it also falsely suggests that it is not so much the responsibility of banks and other users of ratings (or recommendations) to critically assess their value and usefulness. The financial pages of every newspaper contain occasional reports about the unimpressive track records of most analysts; the exceptions are rather due to luck than skill. This shows that it makes no sense to object that the particular use of recommendation terms excludes certain market participants. The stock recommendation bias is nothing but a consistent form of euphemism, and we are all familiar with similar euphemisms from other spheres of life. Moreover, the objection would overestimate the value of analyst recommendations. In finance a great deal of what is called *information* is nothing other than opinions, and opinions typically differ. As we have seen, hardly any trade would be carried out when everyone agrees with the recommendation; for when A buys shares from B, A typically believes that the shares will go up in value, whereas B will typically believe exactly the opposite. Regulation must not contribute to spreading a false sense of security and certainty where things are often nebulous and undetermined. Different systems of rating would, however, do exactly that.

11.4.4 Market concentration

On most accounts, monopoly and oligopoly constitute serious threats to justice. Justice requires, on most accounts, that the market be a level playing field, as excessive barriers to entry discriminate unfairly against smaller and new market participants—or even fail to respect their rights. Consequentialist arguments point out that quality and innovation may suffer when markets become excessively concentrated.

The rating industry is highly concentrated. It is, however, far from clear that this is unfair. While the big three agencies dominate the market, there are around 150 other credit-rating agencies that offer specialist services at the same time. Moreover, it is dubious whether the quality of the ratings would increase by establishing an additional bond-rating agency on European soil, as some commentators have suggested. To the extent that ratings are based on publicly available information, differences in ratings will only be attributed to differences in methodology, which are likely to be very small. To the extent that they are based on private information, there seems to be little room for increasing the number of agencies beyond a certain point of saturation determined by a company's willingness to engage in extended conversation with many different agencies—a willingness correlated not only with the company's stamina, but also with the risk of private information turning public in the hands of rating agency employees of lesser integrity. No company will want to communicate confidential information to a large number of parties. Despite initial appearances, the level of market concentration in the credit-rating industry is, therefore, unproblematic from the point of view of justice.

11.4.5 Impact on national sovereignty

Another, perhaps stronger argument why the distribution of power of the rating agencies may be seen as unfair refers to their alleged influence on national sovereignty. Sinclair's important monograph *The New Masters of Capital*, for instance, laments the negative impact credit-rating agencies have on "national policy autonomy," as their enormous powers provide them with "a means for transmitting policy and managerial orthodoxy to widely scattered governments and corporations" (2008, 71). A negative assessment of the influence of credit-rating agencies on national sovereignty has also been put forward by others, most famously by *New York Times* journalist Thomas Friedman (1995):

> you could almost say that we live again in a two-superpower world. There is the U.S. and there is Moody's. The U.S. can destroy a country by leveling it with bombs; Moody's can destroy a country by downgrading its bonds.

Descriptively this may not be fully accurate, though. To begin with Friedman's claim, there surely is evidence that sovereign ratings are correlated with bond yields, that is, with what a bond owner earns (or loses) on a bond. A bad rating makes it more expensive and difficult to borrow money. But that is wholly unsurprising if poor ratings express higher risks of default, which, as we have seen, they generally do. Of course countries will fear the credit-rating agencies in many cases. The publicity offensive launched by the British government to ensure a high rating of its sovereign debt in 1978 is well documented (Gill 2015), but since governments typically emphasize the social welfare effects of their policy measures at the expense of the financial rewards that bond-holders may enjoy as a result of them (Levy and Pauzner 2014), many governments will be less successful than the British (which, having received help from the International Monetary Fund in 1976, received a stunning AAA rating from Standard & Poor's only two years later).

It may seem that headlines in the financial press such as "Jacob Zuma vows action to prevent South Africa rating downgrade" (England 2016) bolster Sinclair's claim about national sovereignty. But if the South African president ensures that the government will "co-operate with business and curb spending," does that mean that the bond-rating agencies are instrumental in spreading a neo-liberal ideology? Apart from the conceptual difficulties surrounding the definition of *neo-liberalism*, rigorous empirical studies attesting to this claim are so far very scant, nor does the evidence unequivocally point in the direction Sinclair indicates. Soudis (2015), for instance, shows that while there is indeed a tendency towards neo-liberal policy-making, liberalization, and deregulation reforms, it is not true that ratings and downgradings are correlated with the speed and extent of these reforms. Clearly more work has to be done here, because Soudis's analysis does not seem to rule out that countries attempt to *prevent* downgrades by anticipatory deregulation. But as it stands, Sinclair seems to be going a bit too fast.

In addition to that, two normative points are worth making. First of all, the primary reason why the big three rating agencies became so powerful is that power was vested in them by the US government. That Moody's can, in Friedman's words, "destroy a country by downgrading its bonds" is because US investors are bound, by US regulation, to listen to what Moody's, a US credit-rating agency that happens to be one of the three largest worldwide, has to say about the country's creditworthiness. As a result, Moody's power to destroy a country is much more intimately correlated with America's power to "destroy a country by leveling it with bombs" than Friedman's quip suggests. In other words, if the skewed distribution of power across credit-rating agencies did signal injustice, then the injustice would not so much be related to the power of credit-rating agencies as such, but rather derive from global injustices reflected by the skewed distribution of power across nations.

Secondly, to the extent that the ratings offered by the agencies are the result of research that may in principle also be conducted by investors themselves, the agencies are less central in the dynamics to which Sinclair and Friedman refer. It is the investors that require premiums to compensate for additional risks attached to buying debt from countries with high risks of default. I do not deny that the ideology of individual employees of credit-rating agencies may bias their judgments of credit risk. Perhaps through a neo-liberal lens—whatever that may be—certain countries are seen as riskier than they really are, and some are seen as less risky. There seems to be little evidence to demonstrate such a bias, though. In fact, the rating agencies have been more conservative in their judgments of the probability of sovereign default than neo-liberalism would suggest. Polito and Wickens (2015) calculated credit ratings of fourteen European countries using information about their fiscal position only, that is, on their future debt liabilities and on the prospects of using fiscal policy to repay them. Their model turns out to lead to much more pessimistic (or neo-liberal, if you wish) ratings than the ratings from the big three credit-rating agencies: they identify the problems that led to the sovereign debt crisis almost two years earlier than rating agencies. All in all, credit-rating agencies are the messengers, but to the extent that their estimates are compatible with what investors would arrive at themselves, as Polito and Wickens have done, it is a mistake to shoot the messenger.

11.4.6 First Amendment protection

But are the agencies mere messengers? As we have seen, they make it clear that what they offer are "opinions" only, protected by the First Amendment to the US Constitution (freedom of expression); and they style themselves as journalists rather than social scientists (Partnoy 1999). Observing that the revenues of the agencies have increased in the last decade, whereas traditional media are generally in rather poor shape, Poon (2012) argues that credit-rating agencies must not be seen as on a par with the press. The plausibility of that line of argument depends, however, on where the increased revenue comes from. Empirical studies are still scant, but the hypothesis has much to recommend it, that if lawgivers had not made ratings into official stamps of approval for many institutional investors (particularly regarding structured debt), the demand for ratings would have been considerably lower (Benmelech and Dlugosz 2009). (Consider the following analogy: newspaper revenues can be given a significant boost by a government ruling that every citizen must subscribe to one national and one local newspaper; they would not cease to be newspapers, though.)

It surely strikes some regulators as appealing to withdraw First Amendment protection from the rating agencies. This would not be a good idea. It is not the aim of this chapter to develop a fully fledged theory of when regulation interfering with free speech may be justified. One condition, however, seems fairly uncontested, namely, that one may consider regulating speech if the intended audience has difficulty in ascertaining its truth value. The view that certain forms of advertisement are not protected by the First Amendment presupposes, for instance, that consumers are often not in the position to discover whether what manufacturers or salespeople tell them is true. In agreement with Richardson and White (2009), however, the solution recommended here is less rather than more regulation. Justice in financial markets—arguably unlike justice in financial services such as retail banking, insurance, or retirement planning—benefits from using a buyer beware model of investment rather than from more government involvement or the *caveat vendor* principle in retail.

11.5 CONCLUSION

In this chapter I have argued that justice in financial markets is fostered by a modicum of deregulation. In contrast to many policy-makers and political commentators, I see little merit in plans for more intense supervision of the credit-rating industry—or for establishing a credit-rating agency on European soil. Rather, I have shown the unhappy consequences of turning ratings into official stamps of approval: it unjustifiably leads investors to outsource their epistemic responsibilities. Unlike, say, the security of food and drugs or the safety of houses and bridges, the expected risks and returns of financial instruments are hard, indeed often impossible to determine. So far no one has found a method to predict financial markets with a level of accuracy that comes close to common practice in the natural sciences. The image of mathematical whizz-kids populating finance firms is dangerously misguided: from the point of view of theory, their mathematics is fairly trivial, and from the point of view of application, it is often inadequate. Initiatives such as the Dodd-Frank Act suggest that there is a factual basis to the matter of whether a bond-rating agency has used the right methodology to rate a security. This surely may sometimes be the case; but many securities are better called *unratable*—for this would more honestly express the fact that oftentimes predicting the failures and successes of securities is closer to astrology than rocket science.[4]

REFERENCES

Altman, E. 1968. "Financial Ratios, Discriminant Analysis, and the Prediction of Corporate Bankruptcy." *Journal of Finance* 23(4), 589–609.

Atkins, R., and N. Tait. 2011. "Frankfurt Looks at Creating Rating Agency." *Financial Times*, July 27.

Benmelech, E. and J. Dlugosz. 2009. "The Alchemy of CDO Credit Ratings." *Journal of Monetary Economics* 56(5), 617–34.

Boatright, J. R. 2000. "Conflicts of Interest in Financial Services." *Business and Society Review* 105(2), 201–19.

de Bruin, B. 2015. *Ethics and the Global Financial Crisis: Why Incompetence is Worse than Greed*. Cambridge: Cambridge University Press.

Duff, A., and S. Einig. 2015. "Debt Issuer: Credit Rating Agency Relations and the Trinity of Solicitude: An Empirical Study of the Role of Commitment." *Journal of Business Ethics* 129(3), 553–69.

England, A. 2016. "Jacob Zuma Vows Action to Prevent South Africa Rating Downgrade." *Financial Times*, February 16.

Financial Crisis Inquiry Report. 2011. *The Financial Crisis Inquiry Report: Final Report of the National Commission on the Causes of the Financial and Economic Crisis in the United States*. https://www.gpo.gov/fdsys/pkg/GPO-FCIC/pdf/GPO-FCIC.pdf (accessed November 14, 2016).

Friedman, T. L. 1995. "Foreign Affairs: Don't Mess With Moody's." *The New York Times*, pp. A, 19, 1.

Gill, D. J. 2015. "Rating the UK: The British Government's Sovereign Credit Ratings, 1976–8." *Economic History Review* 3, 1016–37.

International Monetary Fund. 2010. *Global Financial Stability Report 2010: Sovereigns, Funding, and Systemic Liquidity*. Washington, DC.

[4] This chapter has benefited from discussions with James Dempsey, Jacques Jacobs, Jens van't Klooster, Marco Meyer, Emmanuel Picavet, Tom Sorell, Dimitrios Soudis, Hugo Thiéfaine, Christian Walter, and Lisa Warenski, as well as audiences in Bayreuth, Cambridge, Frankfurt, Paris, Rotterdam, Utrecht, and Warwick. I owe special thanks to the editor of this volume, Lisa Herzog, for written comments on several drafts of this paper.

Jorion, P. 2009. "Risk Management Lessons from the Credit Crisis." *European Financial Management* 15(5), 923–33.

Jorion, P., and G. Zhang. 2007. "Information Effects of Bond Rating Changes." *Journal of Fixed Income* 16(4), 45–59.

Levy, N., and A. Pauzner. 2014. "Government's Credit-Rating Concerns and the Evaluation of Public Projects." *Journal of Public Economics* 115, 117–30.

Liu, Y., and P. Jiraporn. 2010. "The Effect of CEO Power on Bond Ratings and Yields." *Journal of Empirical Finance* 17(4), 744–62.

Malmendier, U., and D. Shanthikumar. 2007. "Are Small Investors Naive about Incentives?" *Journal of Financial Economics* 85(2), 457–89.

Moody's Investors Service. N.d. *Moody's Terms of Use.* https://www.moodys.com/termsofuseinfo.aspx (accessed February 4, 2016).

Pagano, M., and P. Volpin. 2010. "Credit Ratings Failures and Policy Options." *Economic Policy* 25(62), 401–31.

Partnoy, F. 1999. "The Siskel and Ebert of Financial Markets?: Two Thumbs Down for the Credit." *Washington University Law Quarterly* 77(3), 619–714.

Polito, V., and M. Wickens. 2015. "Sovereign Credit Ratings in the European Union: A Model-based Fiscal Analysis." *European Economic Review* 78, 220–47.

Poon, M. 2012. "Rating Agencies." In *The Oxford Handbook of the Sociology of Finance*, edited by K. Knorr Cetina and A. Preda. Oxford: Oxford University Press, 272–92.

Poor, H. 1860. *History of Railroads and Canals of the United States.* New York: J. H. Schultz.

Richardson, M., and L. White. 2009. "The Rating Agencies: Is Regulation the Answer?" *Financial Markets, Institutions & Instruments* 18(2), 146–8.

Scalet, S., and T. F. Kelly. 2012. "The Ethics of Credit Rating Agencies: What Happened and the Way Forward." *Journal of Business Ethics* 111(4), 477–90.

Securities and Exchange Commission. 2008. *Summary Report of Issues Identified in the Commission Staff's Examinations of Select Credit Rating Agencies.*

Selig, K. 2008. "Teaching Notes: Greed, Negligence, or System Failure? Credit Rating Agencies and the Financial Crisis." The Kenan Institute for Ethics, Duke University. http://kenan.ethics.duke.edu/wp-content/uploads/2012/07/Case-Study-Greed-and-Negligence-notes.pdf (accessed November 14, 2016).

Sinclair, T. J. 2008. *The New Masters of Capital: American Bond Rating Agencies and the Politics of Creditworthiness.* Ithaca: Cornell University Press.

Soudis, D. 2015. "Credit Rating Agencies and the IPE: Not as Influential as Thought?" *Review of International Political Economy* 22(4), 813–37.

Strier, F. 2008. "Rating the Raters: Conflicts of Interest in the Credit Rating Firms." *Business & Society Review* 113(4), 533–53.

US Senate Permanent Subcommittee on Investigations. 2011. *Wall Street and the Financial Crisis: Anatomy of a Financial Collapse.* Washington, DC.

White, L. 2010. "Markets: The Credit Rating Agencies." *Journal of Economics Perspectives* 15, 211–26.

Zhou, C. 2001. "Credit Rating and Corporate Defaults." *Journal of Fixed Income* 11(3), 30–40.

12

Gender justice in financial markets

Roseanne Russell and Charlotte Villiers

12.1 INTRODUCTION

Financial markets have often been represented and treated as gender-neutral domains. Closer scrutiny reveals, however, that the consequences of their operation and the structure of their institutions are in fact deeply gendered. In the post-financial crisis period financial market actors have engaged with gender (or more accurately, "women") explicitly. New empowerment initiatives have allowed women to access financial markets as creditors and entrepreneurs (EmpowerWomen 2016), while various economic actors have spotted the "untapped" potential of women consumers and adapted their practices to pay more attention to their perceived needs (Global Banking Alliance for Women 2016).

One area which has been the subject of intense regulatory and policy attention has been the identity of financial market decision-makers. Across the EU there is an increasing consensus that predominantly male corporate boardrooms are problematic and that boardroom diversity (largely understood as requiring more women directors) is a positive goal. The case for increasing the number of women in company boardrooms has largely been made from two broad standpoints. The first is that it seemingly promises improved business performance when measured in terms of financial profit and better corporate governance. The second argument highlights the benefits of diversity and the "different" perspectives women can bring to corporate decision-making. Whilst there is some recognition of the equality and human rights based arguments for increasing female representation in boardrooms, instrumental diversity and business case arguments have been more broadly supported.

In this chapter we argue that the identity of financial market decision-makers is an important aspect in the move toward financial markets whose institutions, practices, and effects take seriously the idea of gender justice. We diverge from the dominant voices in this debate, however, by suggesting that "diversity" and "business case" arguments lack a secure theoretical and normative foundation. Instead, this chapter offers a revised argument for the importance of gender representation in the considerations of financial market decision-makers based on fair representation for women and others throughout corporations. We conclude by suggesting other reforms to corporate structures and culture that may be required for a more sincerely inclusive business world.

We argue that boardroom diversity is implicated in gender justice but that the recent deepening of interest in the contribution women can make to corporate boardrooms reveals certain tensions. An apparently benign and positive interest by financial market actors in women's representation in decision-making gives the impression of sincere progress toward gender justice that is not reflected in reality. We contend that this turn toward the belief in "women as saviors" is developed from a particular individualistic standpoint of equality that privileges those who can afford to take advantage of the positions of power on offer (the "professional-managerial class" who benefit from "leaning on others" (Gutting and Fraser 2015)). Moreover, it is based on a narrow, essentialist, and instrumental view of women and reflects a normative choice on the part of business and policy-makers to privilege financial capital. More worryingly, the emphasis on the business case undermines women's viewpoints, and pushes their "voice" to the margins. Feminist arguments for equality would appear to be irrelevant within the frameworks of the current debates.

We offer an alternative normative foundation in an attempt to move the debate to a firmer footing and argue that a greater emphasis on social justice feminism is necessary if gender justice in financial market decision-making is realistically to be achieved. Our approach is concerned with improving the prospects of all women in the workplace and improving our economy to create a more egalitarian society for men and women—a more gender-just society.

The chapter is structured as follows: first, in Section 12.2 we describe the financial markets context. Our attention throughout the chapter is focused mostly on the UK and European capital markets. We then go on in Section 12.3 to deal with the origins of the debate on women directors and we analyze the key arguments used to support increasing women's representation in boardrooms. In Section 12.4 we observe and explain the dominance of the business case over the equality claim. In Section 12.5, we argue that there is a need for a more radical feminist agenda that challenges the structures and goals of the political economy and that focuses on social justice for all workers. In Section 12.6 we suggest a way forward toward implementing this approach. We conclude, in Section 12.7, with a statement that a true democratically legitimate approach to gender justice in companies requires a supportive ecosystem, a redistribution of resources, and collective action between unions and feminist activists.

12.2 THE FINANCIAL MARKETS CONTEXT

Since the global financial crisis of 2008 and the period of "austerity" adopted by numerous states as a response to the crisis, increasing attention has been given to the gendered nature of financial markets and the consequences of their operation. Women appear to have endured the worst effects of the austerity measures. For example, UK spending cuts in welfare and public services have had an unequal impact on women because women are more likely to claim welfare benefits, particularly as lone parents, and tend to work in the public sector and make greater use of public services (McKay et al. 2013). The UK Government's budget in 2010 was challenged by the Fawcett Society for contravening the Gender Equality Duty. Although the nature and extent of these effects have varied across countries, Walby points to a number of "complex ways in which women can be affected more than men" (Walby 2009, 7). These include areas such as welfare benefits, health, poverty, and employment. Financial market distributions and the impact of broader economic policy differ for men and women (Prügl 2012, 22).

Income inequality has been described as "the most critical and unsustainable legacy of the neoliberal governing paradigm" (Brodie 2014, 428) and has prompted renewed activism on the part of social groups and movements who agitate for change. As Brodie observes, "The 1 per cent (and the 99 per cent) has become the dominant political motif of the Great Recession" (Brodie 2014, 436). Concerns about sustained and enduring inequality (which has often been linked with gender), coupled with frustration that legislatures and policy-makers have failed to resolve the issue adequately, have prompted renewed engagement in seeking a solution. Indeed Brodie points to the emergence of "cleared discursive and political space to reignite equality claims-making in an expanding field of opposition to the dominant governing paradigm" (ibid., 428).

Amongst the actors occupying this new discursive space are those financial market and global governance institutions that were most heavily implicated in the causes and consequences of the crisis. On one view, reflective engagement by financial market actors is welcome. There is, however, a less benign interpretation. An alternative view is that financial market actors are engaging with gender in essentialist and instrumental ways to further their own ends. Roberts has described three particular "tropes" that have emerged in post-crisis discussions of gender and finance (Roberts 2015, 108). The first she describes as the "financial empowerment trope" (ibid.), centered on ensuring that women (particularly in the Global South) have access to credit to enable or "empower" them to participate in financial markets (ibid., 116–18). Linked to this are the growing plethora of economic empowerment projects driven and coordinated by transnational corporations, such as Unilever's Shakti Project and Goldman Sachs 10,000 Women Global Initiative. The benefits for companies engaging in these empowerment projects are clear. They assist such corporations in:

> harnessing women's business acumen; they help them stabilise their supply chains by optimising women's labour power; and they help them develop a reputation as good corporate citizens in a globalised economy. (Prügl 2015, 626)

Although supporters of such initiatives might point to the opportunities they afford women, they are focused on individual attainment rather than structural change. What Prügl describes as "neoliberalised feminism" "may provide arguments for gender equality and the empowerment of women, but it retains ideological commitments to rationalism, heteronormativity, and genderless economic structures" (Prügl 2015, 619).

A second trope observed by Roberts is described as "womenomics" (Roberts 2015, 109). This engages explicitly with the idea that women are an "untapped market" (ibid., 123) and have the potential to be used as a source of fresh (paid) labor and spending power as consumers. In short, "women are good for business" (ibid.). The third trope identified by Roberts, and the one which offers a useful departure point for our discussion that follows, is the "women as saviors" claim (ibid., 120). At its most reductive, this claim has been played out in discussions of whether we would have had the financial crisis had the Lehman Brothers been the Lehman Sisters (Prügl 2012) and has led to intense attention being paid by corporate and financial institutions to the gendered make-up of their decision-making forums. As Prügl and True have noted:

> The attention to gender equality in business and economic circles is surprising. Men continue to overwhelmingly dominate economic decision-making positions including on corporate boards, as business executives, government financial regulators, trade negotiators and central bankers around the world.
> (Prügl and True 2014, 1138)

In Section 12.3 we explore the development of the boardroom diversity debate.

12.3 THE INTEREST IN FINANCIAL MARKET DECISION-MAKERS: A STUDY OF CORPORATE BOARDROOMS

Since at least 2004 in the UK, there has been a growing interest in the need for boardrooms to include more women directors (DTI 2004). As the organ of the company tasked with shaping its strategic direction and managing its affairs, it is important that those appointed to the role of director have sufficient skill, experience, and integrity to undertake the role successfully.

This imperative finds support in domestic legislation which obliges directors to act in the interests of the company (and not their own interests) (Companies Act 2006, sections 175 and 177, and section 170 especially) and to exercise reasonable care, skill, and diligence (Companies Act 2006, section 174). Concern about boardroom composition has emerged, however, from this standpoint of ensuring that corporate boards are comprised of talented individuals, capable of leading a company to greater success and, in the case of non-executive directors, able to rigorously challenge the actions of the executives. The debate has gathered momentum in the post-financial crisis era as women have been regarded as saviors of the corporate world, representing either an untapped pool of talent, "in touch" with consumers, or as decision-makers who behave differently to men. This is taking place against a backdrop of a highly gendered work environment and a challenge to male dominance. Globalization and restructuring of the economy affect the masculine ideal. The decline of old industries and the transformation of workplaces from manual to more knowledge-oriented tasks have led to a crisis of masculinities. Smart business and finance employees have replaced muscular working men and created more virulent hierarchies between men "with the effect that many men find themselves in precarious situations which are nothing new for women" (Annesley and Scheele 2011, 339). Yet state responses have not been harsh on the men responsible for the crisis and in fact the vulnerability of the male breadwinner has become more visible and has justified government interventions and increases of debts, with a bigger negative impact on women (ibid.). It is in this context that we have seen the "myth of the prudent woman" (Prügl 2012, 31) emerge in discourse around the financial crisis. This is troubling because of its lack of empirical support and because:

> [t]he myth of the prudent woman and her masculine counterpart can be read *as a matter of pure ideology*, a deceptive story to hide capitalist doings after its embarrassing excesses were revealed. (ibid., emphasis added)

It is possibly because of the discomfort felt by feminists at the stereotyping of the prudent woman, together with the unsettling of masculinist power dynamics in corporate boardrooms, that the boardroom diversity debate has generated so much discussion in academic and policy domains. A clear theoretical justification for increasing the number of women directors appears absent. This can be seen in the House of Lords EU Committee Report, *Women on Boards*, which was published just ahead of the publication of the proposed EU Directive in November 2012 (House of Lords 2012). Much of the report concerns whether there should be mandatory quotas for women's boardroom appointments. The conclusion expressed in the Report was that quotas would be inappropriate as a mechanism for increasing the number of women in company boardrooms in Europe. The preferred option was voluntary action by businesses and a "comply or explain" approach to gender recruitment targets, based along the lines of the recommendations set out in the Davies Report published in 2011. The consensus view was that the impact of the Davies Report had been positive and had already shown improvements in the proportion of women in the boardroom. In March 2016 figures show that women hold 26 percent of directorships on FTSE 100 boards and 20.4 percent of directorships on FTSE 250 boards (Sealy et al. 2016, 6, 1). Overall the House of Lords Committee suggested that the European Commission is prematurely attempting to address the issue when measures have been introduced nationally which need time to be more strongly established before judging them to have failed.

The House of Lords relied upon a large body of evidence supplied in response to its consultation questions. It showed a range of opinions about the anticipated proposed Directive. Some respondents supported the introduction of quotas, but arguably the majority favored a variety of softer measures. What stood out most clearly in the evidence provided was a definite pattern of preferences. There was a clear division between those concerned with corporate success and those concerned with women's role in society and decision-making. The respondents who represented business-oriented organizations, including investors, the CBI, directors, and the 30 Percent Club, generally favored the voluntary approach. These were the majority of respondents. Those supporting quotas were predominantly representatives from employment law experts, human rights, and gender, such as the Fawcett Society and the European Women's Network. Fewer of the respondents came from these groups. The majority held the view that quotas do not offer an appropriate solution to the problem. The main reason was that a "one size fits all" response to the problem is not able to meet the specific needs of different organizations and businesses. This is exacerbated at the European level because it ignores the individual circumstances of the different member states. This can lead to imposition of large and unnecessary costs on governments and fails to enable companies to develop individually tailored solutions. The preference was for code requirements to be adhered to on a "comply or explain" basis, giving a consistent corporate governance approach. The idea of "comply or explain" is that whilst generally companies must strive toward meeting the set gender diversity aspirations, if they fail to do so they may be able to explain that by reference to specific and good reasons relevant to their particular circumstances. If they can provide such an explanation this would put such companies into conformance with the gender diversity goals (MacNeil and Li 2006, Moore 2009, Sanderson et al. 2010, Keay 2014). This would give room for companies to maintain their distinctive features. The anti-quota group also tended to favor a variety of softer initiatives such as mandatory reporting on policies and efforts around improving gender representation at the boardroom level. The recent voluntary code on search and recruitment of directors also received welcome. It was argued that recent measures and initiatives need time to get established and failure then would give to the European Commission a stronger evidential basis for imposing quotas.

In other words, it was felt that to introduce quotas now is premature and too soon. A number of respondents also felt that quotas are not sufficiently subtle for tackling the problem of lack of representation and are rather more likely to result in tokenistic appointments for compliance purposes rather than dealing with the underlying cultural problems. They are regarded as a numbers game or to be about political correctness. Moreover, many argued that quotas are patronizing and are likely to cause suspicion that women have been appointed not for their merit but to make up the numbers, which would undermine their achievements and their authority. Furthermore, the supply and demand factor is not necessarily resolved by quotas if the problem is that an insufficient number of women have reached the pipeline required for giving them the experience to step into the role of director. Indeed, the supply and demand problem is partly caused by the lack of turnover of staff at the boardroom level. Many respondents referred to the unfilled pipeline problem and some pointed to the fact of multiple directorships being held by Norwegian women that masks the reality that still not so many women are represented genuinely at this level. In effect, quotas do not deal with the underlying issues of the non-filled pipeline, and nor do they solve the work–life balance for upcoming executives.

What we can see from this outline of the developments in Europe and the UK is that the debate has focused on *how* we achieve more women directors without sufficiently considering the arguments about *why* this is required. In response to this question the business case has been the most influential.

12.4 ANALYSIS OF THE BUSINESS CASE

According to Doldor et al. (2012), "The business case for gender diversity on boards relates to four key dimensions: improving performance, accessing the widest talent pool, being more responsive to the market and achieving better corporate governance." Doldor et al. explain further that the business case for having more women in the boardroom relies on two key arguments: "First, women's drop-out rates in companies are increasing despite the fact that women have similar or higher educational achievements compared to men." Thus, "companies simply fail to draw from the widest pool of available talent. Second, board diversity has been found to correlate with better corporate performance" (ibid., 1).

The chief features of the business case include: involving senior management in human resource planning; enhancing the organization's ability to recruit from a diverse general population; increasing the range and depth of the skills of the workforce; improving staff retention; increasing the appeal of the organization to a wider customer base through offering more nuanced or differentiated services and products; enhancing the organization's reputation in the community; enhancing the organization's ability to predict and respond to customers from diverse backgrounds; or reducing discrimination allegations (Perriton 2009, 222). Other claims include that equal opportunities policies more generally may improve business productivity and/or profits through improved recruitment, improved staff utilization, improved staff morale and employee commitment, greater employee diversity, customer approval, and increased share price (Riley et al. 2013, 217). Yet the effects will be conditional on the characteristics and environment of each organization and so the net benefits are not guaranteed (ibid.).

The business case has provided a basis for some progress with the effect of boardrooms being rebalanced to some degree. In 2010 the percentage of women directors on the boards of the FTSE 100 was 12.5 percent (Davies 2011, 3): by 2016 women had gained 26 percent of FTSE 100 directorships (Sealy et al. 2016, 6). However, this approach has its limits. A major criticism of the business case for diversity is that it does not challenge existing power relations and the established order (Tomlinson and Schwabenland 2010, 104). It is centered on individuals, whereas what is needed is rather an "equal outcomes" approach, focused on social groups. For Dickens, "[t]here is little indication that the depoliticized business-case approach to equality will generate action on what Cockburn calls the 'long agenda; a transformation in access to power and the nature of it'" (Dickens 1994, 15; Cockburn 1989, 220). This is confirmed by Lanning et al. in their recent report for the IPPR on gender equality. They find that individualistic responses dominate in the experience of women in top jobs, and that this does not encourage women to seek changes to working cultures that will benefit other women. Instead, they take on the culture and norms of the organization that promoted them (Lanning et al. 2013, 27–8).

Whilst the argument for diversity has the potential for challenging the nature of organizations as currently construed, in the UK, according to Dickens, the business case arguments for equal opportunities are "more narrowly focused, often pointing out the advantages of particular initiatives, ... in terms of competing in the labour market, enhancing organizational performance and competing in the product market" (Dickens 1994, 9). The narrow focus of the business case is likely to give rise to a selective approach to equal opportunities and so may "serve to confine that action, since it involves a targeting of initiatives to reflect the needs of the employer rather than those of the disadvantaged groups" (ibid., 14).

In fact, it has the effect of subordinating the equality issue to the market. As Perriton argues, "once a financial justification is used as a means of deciding whether to follow a course of action or not, the social issue in question becomes subordinated to the market. The business case discourse takes up all the discursive space available around the debate and drowns out attempts to qualify it" (Perriton 2009, 239).

12.4.1 Why is the business case dominant?

There are three key reasons for the dominance of the business case. First, the voice of business is more strongly represented because corporate actors have been most vocal in the consultations. In the influential report by Lord Davies, *Women on Boards*, the evidence for relying on the business case was largely based on an earlier report by McKinsey and Co. entitled *Women Matter: Gender Diversity, a Corporate Performance Driver*, published in 2007 (McKinsey & Company 2007).[1] The Equality and Human Rights Commission, relying on these two publications, considered the business case for increased diversity at the boardroom level and at executive level to be "substantiated and unequivocal" (Equality and Human Rights Commission 2011). Business case arguments are "based in a normalized Mega-Discourse that enshrines the achievement of organizational economic goals as the ultimate guiding principle and explanatory device for people in organizations" (Litvin 2006). This approach is seen as necessary for obtaining resources and cooperation from top management (Barmes and Ashtiany 2003, 278). In addition, Linda Perriton notes that the dominance of the business case justification can be attributed to the fact that these justifications are heard more often in our society, are given more opportunities to present themselves, monopolize communications, and "make use of strategies of control to ensure their eminence" (Perriton 2009, 240).

Secondly, in a neo-liberal context, the business case and diversity are easier to communicate in business discourse and in public discourse than arguments based on equality. Barmes and Ashtiany suggest that the language of equality and equal opportunities is commonly associated with regulatory interventions and so is eschewed. As the economic considerations are prioritized,

[1] This report has been highly influential and McKinsey & Co. is a global management consulting firm whose mission is to help their clients "make distinctive, lasting, and substantial improvements in their performance": see McKinsey & Co.'s website at: http://www.mckinsey.com/about-us/what-we-do/our-mission-and-values (accessed February 26, 2016). McKinsey has been described as "a major player in the efficiency boom of the 1920s, the post-war gigantism of the 1940s, the rationalization of government and rise of marketing in the 1950s, the age of corporate influence in the 1960s, the restructuring of America in the 1970s, the massive growth in information technology in the 1980s, globalization in the 1990s and the boom-bust-and-clean-up of the 2000s and beyond": see interview with Duff McDonald in Belsky (2013).

the moral justifications are viewed as serendipitous (Barmes and Ashtiany 2003, 278).

The third and more subtle reason is that there is a reluctance to hear the women's voice on these issues, which is symptomatic of a cultural indifference to women's interests. The equality arguments seem to have taken second place despite clear evidence of the insufficiency of existing equality legislation. A frequent rejection of feminism as a broad concept may point to women's issues being regarded as unimportant and to the general subordination of women culturally (Banyard 2010), with the result that, at best, women are instrumentalized in the context of the women directors' debate. Whilst this third reason is not expressly stated, it is evident that women's viewpoints are regularly undermined. For example, in the context of rape allegations "no" appears not always to mean "no" when that word comes from a woman's mouth (Ellison and Munro 2009). In the modern workplace, despite employment protection legislation purporting to protect women, they still do not enjoy equal pay (the median pay gap for full-time employees is 9.4 percent, see ONS 2015, 1) and they suffer sexual harassment. With regards to working parents, the "maternal wall" (Williams 2003) appears as big a barrier to women's participation and progression as ever. For example, the former Equal Opportunities Commission found that the equivalent of 30,000 women each year lost their jobs due to pregnancy or maternity, with around 2 percent being dismissed or made redundant (Equal Opportunities Commission 2005). This affects women with children and without because of the negative perceptions associated with motherhood in the business context.

12.4.2 What results from using the business case?

"The widespread use of the business case discourse has crowded out a range of other ways of thinking about and responding to problems" (Perriton 2009, 240). The business case has raised important questions about how women, diversity, and even feminist movements have been colonized in the pursuit of financial gain. This can be seen outside the boardroom with the growth in women's investment campaigns and in initiatives to develop women's enterprises. In the financial markets industry specifically, it is possible to witness growing emphasis on the supposedly more cautious nature of women that could help avoid some of the trading debacles that arise from the overconfidence of many male investors. A well-known research paper from the US, for example, suggested that men, on average, traded 45 percent more frequently than women, and that hyperactive trading reduced their net returns by 2.65 percentage points a year, compared to 1.72 percentage points for women (Barber and Odean 2001; Belsky 2012). Observations of this nature have encouraged more focus on bringing women into investment activity, particularly since the Great Financial Crisis. For example, there is growing evidence of efforts made toward providing women with targeted financial education (Gaines 2016). Additionally, and more broadly, NGOs and women's groups have often joined with companies in the quest for corporate gain in what Roberts calls "transnational business feminism":

> by which is meant an increasingly large coalition of feminist organizations, capitalist states, regional and international funding institutions, non-governmental organizations (NGOs) and transnational corporations (MNCs) that converge on the need to promote women's equality, particularly in the Global South. (Roberts 2012, 87)

Thus in addition to being too timid, the business case colludes with corporate power to coopt women for its own purpose. Again we see the myth of the prudent woman emerging in response to depictions of the City as being out of control, driven by greed, domination, and the dominance of a particular conception of masculinity (McDowell 1997; McDowell 2010). Some advocates for gender equality highlight its benefits for the economy. Goldman Sachs, for example, has claimed that "economic growth and gender equality form a virtuous circle" (Goldman Sachs 2009, 21). Constructing women as an untapped resource embeds the current neo-liberal capitalist order within the corporate sphere, as women are merely coopted as another resource to be mined rather than using gender as a lens to reveal the deep-seated structural inequalities generated by the current economic and political order. For Roberts,

> [i]t is partly this unproblematic linking of women's interests, development and corporate profitability that makes the business case for gender equality so appealing to such a wide range of social forces. (Roberts 2012, 92)

Eisenstein puts the issue more starkly when she talks of the "dangerous liaison" between feminism and capitalism (Eisenstein 2005, 498), perhaps most clearly revealed in Sandberg's *Lean In* campaign. Similarly, Nancy Fraser has talked about feminism being turned into the "handmaiden of capitalism" and being exploited to contribute to neo-liberalism (Fraser 2013b; Fraser 2009; Fraser 2013a). Efficiency in the corporate context is not a neutral term and it can have a negative impact on women as it is about cost-saving and profit-seeking. It leads to a focus on the interests of shareholders, the majority of whom are men (Computershare 2016 reporting that 61 percent shares are held by men). The German Institute for Economic Research has noted, for example, that 38 percent of women who save report owning insecure investment products that include shares of quoted companies, compared with 45 percent of men (Badumenko et al. 2010). Female participation in the financial markets appears to lag behind that of men, because inter alia they have smaller incomes and the financial services industry does not meet women's needs so well (Paradi and Filion 2015). Thus, if financial markets are dominated by men (as investors), and financial markets increasingly influence corporate strategies in the rest of the economy, this is unlikely to be helpful for broader issues of gender justice. Indeed, women bear the worst cost of the focus on efficiency and capitalist production in the context of workplaces designed around the male body and the male experience (Williams 2010). Moreover, outside of the workplace they are further excluded from participation in the company because they are unlikely to be the holders of financial capital (Sarra 2002, 472). One might object to this approach by questioning why women should have to "earn" equality. This is not equality at all (Holzhammer 2014, 8) but is rather an unfair burden imposed on women in a territory in which they are most disadvantaged.

Overall, the business case has resulted in some change but at a disappointing level even on its own terms. With women only taking up 26 percent of the FTSE 100 boardroom space this is hardly making best use of the talent pool as is claimed in the business case approach. In the financial markets sector, similarly, whilst the numbers, according to a report recently published by New Financial, "are beginning to move in the right direction," there is still quite a lot of disparity and some disappointing pockets remain in particular areas of this sector (Chinwala and Bax 2016). For example, whilst trade bodies within the financial markets industry show around 30 percent female representation in their boardrooms, the executive committees in private equity have representation as low as 7 percent (ibid.). Clearly there is a large disparity in female representation between boards and executive committees. In banks, where there is a 32 percent representation for females in boardrooms, they still only hold 12 percent of the positions in executive committees (ibid.). For the financial sector as a whole, women hold 24 percent of board positions and just 13 percent of executive committee roles (ibid.). Ultimately, the danger of continued reliance on the business case is that women become commodified as a group. One alternative approach is to start by hearing women's voices within companies and through the whole corporate structure.

12.5 REFORM FROM A FEMINIST AND DEMOCRATIC PERSPECTIVE

Hamdani and Buckley point out that direct economic benefits are not necessarily the primary objective of organizations when they aim to comply with institutional demands. Rather, the goal is to seek approval of various institutional stakeholders so as to earn legitimacy and ensure survival. Thus economic gains are not the only indicators that capture the potential benefits of diversity; legitimacy, firm reputation, and goodwill are also important goals. Some businesses may employ a more diverse workforce as a result of being more successful. Therefore, larger, more visible, more profitable businesses that get scrutinized more closely may have stronger incentives to meet demands of various pressure groups to be fair and equitable (Hamdani and Buckley 2011, 37).

There is also a need to reassert the social justice roots of feminism. The reality is that under existing corporate structures much profit comes at the expense of social equality, and companies and financial markets "run counter to democratic ideals and basic principles of socio-economic justice" (Power 2014). Thus, according to Power, "whilst gender battles in business are undoubtedly crucial, they can equally be used as a convenient red herring to distract from the wider, more fundamental need to effect deep, systemic reform in the way capitalist structures operate" (ibid.). She adds that "the debate needs to take conscious account of the continued failures and otherwise ad-hoc benefits of such concepts as 'trickle-down', with the unwarranted faith in market success eventually to provide social and economic progress for all" (ibid.).

Is this the key difference then? That the debate on boardroom quotas, by emphasizing the business viewpoint, has meant that it is not a transformative agenda but one that fits in with a more conservative version of feminism, the "lean-in '1%' feminism" of Sheryl Sandberg that individualizes the debate toward women who seek to have it all rather than seeking to "dismantle the structural barriers to gender equity that still impede most women" (Burnham 2013)? As Burnham observes, "1% feminism is all about the glass ceiling, never about the glass floor. It addresses the concerns, anxieties and prerogatives of the 1%, women who are at or near the top levels of their professions, the corporate world or government. Unfortunately, blind to its own limited field of vision, it tends to speak in the name of all women, universalizing that which is profoundly particular" (ibid.). The key point is that this debate, for feminists, relies on a trickle-down feminism. But "that depends on the benevolence and gender politics of those who make it to the top. It is not about taking collective action or building collective power for change" (ibid.). It is about seeking access to corporate power for a small percentage of women rather than challenging the thinking behind corporate power structures. The fear is that the women who make it to the boardroom will not feel able to lead transformation of existing structures as they may seek to avoid collisions and instead focus on technical expertise tied to their professional identities rather than their gendered identities (Tremblay 2011). Any such parity law might then only effectively benefit a few select women. In Norway the "Golden Skirts" phenomenon highlights these limitations.

One of the outcomes of the debate is that the EU Proposed Directive legislates for non-executive supervisory directors' parity only. But there is an important distinction between executives and non-executives: the real power usually lies with the executive directors, so increasing the number of female non-executives does not necessarily increase the status or power of females in the corporate hierarchy. As Marek Szydlo (2015) observes, "new women members of boards will represent a very similar profile of thinking as the current male members, particularly if these new women members will continue to be recruited from among the business and personal contacts of the current (male) board members... [who] might select women candidates who they know very well and who represent similar thinking and business attitudes as current board members."

Heemskerk and Fennema note that with internationalization the directors being brought in are more likely to be foreign females (Spencer Stuart 2015, noting that 40 percent of women on FTSE 150 boards are non-nationals). They are less likely to participate in national elite business networks, and so are less of a threat to the incumbent corporate elite (Heemskerk and Fennema 2014, 277).

In our view, gender parity is required for a true democracy and requires women not only to vote and have a chance to run for political office, but they must visibly participate in the public institutions of the state (Szydlo 2015, 109). Thus, according to Szydlo, "Because gender parity is necessary to legitimise governance, and because corporations play an important role in economic governance, gender parity must be implemented not only in state institutions, but also in companies (and in other private sector organisations) that participate, together with public authorities, in modern economic governance at the EU and national levels" (ibid.). In this light, achieving gender balance in company boardrooms would lend democratic legitimacy to the system of economic governance and the companies operating within that system (ibid., 110).

While gender balance is a starting point we need to strive toward more representative boardrooms covering other areas such as race, age, class, and disability. In any event, we query how much women in the boardrooms are really influential in the decisions. The problem is exacerbated by multiple directorships, so rewards of equality are not necessarily shared. Women at the top often do not speak up for other women as they either behave like men or blend in and keep a low profile on the board to avoid negative attention. This is the frequent response to the "double-bind" faced by women (Catalyst 2007; O'Connor 2006). However, in Norway, there is evidence that women who have entered boardrooms since the quota law do feel that they have influence and that they are able to assert their opinions. "The women directors report their own behaviour as assertive and active, they have influence on decisions and participate in informal socialising outside the boardroom. Further, they do not experience out-group attitudes toward themselves as a group. They feel they are being respected and listened to, and they are included in information sharing and social interaction with other members of the board" (Ladegard 2013, 150). Elstad and Ladegard also note that an increased ratio of women on the board is also likely to impact positively on their experienced participation and influence (Elstad and Ladegard 2012).

Companies exercise powerful social influence and their decisions affect everyone in society, so we need gender balance in the processes through which such decisions are reached, otherwise such companies are not legitimate (Holzhammer 2014, 5). Management boards have critical social influence and so their leadership is beyond being a private problem of the individual company, but is a problem of democratic magnitude (ibid., 23–4). For the management boards of financial institutions, which have great influence on the economy as a whole, this argument is even stronger. Therefore, women deserve equal representation at all levels, including the very highest of corporate governance. It is not about adding women because of their differentness or because of what they might add; they do not need to prove their worthiness (ibid., 5).

12.6 A WAY FORWARD

The gender of financial market decision-makers is important symbolically and representatively. Putting women at the top might lead to changes throughout the organization, so it becomes a virtuous circle as top women become role models for women at all levels. Those women put at the top face expectations that they will influence structural changes that will help other women to succeed and be empowered. In a similar way, Jacqui True points to the first female President of Chile, Michelle Bachelet, who appointed 50 percent women to her cabinet and introduced a widespread, state-funded child care system, and Hillary Clinton as US Secretary of State who sought to empower women in developing countries through her work in international development (True 2013, 357).

To be clear, the debate is about gender justice, but not only at the top. Much more is required. It also requires attention to the poorly paid workers, those at the bottom of the labor market. Importantly, "equality requires less focus on women's individual rights and opportunities to advance, and more on the collective power and interests of underrepresented groups to influence the decisions that affect their lives" (Lanning et al. 2013, 51). So women lower down the corporate governance hierarchy should be given greater power, as well as women in the boardroom, and the status of lower-paid jobs needs to be improved. "The goal should be democratic renewal across all sectors, regions and occupations" (ibid., 52). As Lanning and others observe:

> The higher levels of women's equality achieved in countries such as Sweden, Norway and Denmark have been won through broad feminist mobilisations, in which trade unions and pressure groups have lobbied alongside feminist politicians for state resources, public institutions and social entitlements to support better choices around work and care, promote shared responsibility, and improve the lives of carers, children and the elderly. (Ibid., 54)

"Whole-istic feminism," as defined by Cynthia Cockburn (Cockburn 2014), is concerned with the need to tackle patriarchy on a number of fronts. From this perspective the debate on boardroom gender quotas might be considered as too narrow. In reality, women are bearing the brunt of austerity with higher job losses as a result of more women in the public sectors, and they frequently suffer worse terms and conditions at work. Thus the debate about women in the boardroom needs to go beyond focusing just on women who may or may not reach the boardroom levels. It is a debate that should be concerned also with power representation across the corporate enterprise and outside it. Women in boardrooms do not just become role models for other women aspiring to those positions, but they should also see within their role the protection of all women including those unlikely to rise beyond the lowest levels within the workplace hierarchy.

Many of the pro quota advocates observe a need for a gender diversity ecosystem within a company as quotas alone will not change a company's culture (House of Lords 2012). Quotas will be part of that ecosystem but they need to be supported by other mechanisms such as reporting requirements and mentoring and networking support for women as they climb the career ladder. Perriton argues that "human beings, even ones that occupy senior positions in business organizations, need to be reacquainted with the 'moral case' for change" (Perriton 2009, 240). She shows that appeal to extrinsic motivation, such as financial benefits, diminishes our motivation to obey moral rules despite the individual and societal benefits that those would result in.

There is arguably a need for feminist movements to collectivize with other social movements. Unions might be a best hope as they seek to protect all workers, men and women of all classes. Lanning and others note that women fared better when unionized (Lanning et al. 2013, 20). There is a need for not just empowerment but also resistance that will run counter to the neo-liberal model, and that will demand redistribution of resources, challenge the operation of markets, organize against state repression, and associate with forms of collective action that involve possibilities of social transformation (Cornwall et al. 2008, 8).

12.7 CONCLUSION

The debates on women's representation in company boardrooms have revealed the prioritization of the business case for greater gender balance. This business case has been pushed more strongly than the equality arguments. Whilst from a business perspective there has been acceptance of the need for more women to participate in boardrooms, and there has been an increase in the number of female directors, we consider, first, that the increase has not been as great as it could be and, more importantly, that emphasis on the business case potentially damages the full democratic capacity of women in the business and political domains. Not only does this business-oriented approach lead to the instrumentalization of women for the purpose of corporate profits and the shareholders' benefit, but also we consider that it effectively commodifies women as a group. More worryingly, we see the preference for the business case as reflecting a more general undermining of women's interests that pervades societies across the globe. Women's voices seem to have gained little recognition over different areas, and the dominance of the business case perpetuates the struggle for women's interests to be noticed.

Within the financial markets sector, and more broadly, we advocate a more social justice and democratically oriented approach to the question of women's representation, not only in the boardroom but throughout the whole corporate structure. Financial markets might in fact offer some levers in this fight. A promising start comes from a group of activist European shareholders who have embarked on a campaign to achieve gender balanced leadership in the companies in which they are investing. The EWSDGE Project has developed a set of recommendations that include adoption of binding quota legislation; positively developing the equal pay provisions in line with transformative equality; getting companies to adopt gender equality cultures and strategies; and changing societal perceptions to strengthen emphasis and improvement of gender balance and equality (EWSDGE 2014–16). This offers a starting point from some of the mainstream corporate governance actors, but more is necessary. Feminist movements are particularly concerned with strengthening women's capacity for democratic participation. From such a perspective the debate about women in the boardroom would focus on the role of directors not only for profit-making but also for improving the culture of companies for the benefit of all the stakeholders, not least the whole workforce. We see the potential of inviting more women into the boardroom as part of a new corporate "ecosystem" that promotes women's interests from top to bottom, inside and outside the company, in the public and the private arena (including the home). We envision a key role for unions joining with the feminist activists to challenge market dominance and to demand a redistribution of resources and of democratic opportunities.

REFERENCES

Annesley, Claire, and Alexandra Scheele. 2011. "Gender, Capitalism and Economic Crisis: Impact and Responses Across Europe." *Journal of Contemporary European Studies* 19(3), 335–47.

Badumenko, Oleg, Nataliy Barasinska, and Dorothea Schäfer. 2010. *Investments: Women Are More Cautious than Men Because They Have Less Financial Resources at Their Disposal.* DIW German Institute for Economic Research, Working Paper No. 1.

Banyard, Kat. 2010. *The Equality Illusion: The Truth about Women and Men Today.* London: Faber & Faber.

Barber, Brad M., and Terrance Odean. 2001. "Boys Will Be Boys: Gender, Overconfidence and Common Stock Investment." *The Quarterly Journal of Economics* 116(1), 261–92.

Barmes, Lizzie, and Sue Ashtiany. 2003. "The Diversity Approach to Achieving Equality: Problems and Pitfalls." *Industrial Law Journal* 32(4), 274–96.

Belsky, Gary. 2012. "Why We Need More Women Traders on Wall Street." *Time,* May 15.

Belsky, Gary. 2013. "Mass Layoffs? Overpaid CEOs? Blame McKinsey!" *Time*, September 10, at http://business.time.com/2013/09/10/mass-layoffs-overpaid-ceos-blame-mckinsey (accessed February 26, 2016).

Brodie, Janine. 2014. "Elusive Equalities and the Great Recession: Restoration, Retrenchment and Redistribution." *International Journal of Law in Context* 10(4), 427–41.

Burnham, Linda. 2013. "1% feminism," *Open Democracy*, April 8 http://www.opendemocracy.net/5050/linda-burnham/1-feminism (accessed February 26, 2016).

Catalyst Inc. 2007. *The Double-Bind Dilemma for Women in Leadership: Damned If You Do, Doomed If You Don't.* New York: Catalyst.

Chinwala, Yasmine, and Laurence Bax. 2016. *Counting Every Woman 2016: Measuring Female Representation on Boards and Executive Committees in European Capital Markets.* New Financial, January.

Cockburn, Cynthia. 1989. "Equal Opportunities: The Short and Long Agenda." *Industrial Relations Journal* 20(3), 213–25.

Cockburn, Cynthia. 2014. "Challenging Patriarchy and Other Power Relations." *Open Democracy*, November 4, at https://www.opendemocracy.net/5050/cynthia-cockburn/challenging-patriarchy-and-other-power-relations (accessed February 19, 2016).

Computershare. 2016. "The Companies Act 2006, Statistics," at http://www-uk.computershare.com/webcontent/doc.aspx?docid=%7Be522af5d-b333-460e-b964-867a92e855e0%7D (accessed February 26, 2016).

Cornwall, Andrea, Jasmine Gideon, and Kalpana Wilson. 2008. "Introduction: Reclaiming Feminism: Gender and Neoliberalism." *Institute of Development Studies Bulletin* 39(6), 1–9.

Davies of Abersoch, Lord. 2011. *Women on Boards.* London: Department for Business, Innovation and Skills.

Department of Trade and Industry. 2004. *Building Better Boards.* London: DTI.

Dickens, Linda. 1994. "The Business Case for Women's Equality: Is the Carrot Better than the Stick?" *Employee Relations* 16(8), 5–18.

Doldor, Elena, Susan Vinnicombe, Mary Gaughan, and Ruth Sealy. 2012. *Gender Diversity on Boards: The Appointment Process and the Role of Executive Search Firms.* Cranfield School of Management: International Centre for Women Leaders.

Eisenstein, Hester. 2005. "A Dangerous Liaison? Feminism and Corporate Globalization." *Science and Society* 69(3), 487–518.

Ellison, Louise, and Vanessa E. Munro. 2009. "Reacting to Rape: Exploring Mock Jurors' Assessments of Complainant Credibility." *British Journal of Criminology* 49(2), 202–19.

Elstad, Beate, and Gro Ladegard. 2012. "Women on Corporate Boards: Key Influencers or Tokens?" *Journal of Management & Governance* 16(4), 595–615.

Equal Opportunities Commission. 2005. *Greater Expectations: Final Report of the EOC's Investigation into Discrimination against New and Expectant Mothers in the Workplace.* Manchester: EOC.

Equality and Human Rights Commission Response to a Consultation Document issued by the Financial Reporting Council. 2011. *Gender Diversity on Boards.* At https://frc.org.uk/Our-Work/Publications/Corporate-Governance/Consultation-Document-Gender-Diversity-on-Boards/Responses-to-Consultation-Document-Gender-Diversit/Equality-and-Human-Rights-Commission.aspx (accessed March 3, 2016).

European Women Shareholders Demand Gender Equality. 2014–16. *Gender Balanced Leadership—European Women Shareholders Pave the Way,* Project Documentation 2014–16, at http://www.ewsdge.eu/wp-content/uploads/2016/02/EWSDGE_Broschuere_engl_72dpi.pdf (accessed October 26, 2016).

Fraser, Nancy. 2009. "Feminism, Capitalism and the Cunning of History." *New Left Review* 56, 98–117.

Fraser, Nancy. 2013a. *Fortunes of Feminism: From State-Managed Capitalism to Neoliberal Crisis.* London: Verso.

Fraser, Nancy. 2013b. "How Feminism Became Capitalism's Handmaiden—and How to Reclaim It." *Guardian,* October 14.

Gaines, Camille. 2016. "Is Financial Education Really Lacking?" *Financial Woman,* at http://financialwoman.com/is-financial-education-for-women-really-lacking (accessed February 29, 2016).

Goldman Sachs. 2009. *The Power of the Purse: Gender Equality and Middle-Class Spending.* Goldman Sachs Global Markets Institute, August 5.

Gutting, Gary, and Nancy Fraser. 2015. "A Feminism Where 'Lean In' Means Leaning On Others." *The New York Times,* October 15.

Hamdani, Maria Riaz, and M. Ronald Buckley. 2011. "Diversity Goals: Reframing the Debate and Enabling a Fair Evaluation." *Business Horizons* 54(1), 33–40.

Heemskerk, Eelke Michiel, and Meindert Fennema. 2014. "Women on Board: Female Board Membership as a Form of Elite Democratization." *Enterprise and Society* 15(2), 252–84.

Holzhammer, Maria M. T. 2014. "The Proposed Gender Equality Directive: Legality, Legitimacy, and Efficacy of Mandated Gender Equality in Business Leadership." *Yearbook of European Laws* 33(1), 433–65.

House of Lords European Union Committee. 2012. 5th Report of Session 2012–12, *Women on Boards*, 9 November, HL Paper 58.

Keay, Andrew R. 2014. "Comply or Explain in Corporate Governance Codes: In Need of Greater Regulatory Oversight?" *Legal Studies* 34(2), 279–304.

Ladegard, Gro. 2013. "Legitimacy, Inclusion and Influence: Investigating Women Directors' Board Experiences." In *Getting Women on to Corporate Boards: A Snowball Starting in Norway*, edited by S. Machold et al. Cheltenham: Edward Elgar, 147–54.

Lanning, Tess, with Laura Bradley, Richard Darlington, and Glenn Gottfried. 2013. *Great Expectations: Exploring the Promises of Gender Equality*. London: IPPR.

Litvin, Deborah R. 2006. "Diversity: Making Space for a Better Case." In *Handbook on Workplace Diversity*, edited by Alison M. Konrad, Pushkala Prasad, and Judith K. Pringle. London: Sage, 75–94.

McDowell, Linda. 1997. *Capital Culture: Gender at Work in the City*. Oxford: Blackwell.

McDowell, Linda. 2010. "Capital Culture Revisited: Sex, Testosterone and the City." *International Journal of Urban and Regional Research* 34(3), 652–8.

McKay, Alisa, Jim Campbell, Emily Thomson, and Susanne Ross. 2013. "Economic Recession and Recovery in the UK: What's Gender Got to Do with It?" *Feminist Economics* 19(3), 108–23.

McKinsey & Company. 2007. *Women Matter: Gender Diversity, a Corporate Performance Driver*. McKinsey & Co., Inc.

MacNeil, Iain, and Xiao Li. 2006. "'Comply or Explain': Market Discipline and Non-compliance with the Combined Code." *Corporate Governance: An International Review* 14(5), 486–96.

Moore, M. T. 2009. "End of Comply or Explain in UK Corporate Governance." *Northern Ireland Legal Quarterly* 60, 85–103.

O'Connor, Marleen. 2006. "Women Executives in Gladiatorial Corporate Cultures: The Behavioural Dynamics of Gender, Ego and Power." *Maryland Law Review* 65(2), 465–503.

ONS. 2015. *Annual Survey of Hours and Earnings, 2015 Provisional Results*. London: ONS, November 18.

Paradi, Judy, and Paulette Filion. 2015. *Financial Advisors Are Failing Women: What Female Clients Really Want and How to Change the Dialogue*. Strategy Marketing, at http://www.investingforme.com/pdfs/reports-studies/Advisors%20Fail%2073%20Women%20.pdf (accessed October 26, 2016).

Perriton, Linda. 2009. "'We Don't Want Complaining Women!' A Critical Analysis of the Business Case for Diversity." *Management Communication Quarterly* 23(2), 218–43.

Power, Steph. 2014. "Proxy Feminism and Gendernomics: What Price Identity Politics in an Age of Austerity?" *New Left Project*, January 8, at http://www.newleftproject.org/index.php/site/article_comments/proxy_feminism_and_gendernomics_what_price_identity_politics_in_an_age_of_a (accessed February 26, 2016).

Prügl, Elisabeth. 2012. "'If Lehman Brothers Had Been Lehman Sisters...': Gender and Myth in the Aftermath of the Financial Crisis." *International Political Sociology* 6(1), 21–35.
Prügl, Elisabeth. 2015. "Neoliberalising Feminism." *New Political Economy* 20(4), 614–31.
Prügl, Elisabeth, and Jacqui True. 2014. "Equality Means Business? Governing Gender through Transnational Public-Private Partnerships." *Review of International Political Economy* 21(6), 1137–69.
Riley, Rebecca, Hilary Metcalf, and John Forth. 2013. "The Business Case for Equal Opportunities." *Industrial Relations Journal* 44(3), 216–39.
Roberts, Adrienne. 2012. "Financial Crisis, Financial Firms... and Financial Feminism? The Rise of 'Transnational Business Feminism' and the Necessity of Marxist-Feminist IPE." *Socialist Studies* 8(2), 85–108.
Roberts, Adrienne. 2015. "Gender, Financial Deepening and the Production of Embodied Finance: Towards a Critical Feminist Analysis." *Global Society* 29(1), 107–27.
Sanderson, Paul, et al. 2010. *Flexible Or Not?: The Comply-or-Explain Principle in UK and German Corporate Governance*. Cambridge: Centre for Business Research, University of Cambridge.
Sarra, Janis. 2002. "The Gender Implications of Corporate Governance Change." *Seattle Journal for Social Justice* 1(2), 457–502.
Sealy Ruth, Elena Doldor, and Susan Vinnicombe. 2016. *The Female FTSE Board Report 2016 Women on Boards: Taking Stock of Where We Are*. Bedford: Cranfield School of Management.
Spencer Stuart. 2015. *Board Index 2015*: at https://www.spencerstuart.com/research-and-insight/2015-uk-board-index (accessed February 26, 2016).
Szydlo, Marek. 2015. "Gender Equality on the Boards of EU Companies: Between Economic Efficiency, Fundamental Rights and Democratic Legitimisation of Economic Governance." *European Law Journal* 21(1), 97–115.
Tomlinson, Frances, and Christina Schwabenland. 2010. "Reconciling Competing Discourses of Diversity? The UK Non-Profit Sector Between Social Justice and the Business Case." *Organization* 17(1), 101–21.
Tremblay, Marie-Soleil. 2011. "Confrontation of Gendered Expertise: A Qualitative Study of Affirmative Action in Boardrooms" at http://elsevier.conference-services.net/resources/247/2182/pdf/CPAC2011_0061_comments.pdf (accessed February 19, 2016).
True, Jacqui. 2013. "Counting Women and Balancing Gender: Increasing Women's Participation in Governance." *Politics and Gender* 9(3), 351–9.
Walby, Sylvia. 2009. "Gender and the Financial Crisis." Paper for UNESCO Project on "Gender and the Financial Crisis," April 9.
Williams, Joan C. 2003. "Beyond the Glass Ceiling: The Maternal Wall as a Barrier to Gender Equality." *Thomas Jefferson Law Review* 26, 1–14.
Williams, Joan C. 2010. *Reshaping the Work-Family Debate: Why Men and Class Matter*. Cambridge, MA: Harvard University Press.

WEBSITES

Empower Women at https://www.empowerwomen.org/en (accessed November 1, 2016).
Fawcett Society: http://www.fawcettsociety.org.uk/2013/02/fawcetts-bid-for-a-judicial-review-of-the-2010-budget-2/ (accessed February 19, 2016).
Global Banking Alliance for Women at http://www.gbaforwomen.org/the-opportunity/ (accessed February 26, 2016).
McKinsey & Co's website at http://www.mckinsey.com/about-us/what-we-do/our-mission-and-values (accessed February 26, 2016).

13

It takes a village to maintain a dangerous financial system

Anat R. Admati

13.1 INTRODUCTION

The financial system is meant to facilitate efficient allocation of resources and help people and businesses fund, invest, save, and manage risks. This system is rife with conflicts of interests. Reckless practices, if uncontrolled by market forces and effective rules, can cause great harm. Most of the time, however, the harm from excessive risk in banking is invisible and the culprits remain unaccountable. They rarely violate the law.

In this chapter I focus on the excessive use of debt in banking that creates unnecessary fragility and distortions. The Great Financial Crisis of 2007–9 exposed the ineffectiveness of the relevant regulations in place at the time. Yet even now and despite the crisis, the rules remain inadequate and flawed. Policy-makers who repeatedly fail to protect the public are not accountable partly because false claims obscure reality, create confusion, and muddle the debate.

It is useful to contrast safety in banking and in aviation. Tens of thousands of airplanes take off, fly, and land daily, often simultaneously within a small geographical area. Yet, crashes are remarkably rare. It takes many collaborating individuals, from engineers and assembly workers to mechanics, airline and airport employees, air controllers, and regulators, to achieve and maintain such safety levels. In banking, instead, there are strong incentives to take excessive risk; banks effectively compete to endanger. The victims are dispersed and are either unaware of the endangerment, misled into believing that the risk is unavoidable or that reducing it would entail significant cost, or they are powerless to bring about meaningful change. Most of those who collectively control the system benefit from its fragility or choose to avoid challenging the system, effectively becoming enablers.

Society's interest in aviation safety is aligned with the incentives of those involved in maintaining it. Crashed planes and dead passengers are visible to the public and easy to understand. Airplane manufacturers and airlines stand to suffer losses from compromising safety. Radars, flight recorders, and other technologies uncover the exact cause of most plane crashes, and those responsible face consequences. Screening procedures try to prevent terrorist attacks. The fear of being directly responsible for deaths prevents individuals involved in maintaining safe aviation from failing to do their part.

In banking, the public interest in safety conflicts with the incentives of people within the industry. Protecting the public requires effective regulations because market forces fail to do so. Without effective regulations, dangerous conduct is enabled and perversely rewarded. Because the harm is difficult to connect to specific policy failures and individuals, it persists. Even if a crisis occurs, the enablers of the system can promote narratives that divert attention from their own responsibility and from the fact that much more can be done at little if any social cost to make the system safer and healthier. The narrative that crises are largely unpreventable shifts attention to emergency preparedness and away from better rules to reduce the frequency of emergencies in the first place.

Compromising safety when accountability is diffuse is not unique to finance. In a recent example, General Motors failed to recall cars with faulty ignition that could cause fatal accidents. Many employees knew about the problem, yet failed to act to prevent the harm. The corporate culture promoted silence, obfuscation, and unaccountability, and there were strong incentives to cut costs and sacrifice safety (see Valukas 2014 for an extensive analysis).

Harm and endangerment might be denied and obscured for extended periods of time. Tobacco companies denied the addictiveness of nicotine and the harm from cigarettes for decades (see e.g. Nestle 2015 and Oreskes and Conway 2010). The US National Football League spent years denying the harm from concussions (see Fainaru-Wada and Fairaru 2013 on the "league of denial"). Companies selling children's products sometimes endanger lives by compromising safety and obscuring known problems even after dangerous products are recalled (Felcher 2001). In some cases, overwhelming evidence eventually exposes the truth, as happened for cigarettes.

Governments have the role of creating and enforcing rules for the safety of roads, buildings, water, air, foods, medicines, etc. When governments fail in this role, the results can be devastating. One example is the preventable nuclear disaster in Japan in 2011. Despite a report that exposed the deep regulatory capture at the root of the disaster, little has changed since (see Ferguson and Janson 2013 and Green 2015). In 2014, the US Department of Veterans Affairs was rocked with a scandal involving phoney wait times that delayed access to treatment and benefits to many eligible veterans. It has struggled with accountability issues since (Boyer 2016). In a recent scandal in the US, lead-contaminated water flowed for months into the town of Flint, Michigan, causing serious and long-lasting health problems for many. State officials had ignored and failed to respond to repeated complaints. Michigan law shields decision-makers from public scrutiny, making it difficult to hold individuals responsible for the harm accountable (Clark 2016).

Designing appropriate rules requires professional expertise. Experts, however, may provide biased or flawed advice. Sometimes experts are paid by interested parties to help tilt the rules in specific ways. Even supposedly neutral academics and other experts may provide poor policy guidance. For example, medical research about drugs and medical devices can get corrupted when pharmaceutical companies are involved in funding research or employ researchers or policy-makers. In one case involving a spinal fusion product, researchers paid by the manufacturer suppressed serious side effects (Meier 2012). In another, members of the Food and Drug Administration (FDA) in the US had direct ties with manufacturers that created conflicts of interest (Lenzer and Epstein 2012).

Flawed claims may resonate with politicians, the media, and the public (see Oreskes and Conway 2010 and the 2014 movie *Merchants of Doubt* and Nestle 2015). In finance, research based on inappropriate assumptions is used to support bad policy without proper scrutiny. Seeing the flaws is often difficult for non-experts. The issues appear complex, the jargon is confusing and the technical details are intimidating. A large group of individuals is involved in creating this situation. As was said in the context of another moral scandal, that of child abuse by Catholic priests: "If it takes a village to raise a child, it takes a village to abuse a child."[1]

Many aspects of the financial system in developed economies are unjust because they allow powerful, better informed people to benefit at the expense of people who are less-informed and less powerful. The injustice can be described from a number of perspectives. First, the system contributes to distortions in the distribution of income and wealth, as some of those who benefit from it are among the most privileged members of society, while those who are harmed include the poorest. Second, by allowing the privatization of profits and the socialization of losses, the financial system distorts basic notions of responsibility and liability. Financial crises affect employment and the economic well-being of many segments of society, but those who benefit most from this system and who enable it tend to suffer the least harm.

[1] This chilling statement is made by a lawyer who represented many victims of sexual abuse by Catholic priests in Boston in the 2015 movie *Spotlight*. Child abuse persisted because abusive priests were reassigned, victims were silent or agreed not to speak publicly about the abuse, and others collaborated to keep the problem hidden from authorities and the public for years. Pervasive child abuse had been covered up in many other locations as well.

The persistence of this unjust system illustrates how democracies sometimes fail to serve the interest of the majority of their citizens.

In the next section, I explain briefly the key issues related to capital regulations. I proceed in Section 13.3 to describe the actions and motivations of those who enable the failure of the regulation. Section 13.4 illustrates how ignorance, confusion, and willful blindness contribute to the situation and how flawed narratives obscure the issues and muddle the debate. I conclude in Section 13.5 with reflection on what might bring about positive change.

13.2 OTHER PEOPLE'S MONEY

Business corporations use money from investors in exchange for financial claims such as debt or shares of equity. Outside banking, it is rare for healthy corporations, without any regulations, to fund more than 70 percent of their assets by borrowing, even though corporate tax codes typically favor debt over equity funding.[2] (Specific ratios depend on how assets and debts are measured.) Profits are a popular source of unborrowed funding, and some highly successful corporations, such as Google or Apple, borrow little.

Heavy borrowing increases the likelihood of costly bankruptcy and creates conflicts of interest that distort decisions when managers and shareholders act in their own interests even if assets get depleted and lenders or others are harmed. Once debt is in place, borrowing can become addictive and excessive as the borrower–lender conflict intensifies. To protect their interests, lenders may charge high interest and attach costly and restrictive loan conditions. As a result, heavy borrowing becomes unattractive for most corporations (see Admati et al. 2013, 2015, Admati and Hellwig 2013a, 2015).

In banking, heavy borrowing is less burdensome than elsewhere, because banks' lenders (such as depositors) are unusually passive and do not impose harsh terms even if banks take significant risk that endangers their ability to pay their debts. Depositors trust that the government (or a deposit insurance fund) will pay them if the bank cannot. Lenders who can seize some of the banks' assets ahead of depositors also feel safe lending to banks under attractive terms.

Since many financial institutions are exposed to similar risks and interact extensively with one another, the financial system can become fragile and prone to crises when institutions are funded almost exclusively with debt.

[2] This preference of debt over equity is highly distortive and has little if any economic justification, particularly for corporations (e.g. Fleischer 2011). Subsidizing debt is particularly perverse in banking, but harmful more generally (Hirshleifer and Teoh 2009, The Economist 2016).

Fears of contagion or "systemic risk" lead governments and central banks to offer supports and bailouts that prevent the default of banks and other institutions. Whereas supports and bailouts prevent default, banks are often allowed to persist in an unhealthy state of distress and possible insolvency for extended periods of time, which distorts their decisions and makes them inefficient or dysfunctional (Admati and Hellwig 2013a, chap. 3, 11). Bailouts and supports help institutions to pay their debt in full, often to counterparties within the financial system itself, as happened with insurance company AIG. There are strong incentives to generate profit by excessive risk-taking and excessive borrowing. Das 2010 describes trading as follows:

> Traders risk the bank's capital.... If they win they get a share of the winning. If they lose, then the bank picks up the losses... the money at risk is not their own, it's all OPM—other people's money.... Traders can always play the systemic risk trump card. It is the ultimate in capitalism—the privatization of gains, the socialization of losses.... Traders are given every incentive to take risk and generate short-term profits.[3]

Explicit and implicit guarantees, combined with tax subsidies of debt, exacerbate and feed banks' already strong addiction to debt. Shareholders and managers avoid the unpleasant consequences of bankruptcy. Without effective regulations, the public perversely subsidizes and rewards excessive borrowing and risk in banking and suffers the harm of the resulting fragile and unhealthy system (Admati and Hellwig 2013a, chaps 4–6, 9, Admati et al. 2015, section 6). An analogy would be subsidizing trucks to drive at reckless speed even as slower driving would cause fewer accidents and be more efficient for the engine, or subsidizing chemical companies to pollute when they have an equally costly clean alternative. Even if some of these subsidies lower the price of chemical products or allow cheaper deliveries, the public pays for the subsidies (thus for any such "benefits") while also suffering the collateral harm of the accidents or pollution.

Excessive fragility and inadequate safety rules have always affected banking. As governments created central banks and deposit insurance and thus allowed banks more privileged access to debt funding, equity levels declined consistently (Hoenig 2016). The problem has gotten more severe in recent decades. Financial innovations such as securitization and derivatives, which can be used to manage risk, have enabled financial firms to take more risk while hiding this fact within the increasingly complex and opaque global system. As privileged access to funding and opportunities to hide risk expanded, regulations and disclosure rules failed to keep up and counter the distorted

[3] Das (2010, 151), in describing the system of incentives for derivatives traders who risk the bank's capital and are able to benefit on the upside and share downside with the bank shareholders, or with the public by playing the "systemic risk trump card."

incentives. These developments, and the risk culture that has evolved in banking since the 1980s, are discussed in, for example, Admati and Hellwig 2013a, Das 2010, Dunbar 2011, Fraser 2015, Hill and Painter 2015, Lewis 1980, 2010, Luyendijk 2015, and Partnoy 2009, 2010.

Institutions considered too big to fail are particularly dangerous because they have an incentive to, and can, become inefficiently large, complex, and opaque. It seems to have become difficult or nearly impossible to manage and regulate them effectively (Admati 2014, Admati and Hellwig 2013a, chaps 8–9, 13, Kay 2015, Norris 2013, Jenkins 2015a, 2015b).[4] Alistair Darling, the British Chancellor of the Exchequer during the Great Financial Crisis, says in his memoir: "[The top management in banks both here and in the US] didn't understand what they were doing, the risks they were taking on, or, often, the products they were selling... [they] failed to understand—or even ask—what was apparently making them so much profit and what were the risks" (quoted in Luyendijk 2015, 154–5).

Small banks also need effective regulations. They too can collectively become inefficient, dangerous, and dysfunctional at the same time, thus harming the economy or needing bailouts. Examples include the Savings and Loans crisis in the US in the 1980s, banks in Japan in the 1990s, and, more recently, in Spain and Italy (Admati and Hellwig 2013a and Treanor 2016).

Contrary to claims by many, the reformed capital regulations are overly complex, dangerously inadequate, and poorly designed. They are not based on a proper analysis of the costs and benefits of different approaches and fail to reflect key lessons from the crisis and the true relevant trade-offs (Admati et al. 2013, Admati and Hellwig 2013a, 2015).[5] International minimum standards allow banks to fund as little as 3 percent of their assets by equity, and the details of how this ratio is determined are subject to lobbying and debate. The measures of financial health used by regulators are unreliable and can lull regulators and the public into a false sense of safety, just as happened prior to the Crisis. They still count on problematic accounting rules, credit ratings, and complex "risk weights" that give the pretense of science while in fact being distortive, political, and counterproductive.[6] Banks are allowed, indeed encouraged, to persist in a permanent state of excessive, inefficient, and dangerous levels of indebtedness.

Many banks failed or needed bailouts during the Great Financial Crisis from investments that regulators had viewed as perfectly safe. In response to

[4] See also Chapters 6 and 7 by Reiff and Cullen respectively in this volume on the problems of legal enforcement in the financial industry.

[5] For materials on these issues, see website entitled "excessive leverage and risk in banking" https://www.gsb.stanford.edu/faculty-research/excessive-leverage (accessed October 27, 2016).

[6] On accounting issues see Partnoy and Eisinger 2013. On models, see Behn et al. 2014, Dowd 2015, and Rajan et al. 2015. Risk weights tend to be biased in favor of governments and against traditional business lending (Admati and Hellwig 2013a, chap. 11).

the design of the regulations, banks had incentives to "innovate" in ways that exacerbated the fragility and complexity of the system. The recent Greek debt crisis is partly the result of bad capital regulations. European banks made excessive loans to the Greek government prior to 2010 using only debt funding. Regulators also still count debtlike securities as "loss absorbing" even though equity provides much more reliable loss absorption at no higher cost to society. Derivatives markets continue to add fragility to the system despite recognition and some attempts at better regulation.[7]

Admati and Hellwig 2013a, chap. 11 provides specific recommendations for improving capital regulations, including steps that can be taken immediately. Our proposals and similar calls by others have led to more discussion of the issues, but the actual impact has been rather small. Society is made to tolerate an inefficient and dangerous system because policy-makers contribute to and fail to counter distorted incentives and ability to endanger.

The main beneficiaries from this situation are managers and executives in banks and other financial institutions, who have access to cheap funding and enjoy magnified profits and bonuses during prosperous periods, often while suffering little on the downside (Admati and Hellwig 2013a, chaps 8–10, Admati 2015, Admati 2012, Bhagat 2017, Bhagat and Bolton 2014, Kay 2015). Auditors, credit-rating agencies, law firms, consultants, and lobbyists are offered many profitable opportunities from overly complex rules.

Those who manage other people's money in institutions such as pension funds and mutual funds also tend to benefit on the upside and have little to lose if they take risks for which their investors or clients are not properly compensated. These institutions may not be run fully in the interests of the small investors whose money they invest (Bogle 2005, Jung and Dobbin 2012), and may prefer to collaborate with banks; indeed, they may be partly owned or sponsored by banking institutions. Other enablers, as discussed later, benefit from the current rules or have reasons to avoid challenging the status quo.

The main losers from this system are taxpayers and the broader public. Those lured into borrowing too much in a credit boom face harsh consequences when boom turns to bust, and the economy is harmed by an unstable financial system that does not allocate resources efficiently (Taylor 2015). The harm, however, is diffused and difficult to connect to actions or inaction by specific individuals, and it persists because of a powerful mix of distorted incentives and pervasive confusion.

[7] Much of the effort to regulate derivatives has focused on forcing at least some of the trade into central clearing houses. However, it is still unclear whether this effort has significantly reduced the overall risk from derivatives; see e.g. Persaud 2015.

13.3 MANY ENABLERS

It takes many collaborating individuals, each responding to their own incentives and roles, to enable a dangerous financial system. Who are the enablers and what are their motivations? As we discuss in this section, enablers work within many organizations, including auditors and rating agencies, lobbying and consulting firms, regulatory and government bodies, central banks, academia, and the media.

The enablers have reasons to defend the system and the regulations and to avoid challenging the financial industry and each other. Their actions, or failures to act, endanger and harm the public even as some of them are charged with protecting the public and most claim and are believed to act in the public interest. Some enablers are confused or misinformed, but as discussed later, the confusion is often willful.

Most companies and organizations employ an auditor, and many regulations require credit ratings from one of very few approved agencies. Four audit firms and three rating agencies are the main providers of these certification services. Regulators and some investors treat auditors and rating agencies as if they were neutral watchdogs interested in producing the best information, but these are in fact profit-seeking companies with little if any accountability to the public, and whose interests are not fully aligned with the public interest. Their consulting business may involve advising regulated institutions about compliance. They also count the regulatory bodies themselves as clients for audits and even consulting.[8] These private watchdogs benefit if they collaborate with rather than challenge their clients. As a result, the information they produce can be distorted and misleading.

Accounting rules and risk models used in regulations allow significant discretion. Exposing fraud in disclosures or flaws in models can be costly for individuals throughout the financial system or within watchdogs and regulatory bodies. Whistleblowers are often ignored or fired, and they are likely to lose career opportunities.[9]

[8] Shah 2015 focuses on distorted incentives in auditing and their work with banks and regulators. Consistent accounts are included in Das 2010 and Luyendijk 2015. Partnoy (2009, 406) says: "regulators gave lots of power to private watchdogs or gatekeepers such as accounting firms, rating agencies, law firms even as their record in assessing and reporting risk has been abysmal. The gatekeepers benefit dramatically and can make more money biasing their reports, hiding risk in footnotes." He also describes how accounting rules for derivatives hide enormous risk. Admati and Hellwig 2013a, chap. 6 discuss the risks lurking around the "fortress balance sheet" of J. P. Morgan Chase. Partnoy and Eisinger 2013 analyze the opaque disclosures of Wells Fargo Bank. Kerr 2011 discusses banks' ability to manipulate regulatory measures. Ramanna 2015 describes the politics of accounting standards setting. On rating agencies, see also White 2010, Morgenson 2016 and Chapter 11 (de Bruin, this volume).

[9] On whistleblowers, see Kenny 2014, Sawyer et al. 2010, Shah 2015, and Cohan 2013. Legal protections for whistleblowers vary across nationality and are sometimes quite poor.

Laws and regulations are written by politicians and regulators within national borders. Because financial markets are highly connected across borders, international bodies attempt to coordinate the rules and set minimal standards, leaving details and implementation to each jurisdiction.[10] In these international bodies, far from the public gaze, politicians and regulators often champion "their" institutions even if their citizens are endangered and harmed.[11]

Regulatory dysfunction is often associated with the notion of "regulatory capture." As Senator Richard Durbin put it in an interview shortly after the Great Financial Crisis: "Banks are still the most powerful lobby on Capitol Hill; and they frankly own the place."[12]

One cause of capture are the "revolving doors" where the same people rotate their roles within institutions in the financial system, politics and regulations, and other organizations, including the media. Connaughton (2012, loc. 459), who worked in policy and as a lobbyist, describes Washington DC as:

> a place where the door between the public sector and the private sector revolves every day. A lawyer at the SEC or Justice Department leaves to take a position at a Washington Law firm; a Wall Street executive takes a position at the Treasury Department. The former will soon be defending the Wall Street executives his old colleagues are investigating; the latter will soon be preventing (or delaying or diluting) any government policy that Wall Street doesn't like.

Government officials and staff routinely proceed to take positions in the financial sector, lobbying or consulting firms, or think tanks sponsored by companies.[13] Government positions are often filled by people currently in the financial sector.[14]

Revolving doors contribute to excessive complexity of regulation, because complexity provides an advantage—and creates job opportunities—to those familiar with the details of the rules. Complexity also opens more ways to obscure the flaws of the regulations from the public and to create the pretense of action even if the regulations are ineffective.[15] Revolving doors do not

[10] Examples include the Basel Committee on Banking Supervision https://www.bis.org/bcbs/ and the Financial Stability Board http://www.fsb.org/.

[11] For description of some of the dynamics in the Basel Committee, see Bair 2012. Admati and Hellwig 2013a, chap. 12 discuss the politics of banking and especially the flawed arguments about global competitiveness and national champions. Mattli and Woods 2009 discuss the global politics of regulation.

[12] Durbin 2009.

[13] See also Lipton and Williams 2016.

[14] Ironically, Alistair Darling, who served in the UK government during the Great Financial Crisis and was quoted earlier saying that top management in banks failed to understand or ask about risks, has recently joined the board of one of the largest banks, following his boss Gordon Brown into a career in banking (Parker and McLanahan 2015). This problem is pervasive in many countries. See Admati and Hellwig 2013a, chap. 12.

[15] On complexity of regulations, capture, and revolving doors see Lucca et al. 2014 and McCarty 2013. On excessive complexity in capital regulations see Admati 2016a, Admati and Hellwig 2013a, chap. 11, Bair 2012, Haldane 2012, Hoenig 2013, and Behn et al. 2014.

ensure, as is sometimes claimed, that people who stay in policy throughout their careers are effective regulators; they might well be at a disadvantage relative to people in the industry. The best regulators are often the few who have worked in the industry and have no plans to return.

Politicians write laws, and they appoint and monitor top regulators. A safe banking system is often not politicians' top priority. Politicians may want banks to provide funding to particular industries and constituents or to help in political campaigns even if these actions put citizens and the economy at excessive risk.[16]

Implicit guarantees, for which the industry does not pay and which are ultimately funded by taxpayers, are particularly attractive for politicians as an invisible form of subsidy. Such guarantees do not appear on budgets and they create the illusion of costing no money. By the time the cost of the guarantees is incurred, politicians may already be re-elected or retired. Such subsidies can be extremely distortive and wasteful, and eventually very costly for citizens. Excessively subsidized sectors of the economy can get bloated and inefficient. Blanket guarantees to large banking institutions are particularly dangerous because banks have significant discretion as to how they use the subsidized funding, and guarantees are an effective license for recklessness, even lawlessness (Admati 2014). Politicians are rarely held accountable for the harmful effect of implicit guarantees combined with poor regulations.

Capture takes many subtle forms in the context of financial regulations. Social connections, shared experiences, and lack of expertise can make policy-makers inclined to accept claims made by financial experts even when the claims are false or misleading. Situations in which policy-makers' worldview is strongly affected by those they interact with have been referred to as "cognitive capture" (Johnson and Kwak 2010), "cultural capture" (Kwak 2013), "social capture" (Davidoff 2010), and "deep capture" (Baxter 2011). Prins 2014 documents the ties between presidents and top bankers.[17]

Regulators and politicians are subject to significant lobbying from interested parties as they set and implement the rules (see e.g. McGrance and Hilsenbarth 2012). Lobbying played a role in reckless lending practices that were key to the Great Financial Crisis of 2007–9 (Igan et al. 2011, Vukovic 2011). Between 1999 and 2012, regulators in the US were less likely to initiate enforcement actions against lobbying banks (Lambert 2015), and lobbies are also involved in drafting laws (Connaughton 2012, Drutman 2015, Lipton and Portes 2013, Mufson and Hamburger 2014). In one case, part of the US

[16] Calomiris and Haber 2015 argue that banking is based on political bargains. Admati and Hellwig 2011, 2013a, chap. 12 discuss some of the politics of banking. Lessig 2012, and Teachout 2014 focus on money and politics in the US.

[17] See also Taub 2014, Omarova 2012, and Wilmarth 2013 on the politics of financial regulations in the US.

financial reform law passed in 2010 was reversed in 2014 as part of a budget law, with the active participation of bank lobbyists in writing the law (Eichelberger 2014). Advisory committees to regulators are often stacked with industry participants (Dayen 2016, Eisinger 2012b).

Economists and other experts become apologists for the status quo and enablers of ineffective policies when they fail to point out problems or, worse, when they provide "scientific" support that contributes to and obscures or justifies flawed rules. Some experts are employed by industry groups or sponsored organizations paid to produce specific research. Drutman (2015, loc. 942) describes how the saturation of the "intellectual environment" with claims made by experts, sometimes with PhDs, can affect policy. Even if it becomes clear later that claims made in a policy debate are false, those who had put forward the claims rarely suffer negative consequences.[18]

Research conducted within government and regulatory bodies can be tainted, especially if key individuals are affected by lobbying or political pressure. Staff economists or other experts are often expected to produce research to support preset policies.[19] Bureaucratic approval processes scrutinize staff research before it becomes public. As a result, approved research tends to promote the "official" narratives, while research whose conclusions would contradict the preferred policy may be suppressed, possibly by the researchers themselves.[20]

Even experts considered neutral, such as academic economists, are not immune to the forces of capture (Zingales 2013, 2015). Their incentives may be colored by the desire for job or consulting opportunities, positions on advisory or corporate or policy boards, prestige, sponsorship of research or conferences, data, and research collaborations. Challenging people within the financial system or other enablers is inconvenient or costly.

The peer-review process in journals and in promotion decisions can also lead researchers to be strategic in how they cite and describe research by others. The content of conferences is often affected by sponsors, thus becoming naturally biased toward speakers and research that would not be critical of sponsors' actions. Enablers can thus control their engagement and avoid being challenged.

[18] Admati et al. 2013, 53ff., describe an example in which flawed claims affected policy regarding an accounting rule change that was first delayed by lobbying, and after the rule was eventually changed, the threats made in the earlier lobby were shown to be wrong. Tetlock 2005 points to the lack of accountability for experts.

[19] A recent paper produced by Bank of England economists, challenged in Admati 2016a and Vickers 2016, appears to be an example.

[20] Luyendijk 2015 discusses the codes of silence throughout the financial sector in London, including among regulators. Of course, it is difficult to assess the extent of this problem with any precision because research that is not published is usually unobservable.

The 2010 movie *Inside Job* illustrated financial ties academics may have with industry (see also Carrick-Haggenbarth and Epstein 2012 and Rampell 2011). Subtle forms of cognitive capture are also relevant. It is easier and more convenient for academics and other experts to find ways to collaborate with the many other enablers and to express themselves vaguely rather than directly contradict the viewpoints favored by policy-makers. When issues appear technical and confusing, claims by people considered "big shots" may resonate or even sound profound to many who do not see their flaws.[21] Making claims that serve the interest of powerful people can pay off, and with enough caveats there is little if any downside risk.

Research might also be colored by ideological and other biases. Economists can engage in "cherry-picking" data and assumptions, thus effectively "reverse engineering" results supporting a desired conclusion. Models in banking have created or promoted myths and narratives that have helped enable and maintain the dangerous system and its inadequate regulation. An analogy would be providing a "scientific explanation" for why people smoke cigarettes by a model that assumes smoking is beneficial to health and ignores the addictiveness and harm of cigarettes. Tobacco companies would obviously want to promote such "research" and policy-makers may cite it in justifying policies that are more tolerant of smoking.

Writing clever mathematical models and elaborate empirical studies is valued and rewarded within economics. The desire to motivate and present research as relevant for the real world and for policy can blind researchers to the possibility that the model's conclusion may depend critically on implausible or false assumptions and thus be inadequate for such applications. Just as a bridge built on faulty assumptions may be prone to collapse, the use of inadequate models in banking regulations can support reckless practices and dangerous and flawed laws and regulations.

In cases like the addiction and health risks of cigarette smoking, overwhelming evidence may eventually expose reality and overcome industry denials. In banking, flawed and unsupported narratives and myths, sometimes dressed in impenetrable mathematics and technical details, are maintained and taken as the basis of flawed empirical analyses.

[21] An example is the claim that banks "produce debt" like car companies produce cars (see Admati and Hellwig 2013a, chap. 10, 2013b, 2015, claims 5–6, which form the basis for the "liquidity narrative" discussed later). Another example is the claim that fragile debt helps banks "discipline" their managers (see Admati et al. 2013, section 5, Admati and Hellwig 2013b, Pfleiderer 2014). As explained in Admati and Hellwig 2013b, these theories give contradictory roles and motives to deposits. Models in banking literature that ignore conflicts of interest and where risk arises from uncontrollable liquidity shocks tend to promote guarantees. With guarantees in place, however, lenders cannot be assumed to collect costly information and monitor managers, as assumed critically in the "debt discipline" theories. See also n. 40.

Some models in banking, for example, assume that risk is out of anybody's control, stemming entirely from "liquidity shocks" or sudden panics. Such models ignore and deny risks that are the result of conflicts of interests and inadequate regulations, where people with more information, power, and control benefit while harming others with less information, power, and control. Other models assume that depositors collect information and monitor bankers' behavior, ignoring the dampening effect of deposit insurance on depositor monitoring incentives, and the possibility that shareholders might do the same and have more incentives to do so. The possibility that banks might increase their reliance on equity is often ignored entirely. Some theoretical models assume, inappropriately, that banks are owned entirely by their managers. Yet others assume that equity funding is scarce and "expensive" for banks even as banks can use their profits as a source of equity and generally have access to the same investors that provide equity to other viable companies. In fact, as discussed earlier, banks have as little equity as they do because the people who control them prefer this situation and because failed markets and regulations allow them get away with it.

Pfleiderer 2014 provides an insightful discussion of the potential misuse of models in finance and economics. Using specific examples from banking and elsewhere he argues forcefully that having a particular model does not necessarily mean we understand anything useful about the economy. Admati et al. 2013, 2015, Admati and Hellwig 2013a, 2013b, 2015, Admati 2016a, 2016b, Kay 2015, Vickers 2016 also challenge models and studies related to banking that make inappropriate assumptions and ignore important parts of reality and basic economic forces. Flawed research and narratives help enablers justify their actions and avoid accountability.

Central banks play a critical role in the financial system and in the economy, and this role has expanded dramatically during and since the Great Financial Crisis. They are often involved in designing and implementing regulations and among their key roles is providing "liquidity supports" to banks and sometimes to other financial institutions so as to prevent defaults. Institutions that have access to such supports are able to borrow more easily than they would otherwise. By providing excessive supports, central banks enable weak, even insolvent "zombie" institutions that are dysfunctional and do not help the economy to persist for extended periods of time. Among the benefits of ensuring that banks are safer and less opaque is that they would be less likely to run into liquidity problems. Because central bank supports are loans, the supports do not reduce indebtedness; if central banks lend at below-market rates, the loans provide hidden subsidies to commercial banks and other firms.

Whereas they are meant to be independent, central banks are subject to political pressure (e.g. Conti-Brown 2016, Nyborg 2016). Their decisions regarding whether and under what terms to provide support are often made with little if any scrutiny. The supports can obscure not only banks' weakness but also the failure of regulators (sometimes within the central bank itself) to intervene early and reduce the likelihood of banks needing supports. Excessive interventions by central banks distort markets, and dysfunctional banks interfere with other central bank objectives (Gambacorta and Shin 2016). These issues are often ignored.

Although financial instability and excessive subsidies to the financial sector distort the broader economy, few business leaders speak up on financial regulations. Some may be unfamiliar with the issues, believe that regulatory reform is not working, or are inclined to view regulations as bad in themselves. Business leaders may also prefer to avoid challenging financial firms or policy-makers whose collaboration may be useful.

Some non-profit groups, as well as a few politicians, regulators, and others, try to provide counterweight to the banking industry and enablers of poorly designed regulations (see e.g. Lowrey 2012), but they are unable to match the enormous resources, power, and collective influence of the industry and its enablers. The details of the regulations are complex, and it takes significant expertise to evaluate the rules and to respond properly to the many claims that are made. Getting access to policy-makers and having an impact on their decisions is challenging.

Democratic governments should ultimately be accountable to citizens. Policy failures can persist, however, if citizens are unaware of the problem, confused about the issues, or powerless to bring about change. Enablers often come from across the political spectrum, leaving citizens few if any choices of effective advocates. Financial regulation is often not a salient topic in political campaigns. Even when there is anger about the financial system (as is the case currently in the US), some key issues are not well understood.

The media can play an important role in informing and educating the public and improving accountability. For example, media has exposed corporate fraud (Dyck et al. 2010), the effect of money on politics (Grim and Blumenthal 2015), how the Fed ignored calls to avoid allowing bank dividends (Eisinger 2012a) and central bank actions that would otherwise remain secret.[22]

News and commentary, however, may get distorted. Most media companies are for-profit businesses. In an extreme example, a newspaper avoided covering a story to protect advertising revenue (Oborne 2015). The interests of media owners, and even their lenders, may also affect coverage (Zingales 2016). Investigative reporting has declined because it can be expensive and adversarial (Starkman 2014).

[22] Ivry et al. (2011) is the result of Bloomberg News fighting in court to obtain detailed information about supports given by the Federal Reserve to hundreds of institutions in 2007–9. Lawmakers were not fully aware of these supports as they debated financial reform.

Most of the time, the impact of private interests on news media is subtle. The same forces that cause cognitive and other forms of capture also operate here. One important factor in news media is reporters' need for access to sources of news and stories, which brings them in frequent contact with those they cover (see e.g. Luyendijk 2015, chap. 9). Publishing negative reports, or asking challenging questions, can interfere with access to stories or interviews. "Balanced" reporting may involve quoting false or misleading statements from industry or enablers (e.g. Oreskes and Conway 2010, Admati and Hellwig 2013a, 2015, n. 3).

Editorial decisions about topics, content, and prominence of news and commentary can have an important impact on public perception and policy. Those who make such decisions face implicit and explicit pressures from individuals and organizations keen to have favorable coverage and prevent unfavorable coverage, and who seek to use the media to promote their image and views. People and institutions with significant power, status, and name recognition tend to be more successful in impacting media. Utterances by "important" individuals are reported as news, and these individuals are interviewed and quoted frequently with little if any scrutiny. Power and status also enable easier access to opinion pages where desired narratives can be promoted.

If the news media gives more access and coverage to the industry and its enablers, and if it echoes rather than challenges flawed claims and fails to clarify issues in investigative reporting or commentary, it helps maintain or exacerbate confusion and diffuse accountability. Sometimes reporters or commentators accept claims made by people considered experts because examining the claims' validity requires expertise that reporters lack. When media is used to explain the issues properly, it can elevate the discussion and help the public.[23]

Media coverage obviously responds to news, evolving voices of important individuals, and political development. For example, in the UK John Vickers, who headed an Independent Commission on Banking in 2011, made news in early 2016 in a series of op-eds and interviews, claiming that the Bank of England is too lenient in its equity requirements for the largest banks (Vickers 2016). Reporting on these developments, Chu 2016 explained the issues. Financial regulations and the excessive political influence of the financial sector are discussed in debates and the media in the 2016 US election (at least in the Democratic party primaries). New voices generate debate on too-big-to-fail banks (Applebaum 2016) and on "financialization" (Foroohar 2016, Emba 2016).

[23] See e.g. media mentioned in http://bankersnewclothes.com/media/ (accessed October 27, 2016).

By contrast, there is virtually no public understanding in Europe of the role of poor banking regulation in encouraging banks in Germany, France, Switzerland, and elsewhere to make excessive and reckless loans to the Greek government over the previous decade by assuming that such loans are perfectly safe and requiring no equity funding to make them. Losses from the excessive lending to Greece will be mostly borne by citizens across Europe, while the banks who had made the loans were effectively bailed out before transferring them to official sector bodies and the ECB (Steil and Walker 2015). The media has not helped bring the role of flawed and dangerous banking regulation to the public's attention. The industry and policy-makers have been able to keep it obscure, thus escaping accountability and preventing or delaying improvements.

13.4 SPIN AND NARRATIVES

The distorted incentives and power of those who control the financial system do not fully explain the failure of financial regulations. Confusion and misunderstandings interact with distorted incentives and play an important role. Miller and Rosenfeld 2010 argue that the Great Financial Crisis was caused by "intellectual hazard," which they define as "the tendency of behavioral biases to interfere with accurate thought and analysis within complex organization, thus interfering with the acquisition, analysis, communication, and implementation of information both within an organization and between an organization and external parties" (ibid., 808; see also Fligstein et al. 2014). The discussion in the previous section illustrated some of the narratives enablers use to justify their actions. The financial system is dangerous and ineffectively regulated largely because the industry and the many enablers get away with their "spin" on reality and on specific issues.

Powerful people are not immune to confusion and to putting trust in people who may be conflicted or misinformed. Anecdotal evidence and discussions with many insiders suggest that "blind spots" about key issues related to banking and finance are pervasive. People are reluctant to question the assumptions behind convenient narratives and to engage with alternative and less convenient ones. They often display "motivated reasoning" (Kahan 2016) and variations of Upton Sinclair's famous quip: "it is difficult to get a man to understand something when his salary depends upon his not understanding it!"[24]

[24] The quote is from *I, Candidate for Governor: And How I Got Licked* (1935). In a Tedx Stanford talk on May 7, 2014, I created three variations on this sentence that are relevant to

Willful blindness (Heffernan 2012, Grossman and van der Weele 2016) is especially pronounced in finance because the harm from excessive risk is abstract and the victims are dispersed and "statistical" (Small and Lowenstein 2003). Enablers can more easily maintain narratives that minimize or deny harm when this harm remains obscured. What people *want* to know becomes at least as important as what they actually know. Codes of silence evolve from collective blindness and an implicit agreement to maintain the silence. We may lie to ourselves and live in hope.[25]

Many false and misleading claims about the health and safety of the financial system, the effectiveness of regulations, and the costs and benefits of different approaches are made by people within the financial system and its enablers. These flawed claims obfuscate reality and create the confusion that allows a bad system to persist.

A frequently made statement is that the system is safer today specifically because there is now *x* percent (e.g. three times) more "capital" in banking relative to the pre-crisis period. Such statements avoid the question whether "safer" means "safe enough" and divert attention from the persistent flaws of the regulations or anyone's responsibility for these flaws. The statements ignore the fact that the actual amounts of equity had been, and still are, dangerously and unjustifiably close to zero, which also means that a multiple of the previous minuscule levels does not make for a large number. The claims divert attention from the serious measurement issues mentioned in the previous sections that still cause "regulatory capital ratios" to provide false reassurances. An analogy would be extolling the reduction of the speed limit for loaded trucks in residential areas from 100 miles per hour to 95 miles per hour without discussing why reckless speed is tolerated and while ignoring the police's difficulty in measuring the speed.[26]

Misleading jargon obscures the issues and excludes many from the discussion. Lanchester (2014, 6) writes that when hearing the economists speak, "it's easy to think that somebody is trying to con you... [or] trying to put up a smoke screen" and expresses the "strong feeling that a lot of the terms... were deliberately obscure and confusing." The jargon can also muddle the debate by suggesting false trade-offs.

this essay. Available at https://www.youtube.com/watch?v=s_I4vx7gHPQ (accessed October 27, 2016).

[25] Grossman and van der Weele 2016 quote the line "living is easy with eyes closed" from the 1967 song "Strawberry Fields Forever." Das 2010, chap. 2, speaks of "the lies that we like to believe." He describes the derivatives sell-side trading floor as a place where lying is pervasive and clients "lie mainly to themselves" (55).

[26] Admati (2015), for example, was written in response to Bernanke (2015), which extols the actions by the Federal Reserve once the crisis broke into the open and since, while minimizing the extent of the regulatory failure prior to the crisis and overstating the progress of regulatory reform after the crisis.

For example, an insidious and pervasive confusion concerns simply the meaning of the word "capital" in banking. Attaching verbs like "hold" or "set aside" to the word "capital" (which is used in a uniquely different way in banking than elsewhere), and comparing capital to "a rainy day fund," suggest to most people that capital is idle cash reserves and that capital regulations prevent banks from making loans, both of which are patently false.[27]

Enablers maintain the confusion inadvertently if they do not actually understand the jargon. Books and media reports routinely contain false explanations. The confusion is entrenched because those who are confused may not realize it and therefore maintain and spread it further. Remarkably, regulators and economists who know better use the same misleading language and often fail to correct false statements and to clarify the issues.

The problem goes much beyond jargon and the meaning of words. A bestselling textbook, written by an academic economist who served in high-level policy positions, includes fallacious statements contradicting material in introductory finance courses.[28] As already mentioned, basic economic forces are often denied and ignored in banking, and models in which risk is assumed to be unpreventable imply that regulations are futile or costly. Financial crises are portrayed as akin to natural disasters, for which emergency supports are the main tool. In fact, as discussed earlier, effective regulations can do much at little social cost to dramatically reduce the incidence and cost of crises and to correct other distortions.

Industry lobbies and policy-makers try to address anger about bailouts by assuring the public that it will be possible for even the largest global institutions to fail without needing bailouts. The focus on making failures palatable diverts attention from doing much more to counter distorted incentives, which would also act to *prevent* failures and crises.

The "failure" of one or many banks and financial institutions entails large collateral harm, as seen in many crises over the years, whoever bears their direct losses. The economy would be disrupted much prior to the actual point of failure, as was seen in 2007–8 (Admati and Hellwig 2013a, chap. 5). It is therefore best to focus on prevention, particularly if it can be done while also correcting other distortions. Trying to make failure palatable is akin to preparing ambulances while tolerating and subsidizing trucks to drive at reckless speed (Admati and Hellwig 2013a, chaps 5, 6, 9, Admati 2014). We do not tolerate reckless driving that endangers lives even if "the industry" pays for the ambulances.

[27] See Admati et al. 2013, section 3.1, Admati and Hellwig 2013a, chaps 1, 6; 2015, Claims 1–2.

[28] The author is Fredric Mishkin from Columbia University, who has served in high-level positions within the Federal Reserve. Admati et al. 2013, section 3 and Admati and Hellwig 2013a, chaps 7–8 explain the issues in detail.

Bankers and some enablers of the system often warn that tough regulations will have "unintended consequences" such as restricting credit and growth. In fact, healthier and safer banks can make loans more consistently and with fewer distortions, and credit suffers when banks have too little equity. The claim also presumes that all lending is good for the economy when excessive credit is typically a precursor to bust and crises. Ironically, such claims are made even as banks seek and are allowed to deplete their equity by making payouts to shareholders that they could have used to make loans.[29]

Another common warning of "unintended consequences" is that tough regulations will "shift activities to the shadow banking system." This claim perversely uses the failure of previous regulations that led the financial system to become extremely complex as an argument against highly beneficial steps.[30] The Great Financial Crisis was in fact an "unintended consequence" of failed regulations that had allowed the massive buildup and hiding of risk in a complex and opaque system. Those who warn about the shadow banking system rarely go on to propose how to tackle the challenge of effective regulation. The warnings appear designed to scare and maintain the status quo.

Admati and Hellwig 2013a is entitled *The Bankers' New Clothes* in reference to the famous story of *The Emperor's New Clothes* by Hans Christian Andersen, where people, including the emperor, his ministers, and observers did not admit that they did not see the emperor's fictional clothes for fear of being exposed as stupid or incompetent.[31] Just as the emperor kept marching, the parade of flawed claims about capital regulations continues. Statements suggesting that "much is being done," "challenges remain," and "we may need to do more in the future" allow enablers to present banks' health and the quality and effectiveness of the regulatory effort in better light than appropriate while vaguely leaving open the possibility of more action at some later point.

In 2013 we started, and periodically update, a list of the flawed claims made just on the issue of capital regulations, with brief explanations of what is wrong with them. The latest version includes thirty-one distinct claims (Admati and Hellwig 2015) and more are likely to be added. Clearing the fog created by flawed claims is critical for improving policy and the system. Otherwise, we will

[29] See Admati et al. 2013, Admati and Hellwig 2013a, 2015, Hoenig 2016, and Gambacorta and Shin 2016. Paul Volcker, former chair of the Federal Reserve, referred to such warnings as "bullshit" (Connaughton 2012, loc. 2290). Jenkins 2011, written by a former banking industry insider who became a regulator, describes the lobbying as "intellectually dishonest" and laments that bankers' lobbying strategy "exploits misunderstanding and fear."

[30] See Admati and Hellwig 2013a, chap. 13; 2015, Claim 28, and Admati 2016a, b, regarding "flawed excuses."

[31] Many experiences motivated the book and advocacy efforts; some are described in the preface of the hardcover and paperback, available at http://bankersnewclothes.com/excerpts/ (accessed October 27, 2016). The book website links to other materials. See also the remarks in Section 13.5.

forever be trapped by the problem cynically described by bankers in the nineteenth century:

> The few who understand the system will either be so interested in its profits or be so dependent upon its favors that there will be no opposition from that class, while the great body of people, mentally incapable of comprehending the tremendous advantage that capital derives from the system, will bear its burdens without complaint, and perhaps without even suspecting that the system is inimical to their interests.[32]

13.5 IS CHANGE POSSIBLE?

Good people can do harm and feel good about themselves, especially when many reinforce one another and remain unaccountable, and when the harm is diffuse, abstract, and invisible As Bandura (2015, 100) puts it: "Collective moral disengagement at the social system level requires a network of participants vindicating their harmful practices." Spreading flawed claims that cannot be definitively contradicted, as lobbyists and enablers often do, is no crime. Distorted incentives, ignorance, and confusion combine for a powerful mix. How might those strong forces be overcome?

First, the public must not be lulled into a false sense of safety and accept flawed narratives. Anger is useful but it must be properly focused. For example, the recent movie *The Big Short* (based on Lewis 2010) has left many viewers scared and angry. That anger was most often focused on unpunished fraud, but the problem is much deeper. Much of what the book and movie describe was legal and the reformed rules still tolerate many of the same practices. Lewis 2016 writes: "*The Big Short* is just a movie, but it's also an invitation, to a huge popular audience, to have a smart and interesting discussion about the place of money and finance in all our lives." Having a smart discussion is difficult when the discussion is muddled by misinformation and confusion.

Some of those who understand that current regulations are ineffective focus on symptoms and overlook steps that can produce huge benefits at small cost. For example, the excessive size of too-big-to-fail institutions is enabled by their privileged access to subsidized debt funding, which creates enormous harm and distortions. These distortions can be addressed at little cost, and the

[32] The text is attributed to a letter from the Rothschild Brothers of London to associates in New York in 1863. The Rothschilds were a major banking family in the eighteenth and nineteenth centuries. There is some dispute about whether the text is genuine or properly dated, but many people familiar with the current system find the content applicable and relevant today.

likelihood of failure would also be reduced, if these institutions were forced to rely much more on equity and thus reduce their dependence on subsidized debt funding.

Complex regulations can create the pretense of tough action while their flaws remain obscured.[33] The confusing spin and narratives make it difficult to distinguish effective from wasteful regulations.

A deeper issue is that although the economy suffers repeatedly from the consequences of excessive borrowing by individuals, corporations, and sometimes governments, many policies encourage and subsidize the use of debt. Senseless tax subsidies of mortgage and corporate borrowing, which are particularly harmful in banking, create large distortions and instability and prolong recessions when credit boom turns to bust (The Economist 2016, Mian and Sufi 2014, Taylor 2015).

Luyendijk 2015 describes his increasing horror as he realized, while interviewing many individuals in the financial sector in London, how distorted the incentives are and how extensive is moral disengagement of those involved. In the last chapter, entitled "The Empty Cockpit," he shares his hesitation about publishing the book. "What's the point of leaving one's readers in powerless fear and outrage?" he asks, but then concludes that publishing the book is valuable because "ignorance, denial or apathy is simply not an option when it comes to a problem of this magnitude and urgency" (261).

As discussed in this chapter, those at the controls of the financial system do not have strong incentives to protect the public; instead they stand to benefit from actions that contribute or tolerate harm and endangerment. Making the financial system safer would require better rules as well as better monitoring of the system, akin to radars in aviation. Yet disclosures in banking remain poor and systems to track financial transactions and contracts have been slow to develop.[34] The main obstacle is not the technical difficulty of controlling risk in banking, but rather the lack of *political will* to do so.

I have been intensely involved in the debate about banking regulation since 2008, first through discussions with colleagues and academic writing, and, starting in 2010, engaging with a broader set of people. The impetus for this deeper involvement came from individuals within regulatory bodies who

[33] For example, the requirement in the US that the largest institutions prepare "living wills" is extremely costly, yet it has produced little if any benefits so far (Admati 2014). Regulatory "stress tests" do not capture the complex interconnections through the system, yet are used to provide false reassurances and allow too-big-to-fail institutions to deplete their equity by making payouts to shareholders (Admati and Hellwig 2013a, chap. 11, Dowd 2015, and Cetina et al. 2016).

[34] For example, there has been some effort to create legal entity identifiers (see https://financialresearch.gov/data/legal-entity-identifier/ (accessed October 27, 2016)) but such systems do not appear to be a priority. Similarly cross-border resolution, a problem known and discussed for decades and essential for addressing global and systemic institutions, is also still intractable, see Admati 2014. Derivatives trading also remains poorly disclosed, as discussed in n. 7.

alerted me that flawed claims are having an important impact on policy and urged me to speak up and help clarify the issues. Many of the references in this chapter reflect efforts to alert policy-makers and the public to the remaining danger and distortions in the financial system and to propose ways to address them.

Over the last eight years I have had numerous private discussions and public encounters with people from within the industry and various enabler categories discussed in this chapter (see also Admati and Hellwig 2013a, prefaces). Some of these engagements have been perfunctory or superficial and seem to have had little impact, but many people have welcomed discussion, engaged genuinely, and provided opportunities for more engagement, even as some of them have maintained their preferred narrative in public.[35]

Luyendijk 2015 classifies the moral attitudes of the people he met within the financial system and describes his reaction to these attitudes. One type he finds ethically most disturbing he calls "cold fish." Cold fish believe anything that is legal is perfectly fine to do. In our economy, responding to incentives without breaking the law is considered the foundation of growth and innovation. This chapter has examined why laws and regulations tolerate and reward unnecessary harm and endangerment in banking and who is responsible.

What I have found surprising, dismaying, and alarming are the behaviors, and in some cases the hypocrisy, of people in charge of protecting the public or who present themselves as acting on behalf of the public, yet who evasively avoid genuine engagement on issues critically related to public safety, who refuse to question their assumptions, and who persist in failing to protect the public and in making flawed claims that help enable harm and endangerment.

There are well-intentioned people in government and elsewhere, including within the financial system itself, who would want to act to promote the public interest, but are often prevented or deterred from doing so by political constraints, institutional policies, and more subtle forms of discouragement. In a system dominated by powerful industry players and supported by powerful enablers, the need to promote institutional objective puts many people in conflict with the public interest. Regulators and financial practitioners may put their careers, status, and prestige at risk if they challenge certain narratives.

Tenured academics, who have the most expertise, job security, and academic freedom to express themselves and to engage in policy without being conflicted, are in a unique position to bring about positive change. Yet, some academics are important enablers of the badly regulated and dangerous financial system. By such behavior as making false statements in textbooks, creating models and narratives with assumptions that distort reality in critical ways, misusing or tolerating the misuse of research to propose or support bad

[35] This chapter reflects my observations and insights from individuals I have engaged with, as well as direct comments on the text from individuals I cannot acknowledge by name.

policy, or making vague and misleading claims whose flaws, often subtle, can be difficult to detect, these economists exacerbate confusion, muddle the debate, and harm instead of promote the public interest. Someone with sufficient background to understand the academic literature, who has been employed by major financial institutions, quipped recently when discussing some statements by academic economists: "with such friends, who needs lobbyists?"[36]

This chapter focused on capital regulation that, if designed and implemented properly, can correct many distortions and protect the public at little social cost and, when successful, can lessen the need for costlier and less effective regulations. Even if this "policy bargain" is improved, however, distorted incentives to commit fraud and to endanger would still be a problem. More radical changes in the structure, compensation practices, and culture of the industry and of regulatory bodies may be essential.[37]

Ultimately, in a functioning democracy political change comes from public pressure, which requires better awareness and understanding. Education is extremely important, so that people become savvier in their own interactions with the financial system, and so they come to see past the fog of confusion.

Entrenched and powerful systems resist change, but a just society must not tolerate a situation in which critically important systems like the financial system are run against the interests of the vast majority. More people must become aware of the problem and understand what is wrong. Then they must demand that policy-makers do better. Change is possible, but it will take a village to repair a financial system.[38]

[36] A thirty-five-year veteran from banking asked me after reading the first version of Admati et al. 2013 in 2010 why we spent so much space debunking the idea that "debt disciplines managers" and added "Is this some academic thing?" Admati and Hellwig 2013b, which includes material omitted from Admati and Hellwig 2013a for being esoteric, provides a more accessible discussion of this academic myth. See also nn. 22 and 40.

[37] For example, Hill and Painter 2015, Bhagat 2017, and Kay 2015 propose changes in the way bankers are compensated to create more personal liability. Kane 2012 and Barth et al. 2012 discuss ways to address regulatory capture. Omarova 2012 advocates inserting public interest directly into the regulatory process to create "tripartism" where policy-makers collaborate with the industry and the public interest is forgotten. King 2016 proposes radical changes in the relations between private banks and central banks. McMillan 2014 outlines a radical plan for the "end of banking" that relies on strong solvency conditions imposed and enforced on all firms to prevent the use of debt to invest in financial assets.

[38] I am grateful to Jon Bendor, John Cochrane, Peter Conti-Brown, Christina Buchmann, Martin Hellwig, Lisa Herzog, David Hirshleifer, Gudrun Johnsen, Tamar Kreps, Martien Lubberink, Paul Pfleiderer, Heiner Schulz, Matthew Zuck, and individuals from within the financial system and various enabling institutions discussed in this chapter for many helpful discussions and comments.

REFERENCES

Admati, Anat R. 2012. "The Great Bank Escape." *Project Syndicate*, December 31.

Admati, Anat R. 2014. "Examining the GAO Report on Expectations of Government Support for Bank Holding Companies." Testimony for hearing of Senate Committee on Banking, Housing and Urban Affairs Subcommittee on Financial Institutions and Consumer Protection, July 31.

Admati, Anat R. 2015. "Where is the Courage to Act on Banks?" *Bloomberg View*, October 12.

Admati, Anat R. 2016a. "Rethinking Financial Regulations: How Confusion Has Prevented Progress." In *Progress and Confusion: The State of Macroeconomic Policy*, edited by Olivier J. Blanchard, Raghuram Rajan, Kenneth S. Rogoff, and Lawrence H. Summers. Cambridge, MA: MIT Press.

Admati, Anat R. 2016b. "The Missed Opportunity and Challenge of Capital Regulation." *National Institute Economic Review*, February, R4–R14.

Admati, Anat R., Peter M. DeMarzo, Martin F. Hellwig, and Paul Pfleiderer. 2016. "Fallacies, Irrelevant Facts, and Myths in the Discussion of Capital Regulation: Why Bank Equity Is Not Socially Expensive." Working paper (original draft August, 2010). http://papers.ssrn.com/sol3/papers.cfm?abstract_id=2349739 (accessed October 27, 2016).

Admati, Anat R., Peter M. DeMarzo, Martin F. Hellwig, and Paul Pfleiderer. 2015. "The Leverage Ratchet Effect." Working paper, http://papers.ssrn.com/sol3/papers.cfm?abstract_id=2304969 (accessed October 27, 2016).

Admati, Anat R., and Martin F. Hellwig. 2011. "Good Banking Regulation Needs Clear Focus, Sensible Rules, and Political Will." Working paper, https://www.gsb.stanford.edu/sites/gsb/files/admati-hellwig_good_regulation.pdf (accessed November 1, 2016).

Admati, Anat R., and Martin F. Hellwig. 2013a. *The Bankers' New Clothes: What's Wrong with Banking and What to Do About It.* Princeton, NJ: Princeton University Press.

Admati, Anat R., and Martin F. Hellwig. 2013b. "Does Debt Discipline Bankers? An Academic Myth about Bank Indebtedness." Working paper, http://papers.ssrn.com/sol3/papers.cfm?abstract_id=2216811 (accessed October 27, 2016).

Admati, Anat R., and Martin F. Hellwig. 2015. "The Parade of Bankers' New Clothes Continues: 31 Flawed Claims Debunked." Working paper, http://papers.ssrn.com/sol3/papers.cfm?abstract_id=2292229 (accessed October 27, 2016).

Applebaum, Binyamin. 2016. "Fed's Neel Kashkari Says Banks Are 'Still Too Big to Fail.'" *New York Times*, February 16.

Bair, Sheila. 2012. *Bull by the Horns: Fighting to Save Main Street from Wall Street and Wall Street from Itself.* New York: The Free Press.

Bandura, Albert. 2015. *Moral Disengagement: How Good People Can Do Harm and Feel Good About Themselves.* London: Worth Publishers.

Barth, James, Gerard Caprio, and Ross Levine. 2012. *Guardians of Finance: Making Regulators Work for Us.* Cambridge, MA: MIT Press.

Baxter, Lawrence G. 2011. "'Capture' in Financial Regulation: Can We Channel it Toward the Common Good?" *Cornell Journal of Law and Public Policy* 21(1), 175–200.

Behn, Markus, Rainer Haselmann, and Vikrant Vig. 2014. "The Limits of Model-Based Regulation." Working paper, http://papers.ssrn.com/sol3/papers.cfm?abstract_id=2523383 (accessed October 27, 2016).

Bernanke, B. S. 2015. *The Courage to Act: A Memoir of a Crisis and Its Aftermath*. New York: WW Norton & Company.

Bhagat, Janjai. 2017. *Bank Capital and Executive Compensation Reform: Preventing the Next Financial Crisis*. Cambridge: Cambridge University Press.

Bhagat, Sanjai, and Brian J. Bolton. 2014. "Executive Compensation, Director Compensation and Bank Capital Requirements Reform." Working paper, http://papers.ssrn.com/sol3/papers.cfm?abstract_id=2442501 (accessed October 27, 2016).

Bogle, John C. 2005. *The Battle for the Soul of Capitalism*. New Haven: Yale University Press.

Boyer, Dave. 2016. "VA Still Plagued by Problems Two Years after Scandal." *Washington Post*, April 3.

Calomiris, Charles W., and Stephen H. Haber. 2015. *Fragile by Design: The Political Origins of Banking Crises and Scarce Credit*. Princeton, NJ: Princeton University Press.

Carrick-Haggenbarth, Jessica, and Gerald A. Epstein. 2012. "Dangerous Interconnectedness: Economists' Conflicts of Interest, Ideology and Financial Crisis." *Cambridge Journal of Economics* 36(1), 43–63.

Cetina, Jill, Mark Paddrik, and Sriram Rajan. 2016. "Stressed to the Core: Counterparty Concentrations and Systemic Losses in CDS Markets." Working paper, https://financialresearch.gov/working-papers/files/OFRwp-2016-01_Stressed-to-the-Core.pdf (accessed October 27, 2016).

Chu, Ben. 2016. "Sir John Vickers Warns on Inadequate Bank Capital." *The Independent*, February 15.

Clark, Anna. 2016, "The Struggle for Accountability in Flint." *Boston Review*, February 6.

Cohan, William. 2013. "Was This Whistleblower Muzzled?" *New York Times*, September 21.

Connaughton, Jeff. 2012. *Payoff: Why Wall Street Often Wins*. Westport, CT: Prospecta Press.

Conti-Brown, Peter. 2016. *The Power and Independence of the Federal Reserve*. Princeton, NJ Princeton University Press.

Das, Satyajit. 2010. *Traders, Guns and Money: Knowns and Unknowns in the Dazzling World of Derivatives*, 2nd edition. Harlow: FT Prentice Hall.

Davidoff, Steven M. 2010. "The Government's Elite and Regulatory Capture." *New York Times*, June 11.

Dayen, David. 2016. "Why Elizabeth Warren Is on the Warpath This Week." *New Republic*, February 26.

Dowd, Kevin. 2015. *No Stress: The Flaws in the Bank of England's Stress Testing Programme*. London: Adam Smith Institute.

Drutman, Lee. 2015. *The Business of America is Lobbying: How Corporations Became Politicized and Politics Became More Corporate*. New York: Oxford University Press.

Dunbar, Nicholas. 2011. *The Devil's Derivatives: The Untold Story of the Slick Traders and Hapless Regulators Who Almost Blew Up Wall Street... and Are Ready to Do It Again*. Cambridge, MA: Harvard Business Review Press.

Durbin, Richard. 2009. "Durbin On Congress: The Banks 'Own The Place'." *Progress Illinois*, April 29.

Dyck, Alexander, Adair Morse, and Luigi Zingales. 2010. "Who Blows the Whistle on Corporate Fraud?" *Journal of Finance* 65(6), 2213–53.

The Economist. 2016. "A Senseless Subsidy: Ending the Debt Addiction." May 16.

Eichelberger, Erika. 2014. "Citigroup Wrote the Wall Street Giveaway the House Just Approved." *Mother Jones*, December 12.

Eisinger, Jesse. 2012a. "Fed Shrugged Off Warnings, Let Banks Pay Shareholders Billions." *ProPublica*, March 2.

Eisinger, Jesse. 2012b. "Fledgling Monitor for Wall St. Risks an Early Compromise." *New York Times*, November 28.

Emba, Christine. 2016. "Has Our Economy Become Too 'Financialized'?" *Washington Post*, April 18.

Fainaru-Wada, Mark, and Steve Fairaru. 2013. *League of Denial: The NFL, Concussions, and the Battle for Truth*. New York: Three Rivers Press.

Felcher, Marla. 2001. *It's No Accident: How Corporations Sell Dangerous Baby Products*. Monroe, ME: Common Courage Press.

Ferguson, Mark D., and Mark Janson. 2013. "Regulating Japanese Nuclear Power in the Wake of the Fukushima Daiichi Accident." *Federation of American Scientists Issues Briefs* May. Washington, DC: Federation of American Scientists.

Fleischer, Victor. 2011. "Tax Reform and the Tax Treatment of Debt and Equity." Testimony to a Joint Hearing of US Senate Committee on Ways and Means and House of Representatives Finance Committee, July 13.

Fligstein, Neil, Jonah Stuart Brundage, and Michael Schultz. 2014. "Why the Federal Reserve Failed to See the Financial Crisis of 2008: The Role of 'Macroeconomics' as Sense-Making and Cultural Frame." Working paper, http://sociology.berkeley.edu/sites/default/files/faculty/fligstein/Why%20the%20Federal%20Reserve%20Failed%20to%20See%20the%20Crisis%20of%202008%20September%2029%202014.pdf (accessed October 27, 2016).

Foroohar, Rana. 2016. *Makers and Takers: The Rise of Finance and the Fall of American Businesses*. New York: Crown Business.

Fraser, Ian. 2015. *Shredded: Inside RBS: The Bank that Broke Britain*. Edinburgh: Birlinn.

Gambacorta, Leonardo, and Hyun Shin. 2016. "Why Bank Capital Matters for Monetary Policy." BIS Working Paper 558, http://www.bis.org/publ/work558.pdf.

Green, Jim. 2015. "Nuclear Zombies: Japan's 'Nuclear Village' is Back in Control." *Australian Business Review*, March 31.

Grim, Ryan, and Paul Blumenthal. 2015. "The Inside Story of How Citizens United Has Changed Washington Lawmaking." *Huffington Post*, February 26.

Grossman, Zachary, and Joel J. van der Weele. 2016. "Self-Image and Willful Ignorance in Social Decisions." *Journal of the European Economic Association*, forthcoming.

Haldane, Andrew G. 2012. "The Dog and the Frisbee." Speech at the Federal Reserve Bank of Kansas City's economic policy symposium, Jackson Hole, Wyoming, August 31.

Heffernan, Margaret. 2012. *Willful Blindness: Why We Ignore the Obvious at Our Peril*. New York: Bloomsbury, USA.

Hill, Claire A., and Richard W. Painter. 2015. *Better Bankers, Better Banks: Promoting Good Business through Contractual Commitment*. Chicago, IL: University of Chicago Press.

Hirshleifer, David, and Siew Hong Teoh. 2009. "Systemic Risk, Coordination Failures, and Preparedness Externalities: Applications to Tax and Accounting Policy." *Journal of Financial Economic Policy* 1(2), 128–42.

Hoenig, Thomas. 2013. "Basel III: A Well Intentioned Illusion." Speech to Association of Deposit Insurers, April 9, Basel.

Hoenig, Thomas. 2016. "A Capital Conflict." Speech to the National Association for Business Economics (NABE) and the Organization for Economic Cooperation and Development (OECD) Global Economic Symposium, Paris, France. May 23.

Igan, Deniz, Prachi Mishra, and Thierry Tressel. 2011. "A Fistful of Dollars: Lobbying and the Financial Crisis." *NBER Macroeconomics Annual* 26(1), 195–230.

Ivry, Bob, Bradley Keoun, and Phil Kuntz. 2011. "Secret Fed Loans Gave Banks $13 Billion Undisclosed to Congress." Bloomberg, November 27.

Jenkins, Robert. 2011. "Lessons in Lobbying." Remarks at the Third Gordon Midgley Memorial Debate, London, November 22.

Jenkins, Robert. 2015a. "How HSBC Chairman Flint Can Restore Accountability at His Bank." *Financial Times*, March 10.

Jenkins, Robert. 2015b. "When Timidity Triumphs…" Speech at Annual Finance Watch Conference, Brussels, November 17.

Johnson, Simon, and James Kwak. 2010. *13 Bankers: The Wall Street Takeover and the Next Financial Meltdown*. New York: Pantheon.

Jung, Jiwook, and Frank Dobbin. 2012. "Finance and Institutional Investors." In *The Oxford Handbook of the Sociology of Finance*, edited by Marin Knorr Cetina and Alex Preda. Oxford: Oxford University Press, 52–74.

Kahan, Dan M. 2016. "The Politically Motivated Reasoning Paradigm." In *Emerging Trends in Social and Behavioral Sciences*. New York: Sage, 1–24.

Kane, Edward J. 2012. "Missing Elements in US Financial Reform: A Kübler-Ross Interpretation of the Inadequacy of the Dodd-Frank Act." *Journal of Money and Banking* 36(3), 654–61.

Kay, John. 2015. *Other People's Money: The Real Business of Finance*. New York: Norton.

Kenny, Kate. 2014. "Banking Compliance and Dependence Corruption: Towards an Attachment Perspective." *Law and Financial Markets Review* 8(2), 165–77.

Kerr, Gordon. 2011. "The Law of Opposites: Illusionary Profits in the Financial Sector." Adam Smith Institute. http://www.thebrokenwindow.net/papers/A/ASI_Law_of_opposites.pdf (accessed November 19, 2016).

King, Mervyn. 2016. *The End of Alchemy: Money, Banking, and the Future of the Global Economy*. New York: Norton.

Kwak, James. 2013. "Cultural Capture and the Financial Crisis." In *Preventing Regulatory Capture: Special Interest Influence and How to Limit It*, edited by Daniel Carpenter and David Moss. Cambridge: Cambridge University Press, 71–98.

Lambert, Thomas. 2015. "Lobbying on Regulatory Enforcement Actions: Evidence from Banking." Working paper, http://papers.ssrn.com/sol3/papers.cfm?abstract_id=2517235 (accessed October 27, 2016).

Lanchester, John. 2014. *How to Speak Money: What the Money People Say—and What It Really Means.* New York: Norton.

Lenzer, Jeanne, and Keith Epstein. 2012. "The Yaz Men: Members of FDA Panel Reviewing the Risks of Popular Bayer Contraceptive Had Industry Ties." *Washington Monthly*, January 9.

Lessig, Lawrence. 2012. *Republic, Lost: How Money Corrupts Congress—and a Plan to Stop It.* New York: Twelve.

Lewis, Michael. 1980. *Liar's Poker.* New York: Norton.

Lewis, Michael. 2010. *The Big Short: Inside the Doomsday Machine.* New York: Norton.

Lewis, Michael. 2016. "Even Michael Lewis Was Surprised Hollywood Bet on *The Big Short.*" *Vanity Fair Magazine*, January.

Lipton, Eric, and Ben Portes. 2013. "Banks' Lobbyists Help in Drafting Financial Bills." *New York Times*, May 23.

Lipton, Eric, and Brooke Williams. 2016. "Researchers or Corporate Allies? Think Tanks Blur the Line." *New York Times*, August 7.

Lowrey, Annie. 2012. "Facing Down the Bankers." *New York Times*, May 30.

Lucca, David, Amit Seru, and Francesco Trebbi. 2014. "The Revolving Door and Worker Flows in Banking Regulation." *Journal of Monetary Economics* 65, 17–32.

Luyendijk, Joris. 2015. *Swimming with Sharks: My Journey into the World of the Bankers.* London: Guardian Faber Publishing.

McCarty, Nolan. 2013. "Complexity, Capacity, and Capture." In *Preventing Regulatory Capture: Special Interest Influence and How to Limit It*, edited by Daniel Carpenter and David Moss. Cambridge: Cambridge University Press, 99–123.

McGrance, Victoria, and Jon Hilsenbarth. 2012. "Fed Writes Sweeping Rules from Behind Closed Doors." *Wall Street Journal*, February 21.

McMillan, Jonathan. 2014. *The End of Banking: Money, Credit, and the Digital Revolution.* London: Zero/One Economics.

Mattli, Walter, and Ngaire Woods. 2009. "In Whose Benefit? Explaining Regulatory Change in Global Politics." In *The Politics of Global Regulation*, edited by Walter Mattli and Ngaire Woods. Princeton, NJ: Princeton University Press, 1–43.

Meier, Barry. 2012. "A Battle Over a Spine Treatment." *New York Times*, September 5.

Mian, A., and A. Sufi. 2014. "What Explains the 2007–2009 Drop in Employment?" *Econometrica* 82(6), 2197–23.

Miller, Geoffrey P., and Gerald Rosenfeld. 2010. "Intellectual Hazard: How Conceptual Biases in Complex Organizations Contributed to the Crisis of 2008." *Harvard Journal of Law and Public Policy* 33(2), 807–40.

Morgenson, Gretchen. 2016. "Ratings Agencies Still Coming Up Short, Years After Crisis." *New York Times*, January 16.

Mufson, Steven, and Tom Hamburger. 2014. "Jamie Dimon Himself Called to Urge Support for the Derivatives Rule in the Spending Bill." *Washington Post*, December 16.

Nestle, Marion. 2015. *Soda Politics: Taking on Big Soda (and Winning).* New York: Oxford University Press.

Norris, Floyd. 2013. "Masked by Gibberish, the Risks Run Amok." *New York Times*, March 21.

Nyborg, Kjell G. 2017. *Collateral Frameworks: The Open Secret of Central Banks.* Cambridge: Cambridge University Press.

Oborne, Peter. 2015. "Why I Resigned from the *Telegraph.*" *Open Democracy UK—Our Kingdom,* February 17. https://www.opendemocracy.net/ourkingdom/peter-oborne/why-i-have-resigned-from-telegraph (accessed November 19, 2016).

Omarova, Soule. 2012. "Bankers, Bureaucrats, and Guardians: Toward Tripartism in Financial Services Regulation." *Journal of Corporation Law* 37, 621–74.

Oreskes, Naomi, and Erik M. Conway. 2010. *Merchants of Doubt: How a Handful of Scientists Obscured the Truth on Issues from Tobacco Smoke to Global Warming.* London: Bloomsbury Press.

Parker, George, and Ben McLanahan. 2015. "Alistair Darling Joins Board of Morgan Stanley." *Financial Times,* December 9.

Partnoy, Frank. 2009. *Infectious Greed: How Deceit and Risk Corrupted the Financial Markets.* New York: Public Affairs.

Partnoy, Frank. 2010. *FIASCO: Blood in the Water on Wall Street.* New York: Norton.

Partnoy, Frank, and Jesse Eisinger. 2013. "What's Inside America's Big Banks." *The Atlantic,* Jan.–Feb.

Persaud, Avinash. 2015. "The Unintended Consequences and Possible Mitigation of the Clearing Mandate for OTC Derivatives." Working paper, http://papers.ssrn.com/sol3/papers.cfm?abstract_id=2643501 (accessed October 27, 2016).

Pfleiderer, Paul. 2014. "Cameleons: The Misuse of Theoretical Models in Finance and Economics." Working paper, http://papers.ssrn.com/sol3/papers.cfm?abstract_id=2414731 (accessed October 27, 2016).

Prins, Nomi. 2014. *All the Presidents' Bankers: The Hidden Alliances that Drive American Power.* New York: Nation Books.

Rajan, Uday, Amit Seru, and Vikrant Vig. 2015. "The Failure of Models that Predict Failure: Distance, Incentives and Defaults." *Journal of Financial Economics* 115(2), 237–60.

Ramanna, Karthik. 2015. *Political Standards: Corporate Interest, Ideology, and Leadership in the Shaping of Accounting Rules for the Market Economy.* Chicago, IL: Chicago University Press.

Rampell, Catherine. 2011. "Buying Influence at Universities." *New York Times* Economix blog, May 12.

Sawyer, Kim R., Jackie Johnson, and Mark Holub. 2010. "The Necessary Illegitimacy of the Whistleblower." *Business and Professional Ethics Journal* 29(1–4), 85–107.

Shah, Atul K. 2015. "The Chemistry of Audit Failure: A Case Study of KPMG." Working paper, Suffolk Business School, http://www.academia.edu/17958528/the_chemistry_of_audit_failure_-_A_Case_Study_of_HBOS_audit_by_KPMG (accessed October 27, 2016).

Small, Deborah A., and George Lowenstein. 2003. "Helping *a* Victim or Helping *the* Victim: Altruism and Identifiability." *Journal of Risk and Uncertainty* 1, 5–16.

Starkman, Dean. 2014. *The Watchdog that Didn't Bark: The Financial Crisis and the Disappearance of Investigative Journalism.* New York: Columbia University Press.

Steil, Benn, and Dinah Walker. 2015. "Greek Fallout: Italy and Spain Have Funded a Massive Backdoor Bailout of French Banks." *Council of Foreign Relations,* July 2. http://blogs.cfr.org/geographics/2015/07/02/greecefallout/ (accessed November 19, 2016).

Taub, Jennifer. 2014. *Other People's Houses: How Decades of Bailouts, Captive Regulators, and Toxic Bankers Made Home Mortgages a Thrilling Business*. New Haven: Yale University Press.

Taylor, Alan M. 2015. "Credit, Financial Stability, and the Macroeconomy." *Annual Reviews of Economics* 7, 309–99.

Teachout, Zephyr. 2014. *Corruption in America: From Benjamin Franklin's Snuff Box to Citizens United*. Cambridge, MA: Harvard University Press.

Tetlock, Philip E. 2005. *Expert Political Judgment: How Good Is It? How Can We Know?* Princeton, NJ: Princeton University Press.

Treanor, Jill. 2016. "Quiet Crisis: Why Battle to Prop Up Italy's Banks Is Vital to EU Stability." *Guardian*, May 10.

Valukas, A. R. 2014. "Report to Board of Directors of General Motors Company Regarding Ignition Switch Recalls." Jenner & Block, Tech. Rep.

Vickers, John. 2016. "The Systemic Risk Buffer for UK Banks: A Response to the Bank of England's Consultation Paper." LSE Financial Markets Group Special Paper 244, April. http://www.lse.ac.uk/fmg/workingPapers/specialPapers/PDF/SP244.pdf (accessed October 27, 2016).

Vukovic, Vuk. 2011. "Political Economy of the US Financial Crisis 2007–2009." *Financial Theory and Practice* 35(1), 91–128.

White, Lawrence J. 2010. "The Credit Rating Agencies." *Journal of Economic Perspectives* 24(2), 211–26.

Wilmarth, Arthur. 2013. "Turning a Blind Eye: Why Washington Keeps Giving in to Wall Street." *University of Cincinnati Law Review* 81(4), 1283–445.

Zingales, Luigi. 2013. "Preventing Economists' Capture." In *Preventing Regulatory Capture: Special Interest Influence and How to Limit It*, edited by Daniel Carpenter and David Moss: Cambridge: Cambridge University Press, 124–51.

Zingales, Luigi. 2015. "Presidential Address: Does Finance Benefit Society?" *Journal of Finance* 70(4), 1327–63.

Zingales, Luigi. 2016. "Are Newspapers Captured by Banks? Evidence from Italy." Promarket blog, May 12. https://promarket.org/are-newspapers-captured-by-banks (accessed October 27, 2016).

General Index

The manufacturer's authorised representative in the EU for product safety is Oxford University Press España S.A. of El Parque Empresarial San Fernando de Henares, Avenida de Castilla, 2 - 28830 Madrid (www.oup.es/en or product.safety@oup.com). OUP España S.A. also acts as importer into Spain of products made by the manufacturer.
Printed and bound by CPI Group (UK) Ltd, Croydon, CR0 4YY
14/09/2026
02216306-0002

Techniques for Lithium Isotope Separation, Laser Cooling, and Scattering

IOP Series in Coherent Sources, Quantum Fundamentals, and Applications

About the Editor

F J Duarte is a laser physicist based in Western New York, USA. His career has covered three continents while contributing within the academic, industrial, and defense sectors. Duarte is editor/author of 15 laser optics books and sole author of three books: *Tunable Laser Optics, Quantum Optics for Engineers*, and *Fundamentals of Quantum Entanglement*. Duarte has made original contributions in the fields of coherent imaging, directed energy, high-power tunable lasers, laser metrology, liquid and solid-state organic gain media, narrow-linewidth tunable laser oscillators, organic semiconductor coherent emission, *N*-slit quantum interferometry, polarization rotation, quantum entanglement, and space-to-space secure interferometric communications. He is also the author of the generalized multiple-prism grating dispersion theory and pioneered the use of Dirac's quantum notation in *N*-slit interferometry and classical optics. His contributions have found applications in numerous fields, including astronomical instrumentation, dispersive optics, femtosecond laser microscopy, geodesics, gravitational lensing, heat transfer, laser isotope separation, laser medicine, laser pulse compression, laser spectroscopy, mathematical transforms, nonlinear optics, polarization optics, and tunable diode-laser design. Duarte was elected Fellow of the Australian Institute of Physics in 1987 and Fellow of the Optical Society of America in 1993. He has received various recognitions, including the *Paul F Foreman Engineering Excellence Award* and the *David Richardson Medal* from the Optical Society.

Coherent Sources, Quantum Fundamentals, and Applications

Since its discovery the laser has found innumerable applications from astronomy to zoology. Subsequently, we have also become familiar with additional sources of coherent radiation such as the free electron laser, optical parametric oscillators, and coherent interferometric emitters. The aim of this book Series in Coherent Sources, Quantum Fundamentals, and Applications is to explore and explain the physics and technology of widely applied sources of coherent radiation and to match them with utilitarian and cutting-edge scientific applications. Coherent sources of interest are those that offer advantages in particular emission characteristics areas such as broad tunability, high spectral coherence, high energy, or high power. An additional area of inclusion are the coherent sources capable of high performance in the miniaturized realm. Understanding of quantum fundamentals can lead to new and better coherent sources and unimagined scientific and technological applications. Application areas of interest include the industrial, commercial, and medical sectors. Also, particular attention is given to scientific applications with a bright future such as coherent spectroscopy, astronomy, biophotonics, space communications, space interferometry, quantum entanglement, and quantum interference.

Publishing benefits
Authors are encouraged to take advantage of the features made possible by electronic publication to enhance the reader experience through the use of color, animation and video, and incorporating supplementary files in their work.

Do you have an idea of a book that you'd like to explore?
For further information and details of submitting book proposals, see iopscience.org/books or contact Ashley Gasque at ashley.gasque@iop.org.

A full list of titles published in this series can be found here: https://iopscience.iop.org/bookListInfo/series-in-coherent-sources-and-applications.

Techniques for Lithium Isotope Separation, Laser Cooling, and Scattering

Ignacio E Olivares
Department of Physics, University of Santiago de Chile, Santiago de Chile, Región Metropolitana, Chile

Patrick Carrazana
Department of Physics, University of California, California, USA

IOP Publishing, Bristol, UK

ISBN 978-0-7503-3839-4 (ebook)
ISBN 978-0-7503-3837-0 (print)
ISBN 978-0-7503-3840-0 (myPrint)
ISBN 978-0-7503-3838-7 (mobi)

DOI 10.1088/978-0-7503-3839-4

Version: 20220901

IOP ebooks

British Library Cataloguing-in-Publication Data: A catalogue record for this book is available from the British Library.

Published by IOP Publishing, wholly owned by The Institute of Physics, London

IOP Publishing, Temple Circus, Temple Way, Bristol, BS1 6HG, UK

US Office: IOP Publishing, Inc., 190 North Independence Mall West, Suite 601, Philadelphia, PA 19106, USA

To my son, Alexander.

—I.O.

Contents

Preface

Techniques for Lithium Isotope Separation, Laser Cooling, and Scattering describes theoretical and experimental techniques for applications of narrow-linewidth tunable lasers to lithium isotope separation, laser cooling, Mie scattering, and Thomson scattering. Albeit the emphasis is from a practical experimental perspective, all the necessary and relevant theory is described in sufficient detail.

Foreword

Laser applications range from the very large to the extremely small, from astronomy to nanoscience. As far as laser applications are concerned, narrow-linewidth tunable lasers are the jewels in the crown. In this regard, *Techniques for Lithium Isotope Separation, Laser Cooling and Scattering* illuminates the story of tunable laser applications to the wonderful fields of laser isotope separation, laser cooling, and light scattering. It does so with an exquisite balance between theoretical elegance and experimental pragmatism. It is particularly significant that the lithium tunable narrow-linewidth diode-laser isotope separation work is based on the first experiments of their kind in the world. As far as the chronology of laser isotope separation experiments, in general is concerned, this work ranks second in the southern hemisphere after uranium enrichment research performed with infrared lasers in Australia. The laser cooling experiments mentioned in this book were the first to be performed in Chile. The scattering sections provide a fresh and elegant perspective on a vintage favorite. I certainly enjoyed reading through the pages of *Techniques for Lithium Isotope Separation, Laser Cooling and Scattering*, I welcome it to our series, it will be a worthy addition to the personal libraries of practicing optical scientists and to numerous physics and engineering libraries around the world.

F J Duarte
Series Editor

Acknowledgements

The authors want to express their thanks to the series editor, Dr F J Duarte, for his constant encouragement and help during the writing of this work. His knowledge of the subject was, without a doubt, essential to help us improve many areas that needed better treatment and his advice was key in achieving a clear understanding of our approach. He also helped us with extensions of deadlines which were difficult to meet given the COVID pandemic and delays due to logistical problems.

Author biographies

Ignacio E Olivares

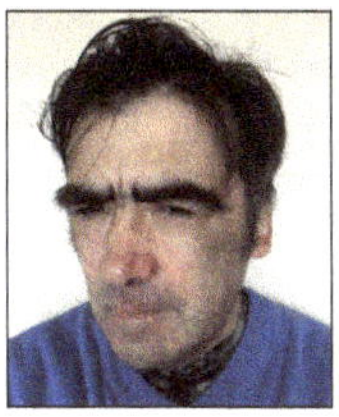

Ignacio E Olivares was born in Viña del Mar, Chile in 1961. He obtained the Bachelor's Degree in Physics in 1984 and his Master's Degree in Physics in 1987, both degrees at the Physics Department, Pontificia Universidad Católica de Chile in Santiago de Chile. In his Masters Degree Thesis he constructed a ruby laser. In 1992 he obtained his promotion Dr.rer.nat. at the Fakultät für Physik und Astronomie der Ruhr Universität Bochum. The main experiment was the construction of a Thomson Scattering experiment for the diagnostic of high density plasmas. In 1992 he returned to Chile and worked for six months at the Physics Department Pontificia Universidad Católica de Chile where he assembled a CW plasma discharge for atomic vapor deposition. Afterwards he was contracted at the Comisión Chilena de Energía Nuclear to lead the project Lithium Laser Isotope Separation. He installed from the ground a laser spectroscopy laboratory and studied laser absorption at lithium vapors, resonance ionization spectroscopy and constructed a laser lithium isotope separation device. He demonstrated the lithium laser isotope separation at a small scale. In 2001 he was hired as an Assistant Professor at the Physics Department, Universidad de Santiago de Chile where he installed a magneto optical trap. He constructed a magneto optical trap and demonstrated for the first time in Chile the laser cooling and trapping of atoms. He was upgraded in 2006 to Associated Professor after writing many articles regarding laser absorption and laser cooling.

Patrick Carrazana

Professor Patrick Carrazana obtained his Bachelor of Science in Physics and his Master's and Doctorate in Physics working in Theoretical Quantum Optics, all in the United States. Practically all of his academic life occurred in the USA. For the last twenty years he has been working in General Relativity with special interests in applications to the studies of the early Universe.

IOP Publishing

Techniques for Lithium Isotope Separation, Laser Cooling, and Scattering

Ignacio E Olivares and Patrick Carrazana

Chapter 1

History of our laser experiments

As Chile is a lithium producer, the use of which is regulated by the Chilean Nuclear Energy Commission, several projects were started in 1993 to improve the use of lithium: study of lithium rechargeable batteries, tritium genesis and lithium isotope separation as a laboratory project. Physics research in Chile is mostly theoretical and we understood that the idea of studying a method of lithium laser isotope separation was a great opportunity to promote and start developing laser and experimental physics in Chile. The project had to start from zero as no previous similar laser facilities existed in Chile. It took some years to import lasers and vacuum equipment and put together all the hardware necessary to develop the laser isotope experiment. We studied first the laser absorption spectroscopy of lithium using a tunable diode laser. Previously, we tried to control the wavelength of CW standing wave dye laser with poor stability and decided to use a tunable diode laser centered at 670 nm. The idea of developing a lithium laser isotope separation method was based on the experimental work of Arisawa *et al* [1], the instructions given by Yamashita [2] and the study of the photoionization cross section of the lithium atom by Karlov *et al* [3]. Our aim was to understand the physics of laser isotope separation and to study the possibility to scale the method to a large scale production. The project took six years. After achieving first results the program was closed and one of us (Ignacio E Olivares) moved to the Universidad de Santiago de Chile starting a project of laser cooling and trapping of rubidium atoms. Although the equipment was totally new and adapted to a different wavelength many techniques that we obtained from laser isotope separation were useful for the magneto optical trap. We also continue studying the absorption of lithium and laser stabilization techniques such as the Pound–Drever–Hall method [4]. We considered that a key experimental technique for lithium isotope separation and for laser cooling is the Pound–Drever–Hall method for laser stabilization. This technique of laser stabilization is discussed in this book.

doi:10.1088/978-0-7503-3839-4ch1

1.1 Laser isotope separation laboratory

The laser isotope separation laboratory was built close to the nuclear reactor facility of the Chilean Nuclear Energy Commission in La Reina, Santiago de Chile. The laboratory was began in 1993 and was fully equipped by 2002. After this the laboratory was dismantled and converted to a Plasma Experimental Physics Laboratory. The main activities of the Chilean Nuclear Energy Commission are related to radio isotopes produced in its experimental reactor. The radio isotopes are mainly used in medicine. The study of lithium isotope separation was an investigation carried out to explore the feasibility of the separation of light atoms and at the present stage was discontinued. Lithium laser isotope separation, utilizing diode lasers, was achieved at the La Reina Laboratory in 2002 [5]. These experiments are described in detail in chapter 10.

1.2 Laser and optics laboratory

The laser and optics laboratory was built in 2002 at the Physics Department of the Universidad de Santiago de Chile, Estación Central. The main funding was obtained from a Millennium Project named Quantum Optics and Information. The goal of the project was to obtain cold atoms for the study of quantum optics experiments. The Millennium group was settled in the University of Concepción and our laboratory was collaborating with this group. We learned how to obtain cold atoms for the first time in Chile [6] and explored the techniques of laser stabilization. We also constructed our own tunable diode laser Littrow cavities for a diode laser centered at 780 nm and initiated the assembly of a laser Littrow cavity for 670 nm. In this case the tunable range should be of the order of at least 20 GHz to observe all the lithium lines. In the case of 780 nm a tunable range of only 10 GHz is enough. So, the challenge of constructing a tunable laser at 670 nm is far more difficult than a 780 nm laser. We understand that there is considerable experience in other countries related to the subject. After completing these experiments we attempted to include other techniques in the laboratory such as the use of pulsed Nd:YAG laser for the study of air pollution in Estación Central, which is a very contaminated part of the city. With the help of personnel in the defense industry (M Inzunza) we obtained discarded Nd:YAG lasers heads with 36 mJ single pulse energy and 6 ms duration. We constructed the power supply for loading the main capacitor and the trigger electronics unit for preionizing the lamps. We replaced the old lamps with similar surplus lamps and adapted the trigger voltage for their operation. This included a change of avalanche diodes with increased breakdown avalanche voltage in the trigger electronics. We also installed photomultiplier tubes and avalanche photodiodes to explore the measurement of short pulses with low energy. This work is not reported here, and our next project is aimed at increasing the capability of our laboratory. In this book we show some previous examples of the use of pulsed ruby lasers for the study of Thomson scattering in high density plasmas. These experiments were performed by Olivares under the supervision of Professor H J Kunze in the Ruhr University Bochum, Germany. Finally we also present a Mie scattering experiment performed by us. Professor Carrazana was a key participant in this project. Our intention was to understand the effect of Mie scattering that is present in air pollution experiments.

1.3 Teaching laboratory: Experimental Physics V

Since 2002 one of us has been teaching optics at the Experimental Physics V Laboratory in Physics Department, Universidad de Santiago. The course is based on the script 'Projects in Optics', by Professor Donald O'Shea, Newport Corporation. The aim of the course is to introduce modern experimental physics techniques to our students. Many of the students have participated as undergraduates in the experiments in the Laser and Optics Laboratory. We show some of the techniques in chapter 3 Optical Detection and Instrumentation. The experiments use state of the art optics, optomechanical components, a helium laser, and a small optical breadboard. All these equipments are of standard use in our research laboratory.

1.4 Advanced laboratory

Since 2004 we have been teaching an advanced laser spectroscopy laboratory course for undergraduate and postgraduate students in the Physics Department. The experiments were carried at the Laser and Optics Laboratory. The course is inspired by a script by Professor K Libbrecht in Caltech and a private communication with him. Other ideas are obtained from communications with Professor W Demtröder in Germany and Professor H Metcalf in New York. Many chapters have been inspired by Libbrecht's course and adapted to our laboratory. In particular chapters 2 and 5.

1.5 Summary

Since 1993 we have been introducing laser experiments in Santiago de Chile. Many of these experiments are related to laser spectroscopy with tunable lasers. The work is intended to help to start an industry based on physics and has helped students to learn modern aspects of experimental physics. The book is mostly aimed at readers who are thinking to take their first steps in the laboratory with simple basic physics experiments.

References

[1] Arisawa T, Maruyama Y, Suzuki Y and Shiba K 1982 Lithium isotope separation by laser *Appl. Phys.* B **28** 73–6

[2] Yamashita M and Kashiwagi H 1979 Method for separation and enrichment of lithium isotopes by laser *US Patent 4149077* https://www.osti.gov/biblio/6303723-method-separation-enrichment-lithium-isotopes-laser

[3] Karlov N V 1977 Measurement of the photoionization cross section of the Li atom at the 2P level *Sov. J. Quantum Electron.* **7** 1305

[4] Black E D 2001 An introduction to Pound–Drever–Hall laser frequency stabilization *Am. J. Phys.* **69** 79–87

[5] Olivares I E, Duarte A E, Saravia E A and Duarte F J 2002 Lithium isotope separation with tunable diode lasers *Appl. Opt.* **41** 2973–7

[6] Olivares I E, Aguilar F and Aguirre-Gómez J 2008 Cold atoms observed for the first time at the Universidad de Santiago de Chile *J. Phys. Conf. Ser.* **134** 012001

Chapter 2

Saturated absorption spectroscopy

A simple technique that is needed for laser isotope separation and for cooling of atoms is laser saturated absorption spectroscopy. The narrow-line spectral feature of many transitions can be resolved using this method. It is also possible to stabilize the laser wavelength by means of locking it to a narrow linewidth atomic transition. In this chapter we explain the method and show with detail numerical examples that will allow a non-expert to describe the obtained spectra.

2.1 Description of saturated absorption spectroscopy

Saturated absorption spectroscopy is a simple technique used to measure the narrow-line atomic spectral feature limited only by the natural linewidth, that is typically 6 MHz or less [1]. A strong laser beam called the pump beam is directed through an optical cell that contains a vapour as shown in figure 2.1. A small part of the pump beam used as a probe beam is sent through the cell in the counter-propagating direction and detected by a simple photodiode.

Precision spectroscopy of the hydrogen atom the simplest atom can be found in [2]

The probe beam can be placed at a small angle or collinear with respect to the pump beam. The laser frequency is scanned close to the atomic resonance. In the case of a two-level atom system the spectral feature is shown in figure 2.2.

The feature is the detected absorption feature when the pump beam is blocked. It shows a Doppler-broadened line which is much broader than the natural linewidth. In the case of weak absorption the feature is a Gaussian profile. The atoms in the vapor move with different velocities in different directions following the Boltzmann velocity distribution. Considering the velocity component of the atoms along the probe beam we see that some atoms move with velocity component in the same direction as the probe beam propagation and others move in the opposite direction. Figure 2.3 is the detected intensity with pump laser, it shows a spike just at the

doi:10.1088/978-0-7503-3839-4ch2

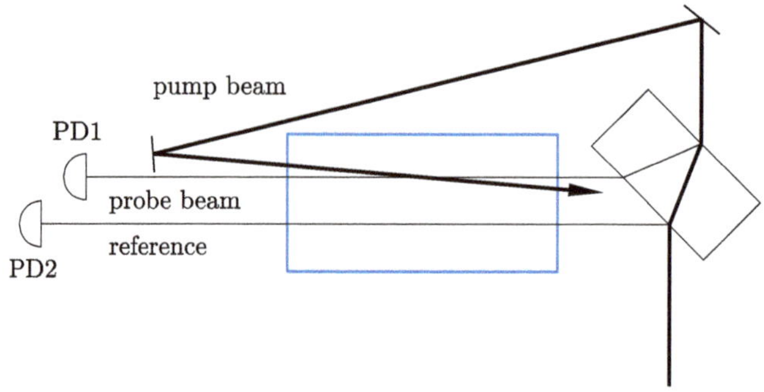

Figure 2.1. Basic setup for saturation absorption spectroscopy. Pump probe experiment.

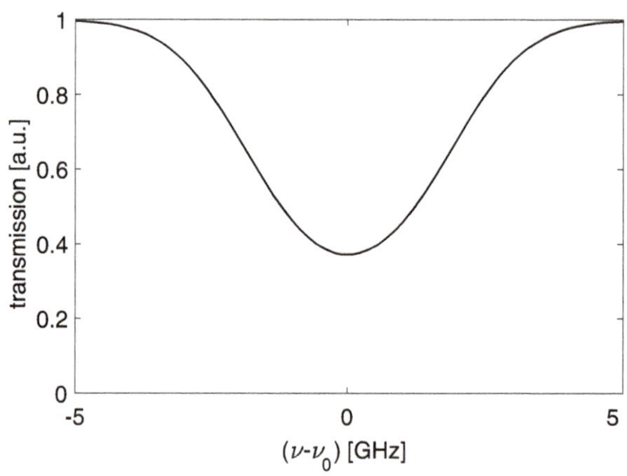

Figure 2.2. Doppler limited spectrum with a Lamb dip.

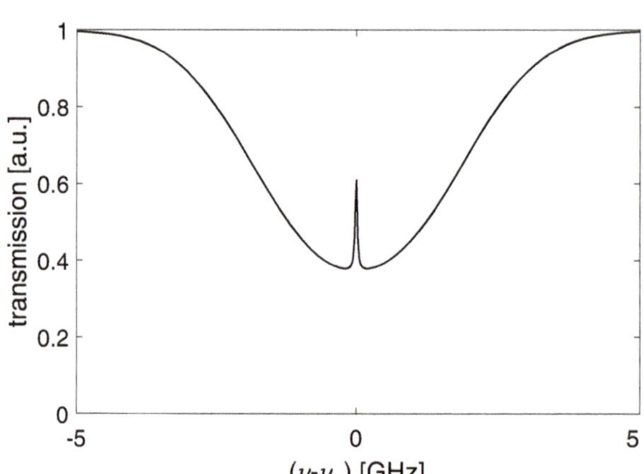

Figure 2.3. Doppler-free spectrum.

atomic resonance frequency, this spike is known as Lamb dip. When the laser is tuned at $\nu_0 - \Delta\nu$, then the probe laser will be absorbed only by atoms with velocity approximately equal to $\upsilon \approx c\Delta\nu_0$ moving toward the probe beam. The beam will not be absorbed by atoms with different longitudinal velocities because they are not in resonance so they don't contribute to absorption. Atoms with zero velocity absorb light from the pump laser and become saturated. The probe laser moves through a saturated transparent group of atoms reducing the absorption and producing the Lamb dip.

2.2 Multi-level atoms

In the case of a three level system with two closely spaced upper levels and one ground level the spectral features presents two ordinary Lamb dips at the resonance frequencies of the associated transitions and one cross over peak situated just between these two dips at the average of these frequencies as shown in figure 2.4.

When the laser is tuned at the cross over frequency it is absorbed by one transition from atoms moving toward the laser and by the other transition of the same atom by the laser beam oriented in the opposite direction. The increase of the population of the upper level caused by the strongest laser (pump beam) produces an increase of the transmission of the probe beam at the cross over frequency. When the system has two closely spaced ground levels and one single upper level the cross over is still half way between the ordinary Lamb dips but it exhibits a reduction of transmission due a process named 'optical pumping' (figure 2.5).

Here the laser is absorbed by one optical transition from atoms moving toward the laser. The atoms decay to the second ground level producing an increase of absorption of the probe laser beam driven in the opposite direction.

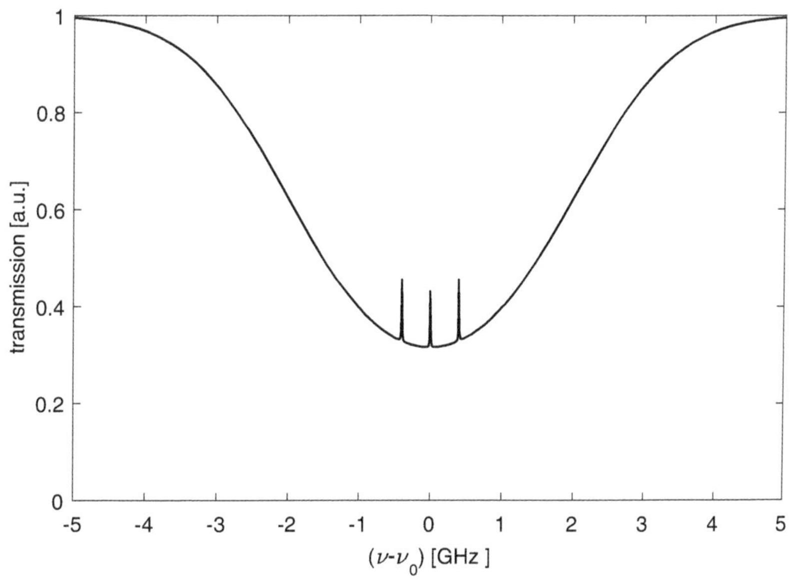

Figure 2.4. Cross over resonances, two excited and one ground states.

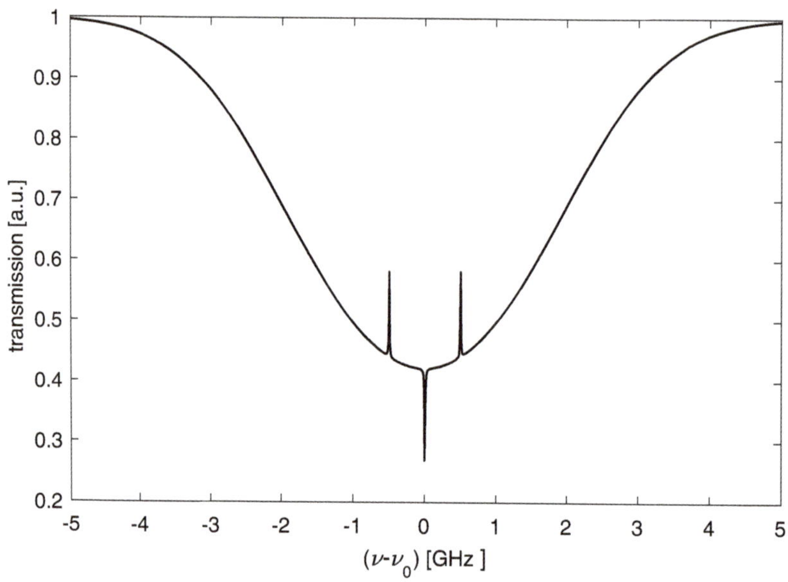

Figure 2.5. Cross over produced by optical pumping.

2.3 The saturated absorption spectrometer

The optical setup of the saturated absorption spectrometer is depicted in figure 2.6. The voltage signal which is a saturated spectra from the probe beam is obtained at the photodiode PD1 as the wavelength is scanned. The signal obtained by the photodiode PD2 can be used as a reference for the Doppler limited spectra. The pump beam is indicated with a broader line. The thinner lines are reflections on both sides of a glass etalon, with approximately 4% of the strong signal. The signal obtained by the photodiode PD2 contains the Doppler-free feature. The pump beam is disposed at a small angle relative to the probe beam direction.

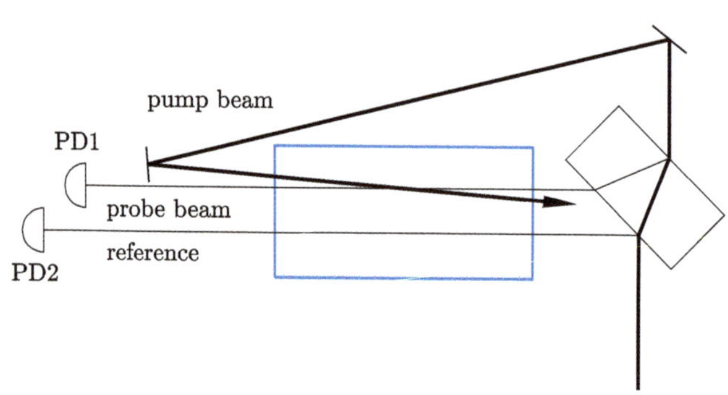

Figure 2.6. Saturated absorption spectrometer.

2.4 Semiquantitative ideas at two-level atoms

The saturated absorption spectra can be calculated with a simplified model for two-level atoms. The differential contribution to the absorption coefficient by atoms with velocity between v and $v + dv$ can be written as

$$d\tau(\nu, v) = (\nu, v) = \tau_0\lambda_0(P_1 - P_2)F(\nu, v)dn(v) \tag{2.1}$$

τ_0 is the optical depth at the center of the resonance, P_1 and P_2 are the relative populations of the ground and excited state respectively,

$$F(\nu, v) = \frac{\Gamma/2\pi}{(\nu - \nu_0 + \nu_0 v/c)^2 + \Gamma^2/4} \tag{2.2}$$

is the normalized Lorentzian absorption profile for atoms with natural linewidth Γ including the Doppler shift and

$$dn \propto \exp(-mv^2/k_B T)dv \tag{2.3}$$

is the Boltzmann distribution for the velocities of the atoms along the beam axis. The transmission of the probe beam through the cell is $\exp(-\tau(\nu))$. In the case that the pump laser is turned off and the probe laser beam intensity is low we see that a few atoms will be excited and most of the atoms will remain in its ground state. In this case we obtained by numerical integration of the absorption coefficient, g_1 and g_2 are the degeneracies of the ground and excited states respectively, and the atom lineshape, with $\delta = (\nu - \nu_0 - \nu_0 v/c)^2$. The minus sign is explained because the pump laser is in the counter-propagating direction in relation to the probe laser. In a stationary state we have $\dot{P}_1 = \dot{P}_2 = 0$ and as $P_1 + P_2 = 1$ so that

$$P_1 - P_2 = 1 - 2P_2; \tag{2.4}$$

considering a stationary state and assuming that $g_1 = g_2$ we have that

$$P_2 = \frac{s/2}{1 + s + 4\delta^2/\Gamma^2} \tag{2.5}$$

where $s = I/I_{sat}$ is the saturation parameter, I is the intensity of the pump laser and

$$I_{sat} = 2\pi^2 hc\Gamma/\lambda^3$$

the saturation intensity.

2.4.1 Excited and ground state populations

In a two-level system it is possible to write rate equations for the population of the excited (2) and ground state (1).

$$1 = P_1 + P_2$$
$$\dot{P}_1 = -\alpha I(P_1 - P_2) + \Gamma P_2$$

In the stationary case the derivative is equal to zero

$$0 = -\alpha I(1 - 2P_2) + \Gamma P_2 \tag{2.6}$$

with

$$\alpha = \alpha_0 \frac{\Gamma/(2\pi)}{\delta^2 + \Gamma^2/4} \tag{2.7}$$

Solving equation (2.6) for P_2 we obtain

$$P_2 = \frac{s/2}{1 + s + 4\delta^2/\Gamma^2} \tag{2.8}$$

where

$$\frac{s}{2} = \frac{2\alpha_0 I}{\pi\Gamma^2} \tag{2.9}$$

At the center of the line we have

$$\boxed{\alpha(\delta = 0) = \frac{2\alpha_0}{\pi\Gamma}} \tag{2.10}$$

and

$$s = \frac{2\alpha(\delta = 0)I}{\Gamma} = \frac{I}{I_{\text{sat}}} \tag{2.11}$$

For example, figure 2.7 was obtained integrating numerically the transmission coefficient of lithium atoms with $\lambda = 671$ nm, $\tau_0 = 0.1$, 0.316, 1, 3.16, and 10 from top to bottom, $s = 10$, $T = 400$ K and $\Gamma = 5.8$ MHz with pump laser

Figure 2.8 shows a zoom of the saturated absorption spectrum.

Figure 2.9 shows the saturated absorption spectrum at different laser power.

2.4.2 Calculating absolute values

The dipole matrix element for the transition strength is obtained from the Wigner–Eckart theorem

$$\begin{aligned} \mu_{if} = |\langle i|D_q|f\rangle| &= e(-1)^{1+L'+S+J+J'+I-M'_F}\langle\alpha' L'\|r\|\alpha L\rangle \\ &\times \sqrt{(2J+1)(2J'+1)(2F+1)(2F'+1)} \\ &\times \begin{matrix} L' & J' & S \\ J & L & 1 \end{matrix} \begin{matrix} J' & F' & I \\ F & J & 1 \end{matrix} \begin{pmatrix} F & 1 & F' \\ M_F & q & -M'_F \end{pmatrix} \end{aligned} \tag{2.12}$$

where

$$\|D\| = \langle\alpha' L'\|r\|\alpha L\rangle \tag{2.13}$$

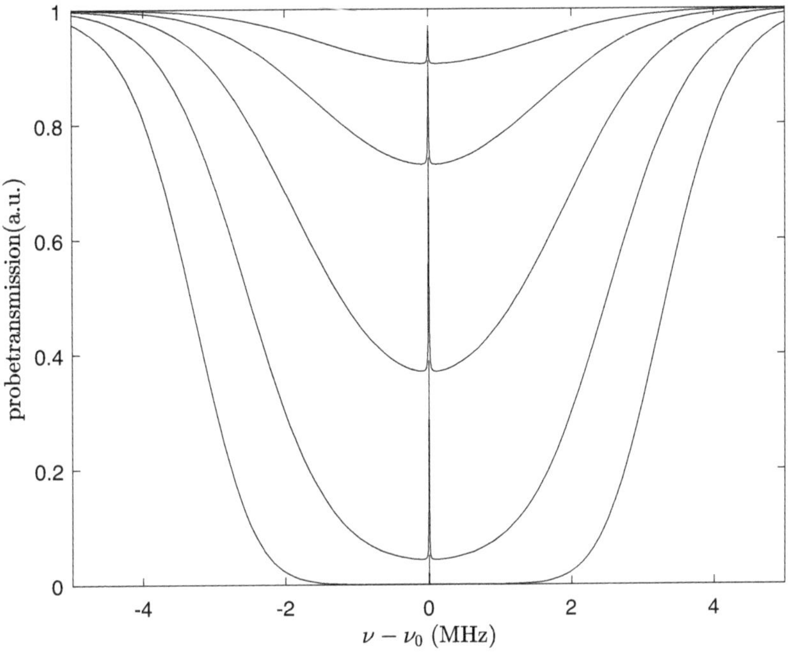

Figure 2.7. Saturated absorption spectrum for $s = 10$ and $\tau_0 = 0.1$, 0.316, 1, 3.16, and 10.

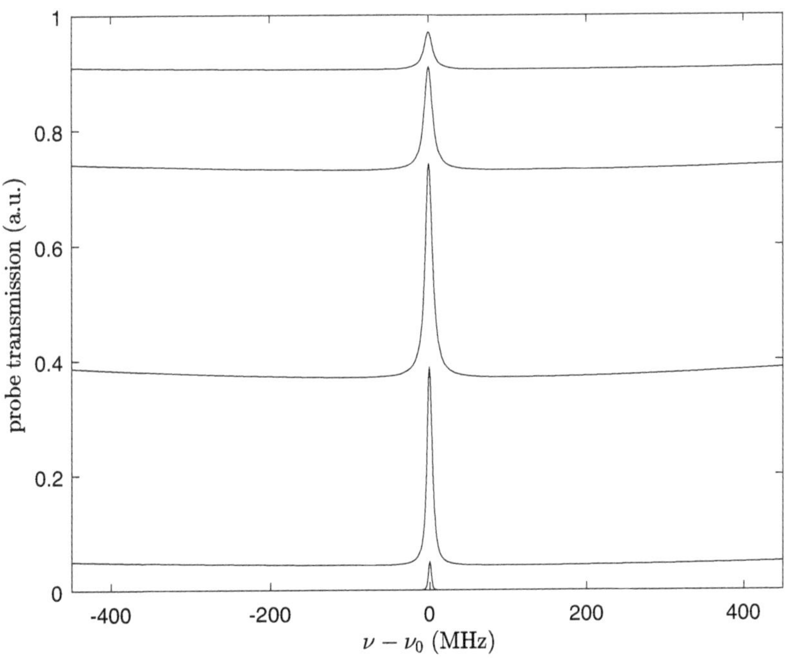

Figure 2.8. Detail of saturated absorption spectrum.

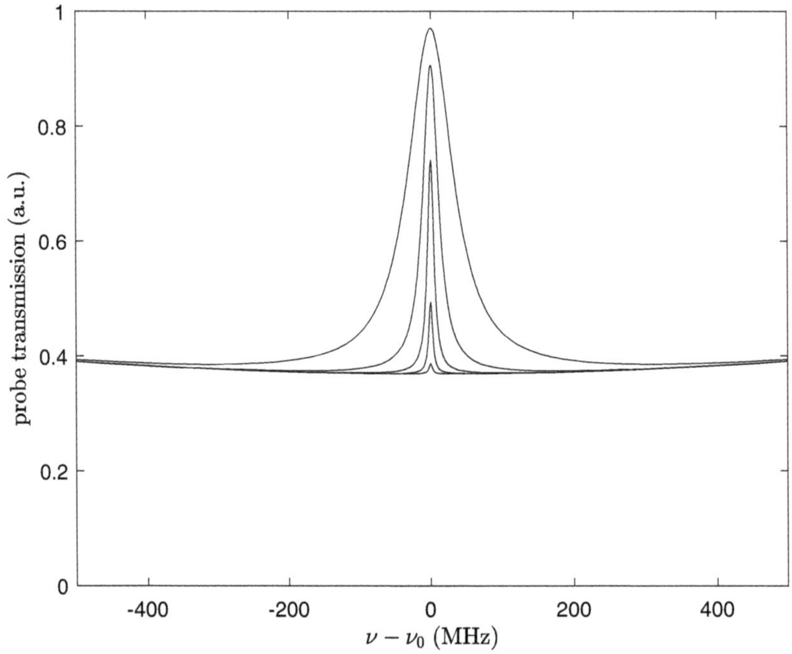

Figure 2.9. Power broadening of saturated absorption spectrum with $\tau_0 = 1$ and $s = 0.1, 1, 10, 100, 1000$.

is the reduced dipole matrix element. The transition strength is calculated using the square of μ_{if}. To obtain numerical results we define the normalized transition strength as

$$N_{ifq} = \mu_{if}^2 / \left\| D \right\|^2 \tag{2.14}$$

and this can be calculated with a Matlab code. The transition strength for each line is normalized again so that the weakest allowed transition becomes an integer. Normalized transition strengths for the ^{6}Li – D_1 ($^2S_{1/2} -^2 P_{1/2}$) line are shown in figure 2.10. The absolute N_{ifq} values can be obtained in this case dividing the values of the diagram by 81. Note that the $F = 3/2$ excited state is shown twice. The transition strength number at the crossing of the left and right circular polarization transitions is valid for both transitions. The transition strength for the σ_- can be obtained by using the values for σ_+ polarization and replaced M by $-M$ s. For example $N_{3,7,+1} = N(6, 8, -1) = 12/81$. Here for $m_F(f = 7) - m_F(i = 3) = +1$ the polarization is right circular and for $m_F(f = 8) - m_F(i = 6) = -1$ the polarization is left circular. In figure 2.10 all polarizations are shown.

The coefficient for spontaneous emission from state $|f\rangle$ to $|i\rangle$ is given by

$$a_{fi} = \frac{4\omega^3 K_e}{3\hbar c^3} \sum_q |\langle i|D_q|f\rangle|^2 \tag{2.15}$$

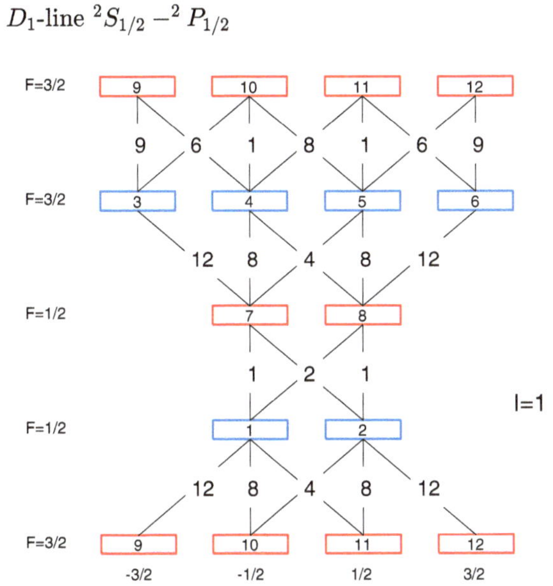

Figure 2.10. Normalized transition strengths for ^{6}Li-D_1 ($^2S_{1/2} -^2 P_{1/2}$) line. The absolute values for the transition strengths N_{ifq} can be obtained in this case by dividing the values of the diagram by 81. It is important to consider that the normalization constant is different for different lines (for example in the case of the D_2 line the normalization constant is 810). Note that the $F = 3/2$ excited state is shown twice. Red rectangles corresponds to excited states and blue rectangles to ground states. The transition strength number at the crossing of the left and right circular polarization transitions is valid for both transitions.

The natural linewidth is

$$\gamma = \tau^{-1} = A_f = \sum_i a_{fi} = \frac{4\omega^3 K_e}{3\hbar c^3(2L_f + 1)}||D||^2 \tag{2.16}$$

Here τ is the lifetime of the transition and $L_f = 1$

$$||D||^2 = \gamma \frac{9\hbar c^3}{4\omega^3 K_e} \tag{2.17}$$

thus $||D||^2 = 1.1778 \times 10^{-57}$. The spontaneous emission coefficients can be written in terms of the normalized transition strength N_{ifq} [3]

$$a_{fi} = \gamma(2L_f + 1)\sum_q N_{ifq} = 3\gamma \sum_q N_{ifq} \tag{2.18}$$

Figure 2.11 shows a diagram for the normalized transition strengths N_{ifq} multiplied by 810. For example $N_{4,14,-1} = 162/810 = 1/5$. The polarization in this example is left circular. The transition is not allowed for $q = 0$ and $q = 1$ polarizations, thus these terms are zero. The spontaneous emission coefficient is $a_{14,4} = \gamma(2L_f + 1)$ $N_{4,14,-1} = 3\gamma 162/810 = 3\gamma/5$.

Exercise: Prove equation (2.16) for example with the excited state 11.

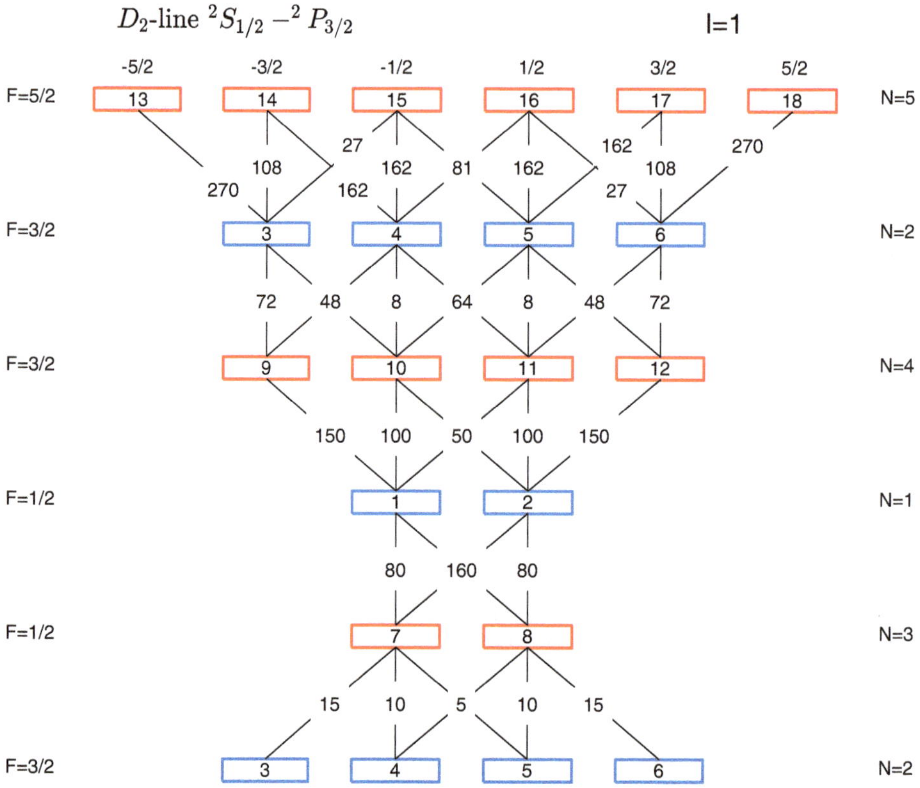

Figure 2.11. Normalized ^{6}Li-D_2 transition strengths. The absolute N_{ifq} numbers, are obtained by dividing the values in the diagram by 810.

2.4.3 Transition rates

The Rabi frequency for each transition for light with intensity I is [3]

$$|\Omega_{if}|^2 = \frac{8\pi I K_e}{c\hbar^2} \sum_q |\langle i|D_q|f\rangle|^2 \tag{2.19}$$

In the case of incident linear polarized light, we only calculated for $q = 0$, i.e. N_{if0}. Here we consider the linear polarized case

$$|\Omega_{if}|^2 = \frac{8\pi I K_e}{c\hbar^2} N_{if0} ||D||^2 \tag{2.20}$$

Defining $\gamma = 2\pi\Gamma$ we have

$$|\Omega_{if}|^2 = \frac{9\lambda^3 \Gamma I}{hc} N_{if0} \tag{2.21}$$

The transition rate for a group of atoms with velocity v is

$$W_{if}(\omega, v) = \frac{1/2|\Omega_{if}|^2\gamma/2}{(\delta_{if} - kv)^2 + \gamma^2/4} \tag{2.22}$$

where $\delta_{if} = \omega - \omega_{if}$ is the laser detuning from resonance, $\omega = 2\pi(\nu_i - \nu_f)$, $\gamma/2$ is the homogeneous broadening, $\gamma/2$ is the natural linewidth, $\omega - (\omega_i - \omega_f)$ is the laser detuning from resonance, and $(\omega_i - \omega_f)$ is the laser angular resonance frequency, $\boldsymbol{v}$ is the mean velocity of the atoms, $\mathbf{k}$ the wavenumber, $K_e = 8.99 \times 10^9$ V m C^{-1} is the Coulomb's constant. Considering that $\omega = 2\pi\nu$ and $k = 2\pi/\lambda$ we can convert $W_{if}(\omega, v)$ to

$$W_{if}(\nu, v) = \frac{1/2|\Omega_{if}|^2 \frac{1}{2\pi}\frac{1}{2}\gamma/2\pi}{\delta^2 + \Gamma^2/4} \tag{2.23}$$

$$W_{if}(\nu, v) = \frac{\frac{1}{4}|\Omega_{if}|^2 \frac{\Gamma}{2\pi}}{\delta^2 + \Gamma^2/4} \tag{2.24}$$

$$\boxed{W_{if}(\nu, v) = \frac{9\lambda^3\Gamma I}{4hc} N_{if0} \frac{\Gamma/(2\pi)}{\delta^2 + \Gamma^2/4}} \tag{2.25}$$

and $\delta = (\nu - \nu_0 - \nu_0 v/c)$. Note that the sign in front of v depends on the direction in which the atom is moving. In our previous work we considered other broadenings writing a more general version of equation (2.22)

$$W_{if}(\omega, v) = \frac{1/2|\Omega_{if}|^2\Gamma_\omega}{(\delta_{if} - kv)^2 + \Gamma_\omega^2} \tag{2.26}$$

Here $\Gamma_\omega = \gamma/2 + \Gamma_L + \Gamma_c + \Gamma_T$, Γ_L is the laser linewidth, Γ_T is the transit time broadening, and Γ_c is the collisional broadening.

2.4.4 Reduction to five levels for the ^{6}Li – D_2 line

It is possible to consider the population of each state in a multiplet to be approximately equal to that of the other states of the same multiplet, which permits us to work with only five levels, each representing a complete multiplet as one state. The optical Bloch equations for the magnetic hyperfine levels are given by [3]

$$\begin{aligned} \dot{\rho}_{ii} &= \sum_f W_{if}(\rho_{ff} - \rho_{ii}) + \gamma_T\left(\rho_{ii}^0 - \rho_{ii}\right) + \sum_f a_{fi}\rho_{ff} \\ \dot{\rho}_{ff} &= \sum_i W_{if}(\rho_{ii} - \rho_{ff}) + \gamma_T\left(\rho_{ff}^0 - \rho_{ff}\right) - \gamma\rho_{ff} \end{aligned} \tag{2.27}$$

where i corresponds to the magnetic ground states and f to the magnetic excited states. As an example we start with the ground $N = 1$ level.

$$\begin{aligned} \dot{\rho}_{1,1} &= (\rho_{7,7} - \rho_{1,1})W_{1,7} + (\rho_{10,10} - \rho_{1,1})W_{1,10} \\ &\quad + a_{7,1}\rho_{7,7} + a_{8,1}\rho_{8,8} + a_{9,1}\rho_{9,9} + a_{10,10}\rho_{10,10} + a_{11,1}\rho_{11,11} \\ \dot{\rho}_{2,2} &= (\rho_{8,8} - \rho_{2,2})W_{2,8} + (\rho_{11,11} - \rho_{2,2})W_{2,11} \\ &\quad + a_{7,2}\rho_{7,7} + a_{8,2}\rho_{8,8} + a_{10,2}\rho_{10,10} + a_{11,11}\rho_{11,11} + a_{12,2}\rho_{12,12} \end{aligned} \tag{2.28}$$

When the populations are distributed among the single states we have

$$\begin{aligned}\dot{\rho}_{1,1} &= \left(\frac{\rho_3}{g_3} - \frac{\rho_1}{g_1}\right)W_{1,7} + \left(\frac{\rho_4}{g_4} - \frac{\rho_1}{g_1}\right)W_{1,10} \\ &\quad + (a_{7,1} + a_{8,1})\rho_3/g_3 + (a_{9,1} + a_{10,10} + a_{11,1})\rho_4/g_4 \\ \dot{\rho}_{2,2} &= \left(\frac{\rho_3}{g_3} - \frac{\rho_1}{g_1}\right)W_{2,8} + \left(\frac{\rho_4}{g_4} - \frac{\rho_1}{g_1}\right)W_{2,11} \\ &\quad + (a_{7,2} + a_{8,2})\rho_3/g_3 + (a_{10,2} + a_{11,11}\rho_{11,11} + a_{12,2})\rho_4/g_4\end{aligned} \tag{2.29}$$

Here the single index of the ρ's and g's correspond to N labels of the reduced whole multiplet states. Adding the equations for the magnetic states at the ground level with $N = 1$ we have

$$\begin{aligned}\dot{\rho}_1 &= \left(\frac{\rho_3}{g_3} - \frac{\rho_1}{g_1}\right)(W_{1,7} + W_{2,8}) + \left(\frac{\rho_4}{g_4} - \frac{\rho_1}{g_1}\right)(W_{1,10} + W_{2,11}) \\ &\quad + (a_{7,1} + a_{8,1} + a_{7,2} + a_{8,2})\rho_3/g_3 \\ &\quad + (a_{9,1} + a_{10,1} + a_{11,1} + a_{10,2} + a_{11,2} + a_{12,2})\rho_4/g_4\end{aligned} \tag{2.30}$$

thus

$$\dot{\rho}_1 = \left(\frac{\rho_3}{g_3} - \frac{\rho_1}{g_1}\right)W_{1,3} + \left(\frac{\rho_4}{g_4} - \frac{\rho_1}{g_1}\right)W_{1,4} + \rho_3\, a_{1,3}/g_3 + \rho_4\, a_{1,4}/g_4 \tag{2.31}$$

and

$$\begin{aligned}W_{1,3} &= \frac{9\lambda^3\Gamma I}{4hc}\left(\frac{16}{81}\right)\frac{\Gamma/(2\pi)}{\delta_{1,3}^2 + \Gamma^2/4} \\ W_{1,4} &= \frac{9\lambda^3\Gamma I}{4hc}\left(\frac{20}{81}\right)\frac{\Gamma/(2\pi)}{\delta_{1,4}^2 + \Gamma^2/4} \\ a_{13}/g_3 &= 3\gamma \cdot 2(80 + 160)/(810 \cdot 2) = 8/9\gamma \\ a_{14}/g_4 &= 3\gamma \cdot 2(150 + 100 + 50)/(810 \cdot 4) = 5/9\gamma\end{aligned}$$

Although the procedure is straightforward it is shown here for the $N = 2$ ground level.

$$\begin{aligned}\dot{\rho}_2 &= \left(\frac{\rho_3}{g_3} - \frac{\rho_2}{g_2}\right)(W_{4,7} + W_{5,8}) \\ &\quad + \left(\frac{\rho_4}{g_4} - \frac{\rho_2}{g_2}\right)(W_{3,9} + W_{4,10} + W_{5,11} + W_{6,12}) \\ &\quad + \left(\frac{\rho_5}{g_5} - \frac{\rho_2}{g_2}\right)(W_{3,14} + W_{4,15} + W_{5,16} + W_{6,17}) \\ &\quad + (a_{7,3} + a_{7,4} + a_{7,5} + a_{8,4} + a_{8,5} + a_{8,6})\rho_3/g_3 \\ &\quad + (a_{9,1} + a_{10,1} + a_{11,1} + a_{10,2} + a_{11,2} + a_{12,2})\rho_4/g_4 \\ &\quad + (a_{13,3} + a_{14,3} + a_{15,3} + a_{14,4} + a_{15,4} + a_{16,4} \\ &\quad + a_{15,5} + a_{16,5} + a_{17,5} + a_{16,6} + a_{17,6} + a_{18,6} + a_{17,5})\rho_5/g_5\end{aligned} \tag{2.32}$$

As $g_1 = 2$, $g_2 = 4$, $g_3 = 2$, $g_4 = 4$, $g_5 = 6$ we have

$$\dot{\rho}_2 = \left(\frac{\rho_5}{6} - \frac{\rho_2}{4}\right)W_{2,5} + \left(\frac{\rho_4}{4} - \frac{\rho_2}{4}\right)W_{2,4} + \left(\frac{\rho_3}{2} - \frac{\rho_2}{4}\right)W_{2,3} + \rho_5 a_{2,5}/g_5 + \rho_4 a_{2,4}/g_4 + \rho_3 a_{2,3}/g_3 \tag{2.33}$$

and

$$\begin{aligned}
W_{2,3} &= \frac{9\lambda^3\Gamma I}{4hc}\left(\frac{1}{162}\right)\frac{\Gamma/(2\pi)}{\delta_{2,5}^2 + \Gamma^2/4} \\
W_{2,4} &= \frac{9\lambda^3\Gamma I}{4hc}\left(\frac{4}{81}\right)\frac{\Gamma/(2\pi)}{\delta_{2,4}^2 + \Gamma^2/4} \\
W_{2,5} &= \frac{9\lambda^3\Gamma I}{4hc}\left(\frac{1}{6}\right)\frac{\Gamma/(2\pi)}{\delta_{2,3}^2 + \Gamma^2/4} \\
a_{23}/g_3 &= 3\gamma \cdot 2(15 + 10 + 5)/(810 \cdot 2) = 1/9\gamma \\
a_{24}/g_4 &= 3\gamma \cdot 2(72 + 48 + 48 + 8 + 64)/(810 \cdot 4) = 4/9\gamma \\
a_{25}/g_5 &= 3\gamma \cdot 2(270 + 108 + 162 + 27 + 162 + 81)/(810 \cdot 6) = \gamma
\end{aligned}$$

In summary the reduced rate equations are given by

$$\begin{aligned}
\dot{\rho}_1 &= W_{13}\left(\frac{\rho_3}{g_3} - \frac{\rho_1}{g_1}\right) + W_{14}\left(\frac{\rho_4}{g_4} - \frac{\rho_1}{g_1}\right) + \gamma\left(\frac{8}{9}\rho_3 + \frac{5}{9}\rho_4\right) \\
&\quad + (\gamma_T + \gamma_{vc})\left(\frac{1}{3} - \rho_1\right) \\
\dot{\rho}_2 &= W_{23}\left(\frac{\rho_3}{g_3} - \frac{\rho_2}{g_2}\right) + W_{24}\left(\frac{\rho_4}{g_4} - \frac{\rho_2}{g_2}\right) + W_{25}\left(\frac{\rho_5}{g_5} - \frac{\rho_2}{g_2}\right) \\
&\quad + \gamma\left(\frac{1}{9}\rho_3 + \frac{4}{9}\rho_4 + \rho_5\right) + (\gamma_T + \gamma_{vc})\left(\frac{2}{3} - \rho_2\right) \\
\dot{\rho}_3 &= W_{13}\left(\frac{\rho_1}{g_1} - \frac{\rho_3}{g_3}\right) + W_{23}\left(\frac{\rho_2}{g_2} - \frac{\rho_3}{g_3}\right) - \gamma\rho_3 - (\gamma_T + \gamma_{vc})\rho_3 \\
\dot{\rho}_4 &= W_{14}\left(\frac{\rho_1}{g_1} - \frac{\rho_4}{g_4}\right) + W_{24}\left(\frac{\rho_2}{g_2} - \frac{\rho_4}{g_4}\right) - \gamma\rho_4 - (\gamma_T + \gamma_{vc})\rho_4 \\
1 &= \rho_1 + \rho_2 + \rho_3 + \rho_4 + \rho_5
\end{aligned} \tag{2.34}$$

In the stationary state the derivatives are zero and it is possible to solve for the ground state and excited state populations.

To solve for the populations in the stationary state all the derivatives are zero. The equation system can be solved using matrix notation as follows

$$A = (M_1 + M_2) \cdot V \tag{2.35}$$

where the absorption and stimulated matrix is given by

$$M_1 = \begin{pmatrix} -\sum_{k=3}^{4} \frac{W_{1k}}{g_1} & 0 & \frac{W_{13}}{g_3} & \frac{W_{14}}{g_4} & 0 \\ 0 & -\sum_{k=3}^{5} \frac{W_{2k}}{g_2} & \frac{W_{23}}{g_3} & \frac{W_{24}}{g_4} & \frac{W_{25}}{g_5} \\ \frac{W_{13}}{g_1} & \frac{W_{23}}{g_2} & -\sum_{j=1}^{2} \frac{W_{j3}}{g_3} & 0 & 0 \\ \frac{W_{14}}{g_1} & \frac{W_{24}}{g_2} & 0 & -\sum_{j=1}^{2} \frac{W_{j4}}{g_4} & 0 \\ 1 & 1 & 1 & 1 & 1 \end{pmatrix} \tag{2.36}$$

and the spontaneous emission matrix is

$$M_2 = \begin{pmatrix} -(\gamma_T + \gamma_{vc}) & 0 & \frac{8}{9}\gamma & \frac{5}{9}\gamma & 0 \\ 0 & -(\gamma_T + \gamma_{vc}) & \frac{1}{9}\gamma & \frac{4}{9}\gamma & \gamma \\ 0 & 0 & -(\gamma + \gamma_T + \gamma_{vc}) & 0 & 0 \\ 0 & 0 & 0 & -(\gamma + \gamma_T + \gamma_{vc}) & 0 \\ 0 & 0 & 0 & 0 & 0 \end{pmatrix} \tag{2.37}$$

the solution of the system are the populations given by

$$V = [\rho_1 \;\; \rho_2 \;\; \rho_3 \;\; \rho_4 \;\; \rho_5 \;\; \rho_6]^T \tag{2.38}$$

where T is the transpose of the row vector giving a column vector and

$$A = \left[-\frac{1}{3}(\gamma_T + \gamma_{vc}) \;\; -\frac{2}{3}(\gamma_T + \gamma_{vc}) \;\; 0 \;\; 0 \;\; 1 \right]^T \tag{2.39}$$

The absorption of the laser light in a vapor with density n and length dx, is given by [4]

$$dI_d(\nu) = h\,\nu_{if}\,n \left(\int_{-\infty}^{\infty} \sum_{if} W_{if}(\nu, v)(\rho_f - \rho_i) F(v) dv \right) dx \tag{2.40}$$

here $i = 1$ and 2 are the reduced ground states and $f = 3$, 4, and 5 are the reduced excited states and d stays for diagnostic. In a numerical calculation, the integral is replaced by a sum and dv can be set to 1 m s^{-1}.

$$F(v) = \left(\frac{m}{2\,\pi\,k_B\,T}\right)^{1/2} \exp\left(-\frac{m\,v^2}{2\,k_B T}\right) \tag{2.41}$$

is the velocity distribution for vapor at temperature T. We can also write

$$\mathrm{d}I_d = -h\,\nu_{if}\,n\,\gamma'\langle\rho_e\rangle\,dx \tag{2.42}$$

and $\gamma' = \gamma + \gamma_T$ and $\rho_e = \rho_3 + \rho_4 + \rho_5$ is the total population for the various excited states. Extending the absorption equations to the Doppler-free saturation spectroscopy, we have

$$dI_d = h\,\nu_{if}\,n\left(\int_{-\infty}^{\infty}\sum_{if} W_{if}(\nu,\,-v,\,I_d)(\rho_f\,-\,\rho_i)F(v)dv\right)dx \tag{2.43}$$

and $\rho_f = \rho_f(\nu,\,v,\,I_p)$ and $\rho_i = \rho_i(\nu,\,v,\,I_p)$ and I_p is the pump intensity.

Exercise: It is possible (and is left as an exercise) to obtain a simple rate equation for a two-level system starting from a multi-level approach by summing all multiplets in stationary state and considering a broadband source. Here E indicates the whole $2p$ excited state and G the whole $2s$ ground state.

$$0 = 2\left(\frac{\rho_E}{18} - \frac{\rho_G}{6}\right)\frac{9\lambda^3\Gamma I}{4hc}\frac{\Gamma/(2\pi)}{\delta^2 + \Gamma^2/4} + 2\pi\Gamma\rho_E \tag{2.44}$$

with $g_G = 6$ and $g_E = 18$. Arranging terms we have

$$0 = \left(\frac{g_G}{g_E}\rho_E - \rho_G\right)\frac{s}{2} + \rho_E(4\delta^2/\Gamma^2 + 1) \tag{2.45}$$

where

$$s = \frac{3\lambda^3 I}{2\pi^2 hc\Gamma} \tag{2.46}$$

and

$$1 = \rho_G + \rho_E \tag{2.47}$$

If $g_E = g_G$ we have

$$\rho_E = \frac{s/2}{1 + s + 4\delta^2/\Gamma^2} \tag{2.48}$$

2.5 Energy level diagram

The energy level diagram (figure 2.12) contains two ground hyperfine levels separated by nearly 228.2 MHz [5]. The excited states of the D_2 line are separated by less than 4.4 MHz. In the case of the D_1 line the separation of the excited states is less than 26.1 MHz.

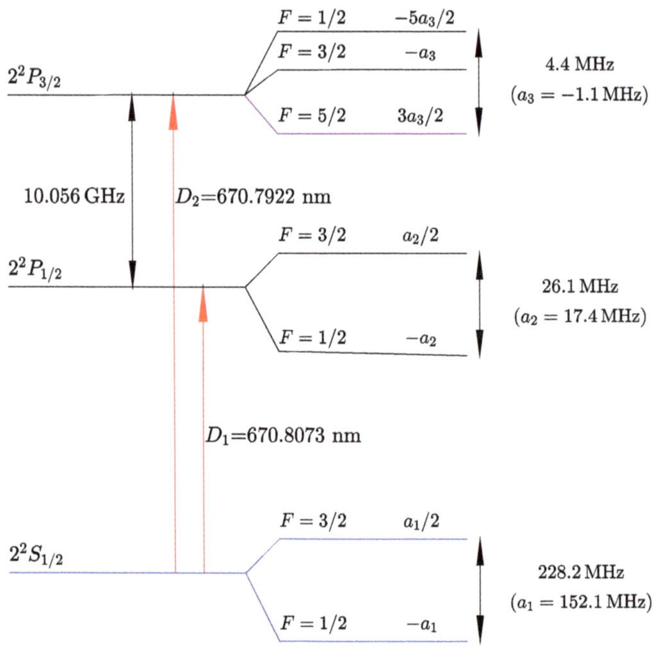

Figure 2.12. Level diagram of the ground $2s$ and excited $2p$ states of ^{6}Li. Energy splittings are not to scale.

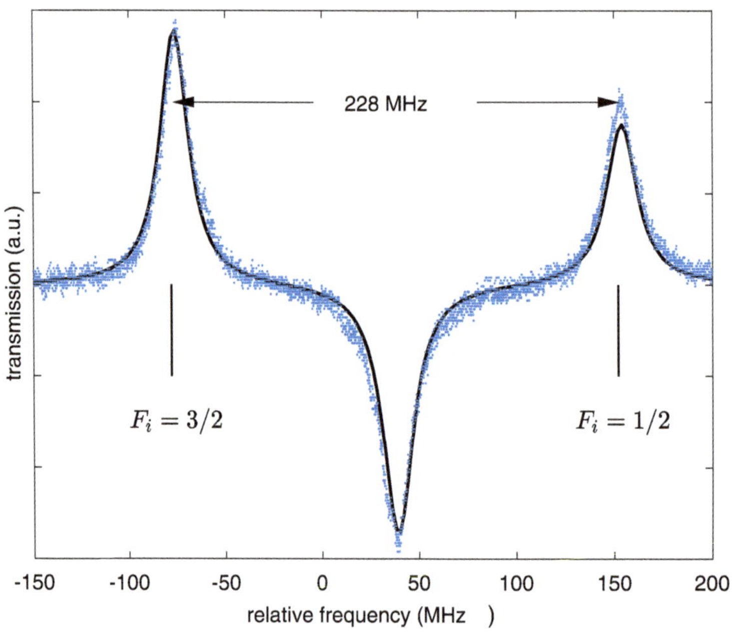

Figure 2.13. ^{6}Li Doppler-free spectrum at low Ar buffer pressure: $P_{\mathrm{Ar}} = 0.0018$ Torr, $I_P = 21$ Wm^{-2}, $n(\mathrm{Li}) = 5 \times 10^9$ cm^{-3}, $T = 375$ °C. Result of the fitting: $\Gamma = 1.5 \times 10^7$ s^{-1}, $\gamma_{\mathrm{vc}} = 2.2 \times 10^6$ s^{-1}.

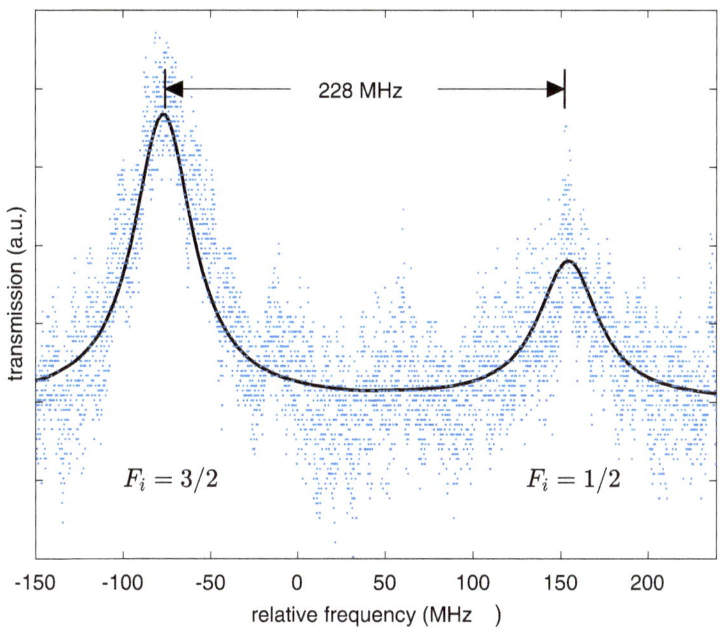

Figure 2.14. ^{6}Li Doppler-free spectrum at low Ar buffer pressure: $P_{\rm Ar} = 0.0018$ Torr, $I_P = 79^{-3}$, $T = 375$ °C. Result of the fitting: $\Gamma = 3.75 \times 10^7$ s^{-1}, $\gamma_{\rm vc} = 7.0 \times 10^7$ s^{-1}.

Figure 2.13 shows a fit of a ^{6}Li Doppler-free line at low pressure buffer gas using equation (2.43).

Figure 2.14 shows a fit of a ^{6}Li Doppler-free line at high pressure buffer gas.

References

[1] Milonni P W and Eberly J H 2010 *Laser Physics* (New York: Wiley)

[2] Hänsch T W, Schawlow A L and Series G W 1979 The spectrum of atomic hydrogen *Sci. Am.* **240** 94–111

[3] Olivares I E, Duarte A E, Lokajczyk T, Dinklage A and Duarte F J 1998 Doppler-free spectroscopy and collisional studies with tunable diode lasers of lithium isotopes in a heat-pipe oven *J. Opt. Soc. Am.* B **15** 1932–9

[4] Loudon R 2000 *The Quantum Theory of Light* (Oxford: Oxford Science) ch 2

[5] Sansonetti C J, Richou B, Engleman R Jr and Radziemski L J 1995 Measurements of the resonance lines of Li 6 and Li 7 by Doppler-free frequency-modulation spectroscopy *Phys. Rev.* A **52** 2682

IOP Publishing

Techniques for Lithium Isotope Separation, Laser Cooling, and Scattering

Ignacio E Olivares and Patrick Carrazana

Chapter 3

Optical instrumentation and detection

In this chapter the main optical hardware used in our experiments is presented. The beam expanders and prisms are described using geometrical optics. The mean interferometers, Michelson and Fabry–Perot, are fully described and a phasor approach to interference is shown. We show also the polarization optics as linear polarizers, polarizing and non-polarizing beam splitter cubes, quarter and half-wave plates. More details on general optics can be found in [1–3].

3.1 Geometrical optics

3.1.1 Laser beam expanders

In many experiments it is necessary to expand a laser beam. As the laser beam diameter is increased, the divergence diminishes and the beam does not change its diameter during the experiment. One of the laser beam expanders is the Keplerian telescope showed in figure 3.1. The first lens (ocular) is a short focal length lens that focuses the incident beam at its focal point that is also the focal point of the second lens (objective). The second lens has a larger focal distance and is placed at the distance f_1 from the focal point F of the first lens. The distance between the lenses is the sum of their focal distances. The magnification of the beam diameter is f_2/f_1

A more compact laser beam expander is the Galilean telescope (figure 3.2). The focal distance of the first lens is negative. The second lens is at a distance f_+ from the focal point from the first lens. The distance between the two lenses is the difference of the absolute values of the focal distances. The magnification of the beam diameter is equal to f_2/f_1.

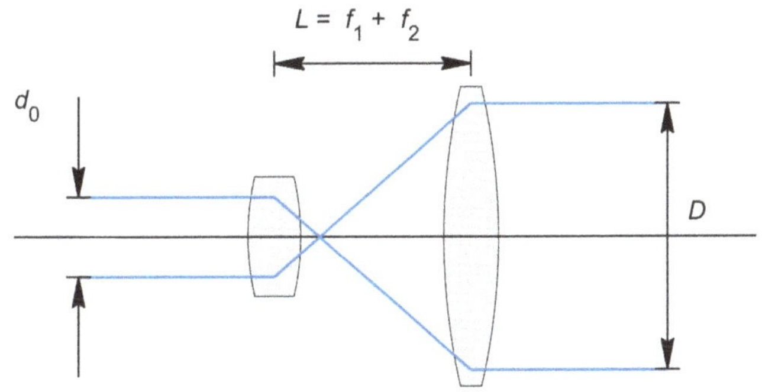

Figure 3.1. Keplerian telescope beam expander.

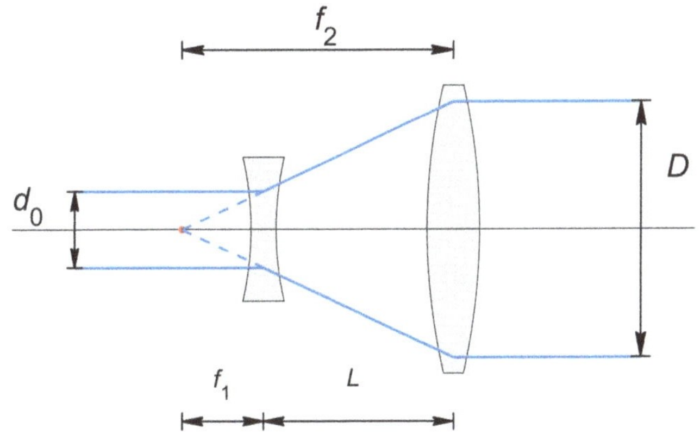

Figure 3.2. Galilean telescope laser beam expander.

3.2 Interference

3.2.1 The Michelson interferometer

A method to measure the change in the laser frequency is the use of a Michelson interferometer (see figure 3.3). The interference pattern of a Michelson interferometer consists of beautiful concentric rings when a point source of light O1 is placed in front of the interferometer and the mirrors are well aligned. The point source O1 can be obtained when the exit lens of a laser beam expander is moved towards the first lens. Two virtual images I3 and I4 act as the source of the interference pattern. It is left as an exercise to obtain the position of the images.

The distance between the point virtual source is $d = 2(L_2 - L_1)$. The maximum and minimum intensity of the interference pattern can be obtained considering the optical path difference from point I_3 and I_4 as seen in figure 3.3.

Considering that we have a maximum of interference on the axis, the first minimum is obtained when the optical path difference is half the wavelength of the incident laser light $\lambda/2$. We have that $\cos\theta = (d - \lambda/2)/d$. For small angles $\cos\theta = 1 - \theta^2/2$ and as $\theta \approx R/L$ and the radius of the central maxima is

$$R = L\sqrt{\frac{\lambda}{2d}} \tag{3.1}$$

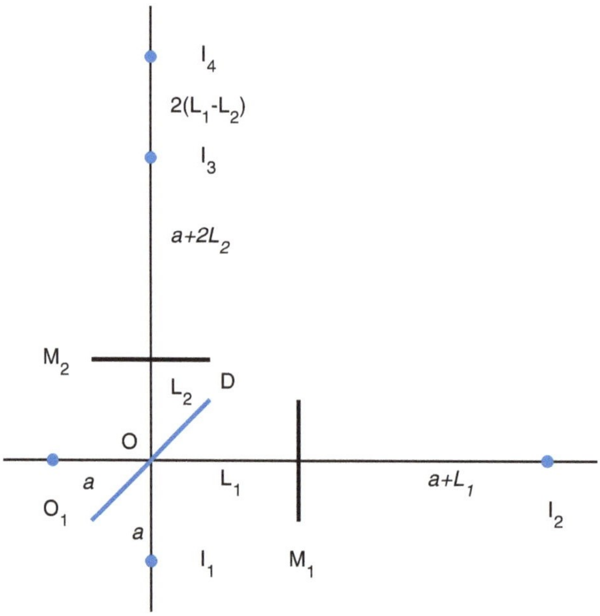

Figure 3.3. Images for ring formation in a Michelson interferometer.

Figure 3.4 shows a detailed diagram of the optical path difference produced by the virtual images in the Michelson interferometer.

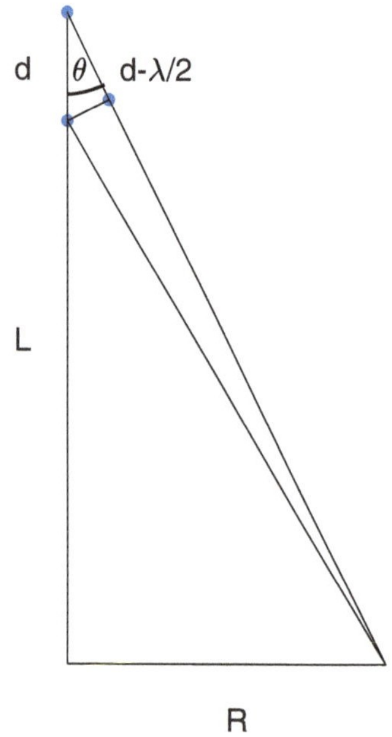

Figure 3.4. Optical path difference.

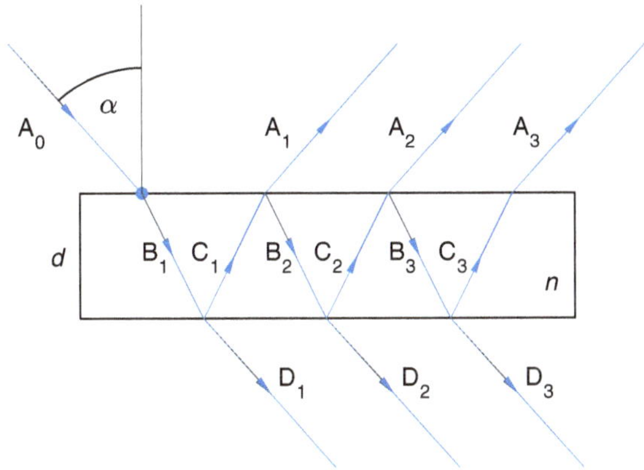

Figure 3.5. Multiple beam interference in a single plate with parallel surfaces.

To measure the change in wavelength it is necessary to determine how much the wavelength has to be changed in order to go from one maxima to the next maxima. The change in wavelength will depend on the relative distance between the mirrors d. For fixed relative distance we have $d = m\lambda$, and the next maximum is achieved when $d = (m + 1)\lambda'$. Isolating m

$$\Delta\lambda = \frac{d}{m(m+1)} \approx \frac{\lambda}{m} \tag{3.2}$$

If $\lambda = 0.7\ \mu\text{m}$, $\Delta\lambda = 0.7$ nm and $m = 10^3$, we have that $d = 0.7$ mm approximately. The setup is useful for observing the change of wavelength of the diode laser with temperature, where the range is on the order of 12 nm. For 0.7 pm the optical path difference has to be 0.7 m (figure 3.5).

$$\Delta\lambda = \frac{\lambda^2}{d}$$

$$\Delta\nu = \frac{c}{\lambda^2}\Delta\lambda$$

$$\Delta\nu = \frac{c}{d}$$

$$\Delta\nu = \frac{c}{2(L_2 - L_1)}$$

The Michelson interferometer is described quantum mechanically using Dirac's *bra ket* notation in [4].

3.2.2 Multiple beam interference in a single plate: demonstration of the Airy relations

When a plane wave $E = A_0 e^{i\omega t - kr}$ falls on a transparent plate covered on both surfaces with highly reflecting coatings, multiple beam interference is produced as seen in figure 3.5. The number of partial waves that participate in the interference depend on the reflectivity of the surfaces. To obtain the reflected and transmitted intensity it is necessary to add the partial waves.

Considering as A_0 the amplitude of the electric field, and R, the reflected amplitude at the first surface is

$$|A_1| = \sqrt{R}|A_0| \tag{3.3}$$

$$\begin{aligned}
|B_1| &= \sqrt{1 - R}|A_0| \\
|C_1| &= \sqrt{R}|B_1| = \sqrt{R(1 - R)}|A_0| \\
|D_1| &= \sqrt{1 - R}|B_1| = (1 - R)|A_0| \\
|A_2| &= \sqrt{1 - R}|C_1| = \sqrt{R}(1 - R)|A_0 \\
|B_2| &= \sqrt{R}|C_1| = R\sqrt{(1 - R)}|A_0 \\
|C_2| &= \sqrt{R}|B_2| = R^{3/2}\sqrt{(1 - R)}|A_0 \\
|D_2| &= \sqrt{1 - R}|B_2| = R(1 - R)|A_0 \\
|A_3| &= \sqrt{1 - R}C_2| = R^{3/2}(1 - R)|A_0 \cdots
\end{aligned} \tag{3.4}$$

it can be demonstrated that for $i \geqslant 2$

$$|A_{i+1}| = R|A_i| \tag{3.5}$$

and for $i \geqslant 1$

$$|D_{i+1}| = R|D_i| \tag{3.6}$$

The optical path difference between adjacent partial waves is given by

$$\Delta s = 2d\sqrt{(n^2 - \sin^2 \alpha)} \tag{3.7}$$

and the phase difference is given by

$$\Delta\varphi = \frac{2\pi}{\lambda}\Delta s + \delta\varphi \tag{3.8}$$

where $\delta\varphi$ is the phase shift produced by the reflection on each surface of the plate. The phase shift $\delta\varphi$ depends on whether the electric field is perpendicular or parallel to the incidence plane. The incidence plane is the plane containing the incident, reflected, and transmitted wave vectors. The parallel electric field is contained in the incident plane, the perpendicular electric field is normal to the plane. It is also possible that the incident electric field is a combination of perpendicular and parallel. For the perpendicular wave E_s, we have a change in the phase of $\delta\varphi = \pi$ for reflection on an optically thicker medium, and $\delta\varphi = 0$, when the wave is reflecting on an optically thinner medium. For the parallel wave E_p, we have that for reflection at an optically thicker medium $\delta\varphi = 0$ for $\alpha < \alpha_B$ and $\delta\varphi = \pi$ for $\alpha_B < \alpha$ and for reflection at an optically thinner medium $\delta\varphi = \pi$ for $\alpha < \alpha_B$, and $\delta\varphi = 0$ for $\alpha_B < \alpha < \alpha_c$. Here α_c is the critical angle for total reflection. For waves that are incident perpendicular to the mirror surface, parallel and perpendicular

Table 3.1. Summary of phase shifts for parallel (||) and perpendicular (⊥) polarized waves.

Polarization	⊥	⊥	⊥	||	||
incident on	$\alpha < \pi/2$	$\alpha < \alpha_c$	$\alpha < \alpha_B$	$\alpha_B < \alpha$	$\alpha_B < \alpha < \alpha_c$
thicker medium	$\delta\varphi = \pi$		$\delta\varphi = 0$	$\delta\varphi = \pi$	
thinner medium		$\delta\varphi = 0$	$\delta\varphi = \pi$		$\delta\varphi = 0$

polarization have the same phase shifts due to reflection. Table 3.1 shows a summary of the phase shift at different incident waves.

Considering nearly perpendicular incidence, which is the case in most applications, we have that $\alpha < \alpha_B$. In this case for the perpendicular wave we have a phase shift $\delta\varphi = \pi$ produced by reflection at the first surface, giving $A_1 = \sqrt{R}A_0e^{i\pi} = -\sqrt{R}A_0$. At the second surface the phase shift $\delta\varphi = 0$ and $A_2 = \sqrt{1-R}|C_1| = \sqrt{R}(1-R)A_0$, for $\alpha < \alpha_B$. For $i \geqslant 2$, $\delta\varphi = 0$. For the parallel wave we have a phase shift $\delta\varphi = 0$ produced by reflection at the first surface, giving $A_1 = \sqrt{R}A_0$. At the second surface the phase shift $\delta\varphi = \pi$ and $A_2 = \sqrt{R}(1-R)A_0e^{i\pi} = -\sqrt{R}(1-R)A_0$. For $i \geqslant 2$, $\delta\varphi = 2\pi$ which is equivalent to $\delta\varphi = 0$.

Exercise: Complete the description for the case $\alpha < \alpha_B$.

Summing the partial waves the sign in front of the sum is plus for parallel and minus for perpendicular polarization.

$$A = \sum_{m=1}^{p} A_m e^{i(m-1)\varphi} = \pm A_0R[1 - (1-R)e^{i\varphi} - R(1-R)e^{2i\varphi} - \cdots] \tag{3.9}$$

The sum gives the amplitude of the total reflected wave

$$A = \pm A_0\sqrt{R}\left[1 - (1-R)\sum_{m=0}^{p-2} R^m e^{im\varphi}\right] \tag{3.10}$$

Using the identities for power series we obtain

$$A = \pm A_0\sqrt{R}\frac{1 - e^{i\Delta\varphi}}{1 - Re^{i\Delta\varphi}} \tag{3.11}$$

The intensity is given by

$$I = c\epsilon_0 AA^* \tag{3.12}$$

and

$$I = I_0 2R\frac{1 - \cos\Delta\varphi}{1 + R^2 - 2R\cos\Delta\varphi} \tag{3.13}$$

where $I_0 = c\epsilon_0 A_0^2$. With the trigonometric identity

$$1 - \cos x = 2\sin^2(x/2) \tag{3.14}$$

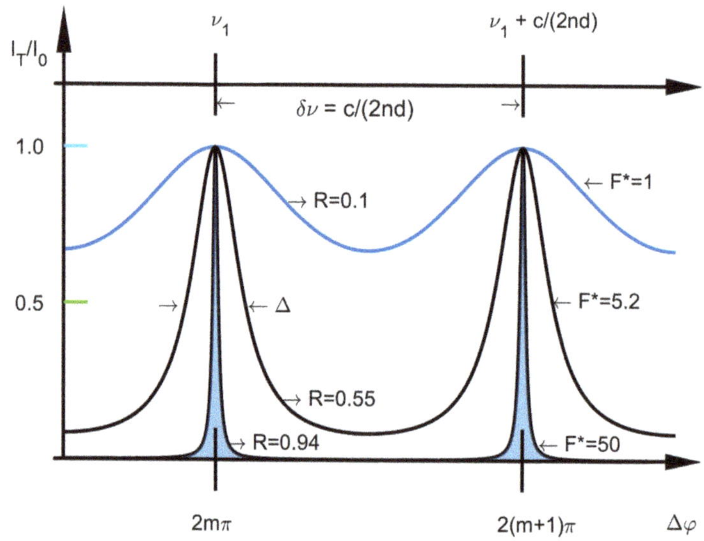

Figure 3.6. Airy equations. Transmission as a function of phase difference.

we obtain

$$I = I_0 \frac{F \sin^2(\Delta\varphi/2)}{1 + F \sin^2(\Delta\varphi/2)} \tag{3.15}$$

for the reflected intensity where

$$F = \frac{4R}{(1 - R)^2} \tag{3.16}$$

With no absorption we have that $R + T = 1$. The Airy formula for the transmitted intensity is

$$I_T = I_0 \frac{1}{1 + F \sin^2(\Delta\varphi/2)} \tag{3.17}$$

figure 3.6 shows an example of the Airy Formulas for different reflectivities.

3.2.3 Multiple beam interference: the Fabry–Perot interferometer

The Fabry–Perot interferometer (FPI) is a measuring instrument based on multiple beam interference. A method to construct a FPI is to coat a plane parallel plate with refraction index n and thickness d on both sides with reflective coatings (see figure 3.7).

In this case, only small changes in the optical path nd, can be achieved by thermal expansion of the plate. Without the coatings, each surface has typically 4% reflectivity for normal glass. Changing the wavelength of the laser will produce intensity changes, called the etalon effect. Another way to asemble a FPI is to install two plates separated by a distance d (see figure 3.8).

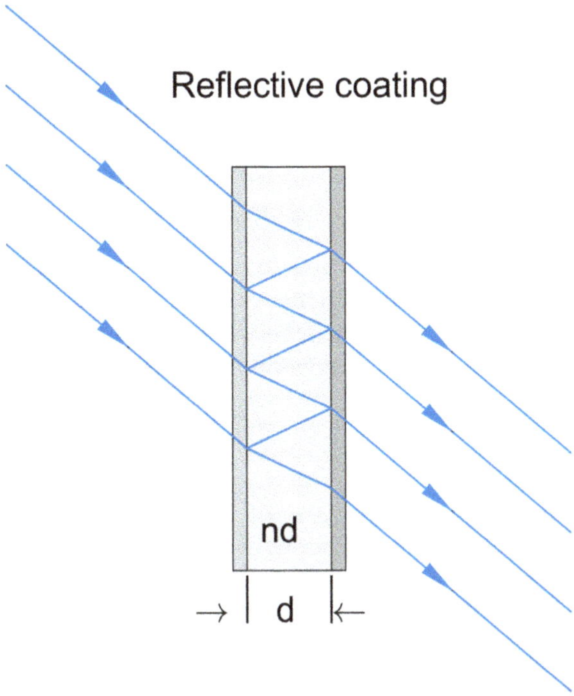

Figure 3.7. Etalon: multiple beam interference in a single plate with parallel surfaces. The surfaces are coated for higher reflectivity.

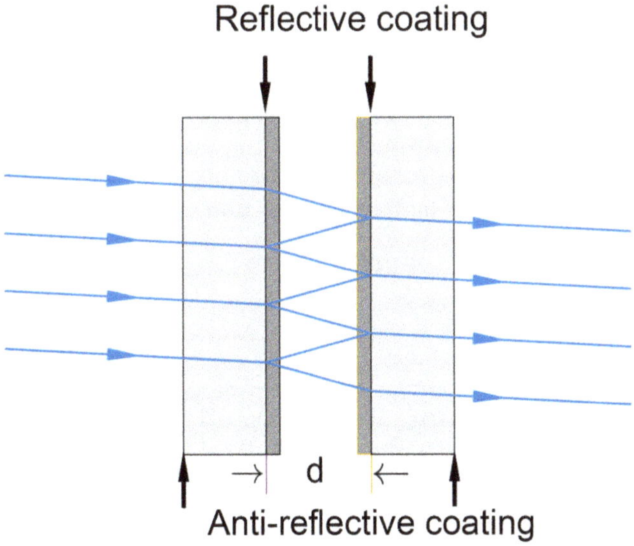

Figure 3.8. Multiple beam interference in two parallel plates. The inner surfaces are reflective-coated and the outer surfaces have anti-reflective coating.

The inner surfaces are reflective-coated and act as highly reflecting mirrors. The external surfaces of the mirrors are coated with anti-reflective coatings. Small changes of the distance between the mirrors can be done with the help of a piezoelectric transducer. The alignment needed to obtain parallel mirrors represents an experimental challenge.

3.2.4 Fabry–Perot interferometer–Airy relations

It is possible to obtain an Airy distribution in two different ways: (a) by changing the wavelength at fixed optical path; (b) by variation of the optical path at fixed wavelength. The *finesse* F^* is the quotient between the free spectral range and the full width at half maximum of the Airy function and is given by

$$F^* = \frac{\delta\varphi}{\Delta\varphi} = \frac{\sqrt{R}}{1 - R} \tag{3.18}$$

For $R = 0.1$, 0.55 and 0.94 the finesse is $F^*=1$, 5 and 50 respectively. The *finesse* is a measure of the number of waves interfering with each other, and in the case of the Fabry–Perot interferometer is related to its resolution.

3.2.5 Confocal scanning Fabry–Perot interferometer

The scanning confocal Fabry–Perot interferometer (figure 3.9) is a nice tool to check if the laser is running in single mode operation particularly when the lasers are turned on. The lasers are correctly adjusted when it is possible to observe single interferometer lines. One of the main features of the Fabry–Perot interferometer is that it can measure with high resolution the spectral content of the laser. The confocal interferometer can detect if the laser is running in single mode. A basic Fabry–Perot consists of two identical spherical mirrors with radius R separated by a distance L. The use of two curved mirrors is convenient as they permit a good match to the Gaussian beam coming from the laser.

Two parameters define the properties of a Fabry–Perot, the free spectral range and the finesse or resolution. The free spectral range (FSR) is defined by

$$\text{FSR} = \frac{c}{4nL} \tag{3.19}$$

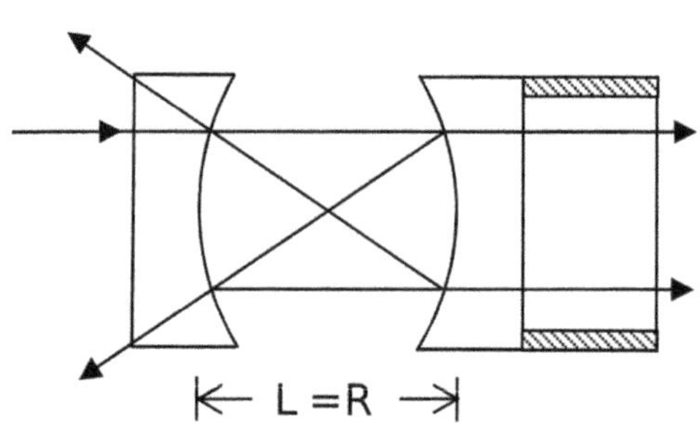

Figure 3.9. Confocal Fabry–Perot interferometer.

where n is the index of refraction of the air between the mirrors, c the speed of light, L the distance between mirrors. Near the center of the mirrors every time the distance between mirrors is changed by a quarter wavelength $\lambda/4$ the same part of the spectrum will be reproduced. The scanning confocal Fabry–Perot used (Toptica Photonics, Model FPI100) has a radius of 75 mm and a $FSR = 1$ GHz. The resolution of the interferometer is given by its finesse

$$\mathrm{F}^* = \frac{\mathrm{FSR}}{\Delta\nu} \tag{3.20}$$

where $\Delta\nu$ is the full with at half maximum of the interference maxima and R reflectivity of the mirrors. The finesse depends on the mirror reflectivity, the losses due to imperfections on the mirror surfaces or dust, and the alignment of the mirrors. In our interferometer the highest finesse reported was $F^* = 240$. A cylindrical piezo-electric transducer (PZT) is attached to one mirror and can move it in small displacements. To displace the mirror a high voltage is applied between the inner and the outer side of the PZT. The interferometer can be used in scanning mode when the laser wavelength is fixed and the piezotransducer is displaced continuously with a ramp function. In this case it is possible to observe the detailed spectra of the laser. Another option is to scan the laser wavelength with a ramp function and the distance between mirrors remains constant. In this case one can observe the laser spectra and change its absolute position in the oscilloscope by applying a constant voltage to the PZT. This option is very useful for finding the resonances needed for cooling.

3.2.6 Adding waves with phasor diagrams

The phasor addition of waves is a very powerful geometrical method to add the amplitudes of several waves. It is very useful for describing the interference pattern and also for obtaining analytical expressions. We shall describe here the graphical phasor procedure for this purpose. Let us consider a sinusoidal wave whose electric field component is given by

$$E_1 = E_0 \sin \omega t \tag{3.21}$$

where E_0 is the wave amplitude and ω is the angular frequency. The sinusoidal wave can be represented graphically by a phasor of magnitude E_0 rotating about the origin counterclockwise with an angular frequency ω. The phasor makes an angle ωt with the horizontal axis. The projection of the phasor on the vertical axis represents E_1, the magnitude of the wave electrical field at some time t. As the phasor rotates in a circle about the origin, the projection E_1 oscillates along the vertical axis. Now consider a second sinusoidal wave whose electric field component is given by

$$E_2 = E_0 \sin(\omega t + \phi) \tag{3.22}$$

This wave has the same amplitude and frequency as E_1, but its phase is ϕ with respect to E_1. The phasor representing E_2 is shown in figure 3.10.

We can graphically obtain the resultant wave, which is the sum of E_1 and E_2, by redrawing the phasors as shown in figure 3.11, in which the tail of the second phasor

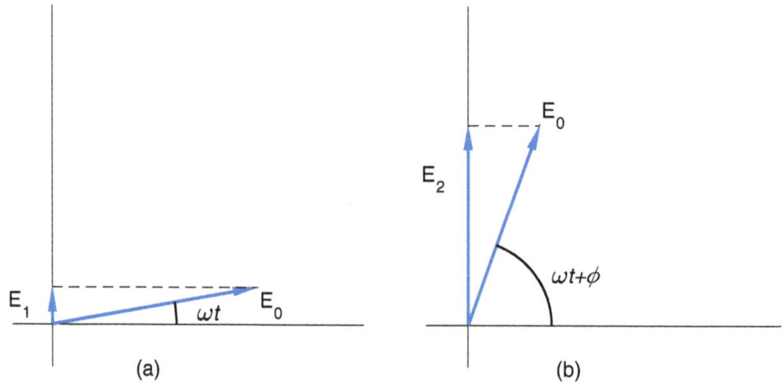

Figure 3.10. (a) Phasor diagram for the wave disturbance $E_1 = E_0 \sin \omega t$. The phasor is a vector of length E_0 rotating counterclockwise. (b) Phasor diagram for the wave $E_2 = E_0 \sin \omega t$.

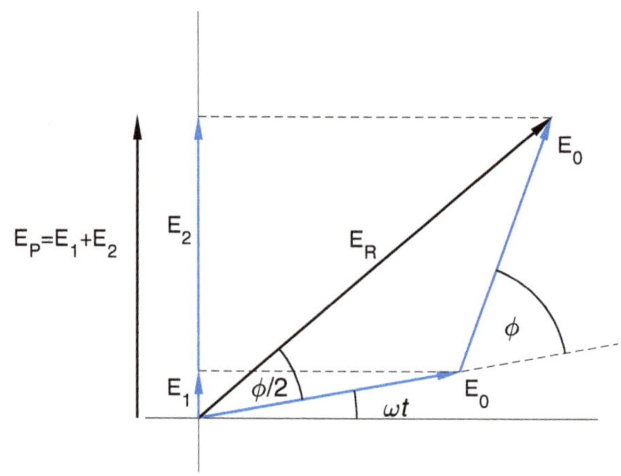

Figure 3.11. The phasor E_R represents the sum of the waves in figure 3.10(a) and (b).

is placed at the tip of the first. As with vector addition, the resultant phasor E_R runs from the tail of the first phasor to the tip of the second. Furthermore, E_R rotates along with the two individual phasors at the same angular frequency. The projection of E_R along the vertical axis equals the sum of the projections of the two other phasors: $E_P = E_1 + E_2$.

3.2.7 Example: adding two waves

To add two waves it is convenient to construct the phasor diagram at $t = 0$ as shown in figure 3.12.

From the geometry of one of the right triangles, we see that

$$\sin \alpha = \frac{E_0}{2R} \tag{3.23}$$

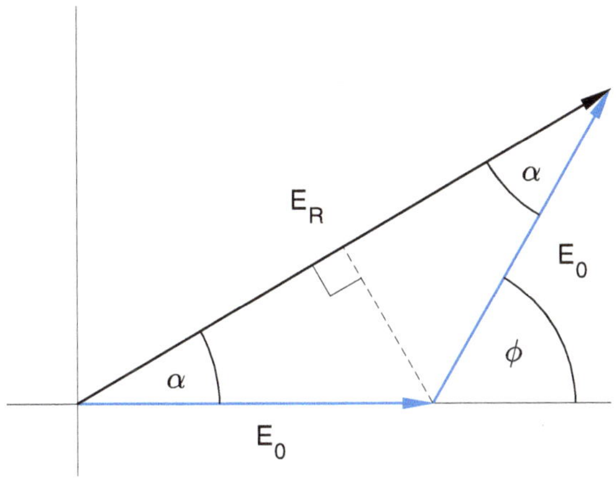

Figure 3.12. The phasor E_R represents the sum of the waves in figure 3.10(a) and (b).

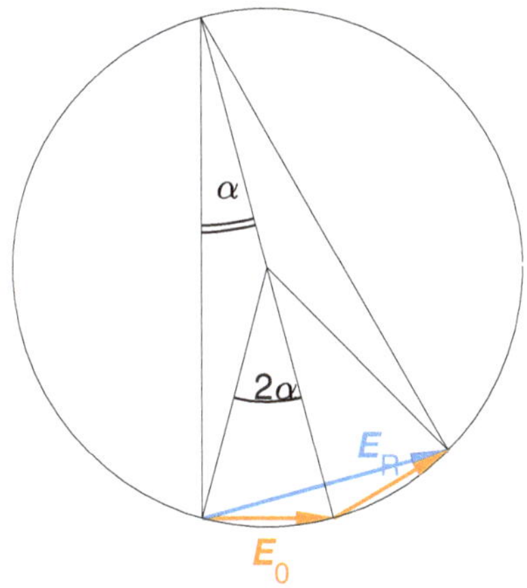

Figure 3.13. Sum of two phasors.

and

$$\sin 2\alpha = \frac{E_R/2}{R} \tag{3.24}$$

where R is the radius of the circumference, $\alpha = \phi/2$ and ϕ the phase difference between the waves. Eliminating R we have

$$E_R = E_0 \frac{\sin 2\alpha}{\sin \alpha} = 2E_0 \cos \alpha \tag{3.25}$$

3.2.8 Geometry for adding N waves

The method of adding phasors can be extended to the addition of more than two waves. For this it is necessary to consider a circle with the phasors contained as secants as seen in figure 3.13, in this case with the sum of two waves.

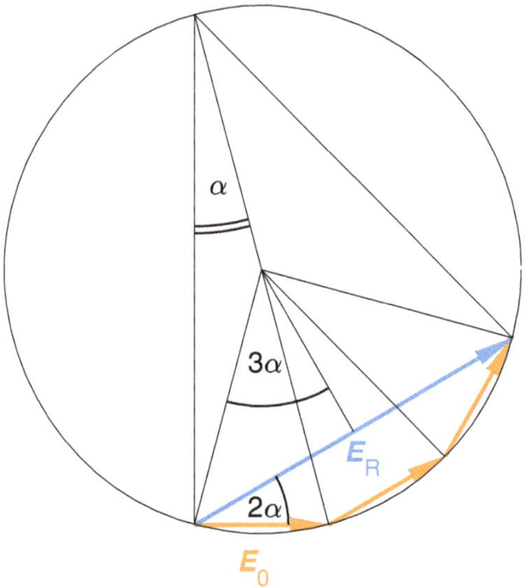

Figure 3.14. Sum of three phasors.

For summing three waves we use the diagram of figure 3.14 and we have $\sin\alpha = E_0/(2R)$, $\sin 3\alpha = (E_R/2)/R$, and

$$E_R = E_0 \frac{\sin 3\alpha}{\sin\alpha} \tag{3.26}$$

For N waves the result can be generalized

$$E_R = E_0 \frac{\sin N\alpha}{\sin\alpha}$$

For infinite partial waves it is necessary to approximate the individual phasors as part of a circumference arc as seen in figure 3.15.

Figure 3.16 shows the sum of different numbers of waves.

Exercise: Using phasor diagrams demonstrate that the intensity of the secondary maxima scales approximately as $1/N^2$ and the width is $180°/(N-1)$.

3.2.9 The diffraction grating

Diffraction gratings (figure 3.17) are normally used to construct spectrometers or monochromators. Depending on the number of slits illuminated, a diffraction grating can be applied for preliminary measurements of the central wavelength of a laser with a resolution of the order of 0.1 nm. It is used to roughly find the central wavelength of a laser diode as a function of temperature. The diffraction grating is also used in a tunable diode laser cavity as the frequency selector. The grating equation can be obtained calculating the path difference between two adjacent rays as seen in figure 3.17. The resolution depends on how many grooves are illuminated,

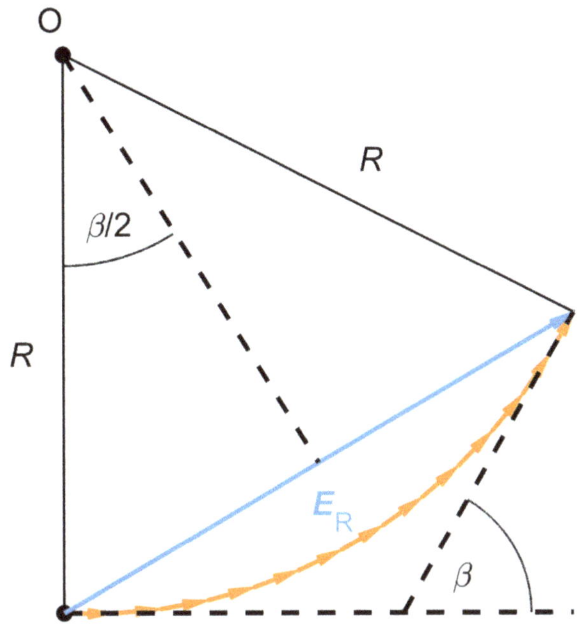

Figure 3.15. Graphical method for the demonstration of the diffraction equation.

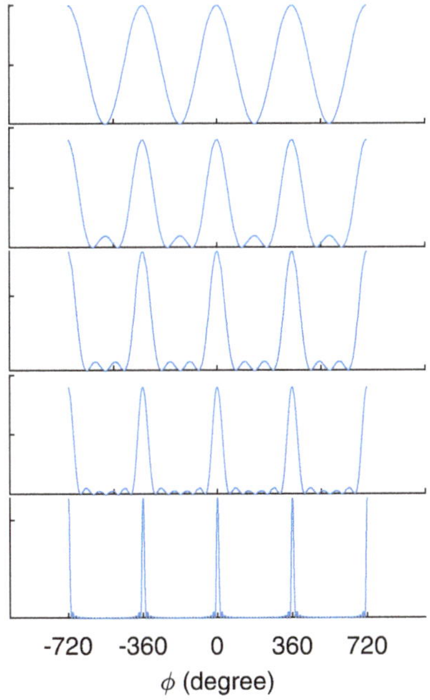

Figure 3.16. From top to bottom, $N = 2$, 3, 4, 6, and 25 waves.

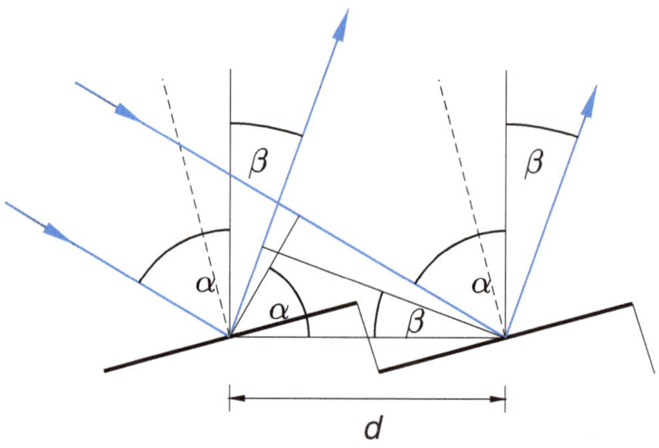

Figure 3.17. Geometry for the grating equation for diffracted light on the opposite side of the incident light.

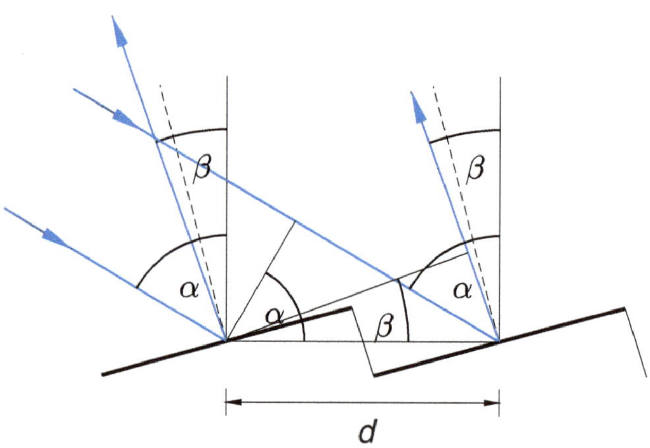

Figure 3.18. Geometry for the grating equation with diffracted light on the same side of the incident light.

i.e., the width of the illuminated region on the grating. The greater the number of waves that interfere, the higher the resolution.

The difference in optical path for the two incident rays is $\Delta s = d(\sin\alpha - \sin\beta)$. Figure 3.18 shows the case of diffracted rays on the left side of the normal.

The general grating equation for maximum interference is

$$m\lambda = d(\sin\alpha \pm \sin\beta) \tag{3.27}$$

where m is an integer. The minus sign is used for constructive interference when β is on the opposite side of α related to the normal and the plus sign is used when β and α are on the same side. α and β are measured from the normal to grating and are both positive. A special case of the grating equation is the Littrow configuration (figure 3.19) when the incident ray is retroreflected and $\alpha = \beta$. Here we have that

$$m\lambda = 2d\sin\alpha \tag{3.28}$$

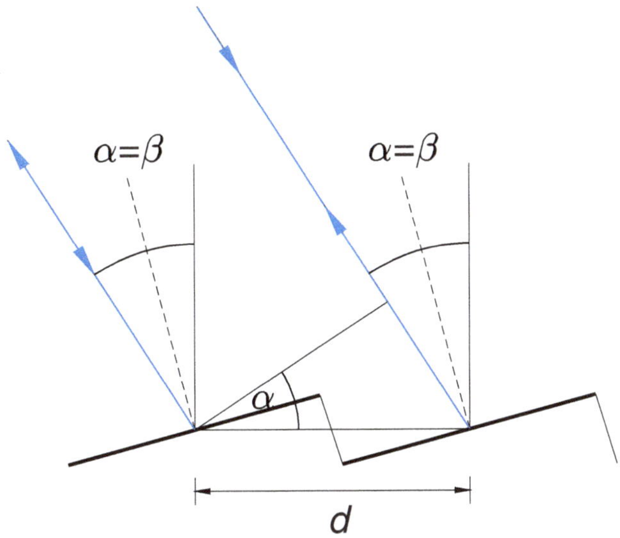

Figure 3.19. Littrow cavity.

For example, if we have a grating with 1800 grooves per mm, $\alpha = 36.7°$ for $m = 1$. No higher m-orders are possible.

3.3 Polarization of light

In this section we will study the linear polarizer, the quarter-wave sheet, and the half-wave sheet. These three elements are necessary to control the intensity and the state of polarization of a wave.

3.4 Linear polarizer and Malus law

Figure 3.20 shows a linear polarizer rotated at an angle θ with respect to the direction of an incident wave linearly polarized along a vertical axis. The drive shaft of the polarizer is turned clockwise by the angle θ

The transmitted intensity is proportional to the square of the transmitted field and is given by the Malus law given by

$$I(\theta) = I_0 \cos^2(\theta) \tag{3.29}$$

where theta is the angle between the direction of the incident electrical field and the polarizer axis. Accurate angle measurements allow the transmitted intensity to be controlled. Figure 3.21 shows a non-polarized beam incident on two linear polarizers. After passing the first polarizer the beam becomes linearly polarized and the intensity becomes half the intensity of the incident beam. The reason for this is that only the field components parallel to the polarizer axis are transmitted. If the second polarizer is crossed no light is transmitted.

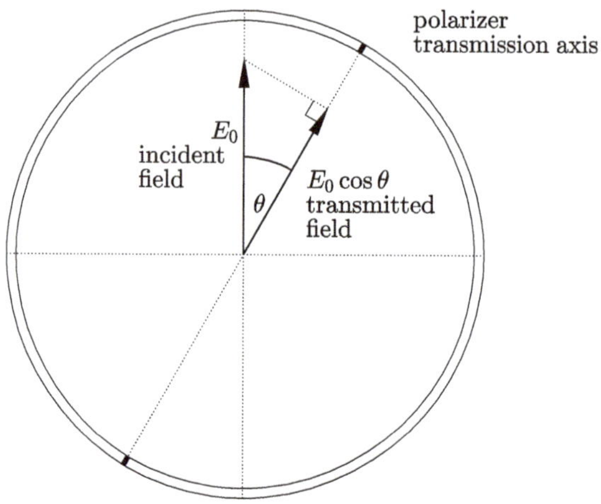

Figure 3.20. Malus Law. The amplitude of the transmitted field is reduced since the scalar component of the incident field is transmitted along the axis of the polarizer. The transmitted field leaves the polarizer with an angle θ with respect to the incident field.

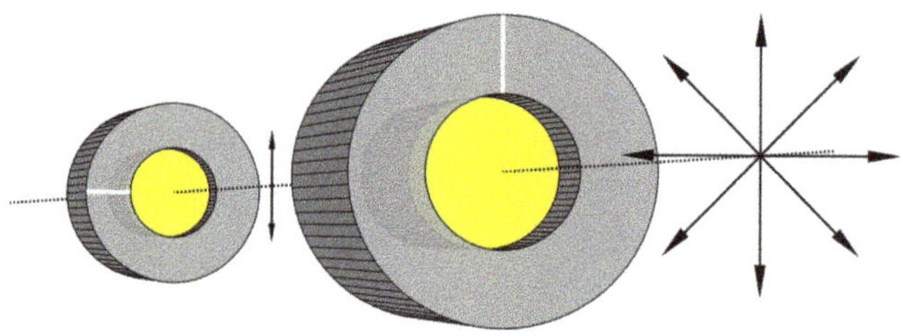

Figure 3.21. Non-polarized light incident on two crossed polarizers.

3.5 The Brewster angle

When a non-polarized wave is incident from a medium with refraction index n_1 on a medium with refraction index n_2, only the component of the field perpendicular to the plane of incidence is reflected when the reflected ray is at 90° from the transmitted ray (figure 3.22). In that case we have that

$$\tan\theta_B = n_2/n_1 \tag{3.30}$$

where θ_B is the Brewster angle. The plane of incidence is the plane that contains the incident, reflected, and transmitted rays. The reason for this can be found when we consider the radiation from an oscillating dipole. The incident field excites the dipoles of the material. It is known that there is no radiation in the direction of the dipole axis, which in this case is in the same direction as the reflected ray.

For $n_2 = 1.5$ and $n_1 = 1.0$ the Brewster is $\theta_B = 56.31°$.

Application: Linear polarizers do not generally have the transmission axis marked. A method to find the transmission axis is to use the partial reflected light off a window or any surface looking at the surface through a polarizer at a nearly Brewster angle. As we know that the light reflected by the surface at Brewster angle is linearly polarized and we

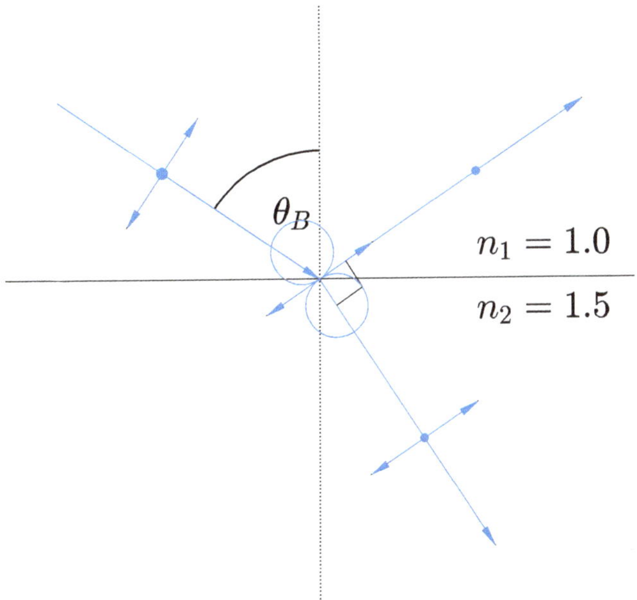

Figure 3.22. Brewster angle.

know its direction, we can find the polarizer axis. By rotating the polarizer, we can find the position where the beam is extinguished. In this case we must use the reflection of the ambient light. **You should not attempt to do this experiment with a laser.**

3.5.1 The quarter-wave plate

A quarter-wave plate is generally used in the laboratory to produce circularly polarized light starting from linear polarized light. The quarter-wave plate is also used to avoid unwanted reflections into the laser cavity. To obtain circularly polarized light it is necessary to rotate the plate or alternatively the field in such a way that the incident linear polarized electrical field vector is oriented at 45° relative to the optical axis of the plate. The optical axis of a quarter-wave plate is parallel to the plate surface. The incident linear polarized electric field can be decomposed into two waves: a vertical and an horizontal wave. In the figure 3.23 the fast axis is the y-axis and it is vertical. The horizontal wave becomes one half-wave retarded after passing the quarter-wave plate (QWP). When observing in the direction of the source the resulting electric field vector is rotating clockwise and the wave is right circular polarized. The electric field for right circular left polarized light can be written as

$$\mathbf{E} = E_0 \sin(kz - \omega t)\hat{\mathbf{x}} + E_0 \sin(kz - \omega t - \pi/2)\hat{\mathbf{y}} \tag{3.31}$$

when the vertical axis is the y-axis. At $z = 0$ we have

$$\mathbf{E} = -E_0 \sin(\omega t)\hat{\mathbf{x}} - E_0 \sin(\omega t + \pi/2)\hat{\mathbf{y}} \tag{3.32}$$

The $\mathbf{E}$-field take the values $-\hat{\mathbf{y}}$, $-\hat{\mathbf{x}}$, $\hat{\mathbf{y}}$, $\hat{\mathbf{x}}$ when ωt take the values 0, $\pi/2$, π and $3\pi/2$.

Figure 3.24 shows a linear polarized wave.

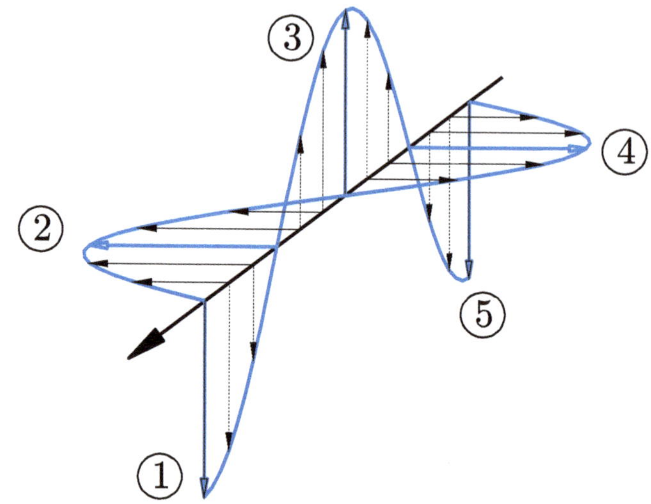

Figure 3.23. Right circular polarized wave. The numbers indicate the order in which the electric field vector is seen by the observer. Here the electric field is rotating to the right when the observer is looking towards the source. Label 1 indicates the electric field vector pointing downwards, label 2 indicates the electric field to the left, and so on until vector 5.

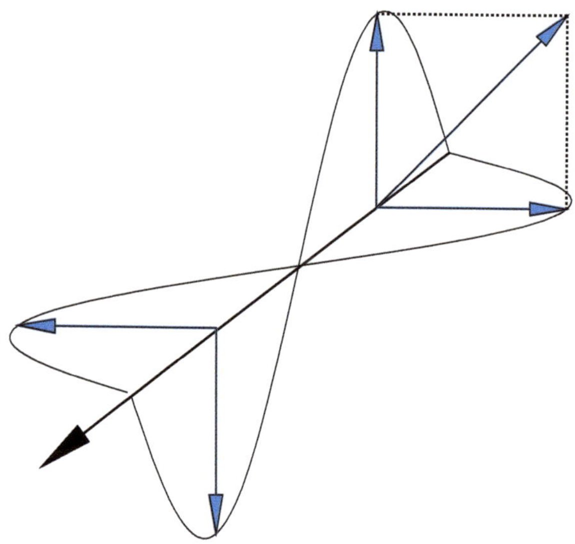

Figure 3.24. Linear polarized wave. As we can see the electric field components are in phase.

3.5.2 How to install a quarter-wave plate

It is possible to find the optical axis of a QWP using a polarizing beam splitter cube (PBSC) and a mirror as seen in figure 3.25. A laser beam is driven through the polarizing beam splitter cube and reflected by a mirror. The PBSC transmits only the horizontal component of the incident electric field. After passing the QWP the

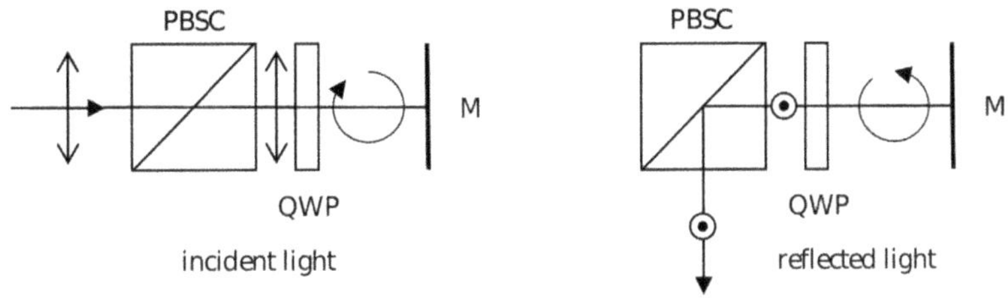

Figure 3.25. Optics isolator based on retarders. Left: the incident beam with horizontal electric field is transmitted through the PBSC. After the QWP the polarization is circular. Right: the reflected beam is retarded twice and the polarization is vertical.

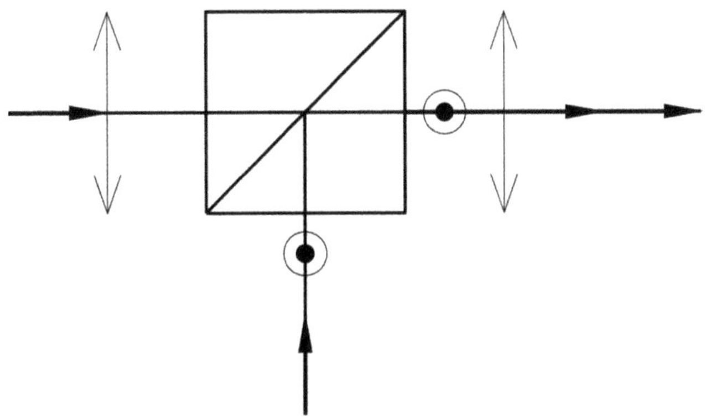

Figure 3.26. Method to combine two beams into one single beam.

polarization becomes circular when the optical axis is oriented at 45° to the incident electric beam. The beam is reflected by the mirror and the QWP produces a vertical polarized beam that is reflected off the polarizing beam splitter cube. The QWP axis can be oriented until maximum light is deviated by the PBSC. Usually the fast axis is marked on the QWP. Right or left circular polarization depends on the direction in which the beam is observed. When observing in the direction of the source the polarization is right circular if the fast axis is oriented at 45° to the right of the incident electric field and left circular if the fast axis is oriented at 45° to the left of the incident electric field.

3.5.3 The half-wave plate

The half-wave plate is mostly used to rotate the electric field in an arbitrary angle. In the particular case that the electric field is oriented at 45° to the optical axis of the plate the field rotates in 90°. The half-wave plate combined with a PBSC can be used to combine two laser beams into a single beam. The horizontal polarized beam passes through the PBSC and a vertical polarized beam is driven through the perpendicular direction and reflected in the same direction as the transmitted beam. We obtain two collinear beams whose electric fields are perpendicular to each other as shown in figure 3.26.

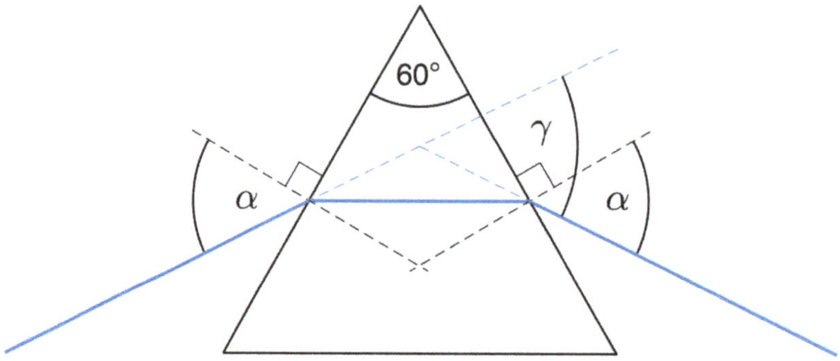

Figure 3.27. Equilateral prism. α is the incidence angle which is measured with respect to the normal. Here, for minimum deviation the exit angle is equal to the incidence angle. The ray is moving from left to right.

3.5.4 Dispersive equilateral prism

When doubling a frequency it is necessary to separate the rays with different wavelengths. A good choice is to use an equilateral prism (figure 3.27).

The index of refraction of an equilateral prism can be obtained from

$$n = \frac{\sin(\gamma/2 + 30^\circ)}{\sin 30^\circ} \tag{3.33}$$

where γ is the angle of minimum deviation. Solving for γ we obtain

$$\gamma = 2(\sin^{-1}(n \sin 30^\circ) - 30^\circ). \tag{3.34}$$

In our experiment we separated a beam with 532 nm from its second harmonic at 266 nm. A suitable prism could be a CaF2 prism (calcium fluoride prism) with n (532 nm) = 1.4354 and n (266 nm) = 1.4621. The refraction indices were obtained using the Sellmeier equation. Note that special attention should be taken in the selection of the prism material as not every prism will transmit in the UV region as for example at 266 nm. We obtain γ(532 nm) = 31.73° and γ(266 nm) = 33.95°. To determine the incidence angle it is easy to demonstrate that for an equilateral prism

$$\gamma = 2\alpha - 60^\circ \tag{3.35}$$

In our example α(532 nm) = 45.86° and α(266 nm) = 46.98°. The generalized prism dispersion theory is given in [5] and [6].

References

[1] Demtröder W 2004 *Experimentalphysik* vol 2 (Berlin: Springer)
[2] Hecht E and Zajac A 1974 *Optics* (Boston: Addison-Wesley)
[3] Serway R A and Jewett J W 2018 *Physics for Scientists and Engineers* (Boston: Cengage)
[4] Duarte F J 2019 *Fundamentals of Quantum Entanglement* (Bristol: Institute of Physics)
[5] Duarte F J and Piper J A 1982 Dispersion theory of multiple-prism beam expanders for pulsed dye lasers *Opt. Commun.* **43** 303–7
[6] Duarte F J 1985 Note on achromatic multiple-prism beam expanders *Opt. Commun.* **53** 259–62

Chapter 4

Vapor generation and vacuum

The techniques and hardware for vacuum, vapor production and connection to sensors for the installation of absorption spectroscopy, resonance ionization spectroscopy, laser isotope separation and laser cooling experiments are described in this chapter. Most of the parts were obtained from vacuum and related companies, other were machined in a mechanical shop. Laser isotope separation needs a turbo pump vacuum (better than 10^{-6} Torr) and laser cooling experiments need a ultra-high vacuum (of the order of 10^{-10} Torr). In this chapter we first describe the laser isotope separation vacuum hardware and then the laser cooling vacuum technique.

4.1 Lithium isotope separation hardware

The experimental setup for laser isotope experiment is shown in figure 4.1. We have tested each part of the hardware separately and obtained partial results before achieving the complete lithium laser isotope separation device. The system includes a heat pipe, a Pierce extractor, a Einzel lens system, a magnetic sector, and a modified Faraday cup system. We also used a lithium ion source to calibrate our system.

Figure 4.2 shows the vacuum facility.

4.1.1 The heat pipe oven

We used the heat pipe oven for the study of the lithium absorption spectroscopy as a stationary vapor and as a lithium beam when it was connected to the lithium isotope separation vacuum chamber. A heat pipe (see figures 4.3, 4.4, and 4.5) is a device which transfers heat by convection of an active or working medium.

The first heat pipe was proposed by Gaugler in 1942: the heat transfer was achieved by evaporating and condensing the working medium using capillarity forces to transfer and circulate the liquid. The invention was used in the area of refrigeration. The main use in high temperature heat transfer was introduced by

doi:10.1088/978-0-7503-3839-4ch4

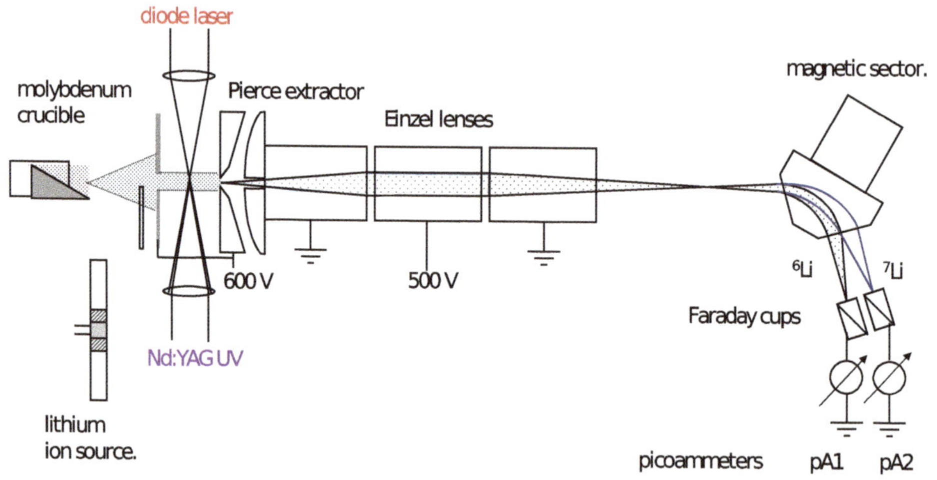

Figure 4.1. Experimental setup for laser isotope separation. Diagram of the mass separator pA1 and pA2, picoammeters.

Figure 4.2. Laser isotope separation setup. From left to right: heat pipe, vacuum chamber with windows for lasers beams (exciter and ionizer laser) and Pierce extractor, vacuum chamber containing ion beam hardware, magnetic sector and Faraday cup ion collectors. It is possible to observe two convections for rough vacuum measurements and a Bayard-Alpert for high vacuum measurement.

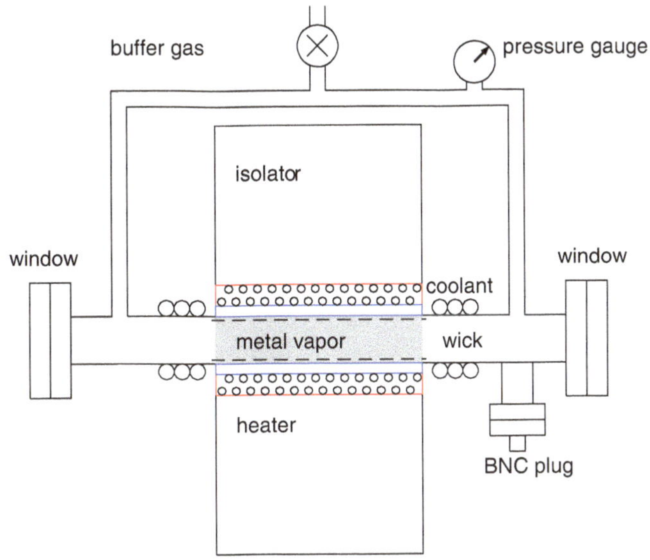

Figure 4.3. Scheme of the heat pipe. Dimensions are not to scale. The wick is a metallic mesh rolled inside the tube. The BNC plug is connected to an electrode inside that permits charges to be collected from the interior. The main feature of the heat pipe is that it keeps the windows clean from lithium metal as the lithium vapor is condensed close to the coolant.

Figure 4.4. Heat pipe oven installed for absorption measurements. The heat pipe has its two windows installed.

Figure 4.5. Heat pipe used as a the source of a lithium beam. The heat pipe is connected to the vacuum line. No buffer gas, and no water was used in this operation mode. The back window is replaced by a flange.

Grover *et al*, in 1963. The main feature is the high degree to which it is isothermal. Vidal and Cooper were the first to use a heat pipe for spectroscopic purposes. They arranged windows at the ends of the tube such that a laser beam could enter and exit the heat pipe passing through the dense metal vapor. A rare gas called a buffer gas was used to confine the metal vapor and prevent fogging of the windows. The gas which can be used are, for example, argon, helium, or neon. Figure 4.3 gives a simplified diagram of the working heat pipe. The central region of the heat pipe is heated by resisting heating with a nichrome wire. The latent heat of evaporation is transferred by evaporating the liquid in the heated region and condensing the vapor in the cooled region of the tube. The liquid is recirculated back to the heated region by capillarity action using as a wick material a metal fine mesh. When the heat pipe is working, the following conditions are observed: (1) evaporation of the liquid phase, (2) transfer of vapor to the low temperature or condensation zone, (3) condensation, (4) transfer of the liquid from the condensation zone to the heated evaporation zone by capillary and bulk forces. In this case the buffer gas (normally a rare gas) is excluded from the central region and the pressure of the central region is determined by the external buffer gas. We filled the heat pipe with a small amount of metallic lithium and used pure argon as a buffer gas. Previously the heat pipe was evacuated with a rotary vane pump. A Swagelok precision gate valve manifold was used to introduce controlled amounts of buffer gas.

The heat pipe oven was also used as a source of neutral atoms for the lithium isotope separation system. In this case no buffer gas was used and no water cooling. The heat pipe was used as the source for a neutral lithium beam.

4.1.2 Lithium ion source

A lithium ion source (beta eucryptite) was used to produce controlled amounts of lithium ions and for calibrating our lithium isotope system. Figure 4.6 shows the installed lithium beta eucryptite ion source. Previous to the building of the lithium isotope separation experiment we tested the beta eucryptite lithium ion cell using a single modified Faraday cup that was placed at some distance in front of the ion cell.

The ion source (figure 4.7) is built with the crystalline compounds Li_2O–Al_2O_3–$2SiO_2$ (β-eucryptite) or Li_2O–Al_2O_3–$4SiO_2$ (spodumene) will when heated above 1000 °C. In our case we used beta eucryptite.

A measurement of the lithium ion current as a function of filament power and emitter temperature is given by [1], and it can be seen in figure 4.8.

Figure 4.9 shows a side view of the ion source holder.

Figure 4.10 shows a front view of the ion source holder.

Figure 4.11 shows a single Faraday plate for ion detection.

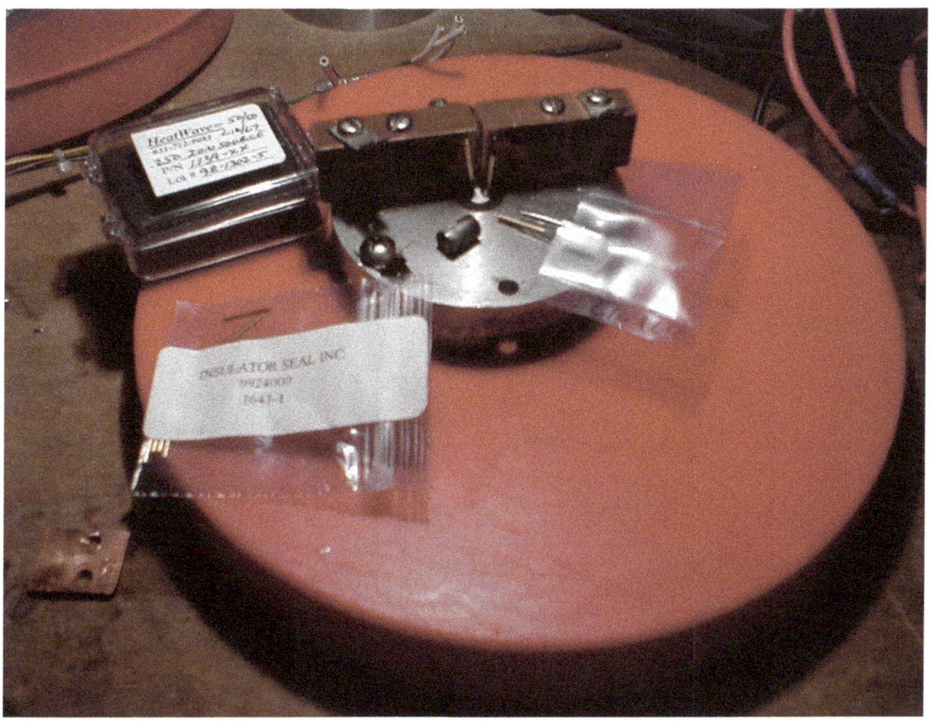

Figure 4.6. Ion source heat wave. The picture shows an installed source, and some sources and connectors.

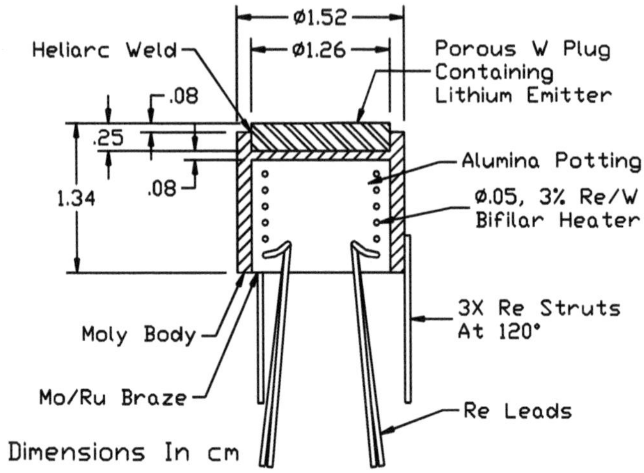

Figure 4.7. Detail of the ion source construction.

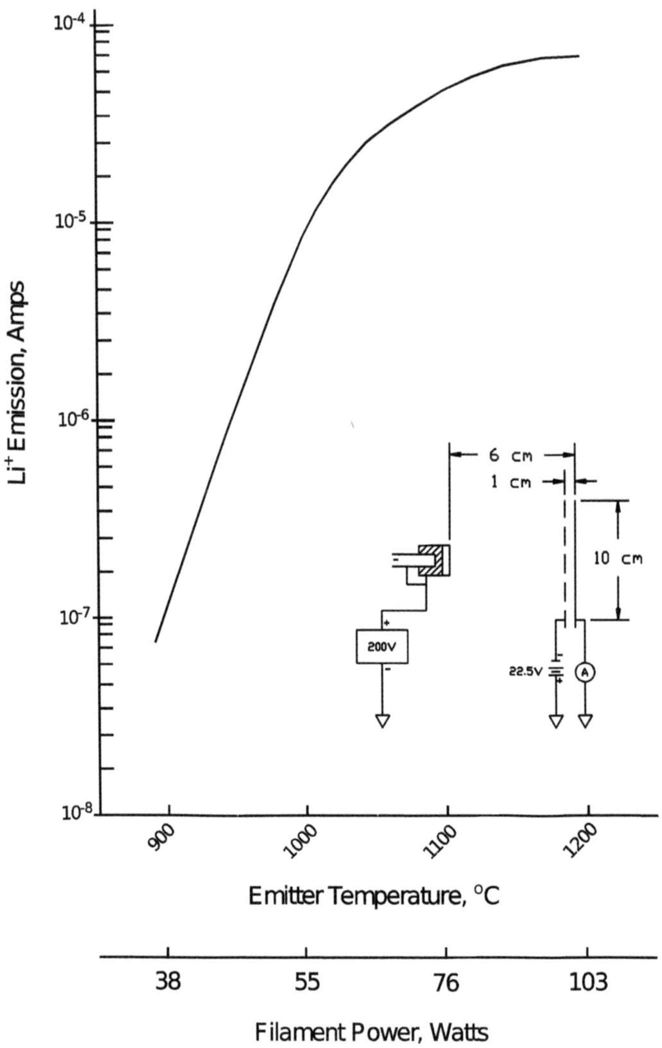

Figure 4.8. Lithium ion source current as a function of the filament power.

Figure 4.9. Side view of lithium ion source holder.

Figure 4.10. Front view of lithium ion source holder.

Figure 4.11. Single Faraday ion detector plate.

4.1.3 Resonance lithium ionization spectroscopy hardware

Before installing the lithium laser isotope system we studied the resonance excitation and ionization of a neutral lithium beam. The experimental setup is shown in figure 4.12.

The lithium beam was collimated through a 5 mm hole. The ions were separated electrostatically by means of a polarized parallel capacitor shown in figure 4.13. The beam of neutral lithium atoms with mass m has a velocity determined by the temperature of the oven

$$v = \sqrt{\frac{k_B T}{m}} \tag{4.1}$$

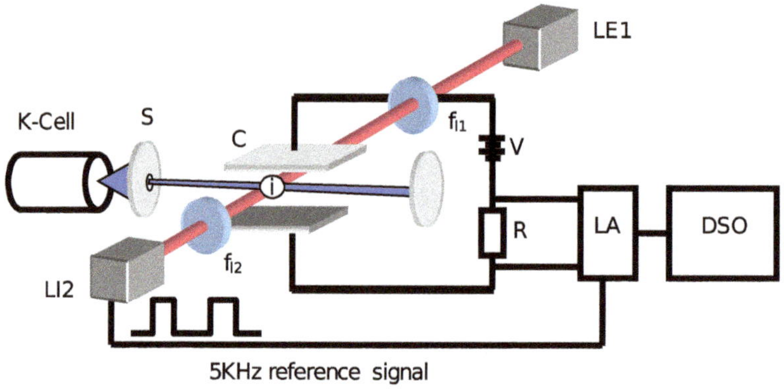

Figure 4.12. Resonance ionization spectroscopy experiment diagram.

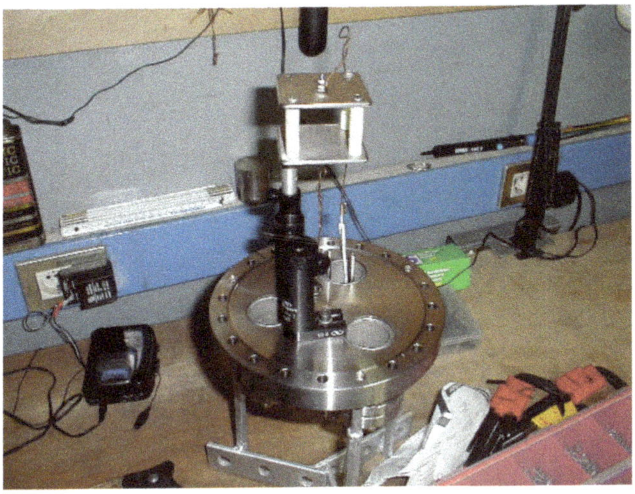

Figure 4.13. Parallel plates for the resonance ionization spectroscopy experiment.

For example for an oven with a temperature of $T = 500$ °C, and ^{6}Li we have $m = 6 \times 1.672\,6231 \times 10^{-27}$, $k_B = 1.380\,664 \times 10^{-23}$ the Boltzmann constant, the velocity is approximately $v = 1031$ m s^{-1}. For calculation of the time needed to reach the negative plate we have to calculate the field for a plane parallel capacitor separated by a distance d held at a potential difference V which is

$$E = \frac{V}{d} \tag{4.2}$$

the acceleration

$$a = \frac{q}{m}\frac{V}{d} \tag{4.3}$$

for $V = 9$ V, $d = 1.84$ cm, $m = 6 \times 1.672\,6231 \times 10^{-27}$ kg, $q = 1.602\,176\,62 \times 10^{-19}$ C we have $a = 7.82 \times 10^9$ m s^{-2} is constant and the time needed for an ion to travel 1.84 cm is

$$t = \sqrt{\frac{2 \times 0.018\,4}{a}} = 2.17\ \mu\text{s} \tag{4.4}$$

Considering a path length of the beam along the capacitor equal to $z = 7.62$ cm, the time to travel this distance with constant velocity $v = 1031$ m s^{-1} is 73.9 μs. The ions have time enough to reach the capacitor plate.

4.1.4 Magnetic sector

The magnetic sector is shown in figure 4.14. It contains a permanent horse shoe magnet and suitable vacuum connections. We used a magnetic sector that was calibrated with different masses up to 12 AMU. The magnetic sector was calibrated

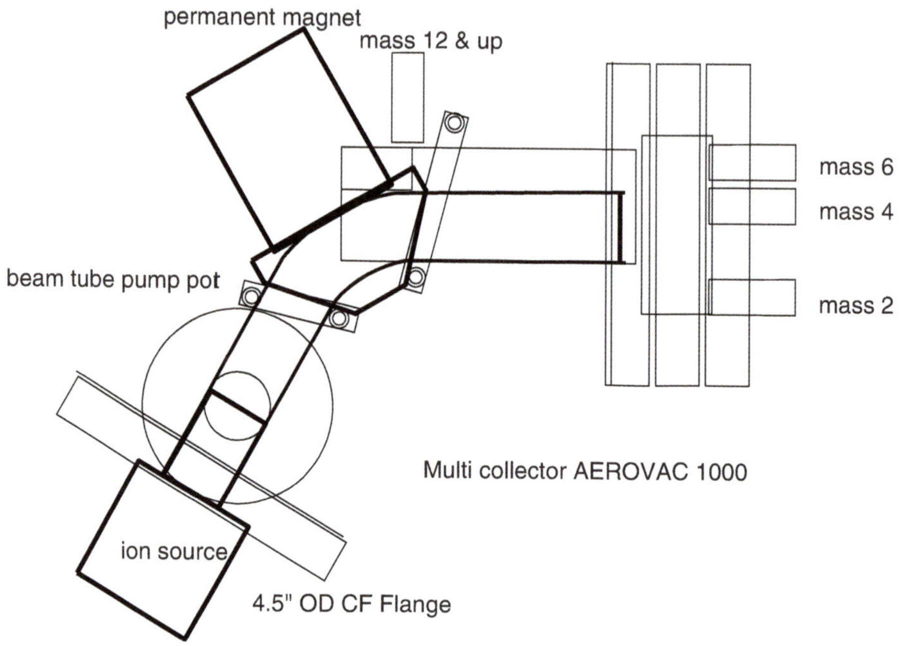

Figure 4.14. Detail of the magnetic sector.

Figure 4.15. Magnetic sector installed. On the right side is the entrance slit.

together with an extraction and, acceleration and focusing system for use with ^{6}Li and ^{7}Li ions. In our case the ion source was a beta eucryptite Li ion source.

Figure 4.15 shows a picture of the magnetic sector installed in the lithium isotope separation device.

Considering a constant magnetic field acting on a ion with velocity v the Newton force law gives

$$qvB = m\frac{v^2}{R} \tag{4.5}$$

The ion entering the magnetic sector will describe a circular orbit with radius of curvature

$$R = \frac{m}{q}\frac{v}{B} \tag{4.6}$$

solving for the magnetic fields strength we have

$$B = \frac{m}{q}\frac{v}{R} \tag{4.7}$$

The velocity of the ion beam that was accelerated by the Pierce extractor is given by

$$qV = \frac{1}{2}mv^2 \tag{4.8}$$

The velocity of the ions entering the magnetic sector is

$$v = \sqrt{\left(\frac{q}{m}\right)2V} = \sqrt{\left(\frac{1.602 \times 10^{-19}}{6 \times 1.673 \times 10^{-27}}\right) \times 2 \times 600} = 1.38 \times 10^5 \text{ ms}^{-1} \tag{4.9}$$

and the magnetic field strength is $B = 54.2$ mT for $R = 16.3$ mm.

4.1.5 Ion charge measurement

To calibrate the magnetic sector we modified a beam profiler consisting in a wire arranged in front of the beam and moved externally by a motor. Figure 4.16 shows the moving wire for ion detection. The wire is connected to a BNC connector which is connected externally to a picoammeter. We determined the position of the 6 and 7 masses from the lecture of the current and the position of the motor.

To measure the isotope separated charge of ^{6}Li and ^{7}Li ions we used two modified Faraday cups consisting in two plane parallel copper plates. Figure 4.17 shows the pair of modified Faraday cups.

4.1.6 Einzel lens array

Figure 4.18 shows the Einzel lens array used to conduct the lithium ions to the entrance of the magnetic sector. The array consists of three aluminum rods. The third rod on the right is attached to the Pierce extractor. Both sides of the Pierce are supported by three small ceramic cylinders. The lens support includes three ceramic rods for electric isolation and two rings that could be adjusted and centered. A good description of ion and electron beams can be found in [2]

Figure 4.16. Ion detection wire.

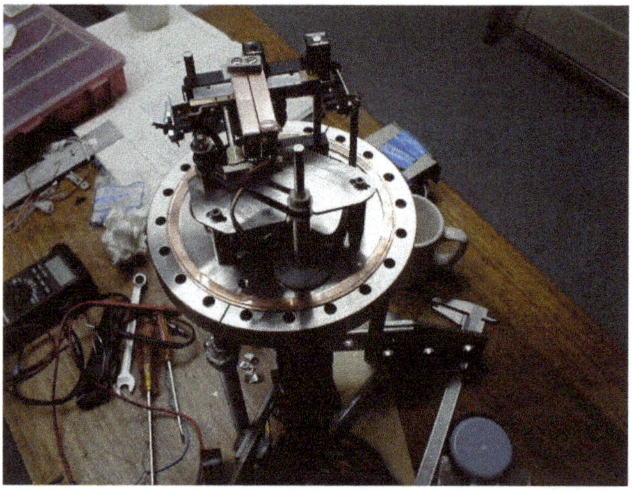

Figure 4.17. Modified Faraday cups.

Figure 4.18. Ion Einzel lens array.

4.2 Preparing the vacuum for laser cooling

To produce cooled atoms it is necessary to have an ultra-high vacuum level with pressures lower than 10^{-7} Pa (10^{-9} Torr). Our vacuum system (figures 4.19 and 4.21) was built with MDC-vacuum pipes with nominal 2.75 inch diameter conflate type flanges made of 308 stainless steel.

The connections between the pipes and other devices were sealed with copper gaskets. Our system consisted of a rotary vane pump, followed by a turbomolecular pump[1] and an ion pump[2]. To measure the low vacuum level up to 1.33×10^{-2} Pa (10^{-4} Torr) we used a convectron[3] gauge. To measure vacuum pressures lower than 1.33×10^{-3} Pa (10^{-5} Torr) we used a Bayard–Alpert gauge[4]. Both gauges were connected to a multi-gauge controller[5]. The ultra-high vacuum was measured alternatively with the indicator of ionic pump controller. The vacuum process started with the onset of the rotary vane pump to obtain a vacuum close to 1.33×10^{-2} Pa (10^{-4} Torr). After obtaining this vacuum pressure we started the turbomolecular pump, to obtain a vacuum close to 10^{-5} Pa (10^{-7} Torr). To obtain lower vacuum pressures the system was heated in a process called baking to

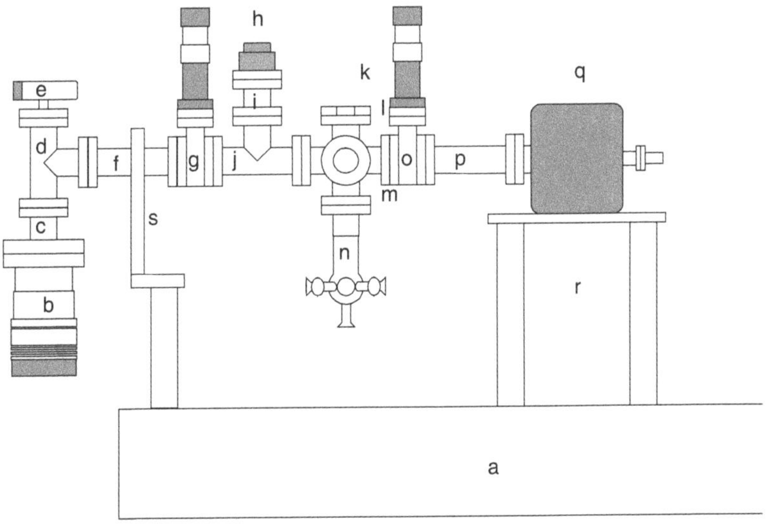

Figure 4.19. Vacuum system for laser cooling: (a) optical table, (b) turbo pump, (c) reduction nipple, (d) tee, (e) convectron gauge sensor, (f) nipple tube, (g) manual gate valve, (h) Bayard-Alpert vacuum gauge, (i) short nipple, (j) tee, (k) window, (l) six way cross, (m) 8 pin electrical feedthrough, (n) laser entrance and observation chamber with seven horizontal windows and one vertical window, (o) manual UHV gate valve, (p) tube, (q) ion pump, (r) aluminum plate ion pump support, (s) holder.

[1] Varian, Model TurboVac V50.
[2] Varian, Model VacIon Plus 20 StarCell.
[3] Granville Phillips, Model 275238.
[4] Varian, 580 Nude ion gauge thoria iridium.
[5] Varian, Model L8350301.

Table 4.1. Components of the vacuum system.

a	optical table	
b	turbomolecular pump	Leybold
c	reduction nipple CF 4.5 to 2.75 inch	MDC-Vacuum, Model 402013
d,j	tee CF 2.75 flange	MDC-Vacuum, Model 404002
e	Convectron vacuum sensor	Granville Phillips
f,p	nipple	MDC-Vacuum, Model 402002
g, o	manual valve for ultra-high vacuum	MDC-Vacuum, Model 302001
h	Bayard-Alpert UHV sensor,	Varian
i	short nipple CF 2.75 flange	MDC-Vacuum, Model 468008
k	window	MDC-Vacuum, Model 450020
l	six way cross	MDC-Vacuum, Model 407002
	blank flange for back side	MDC-Vacuum, Model 110008
m	8 pins electrical feedthrough	MDC-Vacuum, Model 9530001
n	bottle with 7 horizontal windows and one vertical window	home made
q	ion pump	Varian
r	aluminum plate support with posts for ionic pump	home made
s	L form mount for tubing	home made

evaporate the water molecules embedded inside the pipes and chamber. For this we rolled around the pipes and flanges along the vacuum line a heater that was made of a nearly 10 m long AWG26 nichrome wire. To electrically isolate the nichrome wire from the pipes we inserted it into a series of 1 m fiber glass spaghettis that were coupled one by one. To do this we slide the outer part at end of one spaghetti into the inner part of the following. The ionic pump was heated with its own heater, when the pump was switched off. The temperature used in the vacuum process was 120 °C. To reach this temperature we increased the temperature 10 °C every 30 min with a Variac transformer by increasing the current along the nichrome wire. The complete baking process took at least 5 days. The first day was used to reach the 120 °C baking temperature. This temperature was kept constant for the next three days. On the fifth day we initiated the decrease of the temperature at the same rate as at the heating stage, that is a decrease of 10 °C every 30 min. This was a precaution to protect the glass and the glue, because all have different temperature expansion coefficients. To obtain a homogeneous temperature along the vacuum line we made a temperature measurement at different places. For this we installed several thermocouples in some points between the heating wires and the pipes. We also covered the heater with aluminum foil. With the baking of the vacuum line we could reduce the pressure by more than one order of magnitude. The ultimate vacuum was less than 100 nanoPa (1 nanoTorr). Details of the components of the vacuum system are shown in table 4.1.

4.2.1 Observation optical cell: discussion of different methods

Three versions of observation cells were used in our trap. In the first experiment we bored a 30 mm in a 2.75 CF flange that was used for mounting the glass windows. On the flat side we constructed a cell that uses four optical glass plates with 4 mm wall thickness and dimensions 35 × 50 mm. On the top of the cell we glued a 35 × 35 mm optical glass plate. The cell was glued to the flat side of the flange. The plates were glued with a high vacuum Torr seal. The second version consisted of an optical glass cell with outer width ×length ×height wall dimensions 55 × 55 × 52.5 mm and 2.5 mm wall thickness[6]. The cell was glued on the 4.5 inch side of a zero length reducer from nominal conflate flange 4.5 inch to 2.75 inch. We did not remove the edge of the 4.5 inch side so the cell was installed very tightly. This caused the glass to break after some heat up

Figure 4.20. Homemade observation chambers with windows for entrance of laser beams.

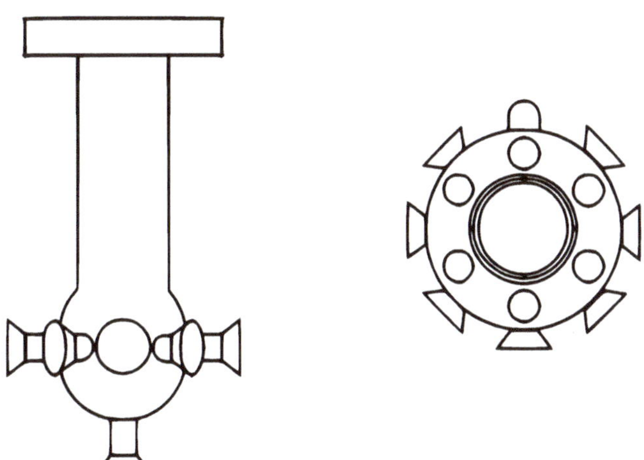

Figure 4.21. Observation chamber with windows for entrance of laser beams. Left: side view, right: top view.

[6] Hellma Cells, Model 704.003-OG.

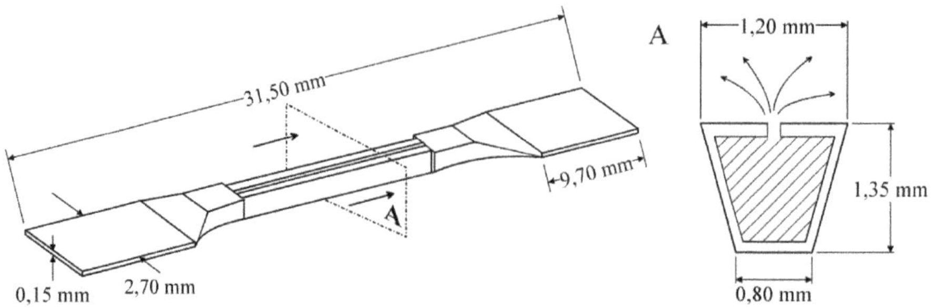

Figure 4.22. Detail of the rubidium getter used for inserting rubidium atoms into the high vacuum.

vacuum procedures. The cell could be repaired several times with the vacuum Torr seal. The first two versions of cells are shown in figure 4.20.

The third version (figure 4.21) consisted of a cell prepared by a glass blower. The cell has a 2.75 inch conflate type adapter and seven optical windows with a 1 inch useful area. This cell was used finally in all laser cooling experiments.

4.2.2 Introduction of neutral atoms using a rubidium getter

Neutral rubidium atoms are introduced into the vacuum chamber by means of a rubidium getter. The getter is a small device that allows the introduction of a small controlled number of atoms into the vacuum. The rubidium is released from the getter as a vapor when a current flows through it. A typical current to release the necessary number of neutral atoms is close to 3.7 A. A diagram of the getter is shown in figure 4.22. The getter is contained in a chamber with a trapezoidal section and released from a small aperture at the upper part. The exit of the getter closes when the getter cools down. The condensation and solidification of the material closes the exit. To start the vapor emission the current should be increased to 8 A during nearly 2 s. To avoid the destruction by melting of the getter due to a high current (like the burning of a fuse) the pulse duration should be controlled precisely. We used a programmable current power supply (Instek, Model PSM-2010) to avoid the destruction by melting of the getter. The power supply was programmed externally with a basic Labview6.0 code that permitted a slow heating of the getter. We programmed the current as follows:5 s at 3 A, 2 s at 8 A, 4 s at 6 A and fixed the current at 3.7 A for the rest of the time. To avoid needlessly opening the vacuum we soldered several getters to pair of pins of an 8 pin conflate flanged power feedthrough. The soldering was made by means of a thermocouple point soldering device. This uses three 5.1 mF, 350 V electrolytic capacitors in parallel. 70 V is enough to solder the parts. We used only one getter for more than 100 hours and it is still working.

References

[1] Heinz O and Reaves R T 1968 Lithium ion emitter for low energy beam experiments *Rev. Sci. Instrum.* **39** 1229–30

[2] Demtröder W 2010 *Experimentalphysik 3: Atome, Moleküle und Festkörper* (Berlin: Springer)

IOP Publishing

Techniques for Lithium Isotope Separation, Laser Cooling, and Scattering

Ignacio E Olivares and Patrick Carrazana

Chapter 5

Diode laser characteristics

This chapter describes the architecture of the tunable diode lasers used in laser isotope separation and laser cooling experiments, and a high repetition rate pulsed Nd:YAG laser used for photoionization. The basic physics of semiconductor lasers is described in many articles such as [1] and [2]. Semiconductor diode lasers are inexpensive, easy to operate, and produce high power tunable narrow bandwidth radiation ($\Delta\nu < 1\text{MHz}$, $\Delta\lambda < 1.5 \times 10^{-6}$ nm). This is because diode lasers have become commonplace in modern research laboratories.

5.1 Littrow grating diode laser cavity

The Littrow configuration, shown in figure 5.1, is the simplest and most popular arrangement for tuning a laser. It is very useful when the tuning range can be small, for example in laser cooling experiments.

In this cavity the grating is aligned such that the first order diffraction from the grating is coupled directly back into the laser while the zeroth-order diffraction is reflected as the output beam. The Littrow configuration is a particular case of the diffraction grating equation

$$\lambda = d(\sin\alpha \pm \sin\beta) \tag{5.1}$$

where $\alpha = \beta$. In this case

$$\lambda = 2d\sin\alpha \tag{5.2}$$

Using the grating in Littrow configuration we find that the lasing wavelength is dependent on the angle of the incident laser beam with respect to the grating. It is possible to roughly adjust the Littrow angle by rotating the grating until the first order is reflected back into the laser diode. A good method is to set the laser current close below the laser threshold and detect the reflected ray by a photodiode. Just

doi:10.1088/978-0-7503-3839-4ch5

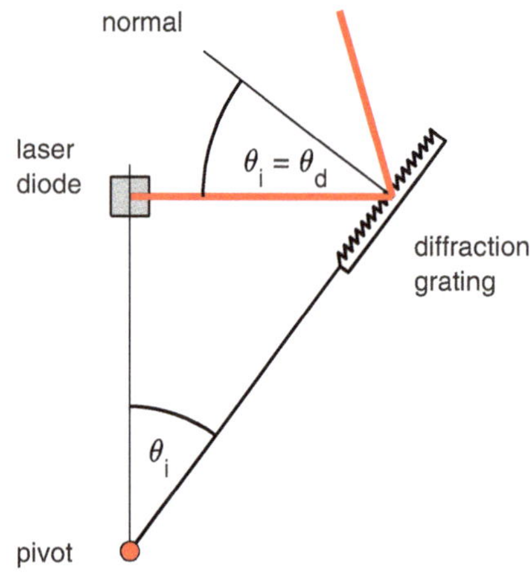

Figure 5.1. Littrow diode laser cavity.

above threshold the diode initiates its laser emission. The optimal angle is obtained when the laser starts its emission caused by the alignment of the grating. Afterwards, the laser can be tuned by finely changing the Littrow angle, e.g. using a piezo electric transducer. The Littrow configuration offers the advantage of high efficiency and power but also faces problems of mode-hopping and beam angular displacement as the grating angle is adjusted. A good method to adjust the laser is to observe the laser spectrum with a scanning Fabry–Perot interferometer. The laser is being correctly adjusted when the laser profile exhibits single mode operation, that is a single feature without additional laser modes.

Problem: Plot the laser frequency distribution that returns to the laser cavity in the Littrow configuration. Hint: fix the angle and change the wavelength. Consider a grating with $N = 1800$ lines per mm an $\lambda_0 = 671$ nm and $d = 0.556\ \mu$ m. Figure 5.2 shows the grating function. The net gain is given by the product of the cavity functions. The grating profile is calculated as a function of the wavelength for given data. To set the laser operating frequency it is necessary to adjust the laser cavity parameters to obtain the highest net gain. Figure 5.2 shows the contributions to the net gain. We considered a grating with 1800 grooves per mm, illuminating 9000 grooves. The length of the external cavity is 1 cm, the length of the diode 0.4 mm and refraction index $n = 3.7$ giving an internal cavity effective length of 1.48 mm.

5.2 Principles of operation of the grazing-incidence grating diode laser cavity

The grazing-incidence grating diode laser cavity also known as the Littman–Metcalf cavity [3–7] has the advantage of a broad bandwidth and a narrow linewidth. The laser is broadly tunable over a large frequency range. The disadvantage is that its construction is more difficult than the Littrow cavity. The original resonators were an adaptation of dye laser designs. A modified Littman–Metcalf laser cavity by New Focus is shown in figure 5.3. The design adapted the cavity to the diode laser gain medium.

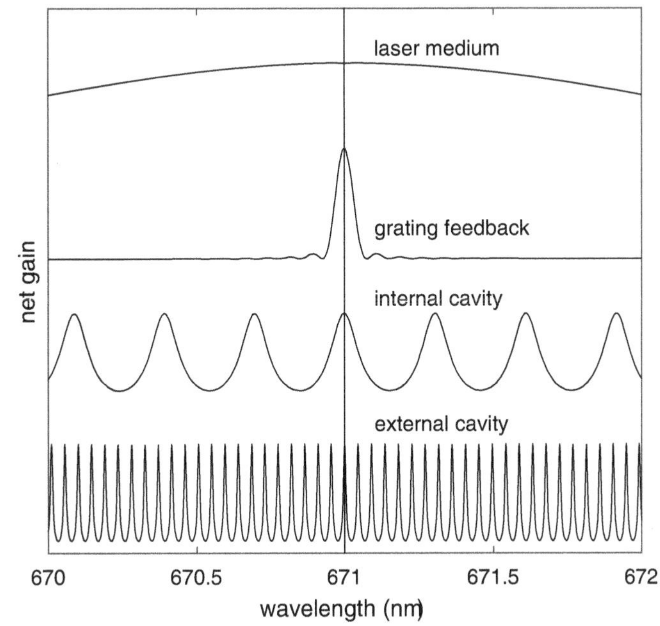

Figure 5.2. Gain functions.

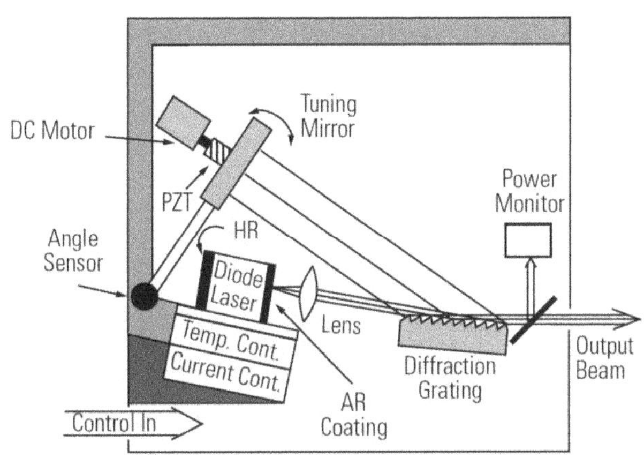

Figure 5.3. Laser focus cavity.

The cavity consisting of a high-reflection coating on one end of the diode laser forms one end of the cavity and a highly reflective tuning mirror forms the other. Starting from the diode, the beam in the cavity passes through a collimating lens and then strikes a diffraction grating at near grazing incidence. The beam is diffracted toward the tuning mirror which reflects the light back on itself for the reverse path. Part of the light from the diode is reflected, not diffracted, by the grating. This portion forms the output beam. The grating functions as a narrow spectral filter. Its passband is only a few gigahertz wide. The high wavelength selectivity results because many lines of the grating are illuminated by the grazing-incidence beam and because the beam is diffracted by the grating twice in each round trip through the cavity. The grating spectral filter is narrow enough to force the laser to operate on only a single longitudinal mode. Different wavelengths diffract off the grating at different angles. However, only one wavelength leaves the grating in a direction that is exactly perpendicular to the surface of the tuning mirror closing the resonant laser cavity. It follows that we can tune the laser by changing the angle of the tuning mirror. In order to maintain resonance on the same mode as we tune the laser, the number of waves in the cavity must be kept constant (even though the wavelength of the light in the cavity is changing). The number of waves in the cavity is maintained by having the tuning mirror rotate around a specific pivot point. The pivot point creates a relationship between the cavity length and the laser wavelength. The laser wavelength is set by the standard law for diffraction of light off a grating: where d is the spacing between grooves in the grating while θ_i and θ_D refer to the incident and diffracted angles of the laser beam measured from a line normal to the surface of the grating. The length, L, of the cavity can be broken into two parts l_1 and l_2 (see figure 5.4). If we call the distance from the pivot point to the place where the beam strikes the grating L, we can see from the figure that: $l_1 = L \sin\theta_i$ and, $l_2 = L \sin\theta_d$. Therefore, the total cavity length is $L(\sin\theta_i + \sin\theta_d)$. Dividing the total cavity length by the wavelength, shows that the total number of waves in the cavity is L/Λ which is a constant. By designing a mechanical system where this condition is maintained over the tuning range of the laser, the cavity can tune mode hop-free over extended wavelength ranges. In the next section we will show how the theory is put into practice by describing the components of the New Focus 6700 series laser system.

Problem: Calculate the optical path inside the cavity. Hint: write the grating equation. Therefore, the total cavity length is

$$s_1 + s_2 = L\sin\theta_i + L\sin\theta_d \tag{5.3}$$

$$\lambda = \Lambda(\sin\theta_i + \sin\theta_d) \tag{5.4}$$

Dividing the total cavity length by the wavelength, shows that the total number of waves in the cavity is

$$N = L/\Lambda \tag{5.5}$$

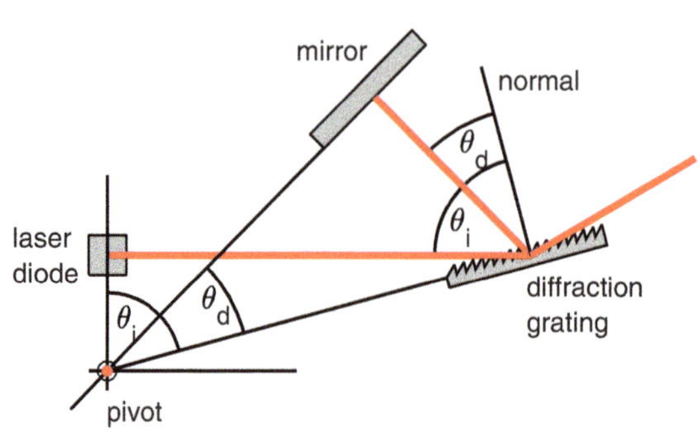

Figure 5.4. Littman–Metcalf diode laser cavity.

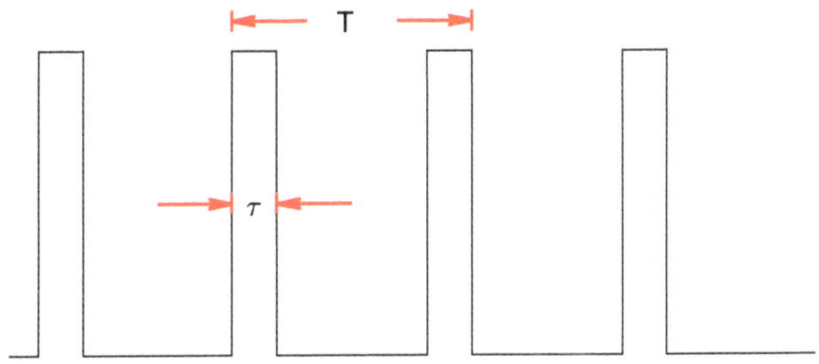

Figure 5.5. Nd:YAG laser train pulses.

which is a constant. By designing a mechanical system where this condition is maintained over the tuning range of the laser, the cavity can tune mode hop-free over extended wavelength ranges.

5.3 Nd:YAG laser

5.3.1 Pulse description

Figure 5.5 shows the a schematics of the pulse train of a Nd:YAG laser.

The average power is the energy of a single pulse times the number of pulses in one second

$$\langle P\rangle = \frac{E}{T} \tag{5.6}$$

where E is the energy per pulse and T the period. For example, if the average power is 15 W, and the laser repetition rate is 5 kHz, we have that $E = 3$ mJ. If the pulse length is $\tau = 100$ ns we have that the peak power is

$$P_{\text{peak}} = \frac{E}{\tau} = \frac{\langle P\rangle T}{\tau} = 30 \text{ kW} \tag{5.7}$$

After doubling the laser to green at 532 nm the average power is typically 2 W and the peak power becomes 4 kW. The laser is doubled intracavity with a KT*P crystal. Afterwards, the green laser was doubled to 266 nm and the typical average power was 200 mW. The peak power of ultraviolet laser light at 266 nm is typically near 400 W.

References

[1] Camparo J C 1985 The diode laser in atomic physics *Contemp. Phys.* **26** 443–77

[2] Wieman C E and Hollberg L 1991 Using diode lasers for atomic physics *Rev. Sci. Instrum.* **62** 1–20

[3] Littman M G and Metcalf H J 1978 Spectrally narrow pulsed dye laser without beam expander *Appl. Opt.* **17** 2224–7

[4] Littman M G 1978 Single-mode operation of grazing-incidence pulsed dye laser *Opt. Lett.* **3** 138–40

[5] Greenhalgh D A and Sarkies P H 1982 Novel geometry for simple accurate tuning of lasers *Appl. Opt.* **21** 3234–6

[6] Harvey K C and Myatt C J 1991 External-cavity diode laser using a grazing-incidence diffraction grating *Opt. Lett.* **16** 910–2

[7] Day T, Luecke F and Brownell M 1993 Continuously tunable diode lasers *Lasers Optronics* **12** 15–8

Ignacio E Olivares and Patrick Carrazana

Chapter 6

Lithium Doppler-free absorption spectroscopy

In this chapter we show the study of the spectra of the $2s$–$2p$ lithium transitions in an atomic-lithium vapor–argon-gas mixture by a Doppler-free saturation amplitude modulation spectroscopy technique. The spectroscopy was carried out with a tunable diode laser. Highly resolved Lamb dips and crossover signals are shown. The experimental Doppler-free spectra were used in conjunction with a density matrix method to yield parameters of spectroscopic interest. These parameters include line broadening and relaxation rates that are due to collisions between isotopic species and argon atoms. In addition, Doppler-limited spectra were used to determine density, concentration, and temperature of the lithium isotopes.

6.1 Introduction

In recent years there has been considerable interest in lithium spectroscopy [1–8]. Studies of Li isotopes by dye laser-based Doppler-free spectroscopy have been published [7, 8]. The availability of semiconductor lasers has considerably facilitated experiments in the field of atomic laser spectroscopy because such lasers offer stable narrow-linewidth emission, excellent tunability, and compactness [9–12]. Specifically, today's diode lasers have linewidths 1000 times smaller than the Doppler width of atomic transitions. Also, diode lasers are stable in the frequency and power domains and can be tuned by electrical, thermal, and optical means [11, 12]. Additionally, because of their compactness and reliability they can substitute for more complicated coherent sources, such as ring dye lasers, especially in applications that require relatively low power. We have recorded and studied Doppler-free and Doppler-limited spectra of Li isotopes by using diode laser-based instrumentation. The diode-laser-generated spectra were recorded as a function of ^{6}Li density, argon pressure, and laser intensity. In particular, we recorded the Doppler-free spectra of the ^{6}Li-D_2 line and resolved its hyperfine structure. We chose this transition of ^{6}Li for

doi:10.1088/978-0-7503-3839-4ch6

study because of the apparent lack of published material on its characteristics and because it represents an intermediate case of difficulty for our experimental facility. To describe the dynamics of atomic excitation under the influence of radiation and collisional processes in the case of narrow laser linewidth and high spectral intensity it is necessary to use the density matrix formalism [13, 14]. We have developed a density matrix approach to describe the Doppler-free and Doppler-limited spectra of Li. The theory is used in conjunction with a numerical method that considers all the sublevels of the hyperfine structure of the Li $2s$–$2p$ transition and the optical pumping and relaxation processes. The hyperfine structure of the ^{6}Li-D_2 line recorded experimentally was successfully matched theoretically by our density matrix approach. We describe the excitation-relaxation dynamics for the special case of ^{6}Li and derive the parameters of experimental interest such as density, concentration, temperature, line broadening, and relaxation rates that result from velocity-changing collisions.

6.2 Experiment

We measured Doppler-limited lines for the $2s$–$2p$ absorption in an Ar-embedded stationary Li vapor produced in a heat-pipe cell. The heat-pipe technology was described previously [15, 16]. This cell permits the heating of Li to 700 °C. The cell should be purged initially and be held at a pressure of 2–3 Torr of Ar, which is used as a buffer gas to avoid deposition of Li onto the windows. The cell includes a Li collection system for reutilization of the Li condensed in the cold regions. The main feature of the heat-pipe oven is that it allows one to obtain an isothermal vapor with constant density and clean windows for absorption measurements. For excitation with narrow-band laser emission we used a cw external-cavity tunable diode laser with a central wavelength of 671 nm, tunable over 12 nm with a power of 6 mW. It has a linewidth of <5 MHz and a wavelength stability of <0.01 nm day^{-1}. The cavity uses a grazing-incidence configuration. The design of the laser cavity includes an external grating that acts as a narrow spectral filter and forces the laser to operate in a single longitudinal mode. We can fine tune the wavelengths by changing the grating angle with a piezoelectric transducer. The center wavelength can also be achieved by control of current, temperature, or both and by picometer setting of the diode laser. Unwanted background radiation is produced by laboratory light and the side modes of the diode laser. The side mode suppression is ~40 dB, and we measured a 3% background compared with that of the unabsorbed signal. We subtracted the background for all the spectra. The laser beam was aligned through the Li vapor and detected by a photodiode and a 400 MHz digital storage oscilloscope. We scanned the spectra by rotating the grating. We measured the wavelengths with a wavemeter. The saturation intensity for the ^{6}Li-D_2 line is obtained when $S_0 = 1$, and in our experiments $\Gamma = 5 \times 10^7$ s^{-1} and $I_s = 206$ W m^{-2}. Based on the fact that the diode laser used in our experiment has a high spectral intensity, we also performed saturation spectroscopy studies. Figure 6.1 depicts the experimental setup.

We scanned the Doppler-free spectra with the diode laser over the D_2 line of ^{6}Li in the heat-pipe oven with the modulated amplitude technique, using a lock-in

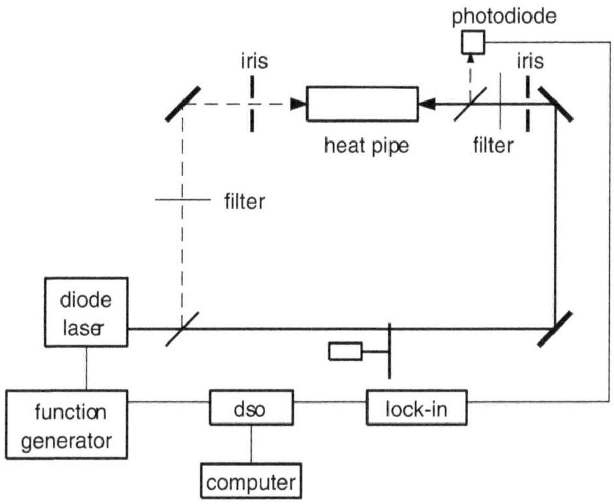

Figure 6.1. Experimental setup for laser spectroscopy of lithium isotopes. Reproduced from Olivares *et al* [17].

amplifier. In the Doppler-limited experiment the lock-in technique was not used. For all experiments we used 95% enriched ^{6}Li. We experimentally removed the broad background of the Doppler-limited profile by using the lock-in technique. The spectra were measured for different Ar pressures and different values for the pump beam I_p. To scan the spectra we used a function generator. We also employed a low scanning frequency (0.1 Hz) to maximize the resolution and to minimize the *RC* distortion and the noise of the spectra. The heat-pipe oven was kept at a low enough temperature (375 °C) to yield high transmittance ($\simeq$0.8) and low density ($n = 5 \times 10^9 \text{cm}^{-3}$), which minimize the effect of radiation trapping and simplify the calculation by producing relatively constant values of I along the heat-pipe oven. Pump intensity I_p was modulated with a chopper at 1046 Hz. With lower frequencies the noise increases, and at high frequencies the populations do not reach steady state during every cycle. The probe beam intensity I_d was 0.8 W m^{-2}. It is convenient to use a low probe intensity to minimize the broadening and the dependence of the spectra on I_d that can be detected with the photodiode without causing its saturation. In this case the intensity Ip should high enough to be above the noise level. The lock-in amplifier was used with time constants low enough to avoid *RC* distortion but high enough to avoid excessive noise. The laser beam was directed into the heat-pipe oven through a 2 mm circular aperture. The power was measured with a powermeter (Newport Model 1815C/818SL) at the exit of the apertures.

6.3 Results

Typical Doppler-limited absorption spectra are shown in figure 6.2.

In addition, spectra of the further cases involving large optical depth are also of interest and are shown in figure 6.3. The circles in these figures represent experimental points, and the curves are theoretical fits from equation (2.40).

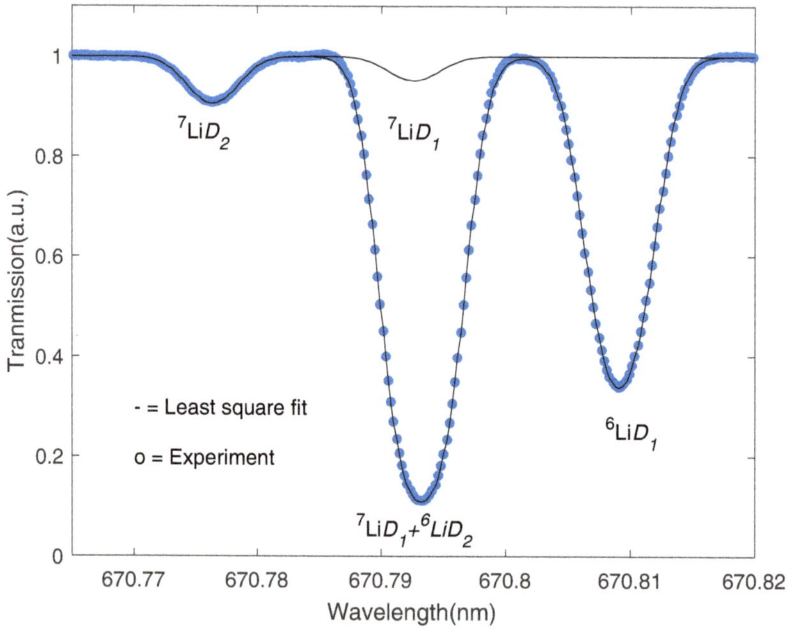

Figure 6.2. Doppler-limited Li lines. Experimental and least square fits for ^{7}Li only and for the sum of ^{6}Li and ^{7}Li. $n(^{7}\text{Li}) = 1.9 \times 10^{9}\ \text{cm}^{-3}$, $n(^{6}\text{Li}) = 4.6 \times 10^{10}\ \text{cm}^{-3}$, $T = 408$ °C, ^{7}Li(4.1%). Reproduced from Olivares *et al* [17].

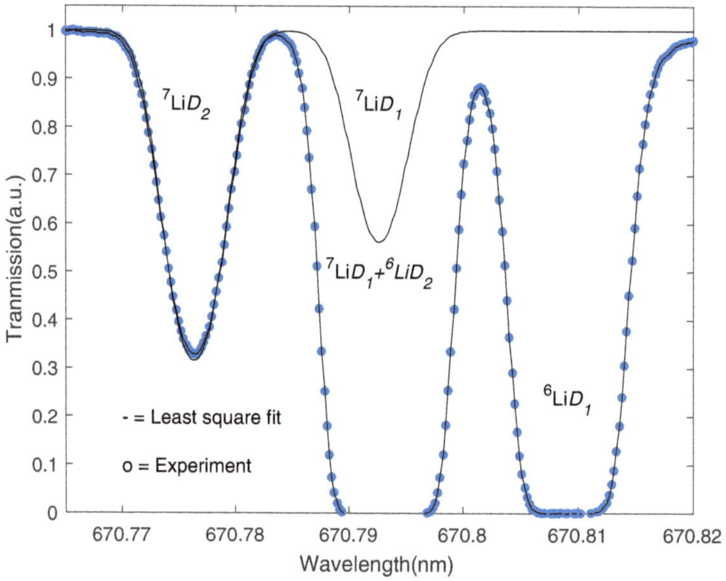

Figure 6.3. Optically thick Doppler-limited Li lines. Experimental and least square fits for ^{7}Li only and for the sum of ^{6}Li and ^{7}Li. $n(^{7}\text{Li}) = 2.5 \times 10^{10}\ \text{cm}^{-3}$, $n(^{6}\text{Li}) = 4.3 \times 10^{11}\ \text{cm}^{-3}$, $T = 549$ °C. Reproduced from Olivares *et al* [17].

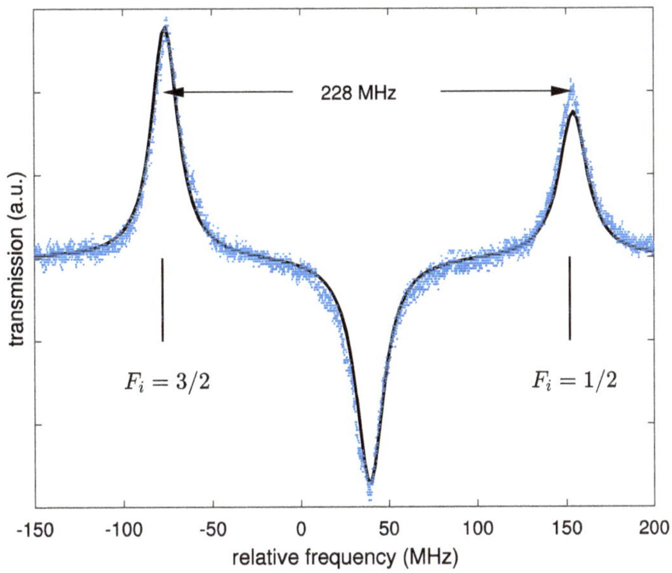

Figure 6.4. ^{6}Li Doppler-free spectrum at low Ar buffer pressure: $P_{Ar} = 0.0018$ Torr, $I_P = 21$ W m^{-2}, n(Li) = 5×10^9 cm^{-3}, $T = 375$ °C. Result of the fitting: $\Gamma = 5.9 \times 10^7$ s^{-1}, $\gamma_{vc} = 4.5 \times 10^6$ s^{-1}. Reproduced from Olivares *et al* [17].

A typical Doppler-free spectrum for the ^{6}Li-D_2 line at low Ar pressure is shown in figure 6.4.

We can observe a crossover signal in this figure at the center of the trace caused by double resonance. The right and left peak lines correspond to the transitions $2s(F = 1/2) - 2p$ and $2s(F = 3/2) - 2p$ hyperfine lines, respectively, separated by 228 MHz [7, 18]. This experimental spectrum shows excellent resolution of the hyperfine structure and is fairly well fitted by our density matrix model. The negative crossover signal is caused when the probe beam is tuned to one of the two transitions of the D_2 line with a common upper level, and the pump beam is tuned to the other. In our case the pump beam tuned to one transition causes an increase in the common upper level that decays to the lower level of the other transition, increasing the population on this level. The second wave (diagnostic beam) is probed on this transition with an increase in the absorption. The effect occurs simultaneously for the two resonant rate groups with equal velocity but opposite direction. The crossover frequency is just halfway between the two hyperfine Lamb dips. In this case the competition between optical pumping and collisional relaxation determines the size of the crossover dip. In the case of low pressure, optical pumping dominates and we have a negative crossover signal. In the case of high Ar pressure the collision process that produces relaxation from the lower filled state to the other lower level (the opposite velocity group) causes an increase of transmission, reducing the crossover signal. This result is shown in figure 6.5 for total reduction.

We obtained from the results of a least-squares fit the values for homogeneous broadening Γ, and the relaxation velocity that is due to the VCC γ_{vc} of the ground state, as a function of the Ar pressure (figure 6.6 and 6.7, respectively).

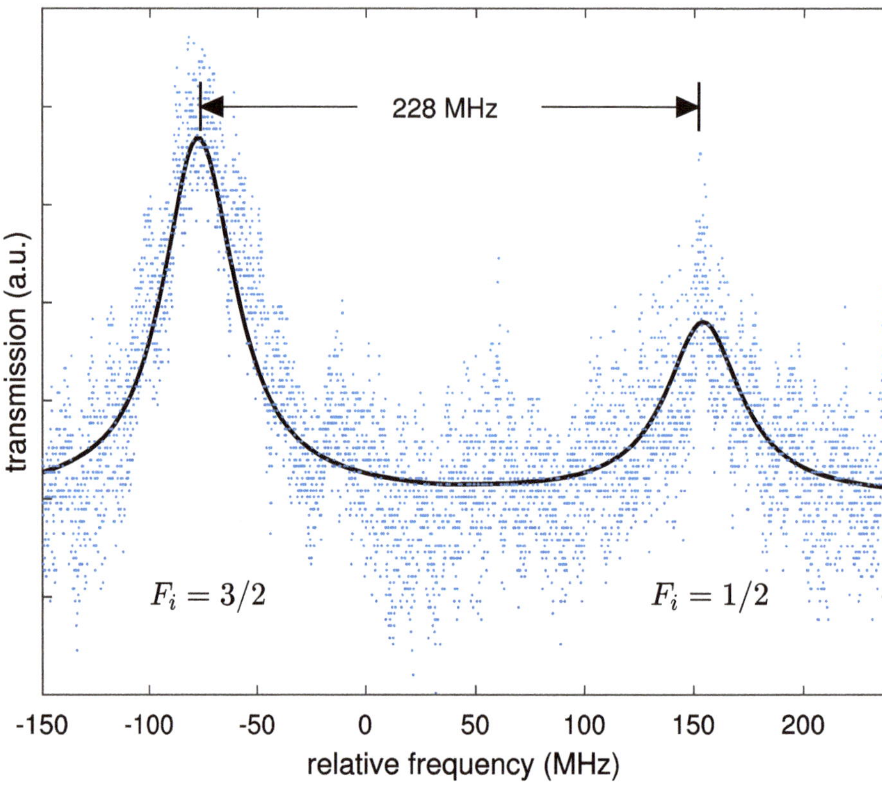

Figure 6.5. ^{6}Li Doppler-free spectrum at high Ar buffer pressure: $P_{\mathrm{Ar}} = 4.46$ Torr, $I_P = 79$ W m^{-2}, $n(\mathrm{Li}) = 5 \times 10^9$ cm^{-3} $T = 375$ °C. Result of the fitting: $\Gamma = 1.5 \times 10^8$ s^{-1}, $\gamma_{\mathrm{vc}} = 2.5 \times 10^7$ s^{-1}. Reproduced from Olivares *et al* [17].

Our model is more accurate at low pressures. At higher pressures a more detailed treatment of the VCC is required [8]. To obtain useful information we calculated the slope as the pressure tends to zero, as this is the case in which the collisional effects behave best. Thus from figure 6.6 we obtain

$$\mathrm{d}\Gamma_\omega = 2.5 \times 10^7 s^{-1}/\mathrm{Torr} \tag{6.1}$$

Thus the collisional broadening FWHM is

$$\mathrm{d}\Delta\nu/\mathrm{d}P/\pi = 8.0\ \mathrm{MHz\ Torr}^{-1} \tag{6.2}$$

at our experimental conditions at 648 K. Inasmuch as the collisional broadening is proportional to $T^{-7/10}$ [19], we rescale our results to 14 MHz Torr^{-1} at 300 K. The value given in the literature is 12 MHz Torr^{-1} [20]. From figure 6.7, the change in the relaxation rate that is due to VCC by the Ar pressure is given by

$$\mathrm{d}\gamma_{\mathrm{vc}}/\mathrm{d}P = 3.2 \times 10^7 s^{-1}\ \mathrm{Torr}^{-1} = 3.3 \times 10^5 s^{-1}\ \mathrm{Pa}^{-1} \tag{6.3}$$

We have that $\gamma_{\mathrm{vc}} = \sigma_{\mathrm{vc}} v_{\mathrm{rel}} n$ and $v_{\mathrm{rel}} = (8k_{\mathrm{B}}T/\pi\mu)^{1/2}$, where $\mu = 8.66 \times 10^{-27}$ kg is the reduced mass for the Li–Ar system. We obtained $\sigma_{\mathrm{vc}} = 1.8 \times 10^{-14}$ cm^2, the range of

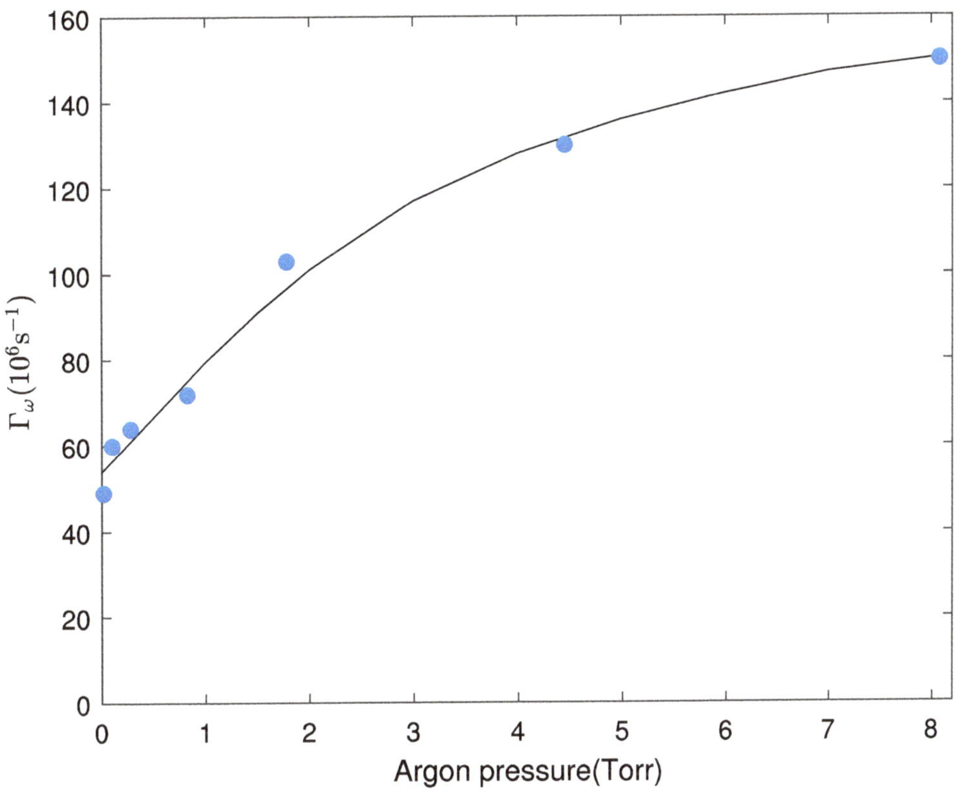

Figure 6.6. Γ_ω versus Ar pressure obtained from fitting of the Doppler-free spectra and extrapolating to $I_p = 0$. Here $\Gamma_\omega = \pi\Gamma$. Reproduced from Olivares *et al* [17].

which from the literature [8] is 1.01–2.4 × 10^{-14} cm^2. For low Ar pressures Γ is given only by natural broadening, transit-time broadening, laser broadening, collisions between Li atoms, and less important relaxation mechanisms not considered here. We obtained values for the transmittance at the center of the D_2 line for ^{6}Li starting from the Doppler-limited spectra discussed above; we show them in figure 6.8.

For each pressure we obtained the expected values for Γ and γ_{vc} by interpolating the curves in figure 6.6 and 6.7. With these values of Γ and γ_{vc} we calculated the transmittance versus intensity curve for each pressure starting from equation (2.43) in the steady state. The value for nx can be obtained from the Doppler-limited absorption measurements described in section 6.2. Figure 6.8 shows good agreement between theoretical and experimental curves; thus the technique to estimate Γ and γ_{vc} is shown to be satisfactory.

6.4 Conclusion

We have measured and resolved the hyperfine structure of the D_2 ^{6}Li line. We also investigated the relaxation processes and applied a numerical technique to study the effect of the vapor conditions on the Doppler-free absorption spectra. These conditions include density, alkali vapor pressure, buffer gas pressure, temperature,

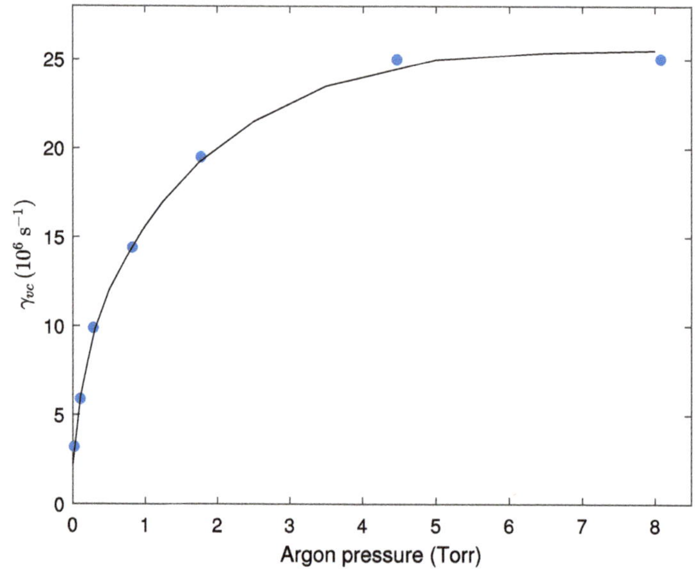

Figure 6.7. γ_{vc} versus Ar pressure obtained from fitting of the Doppler-free spectra and extrapolating to $I_p = 0$. Reproduced from Olivares *et al* [17].

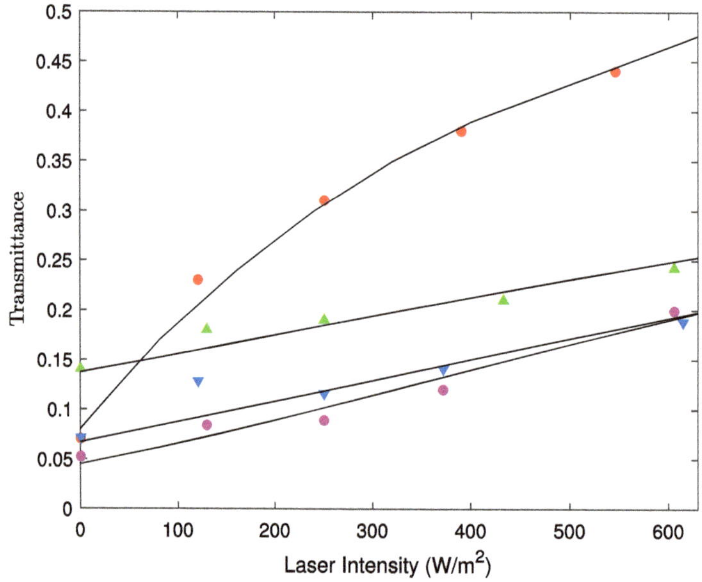

Figure 6.8. Comparison of experimental and theoretical transmittance curves versus laser intensity (calculated starting from the Doppler-free spectra). Line theory, red circles $P = 0.01$ Torr: $\Gamma_\omega = 5.4 \times 10^7$ s^{-1}, $\gamma_{vc} = 2.9\times 10^6$ s^{-1}, magenta circles $P = 0.35$ Torr: $\Gamma_\omega = 6.3 \times 10^7$ s^{-1}, $\gamma_{vc} = 1.0 \times 10^7$ s^{-1}, blue triangles $P = 0.93$ Torr: $\Gamma_\omega = 7.8 \times 10^7$ s^{-1}, $\gamma_{vc} = 1.5 \times 10^7$ s^{-1}, green triangles $P = 2.85$ Torr: $\Gamma_\omega = 1.1\times 10^8$ s^{-1}, $\gamma_{vc} = 2.2 \times 10^7$ s^{-1}. $\Gamma_\omega = \pi\Gamma$. Reproduced from Olivares *et al* [17].

and diode-laser intensity. We found excellent agreement between a theoretical absorption expression derived by density matrix methods and the experimental data of the Doppler-free lines. The method described in this paper is fairly simple; however, the theoretical results depend on secondary calculations, which can be a source of uncertainty. The results reported here further demonstrate that state-of-the art diode lasers are powerful experimental tools for a variety of high-resolution and high-sensitivity laser spectroscopy. We applied these results to derive parameters of spectroscopic interest, such as the line broadening and the relaxation rates that are due to collisions between isotopic species with Ar atoms.

References

[1] Dinklage A, Lokajczyk T, Kunze H J, Schweer B and Olivares I E 1998 In situ density measurement for a thermal lithium beam employing diode lasers *Rev. Sci. Instrum.* **69** 321–2

[2] Brust J, Veza D, Movre M and Niemax K 1995 Collisional excitation transfer between lithium isotopes *Z. Phys. D.* **85** 355–9

[3] Boshier M, Berkeland D, Hinds E and Sandoghdar V 1991 External-cavity frequency-stabilization of visible and infrared semiconductor lasers for high resolution spectroscopy *Opt. Commun.* **85** 355–9

[4] Weidemüller M, Gabbanini C, Hare J, Gross M and Haroche S 1993 A beam of laser-cooled lithium Rydberg atoms for precision microwave spectroscopy *Opt. Commun.* **101** 342–6

[5] Atutov S, Mariotti E, Meucci M, Bicchi P, Marinelli C and Moi L 1994 A 670 nm external-cavity single mode diode laser continuously tunable over 18 GHz range *Opt. Commun.* **107** 83–7

[6] Chen J, Story J G, Tollett J J and Hulet R G 1992 Adiabatic cooling of atoms by an intense standing wave *Phys. Rev. Lett.* **69** 1344

[7] Sansonetti C J, Richou B, Engleman R Jr and Radziemski L J 1995 Measurements of the resonance lines of Li 6 and Li 7 by Doppler-free frequency-modulation spectroscopy *Phys. Rev.* A **48** 2682

[8] Shimkaveg G, Quivers W Jr, Dasari R and Feld M 1993 Direct measurement of velocity-changing collision cross sections by laser optical pumping *Phys. Rev.* A **48** 1049

[9] Wieman C E and Hollberg L 1991 Using diode lasers for atomic physics *Rev. Sci. Instrum.* **62** 1–20

[10] Franzke J, Schnell A and Niemax K 1993 Spectroscopic properties of commercial laser diodes *Spectrochim. Acta B: At. Spectrosc.* **15** 379–95

[11] Zorabedian P 1995 Tunable external-cavity semiconductor lasers *Tunable Lasers Handbook* (New York: Academic) ch 8

[12] Duarte F J 1995 Tunable external-cavity semiconductor lasers *Tunable Lasers Handbook* (New York: Marcel-Dekker) ch 5

[13] Happer W 1972 Optical pumping *Rev. Mod. Phys.* **44** 169

[14] Loudon R 2000 *The Quantum Theory of Light* (Oxford: Oxford Science) ch 2

[15] Vidal C 1973 Spectroscopic observations of subsonic and sonic vapor flow inside an open-ended heat pipe *J. Appl. Phys.* **44** 2225–32

[16] Vidal C and Cooper J 1969 Heat-Pipe Oven: A new, well-defined metal vapor device for spectroscopic measurements *J. Appl. Phys.* **40** 3370–4

[17] Olivares I E, Duarte A E, Lokajczyk T, Dinklage A and Duarte F J 1998 Doppler-freespectroscopy and collisional studies with tunable diode lasers of lithium isotopes in aheat-pipe oven *J. Opt. Soc. Am.* B **15** 1932–9
[18] Arimondo E, Inguscio M and Violino P 1977 Experimental determinations of the hyperfine structure in the alkali atoms *Rev. Mod. Phys.* **49** 31
[19] Hurst G, Payne M, Kramer S and Young J 1979 Resonance ionization spectroscopy and one-atom detection *Rev. Mod. Phys.* **51** 767
[20] Demtröder W 2008 *Laser Spectroscopy* vol 2 (Berlin: Springer)

IOP Publishing

Techniques for Lithium Isotope Separation, Laser Cooling, and Scattering

Ignacio E Olivares and Patrick Carrazana

Chapter 7

Lithium Doppler-limited absorption spectroscopy

We study Doppler-limited laser intensity absorption in a thermal lithium vapor containing ^{7}Li and ^{6}Li atoms in a 9-to-1 ratio using a narrow-linewidth single-longitudinal-mode tunable external cavity diode laser at the wavelength of 670.8 nm. The lithium vapor was embedded in helium or argon buffer gas. The spectral lineshapes were rigorously predicted for D_1 and D_2 for the lithium 6 and 7 isotope lines using reduced optical Bloch equations derived from a density matrix analysis. Here we provide a detailed comparison of the predicted lineshapes of the measured ^{7}Li-D_2, ^{7}Li-D_1, ^{6}Li-D_2 and ^{6}Li-D_1 lines, in the case of high vapor density and with intensity above the saturation intensity. To our knowledge this is the first time that such a detailed comparison is reported in the open literature. The calculations were also extended to saturated absorption spectra and compared to measured Doppler-free ^{7}Li-D_2 and ^{6}Li-D_2 hyperfine lines. We also compare the ^{7}Li-D_2 with the ^{6}Li-D_2 lines. For better understanding of this chapter, the reader should study first chapters 2 and 6.

7.1 Introduction

In the last few decades several new spectroscopic techniques have been developed to study the absorption in neutral vapors utilizing tunable diode lasers. Those include saturated and Doppler-limited absorption spectroscopy, polarization spectroscopy, multiphoton spectroscopy, saturated interference spectroscopy, and heterodyne polarization spectroscopy. Doppler-free and Doppler-limited spectroscopy demands knowledge of the hyperfine structure and the use of density matrix equations. In this regard, the absolute Doppler-broadened absorption by rubidium atoms has been studied theoretically and experimentally for atoms below the saturation intensity [1, 2].

Doppler-free and Doppler-limited lineshape calculations have been performed in detail using density matrix equations only for ^{6}Li-D_2 in [3]. We were able to model,

doi:10.1088/978-0-7503-3839-4ch7

using a two-level approximation only the Doppler-limited spectra of the lines ^{6}Li-D_1, ^{7}Li-D_2, and ^{7}Li-D_1. The Doppler-free spectra cannot be obtained by the same approximation. In this work we extended the analysis to these lithium lines in detail using rate equations that include all the multiplets. Reduced optical Bloch equations for the Zeeman multiplets were obtained starting from Zeeman ^{6}Li-D_2 magnetic sublevels [3] considering the effect of collisions with buffer gas atoms. The method was also extended to the case of ^{85}Rb-D_2 line and was used to calculate the lineshapes in a collisionless rubidium vapor with intensities above saturation [4]. In a previous work, the atom density in lithium beams was studied at low laser intensities [5]. The atom density determination of a given substance requires a carefully selection of the laser conditions such as laser intensity, beam size and shape, and center wavelength in a mode hop free region. Well resolved spectra can be obtained at laser intensities higher than the saturation intensity, where the density determination has to consider the measurement of the laser intensity. At low laser intensities the transmission remains constant and it is possible to obtain absolute measurements without considering laser intensity. In this case, the signal-to-noise ratio of the absorption spectra decreases.

Here, we provide a new set of detailed equations for the absorption of a narrow-linewidth tunable diode laser at the Doppler-broadened ^{7}Li-D_2, ^{7}Li-D_1, ^{6}Li-D_2, and ^{6}Li-D_1 isotopic transitions and verify the validity of these equations with spectral measurements obtained at relative high lithium density and laser intensity above the saturation intensity which is typically 10 W m^{-2}. The absorption equations were also extended to the Doppler-free case and compared to the measured Doppler-free ^{6}Li-D_2 and ^{7}Li-D_2 hyperfine lines with excellent results. The technique described here can also be applied to provide practical and useful equations needed for the description of various other atomic physics experiments such as laser-cooling experiments [6], electromagnetically induced transparency [7], resonance ionization spectroscopy [8], and laser isotope separation [9–11] studies. Absolute absorption spectroscopy can yield the number density of the sample being studied and has many applications in physics, laser and plasma spectroscopy, chemistry, metallurgy, and industry [12–14]. The technique is independent of the absolute intensity measurement at low laser intensities, where the experimental effort should consider the noise suppression or phase sensitive method to increase the signal-to-noise ratio. At higher intensities, where signals are strong and the spectra more defined, it is necessary to consider the absolute measurement of the incident intensity as the transmission depends on the intensity, and the model should account for this intensity dependence. At high vapor pressure it is necessary to use high laser intensity to obtain the transmitted signal.

7.2 Background

The angular momentum for different lithium lines are given in table 7.1 [15, 16], I is the nuclear spin quantum number, J is the quantum number for the electronic angular momentum, which is the sum of the orbital angular momentum L and the electron spin S.

Table 7.1. Angular momentum for different lithium lines [15, 16].

	J_i	J_f	L_i	L_f	I	s
^{7}Li-D_2	0.5	1.5	0	1	1.5	0.5
^{7}Li-D_1	0.5	0.5	0	1	1.5	0.5
^{6}Li-D_2	0.5	1.5	0	1	1	0.5
^{6}Li-D_1	0.5	0.5	0	1	1	0.5

Table 7.2. Transition probabilities for ^{7}Li-D_2 $F' = 2$, $k = 5$, $f = 13 - -17$, $F = 1$, $j = 1$ for $i = 1 - -3$ between ground states i and excited states f, the ground and excited state multiplets are labeled with i and f respectively. m file and m' column correspond to ground and excited magnetic moment of the Zeeman sublevels respectively (this work).

^{7}Li-D_2	i	1	2	3
f	m', m	−1	0	1
13	−2	1/6		
14	−1	1/12	1/12	
15	0	1/36	1/9	1/36
16	1		1/12	1/12
17	2			1/6

The transition probabilities $N_{ifq} = \left| \langle i \mid D_q \mid f \rangle \right|^2 / \| D \|^2$ were calculated in this work for the ^{7}Li-D_2, ^{7}Li-D_1, ^{6}Li-D_2, and ^{6}Li-D_1 hyperfine lines. Here, $\left| \langle i \mid D_q \mid f \rangle \right|^2$ is the matrix element for the dipole moment [3, 4, 17] between the ground states i and the excited states f, $\| D \|^2$ is the reduced dipole matrix element [3], $q = -1, 0, +1$, corresponds to transitions with left circular, linear and right circular polarization respectively when $m' - m = -1, 0, +1$, m and m' are the magnetic moment of the Zeeman sublevels of the ground and excited states respectively. An example for transition probabilities between the ground states $i = 1$–3 corresponding to the ground state multiplet labeled $j = 1$ with total angular momentum $F = 1$, and the excited states $f = 13 - -17$ corresponding to the excited state mutiplet labeled $k = 5$ with $F' = 2$ of the hyperfine lines is shown in tables 7.2, 7.3 and 7.4.

7.3 Experiment

The narrow-linewidth emission is provided by a diffraction grating-tuned external cavity diode laser utilizing a Littman–Metcalf configuration [12, 13] and yielding a linewidth of 100 kHz. The single-transverse-mode, and single-longitudinal-mode, laser emission was directed through a heat-pipe cell (Comstock, Model HP-802) containing a lithium vapor with a total path length inside the vapor of 0.1 m. The temperature was measured by a thermocouple. The heat-pipe cell was evacuated to approximately 13 mPa and filled with a buffer helium gas to avoid lithium vapor

Table 7.3. Reduced transition probabilities N_{j-k} and normalized reduced coefficient a_{j-k}/γ for spontaneous emission.

	j	k	F_j	F_k	N_{j-k}	g_j	g_k	a_{j-k}/γ
^{6}Li-D_2	1	3	0.5	0.5	16/81	2	2	8/9
	1	4	0.5	1.5	20/81	2	4	5/9
	2	3	1.5	0.5	2/81	4	2	1/9
	2	4	1.5	1.5	16/81	4	4	4/9
	2	5	1.5	2.5	2/3	4	6	1
^{6}Li-D_1	1	3	0.5	0.5	2/81	2	2	1/9
	1	4	0.5	1.5	16/81	2	4	4/9
	2	3	1.5	0.5	16/81	4	2	8/9
	2	4	1.5	1.5	20/81	4	4	5/9
^{7}Li-D_2	1	3	1	0	1/9	3	1	1
	1	4	1	1	5/18	3	3	5/6
	1	5	1	2	5/18	3	5	1/2
	2	4	2	1	1/18	5	3	1/6
	2	5	2	2	5/18	5	5	1/2
	2	6	2	3	7/9	5	7	1
^{7}Li-D_1	1	3	1	1	1/18	3	3	1/6
	1	4	1	2	5/18	3	5	1/2
	2	3	2	1	5/18	5	3	5/6
	2	4	2	2	5/18	5	5	1/2

Table 7.4. $F' = 2$ to $F = 2$ transition.

	$F' = 2$					
$F = 2$	j	16	17	18	19	20
i	m/m'	−2	−1	0	1	2
1	−2	14/81	7/81			
2	−1	7/81	7/162	7/54		
3	0		7/54	0	7/54	
4	1			7/54	7/162	7/81
5	2				7/81	14/81

condensation on the heat-pipe windows. Alternatively we used argon as a buffer gas. In the Doppler-limited experiment the laser beam diameter was reduced to 2.4 mm prior to entrance to the heat-pipe. The incident laser power measured with an optical power meter was 2.4 mW and the calculated intensity was 530 W m^{-2}. After passing the heat-pipe cell the beam passed an iris diaphragm with a 2.4 mm diameter. We adjusted the beam direction to ensure maximal signal into the photodiode. The transmitted light was detected with a high speed Si detector. The active area of the detector was 0.8 mm^2, with a 1.0 mm diameter.

The experimental setup of the Doppler-free absorption experiment is depicted in figure 7.1. The diode laser was slowly scanned close to the resonance using a function generator. A strong pump beam (red line) is driven in the opposite direction to the weak diagnostic beam (blue line). Both beams are derived from the same laser and therefore have the same frequency. The pump beam amplitude was modulated with an optical chopper with typical chopping frequencies of 2079 Hz for the ^{7}Li-D_2 line and 1046 Hz for the ^{6}Li-D_2 line. We used a 60 slot disc. A lock-in amplifier was used to remove the background and obtain a Doppler-free absorption signal. The atoms in the heat-pipe have two ground states (separated by the hyperfine interaction) and a set of closely separated excited states. Our Doppler-free absorption signal consists of two ordinary saturated peaks at the two resonance frequencies of the ground states separated by less than the Doppler width, and a middle peak (cross-over), which is at the average frequency value of the two resonance frequencies. In the case of the Doppler-limited absorption experiment the pump beam was blocked and we did not use the lock-in amplifier.

To obtain the absorption spectrum we measured the photodiode signal first with the heat-pipe cell temperature at 450 °C. Simultaneously we measured the voltage ramp of the laser piezo and the Fabry–Perot signal. We let the heat-pipe cool down to 268 °C and measured the transmission with negligible lithium vapor inside the cell when no absorption was observed. This signal was considered as the baseline of the absorption spectrum and was measured simultaneously with the voltage piezo ramp and the interferometer signal. The shape of the baseline is produced by the interference due to the heat-pipe sapphire windows (MDC-Vacuum, Mod. 450002) with 2.7 mm thickness and refraction index approximately n = 1.76 and corresponds to the transmission profile of an etalon with nearly 37 GHz free spectral range. The baseline and the absorption curve have a small slope due to the increasing laser power.

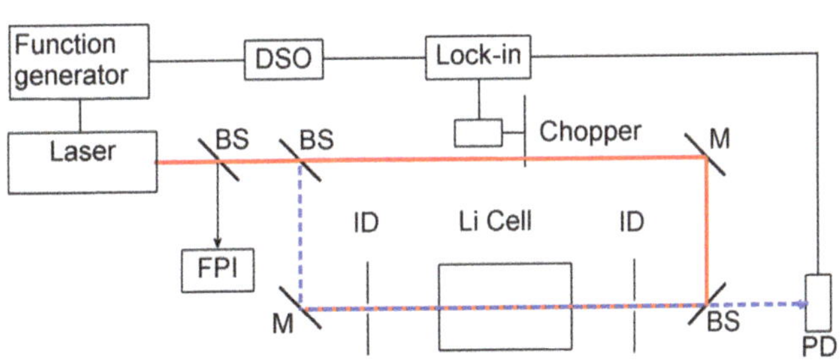

Figure 7.1. Experimental setup of the absorption (Doppler free and Doppler limited) measurements. M is a mirror, BS a beamsplitter, ID the iris diaphragm, PD a photodiode, FPI is a Fabry–Perot interferometer, DSO is a digital storage oscilloscope. The red line corresponds to the intense pump beam and the blue line to the probe beam. Reproduced from [18], copyright (2016) with permission from Springer.

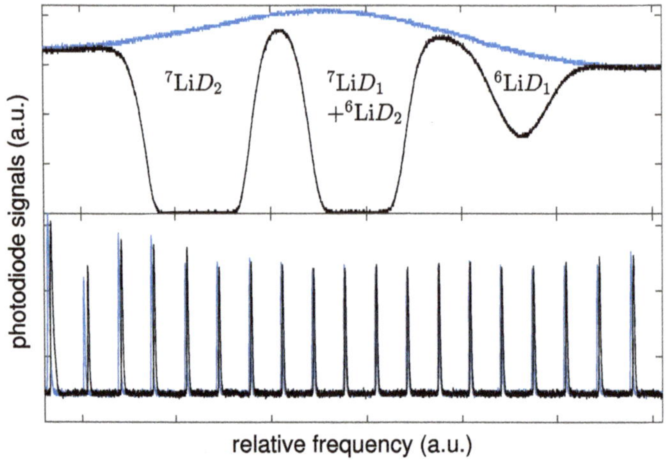

Figure 7.2. Photodiode signal in blue for absorption and in black for baseline recorded simultaneously with Fabry–Perot transmissions. The Fabry–Perot interferograms corresponding to the absorption signal and the baseline are overlapped. Reproduced from [18], copyright (2016) with permission from Springer.

As the laser was not frequency locked we recorded each absorption spectrum, scanning ramp (not shown here), and the interferometer signal simultaneously. A small drift of the baseline frequency regarding the full spectrum was observed in some cases. We corrected this small drift using the Fabry–Perot spectra as references. The absorption line and baseline measurements at 450 °C and 268 °C can be seen for example in figure 7.2. In this example the Fabry–Perot signal corresponding to the baseline and absorption spectrum are overlapped. The transmittance is obtained dividing the absorption spectrum by the baseline.

The lithium gas density and the absorption increase with temperature and depend on the buffer gas pressure. At very low buffer gas pressure the lithium gas density and the absorption diminishes as can be seen in figure 7.3. In this case the pump was extracting more gas from the heat-pipe.

7.4 Results

Figure 7.4 shows the measured transmission of the Doppler-broadened absorption spectrum of lithium isotopes and the theoretical spectrum of the complete line calculated with our new set of density matrix equations. The relative frequency scale was obtained using the values of the line center of the ^{7}Li-D_2 and ^{6}Li-D_1 spectra. The incident laser intensity was 530 W m^{-2}, the heat-pipe cell temperature was 450 °C, and the heat-pipe was filled with 533 Pa of helium as buffer gas.

The lithium density n, the homogeneous broadening Γ, and the relaxation rate due to velocity changing collisions γ_{vc} were obtained from a fit. The density obtained was $n(^7\text{Li}) = 4.6 \times 10^{17}$ m^{-3} and $n(^6\text{Li}) = 5.1 \times 10^{16}$ m^{-3} comparing our experimental spectra with the theoretical and considering abundances of the ^{7}Li and ^{6}Li isotopes in our sample as 10.0% and 90.0% respectively.

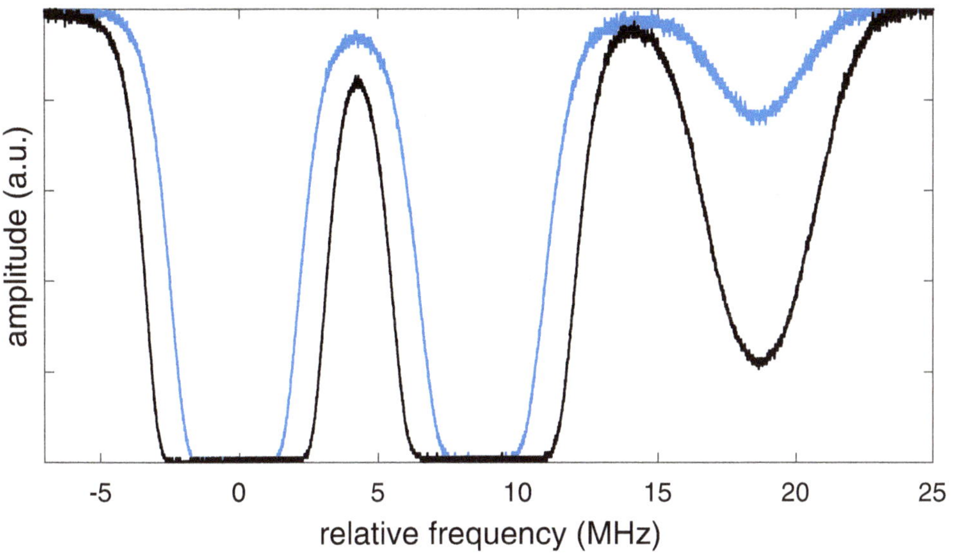

Figure 7.3. Comparison of transmittance at the same temperature (500 °C) and different He buffer gas pressure. Black line 573.3 Pa and blue line 13.3 Pa. Reproduced from [18], copyright (2016) with permission from Springer.

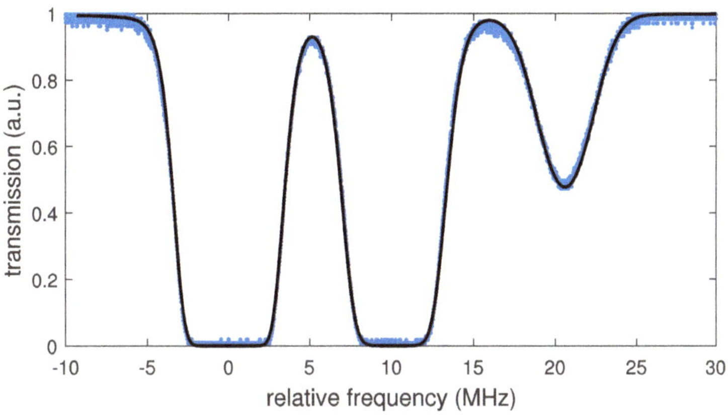

Figure 7.4. Doppler-broadened Li absorption spectrum in red and full theoretical spectrum in black. $\Gamma = 1.2 \times 10^8$, $\gamma_{vc} = 2.4 \times 10^7\ s^{-1}$, $\gamma_T = 3.9 \times 10^5\ s^{-1}$, $n(^7Li) = 4.6 \times 10^{17}\ m^{-3}$ and $n(^6Li) = 5.1 \times 10^{16}\ m^{-3}$ corresponding to the abundances of the ^{7}Li and ^{6}Li isotopes 0.90 and 0.10 respectively. The incident laser intensity was 530 W m^{-2}, the heat-pipe cell temperature was 450 °C, and the heat-pipe was filled with 533 Pa of helium as buffer gas. Reproduced from [18], copyright (2016) with permission from Springer.

In our density matrix approach by fitting the Doppler-limited spectrum we obtained the homogeneous broadening $\Gamma = 1.2 \times 10^8\ s^{-1}$ and the relaxation rate due to velocity changing collisions $\gamma_{vc} = 2.4 \times 10^7\ s^{-1}$ and $\gamma = 1/\tau$ with $\tau = 27.29$ ns the lifetime of the lithium transition, the transit time relaxation rate was $\gamma_T = 3.9 \times 10^5\ s^{-1}$ which is practically negligible compared to γ_{vc}. Thus $\gamma_B \approx 2.4 \times 10^7$. In this experiment the saturation parameter [3, 12]

$$S = \frac{1}{2}\left(1 + \frac{g_e}{g_g}\right)\frac{1}{\gamma_B\Gamma}\frac{\lambda^3 I_0}{2\pi ch\tau} \tag{7.1}$$

was 1.65, where $g_e = 1$ and $g_g = 1$ are the degeneracies of the excited and ground states respectively of the lithium 6 isotope.

The effect of the velocity changing collisions is best observed with saturated absorption spectroscopy. Nevertheless, it is possible to observe the effect of the velocity changing collisions in our Doppler-limited spectra. Inspection of figure 7.4 indicates that the theory for transmission at resonance, given in this paper (solid black line), agrees very well with the experimental data (blue dots). Figure 7.5 shows a saturation curve for the ^{6}Li-D_1 calculated with our theoretical model with $\Gamma = 1.2 \times 10^8$ s^{-1}, $\gamma_{vc} = 2.4 \times 10^7$ s^{-1}, $\gamma_T = 3.9 \times 10^5$ s^{-1} and $n(^6\text{Li}) = 5.1 \times 10^{16}$ m^{-3}. The heat-pipe cell temperature was 450 °C and the helium buffer gas pressure was 533 Pa. The saturation curve consists of the transmittance of the ^{6}Li-D_1 line at resonance as function of laser intensity, and it is shown in figure 7.5. The red asterisk shows the measured transmission which is in perfect agreement with the theoretical curve for the experimental conditions given above.

Figure 7.6 shows a typical Doppler-free spectrum for the ^{7}Li-D_2 line. The probe laser intensity was $I_0 = 30$ W m^{-2}, the pump laser intensity $I_p = 1000$ W m^{-2}, the temperature 408 °C, the argon buffer gas pressure $P_{\text{Ar}} = 33$ Pa and the cell length $L = 0.1$ m. The laser scanning frequency was 551 MHz s^{-1}. The pump laser intensity was modulated with a chopper at 2079 Hz. Comparing the theoretical with the experimental spectra we obtained from the fit of the Doppler-limited spectrum with same experimental conditions the lithium density $n(^7\text{Li}) = 2.7 \times 10^{16}$ m^{-3}, and from the fit of the Doppler-free spectrum the homogeneous broadening $\Gamma = 5.9 \times 10^7$ s^{-1},

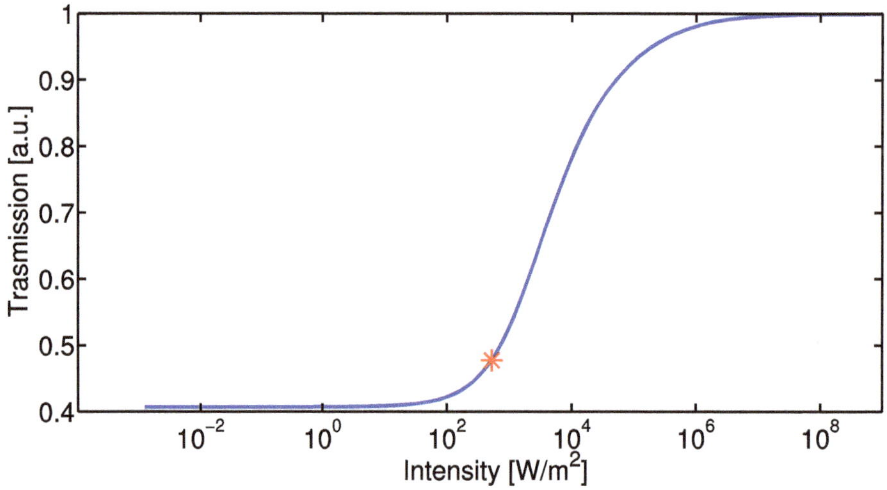

Figure 7.5. Saturation curve with $\Gamma = 1.2 \times 10^8$ s^{-1}, $\gamma_{vc} = 2.4 \times 10^7$ s^{-1}, $\gamma_T = 3.9 \times 10^5$ s^{-1} and $n(^6\text{Li}) = 5.1 \times 10^{16}$ m^{-3} heat-pipe cell temperature 450 °C and helium buffer gas pressure 533 Pa. The red asterisk shows the measured transmission. Reproduced from [18], copyright (2016) with permission from Springer.

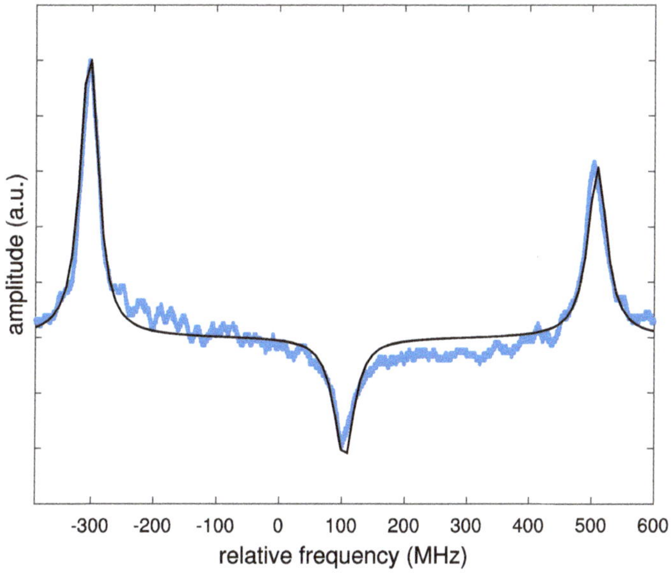

Figure 7.6. Typical Doppler-free spectra for the ^{7}Li-D_2 line. Theory in black and experiment in red. $I_0 = 30$ W m^{-2}, $I_p = 1000$ W m^{-2}, temperature 408 °C, argon buffer gas pressure $P_{Ar} = 33$ Pa and cell length $L = 0.1$ m, $n(^7\text{Li}) = 2.7 \times 10^{16}$ m^{-3}, $\Gamma = 5.9 \times 10^7$ s^{-1}, and $\gamma_B = \gamma_{vc} + \gamma_T = 9.0 \times 10^6$ s^{-1}. Reproduced from [18], copyright (2016) with permission from Springer.

and the relaxation broadening due to transit time and velocity changing collisions $\gamma_B = \gamma_{vc} + \gamma_T = 9.0 \times 10^6$ s^{-1}.

Figure 7.7 shows a typical Doppler-free spectrum for the ^{6}Li-D_2 line using argon as buffer gas. In this case the ^{6}Li isotope concentration was 94.5%. The probe laser intensity was $I_0 = 0.8$ W m^{-2}, the pump laser intensity $I_p = 27$ W m^{-2}, the temperature 375 °C, the argon buffer gas pressure $P_{Ar} = 2.4$ Pa and the cell length $L = 0.1$ m. The pump laser was modulated with a chopper at 1046 Hz. The scanning frequency was 0.5 Hz. Comparing the theoretical spectrum with the experimental we obtained from the fit of the Doppler-limited spectrum with same experimental conditions the lithium density $n(^6\text{Li}) = 5.0 \times 10^{15}$ m^{-3} and from the fit of the Doppler-free spectrum m^{-3}, $\Gamma = 5.9 \times 10^7$ s^{-1}, $\gamma_B = \gamma_{vc} + \gamma_T = 3.5 \times 10^6$ s^{-1}.

7.5 Discussions and conclusions

A set of reduced optical Bloch equations for the ^{7}Li-D_2, ^{7}Li-D_1, ^{6}Li-D_2 and ^{6}Li-D_1 hyperfine lines were obtained and rigorously compared with experimental measurements with excellent results. The derivation starts from the optical Bloch equations applicable to the relative populations of the ground and excited sublevels of the Zeeman multiplets for the case of a single laser beam emission transmitted across a lithium cell. We used the resulting reduced optical Bloch equations to calculate the absorption of a narrow-linewidth tunable diode laser emission in the Doppler-limited case. We found good to excellent agreement between experiment and theory. Furthermore, our fitting parameters were the density, the homogeneous broadening

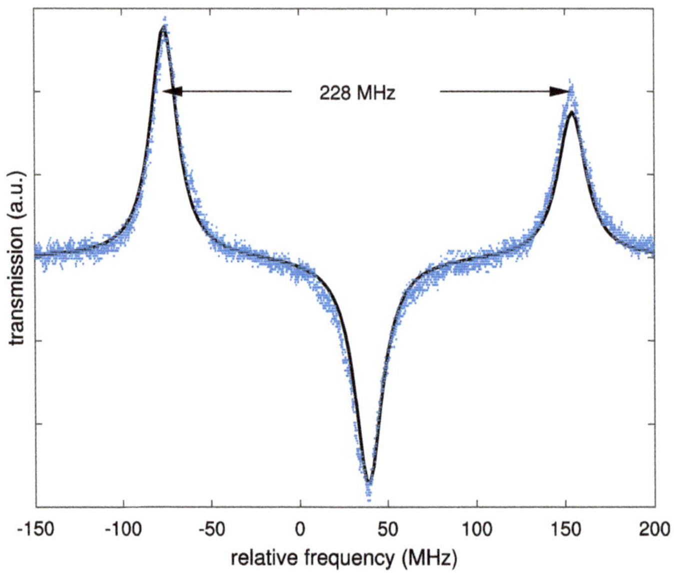

Figure 7.7. Typical Doppler-free spectrum for the ^{6}Li-D_2 line, $P_{Ar} = 2.4$ Pa. Experiment in blue, and fit in black with equations derived in this work. Reproduced from [18], copyright (2016) with permission from Springer.

and the velocity changing collision relaxation rates, other parameters such as intensity and temperature were obtained by measurement. We also fitted the theoretical Doppler-free spectra for ^{7}Li-D_2 hyperfine lines and found excellent agreement with the experimental data.

Parts of this chapter have been reproduced from [18], copyright (2016) with permission from Springer.

References

[1] Siddons P, Adams C S, Ge C and Hughes I G 2008 Absolute absorption on rubidium D lines: comparison between theory and experiment *J. Phys. B: At. Mol. Opt. Phys.* **41** 155004

[2] Siddons P, Adams C S and Hughes I G 2009 Off-resonance absorption and dispersion in vapours of hot alkali-metal atoms *J. Phys. B: At. Mol. Opt. Phys.* **42** 175004

[3] Olivares I E, Duarte A E, Lokajczyk T, Dinklage A and Duarte F J 1998 Doppler-free spectroscopy and collisional studies with tunable diode lasers of lithium isotopes in a heat-pipe oven *J. Opt. Soc. Am.* B **15** 1932–9

[4] Olivares I E 2013 Transmission of tunable diode laser emission, through rubidium vapor, as a function of laser intensity *J. Opt. Soc. Am.* B **30** 945–9

[5] Dinklage A, Lokajczyk T, Kunze H J, Schweer B and Olivares I E 1998 In situ density measurement for a thermal lithium beam employing diode lasers *Rev. Sci. Instrum.* **69** 321–2

[6] Arimondo E 1996 coherent population trapping in laser spectroscopy *Prog. Opt.* **35** 257–354

[7] Harris S E 1997 Electromagnetically induced transparency *Phys. Today* **50** 36–42

[8] Olivares I E and Duarte A E 1999 Resonance ionization spectroscopy in a thermal lithium beam by means of diode lasers *Appl. Opt.* **38** 7481–5

[9] Olivares I E, Duarte A E, Saravia E A and Duarte F J 2002 Lithium isotope separation with tunable diode lasers *Appl. Opt.* **41** 2973–7
[10] Arisawa T, Maruyama Y, Suzuki Y and Shiba K 1982 Lithium isotope separation by laser *Appl. Phys.* B **28** 73–6
[11] Duarte F J and Piper J A 1984 Narrow linewidth, high prf copper laser-pumped dye-laser oscillators *Appl. Opt.* **23**
[12] Demtröder W 2013 *Laser Spectroscopy: Basic Concepts and Instrumentation* (Berlin: Springer)
[13] Zorabedian P 1995 Tunable external-cavity semiconductor lasers *Tunable Lasers Handbook* (New York: Academic) ch 8
[14] Duarte F J 2008 *Tunable Laser Applications* 2nd edn (New York: CRC Press)
[15] Das D and Natarajan V 2007 Absolute frequency measurement of the lithium D lines: precise determination of isotope shifts and fine-structure intervals *Phys. Rev.* A **75** 052508
[16] Sansonetti C J, Richou B, Engleman R Jr and Radziemski L J 1995 Measurements of the resonance lines of Li 6 and Li 7 by Doppler-free frequency-modulation spectroscopy *Phys. Rev.* A **52** 2682
[17] Cowan R D 1981 *The Theory of Atomic Structure and Spectra* (Berkeley: University of California)
[18] Olivares I E and González I A 2016 Diode laser absorption spectroscopy of lithium isotopes *Appl. Phys. B* **122** 1–7

Ignacio E Olivares and Patrick Carrazana

Chapter 8

Rubidium absorption spectroscopy

In this chapter we show a laser intensity absorption experiment at the wavelength of 780 nm, in neutral rubidium vapor using a tunable external cavity diode laser close to the ^{85}Rb $-$ D_2 line. The dependence of laser transmission, as a function of laser intensity, was calculated using the optical Bloch equations described previously and compared with the experiment. The calculations were extended to the saturated absorption case and compared to saturated absorption spectra.

8.1 Introduction

Recently, there has been increased interest in the study of the diode laser absorption in rubidium vapor. Absolute Doppler-broadened absorption has been studied theoretically and experimentally below the saturation intensity [1, 2]. A rubidium vapor laser, pumped by a diode laser, has been demonstrated and kinetic equations have been used to describe the laser emission [3, 4]. Also, line shape calculations in lithium and rubidium have been done using density matrix equations [5, 6]. In a previous work, atom density in lithium beams has been obtained at low laser intensities [7]. Atom density determination of a given substance requires a carefully selection of the laser conditions. Well-resolved spectra can be obtained at laser intensities higher than the saturation intensity, which is 2 mW cm^{-2} for rubidium, but the density determination has to consider the laser intensity. At low laser intensities the transmission remains constant giving an absolute measurement. In this case the method does not require the measurement of the laser intensity, but the signal-to-noise ratio of the absorption spectra decreases. To improve the signal-to-noise ratio the laser beam diameter should be increased, or methods such as phase sensitive detection or boxcar averaging should be used, thus increasing the complexity of the experiment. In this work we study laser intensity transmission at the center of the ^{85}Rb line based on density matrix calculations. The aim of this work is to

doi:10.1088/978-0-7503-3839-4ch8

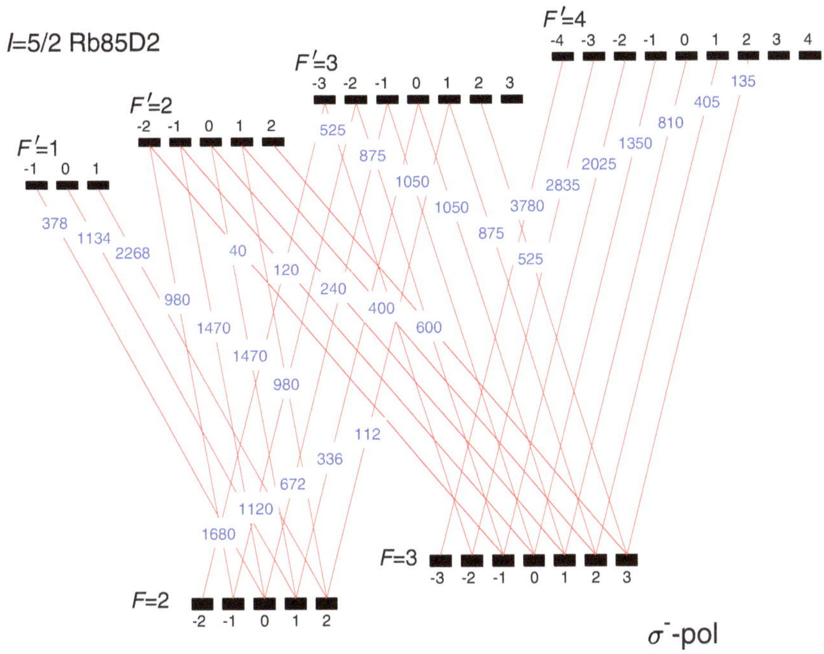

Figure 8.3. ^{85}Rb-D_2 transitions for a left circular polarized incident wave. In this case $\Delta m_F = m_{F_f} - m_{F_i} = -1$.To obtain absolute normalized transition strengths $N_{ifq} = \left| \left\langle i|D_q|f \right\rangle \right|^2 / \| D \|^2$ the values in the diagram should be divided by the normalization constant 11 340.

$$\sum_k a_{k,1}\frac{\rho_k}{g_k} = \gamma\left(\rho_3 + \frac{7}{9}\rho_4 + \frac{4}{9}\rho_5\right)$$
$$\sum_k a_{k,2}\frac{\rho_k}{g_k} = \gamma\left(\frac{2}{9}\rho_4 + \frac{5}{9}\rho_5 + \rho_6\right) \tag{8.1}$$
$$a_{fi} = 3\gamma\sum_q N_{ifq}$$

here for example for $j = 1$ to $k = 3$ we have

$$\sum_{i=1}^{5}\sum_{f=1}^{3} a_{fi}\rho_{ff} = 3\gamma\sum_{i=1}^{5}\sum_{q} N_{ifq}\frac{\rho_3}{g_3} \tag{8.2}$$

and the detailed arithmetics gives

$$\begin{aligned}\sum_{i=1}^{5}\sum_{f=1}^{3} a_{fi}\rho_{ff} &= 3\gamma(1134 + 1512 + 1134 \\ &\quad + 2268 + 1134 + 378 \\ &\quad + 378 + 1134 + 2268)/11340\frac{\rho_3}{3} \\ &= \gamma\rho_3\end{aligned} \tag{8.3}$$
$$W_{j,k} = \frac{9\lambda^3\Gamma I}{4hc}N_{j,k,0}\frac{\Gamma/(2\pi)}{\delta_{j,\,k}^2 + \Gamma^2/4}$$

where $N_{1,3,0} = 1/3$, $N_{1,4,0} = 35/81$, $N_{1,5,0} = 28/81$, $N_{2,4,0} = 10/81$, $N_{2,5,0} = 35/81$, and $N_{2,6,0} = 1$. Here the subscripts $j = 1$ and 2 correspond to the $5^2S_{1/2}$ ground levels with $F = 2$ and 3, respectively, and the subscripts $k = 3$ to 6 correspond to the $5^2S_{3/2}$ excited levels with $F = 1$ to 4, respectively.

$$\begin{aligned}
\dot{\rho}_1 &= W_{1,3}\left(\frac{\rho_3}{g_3} - \frac{\rho_1}{g_1}\right) + W_{1,4}\left(\frac{\rho_4}{g_4} - \frac{\rho_1}{g_1}\right) + W_{1,5}\left(\frac{\rho_5}{g_5} - \frac{\rho_1}{g_1}\right)\\
&\quad + \gamma\left(\rho_3 + \frac{7}{9}\rho_4 + \frac{4}{9}\rho_5\right) + \gamma_T\left(\frac{5}{12} - \rho_1\right)\\
\dot{\rho}_2 &= W_{2,4}\left(\frac{\rho_4}{g_4} - \frac{\rho_2}{g_2}\right) + W_{2,5}\left(\frac{\rho_5}{g_5} - \frac{\rho_2}{g_2}\right) + W_{2,6}\left(\frac{\rho_6}{g_6} - \frac{\rho_2}{g_2}\right)\\
&\quad + \gamma\left(\frac{2}{9}\rho_4 + \frac{5}{9}\rho_5 + \rho_6\right) + \gamma_T\left(\frac{7}{12} - \rho_2\right)\\
\dot{\rho}_3 &= W_{1,3}\left(\frac{\rho_1}{g_1} - \frac{\rho_3}{g_3}\right) - (\gamma + \gamma_T)\rho_3\\
\dot{\rho}_4 &= W_{1,4}\left(\frac{\rho_1}{g_1} - \frac{\rho_4}{g_4}\right) + W_{2,4}\left(\frac{\rho_2}{g_2} - \frac{\rho_4}{g_4}\right) - (\gamma + \gamma_T)\rho_4\\
\dot{\rho}_5 &= W_{1,5}\left(\frac{\rho_1}{g_1} - \frac{\rho_5}{g_5}\right) + W_{2,5}\left(\frac{\rho_2}{g_2} - \frac{\rho_5}{g_5}\right) - (\gamma + \gamma_T)\rho_5\\
1 &= \rho_1 + \rho_2 + \rho_3 + \rho_4 + \rho_5 + \rho_6
\end{aligned}$$

To solve for the populations in stationary state all the derivatives are zero. The equation system can be solved using matrix notation as follows

$$A = (M_1 + M_2) \cdot V \tag{8.4}$$

where the absorption and stimulated matrix is given by

$$M_1 = \begin{pmatrix}
-\sum_{k=3}^{5}\frac{W_{1k}}{g_1} & 0 & \frac{W_{13}}{g_3} & \frac{W_{14}}{g_4} & \frac{W_{15}}{g_5} & 0\\
0 & -\sum_{k=4}^{6}\frac{W_{2k}}{g_2} & 0 & \frac{W_{24}}{g_4} & \frac{W_{25}}{g_5} & \frac{W_{26}}{g_6}\\
\frac{W_{13}}{g_1} & 0 & -\frac{W_{13}}{g_3} & 0 & 0 & 0\\
\frac{W_{14}}{g_1} & \frac{W_{24}}{g_2} & 0 & -\sum_{j=1}^{2}\frac{W_{j4}}{g_4} & 0 & 0\\
\frac{W_{15}}{g_1} & \frac{W_{25}}{g_2} & 0 & 0 & -\sum_{j=1}^{2}\frac{W_{j5}}{g_5} & 0\\
1 & 1 & 1 & 1 & 1 & 1
\end{pmatrix} \tag{8.5}$$

and the spontaneous emission matrix is

$$M_2 = \begin{pmatrix} -\gamma_T & 0 & \gamma & \frac{7}{9}\gamma & \frac{4}{9}\gamma & 0 \\ 0 & -\gamma_T & 0 & \frac{2}{9}\gamma & \frac{5}{9}\gamma & \gamma \\ 0 & 0 & -(\gamma+\gamma_T) & 0 & 0 & 0 \\ 0 & 0 & 0 & -(\gamma+\gamma_T) & 0 & 0 \\ 0 & 0 & 0 & 0 & -(\gamma+\gamma_T) & 0 \\ 0 & 0 & 0 & 0 & 0 & 0 \end{pmatrix} \tag{8.6}$$

the solution of the system are the populations given by

$$V = [\rho_1 \ \ \rho_2 \ \ \rho_3 \ \ \rho_4 \ \ \rho_5 \ \ \rho_6]^T \tag{8.7}$$

where T is the transpose of the row vector giving a column vector and

$$A = \left[-\frac{5}{12}\gamma_T \ \ -\frac{7}{12}\gamma_T \ \ 0 \ \ 0 \ \ 0 \ \ 1\right]^T \tag{8.8}$$

For the absorption equations to the Doppler-free saturation spectroscopy considering the magnetic states (as seen before) we have

$$dI_d = h\,\nu_{if}\,n\left(\int_{-\infty}^{\infty}\sum_{if} W_{if}(\nu, -v, I_d)(\rho_f - \rho_i)F(v)dv\right)dx \tag{8.9}$$

and $\rho_f = \rho_f(\nu, v, I_p)$ and $\rho_i = \rho_i(\nu, v, I_p)$ and I_p is the pump intensity.

Following our level reduction we obtain

$$dI_d = h\,\nu_{jk}\,n\left(\int_{-\infty}^{\infty}\sum_{jk} W_{jk}(\nu, -v, I_d)\left(\rho_k/g_k - \rho_j/g_j\right)F(v)dv\right)dx \tag{8.10}$$

Figure 8.4 shows the energy level diagram with the corresponding multiplet numbers.

The vapor pressure for temperature T below 40 °C is given by

$$\log_{10}P_{\text{vapor}}\,(\text{Torr}) = 2.881 + 4.857 - 42\,157/T\ (\text{K}) \tag{8.11}$$

To obtain the vapor density we used the gas law equation and consider the natural abundance of the ^{85}Rb isotope, which is 72.17%.

8.3 Experiment

In these experiments, we have measured the transmittance at the resonance of a Doppler-broadened line shape for increasing incident laser intensities. The setup of the absorption experiment is depicted in figure 8.5

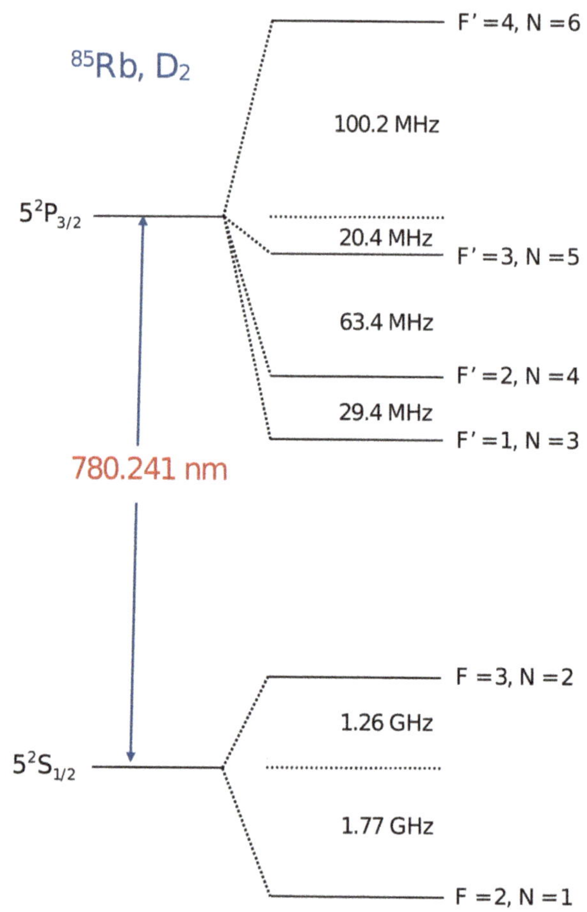

Figure 8.4. Energy level diagram ^{85}Rb. Reproduced from [13] with permission.

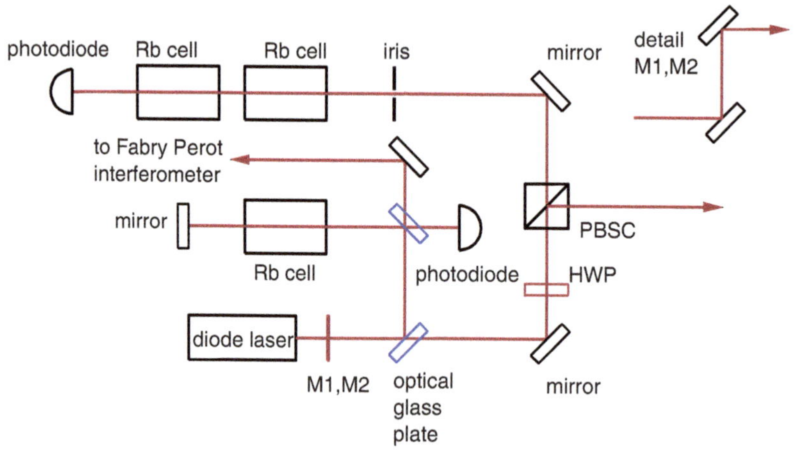

Figure 8.5. Setup of the absorption experiment. Reproduced from [13] with permission.

An external cavity tunable diode laser [14, 15] with a 60 dB optical isolator was directed through two 10 cm cells filled with rubidium vapor at room temperature, giving a total path length inside the vapor of 20 cm. To adjust the laser power to the desired values, we used a half-wave plate followed by a polarizing beam splitter cube and a neutral density dual filter wheel that was installed between the second mirror and the rubidium cell. The incident laser power was measured with an optical powermeter. The transmitted light was detected with a high-speed Si detector. The active area of the detector is 0.8 mm^2 with 1.0 mm diameter. After passing the Rb cells the beam was oriented with a mirror at 90° to the photodiode (PD). We adjusted the mirror screws to ensure maximal signal into the PD. To measure the maximal intensity of the laser profile we installed a diamond paper in the path of the beam and a digital camera behind the paper to obtain a digital picture of the laser spot. We calculated the relative power of the pixels at maximum signal and determined the area of one pixel from the picture by carrying out a scaling procedure. The incident intensity was obtained by dividing the power at one pixel at maximum power by the area of one pixel. This method allowed us to measure even when the laser profiles were noisy. The temperature was measured with a thermistor close to the first rubidium cell. The temperature varied between 17.2° C and 17.7° C during the whole measurement. We considered no collisions and the laser linewidth $\Gamma_L = 5$ MHz. The transit time relaxation rate was $\gamma_T = 8.97 \times 10^4$ s^{-1}. We also measured the saturated absorption spectrum. The setup of the saturated absorption experiment is depicted in figure 8.6.

The rubidium cell temperature was 20.5° C. The diameters of the pump laser and probe laser were 1.91 and 1.85 mm, respectively. In this case we used a detector with diameter 2.5 mm, which was larger than the beam diameter. The profiles were

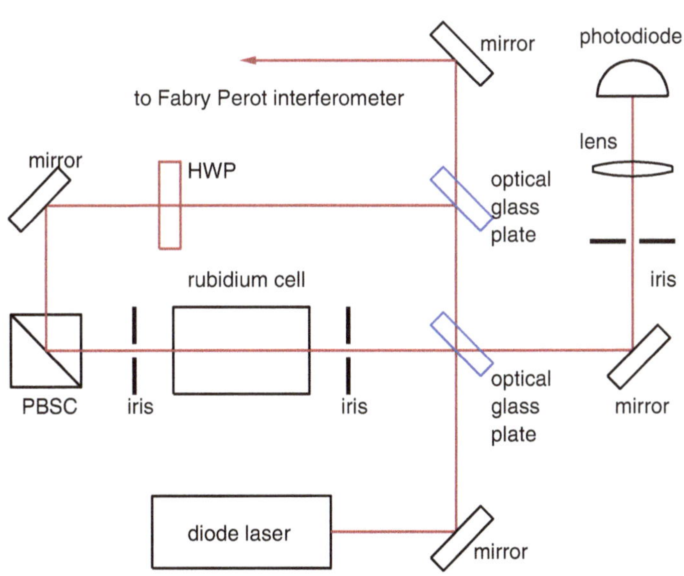

Figure 8.6. Setup saturation experiment. Reproduced from [13] with permission.

circular and their diameters were measured after passing the iris diaphragms. The pump and the probe intensities before entering the cell were $I_p = 8.17$ mW cm^{-2} and $I_2 = 0.244$ mW cm^{-2}, respectively. The cell length was 70 mm. The power of the laser pump laser before entering the cell was 252 μW and after the cell it was the 76 μW. The probe power measured before entering the cell was 6.55 μW. We considered an attenuation of 0.08 due to the reflectivity of the glass of the windows and the attenuation of the pump beam while passing the cell. The cell was partitioned into seven parts, each 1 cm in length. The entrance intensity of each cell considering the glass reflectivity and an exponential intensity decay along the cell was 8.013 mW cm^{-2}, 6.760 mW cm^{-2}, 5.704 mW cm^{-2}, 4.812 mW cm^{-2}, 4.060 mW cm^{-2}, 3.425 mW cm^{-2}, and 2.890 mW cm^{-2}. We considered no collisions and the laser linewidth $\Gamma_L = 5$MHz. The transit time relaxation rate was $\gamma_T = 8.97 \times 10^4$ s^{-1}.

8.4 Results

The measured transmission at resonance (maximal absorption) in the case of the Doppler-broadened absorption spectrum with increasing laser power is shown in figure 8.7.

For intensities over 100 mW cm^{-2} the vapor becomes completely saturated and the transmission approaches one. For laser intensities below 1 mW cm^{-2} the transmission becomes constant. As illustrated in figure 8.7, the theoretical transmission at resonance fits well with the experiment: this is the first principal result of

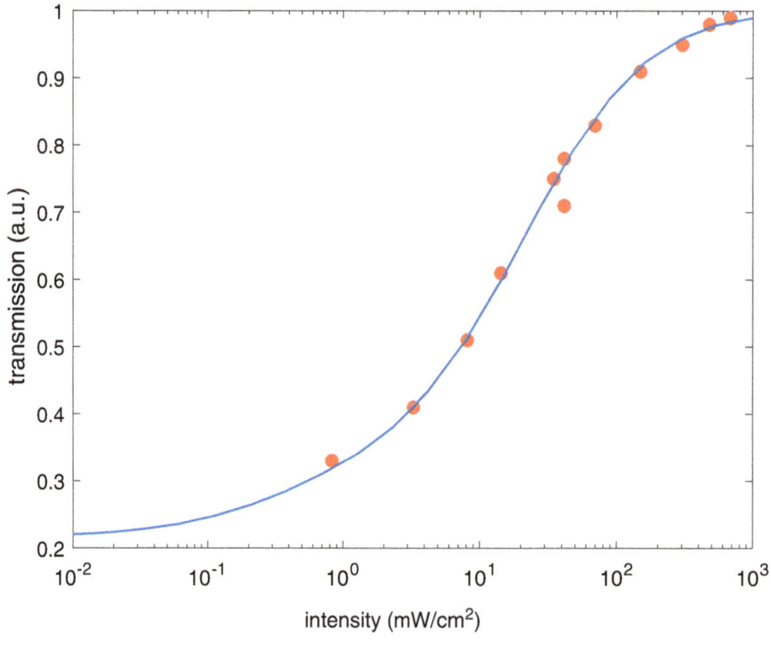

Figure 8.7. Saturation curve for a rubidium vapor. Reproduced from [13] with permission.

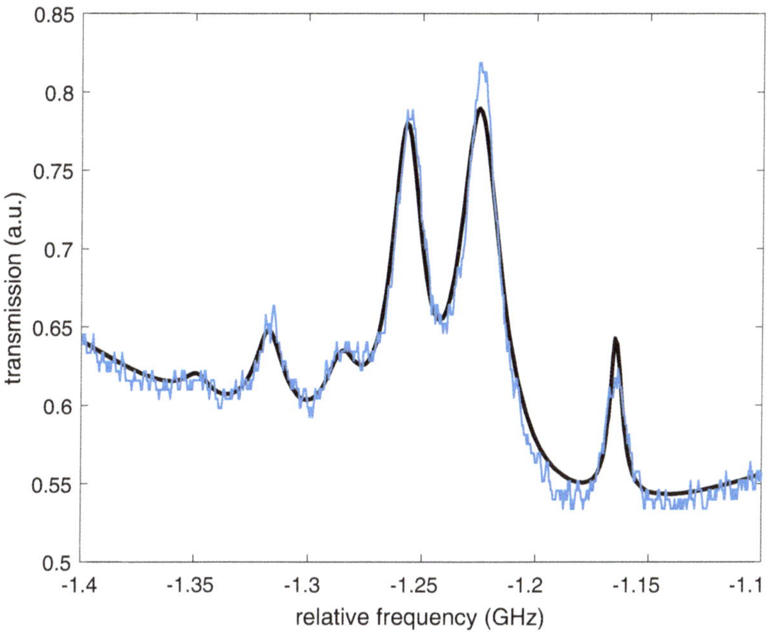

Figure 8.8. Doppler-free spectrum, $T = 20.5$ °C, $\Gamma = 5$ MHz. Reproduced from [13] with permission.

this study. A typical saturated absorption spectrum for the ^{85}Rb-D_2 line is shown in figure 8.8.

We can observe a crossover signal in this figure caused by double resonance. From left to right, the first, third, and sixth peak lines correspond to the transitions $5^2S_{1/2}F = 3$ to $5^2P_{3/2}F' = 2$; 3; and 4 hyperfine lines, respectively. The second, fourth, and fifth peaks from left to right correspond to the crossover signal between $5^2S_{1/2}F = 3$ to $5^2P_{3/2}F' = 2$, and 3 lines, $5^2S_{1/2}F = 3$ to $5^2P_{3/2}F' = 2$ and $F' = 4$ lines, and between $5^2S_{1/2}F = 3$ and $F' = 3$, and 4 lines, respectively. This experimental spectrum shows excellent resolution of the hyperfine structure and is fairly well fitted by our density matrix model: this is the second principal result of this study. The positive crossover signals are caused when the probe beam is tuned to one of the two transitions of the D_2 line with a common lower level, and the pump beam is tuned to the other.

8.5 Discussion and conclusion

Reduced optical Bloch equations for the ^{85}Rb-D_2 hyperfine lines were obtained starting from the optical Bloch equations for the relative populations of the ground and excited sublevels of the Zeeman multiplets for the case of a single laser beam emission transmitted across a rubidium cell. We used the obtained reduced optical Bloch equations to calculate the absorption of a tunable diode laser emission in the Doppler-limited case and we calculated the transmission at resonance as a function of the laser intensity. We found good to excellent agreement between experiment and theory. To confirm our results we measured a saturated absorption spectra with controlled experimental conditions and extended the use of the reduced optical equations to calculate the saturated absorption spectra. Here, we found excellent agreement between theory and experiment. Additionally, the fit parameters were obtained by measurement, confirming the validity of our reduced Bloch equations.

8.6 Transitions

The values for the normalized dipole matrix elements $N_{ifq} = \left| \langle i|D_q|f \rangle \right|^2 / \| D \|^2$ for each transition of ^{85}Rb are shown in tables 8.1–8.5.

Table 8.1. $F' = 2$ to $F = 2$ transition.

	$F' = 2$					
$F = 2$	j	16	17	18	19	20
i	m/m'	−2	−1	0	1	2
1	−2	14/81	7/81			
2	−1	7/81	7/162	7/54		
3	0		7/54	0	7/54	
4	1			7/54	7/162	7/81
5	2				7/81	14/81

Table 8.2. $F' = 3$ to $F = 2$ transitions.

	$F' = 3$							
$F = 2$	j	21	22	23	24	25	26	27
i	m/m'	−3	−2	−1	0	1	2	3
1	−2	4/27	4/81	4/405				
2	−1		8/81	4/405	4/135			
3	0			8/135	4/45	8/135		
4	1				4/135	32/405	8/81	
5	2					4/405	4/81	4/27

Table 8.3. $F' = 2$ to $F = 3$ transitions.

	$F' = 2$					
$F = 3$	j	16	17	18	19	20
i	m/m'	−2	−1	0	1	2
6	−3	10/189				
7	−2	10/567	20/567			
8	−1	2/567	16/567	4/189		
9	0		2/189	2/63	2/189	
10	1			4/189	16/567	
11	2				20/567	10/567
12	3					10/189

Table 8.4. $F' = 3$ to $F = 3$ transitions.

	$F' = 3$							
$F = 3$	j	21	22	23	24	25	26	27
i	m/m'	−3	−2	−1	0	1	2	3
6	−3	5/36	5/108					
7	−2	5/108	5/81	25/324				
8	−1		25/324	5/324	5/54			
9	0			5/54	0	5/54		
10	1				5/54	5/324	25/324	
11	2					25/324	5/81	5/108
12	3						5/108	5/36

Table 8.5. $F' = 4$ to $F = 3$ transitions.

	$F' = 4$									
$F = 3$	j	28	29	30	31	32	33	34	35	36
i	m/m'	−4	−3	−2	−1	0	1	2	3	4
6	−3	1/3	1/12	1/84						
7	−2		1/4	1/7	1/28					
8	−1			5/28	5/28	1/14				
9	0				5/42	4/41	5/42			
10	1					1/14	5/28	5/28		
11	2						1/28	1/7	1/4	
12	3							1/84	1/12	1/3

References

[1] Siddons P, Adams C S, Ge C and Hughes I G 2008 Absolute absorption on rubidium D lines: comparison between theory and experiment *J. Phys. B: At. Mol. Opt. Phys.* **41** 155004

[2] Siddons P, Adams C S and Hughes I G 2009 Off-resonance absorption and dispersion in vapours of hot alkali-metal atoms *J. Phys. B: At. Mol. Opt. Phys.* **42** 175004

[3] Krupke W F 2012 Diode pumped alkali lasers (DPALs)—A review (rev1) *Prog. Quantum Electron.* **36** 4–28

[4] Ya-Juan W, Bai-Liang P, Qi Z and Jing Y 2011 A kinetic model for diode pumped rubidium vapor laser *Opt. Commun.* **284** 4045–8

[5] Bhattacharyya D, Dutta B K, Ray B and Ghosh P N 2004 Line shape simulation and saturated absorption spectroscopic measurement of Rb–D2 transition *Chem. Phys. Lett.* **389** 113–8

[6] Olivares I E, Duarte A E, Lokajczyk T, Dinklage A and Duarte F J 1998 Doppler-free spectroscopy and collisional studies with tunable diode lasers of lithium isotopes in a heat-pipe oven *J. Opt. Soc. Am.* **B 15** 1932–9

[7] Dinklage A, Lokajczyk T, Kunze H J, Schweer B and Olivares I E 1998 In situ density measurement for a thermal lithium beam employing diode lasers *Rev. Sci. Instrum.* **69** 321–2

[8] Olivares I, Cuadra J, Aguilar F, Aguirre Gomez J and Duarte F 2009 Optical method using rotating Glan–Thompson polarizers to independently vary the power of the excitation and repumping lasers in laser cooling experiments *J. Mod. Opt.* **56** 1780–4
[9] Arimondo E 1996 coherent population trapping in laser spectroscopy *Prog. Opt.* **35** 257–354
[10] Olivares I E and Duarte A E 1999 Resonance ionization spectroscopy in a thermal lithium beam by means of diode lasers *Appl. Opt.* **38** 7481–5
[11] Olivares I E, Duarte A E, Saravia E A and Duarte F J 2002 Lithium isotope separation with tunable diode lasers *Appl. Opt.* **41** 2973–7
[12] Demtröder W 2008 *Laser Spectroscopy* vol 2 (Berlin: Springer)
[13] Olivares *et al* 2013 Transmission of tunable diode laser emission, through rubidium vapor, as a function of laser intensity *JOSA B* **30** 945–9
[14] Zorabedian P 1995 Tunable external-cavity semiconductor lasers *Tunable Lasers Handbook* (New York: Academic) ch 8
[15] Duarte F J 2008 *Tunable Laser Applications* 2nd edn (New York: CRC Press)

Techniques for Lithium Isotope Separation, Laser Cooling, and Scattering

Ignacio E Olivares and Patrick Carrazana

Chapter 9

Lithium resonance ionization spectroscopy

In this chapter we describe the method used to selectively ionize lithium isotopes. We used a semiconductor diode laser and a Q-switched Nd:YAG laser with fourth-harmonic generation at 266 nm for ionizing neutral atoms in a lithium beam. The method uses a two-step photoionization scheme. The number of measured ions is compared with an estimate from the diode laser absorption measurement. The estimate uses a set of precisely solved rate equations. At high laser intensity saturation effects on absorption are observed. Transit time relaxation and detailed calculations of the ionization levels are described here.

9.1 Introduction

Resonant ionization spectroscopy (RIS) of lithium metal vapor by laser radiation tuned to the first resonance lithium lines has been widely investigated in recent years [1–5]. The method is considered to be useful for isotope separation because of its high selectivity. In recent publications [6, 7] we reported on optical absorption at the first excited states in Doppler-limited and Doppler-free cases by using a tunable diode laser in neutral lithium vapor. The absorption was described by means of a numerical procedure based on the rate equation formalism that takes into consideration all the hyperfine sublevels, optical pumping, and relaxation processes. Here we present a simple method to resolve fully the photoionization spectra at the ^2P level by radiation at $\lambda = 670.8$ nm for selective excitation of the $2s$–$2p$ transition. A tunable diode laser and fourth-harmonic generation Nd:YAG laser that emits at $\lambda = 266$ nm were employed for the ionization process. For our experiment we used a well-collimated lithium beam and a narrow linewidth laser for selective excitation of ^{6}Li and ^{7}Li lines. We explain the diminished photocurrent caused by relaxation mechanisms by using the saturation absorption curve for diode laser excitation.

doi:10.1088/978-0-7503-3839-4ch9

9.2 Background

Inasmuch as both lithium isotopes have a fine structure at the $2p$ level, lithium atoms in the ground state ($S_{1/2}$) can be excited selectively to any of the doublet states $2P_{1/2}$ and $2P_{3/2}$ which are separated by 0.0151 nm by use of a narrow linewidth laser and a well-collimated atomic beam. The energy level diagram for lithium isotopes illustrating UV and red radiation is shown in figure 9.1.

The wavelengths of the $2s$–$2p$ transitions have been assigned as corresponding to 670.7764 nm for the ^{7}Li-D_2 line and 670.7915 nm for the ^{7}Li-D_1 line. The $2s$–$2p$ transitions for ^{6}Li-D_2 and for ^{6}Li-D_1 lines were assigned to 670.7922 and 670.8073 nm, respectively [9]. Inasmuch as the energy of these excited states is approximately 1.84 eV and the ionization potential is approximately 5.39 eV, the energy required to ionize the lithium atoms from the $2p$ level corresponds to wavelengths shorter than 350 nm. Thus a 266 nm wavelength will reach ionization from any previous selectively excited $2p$ level [1, 3]. The number of ions at the end of a laser pulse can be estimated from density matrix calculations for the ground-excited-ionization continuum system. The following rate equation was obtained in a two-step photo-ionization system in which no collisions occur: [4, 10]

$$\begin{aligned}\dot{\rho}_{00} &= W(\rho_{11} - \rho_{00}) + \gamma\rho_{11} \\ \dot{\rho}_{11} &= W(\rho_{00} - \rho_{11}) - \gamma\rho_{11} - \Gamma_i\rho_{11} \\ W &= \frac{1/2\Omega^2\Gamma}{\Gamma^2 + [(\omega - \omega_0) - \mathbf{k}\cdot\mathbf{v}]^2}\end{aligned} \quad (9.1)$$

where ρ_{00} and ρ_{11} are the populations of the ground and each excited state of the considered isotope respectively; $\gamma = 1/\tau$ is the spontaneous decay rate, where τ is the lifetime of the excited state that is 27 ns for lithium; W is the transition rate from

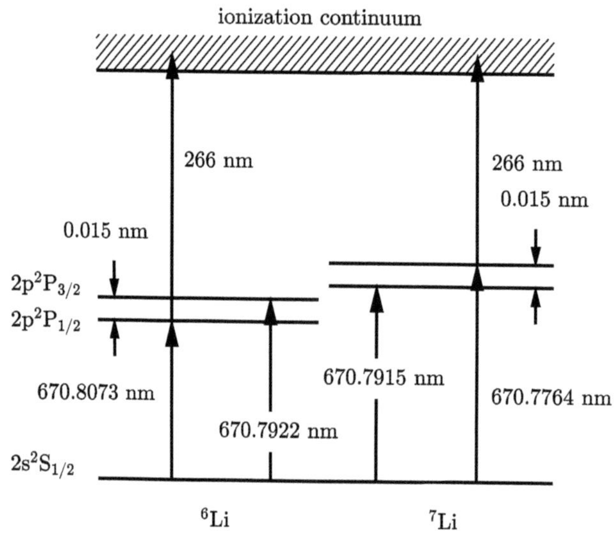

Figure 9.1. Lithium energy level diagram. Reproduced from [8] with permission.

the ground to the excited state [7]; $\Gamma_i = \sigma_i I_i/(h\nu_i)$ is the ionization transition rate; I_i is the intensity of the ionizing laser in Watts per square meter; n_i is its frequency in Hertz; σ_i is the cross section for ionization in square meters; ω is the angular frequency in Hertz of the laser that was used for excitation; ω_0 is the angular transition frequency in Hertz; k is the wave vector of the excitation radiation in inverse meters; v is the velocity of the atoms in meters per second; Γ is the total homogeneous broadening in Hertz; and Ω is the Rabi frequency in Hertz. Homogeneous broadening is a function of the transition rates and other broadening effects [5] according to $\Gamma = \gamma/2 + \Gamma_i + \Gamma_L$, where Γ_L is the linewidth of the exciting laser. This system of homogeneous linear rate equations with constant coefficients was solved, neglecting the hyperfine structure of the ground level. The numerical procedure that describes the hyperfine structure was described previously [6]. The solution of equation (9.1) is given by

$$\begin{aligned} \rho_{00}(t) &= A\exp(\lambda_1 t) + B\exp(\lambda_2 t) \\ \rho_{11}(t) &= C\exp(\lambda_1 t) + D\exp(\lambda_2 t) \\ \lambda_{12} &= -b \pm \sqrt{b^2 - c} \\ b &= W + \frac{1}{2\tau} + \frac{\Gamma_i}{2} \\ c &= W\Gamma_i \end{aligned} \tag{9.2}$$

where

$$\begin{aligned} A &= \frac{1}{\lambda_1 - \lambda_2}[-(W + \lambda_2) + \rho_{11}(0)(2W + \gamma + \lambda_2)] \\ B &= \frac{1}{\lambda_1 - \lambda_2}[(W + \lambda_1) - \rho_{11}(0)(2W + \gamma + \lambda_1)] \\ C &= \frac{1}{\lambda_1 - \lambda_2}[W - \rho_{11}(0)(2W + \lambda_1)] \\ D &= \frac{1}{\lambda_1 - \lambda_2}[-W - \rho_{11}(0)\lambda_2] \\ 1 &= \rho_{00}(0) + \rho_{11}(0) \end{aligned} \tag{9.3}$$

We obtain the ionization probability (number of ions divided by the total number of atoms) at a time t by averaging over the velocity distribution as

$$P_i(t) = \left\langle 1 - \rho_{00}(t) - \rho_{11}(t) \right\rangle \tag{9.4}$$

Thus the number of ions obtained in volume V with length X perpendicular to the direction of the laser beam after an irradiation pulse with duration t is given by

$$N_i = \rho V \frac{1}{X} \int_0^X \left[\int_0^t P_i\left(t'\right) dt' \right] dx, \tag{9.5}$$

where ρ is the initial density of neutral atoms inside this region. We believe that t is sufficiently short so that no atoms enter or leave the region with length X. This condition applies when $t \ll T_t$, where T_t is the transit time [6], which is typically 500 ns for a 1 mm path. Inasmuch as the neutral lithium beam moves at thermal velocities, the laser beams are disposed perpendicular to the lithium beam direction, and the repetition rate of the laser pulses is low enough in our experiments, so that the ionized atoms leave the ionization region before the next ionizing pulse arrives. Integrating equations (9.1) and inserting them into equations (9.4) and (9.5) yield

$$N_i = \rho V \Gamma_i \frac{1}{X} \int_0^X \left[\int_0^t \left\langle \rho_{11}(t') \right\rangle dt' \right] dx, \tag{9.6}$$

When we use a cw laser for excitation and the ionizing laser pulse has low power, we can assume that the number of excited atoms $\left\langle \rho_{11} \right\rangle$ remains nearly constant in time:

$$N_i = \rho V \Gamma_i t \frac{1}{X} \int_0^X \left\langle \rho_{11}(t) \right\rangle dx \tag{9.7}$$

The loss of excitation power along irradiation path X is given by [6]

$$\mathrm{d}I = -\, h\nu\rho \frac{1}{\tau} \left\langle \rho_{11} \right\rangle dx \tag{9.8}$$

The absorption of the ionization laser power was neglected because the ionization cross section is low. Integrating equation (9.8) and using equation (9.7) and the definition of Γ_i, we obtain

$$N = \frac{A\tau\sigma_i(I_0 - I)}{h^2 \nu_e \nu_i} \tag{9.9}$$

where A is the area normal to where the two lasers coincide when they are parallel, I_0 is the incident intensity, and I is the transmitted intensity of the exciting laser. Then the number N_i of ions collected at the end of a laser ionizing pulse for low UV laser intensity is given by

$$N = \alpha P_e P_i (1 - T)/A \tag{9.10}$$

where $\alpha = \sigma_i \tau T_{\mathrm{UV}}/(h^2 \nu_e \nu_i)$=17 100 W m^{-2} for $T_{\mathrm{UV}} = 200\ \mu$s, $c/\nu_i = 266$ nm, P_i is the average UV laser power, P_e is the exciting laser power, T is the transmittance of the exciting laser at area A where both lasers coincide in the interaction region $\sigma_i = 7 \times 10^{-22}$ m^2 is the ionization cross section [5] T_{UV} is the period of the UV laser pulses of the ionizing laser, h is Planck's constant, and ν_e, ν_i are the excitation and ionization frequencies respectively. The transmittance is given approximately by Beer's law:

$$T \approx \exp(\sigma n x) \tag{9.11}$$

where n is the lithium density, x is the length of the lithium beam path, and σ is the absorption cross section given by

$$\sigma = \frac{\sigma_0}{\sqrt{1 + S_0}} \tag{9.12}$$

where S_0 is the saturation parameter and σ_0 is the cross section at low laser intensity that is a Gaussian function as a result of Doppler broadening. Taking into consideration the dependence of S_0 on A [6] and equation (9.10) and approximations (9.11) and (9.12), for a high saturation parameter and high transmittance we have $N = 1/\sqrt{A}$, where A is the focusing area. Thus the number of ions increase when the lasers are well focused. However, it is not convenient to focus more than the saturation intensity for ionization, which, for the UV, is 50 GW m^{-2}. We obtained the value of the saturation ionizing intensity by solving equations (9.1)–(9.3), where the excitation and stimulated emission transition probabilities are considered functions of the atom velocity and laser frequency.

9.3 Experiment

The experiment is shown in figure 9.2.

We formed a beam of lithium atoms by evaporating metallic lithium from a molybdenum crucible in a Knudsen cell (Comstock Model KMB237/6). The vapor passed through a 1 mm collimator and the beam was recollimated at 5 cm from the crucible aperture. The Knudsen cell is equipped with a shutter that can be used to interrupt the beam whenever necessary. The Knudsen cell can reach 630 °C with a stability of approximately 1 °C min^{-1}. For excitation with a narrow-band laser, we used a cw external-cavity tunable diode laser (New Focus Model 6202) with a central wavelength of 671 nm, tunable over 12 nm, and a linewidth of <5 MHz. This laser was focused into the lithium beam, but for ionization we focused the fourth harmonic of a Nd: YAG laser (LeeLaser Model 815TQ) deployed in the counter-propagating direction. Typical power densities of the exciting and ionizing laser are 60 kW m^{-2} at 671 nm and 1 GW m^{-2} at 266 nm, respectively. The Nd:YAG laser has a 5 kHz repetition rate and 120 ns pulse width with a KTP* crystal intracavity to produce the green output. We used a temperature-stabilized KD*P crystal (Inrad Model 5-301) to produce the fourth-harmonic generation at 266 nm and a dispersive quartz prism to separate the green from the UV radiation. Laser produced ions were deflected and collected by means of a plane-parallel capacitor inside a vacuum chamber at the irradiation zone, which was polarized by 7 V. For voltages greater than 4 V, all the ions are collected. We measured the photoion current by using the amplitude-modulated lock-in technique. The voltage signal in a 47 kV load was

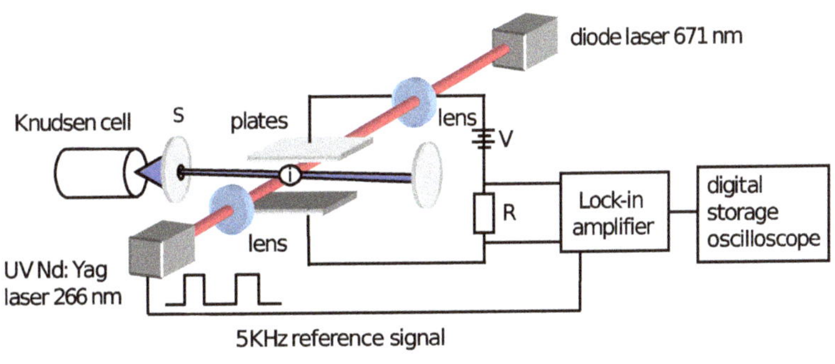

Figure 9.2. Resonance ionization spectroscopy experiment diagram. Reproduced from [8] with permission.

amplified with a lock-in amplifier (Stanford Research Model SR510), and the amplified signal was measured with a digital storage oscilloscope (LeCroy Model 9310A). We used a square 5 kHz function from the Nd:YAG trigger as the reference signal. The diode laser wavelength was scanned slowly over the lithium transitions at 1 GHz s^{-1} by means of a function generator (Tektronix Model CFG100). The collected number of ions N that was measured after each ionizing laser UV pulse is given by

$$N \approx kT_{\mathrm{UV}}V_M/(eR) \tag{9.13}$$

where k is a proportionality constant, T_{UV} is the period of the Nd:YAG laser pulses, V_M is the voltage measured at load R by the lock-in amplifier when the phase was optimized, and e is the electron charge. The approximation and the value of k were obtained from the lock-in specifications and the signal conditions. The length of the ionization pulse after resistance-capacitance distortion was of the order of 30 μs. To measure the transmittance it is necessary to open the shutter of the Knudsen cell for absorption and to close it to obtain the baseline for zero absorption.

9.4 Results

A typical recorded resonance ionization spectrum is shown in figure 9.3

This spectrum shows saturation effects on the $^7\mathrm{Li}D_2$ line as a result of optical pumping between ground states produced by the diode laser. This effect can be observed as a diminished photoion current. The hyperfine structure can also be seen in figure 9.3 because of the narrow linewidth of the diode laser and the collimation of the lithium beam. The lithium beam flux is given by $F = n\phi v$, where density n is

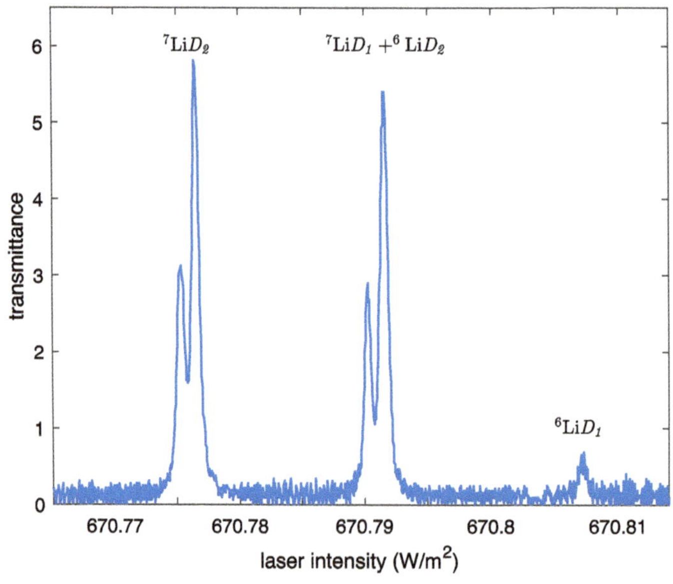

Figure 9.3. Typical resonance ionization spectrum for the ^{6}Li and ^{7}Li isotopes. Reproduced from [8] with permission.

calculated from the absorption spectra, ϕ is the cross section of the lithium beam that can be obtained from fluorescence measurements [7], and v was calculated from the temperature with the kinetic gas theory. We have estimated a flux of 10^{15} atoms/s and confirmed the estimate with the measurements obtained with a quartz film thickness meter (Bal-Tec Model QSG060). By using a well-collimated laser beam we measured the transmittance of the $^7\mathrm{Li}D_2$ spectral line at 670.7764 nm as a function of the intensity of the excitation light. For this measurement, the diode laser wavelength was fixed and the Nd:YAG laser was off. The saturation curve that we obtained is shown in figure 9.4.

It can be adjusted by means of a numerical procedure that has been described elsewhere. The fit parameter is the transit time relaxation rate γ_T We obtained $\gamma_T = 5 \times 10^5\ \mathrm{s}^{-1}$ from the fitting. This value is in good agreement with the inverse of the transit time calculated as X/v, where X is the length of the atom's path across the laser beam, which is the 3 mm diameter beam, and v is the 1800 m s^{-1} velocity of the lithium atoms. The saturation parameter is approximately ten times larger than for a two-level atom, which can be explained by the presence of the various ground sublevels in lithium, where additional pumping can occur. The optical pumping could be altered by collisions between atoms, but in our case the collisions are negligible because of the large 3 m mean free path that we obtained by using a high vacuum and a low lithium density. For the same reason other relaxation mechanisms were also neglected. As an example of the RIS measurements the temperature of the Knudsen cell was set at T = 633 °C, the incoming power of the diode laser was

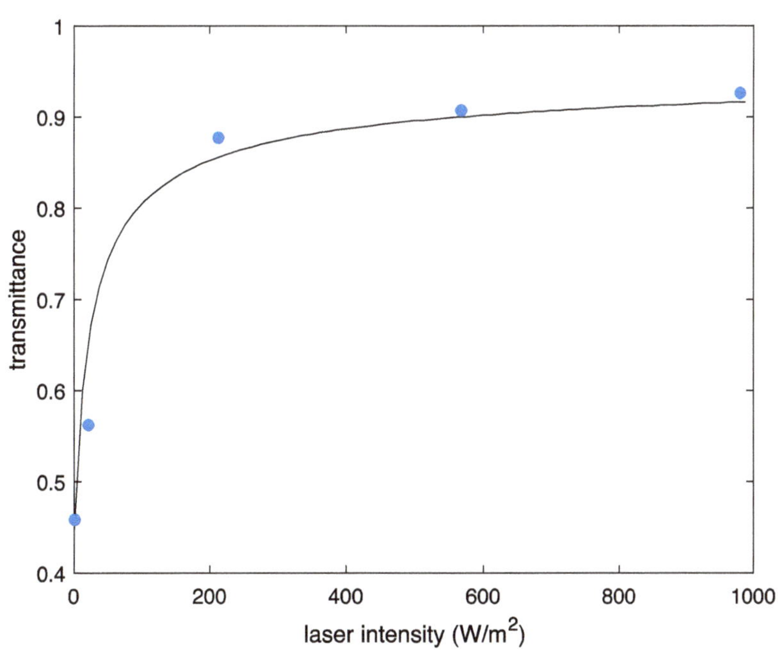

Figure 9.4. Saturation curve for the absorption of the $^7\mathrm{Li}$-D_2 line at 670.7764 nm. Reproduced from [8] with permission.

$P_e = 2360\ \mu W$, and at the exit we measured $P_e = 2220\ \mu W$ with an optical powermeter (Newport Model 818). The resolution determined experimentally for this powermeter was better than 0.75% at the microwatt level. The ionizing UV power P_i was a 15 mW average, which was focused at an area of $A = 7.5 \times 10^{-9}\ m^2$. The red light was focused with an $f = 0.25$ m lens and the UV light with an $f = 0.58$ m lens. Inasmuch as the shape of the diode laser light is elliptical and is larger than the circular UV laser spot, the two lasers do not coincide completely. So we used only the 0.25 part of the red light power. The proportionality constant of approximation (9.13) we obtain $k = 1.9$ and $V_M = 17.8\ \mu V$. Using approximation (9.13) and these values for k and V_M, we obtained the measured ions per pulse $N = (9 \pm 1) \times 10^5$, and the estimated number of ions per pulse was $N = (12 \pm 3) \times 10^5$ when we took into consideration equation (9.10) and the values of P_e incident, P_e transmitted, A, and the fraction of the red light in the ionization zone. The total error of the value of N in each case was obtained by means of the error propagation theory and the given standard deviation error of each variable. In a second case that involved an incident diode laser power of $P_e = 3750\ \mu W$ and a transmitted power of $P_e = 3550\ \mu W$, we determined $N = (1.9 \pm 0.5) \times 10^5$ ions per pulse by use of equation (9.10). This value should be compared with the $N = (1.5 \pm 0.2) \times 10^5$ ions per pulse derived from the measurement and from the approximation given in equation (9.13).

9.5 Discussion and conclusion

We have demonstrated a simple method to measure the RIS spectra of lithium isotopes using a narrow linewidth tunable diode laser for the excitation. We found good agreement between the estimation of the produced ions beginning with transmittance measurements and photoion current measurements. Saturation of the recorded photoion spectra was produced by the diode laser. We investigated the saturation by measuring the transmittance at different laser intensities, fitted with the numerical procedure reported in [6]. This procedure includes the hyperfine structure of the levels and optical pumping and uses the transit time relaxation rate as a fit parameter.

References

[1] Arisawa T, Maruyama Y, Suzuki Y and Shiba K 1982 Lithium isotope separation by laser *Appl. Phys.* B **28** 73–6

[2] Karlov N V, Krynetskiĭ B and Stelmakh O M 1977 Measurement of the photoionization cross section of the Li atom at the 2P level *Sov. J. Quantum Electron.* **7** 1305

[3] Yamashita M and Kashiwagi H 1979 Method for separation and enrichment of lithium isotopes by laser *US Patent* 4149077 https://www.osti.gov/biblio/6303723-method-separation-enrichment-lithium-isotopes-laser

[4] Payne M, Deng L and Thonnard N 1994 Applications of resonance ionization mass spectrometry *Rev. Sci. Instrum.* **65** 2433–59

[5] Hurst G, Payne M, Kramer S and Young J 1979 Resonance ionization spectroscopy and one-atom detection *Rev. Mod. Phys.* **51** 767

[6] Olivares I E, Duarte A E, Lokajczyk T, Dinklage A and Duarte F J 1998 Doppler-free spectroscopy and collisional studies with tunable diode lasers of lithium isotopes in a heat-pipe oven *J. Opt. Soc. Am.* B **15** 1932–9
[7] Dinklage A, Lokajczyk T, Kunze H J, Schweer B and Olivares I E 1998 In situ density measurement for a thermal lithium beam employing diode lasers *Rev. Sci. Instrum.* **69** 321–2
[8] Olivares 1999 Resonance ionization spectroscopy in a thermal lithium beam by means of diode lasers *Applied Optics* **38** 7481–5
[9] Sansonetti C J, Richou B, Engleman R Jr and Radziemski L J 1995 Measurements of the resonance lines of Li 6 and Li 7 by Doppler-free frequency-modulation spectroscopy *Phys. Rev.* A **52** 2682
[10] Ackerhalt J R and Shore B W 1977 Rate equations versus Bloch equations in multiphoton ionization *Phys. Rev.* A **16** 277

Ignacio E Olivares and Patrick Carrazana

Chapter 10

Lithium isotope separation

A lithium laser isotope separation experiment is performed with a visible tunable-diode laser and a UV laser. The method considers a two-step excitation-ionization scheme. The narrow-linewidth and tunability of the diode laser combined with a magnetic sector allows the resonance ionization spectra of the ^{7}Li-D_1 and ^{6}Li-D_2 line to be measured independently. The system includes a compact mass selector that consists of a precision magnet sector combined with an ion beam designed for light ions such as lithium.

10.1 Introduction

Lithium enriched isotopes are important for fission and fusion reactors. The laser isotope-separation method is considered, to be very attractive due to the high selectivity that can be obtained [1–6]. In this chapter we show a two-step selective photoionization method with commercial tunable-diode lasers, that can be used for nearly all the elements of the periodic table [7]. The method can also be used for ultra-sensitive trace-element analysis [8]. In this chapter we present a study of laser isotope separation in lithium with a simple, compact tunable-diode laser, with excellent spectral characteristics. The overall method allows the complete separation of the different isotopes, even in the case where the lines of the different isotopes overlap. We also present an experimental method consisting of a mass selector that includes a magnetic sector. A fairly detailed description of this relatively simple, compact, and inexpensive apparatus for separating lithium isotopes is given in this chapter.

Tunable lasers that can be chosen for laser isotope separation include the cw dye lasers [9] and narrow-linewidth copper-vapor-laser CVL-pumped-dye lasers [10–13]. Dye lasers are relatively complex and require fairly sophisticated engineering to build and maintain them. One advantage is that they can yield relatively high CW powers in a single-longitudinal mode. Even higher average powers are available from narrow-linewidth CVL-pumped pulsed-dye lasers. However, this class of laser, although very

doi:10.1088/978-0-7503-3839-4ch10

desirable for this type of application, has been demonstrated and operated only in a handful of laboratories around the world [10–14]. An initial alternative is to use tunable external-cavity semiconductor lasers [15, 16]. These lasers are relatively inexpensive, easy to operate, compact, and yield narrow-linewidth single-longitudinal-mode emission. For a laboratory with limited resources it is a good option to use well suited tunable-diode lasers as a coherent source. Our approach described here was designed for the selective excitation of light atoms as lithium specifically for spectroscopic applications. A scaling of the method to large isotope separation device requires higher laser power, higher lithium production and it will have some limitations due to the sensibility and international regulations of the subject.

10.2 Background

The upper limit for the number of ions produced by the lasers at the end of a laser-ionizing pulse can be obtained with the result of an absorption measurement [17]

$$N_i = \alpha P_i P_e (1 - T)/A \tag{10.1}$$

where $\alpha = \sigma_i T_{\mathrm{UV}}/(h^2 \nu_e \nu_i) = 17\,100\mathrm{m}^2\,\mathrm{W}^{-2}$, P_i is the averaged UV power, P_e is the exciter power, T is the exciter transmittance at the coincidence area A of both lasers in the interaction region, $\sigma_i = 7 \times 10^{22}\ \mathrm{m}^2$ is the ionization cross section [7], T_{UV} is the period of the UV laser pulses of the ionizing laser, h is the Planck's constant, and ν_e, ν_i are the excitation and ionization frequencies, respectively. The density n of the different isotopes can be obtained with the integral of the absorption coefficient over each line as described elsewhere [18] when the laser intensity is sufficiently low.

10.3 Lithium isotope separation experimental setup

The schematics of the experimental setup is depicted in figure 10.1. A beam of lithium atoms enters an optical cell through an entrance aperture. At the optical cell an

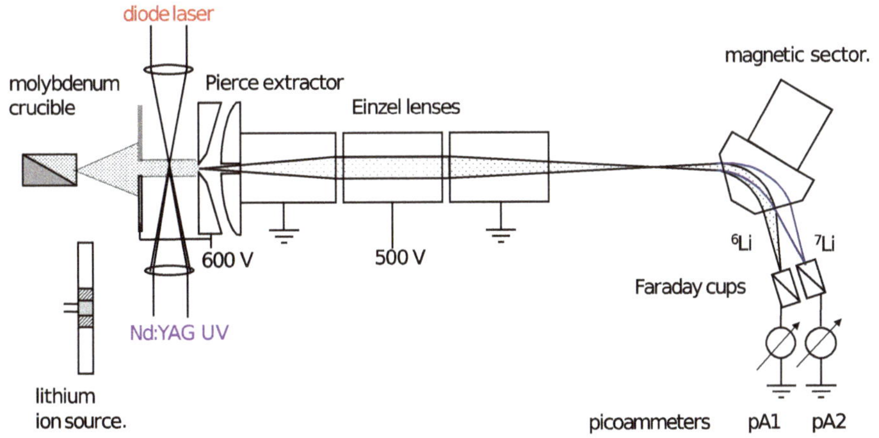

Figure 10.1. Experimental setup for laser isotope separation. The lithium ion source can replace the molybdenum crucible and be attached to the entrance slit for calibration of the mass selector. Reproduced from Olivares *et al* [19] with permission.

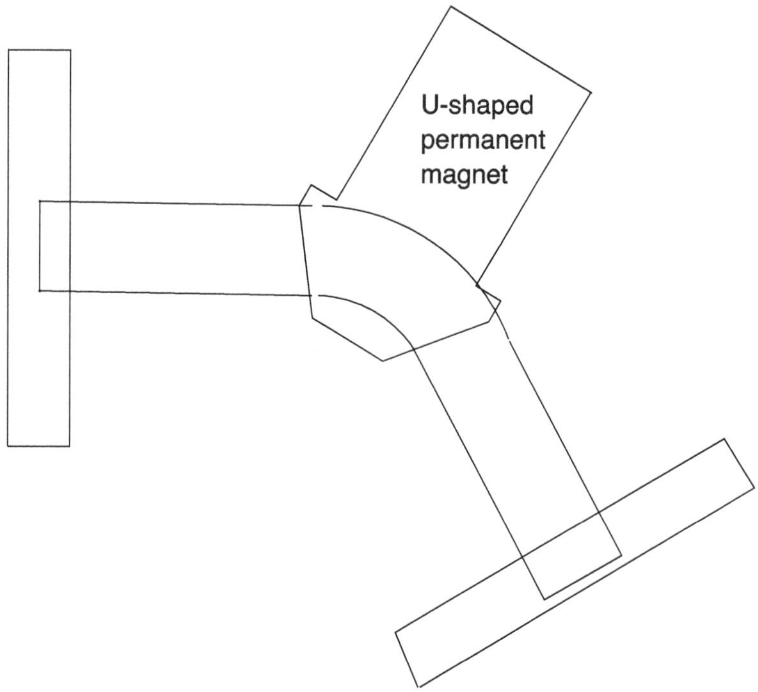

Figure 10.2. Basic diagram of the mass sector including vacuum manifold.

excitation volume is created by focusing two transverse laser beams of different frequencies, which provide the two-step excitation energy necessary for selective photoionization. Specifically, the lithium beam is illuminated by a focused UV laser beam and a spatially coincident focused tunable-diode laser. Following the illumination volume the doubly-excited lithium atoms enter a Pierce extractor and proceed to a set of Einzel lenses. The divergent doubly-excited lithium beam then enters a magnetic sector (figure 10.2) of a mass selector. At this stage the atom beam is separated into two subbeams corresponding to the ^{6}Li and ^{7}Li isotopes. Each of the isotopic subbeams continues to a separate Faraday cup, where the picocurrent is measured.

10.4 Laser system

The CW tunable-diode laser used in these experiments was a commercial device EOSI Model 2010, Environmental Optical Sensors, Inc., Boulder, Colorado configured in a Littrow grating cavity [15, 16]. The tuning range of this laser is 25 nm centered at 672 nm. This laser emits in a single-longitudinal mode at a linewidth of 100 kHz. The beam divergence is diffraction limited at an output power of 9 mW. This laser was tuned with an electronically controlled servomechanism that rotates the grating. This servomechanism includes a piezoelectric transducer driven by a slow triangular wave generator[1]. The time to scan one complete spectrum was about

[1] HP Model 3310B, Hewlett Packard Corp.

15 min in order to get enough resolution at the ionization spectra. The emission wavelength was monitored with an optical wavemeter[2]. As noted by previous authors [15–18] tunable semiconductor lasers are ideally suited for this type of spectroscopic task, given their remarkable stability and the absence of thermal and other media-related instabilities that tend to introduce short-term wavelength drifts that require sophisticated control systems. The tunable-diode laser was focused into the neutral lithium beam with a $f = 0.25$ m lens, while for ionization of the excited atoms we focused the fourth harmonic of a Nd:YAG laser[3] deployed in the counter-propagating direction with a fused silica $f = 0.58$ m lens. Typical average power densities of the exciter and ionizer at the focus were 35 W cm^{-2} at 671 nm and 125 W cm^{-2} at 266 nm, respectively. The Nd:YAG laser has a 5 kHz repetition rate with a KTP* intracavity crystal to produce the green output. We used a temperature-stabilized KD*P crystal[4] to produce the FHG at 266 nm and a dispersive quartz prism to separate the green from the UV radiation. To increase the UV power density we used a $f = 0.2$ m lens to focus the green into the KD*P crystal and a $f = 0.2$ m fused silica lens to recollimate the beam. We measured the UV pulse length with a photodiode[5] obtaining 80 ns at FWHM. We measured the focusing area of the red and UV laser using an ICCD[6] at different positions near the focal point. We obtained $A = (11.8 \pm 1.3) \times 10^{-9}\ m^2$ for the red laser and $A = (16.8 \pm 0.7) \times 10^{-9}\ m^2$ for the UV, respectively. In this case we are using only the 71% of the UV light for ionization.

10.5 Isotope separation apparatus

The beam of lithium atoms (figure 10.1) was produced through an evaporation of metallic lithium from a heat-pipe cell[7]. The heat-pipe used here can reach a temperature of 800 °C with a stability better than 1 °C min^{-1}. A detailed description is given elsewhere [20, 21]. One end of the heat-pipe was closed, and the other end was opened and connected to a vacuum chamber containing a mass selector. The aperture used to collimate the beam has a 0.5 cm diameter. The collimator and the Pierce extractor [22] were held at the same positive potential. The region between them is used as the laser-excitation volume region. The Pierce extractor yields a divergent ion beam that is focused with an Einzel lens system into the entrance of a mass selector. This mass selector was made in-house and is comprised of an ion gun and a magnetic sector. To calibrate the mass selector we have used a lithium ion source (figure 10.3).

The lithium ion source can be placed behind the Pierce extractor for nonselective ion production and calibration of the mass separator. Our lithium ion cell[8] is a

---

[2] Burleigh Model WA4500, Burleigh Instruments.
[3] Nd:YAG laserl Lee Laser Model 815TQ, Lee Laser, Inc.
[4] Inrad Model 5-301.
[5] Model FND100Q,EGG Optoelectronics.
[6] Model 576EMGRB, Princeton Instruments.
[7] Model HP-802, Comstock Inc.
[8] STD 250x, HeatWave Labs, Inc.

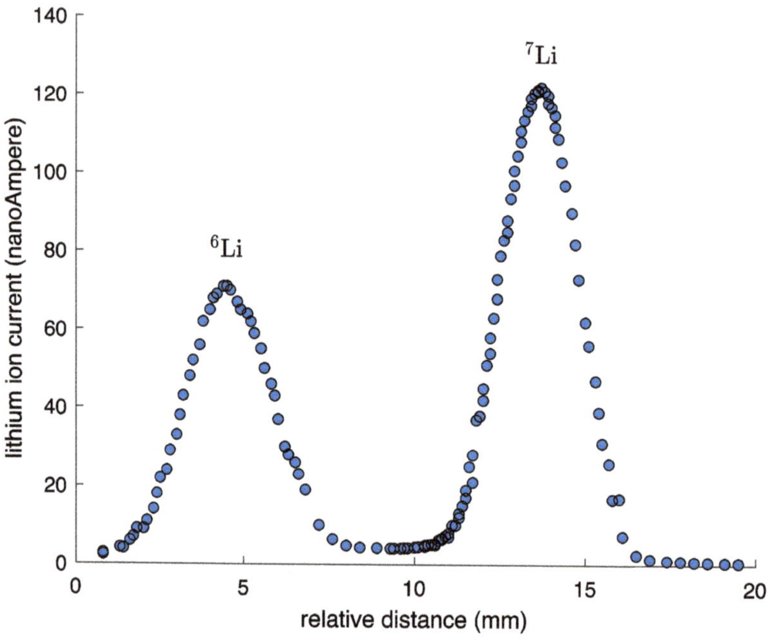

Figure 10.3. Mass spectrum of mixed ^{7}Li–^{6}Li beta-eucryptite source. The mass spectrum was obtained with a copper wire that was moved inside the vacuum. The wire was connected to a picoammeter. Reproduced from Olivares *et al* [19] with permission.

ceramic beta-eucryptite source containing a 30%/70% mixture of ^{6}Li and ^{7}Li isotopes. The construction and performance of these cells has been disclosed elsewhere. We also tested our system with pure ^{6}Li and ^{7}Li cells. The Pierce voltage V_p determines the ion-beam energy. Using the relationship that mass is proportional to the inverse of the applied voltage at a given magnetic field strength and geometry, we can estimate the required V_p. The most convenient value was obtained experimentally at 572 V with a stabilized high-voltage power supply[9], after focusing the beam at the entrance of the sector. To obtain a well-focused beam we have used a beam profile monitor[10] and adapted the length of the vacuum chamber to the position of the optimum focus. This focal point is 15 cm from the exit of the ion gun. The best focusing voltage V_f was held at 464 V and was determined experimentally by the position of the entrance slit of the magnetic sector. To measure the mass spectrum we employed a 2.5 mm section copper wire that was moved by a gear system connected to a rotary-motion feedthrough with a stepper motor[11]. The ion current reaching the wire was measured by a picoammeter[12], and recorded with a digital-storage oscilloscope[13] By using a mixed cell we were able to obtain a mass

[9] Model EH05P20, Glassman High Voltage, Inc.
[10] Model BPM80, Natural Electrostatics Corporation.
[11] Model BRM275-03, MDC.
[12] Model 485, Keithley Instruments, Inc.
[13] Model 9314, LeCroy Corp.

spectrum at one scan of the wire. The positions of the isotopes and the resolution were obtained from the barrel graduation. With this result we could replace the wire at the exit of the sector by two 9 mm wide copper plates separated by 1 mm. The size and position of the plates were determined from the mass spectrum. We adjusted the position of the plates by measuring the current with the ion cell again. In this manner we obtained a collector suitable for mass 6 and mass 7 isotopes. In the experiments, where the ions were produced by the lasers, the ion cell was removed and replaced by the neutral beam and collimator described above. The lasers were focused just behind the Pierce element. The rms value of the current at the ^{7}Li collector was measured with a picoampermeter[14] connected with a general purpose interface bus to a personal computer and recorded with a Labview 5.0 application. The current of the ^{6}Li isotope was recorded simultaneously with the same software and interface with a more sensitive picoampermeter[15]. The time required by our system to take the data for each pair of current values was 652 ms. The total number of ions produced at the ionization area were obtained from an absorption measurement and compared with the ions collected at both plates behind the magnetic sector. In this case the transmittance was measured at saturation with the same laser intensity that was used at the current measurement. This was done at resonance and slightly off resonance to avoid etalon effects. To determine the density of neutral lithium atoms we removed the focusing lens and reduced further the intensity by means of a neutral density filter. The spectrum was recorded with an optical power meter[16] and a digital-storage oscilloscope[17]. The background light was subtracted. The absorption path length was determined from fluorescence measurements [23].

10.6 Experimental overview

The overall experimental setup described in the sections 10.4 and 10.5 fits in the space provided by two 1.21 × 2.43 m commercial optical tables with a total utilized surface area of approximately 4.5 m^2. The main two items contributing to this reduced area are the tunable-diode laser and the in-house mass separator. The tunable-diode laser is only a fraction of the size of an alternative cw dye laser or a CVL pumped-dye laser. The high-stability precision magnet comprising the mass selector was designed specifically for applications involving light atoms such as lithium. As such, it is only a small fraction of the size of a conventional commercial mass spectrometer. Ease of operation is a further experimental advantage.

10.7 Results

In these experiments a beam of lithium atoms is produced and illuminated by a two-step selective-laser excitation process. Following passage through a mass-selection apparatus two detectors, Faraday cup 1 and Faraday cup 2, are used to collect the

[14] Keithley Model 485.
[15] Keithley Model 595.
[16] Model 1815C, Newport Corp.
[17] LeCroy Model 9314A.

spatially separated isotopes ^{7}Li and ^{6}Li, respectively. Spatial separation is shown, through a mass spectrum, in figure 10.3. For our experimental conditions we have a resolution of $\Delta M/M = 3$, which is enough to separate the isotopes of interest.

The isotopic beam detected in Faraday cup 1 gives origin to the resonance ionization mass spectrum of the ^{7}Li-D_1 and ^{7}Li-D_2 resolved in doublets (figure 10.4).

Note that this spectrum is clear, well resolved, and typical of only this isotope. The isotopic beam detected in Faraday cup 2 gives origin to the resonance ionization mass spectrum of the ^{6}Li-D_1 and ^{6}Li-D_2 lines (figure 10.5). Note that this spectrum is characterized by the lower intensity peaks, which correspond to this particular isotope exclusively. For comparison purposes the reader can observe the mixed, or combined, high-resolution spectrum of ^{7}Li and ^{6}Li given elsewhere. Albeit rather insignificant, the average value for the background signal was subtracted in each case from the measured spectra. This average background level was measured when the lithium was cold (heat-pipe cell off) obtaining 0.87 pA and 0.12 pA at the ^{7}Li and at the ^{6}Li collector plate, respectively. This background level is deemed to have a negligible effect on the overall signal. The hyperfine structure of the isotopes can be distinguished owing to a reduction in the Doppler width produced by the collimation and expansion of the vapor [24]. The transmittance T of each hyperfine line of the ^{7}Li-D_2 line was 0.991 and 0.996, respectively, and the ionization laser power was $P_i = (15 \pm 1)$ mW. In each case we considered the losses at the windows. For these parameters equation (10.1) can be used to estimate the upper limit for the number of ions. In this case those upper

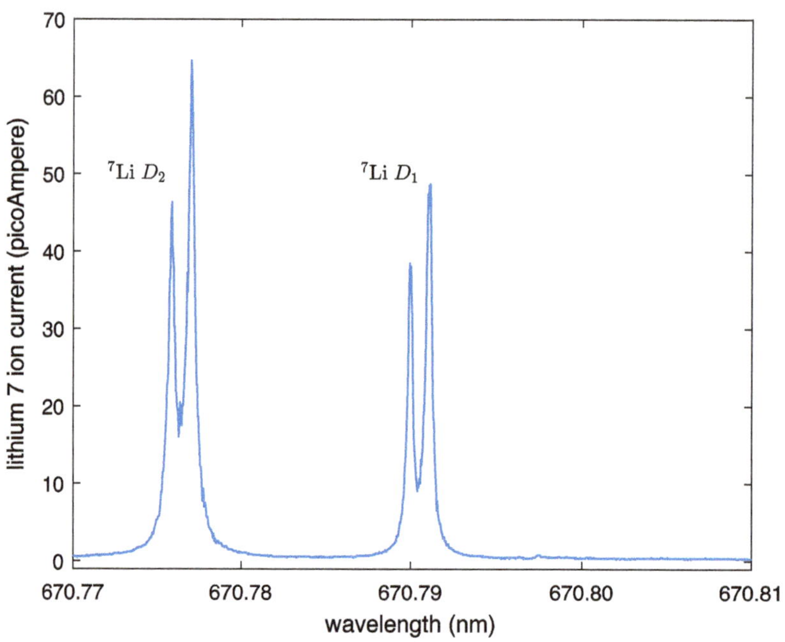

Figure 10.4. Resonance ionization mass hyperfine spectrum recorded at the Faraday cup 1. Reproduced from Olivares *et al* [19] with permission.

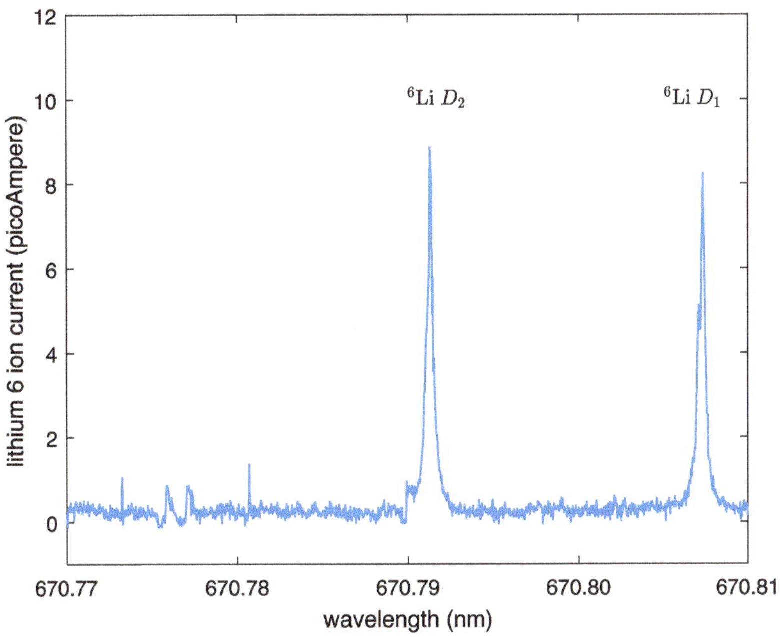

Figure 10.5. Resonance ionization mass hyperfine spectrum recorded at the Faraday cup 2. Reproduced from Olivares *et al* [19] with permission.

limits are estimated to be $N_1 = 8.56 \times 10^5$ and $N_2 = 3.83 \times 10^5$ at the peaks of the lines, respectively. The density of the neutral lithium beam was determined from the absorption spectra. In this measurement the intensity of the laser used for excitation was kept low enough to avoid saturation effects and optical pumping 1 W cm $^{-2}$ is convenient. At 780 °C the density of the beam was $n = 2.5 \times 10^{16}$ m^{-3} with a lithium beam diameter of 0.005 m. The collimator installed behind the Pierce extractor has the important function of efficiently repelling the thermal ions arriving from the heat-pipe cell, which could contribute to an increase of the background signal at the spectra, giving a loss of selectivity. Selectivity also could be reduced by collision effects among atoms or ions as excitation transfer, but these effects are quite negligible owing to the low lithium density, which gives a mean free path 1n of the order of 10 m or more, depending on the cross section value of each collision process. The ionization by electrons can also affect the selectivity, but this effect is absent because the Pierce extractor repels the electrons of the beam. An additional nonselective effect is the direct ionization of the lithium clusters produced by the UV; this effect can be measured with the experimental arrangement of our previous work. This corresponds to 104 clusters pulse or less. These clusters are filtered by the mass selector and do not contribute to the picocurrent signal. In these experiments we observe a negligible background signal, and the spectral lines ^{7}Li-D_2, depicted in figure 10.4, and ^{6}Li-D_1 depicted in figure 10.5, appear free of the simultaneous signal from the other isotope. This indicates a high selectivity during the resonant ionization process.

10.8 Discussion and conclusion

In these experiments we have recorded a high-resolution spectrum corresponding to ^{7}Li in one Faraday cup detector, whereas the spectrum corresponding to ^{6}Li was recorded in a second Faraday cup detector. These two detectors were separated spatially from each other. This spatial mass separation was a result of the selective two-step laser excitation, using a UV laser beam and a visible tunable-diode laser, of an atomic beam of lithium that propagated through a relatively simple mass selector. The intensity ratio and wavelength characteristics of the two separated hyperfine spectra are consistent with known spectroscopic data. To our knowledge this is the first report of the laser isotope separation of lithium utilizing a tunable-diode laser. The application of this tunable-diode laser in conjunction with a simple, and compact, mass selector contribute significantly towards the ease of use and the overall compactness of the experimental apparatus for lithium isotope separation experiments in light atoms.

References

[1] Arisawa T, Maruyama Y, Suzuki Y and Shiba K 1982 Lithium isotope separation by laser *Appl. Phys.* B **28** 73–6

[2] Karlov N V, Krynetskiĭ B and Stelmakh O M 1977 Measurement of the photoionization cross section of the Li atom at the 2P level *Sov. J. Quantum Electron.* 1305

[3] Yamashita M and Kashiwagi H 1979 Method for separation and enrichment of lithium isotopes by laser *US Patent* 4149077 https://www.osti.gov/biblio/6303723-method-separation-enrichment-lithium-isotopes-laser

[4] Payne M, Deng L and Thonnard N 1994 Applications of resonance ionization mass spectrometry *Rev. Sci. Instrum.* **65** 2433–59

[5] Shaw R W, Young J P, Smith D H, Bonanno A S and Dale J M 1990 Hyperfine structure of lanthanum at sub-Doppler resolution by diode-laser-initiated resonance-ionization mass spectroscopy *Phys. Rev.* A **41** 2566

[6] Shaw R W, Young J P and Smith D H 1989 Diode laser initiated resonance ionization mass spectrometry of lanthanum *Anal. Chem.* **61** 695–7

[7] Hurst G, Payne M, Kramer S and Young J 1979 Resonance ionization spectroscopy and one-atom detection *Rev. Mod. Phys.* **51** 767

[8] Bekov G I, Letokhov V S and Radaev V N 1989 Laser photoionization spectroscopy for ultrasensitive trace element analysis *Fresenius Z. Anal. Chem.* **335** 19–24

[9] Hollberg L 1990 CW dye lasers *Dye Laser Principles, with Applications* (San Diego, CA: Academic) ch 5

[10] Duarte F J and Piper J A 1984 Narrow linewidth, high prf copper laser-pumped dye-laser oscillators *Appl. Opt.* **23** 1391–4

[11] Bass I L, Bonanno R E, Hackel R P and Hammond P R 1992 High-average-power dye laser at Lawrence Livermore National Laboratory *Appl. Opt.* **31** 6993–7006

[12] Singh S, Dasgupta K, Kumar S, Manohar K, Nair L and Chatterjee U 1994 High-power high-repetition-rate copper-vapor-pumped dye laser *Opt. Eng.* **33** 1894–904

[13] Maruyama Y, Kato M and Arisawa T 1996 Effects of excited-state absorption and amplified spontaneous emission in a high-average-power dye laser amplifier pumped by copper vapor lasers *Opt. Eng.* **35** 1084–7

[14] Sugiyama A, Nakayama T, Kato M, Maruyama Y and Arisawa T 1996 Characteristics of a pressure-tuned single-mode dye laser oscillator pumped by a copper vapor laser *Opt. Eng.* **35** 1093–7

[15] Zorabedian P 1995 Tunable external-cavity semiconductor lasers *Tunable Lasers Handbook* (New York: Academic) ch 8

[16] Duarte F J 1995 Tunable external-cavity semiconductor lasers *Tunable Lasers Handbook* (New York: Marcel-Dekker) ch 5

[17] Olivares I E and Duarte A E 1999 Resonance ionization spectroscopy in a thermal lithium beam by means of diode lasers *Appl. Opt.* **38** 7481–5

[18] Olivares I E, Duarte A E, Lokajczyk T, Dinklage A and Duarte F J 1998 Doppler-free spectroscopy and collisional studies with tunable diode lasers of lithium isotopes in a heat-pipe oven *J. Opt. Soc. Am.* B **15** 1932–9

[19] Olivares *et al* 2002 Lithium isotope separation with tunable diode lasers *Appl. Opt.* **41** 2973–7

[20] Vidal C 1973 Spectroscopic observations of subsonic and sonic vapor flow inside an open-ended heat pipe *J. Appl. Phys.* **44** 2225–32

[21] Vidal C and Cooper J 1969 Heat-Pipe Oven: a new, well-defined metal vapor device for spectroscopic measurements *J. Appl. Phys.* **40** 3370–4

[22] Heinz O and Reaves R T 1968 Lithium ion emitter for low energy beam experiments *Rev. Sci. Instrum.* **39** 1229–30

[23] Dinklage A, Lokajczyk T, Kunze H J, Schweer B and Olivares I E 1998 In situ density measurement for a thermal lithium beam employing diode lasers *Rev. Sci. Instrum.* **69** 321–2

[24] Demtröder W 2013 *Laser Spectroscopy: Basic Concepts and Instrumentation* (Berlin: Springer)

IOP Publishing

Ignacio E Olivares and Patrick Carrazana

Chapter 11

Laser cooling

Our first experiments in a magneto optical trap were performed and published in 2008 [1, 2]. A brief review of the experimental methods can be found in [3–5]. The physics of a cloud of cold atoms is well described by Metcalf *et al* [6]. In this chapter we explain our approach to the construction of the magneto optical trap. Our experiments are based on the construction described by Wieman *et al* [7] and Rapol *et al* [8]. We followed the guidelines given in these articles but used state of the art equipment to obtain reliable results in our initial attempts to obtain a cloud of cold atoms. The only initial exception was a self-made optical glass cell that was considered inexpensive. Subsequently, it was replaced by a more technically advanced cell that permitted us to improve the observational capability of the system. We describe here an experiment that proved the stability of the cloud and the optical method to vary the laser intensity of the pump and trap beams. Finally, we study the influence of laser intensity imbalance on cloud formation and give values for the threshold intensity of each laser that supports cloud formation.

11.1 The pump and the probe laser

Tunable diode lasers are particularly well suited to induce cooling in rubidium near 780 nm (see, e.g., [9–11]. In these experiments we use two grating-tuned semi-conductor lasers: a cooling laser (also known as the trapping laser) and a repumping laser (also known as a hyperfine pumping laser). The cooling laser is tuned to the $5S_{1/2}F = 3 \rightarrow 5P_{3/2}F' = 4$ transition of ^{85}Rb while the repumping laser is tuned to the $5S_{1/2}F = 2 \rightarrow 5P_{3/2}F' = 3$ transition of ^{85}Rb. Most tunable diode lasers used in laser cooling experiments, and commercially available diode laser systems for this application, are of the 'open cavity' class with the diffraction grating either deployed in Littrow configuration or grazing-incidence configuration. These lasers are susceptible to external optical coupling, thus requiring the use of optical isolators.

doi:10.1088/978-0-7503-3839-4ch11

A solution is to employ 'closed cavity' configurations where the output is taken in a traditional manner via an output coupler mirror [12, 13]. However, these lasers tend to be more expensive and are not widely available in their semiconductor versions. An additional limitation associated with these open cavity semiconductor tunable laser sources is the inherent interdependence of the operating current and temperature, which severely limits the ability to vary the laser intensity whilst maintaining oscillation at a specific laser wavelength. Thus, in order to vary the laser intensity at will, while maintaining narrow-linewidth oscillation at a desired frequency, it is necessary to use independent external methods that do not interact with the laser. Glan–Thompson polarizers have been previously used as output coupler mirrors in narrow-linewidth tunable laser oscillators [14]

The pump and probe lasers used in our experiments are Littrow cavity diode lasers[1] delivering about 50 mW of single longitudinal mode emission near 780 nm at a laser linewidth of nearly 1 MHz. Each laser was protected with a 60 dB optical isolator. The optical isolators were placed inside the laser case after the grating. The use of the optical isolators is essential to obtain a reproducible magneto optical trap as it is very difficult to avoid reflections back into the laser. These reflections can destroy the single mode emission of the lasers.

The lasers are stabilized with the Pound–Drever–Hall (PDH) method. The PHD system includes a proportional, integral, differential unit (Toptica Photonics PID 110) and PDH detectors (Toptica Photonics PDD 110). Each laser was protected with a 60 dB optical isolator (Model FI-790-TV, Linos).

11.2 Energy level diagram-laser cooling

The energy level diagram (figure 11.1) contains two ground hyperfine levels separated by nearly 3 GHz and four excited levels separated by less than the Doppler broadened line. As the atoms pumped by the cooling laser from the $F = 3$ level into the $F' = 4$ level decay into the $F = 2$ level it is necessary to optically pump the atoms from this level back to the $F = 3$ level through the $F' = 3$ level. This is done by the repumping laser.

11.3 Finding the spectral lines for repumping and cooling laser

To find the spectral lines for the repumping and cooling lasers it is necessary to measure the whole absorption spectrum from the rubidium atoms in the cell using a photodiode. The experimental setup for measuring the saturated absorption spectrum is depicted in figure 11.2.

Part of the light is driven to a scanning confocal Fabry–Perot interferometer (FPI not shown here). The FPI signal gives a diagnostic of the single mode operation of the laser. To obtain the central wavelengths, it is necessary to find the bias current and set the temperature of each laser. Afterwards the laser wavelength should be scanned at nearly 10 to 20 GHz around the resonance frequency. This is done driving the piezo element attached at the grating at large amplitudes. This procedure

[1] Toptica Photonics, Model DL100.

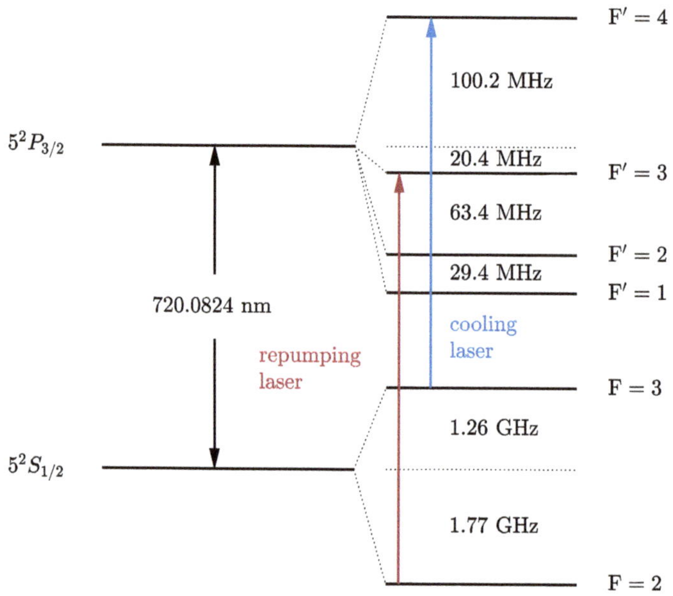

Figure 11.1. Energy level diagram for Rb85.

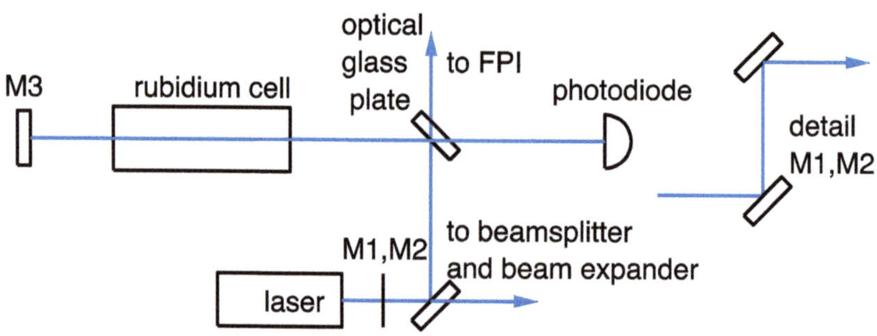

Figure 11.2. Detail of the saturated absorption spectrometer for the MOT.

should be followed for each laser. The complete rubidium spectrum is shown in figure 11.3

A typical detailed absorption spectra of rubidium with the repumping and cooling lines is shown in figure 11.4 and recorded in two different oscilloscopes. The spectra corresponds to a zoom of the whole spectrum shown in figure 11.3.

11.4 Description of the Pound–Drever–Hall method for frequency stability of the pump and probe lasers

The setup of a cold atom cloud requires fixed cooling and repumping laser frequencies. It is possible to obtain the cloud of cooled atoms without stabilizing the laser, but it makes the work more difficult. The PDH method permits the stability of the frequency of the laser frequencies close to the resonances. Figure 11.5 shows the optical setup of the PDH detector.

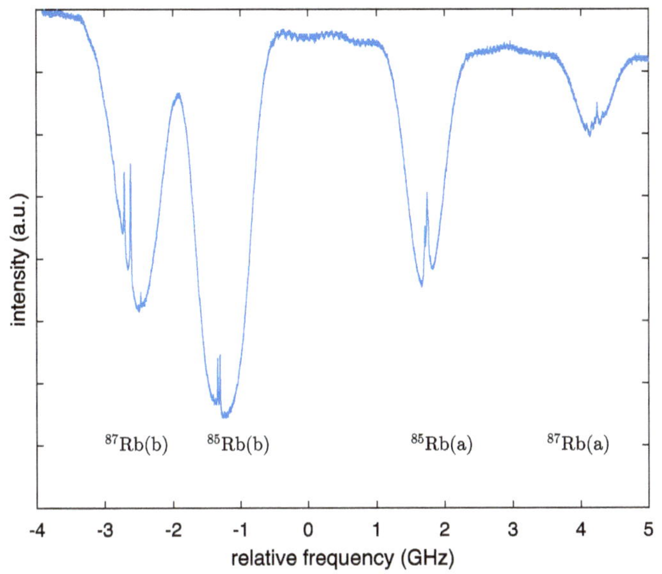

Figure 11.3. Complete spectrum of rubidium lines as seen in the oscilloscope.

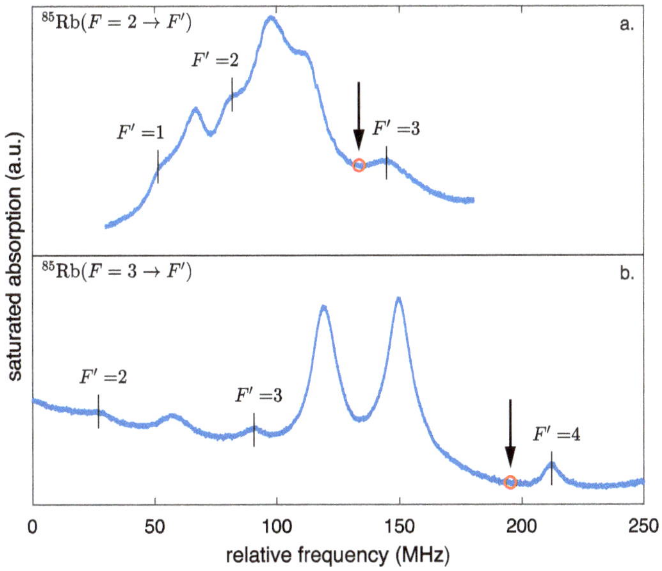

Figure 11.4. Detailed saturated absorption spectra for the magneto optical trap: (a) repumping laser; (b) cooling laser. The red circles indicate the frequency to which the laser have to be locked with the Pound–Drever–Hall method. Peaks between transitions are cross overs. Lamb dips are useful to identify the lines.

A diode laser is collimated by a aspheric lens of short focal distance and its wavelength controlled by a grating that reflects its first diffraction order back into the laser cavity. The wavelength is roughly adjusted by rotating the grating. A piezo electric transducer (PZT) can produce fine angular displacements of the grating and

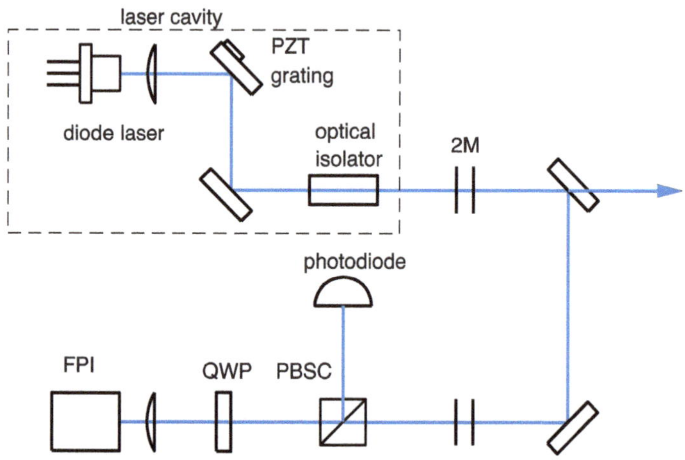

Figure 11.5. Detail Pound–Drever–Hall detector MOT.

control the frequency of the lasers single mode emission at the MHz level. An optical isolator installed in front of the laser permits to avoid unwanted back reflections into the laser cavity. These reflections could destroy the single mode emission of the laser. Laser exiting the optical isolator is driven to the confocal scanning Fabry–Perot interferometer. Two mirrors (2M) lifted the laser to 15 cm from the optical top. The beam was conducted by means of an optical glass divider, a mirror and a pair of mirrors that placed the beam at the level of the interferometers axis. The beam passes a polarizing beam splitter cube, a quarter wave plate and was focused with an $f = 200$ mm lens to the interferometer. The light reflected from the interferometer becomes horizontally polarized after passing the quarter wave plate twice and was reflected by the polarizing beam splitter cube into a fast photodiode. The reflected electric field from a Fabry–Perot interferometer is given by

$$E_r = \frac{(1 - e^{i\delta})\sqrt{R})}{1 - Re^{i\delta}} E_i \tag{11.1}$$

where R is the mirror reflectivity and $\delta = 2\pi\Delta\omega/\Delta\omega_{\mathrm{FSR}}$. The laser is modulated at a frequency $\Omega/2\pi = 20$ MHz The incident laser amplitude can be written as a carrier with two weak sidebands as

$$I(\omega) = J_0^2(\beta)L(\omega;\, \omega_0) + \sum_{n=1}^{\infty} J_n^2(\beta)[L(\omega;\, \omega_0 + n\Omega) + L(\omega;\, \omega_0 - n\Omega)]$$

where β is the modulation amplitude,

$$L(\omega) = \frac{\Gamma/(2\pi)}{(\omega - \omega_0)^2 + \Gamma^2/4} \tag{11.2}$$

is a Lorentzian function, and Γ the laser linewidth. A modulated spectra for $\Omega/2\pi = 20$ MHz modulation frequency and laser linewidth and $\Gamma = 10$ MHz is depicted in figure 11.6.

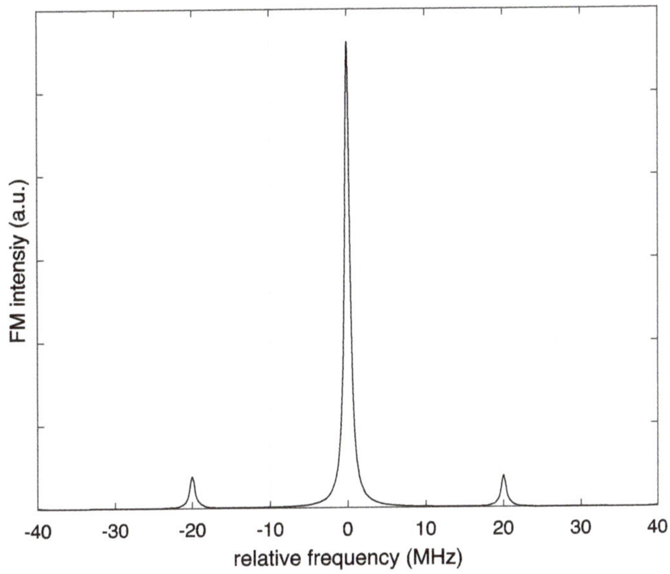

Figure 11.6. Theoretical frequency modulated spectrum. $\beta = 0.5$, $\Omega/(2\pi) = 20$ MHz, $\Gamma = 5 \times 10^6$ s^{-1}.

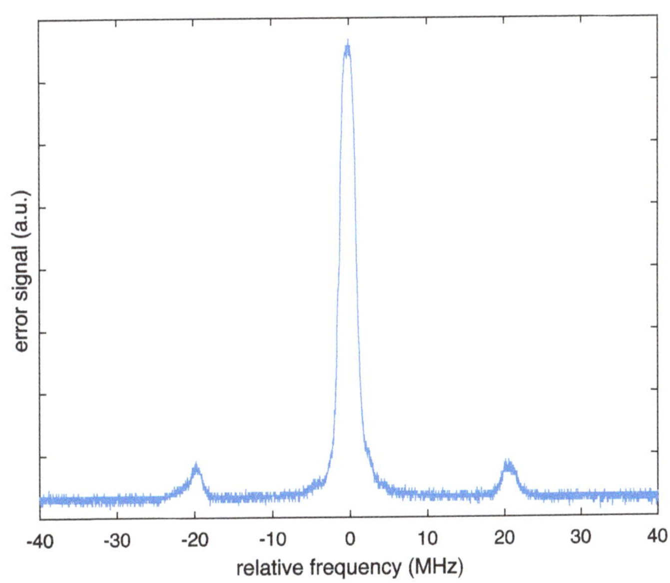

Figure 11.7. Frequency modulated laser spectrum. Sidebands at 20 MHz on both sides of the central laser wavelength.

Two sidebands can be found on each side of the central feature (figure 11.7). The signal produced by the fast photodiode is mixed with the modulation sinusoidal signal. The error function (figure 11.8) is obtained when the product of these two functions is passed through a low pass filter. Our experimental error function is shown in figure 11.9

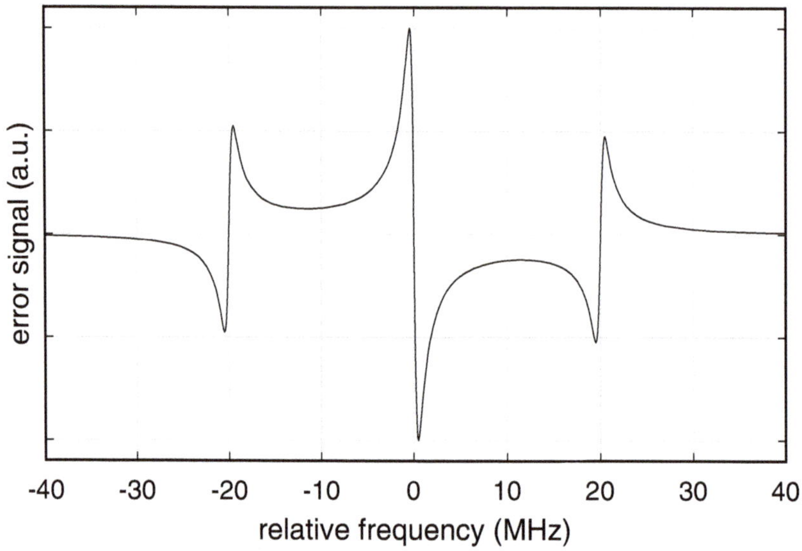

Figure 11.8. Error function considering a FSR = 1 GHz, finesse = 500 and 20 MHz modulation.

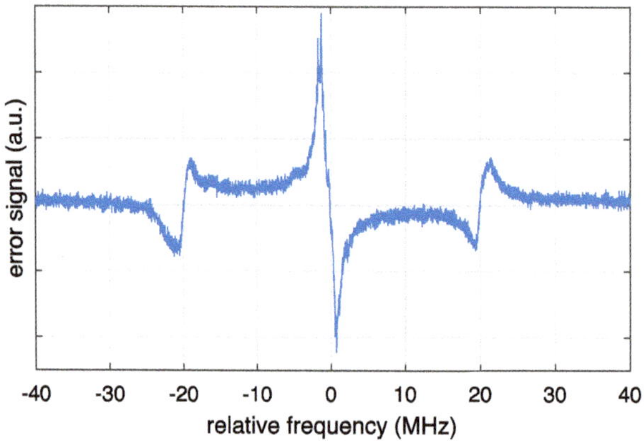

Figure 11.9. Experimental error function.

11.5 Installing the MOT optics

The optics and laser requirements needed to observe laser cooling in atomic vapors, via the use of a magnetic optical trap (MOT), are well-known in the literature (see, e.g., [15]). The lasers and part of our MOT optics was purchased from Toptica Photonics and it is shown in figure 11.10. The reader should analyze the configuration presented here that was done for simplicity and can check easily to determine right or left polarization. Other configurations can be also explored.

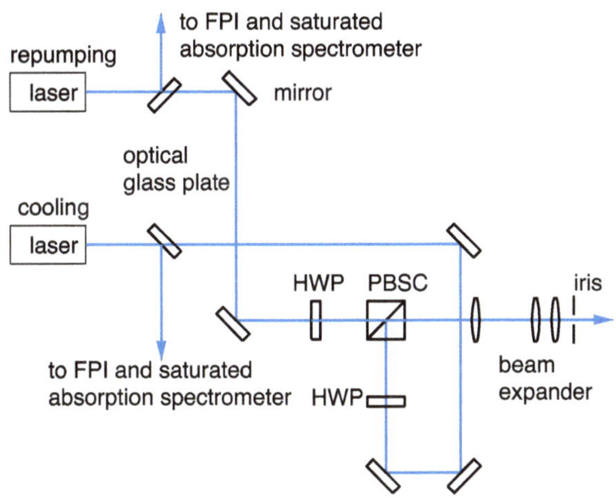

Figure 11.10. Experimental setup for combining and expanding cooling and repumping laser cooling.

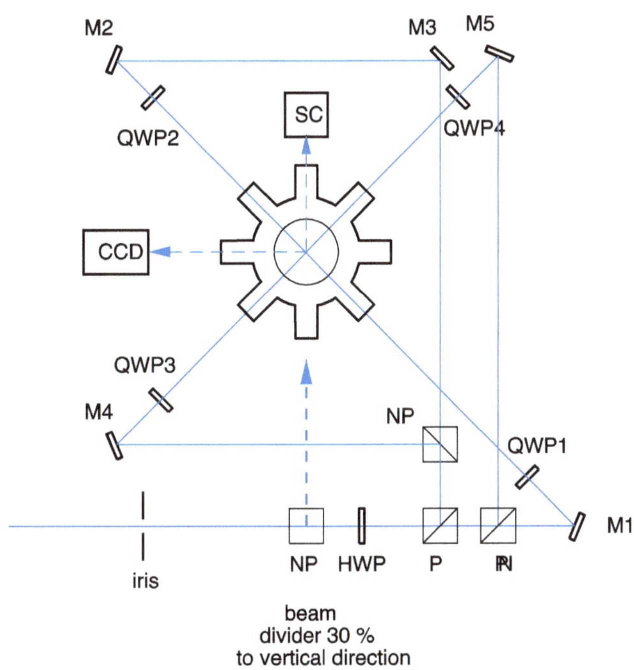

Figure 11.11. Horizontal polarizing arrangement for circular light.

11.6 Polarizing optics: left and right circulating light

The polarizing optics in the plane of the optical table is shown in figure 11.11 The vertical arrangement for the polarizing optics is shown in figure 11.12.

Two laser beams with opposite helicity polarizations impinge on an atom from opposite directions. The magnetic levels of the atoms are shifted by the magnetic field which changes with position. The net result is a position-dependent force that pushes the

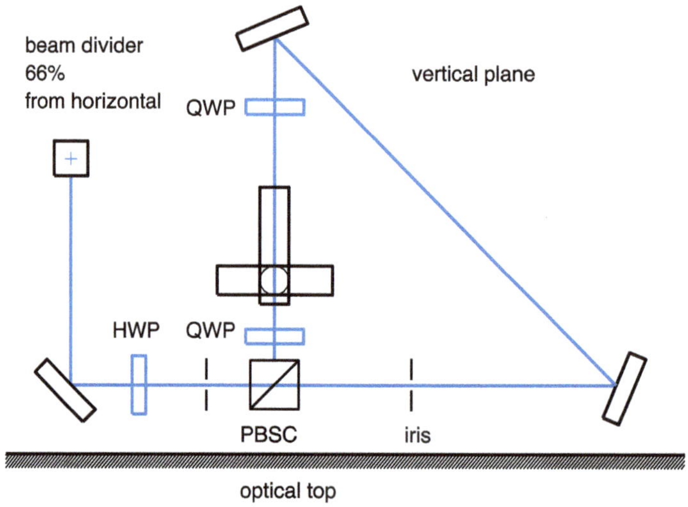

Figure 11.12. Vertical polarizing arrangement for circular light.

atoms into the center of the magneto optical trap. In our experiment we used 1 inch diameter multiple order quarter wave plates[2] and 1 inch diameter multiple order half wave plates[3]. It is desirable that the wave plates are installed in optical rotating mounts[4]. In our case we used fixed mounts that were constructed by us. Multiple order wave plates are designed for a specific wavelength. In our case the required wavelength was 780 nm. A linear polarized beam incident on a multiple order quarter wave plate produces circular polarized light when the electrical field of the incident laser is oriented at 45° with respect to the optical axis of the quarter wave plate. One of the vector components of the E-field is parallel to the optical axis and the other perpendicular to it. A good method to check the orientation of optical axis of a quarter wave plate is to construct an optical isolator as described previously. Incident light coming from the left side with its polarization vector parallel to the plane of the paper passes the polarizing beam splitter cube and continues through the quarter wave plate. When the optical axis of the plate is rotated in 45° with respect to the electrical field the wave becomes circular. The reflected light turns perpendicular to the plane of the paper, and becomes fully reflected by the polarizing beam splitter cube. With the aid of a photodiode it is possible to find the largest reflected signal by rotating the quarter wave plate slightly back and forth. The optical axis of the half wave plate can be found using the linear incident laser light and a polarizing beam splitter cube. When this plate is rotated 45° relative to the incident field, the field rotates 90°. In general when the half wave plate is rotated at an angle, the electrical field rotates at the double angle. This can be used to obtain a transmission of 0.4 and reflectivity of 0.6. This is normally correct, but the transmitted E-fields are slightly rotated to vertical or horizontal orientations.

[2] CVI—Melles Griot, Model QWPM-780-10-4.
[3] CVI—Melles Griot, Model QWPM-780-10-230.
[4] Thorlabs, Model RSP1.

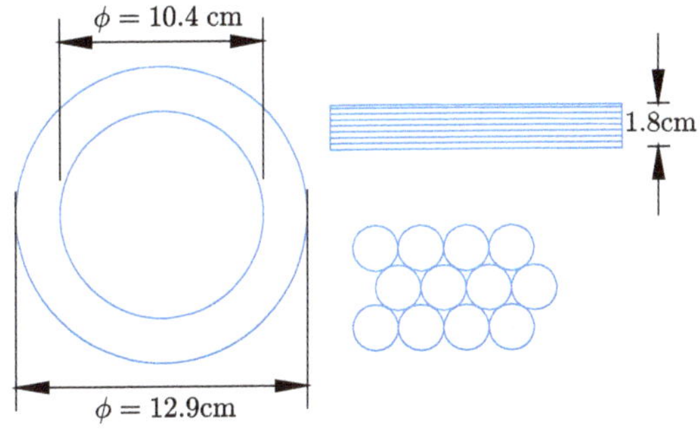

Figure 11.13. Anti-Helmholtz coils.

11.7 Anti-Helmholtz coils: magneto optical trap

The force acting on the atoms in the magneto optical trap depends on the position. It is larger for atoms that are more distant from the center of the trap. The MOT coils consists in two copper solenoids with the same dimensions and number of windings. The coils are disposed in anti-Helmholtz configuration one over the other. Figure 11.13 shows a diagram of the coils.

The current in one coil flows in the opposite direction with respect to the other coil. It is recommended [7] to have a variable magnetic field gradient with a maximum of 0.2 T m^{-1}. We normally used between 0.10 and 0.15 T m^{-1}. We used a 1.15 mm diameter (AWG 17), enameled copper wire. Each coil has 196 windings ordered in 14 sheets with 14 windings per sheet. To drive the coils we used two 5 A variable current supplies.

11.8 Observation of the cloud with NIR camera

Our first result with our homemade chamber is shown in figure 11.14

Figure 11.15 shows a near infrared photo of the atomic cloud. The photo was obtained with a modified camera where the NIR filter was removed.

11.9 Analog control of laser intensities with a Glan–Thompson polarizer

In this section we explain the use of a simple optical method, based on rotating Glan–Thompson polarizer (RGTP) prism pairs to control the laser intensity incident on the rubidium MOT at the experimenter's will. This method was previously demonstrated in industrial laser printers [16, 17] and is applied here in a manner compatible with the propagation optics of the MOT configuration. The optical configuration including the RGTP, and a polarizing beam splitter (PBS), is depicted in figure 11.16.

With this arrangement, the laser intensity is varied independently of the operating current and temperature of the lasers, thus allowing the emission frequency to be controlled by the dispersive optics of the cavity. An additional benefit of this technique is that it provides a further, albeit partial, optical isolator to protect the laser from external optical coupling. In this regard, in any angular position other than that required for maximum transmission, a counter propagating radiation is attenuated.

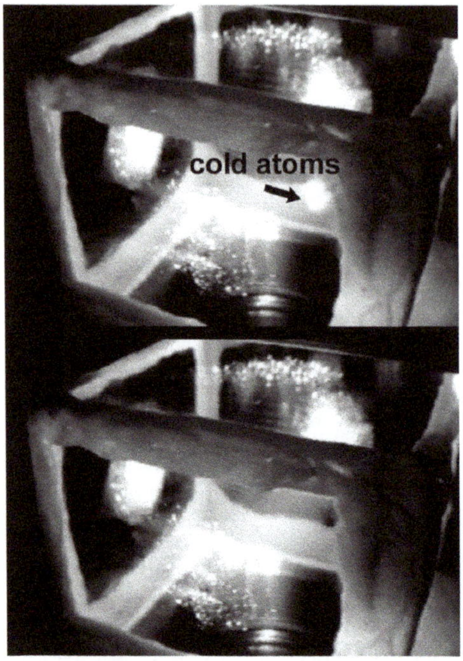

Figure 11.14. Photo of our first cold atom cloud taken with a modified camera (the NIR filter was removed). Reprinted with permission from Olivares I E 2006 Photos of the cloud of cooled atoms experiment, Physics Department, Universidad de Santiago de Chile.

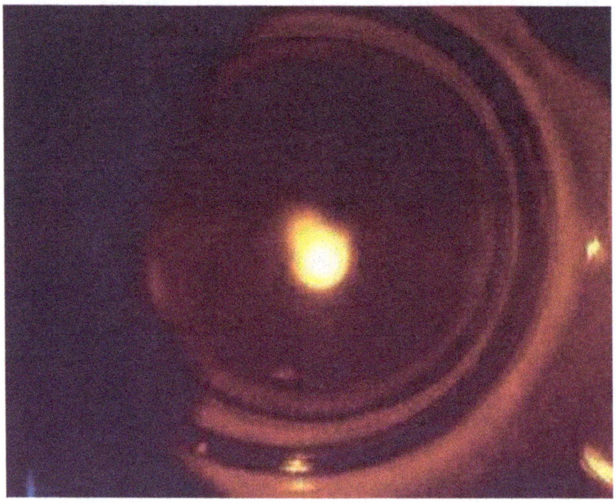

Figure 11.15. Photo of the cold atom cloud taken with a modified camera (the NIR filter was removed). The cloud is at the center of the image. The chamber entrance tube can be observed. Reprinted with permission from Olivares I E 2006 Photos of the cloud of cooled atoms experiment, Physics Department, Universidad de Santiago de Chile.

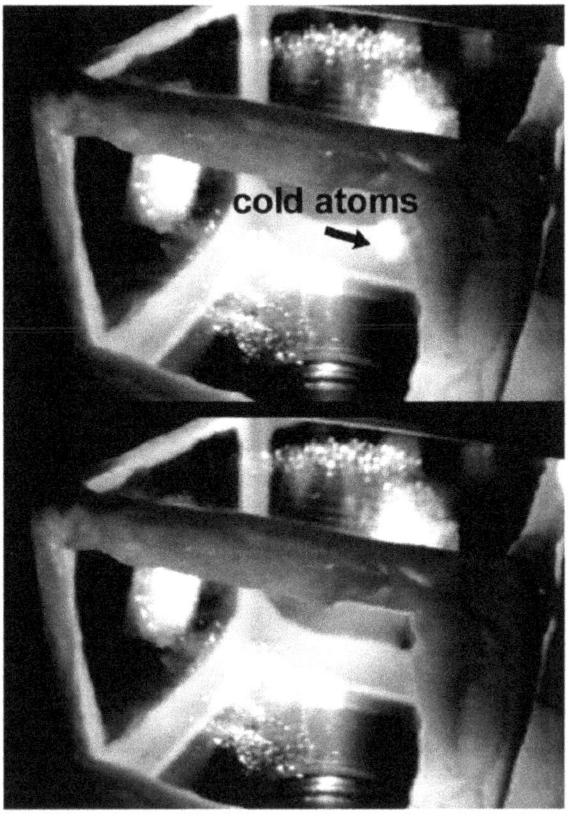

Figure 11.16. Schematics of the laser cooling optics: laser 1 is the cooling laser; laser 2 the repumping laser, Pound–Drever–Hall stabilization systems are associated with lasers 1 and 2; RGTP1 is the rotating Glan–Thompson polarizer associated with laser 1; RGTP2 is the rotating Glan–Thompson polarizer associated with laser 2. In this diagram, the RGTPs are depicted for maximum transmission of emission polarized perpendicular to the plane of propagation. Rotation by $\pi/2$ radians of the RGTP (as shown in figure 11.16) extinguishes the transmission of the laser emission. The two expanded laser beams proceed to split into six beams to illuminate the three axes of the MOT (two horizontal axes and one vertical axis). Laser powers are monitored prior to the entrance of the beam expander. This particular configuration is optimized to allow the variation of laser 2 power while keeping laser 1 constant.

The rotating Glan–Thompson extra cavity technique described here, to vary the intensity of the laser beams, to the best of our knowledge has not been previously disclosed in the context of laser cooling experiments, as can be established by perusing well-known reviews on the subject [6, 18, 19] and the recent literature. A successful and widely used method applied to control, extra cavity, the intensity of laser beams in laser cooling experiments, is acousto-optic modulation (AOM) (for recent references see, e.g., [20, 21]. However, as partially explained in [16], from an engineering perspective, AOMs are relatively expensive, exhibit transmission limitations, energy density limitations, and require sophisticated electronics for control. Rotating Glan–Thompson polarizers provide a simple, efficient, and optically rugged alternative, to vary at will the intensity of transmitted laser beams as disclosed in 2001 [16].

The Glan–Thompson polarizers used in these experiments are antireflection coated on the surface facing the laser and provide an extinction ratio of $\sim 5 \times 10^{-5}$. To explain how the optics work we arbitrarily chose to illustrate the mechanics of extra cavity power variation in the L2 beam while the power of the L1 beam was kept constant as seen in figure 11.16.

The outputs of both lasers are initially polarized perpendicular to the plane of propagation and both RGTPs are set for maximum transmission. Under this configuration, the repumping laser (L2) beam polarization is rotated by $\pi/2$ radians by the half wave plate prior to the PBS, which ensures that only polarization parallel to the plane of propagation proceeds towards the MOT optics. As RGTP2 is rotated from its maximum transmission angle, the intensity of the transmitted beam, at the PBS, is diminished. On the other hand, the cooling laser (L1) beam polarization remains unchanged towards the PBS, which now ensures that only polarization perpendicular to the plane of propagation proceeds toward the MOT optics. Thus, the combined beam entering the BE contains two collinear beams polarized orthogonally to each other. An optional refinement consists of adjusting the half wave plate to compensate for minor rotations of the transmitted E-field due to the rotation of the RGTP. However, this is optional, since the results pertinent to the visibility of the Rb cloud are very close regardless of the refinement. The MOT itself, which includes a getter [8], is of a standard three intersecting optical axes design [9] with two of its axes in a cross configuration, in the horizontal plane, while the third axis is perpendicular to the horizontal plane of propagation and intersects the two horizontal axes at the center. As far as the MOT optics is concerned, it should be mentioned that the expanded, collinear, laser beams have a diameter of 12 mm and that an effort was made to balance as much as possible the powers of L1 and L2 in each of the optical paths toward the three-axes MOT. To this end, the optics are designed to deliver 1/6 of the power of each laser to each optical path toward the cell. In practice, however, balance was achieved in half, that is three, of the optical paths. In the other optical paths, the repumping laser has about half the power of the cooling laser in two of the beams. The greatest imbalance is present in the third unbalanced path (in the upward direction) where the cooling laser had only about 1/5 the power of the repumping laser. For the downward optical path the powers were balanced.

11.10 Results

For conditions relating to both lasers at maximum brightness (48 mW) the observed cloud of cold rubidium atoms is shown in figure 11.17.

The same cloud can displayed in a three dimensional intensity versus position plot as seen in figure 11.18.

The results of laser power imbalance are summarized in table 11.1. The cloud brightness as a function of the repumping laser is shown in figure 11.19.

As the repumping laser (L2) is kept at 48 mW the transmitted overall power from the cooling laser (L1) can be decreased by a factor of 5 while the cloud of rubidium atoms is diminished in brightness but is still faintly visible. On the other hand, as the cooling laser (L1) is kept at 48 mW, the transmitted overall power from the repumping laser (L2) can

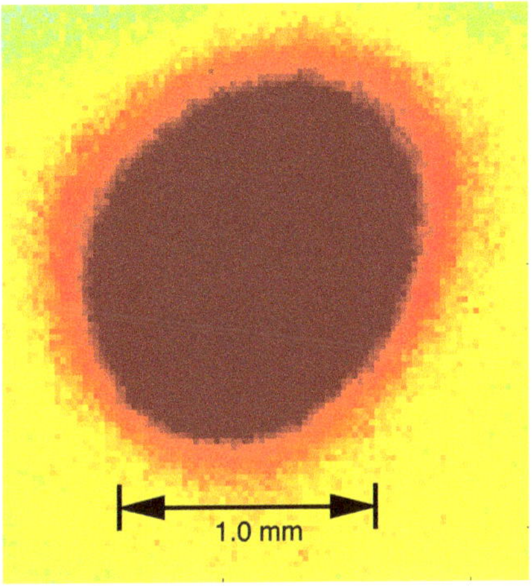

Figure 11.17. Cloud of cooled rubidium atoms observed at maximum power for the cooling laser 1 and the repumping laser 2.

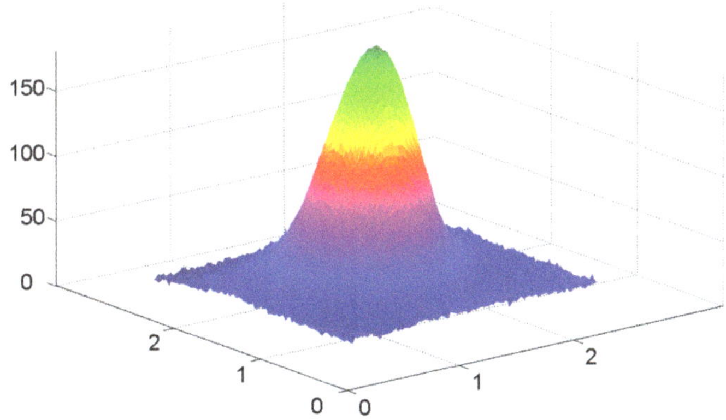

Figure 11.18. This cloud is 2.18 mm in diameter at its full width and 0.75 mm at its FWHM. The acquisition time is 48 ms.

Table 11.1. While the power of L1 is varied L2 is maintained at its maximum and vice versa.

Angular position of RGTP	Laser power	Power ratio	Visibility of cold cloud
θ (RGTP1)	L1		
0°	48 mW	1	Maximum (figures 11.17 and 11.18)
47°	10 mW	~1/5	Minimum
θ (RGTP2)	L2		
0°	48 mW	1	Maximum (figures 11.17 and 11.18)
76°	103 μW	~1/466	Minimum (figure 11.20)

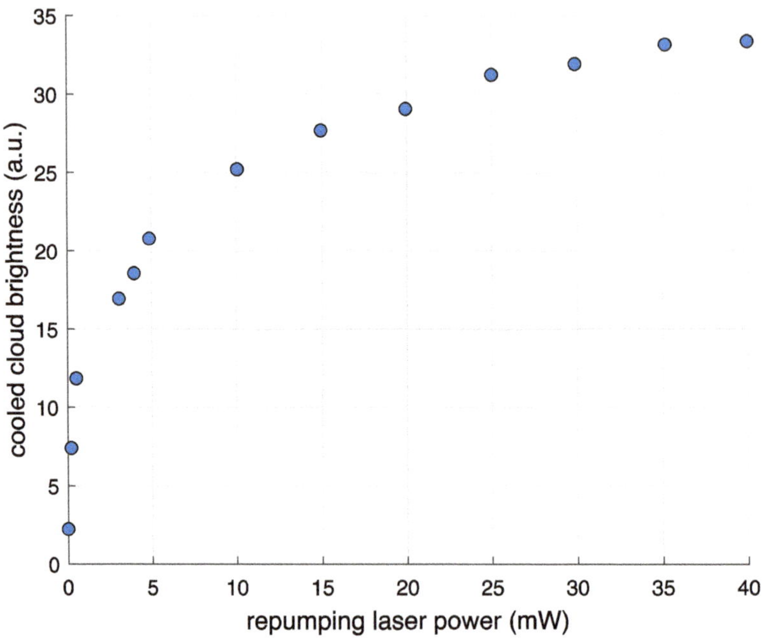

Figure 11.19. Cloud brightness as a function of repumping laser (L2) power. This variation in laser power is achieved following rotation of the RGTP2 by 80°.

be decreased by a factor of 466 while the cloud diminishes in brightness but is still faintly visible. These results mean that in the upwards vertical beam the cooling laser has 1/25 the power of the repumping laser. Further, in two of the horizontal beams the repumping laser is reduced to 1/932 the power of the cooling laser. The brightness of the Rb cloud, as a function of the repumping laser power, is depicted in figure 11.20.

It should be noted that attenuation of the repumping laser power, from nearly 50 mW to microwatt levels, requires rotation of RGTP2 by nearly 80°.

11.11 Discussion

In this chapter we explain a design of a MOT based on experimental setups described in the literature and adapted it for non-expert experimentalists in the area. We describe the critical aspects of the laser and optical details. Our description is useful for undergraduate or postgraduate students who want to cool and trap atoms. We demonstrate a simple technique, consisting of the rotation of Glan–Thompson polarizers, to independently control at will the narrow-line-width laser powers illuminating the cooled ^{85}Rb cloud. This is easily done extra cavity without altering the frequency, power, or tuning performance of the grating-tuned diode lasers. We also established that the difference in power between the cooling and the repumping beam can be enormous. Indeed, the power of the repumping laser was reduced, by more than a factor of 400, relative to the power of the cooling laser, with the cloud diminishing but still in its threshold of visibility

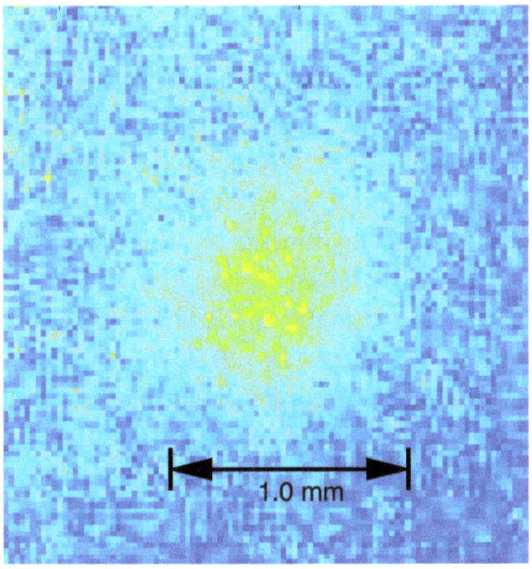

Figure 11.20. Cloud of cooled rubidium atoms observed at maximum power for the cooling laser (1) and threshold power (103 μW) for the repumping laser (2). This cloud is 1.35 mm in diameter at its full width. The acquisition time is 870 ms.

(figure 11.20). Further, in two of the beams facing the cell the power of the repumping laser was reduced by as much as a factor of 932 relative to the cooling laser with the cloud still visible. This has been done with relative ease using an opto-mechanical method that is completely independent of the current-temperature operational parameters of the lasers. In addition, this method of laser power control adds extra means of protecting the 'open cavity' lasers by reducing the magnitude of possible counter propagating radiation. The enormous imbalance in power, between the cooling and repumping lasers, allowed by the ^{85}Rb cloud appears to be permitted, at least in part, by the relatively large laser powers available in the present experimental configuration. These results indicate that only a very small fraction of atoms at the hyperfine transition need to be excited thus broadening the range of the excitation parameters for laser cooling experiments. Although relatively modest power differences have been previously reported [22], to our knowledge the results disclosed in this chapter represent the largest power differences disclosed so far in the laser cooling literature.

A simple optical technique consisting of the rotation of Glan–Thompson polarizers is applied to independently vary and control the power of the cooling laser and the repumping laser in laser cooling experiments of ^{85}Rb. For our experimental conditions, which include initial laser powers of approximately 48 mW (for each laser), it was observed that the atom cloud was still visible after reducing the power of the cooling laser to $\sim$10 mW while keeping the power of the repumping laser at its initial level. On the other hand, the atom cloud maintained visibility after reducing the power of the repumping laser to $\sim$103 μW while keeping the power of the excitation laser at its initial level. In both cases the power variation of the lasers is achieved without altering the frequency or tuning characteristics of the lasers.

References

[1] Olivares I E, Aguilar F and Aguirre-Gómez J 2008 Cold atoms observed for the first time at the Universidad de Santiago de Chile *J. Phys. Conf. Ser.* **134** 012001
[2] Olivares I, Cuadra J, Aguilar F, Aguirre Gomez J and Duarte F 2009 Optical method using rotating Glan-Thompson polarizers to independently vary the power of the excitation and repumping lasers in laser cooling experiments *J. Mod. Opt.* **56** 1780–4
[3] Milonni P W and Eberly J H 2010 *Laser Physics* (New York: Wiley)
[4] Olivares I E 2013 Transmission of tunable diode laser emission, through rubidium vapor, as a function of laser intensity *J. Opt. Soc. Am.* B **30** 945–9
[5] Olivares I E 2008 Lithium spectroscopy using tunable diode lasers in *Tunable Laser Applications* 2nd edn (New York: CRC Press)
[6] Metcalf H J and van der Straten P 1999 *Laser Cooling and Trapping* (Berlin: Springer)
[7] Wieman C, Flowers G and Gilbert S 1995 Inexpensive laser cooling and trapping experiment for undergraduate laboratories *Am. J. Phys.* **63** 317–30
[8] Rapol U D, Wasan A and Natarajan V 2001 Loading of a Rb magneto-optic trap from a getter source *Phys. Rev.* A **64** 023402
[9] Wallace C D, Dinneen T P, Tan K Y N, Kumarakrishnan A, Gould P L and Javanainen J 1994 Measurements of temperature and spring constant in a magneto-optical trap *J. Opt. Soc. Am.* B **11** 703–11
[10] Pruvost L, Serre I, Duong H T and Jortner J 2000 Expansion and cooling of a bright rubidium three-dimensional optical molasses *Phys. Rev.* A **61** 053408
[11] Booth J L, Van Dongen J, Lebel P, Klappauf B G and Madison K W 2007 Dual-channel amplification in a single-mode diode laser for multi-isotope laser cooling *J. Opt. Soc. Am.* B **24** 2914–20
[12] Zorabedian P 1995 Tunable external-cavity semiconductor lasers *Tunable Lasers Handbook* (New York: Academic) ch 8
[13] Duarte F J 2008 *Tunable Laser Applications* 2nd edn (New York: CRC Press)
[14] Duarte F J 1994 Solid-state multiple-prism grating dye-laser oscillators *Appl. Opt.* **33** 3857–60
[15] Webb C E and Jones J D C 2004 *Handbook of Laser Technology and Applications: Laser Design and Laser Systems* (New York: CRC Press)
[16] Duarte F J 2008 Interferometric imaging *Tunable Laser Application* 2nd edn (New York: CRC Press) ch 12
[17] Duarte F J 2015 *Tunable Laser Optics* 2nd edn (New York: CRC Press)
[18] Metcalf H J and van der Straten P 2003 Laser cooling and trapping of atoms *J. Opt. Soc. Am.* B **20** 887–908
[19] Foot C J *et al* 2005 *Atomic Physics* vol 7 (Oxford: Oxford University Press)
[20] Schnelle S K, Van Ooijen E D, Davis M J, Heckenberg N R and Rubinsztein-Dunlop H 2008 Versatile two-dimensional potentials for ultra-cold atoms *Opt. Express* **16** 1405–12
[21] Arikawa M, Honda K, Akamatsu D, Yokoi Y, Akiba K, Nagatsuka S, Furusawa A and Kozuma M 2007 Observation of electromagnetically induced transparency for a squeezed vacuum with the time domain method *Opt. Express* **15** 11849–54
[22] Ovchinnikov Y B 2005 Compact magneto-optical sources of slow atoms *Opt. Commun.* **249** 473–81

IOP Publishing

Techniques for Lithium Isotope Separation, Laser Cooling, and Scattering

Ignacio E Olivares and Patrick Carrazana

Chapter 12

Mie scattering

In this chapter we revisit Mie scattering theory and experimental techniques using calibrated spherical particles, a 1 mW helium neon with a wavelength 632.8 nm laser, and an 80 mW tunable diode laser tuned at 780 nm. Our experiments allowed us to measure the size of microscopic dielectric spherical particles immersed in purified water with spheres with a nominal diameter of 5.2 ± 0.15 μm. The experiments consisted of measuring the distribution of the scattered light intensity. We included a modest amount of theory to describe the distribution of the scattered light intensity. We considered a set of spheres with different diameters, in our case a distribution of sphere diameters with mean diameter 5.2 μm and standard deviation 0.15 μm. Our measured Mie scattering angular distribution accounts for the effect of the diameter distribution, which we assume to be a Gaussian distribution. Our results indicate that there is a very good agreement between experiment and theoretical predictions. The technique we offer here is found to be useful to familiarize technicians, undergraduate and graduate students that have a basic instruction in electromagnetic theory.

12.1 Introduction

The purpose of this chapter is to introduce the subject of laser light Mie scattering by spherical particles with diameters much larger than the wavelength of the laser. Mie scattering is important in so many areas of applied current research even if the reader has not yet studied Maxwell's equations in detail. Despite the fact that Maxwell's theory is basic to the understanding of, e.g., atmospheric light transmission, we are of the opinion that many engineering, physics, chemistry, and even biology professionals would benefit by grasping the fundamental principles of this important research tool by carrying out an experiment that measures the spatial intensity of the scattered light incident on spherical polystyrene spheres immersed in purified water. Our work [1] is inspired by that of Mie [2], Wiener, Rust and Donelly [3] and is based on the collective experience of the

doi:10.1088/978-0-7503-3839-4ch12

research of Cox, De Weerd and Linden [4], Stratton [5], Van de Hulst [6], Kerker [7], and Bohren and Huffman [8]. Rather than developing the full theory of light scattering we concentrate on simply using established results as found in, e.g., [8]. Thus we introduce the minimum number of equations that would allow the reader to use data from the experiment to develop results for the Mie theory of the intensity of scattered light from a spherical particle to a given angle—the angular scattered distribution. Of course, those readers who have the mathematical background of vector calculus, partial differential equations, etc, are welcome to study details of the theory in, e.g., [3]. Using measurements based on light scattering and extinction experiments, it is possible to measure several parameters associated with characteristics of particles immersed in, e.g., fluids. Thus measurements of size, shape, and concentration of particles can be obtained when such particles are in turbid materials. In meteorology, LIDAR (Light Detector And Ranging) techniques have been used to analyze the backscattered light from particles present in our atmosphere [9]. Medical applications have benefited from the use of pulsed laser radiation in the treatment of preference used in several medical conditions associated with human skin, [10]. Marine biology has also been investigated to characterize marine plankton using the laser light scattered by the plankton particles in the ocean [11]. A dust model for light scattering in the halo of the irregular II galaxy M82 has been proposed by Abadi and Bohren by assuming that the Galaxy is moving through an intergalactic dust cloud [12]. The theoretical result for the light intensity scattered by a spherical particle to a given angle is given by the Mie theory. The solution is obtained by solving the problem of a plane electromagnetic wave incident on a uniform, uncharged sphere of arbitrary refractive index and radius. In a solution of scattered spheres where the concentration of spheres is not very high (in our experiment the concentration used was approximately 2.45×10^{-5} particles per mL), we can make the approximation that their collective scattering is the result from a large number of independent scatterers. In this view, the scattering curve would be a multiple of the curve for a single sphere. Thus, a concentration of such spheres is thought to be in the 'single scattering regime'. The Mie theory gives us a theoretical expression for the intensity of light scattered from a spherical particle to a given angle—the angular scattered distribution. The theoretical expression is derived by many authors in great detail in the works of Stratton [5], van de Hulst [6], Kerker [7], and Bohren and Huffman [8]. In this work we used the notation and conventions used by Bohren and Huffman. We study the Mie scattering equations for the interaction of a laser field with dielectric spheres whose diameters are much larger than the wavelength of the laser. The scattering intensity was measured for different angles by nominal 5.2 μm diameter spheres suspended in purified water. The spheres are made by Thermo Scientific with an index of refraction of 1.59 at a wavelength of 589 nm and, even though they are old we assume they are perfectly spherical. We wrote a Matlab code named MIEGEOMETRY that calculates a vector with 501 scattering angles corresponding to 0° to 50° deviation angles in 0.1° steps. The scattering angle is the angle inside solution while the deviation angle is the measured angle. Here we used very basic geometrical optics knowledge, e.g., Snell's law and consider the cell water–glass–air interface. See figure 12.1.

We wrote a second Matlab code named MIECODE that calculates the scattering function for the scattering angles. The MIECODE uses the special functions and the

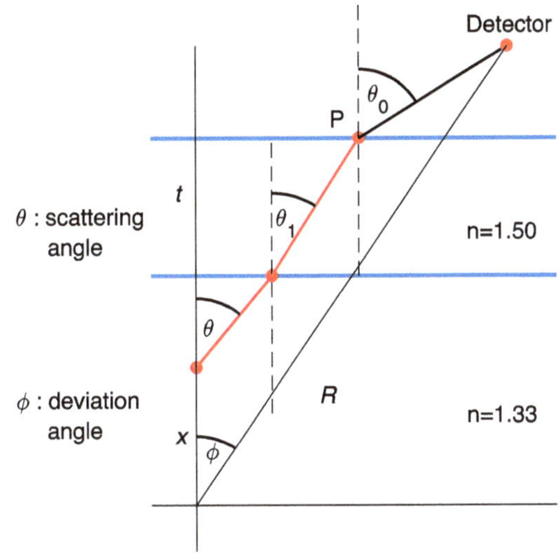

Figure 12.1. Diagram for construction of the MIEGEOMETRY code.

a_n and b_n coefficients as subroutines or Matlab functions. We show the minimum number of equations needed to calculate the scattering intensity for different angles. Since our spheres have a nominal diameter of 5.2 ± 0.15 μm, we considered the Mie scattering by a set of spheres with different diameters in our case a distribution of sphere diameters, with mean diameter 5.2 μm, and standard deviation 0.15 μm. Our work describes the effect on the intensity curve caused by an ensemble of particles of different sizes whose diameters are widely Gaussian distributed around a central value, in this case with a standard deviation of 0.15 μm. We used the Matlab program GAUSSIAN to consider the Gaussian diameter distribution. In this sense this work is a new contribution as it extends the range of study given in previous works that consider an ensemble of particles with a lower diameter distribution considered as a single diameter case. The use of a single mode and single polarized laser diminishes the experimental difficulty, because a random polarized laser presents intensity fluctuation after passing through the polarizing filter or Glan-laser polarizer. We have no need to measure the entrance intensity. Another novel contribution is the use of different wavelengths. We also wrote a program we called CHISQUARE to find the best fit. The program require the calculation of the fit with different mean value diameters in order to find the best fit. The technique showed in this work can be used to measure size distributed 'real-life' spheres as in aerosols.

12.2 Theory

The Mie scattering theory has been explained elsewhere by Bohren and Huffman [8]. The scattered electric and magnetic fields are given by

$$\mathbf{E}_s = \sum_{n=1}^{\infty} E_n(ia_n\mathbf{N}^{(3)}_{e1n} - b_n\mathbf{M}^{(3)}_{o1n}) \tag{12.1}$$

and

$$\mathbf{H}_s = \frac{k}{\omega\mu}\sum_{n=1}^{\infty} E_n(ib_n\mathbf{N}^{(3)}_{oln} + a_n\mathbf{M}^{(3)}_{eln}) \tag{12.2}$$

where the upper index (3) indicates radial dependence by the first (outgoing wave) Hankel function and

$$E_n = E_0 i^n \frac{2n+1}{n(n+1)} \tag{12.3}$$

and where the N's and M's are given by

$$\begin{aligned}\mathbf{N}^{(3)}_{eln} &= n(n+1)\cos\phi P_n^1(\cos\theta)\frac{h_n^{(1)}(\rho)}{\rho}\hat{\mathbf{e}}_r \\ &+ \cos\phi\frac{dP_n^1(\cos\theta)}{d\theta}\frac{1}{\rho}\frac{d}{d\rho}[\rho h_n^{(1)}(\rho)]\hat{\mathbf{e}}_\theta \\ &- \sin\phi\frac{P_n^1(\cos\theta)}{\sin\theta}\frac{1}{\rho}\frac{d}{d\rho}[\rho h_n^{(1)}(\rho)]\hat{\mathbf{e}}_\phi\end{aligned} \tag{12.4}$$

$$\begin{aligned}\mathbf{M}^{(3)}_{oln} &= \cos\phi\frac{P_n^1(\cos\theta)}{\sin\theta}h_n^{(1)}(\rho)\hat{\mathbf{e}}_\theta \\ &- \sin\phi\frac{dP_n^1(\cos\theta)}{d\theta}h_n^{(1)}(\rho)\hat{\mathbf{e}}_\phi\end{aligned}$$

$$\begin{aligned}\mathbf{N}^{(3)}_{oln} &= n(n+1)\sin\phi P_n^1(\cos\theta)\frac{h_n^{(1)}(\rho)}{\rho}\hat{\mathbf{e}}_r \\ &+ \sin\phi\frac{dP_n^1(\cos\theta)}{d\theta}\frac{1}{\rho}\frac{d}{d\rho}[\rho h_n^{(1)}(\rho)]\hat{\mathbf{e}}_\theta \\ &+ \cos\phi\frac{P_n^1(\cos\theta)}{\sin\theta}\frac{1}{\rho}\frac{d}{d\rho}[\rho h_n^{(1)}(\rho)]\hat{\mathbf{e}}_\phi\end{aligned} \tag{12.5}$$

$$\begin{aligned}\mathbf{M}^{(3)}_{eln} &= -\sin\phi\frac{P_n^1(\cos\theta)}{\sin\theta}h_n^{(1)}(\rho)\hat{\mathbf{e}}_\theta \\ &- \cos\phi\frac{dP_n^1(\cos\theta)}{d\theta}h_n^{(1)}(\rho)\hat{\mathbf{e}}_\phi;\end{aligned} \tag{12.6}$$

$\phi = 0$ for incident laser horizontal polarization, $\phi = \pi/2$ for vertical polarization, and $\phi = \pi/4$ for unpolarized field. $h_n^{(1)}$ are spherical Hankel functions of the first kind, and P_n^1 are associated Legendre functions of degree n and order 1. The subscripts e and o denote extraordinary and ordinary waves respectively. The coefficients of the fields E's and H's are given by

$$
\begin{aligned}
a_n &= \frac{\mu m^2 j_n(mx)[xj_n(x)]' - \mu_1 j_n(x)[mxj_n(mx)]'}{\mu m^2 j_n(mx)[xh_n^{(1)}(x)]' - \mu_1 h_n^{(1)}(x)[mxj_n(mx)]'} \\
b_n &= \frac{\mu_1 j_n(mx)[xj_n(x)]' - \mu j_n(x)[mxj_n(mx)]'}{\mu_1 j_n(mx)[xh_n^{(1)}(x)]' - \mu h_n^{(1)}(x)[mxj_n(mx)]'};
\end{aligned}
\tag{12.7}
$$

the size parameter is given by $x = ka = 2\pi Na/\lambda$, $m = k_1/k = N_1/N$, and $\rho = kr = 2\pi N_1 r/\lambda$, a is the sphere radius, μ and μ_1 are the magnetic permeability of the sphere and the surrounding medium respectively. In our case we used for the sphere and surrounding medium the permeability of free space $\mu_0 = 4\pi \times 10^{-7}$. For other materials it may be different.

The prime indicates differentiation with respect to the argument in parenthesis. N_1 and N are the refraction index of the medium and the particle respectively, j_n are spherical Bessel functions of the first kind. The scattering intensity is proportional to the Poynting vector $I = \mathbf{S} \cdot \hat{\mathbf{e}}_r = (\mathbf{E}_s \times \mathbf{H}_s^*) \cdot \hat{\mathbf{e}}_r$. The asterisk stands for complex conjugate. Since we approximated the Poynting vector to be in the same direction as the radial unit vector $\hat{\mathbf{e}}_r$, we neglected the $\hat{\mathbf{e}}_r$ components of the electric and magnetic field in our code. We summed first over 40 terms of the series to obtain one single three-component vector for the electric and a second vector for the magnetic field. Afterwards we carried out the cross product of the total electric field and the complex conjugate of the magnetic field. The convergence of the series was checked up to 100 terms at different scattering angles. Figure 12.2 shows a set of plots for the intensity as a function of the summation index n

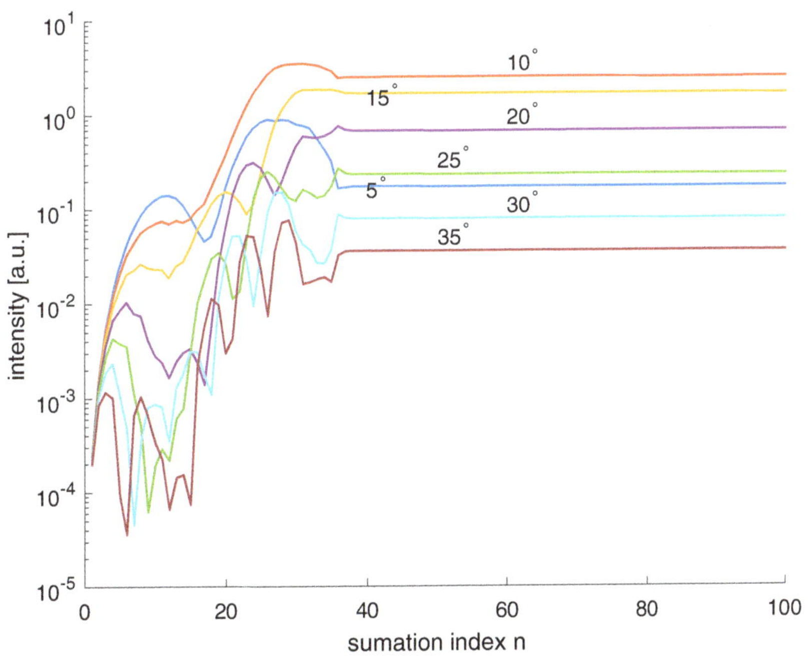

Figure 12.2. Convergence test at different angles for spheres with diameter $2a = 5.2$ μm, laser wavelength $\lambda = 632.8$ nm, laser vertical polarization, cell-detector distance 15 cm, sphere refraction index $N = 1.5872$. For summation index $n > 35$ the intensity converges to a constant value. Reproduced from Olivares and Carrazana [1] with permission.

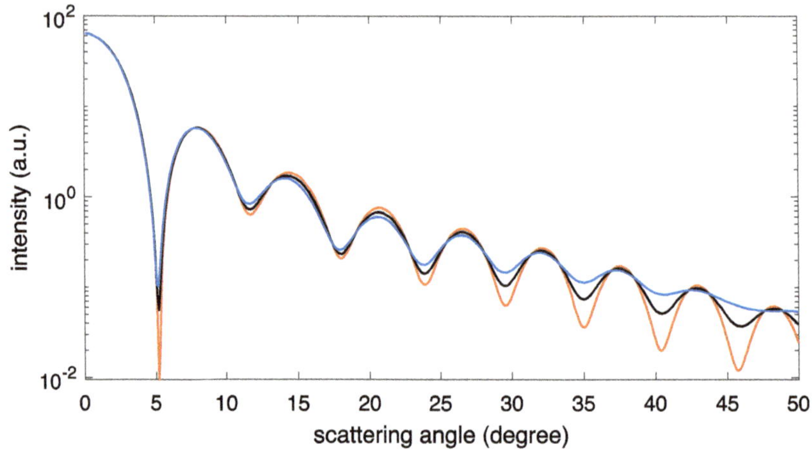

Figure 12.3. Theoretical Mie scattering function for vertical (orange), horizontal (blue) and unpolarized (black) incident laser light. The scattering parameters are $\lambda = 632.8$ nm, sphere refraction index $N = 1.5872$, $r = 15.0$ cm, single sphere diameter $2a = 5.2$ μm. The theoretical Mie scattering function shown are not corrected for deviation by the water–glass-air interface. The interfaces are not considered in the calculation of the scattering function here. The scattering angle is the measured angle as seen from a detector as it would be immersed in the water-sphere solution. Reproduced from Olivares and Carrazana [1] with permission.

for values between $n = 1$ and $n = 100$. Each plot was made for a different angle between 5° and 35° with 5 degree steps obtaining a non-uniform oscillation for $n < 36$ with $\lambda = 632.8$ nm, and for $n < 30$ with $\lambda = 780.0$ nm. Beyond this value we obtained a constant function. This behavior arises from the properties of the special functions.

Figure 12.3 shows a theoretical scattering function example. The code was written in Matlab R2020 and was run on a commercial laptop (Lenovo, IdeaPad S340). The calculation of the complete scattering function for 500 different scattering angles separated by 0.1 degree takes 12.75 s.

We considered the refraction of the scattered light transmitted through the water–glass interface and through the glass to air interface and calculated the average of the scattering angles of ten scatterers which are equally spaced along the scattering line path inside the cell for each deviation angle. The scattering line path is the illuminated region inside the cell by the laser. The deviation angle is the measured angle. The intensity was calculated with the corresponding scattering angle. For example, for a deviation angle of 18.1° the corresponding scattering angle is 24°. In our experiment we used spheres with a wide distribution of diameters. Figure 12.4 shows the scattering curve for three different diameters and the result of averaging the three intensities decreasing the contrast of the theoretical curves. In this case the effect of refraction on the water–glass–air interface was included. We assume that the diameters of the particles are distributed as a Gaussian distribution given by

$$n(D) = \frac{1}{\sigma\sqrt{2\pi}} \exp\left\{ -\frac{1}{2}\left(\frac{D - D_0}{\sigma}\right)^2 \right\} \tag{12.8}$$

where D is the diameter of a class of n particles with the same diameter, D_0 is the mean value of the diameter, and σ the standard deviation.

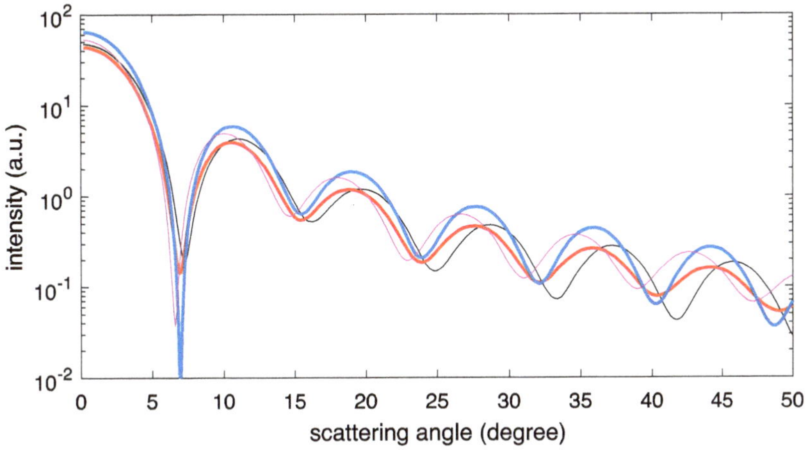

Figure 12.4. Vertical polarization. Distance from the center of the cell to detector $r = 15$ cm, sphere index of refraction $N = 1.5872$, $\lambda = 632.8$ nm. The orange line is the sphere diameter $2a = 5.1$ μm, the blue solid line $2a = 5.2$ μm, the black line $2a = 5.3$ μm, the red solid line is the average of three lines. Reproduced from Olivares and Carrazana [1] with permission.

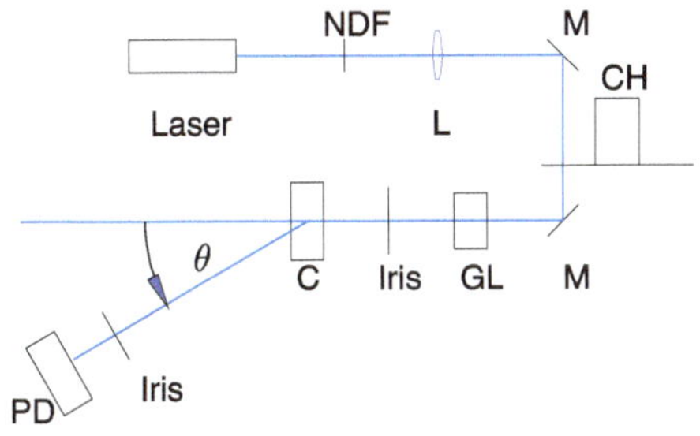

Figure 12.5. Experimental setup. NDF neutral density filter, M mirror, CH chopper, GL Glan-laser polarizer, PD photodiode, L lens with $f = 200$ mm focal length. Reproduced from Olivares and Carrazana [1] with permission.

12.3 Experiment

We followed the experiment done by Wiener *et al* [3] with relevant changes. We replaced a random polarized laser by a linear polarized laser thus reducing the intensity fluctuations due to mode hopping. We used spheres whose diameters were widely distributed around 5.2 μm. In our experimental setup it is not necessary to measure the entrance intensity. Figure 12.5 shows our experimental setup. In our experiment it is not needed to consider scattering light arriving from the side of the cell as our cell front side is large enough.

A nominal 2.0 mW linear polarized helium neon laser (HNL020L-EC, Thorlabs) with wavelength 632.8 nm, and with minimum polarization ratio 500:1 was driven by two mirrors installed firmly on an optical table. The laser has a power stability of ± 2.5% in 8 h. Vertical or horizontal polarization were obtained by rotating the laser rod around its optical axis. We checked the polarization with a Glan-laser polarizer (MGLA12, Karl Lambrecht Company). We introduced the Glan-laser polarizer between the second mirror and the glass cell. In our case the transmission direction of the polarizer is marked on the Glan holder. A method to verify the transmission axis of the polarizer is to observe the reflections off a window at nearly Brewster angle, by looking through the polarizer to the window. Considering that the reflected s-wave is vertically polarized related to the floor, the transmission axis is determined when minimum light is observed, i.e., when the transmission axis of the polarizer is perpendicular to the vertical direction. We rotated the laser to obtain pure vertical or horizontal polarization that were checked with the Glan-laser polarizer. In our case the vertical polarization means perpendicular to the mirror plane of incidence (s-wave) and horizontal polarization means parallel to the mirror plane of incidence (p-wave). The plane of incidence is the surface that contains the incident and reflected ray. In the case of pure s-waves or p-waves any changes of polarization state were observed. The polarization could change if the laser polarization is a mixture of both s- and p-states as the mirrors have different reflectivities depending on the incident polarization of the laser. In our experiment we used pure vertical or pure horizontal polarization. We installed a neutral density filter in front of the laser obtaining 1.7 mW laser optical power. The power was measured with an optical power meter plus head (Model 840+818SL, Newport). A plano-convex lens with $f = 200$ mm focal length was installed after the filter to collimate the beam. The beam diameter in the cell was nearly 1.0 mm. A dovetail optical rail (RLA2400, Thorlabs) was connected to a manual rotation stage (Model RP01, Thorlabs). A photodiode (Model DET10A, Thorlabs) was mounted 40 mm behind an iris diaphragm (ID25, Thorlabs) on the rail and at 150 mm from the center of rotation of the rail. The iris diaphragm diameter was set at 8.0 mm. The rail was rotated around the center of the glass cell which was installed above the center of the rotation stage. The glass cell dimensions were $16 \times 46 \times 50$ mm and the cell wall thickness was 3 mm. We used an optical chopper (MC1000A, Thorlabs). The chopping frequency was 200 Hz. The signal from the photodiode was measured with a lock-in amplifier (SR510, Stanford Research Systems). We used polystyrene non-ionic spheres (N37460, Thermofisher). The sphere mean diameter measured by the manufacturer with transmission electron microscopy was $2a = 5.2\ \mu$m, the standard deviation of the diameter is 0.15 μm, the percentage of solids is 3.8% w/v, the given refraction indices are $n_1 = 1.6020$ at 486 nm and $n_2 = 1.5905$ at 589 nm. Using the empirical Cauchy relation

$$n(\lambda) = A + \frac{B}{\lambda^2} + \frac{C}{\lambda^4} + \cdots \tag{12.9}$$

where n is the refraction index, λ is the wavelength, A, B, and C are coefficients that can be obtained for a material by fitting the equation to measure refractive indices at known wavelengths we can determine the refractive indices at the two wavelengths we are using. The term proportional to λ^{-4} is neglected in our work. The Cauchy relation is valid in regions of normal dispersion in the visible and near infrared wavelength region. The use of this equation, using the previous given n_1 and n_2

indices of refraction, allows us to calculate A and B and obtain the refraction index $N = 1.5872$ at 632.8 nm and $N = 1.5799$ at 780.0 nm. The spheres are five years old, that is three years older than the duration specified by the manufacturer. We used one drop in 100 ml and shook the solution to obtain a uniform sphere distribution. We used a generic 5 ml syringe without a needle. The syringe was purchased in a veterinary drugstore. Our syringe gives typically 20 drops per ml, which is 0.05 ml per drop when the needle is removed. We obtained this value by counting 20 drops and reading the syringe scale. The polystyrene sphere concentration given by the manufacturer is 4.9×10^8 particles per mL, giving 2.45×10^7 particles per 0.05 ml drop. We mixed the drop with 100 ml of pure water to obtain a concentration of 2.45×10^5 particles per mL. Adding a syringe needle it is possible to get smaller drops, e.g., with half the volume, that is 40 drops per ml. We measured the intensity for deviation angles between 4° and 45°. Afterwards we repeated the scattering experiment with a 780 nm vertically polarized tunable diode laser (Toptica Photonics, DLL100). Two days after starting the experiment some spheres could be seen with the naked eye at the bottom of the cell. We measured again the intensity as a function of deviation angle and obtained a flat slow decreasing curve that may be attributed to much smaller solids suspended in the water. We think of this curve as giving us the 'background'. The background was measured two days later giving an overall smaller intensity. As the background is time dependent it can be considered as a dynamic background. The dynamic background may be caused by Rayleigh scattering at smaller particles that take more time to reach the bottom of the cell than the $2a = 5.2\ \mu$m spheres under study. We intentionally dismissed the subtraction of the background as we consider that this subject can be considered in a further study. By subtracting the background the contrast of the experimental data increases, but it is difficult to determine the correct background.

12.4 Results

Figure 12.6 shows the measured scattering intensity as a function of deviation angle, for vertical laser polarization and wavelength 632.8 nm. The theoretical scattering function was obtained as the average of 81 scattering functions calculated for different diameters separated by 0.01 μm distributed by a Gaussian distribution around a sphere diameter of 5.2 μm, and standard deviation 0.15 μm. We added weighted scattering functions for spheres with diameters between 4.8 μm and 5.6 μm. The scattering functions were weighted by the Gaussian distribution. The sum was divided by the normalization factor and multiplied by an arbitrary constant. In figure 12.6 we added the theoretical scattering curve for single 5.2 μm diameter spheres. The contrast is larger than in the case of widely distributed diameters. The theoretical curve has a sharp dip for lower angles, while the measured data shows a smoother dip. Our finite angular resolution is of the order of 1° and our apparatus is not able to resolve the sharp dip. At higher angular regions our data fit the scattering curve well. A second source of error is stray light produced by multiple reflections on the glass surfaces and other components that increase the relative intensity on the detector for measurements at lower angles in which the measuring line-of-sight is

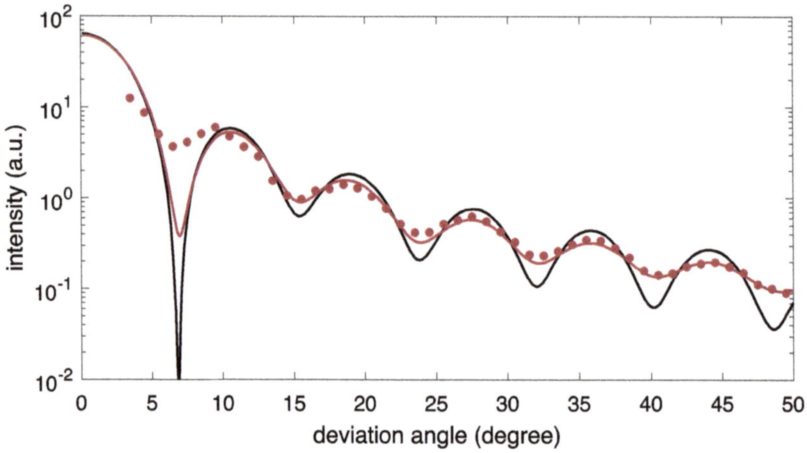

Figure 12.6. Vertical polarization. Manufacturer specified parameters: sphere diameter $2a = 5.2 \pm 0.15$ μm measured with transmission electron microscopy, sphere index of refraction $N = 1.5872$, center of cell to detector distance $r = 15.0$ cm, $\lambda = 632.8$ nm. The dots are measured intensity. The red line is the theoretical curve for the average of 81 diameter Gaussian distributed spheres. The black line theoretical curve for single 5.2 μm diameter spheres. Reproduced from Olivares and Carrazana [1] with permission.

closer to the laser beam. To avoid this effect, it would be necessary to use antireflective coating on the glass cell surfaces, to introduce a small tilt to the cell, or to give a small angle to the inner surfaces of the cell. Other differences could be caused by the movement of the particles in an out of the laser beam interaction volume. The best fit for the center value of the sphere diameter is 5.21 ± 0.03 μm using the chi-square method and considering a Gaussian standard deviation of 0.15 μm for the sphere diameter. Figure 12.7 shows the result of the chi-square method for vertically polarized light, $N = 1.5872$, center of cell to detector distance $r = 15.0$ cm, and $\lambda = 632.8$ nm. We compared the intensity scattering curve for the center diameter value given by the manufacturer's as 5.2 μm, and the best fit value 5.21 μm; the difference is negligible. Our experimental error is mostly determined by our poor angular resolution of the order of nearly 1°, and the instrumental resolution of the engraved angular scale of our manual rotation stage (Thorlabs, Model RP01) which is 1°. Figure 12.8 shows the experimental data and the theoretical intensity profile as a function of deviation angle for incident laser with horizontal polarization and same experimental conditions as in figure 12.6. The theoretical profile uses the diameter obtained with vertical polarization, and the fitting is good. There is a small difference for the intensity profile between vertically polarized light and horizontally polarized light that can be measured experimentally. The relative intensity is the voltage measured with the lock-in amplifier. Figure 12.9 shows the measured and theoretical scattering function with the previously described set of distributed spheres and a vertically polarized 780 nm laser. The distance between maxima increases when increasing the wavelength according to theory.

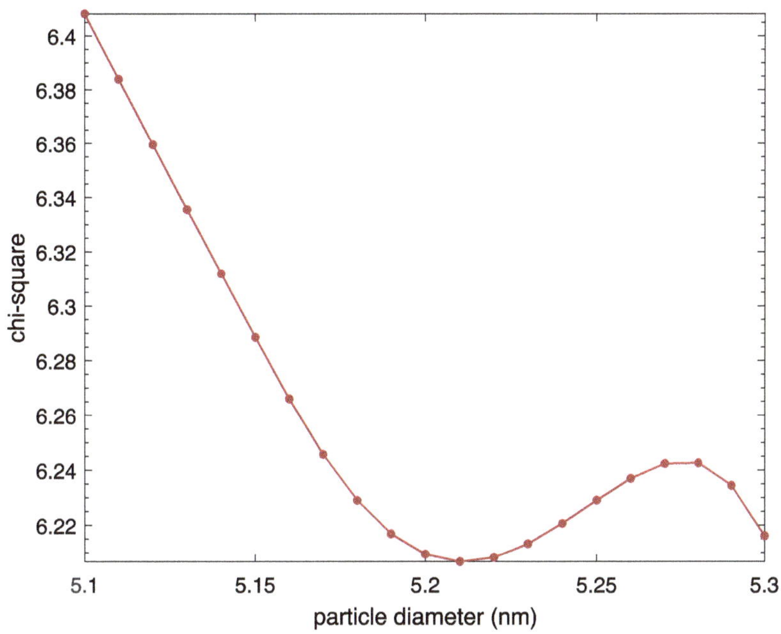

Figure 12.7. Chi-square function as a function of the center value of the sphere diameter distribution. The best fit is the minimum of the chi-square function at 5.21 ± 0.03 μm. Vertical polarization, $N = 1.5872$, center of cell to detector distance $r = 15.0$ cm, and $\lambda = 632.8$ nm. Reproduced from Olivares and Carrazana [1] with permission.

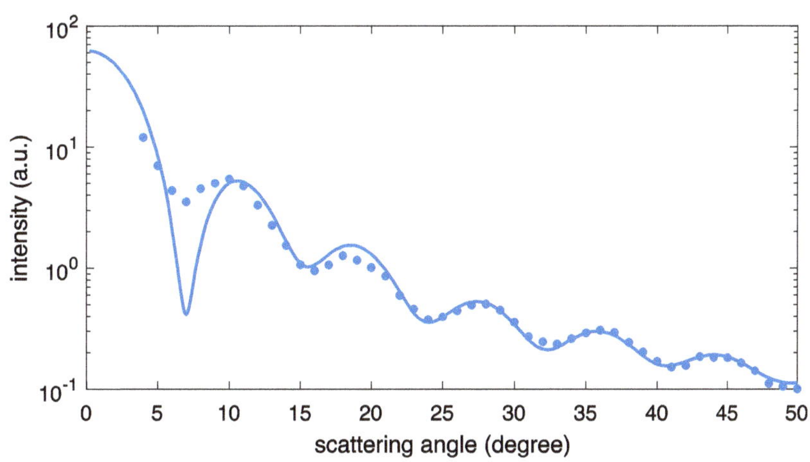

Figure 12.8. Horizontal polarization. Manufacturer specified parameters: sphere diameter $2a = 5.2 \pm 0.15$ μm measured with transmission electron microscopy, sphere index of refraction $N = 1.5872$, center of cell to detector distance $r = 15.0$ cm, $\lambda = 632.8$ nm. The dots are the measured intensity. The blue line is the theoretical curve for the average of 81 diameter Gaussian distributed spheres with given parameters. Reproduced from Olivares and Carrazana [1] with permission.

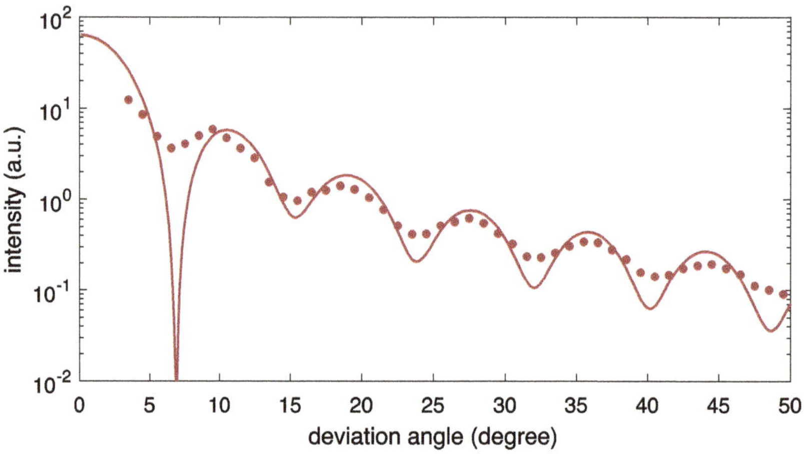

Figure 12.9. Vertical polarization. Manufacturer specified parameters: sphere diameter $2a = 5.2 \pm 0.15$ μm measured with transmission electron microscopy, sphere index of refraction $N = 1.5872$, center of cell to detector distance $r = 15.0$ cm, laser wavelength $\lambda = 780.0$ nm. The dots are the measured intensity. The red line is the theoretical curve for the average of 81 diameter Gaussian distributed spheres with given parameters. Reproduced from Olivares and Carrazana [1] with permission.

12.5 Discussion and conclusions

We revisited the Mie scattering theory and compared it with experiment using nominal $2a = 5.2 \pm 0.15$ μm diameter spheres. We reported a novel Mie scattering experiment for a set of widely Gaussian distributed spheres. We measured the Mie scattering curve at two different wavelengths at 632.8 nm and 780 nm. We compared the experimental data with the theoretical scattering intensities using manufacturer nominal diameter that were measured with transmission electron microscopy. Our theoretical calculation considers a set of particles of different diameters distributed around a center value. We found good to excellent agreement between theory and experiment. Small differences between the measured and theoretical scattering curve are attributed to dynamic background Rayleigh scattering caused by much smaller solids present in the original sphere solution. We dismissed the background as we consider it a matter for further studies. We improved previous reported experiments by using a linear polarized laser instead of a random polarized laser diminishing the intensity fluctuations due to mode hops. We established and showed the set of minimal self-consistent equations needed to describe the experimental data and show close agreement between theory and experiment, which is further verified by a chi-square test. We found the diameter of our spheres have a center value to be $2a = 5.21 \pm 0.03$ μm and a standard deviation 0.15 μm.

References

[1] Olivares I E and Carrazana P 2020 Mie scattering revisited: study of bichromatic Mie scattering of electromagnetic waves by a distribution of spherical particles *Rev. Sci. Instrum.* **91** 1–6

[2] Mie G 1908 Beiträge zur Optik trüber Medien, speziell kolloidaler Metallösungen *Ann. Phys.* **330** 377–445
[3] Weiner I, Rust M and Donnelly T D 2001 Particle size determination: an undergraduate lab in Mie scattering *Am. J. Phys.* **69** 129–36
[4] Cox A J, DeWeerd A J and Linden J 2002 An experiment to measure Mie and Rayleigh total scattering cross sections *Am. J. Phys.* **70** 620–5
[5] Stratton J A 1941 *Electromagnetic Theory* (New York: McGraw-Hill)
[6] van de Hulst H C 1957 *Light Scattering by Small Particles* (New York: Wiley)
[7] Kerker M 2013 *The Scattering of Light and Other Electromagnetic Radiation: J. Phys. Chem.: AJ. Phys. Chem.: A Series of Monographs* vol 16 (New York: Academic)
[8] Bohren C F and Huffman D R 2008 *Absorption and Scattering of Light by Small Particles* (New York: Wiley)
[9] Tuchin V V 2002 *Handbook of Optical Biomedical Diagnostics* (Bellingham, WA: SPIE Optical Engineering Press)
[10] Anderson R R and Parrish J A 1983 Selective photothermolysis: precise microsurgery by selective absorption of pulsed radiation *Science* **220** 524–7
[11] Shao B, Jaffe J S, Chachisvilis M and Esener S C 2006 Angular resolved light scattering for discriminating among marine picoplankton: modeling and experimental measurements *Opt. Express* **14** 12473–84
[12] Abadi H I and Bohren C F 1977 A dust model for M82-Constraints on the nature of intergalactic dust *Astron. Astrophys.* **60** 125–30

Chapter 13

Thomson scattering

In this chapter we show Thomson scattering spectra of single gas plasmas. The experimental techniques and Thomson scattering equations are described. It is demonstrated that the collisionless theory of Salpeter can be fitted rather well to the ion feature of collective Thomson scattering on dense plasmas in equilibrium for elements up to argon.

13.1 Introduction

The ion feature of collective Thomson scattering is now widely used for the diagnostics of dense plasmas as produced in Z-pinches [1] or by lasers for inertial confinement fusion [2]. Plasma parameters are obtained spatially resolved and even with high time resolution when fast streak cameras are employed. Prerequisite is certainly the reliable theoretical description of the spectral features, which in many experiments are complex due to the presence of multiple ion species, drifts, instabilities, and steep gradients in density and temperature within the scattering volume. Furthermore, at high densities ion–ion collisions will influence the shape [3, 4]. In this study we show how well the collisionless theory of Salpeter still describes the ion feature reflecting the ion acoustic modes in plasmas of densities of up to 6×10^{18} cm, when the plasma is homogeneous and in equilibrium.

13.2 Theory

The differential cross-section for scattering by a plasma is of the form

$$\frac{d^2\sigma}{d\Omega_s d\omega_s} = r_e^2 \sin^2\varphi \; S(\mathbf{k}, \omega) \tag{13.1}$$

where the first two factors give scattering characteristic of the single electron (r_e is the classical electron radius and ϕ the angle between the direction of the electric field vector of the incident wave and the direction of observation), and $S(\mathbf{k}, \omega)$ is the dynamic form factor containing the properties of the whole ensemble of electrons. The scattering parameter is given by

$$\alpha = \frac{1}{k\lambda_D} \tag{13.2}$$

where λ_D is the Debye length and k the absolute value of the scattering vector given by the difference of the wave vectors of incident and scattered wave, $k = |\mathbf{k}_s - \mathbf{k}_0|$. When the scattering parameter is increased the scattered spectrum starts to reflect the collective properties of the plasmas. A narrow central part mirrors collective properties of the ions and is called the ion feature, and two side bands reflect those of the electron's electron feature. In Salpeter's approximation the dynamical form factor takes a relatively simple analytical form [5, 6] and splits into the two features,

$$S(\mathbf{k}, \omega) = S_e(\mathbf{k}, \omega) + S_i(\mathbf{k}, \omega) \tag{13.3}$$

With the shape function

$$\Gamma_\alpha(x) = \frac{\exp(-x^2)}{|1 + \alpha^2 W(x)|^2} \tag{13.4}$$

$S(\mathbf{k}, \omega)$ becomes

$$S_e(\mathbf{k}, \omega)\, \mathrm{d}\omega = \Gamma_\alpha(x_e)\, \mathrm{d}x_e \quad \text{and} \quad S_i(\mathbf{k}, \omega)\, \mathrm{d}\omega = \frac{Z\alpha^4}{(1 + \alpha^2)^2} \Gamma_\beta(x_i)\, \mathrm{d}x_i \tag{13.5}$$

$$x_e = \frac{\omega}{k\sqrt{(2k_\mathrm{B}T_e)/m_e)}} \quad \text{and} \quad x_i = \frac{\omega}{k\sqrt{(2k_\mathrm{B}T_i)/m_i}} \tag{13.6}$$

$W(x)$ is the plasma dispersion function and β is given by

$$\beta^2 = Z \frac{\alpha^2}{1 + \alpha^2} \frac{T_e}{T_i} \tag{13.7}$$

For the determination of the electron density the absolute calibration of the system is usually done by means of Rayleigh scattering. For that purpose the vacuum chamber is filled with a suitable gas. The scattering volumes for Rayleigh and Thomson scattering are identical. By comparison of Thomson and Rayleigh scattering signals the product $n_e S_i(\mathbf{k})$ simply becomes

$$n_e S_i(\mathbf{k}) = n_R \left(\frac{\sigma_R}{\sigma_{TH}}\right)\left(\frac{W_S}{L_S}\right)\left(\frac{L_R}{W_R}\right) \tag{13.8}$$

W_S and W_R are the signals of Thomson and Rayleigh scattering, L_S and L_R are the intensities of the incident laser beam in both experiments, and σ_{TH} and σ_R are the respective cross-sections. The density of the gas molecules is obtained from the gas pressure by $n_R = p/k_\mathrm{B}T$ and the form factor by integration over the frequency, i.e., by summation of the signals in the pixels of the detector. In the above approximation

$$S_i(\mathbf{k}) = \frac{Z\,\alpha^4}{(1 + \alpha^2)[1 + \alpha^2 + Z\alpha^2(T_e/T_i)]}$$

13.3 Thomson scattering experiment

The scattering experiments were performed on plasmas which were produced in the Bochum gas liner pinch facility [7]. This is a dynamic z-pinch provided with two independently operating fast electromagnetic valves. The first valve injects the working gas into the vacuum chamber next to the inner wall of a 18 cm diameter glass cylinder. In this vessel the two electrodes are placed 5 cm apart. The second valve permits the entrance of a small amount of test gas in the center of the discharge; usually the emission of these ions is the goal of spectroscopic studies. Before the main discharge the working gas is pre-ionized by a discharge of a 50 nF capacitor from 50 needle electrodes placed in a circle 2 mm below the lower electrode (anode). Electrons and UV-radiation produced by this discharge flow through small holes in the anode and pre-ionized gas. The pre-ionizing pulse is followed with some delay by the main discharge of a 10 μF capacitor bank. This is typically charged to voltages between 25 and 35 kV. The best experimental condition was found at 27 kV for our studies. The main discharge of the capacitor bank is switched by a rail gap. The current rises to a maximum of 250–500 kA in 1.5 μs depending on the voltage. The plasma accelerates radially inward to the center of the cylinder due to a magnetic piston, producing a high density and temperature plasma at the center after stagnation. The best conditions are when the maximum current is next to the maximum density. Figure 13.1 shows a scheme of the Thomson scattering setup

For scattering a 2 J Q-switched ruby laser (Korad, model K1) with a 35 ns pulse duration is available. The beam shaping and relaying optics are based on a Keplerian-telescope configuration. The ocular (entrance lens L1) of the telescope was initially a positive $f = 300$ mm lens that produced an ionized plasma at the focus. We replaced this lens by a positive $f = 500$ mm lens. It is possible that due to the high energy densities at the focus deviation of the ray could occur producing

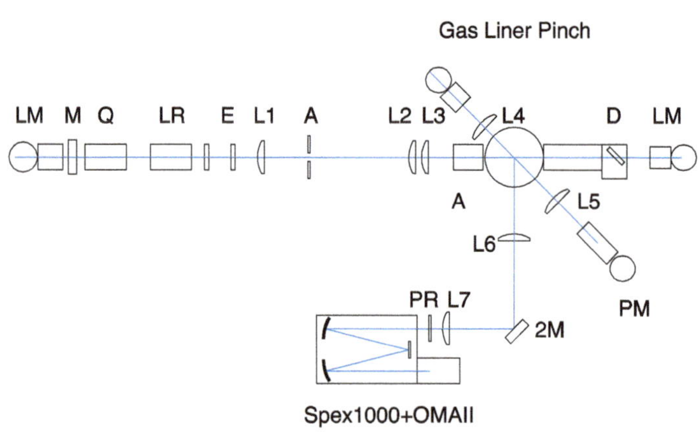

Figure 13.1. Diagram of the Thomson scattering experiment. LM: laser monitor with a FND100 avalanche photodiode, M: mirror, Q: Q-switch, E: etalon, A: aperture, D: beam dump, PM: plasma monitor, Jobin Yvon spectrometer+FND100, 2M: two folding mirror system for rotating the image of the scattering volume, PR: polarizing filter + red filter, L1 to L7 plane convex lenses with focal distances $f_1 = 500$ mm, $f_2 = 1000$ mm, $f_3 = 665$ mm, $f_4 = 50$ mm, $f_5 = 150$ mm, $f_6 = 500$ mm, and $f_7 = 500$ mm respectively. The diagram is not to scale.

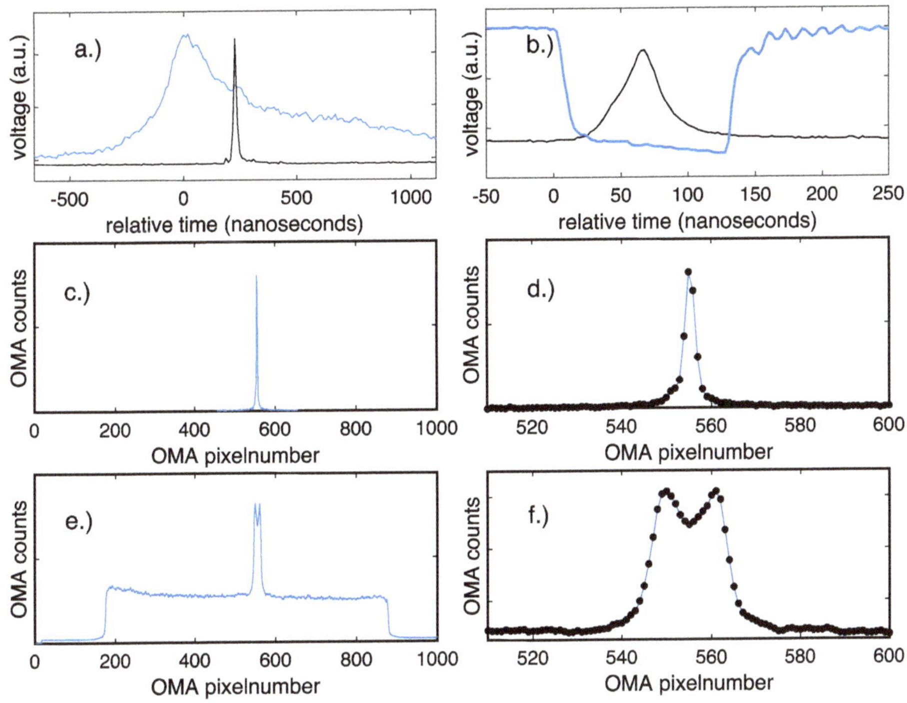

Figure 13.2. Minimum set of measurements for Thomson scattering plasma diagnostics: (a) oscilloscope plasma and laser monitor, (b) oscilloscope OMA gate and laser monitor, (c) Rayleigh scattering spectrum, (d) expanded Rayleigh scattering spectrum, (e) Thomson scattering spectrum, (f) expanded Thomson scattering spectrum. Wavelength resolution is 0.02 nm per pixel.

misalignment of the scattering light. To improve this problem a Galilean expander telescope would be a better choice. The expanded beam was focused at the center of the chamber and its diameter there was about 1 mm. The collecting optics were placed perpendicular to the laser beam, also based on a Keplerian-telescope configuration. The image of the scattering volume is formed at the entrance slit of a 1 m $f/10$ Czerny-Turner mount monochromator (Spex, model 1704). As the slit is vertical, two mirrors in the collecting beam path are added that rotate the image of the scattering volume in order to obtain the maximum scattered signal into the spectrograph. The first mirror directs the light vertically down and the second mirror placed below reflects the light horizontally into the monochromator. To improve the signal-to-noise ratio an interference filter and a red filter are included in the path of the collecting optics. At the exit of the monochromator an optical multichannel analyzer (Princeton Instruments, model OMAII) is used as detector. Wavelength calibration was done using two lines at 703.1 nm and 692.9 nm of a neon spectral lamp (Osram, model Ne10). For a 1200 lines per mm grating with a blaze wavelength of 1000 nm, for example, the linear reciprocal dispersion in second order was thus determined to 0.006 3 nm per pixel for the above wavelength interval. Figure 13.2 shows the set of measurements needed to obtain plasma parameters with Thomson scattering.

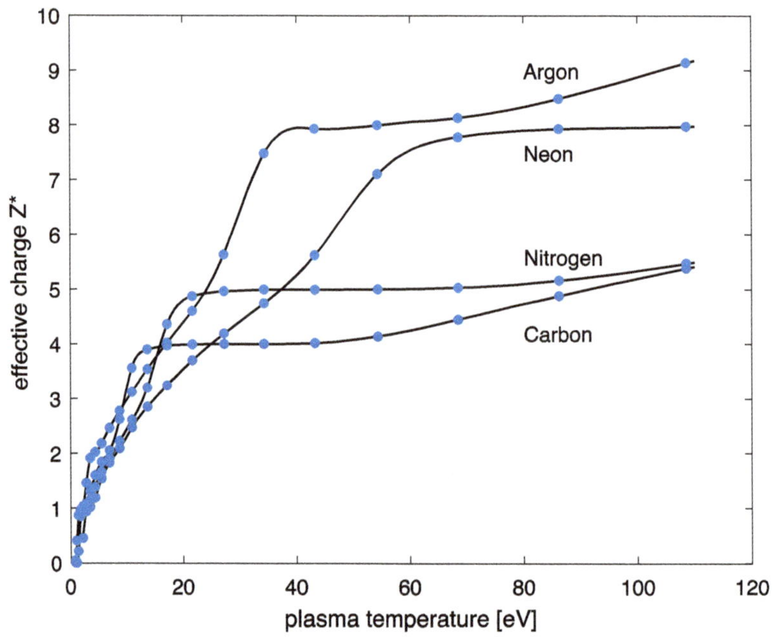

Figure 13.3. Effective charge as a function of plasma temperature.

The OMA is used in the triggered intensified gate mode with variable gate time. In our studies we employed typically a 100 ns duration gate pulse, which was enough to capture the 35 ns laser pulse. To obtain the best Thomson scattering signal, the gate trigger pulse and Pockels-cell trigger of the laser pulse were obtained from the same source. The coincidence of the pulses at the OMA was achieved by adjusting the lengths of 50 Ohm coaxial cables. As a reference signal we used the light of the plasma continuum that was recorded by a fast avalanche photodiode (EGG, Model FND100). The performance test of the system was initially done by carrying out Rayleigh scattering experiments. It was crucial to cover the whole system with black cloth in order to eliminate stray light completely. For the calibration by Rayleigh scattering we used propane (C_3H_8) at a pressure of 300 mbar. Figure 13.2 shows the set of measurements needed to obtain plasma parameters with Thomson scattering. The effective charge Z of the ions naturally had to be included. For hydrogen and helium plasmas it was set to $Z = 1$ and $Z = 2$, respectively. For neon and argon Z is given as a function of the electron temperature in the corona model by Arnaud and Rothenflug [8], and this dependence was included in the fit code. Figure 13.3 shows some examples of effective charge as a function of temperature for different ions.

13.4 Results

Dense plasmas were produced with pure H_2, He, Ne and Ar as working gas, no test gas injection along the axis. The left side of figure 13.4 shows typical well-resolved scattering spectra of the ion feature, after the continuum background has been subtracted. The spectra were selected after stagnation on the axis when

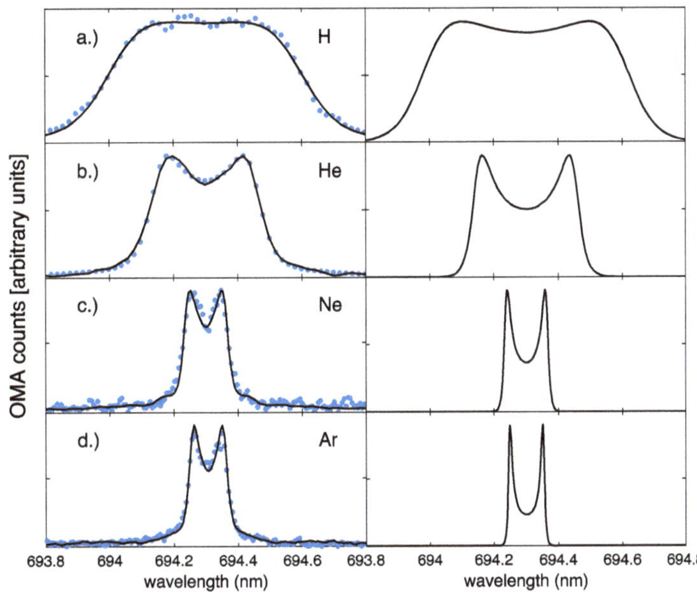

Figure 13.4. Left: Thomson scattering spectra of collisionless plasmas at optimal conditions of the gas liner pinch: experimental spectra (red dots), best fit including the instrumental function, i.e., the convolution of best theoretical curve with the instrumental function (blue). (a) hydrogen: 0.02 nm per pixel, $n_e = 0.62 \times 10^{18}\ \mathrm{cm}^{-3}$, $T_e = T_i = 22$ eV, $Z = 1$; (b) helium: 0.02 nm per pixel, $n_e = 6.05 \times 10^{18}\ \mathrm{cm}^{-3}$, $T_e = T_i = 16$ eV, $Z = 2$; (c) neon: 0.0064 nm per pixel, $n_e = 0.55 \times 10^{18}\ \mathrm{cm}^{-3}$, $T_e = T_i = 12$ eV, $Z = 2.6$; (d) argon: 0.0064 nm per pixel, $n_e = 0.96 \times 10^{18}\ \mathrm{cm}^{-3}$, $T_e = T_i = 14$ eV, $Z = 3.6$. Right shows only the best theoretical curve. Reproduced from Olivares and Kunze [9] with permission of AIP Publishing.

thermalization was complete, i.e., $T_e = T_i$. The recorded spectra (circles) were fitted with theoretical spectra according to equations (13.4)–(13.8) after these had been convolved with the instrument function, which was given by the shape of the Rayleigh scattered signal. For the least square fit procedure the primary parameters were density and temperature.

Figure 13.5 shows an asymmetrical Thomson scattering spectrum.

Figure 13.6 shows density and temperature as a function of time at conservative Gas Liner Pinch voltage and work gas pressure. The dispersion of results is connected with plasma instabilities and electrical jitter.

13.5 Conclusion

We describe a Thomson scattering experiment and the equations needed to describe the spectra. Thomson scattering was performed on dense plasmas of hydrogen, helium, neon and argon. It is shown that up to densities of the collisionless theory of Salpeter the experiment still describes well the ion feature including the valley between the two peaks of the ion acoustic modes, when the plasma is homogeneous and in equilibrium.

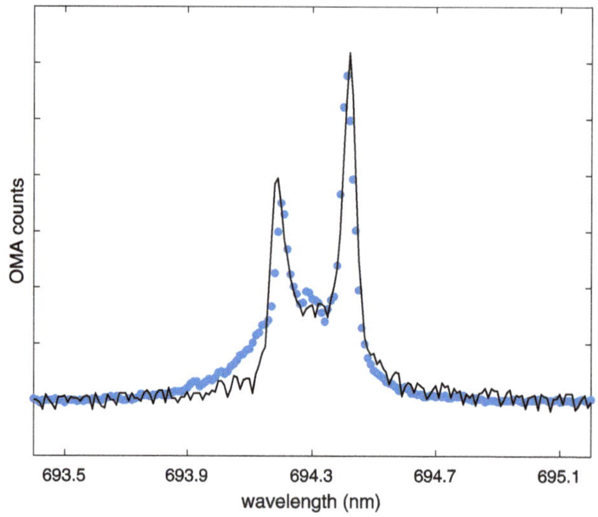

Figure 13.5. Asymmetrical Thomson scattering spectrum with electron drift velocities. Work gas argon, $n_e = 5.2 \times 10^{18}$ cm^{-3}, $T_e = T_i = T_{\mathrm{Ar}} = 50$ eV, $Z^{*}=8$, $x_d = -0.012$, spectrometer grating in second order with resolution 0.0638 Å/pixel.

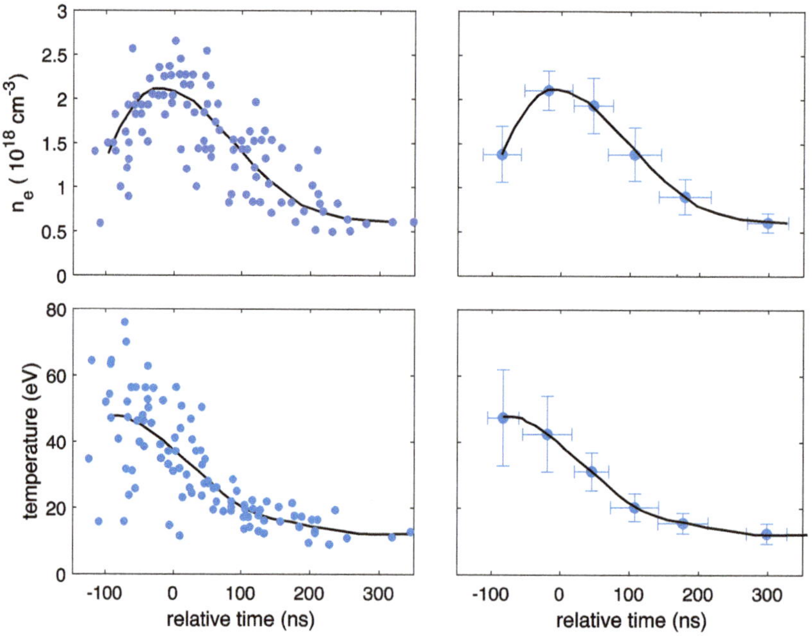

Figure 13.6. Left: density and temperature measurements obtained from Thomson scattering experiments for a pure hydrogen plasma with 35 bar initial pressure in the supply volume and 27 kV load tension. The time position of the laser pulse was measured relative to the maximum of the plasma monitor. The maximal compression takes place 100 ns before maximum voltage of the plasma monitor. Here the relative time scale is shown so that the maximum plasma compression takes place at $t = 0$. Right: average of groups of 10 similar plasma monitor signals.

References

[1] Wrubel T, Büscher S and Kunze H 2000 Radially and axially resolved Thomson scattering in a Gas-Liner Pinch *Plasma Phys. Control. Fusion* **42** 519
[2] Glenzer S H *et al* 1999 Thomson scattering from laser plasmas *Phys. Plasmas* **6** 2117–28
[3] Zhang Y, DeSilva A and Mostovych A 1989 Density fluctuation spectra of a collision-dominated plasma measured by light scattering *Phys. Rev. Lett.* **62** 1848
[4] Myatt J F, Rozmus W, Bychenkov V Y and Tikhonchuk V T 1998 Thomson scattering from ion acoustic waves in laser plasmas *Phys. Rev.* E **57** 3383
[5] Salpeter E E 1960 Electron density fluctuations in a plasma *Phys. Rev.* **120** 1528
[6] Sheffield J 1975 *Plasma Scattering of Electromagnetic Radiation* (New York: Academic)
[7] Büscher S, Wrubel T and Kunze H 2000 Technical setup and physical properties Technical setup and physical properties of a Gas-Liner Pinch *Nukleonika* **45** 167–72
[8] Arnaud M and Rothenflug R 1985 An updated evaluation of recombination and ionization rates *Astron. Astrophys. Suppl. Ser.* **60** 425–57
[9] Olivares I E and Kunze H J 2006 Measurement of the ion feature of collective Thomson scattering in collisionless plasmas *J. App. Phys.* **99** 123305

IOP Publishing

Ignacio E Olivares and Patrick Carrazana

Chapter 14

Thomson scattering with impurities

Measurement of the scattered light spectrum from hydrogen plasmas containing small amounts of heavy impurity ions confirms the predictions of theory that the low-frequency ion-acoustic scattered light feature consists of the normal profile due to scattering from a pure hydrogen plasma, with a narrow peak superimposed that is attributed to the impurity. The intensity of the impurity peak scales as the square of a mean charge Z. Measurements are reported for electron densities of $1–3 \times 10^{18}$ cm^{-3} and electron temperatures ranging from 10 to 80 eV.

14.1 Introduction

Analysis of the spectrum of light scattered by a plasma when it is illuminated by a strong monochromatic source of electromagnetic radiation can yield much information about the plasma [1, 2] including electron and ion temperatures and densities, local electron and ion velocities, and amplitude and frequency spectra of nonthermal density fluctuations. In this work, we have investigated the use of light scattering to determine the density, temperature, and state of ionization of heavy impurity ions in a hydrogen plasma. There has been recent interest in measuring the ion temperature of hot confined plasmas in tokamaks, using the scattering of far-infrared or microwave radiation from the low-frequency ion-acoustic fluctuations. Impurities may strongly influence this spectrum, so it is of interest to make comparisons of the measured spectra of plasmas containing known impurities with theory. Our purpose has been to verify the theory as proposed by Evans [3] for such mixtures, and to evaluate the possibility for use of high resolution scattering to measure impurity content. Previously, proposals for the measurement of impurity content of plasmas by light scattering have been made that use observation of the intensity at the line center for two scattering angles [4], or that measure the integrated scattered light intensity for two scattering angles. Observations of the

doi:10.1088/978-0-7503-3839-4ch14

low-frequency spectrum of scattered light from plasmas containing impurities have been previously reported by Kasparek and Holzhauer [5] but a systematic experimental study of the effects of heavy impurities on the scattered light spectrum does not appear to have been made, at least not to this date. Experiments were performed in a gas-liner Z-pinch device, which allows the introduction of controlled amounts of impurity ('test') atoms into a pure hydrogen (or other 'working gas') plasma. The low-frequency spectrum of electron density fluctuations was resolved for plasmas in which the scattering parameter $\alpha = 1/k\lambda_D$ was well above unity. Here, $k = 4\pi \sin(\theta/2)/\lambda$, is the plasma density fluctuation wave number, θ the scattering angle, λ, the laser wavelength, and $\lambda_D = (k_B T/4\pi n e^2)^{1/2}$ is the Debye length. Under the conditions of the experiment, the scattered light spectrum represents the spectrum of density fluctuations due to thermally excited ion-acoustic waves. No attempt was made in this work to observe the fluctuations due to high-frequency electron plasma oscillations [6, 7].

14.2 Different kind of ions in plasma

To generalize the form factor in the case that many different types of ions are present in the plasma we consider that each kind of ion and electron has a Maxwell distribution. The different ions and electrons are connected by the Poisson equation. The resulting form factor is

$$S = \frac{|1 - \sum_j G_j|^2 F_e + |G_e|^2 \sum_j b_j F_j}{|1 - G_e - \sum_j G_j|^2} \tag{14.1}$$

with $b_j = Z_j^2 N_j / N$ and $N = \sum_j N_j Z_j$. Z_j is the effective type j ion charge and N_j the number of these ions per unit volume. F_e and F_i are the velocity distributions of the electrons and ions respectively. In thermodynamical equilibrium these are Maxwell distributions $F_e = \exp(-v^2/a^2)/(\pi a^2)^{3/2}$ and $F_i = \exp(-v^2/b^2)/(\pi b^2)^{3/2}$, and $a = (2k_B T_e/m_e)^{1/2}$ and $b = (2k_B T_i/m_i)^{1/2}$ are the average thermal velocities. The dielectric susceptibilities are defined by

$$G_e = \alpha^2 W G_i = -Z\frac{T_e}{T_i}\alpha^2 W \tag{14.2}$$

and

$$\begin{aligned} W(x) &= R(x) + iI(x) \\ R(x) &= 1 - 2x\exp(-x^2)\int_0^x \exp(t^2)dt \\ I(x) &= 1 - \sqrt{\pi}\exp(-x^2) \\ x &= \frac{\omega}{kv} \end{aligned} \tag{14.3}$$

W is the *plasma dispersion function* given by Fried and Conte [8] Notice that the plasma spectrum for a plasma with different types of ions is not the linear superposition of the spectra of the individual ion sorts. The form factor is given by

$$S(\alpha, x) = \frac{\pi^{-\frac{1}{2}}\left\{\left[\frac{1}{\alpha^2} + \sum b_j \frac{T_e}{T_j} R(a_j x)\right]^2 + \left[\sum b_j \frac{T_e}{T_j} I(a_j x)\right]^2\right\} a_e \exp(-a_e^2 x^2)}{\left[\frac{1}{\alpha^2} + R(a_e x) + \sum b_j \left(\frac{T_e}{T_j}\right) R(a_j x)\right]^2 + \left[I(a_e x) + \sum b_j \left(\frac{T_e}{T_j}\right) I(a_j x)\right]^2} + \frac{\pi^{-\frac{1}{2}}\{[R(a_e x)]^2 + [I(a_e x)]^2\} \sum b_j a_j \exp(-a_j^2 x^2)}{\left[\frac{1}{\alpha^2} + R(a_e x) + \sum b_j \left(\frac{T_e}{T_j}\right) R(a_j x)\right]^2 + \left[I(a_e x) + \sum b_j \left(\frac{T_e}{T_j}\right) I(a_j x)\right]^2} \tag{14.4}$$

where

$$a_e = \sqrt{\frac{m}{M_1}}\sqrt{\frac{T_1}{T_e}} = \frac{\text{thermal velocity of the main ions}}{\text{thermal velocity of the electrons}}$$
$$a_j = \sqrt{\frac{M_j}{M_1}}\sqrt{\frac{T_1}{T_j}} = \frac{\text{thermal velocity of the main ions}}{\text{thermal velocity of the other j} - \text{ions}} \tag{14.5}$$

The frequency shift can be written as function of kv_1, and v_1 is the thermal velocity of the main ions

$$x = \frac{\omega}{kv_1} = \frac{\omega}{k}\sqrt{\frac{M_1}{2k_B T_1}} \tag{14.6}$$

and k_B is the Boltzmann constant.

The Thomson scattering spectra of plasmas with impurities include a central peak, which is produced by the heavier atoms. The height of these peaks depends on the impurity concentration and mass. Figure 14.1 shows an example for a hydrogen plasma with carbon, nitrogen, and argon impurity ions with same density and temperature.

14.3 Experiment

The experiment was fully described in chapter 13. The difference is that a test gas was inserted in the center of the plasma column.

14.4 Results: Thomson scattering spectra with impurity ions

Typical examples of Thomson scattering spectra with impurities are shown in figure 14.2 The initial values for electron density and temperature are obtained with the assumption that the plasma does not contain any contamination using a graphical process. For an exact fit, the theoretical Thomson spectrum is used with equation (14.4) and calculated with the initial values of the graphical procedure, with the instrumental function folded and compared with the experimental Thomson scattering spectrum. Afterwards a tentative value for the concentration

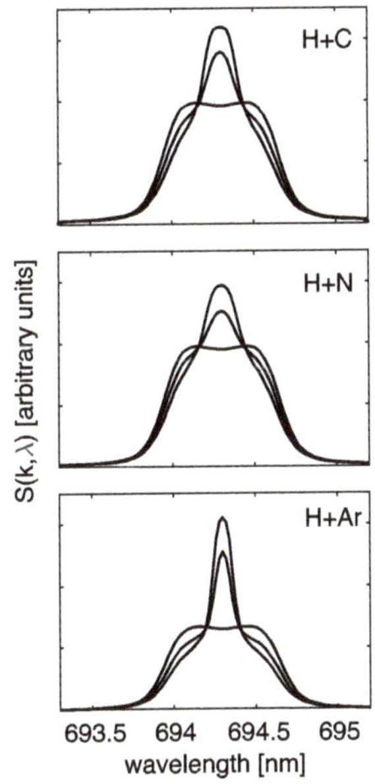

Figure 14.1. Thomson scattering spectra for hydrogen plasmas with carbon, nitrogen, and argon impurities. The theoretical profile was folded with the instrumental function consisting of the experimental Rayleigh-scattering spectrum. All the spectra were calculated with same density and temperature. The impurity concentration was 0%, 2% and 5% in each case.

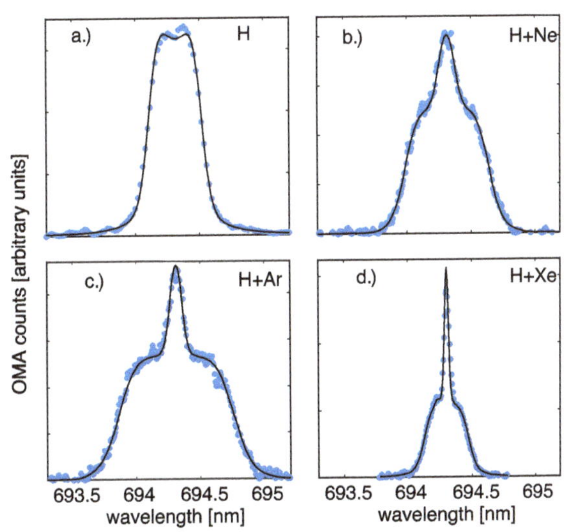

Figure 14.2. Measured spectra from hydrogen plasma [1]: (a) without impurities [2]: $T_e = T_i = 8.7$ eV, $n_e = 2.05 \times 10^{18}$ cm^{-3}, $Z^* = 1$, (b) with 2.3% neon, $T_e = T_{i1,2} = 24.3$ eV, $n_e = 1.9 \times 10^{18}$ cm^{-3}, $Z^* = 4$, (c) with 0.37% argon, $T_e = T_{i1,2} = 47.3$ eV, $n_e = 1.6 \times 10^{18}$ cm^{-3}, $Z^* = 8$, (d) with 5% xenon, $T_e = T_{i1,2} = 17.5$ eV, $n_e = 2.5 \times 10^{18}$ cm^{-3}, $Z^* = 4$. The continuous line is the best fit. Instrumental function and Rayleigh calibration were considered. Reproduced from DeSilva *et al* [9] with permission of AIP Publishing.

of the impurity is inserted in equation (14.4). The procedure was repeated with the new initial values until an optimal fitting is obtained.

14.5 Conclusion

The results of these measurements show good agreement with the theory of Evans. The existence of a well-defined peak in the scattered light profile that can be attributed to the impurity species is confirmed, and the data show good agreement with theory.

References

[1] Kunze H J 1968 The laser as a tool for plasma diagnostic *Plasma Diagnostics* (Amsterdam: North-Holland)

[2] Sheffield J 1975 *Plasma Scattering of Electromagnetic Radiation* (New York: Academic)

[3] Evans D E 1970 The effect of impurities on the spectrum of laser light scattered by a plasma *Plasma Phys.* **12** 573

[4] Evans D and Yeoman M 1974 Spatially resolved measurement of impurities and the effective charge Z_{-} in a tokamak plasma *Phys. Rev. Lett.* **33** 76

[5] Kasparek W and Holzhauer E 1983 CO2-laser scattering from thermal fluctuations in a plasma with two ion components *Phys. Rev.* A **27** 1737

[6] Finken K H and Ackermann U 1981 The Gas-Liner Pinch—a new spectroscopic light source *Phys. Lett.* A **85** 278–80

[7] Finken K H and Ackermann U 1982 Plasma composition in a Gas-Liner Pinch *J. Phys. D: Appl. Phys.* **15** 615

[8] Fried B D and Conte S D 1961 *The Plasma Dispersion Function: The Hilbert Transform of the Gaussian* (New York: Academic)

[9] DeSilva A W, Baig T J, Olivares I and Kunze H J 1992 The effects of impurity ions on the scattered light spectrum of a plasma *Physics of Fluids B: Plasma Physics* **4** 458–64

www.ingramcontent.com/pod-product-compliance
Ingram Content Group UK Ltd.
Pitfield, Milton Keynes, MK11 3LW, UK
UKHW051852100926
8556IPUK00005B/579

9 780750 338370